SmartStart Guitar

by Jessica Baron Turner

What Is SmartStart Guitar?

SmartStart Guitar teaches you to sing and play the guitar by ear right from the beginning. It is easy, rewarding, and very creative. Young students succeed with SmartStart Guitar and so can you. The strategy is simple...you learn to make music by building one new skill at a time.

- When you play SmartStart Guitar, your instrument is tuned to a special tuning called "SmartStart G."
- You will learn many ways of strumming the strings of the guitar. Strumming means dragging your fingers or a pick across the strings in a regular rhythm like walking.
- You'll learn the "Marching Strum," the "Horseback Strum," the "Two-Step Strum," the "Waltz Strum," and more.
- Before long, you'll be playing and singing many songs on the guitar.

How Do I Use This Book?

- Take your time with each lesson.
- Before you begin practicing, read page 29, " 'SmartStart' A Practice Plan."
- Each time you achieve a new skill, celebrate by giving yourself a sticker on the "SmartStart Milestones Chart" on pages 30 and 31.
- Trust yourself and have fun!

How Do I Use the CD or Video?

SmartStart Guitar is available in both Book/CD and video formats*. Next to songs and very important parts of lessons, you will see a number inside a diamond ◆1◆ . That number tells you where on your CD or video you can hear and/or see a demonstration of the information. Forward your CD or video to the matching number to hear how songs should sound. Whenever you want to do something over, rewind the recording to the right spot and start again.

*Please see your local music dealer to order the Smartstart Video (order no. 00641365).

LESSON ONE: What's What

Before you begin learning to play, it's important to know what to call the parts of your instrument and how each one works.

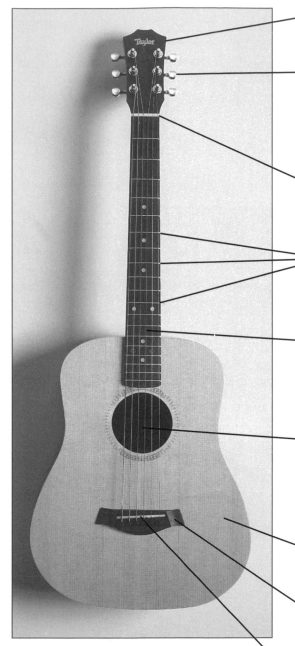

HEAD – The head of the guitar holds the tuners.

TUNERS – There are six tuners on a guitar. One holds the end of each string. Turning them raises or lowers the sound of the string.

NUT – The nut has six little grooves that guide the strings.

FRETS – Strings are pressed between the frets to sound different pitches.

FINGERBOARD – The frets sit on the fingerboard. You press your fingertips down on the strings against the fingerboard to make music.

SOUND HOLE – Also called the "mouth." You strum the strings over the sound hole for a big, bold sound.

BODY – The "body" of the guitar.

BRIDGE – This holds the saddle. Attach your guitar strings here.

SADDLE – This guides the strings and lifts them up above the fingerboard.

LESSON TWO: Look Before You Leap

WHICH PERSON IS HOLDING THE RIGHT SIZED GUITAR?

Answer: The person holding the guitar on the right (Baby Taylor) is ready to play!

What Is the Correct Way to Sit When I Hold a Guitar?

To sit correctly and hold the guitar, follow these steps:

- Sit up straight.
- Place your feet flat on the floor or on a foot stool. Your right thigh must be level to prevent your guitar from slipping.
- Look at the way the person on the right is holding the guitar.
- Put your guitar over your right thigh.
- Reach your right arm over the big hump on the guitar. Rest your elbow on top.
- Let your right hand cover the strings over the sound hole.

What Is the Correct Way to Hold the Guitar?

With your left hand, hold the neck of the guitar just below the head of the guitar. If your left elbow can relax and bend, the neck is the right length for you.

Where Is Thumbo?

Fit your hands over the drawings of the hands below. Read the word above each fingertip to find the name of each finger.

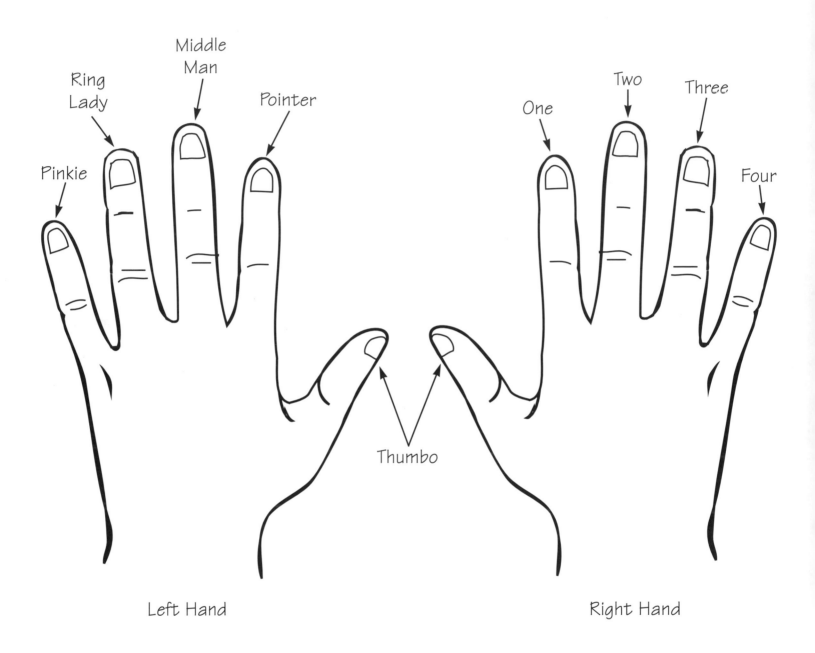

Left Hand

Right Hand

Single letters are used to refer to the fingers on the left hand. Here they are:

P = Pointer   M = Middle Man   R = Ring Lady   p = Pinkie

QUICK TIP: Keep your fingernails short. This will make it easier to press the strings down.

◆ LESSON THREE: Tuning Your Guitar

How Do I Tune My Guitar?

Your guitar has six strings and each one makes its own special sound. The lowest sound is made by playing string 6; the highest sound is made by playing string 1. When we tune, we'll call the strings by their letter names. At all other times, we'll call strings by their number names.

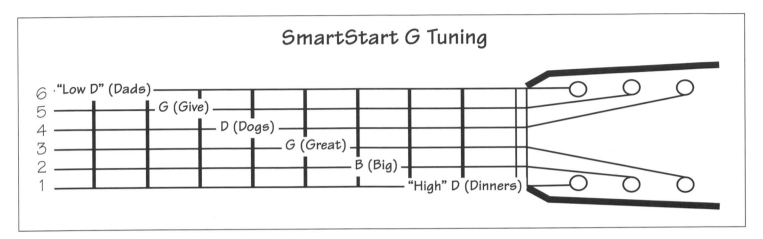

SmartStart G Tuning

6 ·"Low D" (Dads)
5 — G (Give)
4 — D (Dogs)
3 — G (Great)
2 — B (Big)
1 — "High" D (Dinners)

Dads Give Dogs Great Big Dinners

- The letter names of the strings in SmartStart G Tuning are D, G, D, G, B, D.
- Tune each string to the correct note by matching it with the sound on the recording, a pitch pipe, tuner, or a piano.
- Begin tuning at the sixth string and work up to the first string.
- Take your time. Listen closely.

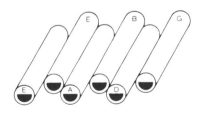

Guitar Pitch Pipe

Tuner

LESSON FOUR: The Steady Beat

Take a few minutes and try these easy exercises. They'll help you feel, play, and sing the steady beat.

Swaying to the Beat

Sing the song "Twinkle, Twinkle, Little Star." Sway your body side to side on each word while you sing. Now you are moving to the steady beat. To see exactly where each beat occurs in the song, look for the strum arrow (↓) below a word. Every song in this book has arrows that point to the steady beat and strum pattern.

Look Ma, No Hands!

SmartStart G tuning makes a pretty sound called a "G chord." A chord is a group of notes that belong together. The G chord contains the notes, G, B, and D. You can play the G chord without pressing down on any strings. Just strum!

◆₂ TWINKLE, TWINKLE, LITTLE STAR

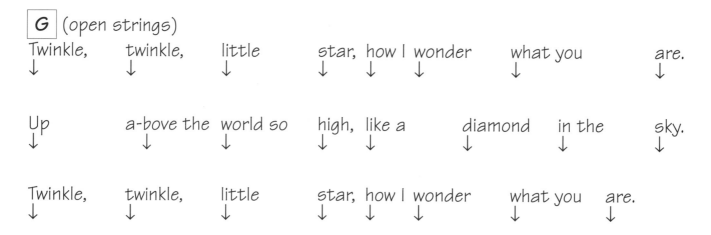

LESSON FIVE: The Marching Strum

This strum feels just like marching "left, right, left, right" on the steady beat. To play it, just follow these steps:

- Put the Thumbo of your right hand on top of the sixth string, over the sound hole.

- Bring Thumbo down gently across all six strings.

- Let the weight of your hand guide it down when you strum.

- Place Thumbo on the sixth string and strum down across the strings every time you see an arrow and a new beat begins. Make your strumming strong and even, like marching steps.

Play the Marching Strum while you sing "Are You Sleeping?" You can turn on your recording and play along with Jessica. When you make a mistake, don't worry — just keep strumming.

"Are You Sleeping?" is called a "round" because the melody goes around and around. Two people or more can sing the song by starting at different times and making pretty harmonies. Just listen to the recording.

◆ ❸ ARE YOU SLEEPING?
Marching Strum; SmartStart G Tuning

G

Are you   sleeping,   are you   sleeping,   Brother   John?   Brother   John!
↓   ↓   ↓   ↓   ↓   ↓   ↓   ↓

Morning bells are ringing, morning bells are ringing. Ding, dong, ding! Ding, dong, ding!
↓   ↓   ↓   ↓   ↓   ↓   ↓   ↓

LESSON SIX: Strum With A Flatpick!

A flatpick is made of plastic. You hold it between your thumb and first finger. It touches the strings when you strum. It can make the guitar sound loud and bright.

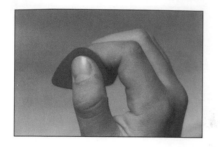 

How Do I Hold a Flatpick?

Pinch the pick between Thumbo of your right hand and the top joint of your Pointer. The most important thing is to hold the flatpick firmly.

How Do I Strum with the Flatpick?

- Bring the pointy tip of the flatpick to the top of the sixth string, over the sound hole.
- Strum down firmly and smoothly so the sound of each string blends into the next one (make one long sound, not six choppy ones). Now do that again. Congratulations! You can strum with a flatpick.

Now let's sing some songs while flatpicking the Marching Strum in SmartStart G.

◆ THIS OLD MAN

Marching Strum; SmartStart G Tuning

G

This old	man,	he played	one,	he played	knick knack	on my	thumb,	with a
↓	↓ ↓		↓	↓	↓	↓	↓	

knick knack	paddy whack,	give the dog a	bone. This old	man went	rolling	home.
↓	↓	↓	↓ ↓	↓	↓	↓

Additional Lyrics

2. ... shoe   3. ... knee   4. ...door   5. ... hive   6. ... sticks   7. ... heaven

Changing Keys with a Capo

A *capo* is a kind of clamp that fits over the guitar neck and presses all the guitar strings down along one fret. When a song feels too low for your voice, put the capo on and raise the sound, or key.

Where Should I Put the Capo?

- Always put the capo just to the left of a fret on the wood, not the metal.
- If you want to sing a *little higher*, put the capo on the first or second fret.
- If you want to sing *even higher*, put the capo on the fourth or fifth fret.

How Do I Play When the Capo Is on the Guitar?

When the capo is on the guitar, imagine that it is really the nut, moved to a new place. Make your chords on the side of the capo closest to the body of the guitar. Your fingertips should be the same distance from the capo as they usually are from the nut.

❖ 5 OLD JOE CLARK

Marching Strum; SmartStart G Tuning

- New Lyrics by
Jessica Baron Turner

G

Old Joe   Clark he   had a   dog,   chewed a   smelly   shoe.
↓   ↓   ↓   ↓   ↓   ↓   ↓

That darn   dog had   such bad   breath, he   made the   cat say   pee-uuu!
↓   ↓   ↓   ↓   ↓   ↓   ↓   ↓

'Round and   'round, Old Joe   Clark,   'round and   'round I   say.
↓   ↓   ↓   ↓   ↓   ↓

'Round and   'round, Old Joe   Clark,   give that   dog   away.
↓   ↓   ↓   ↓   ↓   ↓

❖ 6 ROW, ROW, ROW YOUR BOAT*

Marching Strum; SmartStart G Tuning

G

Row,   row,   row   your   boat   gently   down   the   stream.
↓   ↓   ↓   ↓   ↓   ↓   ↓   ↓   ↓

Merrily,   merrily,   merrily,   merrily,   life   is   but   a   dream!
↓   ↓   ↓   ↓   ↓   ↓   ↓   ↓   ↓

*This is a round. Listen to the recording or watch the video to hear where to start your round.

LESSON SEVEN: Your Second Chord — Easy D

The D chord contains notes D, F#, and A. Easy D is the simplest kind of D chord to play. It also contains a C note. With Easy D, you can play many songs. Use the photo and diagram below to help you place your fingers.

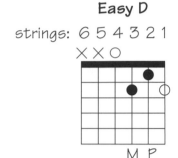

Easy D

strings: 6 5 4 3 2 1

- An 'x' means don't play that string.
- An 'o' means play the open string.
- A dot means put your finger here.
- The letter tells you which finger to put on the dot.

❼ How Do I Play Easy D?

- Put the tip of your first finger (Pointer) on the second string, between the nut and the first fret. This finger is "in the first fret."
- Put the tip of your second finger (Middle Man) on the third string between the first and second frets. This finger is "in the second fret."
- Strum the top four strings (strings 1-4) and listen. You are playing Easy D, your second chord! Even when you strum all six strings, the chord sounds pretty.

QUICK TIP: Look at the photograph above. The child's fingers are curved and only the fingertips are touching the strings. Check to make sure that your fingertips are not touching a metal fret. Press down *firmly* and the strings will sound clear. If your fingers flatten out, the strings will sound muffled.

How Can I Get Better at Playing Easy D?

Here's a fun game called "Fingers On! Fingers Off" which will help you play and change chords. Whenever you learn a new chord, come back to this game again.

◆8 Fingers On! Fingers Off!

1. Place two little stickers on the fingerboard of your guitar to show exactly where your fingers belong when they play Easy D (or any other chord you're learning).

2. Strum across all six open strings, and count out loud up to six while
    you strum: 1 - 2 - 3 - 4 - 5 - 6
    ↓   ↓   ↓   ↓   ↓   ↓

3. When you get to six, press your fingers down on Easy D and *keep strumming* and counting up to six again.

4. When you finish six, raise your fingers and strum the open strings five times. Then play Easy D and strum five more times.

5. Now try this with four strums, then three strums, and two strums until you strum the open strings once and Easy D once! Then build back up by adding a strum in each round until you get to six again.

With Easy D, you can sing and play "Old MacDonald Had a Farm."

◆9 OLD MACDONALD HAD A FARM
Marching Strum; SmartStart G Tuning

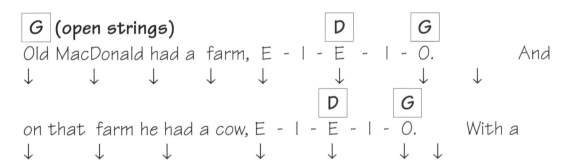

G (open strings)   D   G
Old MacDonald had a farm, E - I - E - I - O.   And
↓   ↓   ↓   ↓   ↓   ↓   ↓   ↓

                                    D   G
on that farm he had a cow, E - I - E - I - O.   With a
↓   ↓   ↓   ↓   ↓   ↓   ↓

moo - moo here and a moo - moo there, here a moo, there a moo, everywhere a moo - moo.
↓   ↓   ↓   ↓   ↓   ↓   ↓   ↓

                      D   G
Old MacDonald had a farm, E - I - E - I - O.
↓   ↓   ↓   ↓   ↓   ↓   ↓

LESSON EIGHT: The Horseback Strum

Have you ever taken a pony ride or skipped? Remember how that feels? You feel a long beat followed by a short one. Skip around or pretend you're galloping around the room. That's the *horseback beat*.

How Do I Play the Horseback Strum?

- First, strum down for the long beat.
- Next, play the short beat by strumming the other way...up!
- When you strum down, say "loooong" and when you strum up, say "short!" Practice until you're playing a nice lazy rhythm — like riding a slow horse.

What Songs Can I Play with the Horseback Strum?

You can give any song a Country and Western feel if you play it with this strum. Put a little "giddy-up" into the popular cowboy song below with the Horseback Strum.

QUICK TIP: Every single beat gets both a down-and-up Horseback Strum. The numbers below the strum arrows show you where the beats are.

⑩ BUFFALO GALS

Horseback Strum; SmartStart G Tuning

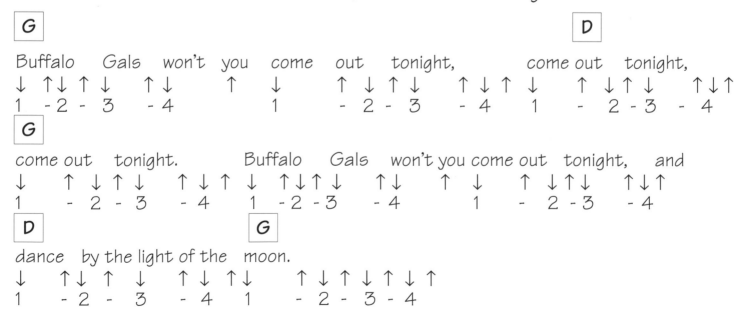

LESSON NINE: The Two-Step Strum

How Do I Play the Two-Step Strum?

- Pick just the sixth string (or the lowest string in the chord)
- Now strum down the rest of the strings.
- Bring your pick back up to the sixth string again, pluck it, then strum down across the remaining strings like before.
- When you play the Two-Step Strum smoothly, try picking the fifth string first (instead of the sixth). It sounds better when you play the "G" chord.

QUICK TIP: Keep plucking and strumming while you count "one, two, one, two." Practice will help you make the two actions sound and feel smooth.

What Songs Can I Play with the Two-Step Strum?

The Two-Step Strum is peppy, so play it with a lively song. The beats of the song you choose must come in groups of two or four.

11 MICHAEL FINNEGAN
Two-Step Strum; SmartStart G Tuning

P = pluck low string in chord

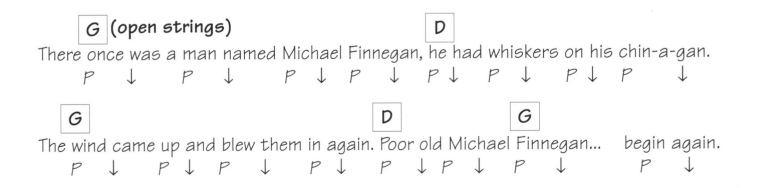

G (open strings)   D
There once was a man named Michael Finnegan, he had whiskers on his chin-a-gan.
  P   ↓   P   ↓   P ↓ P   ↓   P↓   P   ↓   P↓ P   ↓

G   D   G
The wind came up and blew them in again. Poor old Michael Finnegan...   begin again.
  P   ↓   P ↓ P   ↓   P ↓   P   ↓ P ↓   P   ↓   P   ↓

LESSON TEN: Your Third Chord — Easy C

Look at the photograph. Easy C looks a lot like Easy D. In fact, Pointer stays in the same place for both chords! That means you'll only move Middle Man to play the new chord.

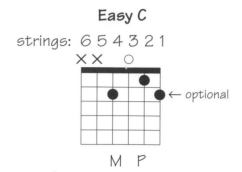

⑫ How Do I Play Easy C?

- First, play Easy D.
- Next take your second finger (Middle Man) off the third string.
- Move Middle Man to the fourth string and keep it in the second fret.
- Strum down across the strings and listen to Easy C!
- If you want to play a regular C chord, try adding Ring Lady to the first string in the second fret.

⑬ KUM-BAH-YAH
Marching Strum; SmartStart G Tuning

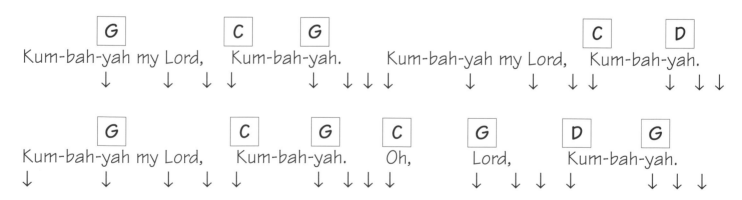

Additional Lyrics

2. Someone's singing...   4. Someone's praying...
3. Someone's crying...   5. Someone's smiling...

14 SHE'LL BE COMIN' 'ROUND THE MOUNTAIN

Two-Step Strum; SmartStart G Tuning

G

She'll be comin' 'round the mountain when she comes.
P ↓ P ↓ P ↓ P ↓ P ↓ P ↓ P ↓

D

She'll be comin' 'round the mountain when she comes.
P ↓ P ↓ P ↓ P ↓ P ↓ P ↓ P ↓ P ↓

G **C**

She'll be comin' 'round the mountain. She'll be comin' 'round the mountain.
P ↓ P ↓ P ↓ P ↓ P ↓ P ↓ P ↓ P ↓

G **D** **G**

She'll be comin' 'round the mountain when she comes.
P ↓ P ↓ P ↓ P ↓ P ↓ P ↓ P ↓ P ↓

Additional Lyrics
2. She'll be driving six white horses...
3. Oh we'll all go out to meet her...
4. She'll be wearing red pajamas...
5. Oh we'll all have chicken and dumplings...

15 WHEN THE SAINTS GO MARCHING IN

Two-Step Strum; SmartStart G Tuning

G

Oh when the saints, go marching in. Oh when the
P ↓ P ↓ P ↓ P ↓ P ↓ P ↓ P ↓ P ↓

D **G**

saints go march - ing in. Oh Lord, I want to be in that
P ↓ P ↓ P ↓ P ↓ P↓P↓P↓ P ↓P ↓ P ↓ P↓P↓

C **G** **D** **G**

number, when the saints go march - ing in.
P ↓ P ↓ P ↓ P ↓ P ↓ P ↓ P ↓ P ↓ P ↓ P↓P↓P

LESSON ELEVEN: The Waltz Strum

The *Waltz Strum* has three beats, 1-2-3. The beats are even, but the first beat is strummed a little louder than the next two. This helps you feel the beginning of each new group of three beats. The first beat is called the *downbeat*. Use the following game to help you count in groups of three.

Clapping and Slapping to the Beat

- Slap your thighs with the palms of your hands and say "one."

- Clap your two hands together twice and say two," then "three."

- Repeat these steps until you feel that 1-2- 3 rhythm. Now speed up!

Is There More Than One Way to Play the Waltz Strum?

There are many. Strumming down three times is the easiest, but here are two more:

1. Play the Two-Step Strum but add one more down strum at the end. We'll call this the "Three-Step Strum."

2. Combine downstrums and upstrums in groups of three. See for yourself how they sound and feel. Down, up, down is a nice strum. So is down, down, up.

Practice playing the Waltz Strum and changing chords before you play it with a song. Remember to take your time and relax.

What Songs Can I Play with the Waltz Strum?

Since the Waltz Strum has three beats, use it for songs that have three or six beats per measure. In the songs below, the downbeats are darker to remind you to strum harder.

🔶16 ON TOP OF OLD SMOKY

Three-Step Strum; SmartStart G Tuning

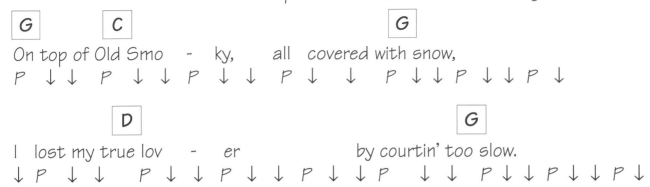

Do you know the words to the funny version of this song? It's called "On Top of Spaghetti."

🔶17 SWEET BETSY FROM PIKE

Three-Step Strum; SmartStart G Tuning

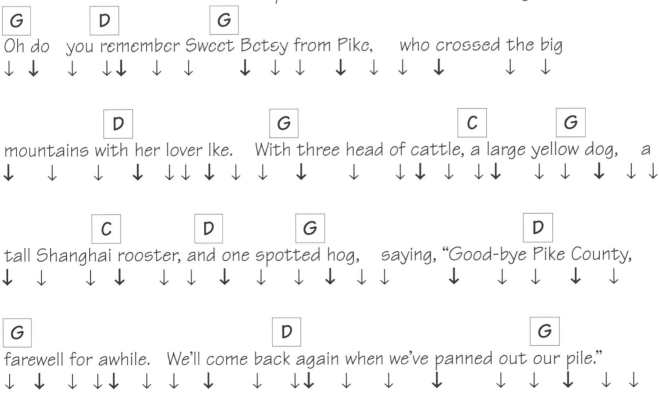

LESSON TWELVE:

E Minor And Intermediate D

Congratulations! Your fingers are good enough at playing chords to learn new positions. Take your time and remember to play "Fingers On! Fingers Off!"

Em

strings: 6 5 4 3 2 1

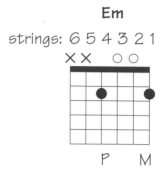

◆18 How Do I Play E Minor?

- Place Pointer on the fourth string in the second fret.
- Now, place Middle Man on the first string in the second fret.
- When your fingers are curved, press down with your fingertips and strum (strings 1-4 only). You are playing E minor, which is written "Em."

You're ready to play a chord with Ring Lady now.

Intermediate D

strings: 6 5 4 3 2 1

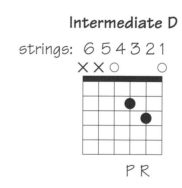

◆19 How Do I Play Intermediate D?

- Begin by playing Em.
- Lift Middle Man off of the first string.
- Now put Ring Lady on the second string, in the *third* fret.
- Now strum Intermediate D!

◆20 JOSHUA FOUGHT THE BATTLE OF JERICHO
Marching Strum; SmartStart G Tuning

REFRAIN

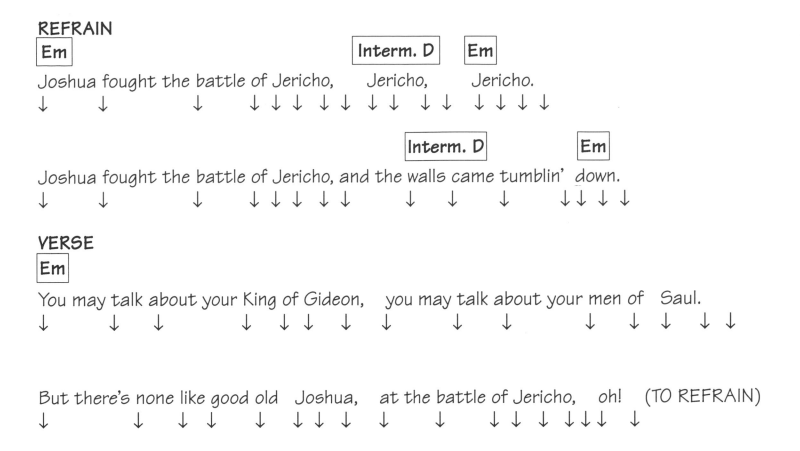

Em / Interm. D / Em

Joshua fought the battle of Jericho, Jericho, Jericho.
↓ ↓ ↓ ↓ ↓ ↓ ↓ ↓ ↓ ↓ ↓ ↓ ↓ ↓ ↓ ↓ ↓

Interm. D / Em

Joshua fought the battle of Jericho, and the walls came tumblin' down.
↓ ↓ ↓ ↓ ↓ ↓ ↓ ↓ ↓ ↓ ↓ ↓ ↓ ↓

VERSE

Em

You may talk about your King of Gideon, you may talk about your men of Saul.
↓ ↓ ↓ ↓ ↓ ↓ ↓ ↓ ↓ ↓ ↓ ↓ ↓ ↓

But there's none like good old Joshua, at the battle of Jericho, oh! (TO REFRAIN)
↓ ↓ ↓ ↓ ↓ ↓ ↓ ↓ ↓ ↓ ↓ ↓ ↓ ↓ ↓

◆21 SHADY GROVE
Two-Step Strum; SmartStart G Tuning

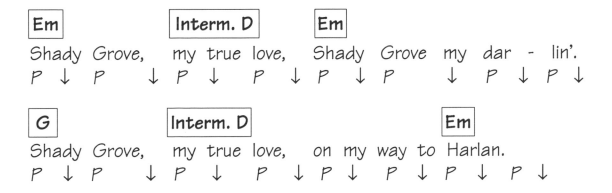

Em / Interm. D / Em

Shady Grove, my true love, Shady Grove my dar - lin'.
P ↓ P ↓ P ↓ P ↓ P ↓ P ↓ P ↓ P ↓

G / Interm. D / Em

Shady Grove, my true love, on my way to Harlan.
P ↓ P ↓ P ↓ P ↓ P ↓ P ↓ P ↓ P ↓ P ↓

Additional Lyrics
Shady Grove, my true love, standin' in the door.
Shoes and stockings in her hand, barefeet on the floor.

❖²² LESSON THIRTEEN: Standard Tuning

Use the directions below to tune your guitar from SmartStart G to standard tuning.

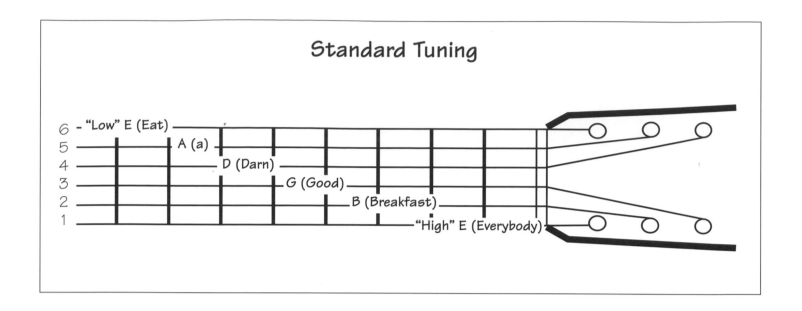

- Get your pitch pipe, tuner, or go to a piano.

- Tune the sixth string up from "low" D to "low" E.

- Tune the first string up from "high" D to "high" E.

- Tune the fifth string up from G to A.

- Check the pitches of strings 4 (D), 3 (G), and 2 (B) to be sure they are still in tune.

LESSON FOURTEEN: Two New Chords

To learn your first chords in standard tuning, let's begin by turning what you already know into something new. If you play Easy C in standard tuning, it sounds very different. That's because you are now playing notes of a new chord. This chord is called Am7.

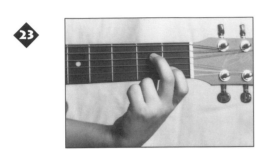

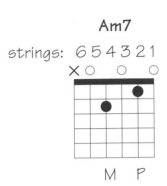

Am7

strings: 6 5 4 3 2 1

M P

Now let's play A minor (Am). Look at the diagrams and follow the directions below.

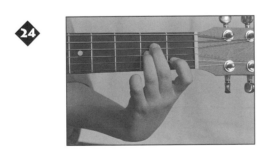

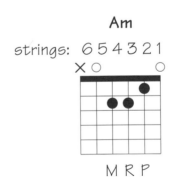

Am

strings: 6 5 4 3 2 1

M R P

How Do I Play Am?

- Begin by playing Am7.
- Now, place Ring Lady below Middle Man on the third string. Both Ring Lady and Middle Man belong in the second fret. Now you are playing A minor (Am).

LESSON FIFTEEN: Two More New Chords

Now put your new chords to work to make *two more chords*: E7 and E.

How Do I Play E7 and E?

E7

strings: 6 5 4 3 2 1

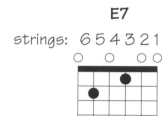

M P

- To play E7, first play Am7.
- Keep your fingers in the same frets, but move each one up onto the string above it. Your fingertips should be on the fifth and third strings.
- Strum down and listen to E seven (E7).

E

strings: 6 5 4 3 2 1

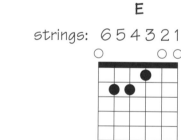

MRP

- To play E major (E), place Ring Lady below Middle Man on the fourth string, in the second fret. It looks a lot like A minor.

What Songs Can I Play Using My New Chords?

Many. Below are two you can play and sing right away. First practice switching from chord to chord by turning back to page 11 and playing "Fingers On! Fingers Off!"

◆27 HEY, HO! NOBODY HOME
Marching Strum; Standard Tuning

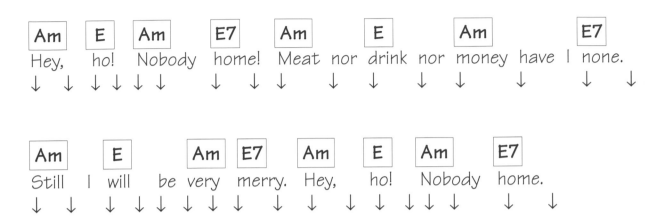

Am	E	Am	E7	Am	E	Am	E7
Hey,	ho!	Nobody	home!	Meat	nor	drink	nor	money	have	I	none.

↓ ↓ ↓ ↓ ↓ ↓   ↓ ↓ ↓   ↓   ↓   ↓   ↓   ↓   ↓   ↓

| Am | E | Am | E7 | Am | E | Am | E7 |
Still I will   be very merry. Hey,   ho!   Nobody home.
↓ ↓   ↓ ↓ ↓ ↓ ↓ ↓   ↓   ↓ ↓   ↓ ↓ ↓ ↓ ↓   ↓   ↓

Now that you can play Am, E, and E7, it's time to hear how they sound on a song you already know!

◆28 JOSHUA FOUGHT THE BATTLE OF JERICHO
Marching Strum; Standard Tuning

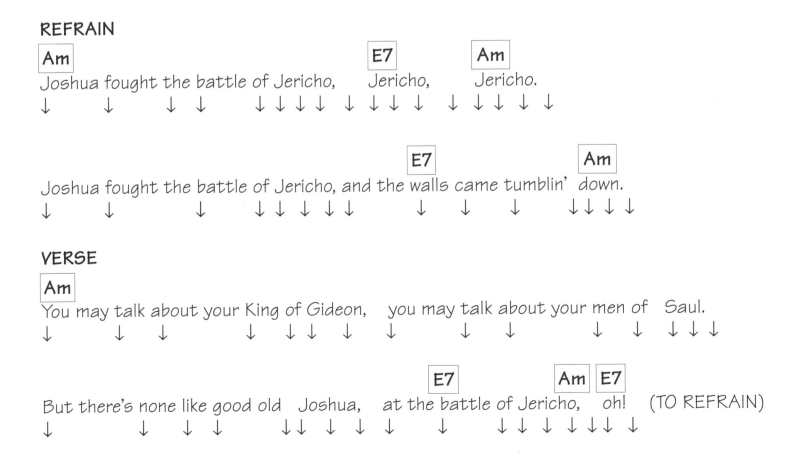

REFRAIN

Am   E7   Am
Joshua fought the battle of Jericho,   Jericho,   Jericho.
↓   ↓   ↓ ↓ ↓↓↓↓ ↓ ↓↓↓ ↓ ↓↓↓↓

                                        E7   Am
Joshua fought the battle of Jericho, and the walls came tumblin' down.
↓   ↓   ↓   ↓↓↓↓ ↓   ↓   ↓   ↓ ↓↓↓↓

VERSE

Am
You may talk about your King of Gideon,   you may talk about your men of Saul.
↓   ↓   ↓   ↓   ↓ ↓↓↓ ↓   ↓   ↓   ↓   ↓ ↓ ↓↓↓

                                        E7   Am E7
But there's none like good old Joshua, at the battle of Jericho, oh!   (TO REFRAIN)
↓   ↓   ↓ ↓ ↓   ↓↓ ↓ ↓ ↓   ↓   ↓   ↓↓ ↓↓↓↓ ↓

LESSON SIXTEEN:

More Chords In Standard Tuning

Congratulations! If you followed the lessons in this book, you are ready to learn many new chords, one at a time.

To get a smart start in standard tuning, learn the new chords in this order. Your muscles will stretch a little more for each one.

Em

strings: 6 5 4 3 2 1

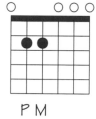

P M

- First play E major.
- Now lift Pointer off the third string.
- You are playing E minor (Em).

D

strings: 6 5 4 3 2 1

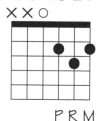

P R M

- Begin by playing Intermediate D.
- Add Middle Man to the first string in the second fret.

31 THE DRUNKEN SAILOR

Marching Strum; Standard Tuning

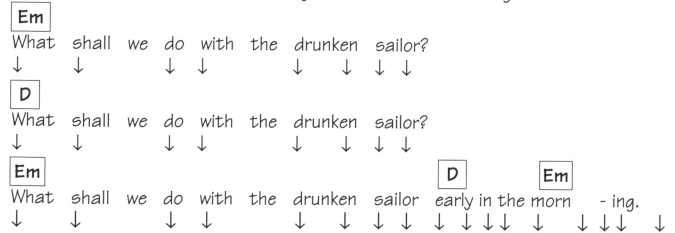

Em							
What	shall	we	do	with	the	drunken	sailor?
↓	↓		↓	↓		↓	↓ ↓

D							
What	shall	we	do	with	the	drunken	sailor?
↓	↓		↓	↓		↓	↓ ↓

Em   **D**   **Em**

What shall we do with the drunken sailor early in the morn - ing.
↓ ↓ ↓ ↓ ↓ ↓ ↓ ↓ ↓ ↓ ↓ ↓ ↓ ↓ ↓

24

Now your fingers are ready to reach for new chords. Read the diagrams below and try the chords one at a time. Remember, they get easier the more you practice.

Dm

strings: 6 5 4 3 2 1

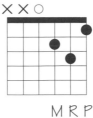

M R P

- Begin with Intermediate D.
- Now lift Pointer up and put Middle Man in Pointer's old place.
- Add Pointer to the first string in the first fret.

C

strings: 6 5 4 3 2 1

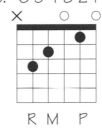

R M   P

- Play Am 7.
- Add Ring Lady to the fifth string in the second fret.
- This is advanced C.

F

strings: 6 5 4 3 2 1

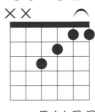

R M P P

- Begin by playing C.
- Bring Middle Man down from the fourth string to the third.
- Bring Ring Lady down from the fifth string to the fourth.
- Roll Pointer on its side and press down on strings one and two at the same time.

G

strings: 6 5 4 3 2 1

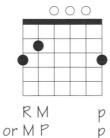

R M   p
or M P   p

- Place Pointer on the fifth string in the second fret.
- Put Middle Man on the sixth string in the third fret.
- Place Pinkie on the first string in the third fret.

🔶36 I'VE BEEN WORKING ON THE RAILROAD

Horseback Strum; Standard Tuning

C   **F**   **C**
I've been working on the rail - road, all the live - long day.
↓↑↓↑   ↓   ↑   ↓   ↑   ↓↑↓↑ ↓↑↓↑ ↓↑↓↑ ↓ ↑ ↓ ↑ ↓ ↑ ↓ ↑ ↓ ↑ ↓ ↑

C   **Dm**   **G**
I've been working on the rail - road, just to pass the time a - way.
↓↑↓↑   ↓   ↑   ↓   ↑   ↓↑↓↑ ↓ ↓ ↑ ↓   ↑   ↓↑↓ ↑   ↓ ↑ ↓↑↓↑↓↑↓↑↓↑

G   **C**   **F**   **E7**
Can't you hear the whistle blow - in'? Rise up so early in the morn.
↓↑↓ ↑   ↓   ↑   ↓   ↑   ↓↑↓↑ ↓↑↓↑↓↑ ↓ ↑ ↓ ↑ ↓ ↑ ↓↑↓↑↓↑↓↑

F   **C**   **G**   **C**
Can't you hear the captain shout - ing "Di - nah, blow your horn!"
↓↑↓↑   ↓   ↑ ↓ ↑   ↓↑↓↑   ↓↑↓↑ ↓↑↓↑ ↓ ↑↓↑ ↓↑↓↑↓↑↓↑

C   **F**
Dinah won't you blow,   Dinah won't you blow
↓↑   ↓   ↑   ↓↑↓↑↓↑   ↓   ↑   ↓   ↑↓↑

G   **C**
Dinah won't you blow your ho - o - orn?
↓↑   ↓   ↑   ↓ ↓ ↓ ↑ ↓ ↑ ↓↑↓↑↓↑

C   **F**
Dinah won't you blow,   Dinah won't you blow
↓ ↑ ↓   ↑ ↓↑↓↑↓↑   ↓   ↑   ↓↑↓↑

G   **C**
Dinah won't you blow your horn?
↓ ↑ ↓   ↑   ↓ ↑ ↓ ↑ ↓ ↑↓↑↓↑↓↑

C   **G**
Someone's in the kitchen with Di - nah, someone's in the kitchen I kno - o - o - ow.
↓   ↑   ↓↑↓↑ ↓ ↑   ↓↑ ↓↑↓↑↓↑↓↑ ↓   ↑   ↓↑ ↓ ↑ ↓↑↓↑ ↓↑↓↑↓↑

C   **F** **G**   **C**
Someone's in the kitchen with Di - nah, Strumming on the old ban-jo and sing-ing
↓   ↑   ↓↑↓↑ ↓↑   ↓↑ ↓↑↓↑↓↑↓↑↓   ↑   ↓↑ ↓↑ ↓↑ ↓↑↓↑↓↑↓↑↓↑

C   **G**
Fee, fi, fid - dle - ee - aye - oh, fee, fi, fid - dle - ee - aye - ooh - oh - oh - oh.
↓↑↓↑ ↓↑↓↑↓   ↑ ↓↑↓ ↑↓↑↓↓↑ ↓↑   ↑   ↓↑ ↓↑ ↓↑ ↓↑↓↑

C   **F**   **G**   **C**
Fee, fi, fid - dle - ee - aye - oh! Strumming on the old ban - jo!
↓↑↓↑ ↓↑↓↑↓   ↑↓↑↓ ↓ ↑ ↓↑↓↑ ↓   ↑   ↓ ↑ ↓↑↓↑ ↓↑↓↑↓↑↓↑

37

A7

strings: 6 5 4 3 2 1

P R

- Put Pointer on the fourth string in the second fret.
- Add Ring Lady to the second string in the second fret.

 38

A

strings: 6 5 4 3 2 1

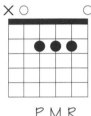

P M R

- Play A7.
- Add Middle Man to the third string in between Pointer and Ring Lady.

 39

B7

strings: 6 5 4 3 2 1

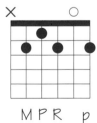

M P R   p

- Begin by playing E major (E).
- Keep Middle Man in place while you move Pointer up to the fourth string and Ring Lady down to the third string.
- Add Pinkie to the first string in the second fret.

◆⁴⁰ MY BONNIE

Waltz Strum; Standard Tuning

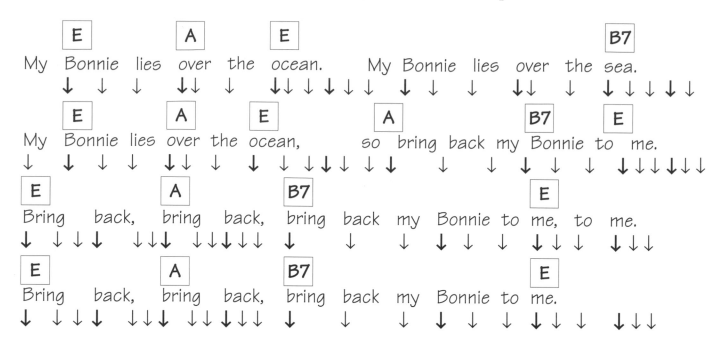

E   A   E   B7
My Bonnie lies over the ocean. My Bonnie lies over the sea.

E   A   E   A   B7   E
My Bonnie lies over the ocean, so bring back my Bonnie to me.

E   A   B7   E
Bring back, bring back, bring back my Bonnie to me, to me.

E   A   B7   E
Bring back, bring back, bring back my Bonnie to me.

More on Notes, Chords, Keys, Measures, and Time Signatures

There are hundreds of other chords you can learn to play on the guitar. Some of these are called *barre chords*. These require Pointer on your left hand to be very strong. The **Hal Leonard Guitar Method**, the **Wolf Marshall Guitar Method**, or Hal Leonard's **FastTrack** series would be a good place to start learning these chords. These books will also show you more about written music and music theory.

LESSON SEVENTEEN:
"SmartStart" A Practice Plan

- If you keep your guitar handy, you'll play it more often. So put your guitar where you can see it.

- The muscles in your arms and hands work like all the other muscles in your body. The more often you practice, the stronger and faster they act, and the more easily they stretch.

- It is good to play each day because you'll learn quickly and develop calluses. A callus is an extra layer of skin that you can't see, but it protects your fingertips. The sooner you get calluses, the better your fingertips will feel. If you have a busy schedule, set a regular practice time such as before school, after you finish your homework, or before you go to bed.

- At first, practicing between five and ten minutes a day is enough. If your fingertips feel too tender, then stop. They'll get tougher if you practice a little every day.

- After your fingertips have calluses, practice fifteen minutes or more at least every other day. The more regularly you practice, the more you and your hands will remember. Make friends with your mistakes and have a good time.

- On the next page is a chart of SmartStart Milestones to celebrate how much you've learned. Check the chart after each practice and reward yourself with a sticker when you reach a new milestone!

SmartStart MILESTONES

Here is a chart of important steps to leaning to play SmartStart Guitar. You can keep track of your progress by writing the date next to each milestone you reach. It's always good to celebrate your accomplishments, so there's room for you to put a sticker next to each one!

Milestone	Date Accomplished	Sticker
1. I know the names of the parts of the guitar and what to call the fingers on each of my hands.		
2. I can sit, hold and strum the guitar.		
3. I can sing and play a song on the guitar in SmartStart G tuning.		
4. I can raise or lower the key of a song by using a capo.		
5. I can strum the Marching Strum on the guitar with a flatpick while singing a song.		
6. I can play Easy D.		
7. I practice the guitar regularly.		
8. I am getting calluses.		
9. I can play the Horseback Strum with a flatpick while changing between SmartStart G and Easy D chords.		
10. I can play the Two-Step Strum.		
11. I can play and sing a song with SmartStart G and Easy D while flatpicking the Two-Step Strum.		

Milestone		Date Accomplished	Sticker
12.	I can play Easy C.		
13.	I can change from SmartStart G to Easy D to Easy C while playing the Marching Strum.		
14.	I can change from SmartStart G to Easy D to Easy C while playing the Horseback Strum.		
15.	I can sing and play a song with SmartStart G, Easy D, and Easy C while playing the Two-Step Strum.		
16.	I can play the Waltz Strum at least two different ways.		
17.	I can sing and play a song with SmartStart G, Easy D, and Easy C while playing the Waltz Strum.		
18.	I can play Em.		
19.	I can change from Easy D to Easy C to Em.		
20.	I can play Intermediate D.		
21.	I can change from Easy D to Easy C to Em to Intermediate D.		
22.	I can sing and strum a song with Em and Intermediate D.		
23.	I can switch from SmartStart G tuning to standard tuning.		
24.	I can play new chords and songs in standard tuning.		
25.	I feel good when I play the guitar.		

ABOUT THE AUTHOR

Jessica Baron Turner is a teacher, musician, writer, and a mom. Children and adults love her work because it encourages them to learn at their own pace and follow their creative instincts. Like her co-authored 1995 award-winning book, **Let's Make Music** (Hal Leonard Corporation.), **SmartStart Guitar** provides simple step-by-step lessons that help beginners achieve success after success. Her unique approach is founded on the notion that, just as we learn to speak before we learn to read, we also make music naturally long before we are ready to learn theory. **SmartStart Guitar** is designed to get you playing and singing right away while you build one new skill at a time.

Mrs. Turner holds a Bachelor of Arts degree in Child Development with an emphasis in learning styles, disabilities, and strategies. She has a Masters degree in Marriage, Family, and Child Counseling, and has been teaching guitar since 1974. She lives with her husband, luthier Rick Turner, and their son Elias in Santa Cruz, California.

"Many novels and books about St. Paul have told in marvelous detail what he *did* and accomplished in his life and missionary journeys. I am concerned with what he *was*, a man like ourselves with our own despairs, doubts, anxieties and angers and intolerances, and 'lusts of the flesh.' Many books have been concerned with the Apostle. I am concerned with the man, the human being, as well as the dauntless saint."

—TAYLOR CALDWELL

"RANKS HIGH FOR SHEER ENTERTAINMENT"

—*Fort Worth Star-Telegram*

"TOTALLY ENGROSSING, TOTALLY REAL"

—*Illinois Journal-Register*

Fawcett Crest and Gold Medal Books
by Taylor Caldwell:

GREAT
LION
OF
GOD

Taylor Caldwell

FAWCETT CREST • NEW YORK

GREAT LION OF GOD

THIS BOOK CONTAINS THE COMPLETE TEXT
OF THE ORIGINAL HARDCOVER EDITION.

Published by Fawcett Crest Books, a unit of CBS Publications,
the Consumer Publishing Division of CBS Inc.,
by arrangement with Doubleday & Company, Inc.

ISBN: 0-449-24096-7

Selection in Reader's Digest Condensed Books, April 1970
Selection of the Doubleday Book Club, August 1970
Selection of the Literary Guild, November 1970

Printed in the United States of America

19   18   17   16   15   14   13   12   11

For Judge Edward L. and Janet L. Robinson,
with affection

Any resemblance between the world of St. Paul or Tarsus and the world of today is purely historical.

GREAT
LION
OF
GOD

Foreword

MANY years of intensive study have gone into this novel about one of the most passionate, intelligent, urban and dedicated Apostles of early Christianity, Saul of Tarshish, or, as the Romans called him, Paul of Tarsus, the intellectual Pharisee and lawyer and theologian, and, finally, the Apostle to the Gentiles.

Saul has had more influence on the Western world and Christianity than most of us know, for Judeo-Christianity, which he sedulously spread throughout the world, is the bedrock of modern jurisprudence, morals and philosophy in the West, and which, through their spiritual and mental power and industry and justice, have literally over the past two thousand years truly created a new society, and advanced the cause of freedom. As we all know, it was Moses who cried, "Proclaim liberty throughout the land, unto the inhabitants thereof!" It was the first time in human history that such a proclamation was uttered, and Saul of Tarshish proclaimed it anew and vehemently. Liberty, above all, has been the most profound ideal of Judeo-Christianity, liberty of mind and soul and body, a new concept among men. It is no wonder, then, that the foes of freedom first attack religion, which liberated mankind.

It may cheer many—and depress others—to realize that man never really changes, and the exact problems of Saul's world are the same that confront us today. Cheer, in that man has an indomitable way of surviving his governments and his tyrants and surmounting them, and depressing that he never learns from his own experiences. As Aristotle said, long before Christ, a people who do not learn from history are doomed to repeat it. It is obvious that we are repeating it today.

Solomon said, "There is nothing new under the sun."

The Roman empire was declining in the days of Saul of Tarshish as the American Republic is declining today —and for the very same reasons: Permissiveness in society, immorality, the Welfare State, endless wars, confiscatory taxation, the brutal destruction of the middle-class, cynical disregard of the established human virtues and principles and ethics, the pursuit of materialistic wealth, the abandonment of religion, venal politicians who cater to the masses for votes, inflation, deterioration of the monetary system, bribes, criminality, riots, incendiarisms, street demonstrations, the release of criminals on the public in order to create chaos and terror, leading to a dictatorship "in the name of emergency," the loss of masculine sturdiness and the feminization of the people, scandals in public office, plundering of the treasury, debt, the attitude that "anything goes," the toleration of injustice and exploitation, bureaucracies and bureaucrats issuing evil "regulations" almost every week, the centralization of government, the public contempt for good and honorable men, and, above all, the philosophy that "God is dead," and that man is supreme.

All this Saul of Tarshish confronted in his own world, where the word "modern" was deeply cherished. There is a common fallacy that the early Church was one, loving and fervent and devoted and without contention or controversy, united and dedicated. On the contrary! Christ had not been resurrected two years before dissension and protest and dissent wracked the young Church almost to oblivion. As Saul said, "There is not an obscure little bishop or deacon in some dusty little town who does not have his own interpretation." These small men also had a multitude of followers who heartily disagreed with—and fought—other Christians, and the bitterness was intense. For many years that bitterness was powerful between St. Peter and St. Paul, and almost destroyed the Church. How they were reconciled is an amusing story in itself—but they never really loved each other! In short, they were all too human and we can all understand them, and as humanity finds itself lovable we can find these two ardent and determined contestants lovable, too.

There is another fallacy, too, that all Christians were "holy martyrs" in a naughty world, and were as pure and long-suffering as lambs. On the contrary, again! They were often insufferable and intolerant of the world about them, and deliberately provoked "the heathen," and made themselves generally obnoxious. They were not persecuted, as it has been too long assumed, "for their faith," for the Roman world was cynical and totally tolerant of all religions and devoted to none. But the early Christians brought themselves dangerously to the attention of the ruling authorities in Rome and in Rome-dominated Israel by their loud and public objections to practically everything, including the "heathen" temples. They were also guilty of invading those temples during religious ceremonies and shouting, "Woe!" and overturning statues and taking over pulpits and denouncing ruling authorities and the Establishment—and where have we heard that since? On the other hand, the Faith was advanced not by these militants who thought Our Lord was about to return the next hour or the next day and set them up in glory and as absolute rulers over the world, but by quiet and devoted and intelligent and peaceful men working often in solitude and in prayer. The militant Christians—who almost destroyed the infant Church with their dissents and protests and belligerence—had already forgotten that Our Lord had said, "I am no divider of men. My Kingdom is not of this world," and "Render unto Caesar the things which are Caesar's and to God the things which are God's." Alas, like so many millions of us living today, they believed that the establishment of the Kingdom of God meant material affluence—for themselves, and power. It is curious that the militant are rarely spiritual, and are concerned only selfishly with advantages in the world, and the "punishment" of "enemies."

There is one cheerful thought that emerges: The Church survived its external enemies—which were the least important—and its internal enemies, which were the most disastrous and powerful. So, as the Church is torn by loud "innovators" today, and "dissent," and "modernism," to the anxiety and sometimes despair of the truly faithful, so it was in the past, and by its internal rather than external enemies. And as the Church survived then, so it will survive now, finally purged of the "dissenters" who were never truly aware of their Faith and never, in their hearts, fully accepted it. (When I speak of the Church, I speak of all Christian churches, of course.)

There is also the depressing thought: We never learn from the past.

Judeo-Christianity is facing its greatest test of history in these days, for in a great and terrible measure it has become secular and preaches "the Social Gospel" rather than the Gospel of Christ. Christ was not concerned with this world, which now so engrosses those who claim to be His followers, and repeatedly said that He would "create a new world." *He,* you will notice, *not we.* He was not preoccupied with "social problems" and injustices. He constantly preached that justice and mercy would flow from a changed heart, and love, not by man's laws and ordinances.

Man's nature cannot be changed in any particular—except by the power of God, and religion. All the "education" in secular institutions and all the secular exhortations will never succeed in civilizing man. As Christ said, "Who, *by taking thought,* can add one cubit to his stature?" No one, of course.

In this novel I have capitalized the pronoun of Divinity when the speaker speaks of God and Our Lord in faith and acceptance, and have kept the pronoun uncapitalized when the speaker or writer is skeptical or unconvinced or unaccepting. Many novels and books about St. Paul have told in marvelous detail what he *did* and accomplished in his life and missionary journeys. I am concerned with what he *was,* a man like ourselves with our own despairs, doubts, anxieties and angers and intolerances, and "lusts of the flesh." Many books have been concerned only with the Apostle. I am concerned with the man, the human being, as well as the dauntless saint. I am also interested in what influenced him in his childhood and early life as a Roman citizen and Roman lawyer, as well as a Pharisee Jew of great learning and enormous intellect, and abiding faith. That is why I halted at his last leaving of his beloved country, Israel. We all know his journeys after that and his martyrdom in Rome, but the last sight of his dear country ends, I hope, the novel on a poignant note. Death is not more moving to a man than the final vision of his native land, which he is leaving forever, and his own people.

If I can influence, in this book, only ten people who

will follow the advice of Our Lord to "study the Scriptures," both the Old and the New Testaments, I will feel I have succeeded. Therefore, I dedicate this book *"Urbi et Orbi."*

TAYLOR CALDWELL

Part One

For he was a veritable lion, a red lion, the great lion of God.

—*St. Augustine*

d smit transparett tilge Het large blue eyes, as vivid
as any Greek sky, had both an innocent and a discontented expression, looking and restless, and fluttering
a husband considered

Chapter 1

"HE is very ugly," said his mother. "My brothers are all
handsome, and my mother was celebrated for her beauty,
and I am not, myself, unprepossessing. How is it possible that I gave birth to so repulsive a child?"

"Be thankful we have a son," said her husband. "Did
you not give birth to dead girls before this? We have a
son."

"You speak as a Jew," said the child's mother, with a
flick of her white and delicate hand. "But we are Roman
citizens also, and our conversation is conducted in Greek
and not in barbarous Aramaic." She contemplated the
child in his cradle with increased melancholy and some
aversion, for she had Hellenic pretensions and had written
some poetry in Grecian pentameters. Her father's friends
had remarked on her taste and had mentioned Sappho.
Her father, a scholar himself, had been gratified.

"We are still Jews," said Hillel ben Borush. He stroked
his fair beard and looked down at his son. A son was a
son, even if hardly beautiful. Too, what was beauty in
the eyes of God, blessed be His Name, at least physical
beauty? There was considerable controversy, especially in
these days, as to whether a man possessed a soul or not,
but had there not always been this controversy even
among the devout? A man's function was to glorify God,
and whether or not he possessed a soul was irrelevant.
Hillel found himself hoping that his newborn son had a
lovely soul, for certainly his appearance did not inspire
his nurses to raptures. But, what was a body? Dust, dung,
urine, itches. It was the light within which was important,
and it was not significant if that light endured after
death, or if the soul was blinded eternally in the endless
night of the suspired flesh. Let the old men ponder uneasily, and hope.

Deborah sighed. Her exquisite auburn hair was only
partly concealed by her veil, which was of the lightest

and most transparent silk. Her large blue eyes, as vivid
as any Greek sky, had both an innocent and a discontented expression, seeking and restless, and fluttering in
thick reddish lashes. Everyone but her husband considered
her very cultured, and an impressive matron. Hillel ben
Borush was a fortunate man, said his friends, for Deborah bas Shebua had brought him a magnificent dowry
—and he only a poor scholar, and his wife was famous
for her grace, charming smile, learning and style, and
had been educated by private tutors in Jerusalem, and
was the delight of her father's eyes. She was tall and
winsome and had a lovely bosom and the hands and
feet of a Greek statue, and her garments draped themselves about her figure as if grateful for the lovely opportunity. She was nineteen years old and had given birth
to three children, the first two dead at birth, and girls,
and the third surviving, a son, now in his cradle.

She had a very pale and oval face and her complexion
was like marble and her mouth was a folded rose, her
chin firm and dimpled, her nose daintily carved. Her
stola, arranged in the Roman fashion, was blue with
golden embroidery, and her feet were shod in gilded
leather sandals. She seemed to carry about her a veritable
aura of beauty, a shadow of lucent light. A young Roman
of great family and of a rich and ancient house had
sought her hand in marriage, and she had desired him
also. But tiresome superstitions and prejudices had eventually intervened, and she had been bestowed on Hillel
ben Borush, a poor young man famous for his piety and
learning, and of an old and honored house.

Alas, thought Deborah, that even her cosmopolitan
father had let dead traditions prevail. How most unfortunate for the young! The old refuse to believe that
the world changes and the musty gods die, and the
temples fall in on themselves in rubble and the altars
are overthrown and the names upon them obliterated, and
the worshipers are no more. She, herself, was a victim
of tradition and arcane ideas now rejected. She had been
born before her time. But it was possible that her son
would live in a new world of urbane laughter and enlightenment, in an environment where man's sole pre-
eminence in creation was established, as the cultivated
Greeks now asserted. The very idea of a God was tedious

and absurd in these sophisticated days, and embarrassing. It could not be reconciled with objective phenomena. She, Deborah, was determined that her son's mind would not be filmed over with superstitions, like an old mirror clouded with antiquated dust and the smearings of unwashed hands.

"Saul," said Hillel ben Borush.

"Eheu!" cried Deborah. "Saul! It is not a distinguished name, to our friends."

"Saul," said Hillel. "He is a lion of God."

Deborah considered, her ruddy brows drawn together. She hastily relaxed them, for frowning brought wrinkles which even honey and almond meal could not lighten. She was a lady, and ladies do not dispute violently with husbands, no matter how foolish. "Paulus," she said. "Surely there can be no objection, my husband. Paulus is the Roman translation."

"Saul ben Hillel," said the father.

"Paulus," said Deborah. She smiled musingly. It had an aristocratic sound, Greek as well as Roman.

"Saul of Tarshish," said Hillel.

"Paulus of Tarsus," said Deborah. "Only barbarians call Tarsus Tarshish."

Hillel smiled, and his smile was gentle and winning even to his young wife, for it was filled with tenderness as well as amusement. He put his hand on her shoulder. One must humor women. "It is the same," he said. He thought Deborah enchanting. He also thought her stupid. But that, regrettably, was doubtless due to having been born to Sadducee parents, who were very shallow and unlearned in the matters which were pleasing to God, and to please God was the reason a man was born and lived and had his being. There was none else. He often pitied the Sadducees, whose lives were firmly fixed in a secular world and who accepted nothing that could not be proved by their five senses, and who mistook mere learning for intellect, and sophisticated prattle for knowledge. It must be, he thought, like a man being born unable to detect the infinite hues and colors and tints of the world, and so had been robbed of mystery and delight and the endless joy of conjecture and meditation, and the majesty of wonder. He often marveled how men could endure a world without God. Such a world was populated only with animals, whose lives are meaningless.

"Of what are you thinking?" said Deborah with suspicion, for she disliked her husband's expression when he was communing with himself. It made her uneasy and too conscious of her youth in comparison with his thirty years.

"I am a Pharisee," he replied, "and we believe in reincarnation. So I was comtemplating our son's former existence, and from whence he came, and why he is here with us now."

Deborah arched her pretty brows in scorn. "That is nonsense," she said. "He is flesh of our flesh and bone of our bone, and spirit of our spirit, and there was none like him before, nor will there ever be again one like him."

"True," said Hillel ben Borush. "God never repeats Himself, no, not even in a leaf or a blade of grass. All souls are unique from the beginning, but that does not deny that if they are eternal—as we assert—their lives must be eternal also, moving from flesh to flesh as God wills. The acquisition of knowledge never ends. Its imperative is not ended in the tomb."

Deborah yawned. Tomorrow she must go to the Temple for the presentation of her son, and the thought annoyed her. It is true that the Sadducees also obeyed the ancient law, but they laughed at it secretly, though honoring it as a tradition. How could she explain the ceremony to her Greek and Roman friends in Tarsus? They would be amused. She discontentedly smoothed a fold in her stola, and looked with a small resentment at her son.

Hillel knew why she had been bestowed upon him. The Sadducees might not believe in any life everlasting, or even in a God, and were purely secular and worldly, but they were often insistent on their daughters marrying a pious man. They were like men who prudently invested in what they sheepishly considered might eventually prove a good investment. Or they gave their daughters as hostages to a God in Whom they did not believe, but Who might astoundingly exist, and Who was rumored to be wrathful.

Hillel had large and shimmering brown eyes, a white

and ascetic face, a prominent nose like the Hittites, a golden beard and golden brows, and a domed forehead from which rose the gilded crest of his hair, partly covered now with the skullcap which exasperated Deborah. He had broad shoulders and strong white hands and sturdy legs, but he was not so tall as his wife. This also made her discontented. Had not a Grecian gentleman bowed to her once and quoted Homer: "Daughter of the gods, divinely tall, and most divinely fair!" Hillel also wore those foolish curls in front of his ears and invariably his prayer shawl —or so it seemed to young Deborah—for he was constantly praying. The ceremonies of Judaic life were profoundly baffling to her, as well as almost completely unknown. Times changed; the world moved; the truths of yesterday were the laughter of today. God was a quaint hypothesis, interchangeable with the gods of Greece and Rome, with a slight flavor of Babylon and Egypt. It was a serene and laughing household in Jerusalem, where Deborah had been born, a cosmopolitan household. She regretted leaving it for this household where Pharisees moved and debated gravely and looked at her with covert disapproval and averted eyes, almost as if she were a member of the Ionian courtesans, like Aspasia.

Once Deborah had said to her husband, "Do you consider me another Aspasia?" She never understood why he had burst into the wildest laughter she had ever heard, and had then embraced her tenderly and had said, "No, my darling. I should never call you an Aspasia."

A peacock screeched furiously outside. He was very jealous of the black swans in the spring-fed pond in the garden, for he knew that they were greatly admired. Hillel winced; he had sensitive hearing. He said with an absent sense of caution, "That creature sounds like an ill-tempered woman. He has awakened the child."

Deborah felt a thrill of unkindness toward her husband for this remark, which denigrated her sex. She lifted her head with hauteur and said, "Then I will remove my disturbing presence also, so you will not be reminded of women."

"Deborah," said Hillel, but Deborah could move like a child and she was gone in an instant through the light and shadow of the columns outside, which guarded the outdoor portico. Hillel sighed, and smiled. He was

always offending Deborah, who was an adorable small girl
—he never thought of her as an adult woman. He had
heard from his bookshop that a little known manuscript
of one of Philo of Larissa's earlier works had been discovered a year ago, and copies were expected in Tarsus.
He would send for one tomorrow; it would please Deborah, and, alas, it would flatter her. She would not understand a single word, poor pretty child. On the other
hand, she had admired a necklace of fiery opals she had
seen in her jeweler's shop, though had prudently caviled
at the price. Which should it be? Philo of Larissa or
the opals? Hillel, in mercy, decided on the jewels. Two
heavily laden ships had made their way from Cilicia to
Rome without encountering the enthusiastic and ubiquitous Cilician pirates—who had not been entirely destroyed
by Julius Caesar and his successors—and Hillel had been
heavily invested in those vessels and their cargo. He had
made a handsome profit. Therefore, Deborah would have
her fine opals.

The peacock screeched again, and the child in his ivory
and ebony cradle complained. The nursery was filled with
the newly awakened scent of the night-blooming jasmine,
though the sun had not yet set and its reddish light struck
on white marble wall and on the white and black marble
floor. The shadow of a palm tree blew against the wall
nearest the young child, and he quickly turned his head
and gazed at it, and Hillel marveled. A child so young,
so newly born, and he saw! It was said that an infant
did not truly see anything but light and shadow before
he was two months old, but of a certainty this child not
only saw but comprehended. Hillel did not in the least
feel fatuous and too fond as he bent over the cradle
and clucked at his son. "Saul," he said, in the softest
voice. "Saul?"

The boy had not yet been named in the Temple, but
a man held his son's name in his heart before that. Hillel
and the infant were alone in the large and gleaming nursery. Hillel's face and golden beard shone as if the light
of his own spirit illuminated it. He felt a passionate love,
and immediately murmured a prayer, for above all one
must love one's God with all one's heart, mind and soul,
and that love must surpass any human love for any human creature. Hillel hoped for a moment that he had

not offended his omnipresent God nor incurred His wrath, which could fall upon this innocent morsel in his cradle.

The child turned his head quickly again and looked up at his father, who leaned over him. As Deborah had said, he was not beautiful; he was almost ugly. He was smaller than the average baby, even at his age, yet he had a broad and sturdy body, naked except for the cloth about his loins, and that body was not fair as were the parents' but slightly ivory in tint as if he had been exposed to the sun. The nursemaids had mentioned a young Hercules, which had pleased Deborah, but Hillel thought of David, the warrior king. The muscles of the little chest were strong and visible under the sweating skin, like minute plates of armor, and the arms were the arms of a soldier. The legs, equally strong, were, however, bowed like one who has ridden a horse since childhood. The toes flexed vigorously and with a kind of rhythm, as did the square little fingers. They seemed to move with purpose, and not aimlessly, thought Hillel.

He had a round head, virile and solid, but overlarge for his body, and big red ears. Unfortunately, his hair, thick and coarse, was even redder. It was not a charming tint, as was the hair of Deborah. It was that particular shade of raw and audacious color which usually aroused mistrust among superstitious Jews. Moreover, it grew far down the wide powerful cliff which was the child's forehead, and this gave him a pugnacious appearance, like an irritable Roman.

The effect of irritability was enhanced by his most peculiar eyes. They were round, huge and commanding, under the red brows—which almost met across a nose even more suggestive of a Hittite's than Hillel's. (At least, thought Hillel, it is not a cherry of a nose like a peasant's.) But the startling impression of the eyes lay mostly in their color, a curiously metallic blue, like the glitter on a polished dagger. The blue was concentrated as well as intense, and the auburn lashes, long and shining, did not diminish it. There was a strenuousness and force in the eyes, not childlike, not wholly innocent, but aware and stern. Hillel, though a Pharisee, did not entirely believe in the transmigration of souls, but he wondered now, as he had often wondered lately. Saul's eyes were not an infant's eyes. They met his, he was certain, with conjecture and recognition. "Who are you, my son?" he whispered, with uneasiness. "From whence did you come? What is your fate?"

The child stared at him, but not blankly. The mouth, the wide thin mouth like an exasperated man's, stirred, but no sound came from it. Then it set itself tightly, and the child looked away from his father and contemplated the dance of vivid light and shadow between the columns of marble. He seemed to be reflecting. Hillel felt a little awed. What moved in that infant brain, what thoughts, what dreams, what determinations, what memories? The small chin, firm and dimpled and puissant, appeared to gather itself together with resolution. Saul withdrew himself.

Gaia, the little Grecian nursemaid who was Deborah's own servant, came briskly through the farther bronze door into the nursery, her sandals clattering quickly on the stone. She was hardly more than a child herself, but very competent, with her flowing light brown hair and pale eyes and merry face and lilting step. She wore a long thin tunic of a rosy cloth, bound with blue ribbons about her slender waist. She bowed to Hillel, who raised his hand in automatic blessing though the girl was a heathen, and he greeted her kindly.

"The nurse awaits the child, Master," she said. Hillel had had the vision of Deborah suckling her son, but Deborah had decided otherwise. No Greek or Roman lady suckled children any longer, nor did enlightened Jewish ladies who had duties and responsibilities beyond the mere demands of the body. Hillel had been extremely disappointed. He thought the picture of a mother nursing her infant the most beautiful in the world. Certainly his own mother had suckled her children and he remembered the warmth and tenderness in the nursery and the crooning and the evening light caught in his mother's hair, and the round morning freshness of her body. He had raised no complaint to Deborah, who at this hour was furbishing her mind in the library, for he was too kind and gentle a man. He knew this, and deplored it. The old patriarchs had been held in awe by their wives and their daughters in the past, but alas, Hillel was no patriarch.

So, without a word he watched little Gaia gather up

the infant in her arms and he heard her remark about the condition of his napkin, which the other nursemaid had apparently neglected, and she rolled him deftly in the linen sheet and carried him out. As the girl reached the door the boy suddenly uttered a loud strange cry, not a childish wail or a whimper, but a humiliated and disgusted cry. He seemed almost to be saying, "I detest my present state and weakness, and I shall not long endure it!"

I am fanciful, like all new and proud fathers, thought Hillel, and he went out into the outdoor portico and then stepped down into the gardens. It was time for his evening prayers in the warm and scented silence. As a pious Jew, he knew that these prayers should be prayed in a synagogue, but he and Deborah lived in the house her father had bought for them in the far suburbs of Tarsus. ("My daughter is of a delicate constitution.") There was no synagogue under less than an hour's energetic walking, and Hillel was just recovering from malaria which left his strong legs somewhat weak, and his heart palpitated on effort. He was not a horseman, and he disliked effete litters, and though he owned a large car and a smaller chariot he disliked them little less than he did the litters. A man was made for walking. He would not have rejected a humble ass, but this Deborah would not endure, and Hillel was a man of peace. Men might talk of the unbending patriarchs but husbands were not so valorous.

Hillel looked about in the calm and luminous early evening. His house, in the suburbs of Tarsus, was held in constant quietude, a tranquil hush, even when the slaves and other servants were working busily or laughing or singing—for it was a happy household. Even the discordant cries of peacocks and swans and birds of prey sounded musically here, part of the murmurous background of palms and citrons and karobs and sycamores and fragrant shrubs, and a gentle benignity appeared to pervade during the hot spring storms, and the roaring summer thunder. The house and its extensive and beautiful grounds appeared protected, and this was remarked on by Greek and Roman friends who laughingly vowed that Hillel was under the loving guardianship of woodland deities and fawns and nymphs. Certainly the house was in a hollow section of land, verdant, fed by springs and little rills even during the driest seasons, and in the fertile and luxurious valley of Issus, that fruitful vast area in Cilicia Pedias, which had been joined to Syria and Phoenicia by Julius Caesar.

The country estate rolled in the softest green waves about the house, crowned by copses of thick dark emerald trees which made cool hollows of refuge during the hottest days, throwing their shadows on dense grass and formal beds of flowers and small red paths or graveled footways. Here fountains, bright amber in sunlight, hissed and gurgled, the illuminated waters pouring from gleeful marble hands or from horns of plenty or even from the mouths of exotic little beasts. (There had been a small statue of a little boy in one of the fountains from which the water arched, but Hillel had decided, in his Pharisee sense of what was obscene, to have it removed, to Deborah's annoyance.) Hillel, in keeping with the Ten Commandments, would have had the "graven images" removed from the fountains and grounds—images erected by the former Roman owner—but here Deborah tearfully and vehemently prevailed, and became so agitated that Hillel, always the compromiser, yielded. He also compromised by not looking at the graceful statues in grottos and arbors and fountains, and avoiding direct confrontation with their classic and beautiful faces, but sometimes his naturally perceptive and appreciative eye wandered involuntarily. When sternly reproached by his more rigidly religious friends, he would laughingly change the subject. Unlike the gentle men, he could infuse a tone of quiet authority and character into his voice, which silenced even the most choleric or rebellious, and his brown eye would glow with a fixed and steady coldness. Once halted by this, the quarreler would never again contend for his own views or rebuke or criticize his host or master, but forever afterwards would hold Hillel not only in respect but in some fear.

A great natural pond lay in the very center of the grounds, flashing blue and purple under the sun, and becoming a shield of silver under the moon. Here floated the arrogant black and white swans, and the curious and highly colored ducks from China, seemingly made of angular painted wood, who occasionally disputed lordship with the swans over the water. During the migration periods of red-legged white storks flying to Africa or returning, these fowls would often halt at the pond to devour the fish with which it was sedulously stocked, and the singing frogs, and the clouds of insects. The regal peacocks drank here, and jeered at the swans, and so did the small denizens of the land. Fed by clear springs, and released into tiny brooks and rivulets—which freshened the earth—the pool was always clear and pure, with its rocky little walls in which blue and gold and crimson flowers, and even ferns, grew with colorful abandon. Sometimes the slaves waded here on hot evenings, to the combined indignation of the usually quarreling inhabitants, catching iridescent fish in their young hands and then releasing them with laughter. The former owner, who had visited the Orient, had erected a very complex and ornate little arched bridge over the narrowest part of the pond—which had the shape of a pear—and it gave an exotic touch to an otherwise too formal setting. Dragon shapes and serpents and vines twined together in the teak of the bridge, and the animal shapes had eyes of silver or lapis lazuli, and the minute fruit of the vines were delicately fashioned of jade or yellow stone. The younger slaves would often lie on the arch of the bridge to examine with wonder and delight, freshly discovering new intricacies of the artist's work, and marveling over inlays of carved ivory.

There were small awninged retreats under the thick trees for refreshment, striped in blue or red or green, and Hillel came here to meditate after a twinge of conscience following his admiration of beauty. Deborah could also retire here with her friends from the city and from nearby estates, decorously to sip spiced or perfumed wine and partake of fine little cakes and fruit. When Hillel would hear their high and tripping voices he would flee, though Deborah would later speak of discourtesy and the duties of a host. Hillel had a wise way of avoiding women.

The estate had cost Deborah's father a considerable fortune, which he was not averse to discussing with Hillel, and he had furnished it with slaves and other servants and had sent one of his best cooks to serve his daughter. "One must remember that my child, my sweetest only daughter, is accustomed to refinement and comfort, and could not tolerate privation." This was accompanied by a meaning hard glance over the affectionate smile, and the father-in-law would consider that he had instilled meek acceptance in Hillel. But Hillel, the tolerant compromiser, would smile inwardly.

So Hillel, this early evening, stood in his flowering, green and pleasant gardens, folded his hands and murmured aloud, "Hear, O Israel! the Lord our God, the Lord is One! O, King of the Universe, Lord of lords, we praise You, we bow before You, we glorify You, for there is none else."

He pondered on that with his usual awe. "There is none else." The endless universes were pervaded with God's grandeur. The uttermost star was charged with His glory. The worlds—endless like the sands of the sea—sang His praises. The smallest golden wild flower, clinging to the rocky side of the pool, dumbly, through its color and life and vitality announced His power over the smallest and the humblest, as well as the most majestic, and His invincible life, His omnipresence, His circumambient pervasion. Each blade of grass reflected His occupancy. His altars were not only in the Temple and the synagogue, but in every morsel of earth, in the silver bark of trees, in the clattering fronds of palms, and in the rainbowed darting light of the wings of birds and insects. His voice was in the thunder, the spark of His wrathful eye in the lightning, the movement of His garments in the winds. His breath stirred trees and bent grasses. His footsteps revealed stone and mountains. His was the cool shade, the clusterings of shadows, the cry of innocent beings, the rising evening mist, the sudden exhalations of cooling flowers, the scent of freshness of ground and water. "There is none else." Nothing existed but God.

Hillel's heart swelled with passionate exaltation. All exulted in God and acknowledged Him—except man. All obeyed His slightest command implicitly—except man. All lived in beauty—except man. All bowed before Him, existing only in Him—except man. Man was the outlaw, the rebel, the distorted shape that scarred the earth, the voice that silenced the music of Eden, the hand that raised up obscenities and blasphemies. Man was the pariah dog, the moral leper in this translucent mirror of Heaven. He was the muddier of crystal waters, the despoiler of forests, the murderer of the innocent, the challenger against God. He was the assassin of the saints and the prophets, for they spoke of what he would not hear, in the darkness of his spirit.

Hillel preferred to think well of his fellow man, being compassionate and often reflecting on the sorrows and the murky predicament of humanity, but he could not always delude himself that man was worthy to be alive. When he found himself in this crepuscular misery—as he did this evening—a misery mysterious in its source—he would remind himself of the prophecies concerning the Messias, and quote the words of Isaias regarding Him: "He will deliver His people from their sins."

The few Sadducees whom Hillel knew and whom he welcomed in his house, smilingly laughed at him when he confessed—after an extra cup of wine—that he "felt" something divine had "moved" upon the world, that a powerful event had already taken place which would change the face of history and revitalize man with the Voice of God. "It is your voluntary seclusion," they would tell him, with fondness. "This world is of rock and substance and the power of Rome, and it is reality, fixed in space, and only madmen deny reality. Abandon the stars, my friend, and the Kabalah, and prophecies made by ancient prophets smelling of dung and goat's-hair garments and sweat. They lived in a simpler day. Today the world is complex and civilized and filled with great cities and commerce and the arts and the sciences. Man has come of age. He is a sophisticated being, a citizen of the Roman world, at least by existence if not by fiat. He knows all that there is to be known. He is no longer the prey of jejune fantasies and hopes and delusions. He knows what the stars are. He knows what matter is. He knows his place in the universe. He is no longer superstitious, except in a mild manner, like the Romans. He feels no terror for natural phenomena—he understands it. He has his universities, his schools, his wise teachers. Few Jewish maidens there are, these days, who dream of giving birth to the Messias, for they know there will be no Messias, and that that delusion was only the wistfulness of innocent, ancient men. We still honor those men's childish wisdom, and find it remarkable, considering that they had no access to our libraries and our schools. But it was the wisdom of most ingenuous men, who knew nothing of the cities and the roaring world of today."

"A virgin shall give birth—" But no one spoke of that these days, except a few old Pharisees among Hillel's friends, and even they spoke of it as an event still shrouded in time and possibly only a mystical hope. Hillel felt alone. At midnight, he found himself pondering on his peculiar surety that something had, indeed, moved on the face of the world and that all creation was holding its breath.

Once Hillel said to an old man whom he honored in Tarsus, an old Jew bent with years but with the mind of a leaping youth, "I have heard from my female cousin in Jerusalem, who is—I do not regret to say—married to a burly Roman centurion. A good man; I have dined in his house; he adores my cousin and defers to her, which, in some minds makes him less a man, but I have never believed that it was a proof of manhood to despise women. In many ways he possesses a rough wit and much shrewdness, and contrary to popular belief that all Romans are monsters, he is very kindly and has much humor." Hillel spoke diffidently, while his guest frowned at this doubtless exaggerated view of the Roman conquerors of God's Holy Land.

"He is also superstitious," Hillel continued. "He had been married to Hannah for six years, but God had not seen fit to bless them with a son though they have four rosy little daughters and I long for such, myself. This was a sore sorrow to Hannah, though Aulus seemed singularly and happily resigned. However, four years ago, after the winter solstice when the Romans were celebrating their boisterous Saturnalia even in Jerusalem—they are restrained, however, on command of Caesar Augustus who is a sensible man—Hannah gave birth to a son. Aulus was consoling some of his men in a watchtower high over Jerusalem, for they, that night, were on duty and could not join the final night of the festivities, which he assured me are the most—pleasant—of all. It was a fine cold night, and Aulus was gazing in the direction of Bethlehem, the birthplace of King David, and all the stars were sharply visible."

Hillel had glanced apologetically at his old visitor who

was accepting more wine from a slave and who revealed traces of ennui. Candidly, he was yawning.

"A messenger came to Aulus to tell him of the birth of his first son, and Aulus immediately poured wine for his bereft men and declared a festivity of their own in the tower. He was partaking of his third goblet of wine when he chanced to glance in the direction again of Bethlehem, and then he saw a most amazing thing."

"He was drunk," said the guest. "I know these Romans. They are always drunk."

Hillel was a little vexed. "Was it not David who said, 'Oil to make the countenance shine, and wine to make the heart of man glad?' He counted these as excellent gifts of God, and not to be rejected. Aulus is a prudent man. I have seen him drunk but five times."

The guest snorted. "There are abjurations in the Holy Books against drunkenness. There is the case of Noë. What does your friend know of Noë?"

Hillel said, "I was not speaking of Noë. Aulus looked at the bright cold sky over Bethlehem on its hills and he saw a most remarkable sight. Among the stars was a star such as men have never seen before, brilliant and huge as a full moon and restless, turning and burning with a white fire, and moving as if with purpose."

"Your Aulus was indeed drunk, or he had observed what the astrologers call a nova—a new star. It is a phenomenon not unusual."

"Stars do not destroy themselves in one burst of flame in a twinkling," said Hillel, with a light flush on his fair cheek at this dismissal of his exciting story. "And if a nova appears, it is at least visible on successive nights for a considerable time. It is true that the star endured for a number of days, and then disappeared, but not in a fading or diminishing. It ended abruptly as if its mission was accomplished. For, you see, my dear old friend, it ceased its movements on that first night and remained suspended like a mighty cluster of great stars over a certain spot. It remained fixed, vivid and unchanging, at rest, until it disappeared as quickly as it had appeared. I heard that the light of it was so powerful and intense that it cast shadows as defined as full moonlight on the earth, and occasioned much awe and fear in the surrounding country."

"I, too," said the guest, shrugging, "have relatives in

Jerusalem, and they did not see this astonishing star."

"It was midnight, or later," said Hillel, "and how many are there now among men who lift their eyes from the world and consider the stars?"

"True," said the guest.

"Aulus was convinced that a great hero had been born," said Hillel, "a great warrior, though he doubted that this had occurred in Bethlehem, a poor little farming and market town. Hannah, on being told of this by her husband, declared it heralded the birth of their son."

The guest raised exasperated eyes to the ornate ceiling of the dining room, and groaned, "The fantasies of women! Now your revered young cousin will declare she gave birth to the Messias!"

"No," said Hillel, still somewhat vexed, but smiling now. "Hannah is not so vainglorious, and she has also known a man. She is inclined to believe in a prophet though not in one of Aulus' heroes."

"There must have been several thousand infants born on that night in Jerusalem and Bethlehem," said the guest. "Who is the prophet, or the hero?"

Hillel stared at his folded hands, which he was resting on the white linen of the dining cloth. "I do not know," he murmured. "But when I received Hannah's letter a most mysterious joy seized me, an exaltation, and this I do not understand. It was as if an angel had touched me."

The guest chortled rustily and shook his head. "I have heard from your father and your grandfather, Hillel ben Borush, that you were always a mystical boy, and that you implored to be introduced to the hidden wisdom of the Kabalah. It is my opinion that this was a mistake, and I trust you will forgive me. It is only the calm and detached mind which should be introduced to the Kabalah, the cold if thoughtful mind, and perhaps even the skeptical, but of a certainty not the emotional and susceptible."

Hillel had been angered at this dryly amused dismissal of his story and so had changed the subject. He had also felt foolish and demeaned. He spoke of it no longer to anyone. But he thought frequently of the star. Some fear, some reticence, had prevented him from writing others in Jerusalem about the star, notably his relatives, for he did not wish to be disillusioned. This also surprised him, for he was a man who deplored illusions in others and had a gentle disdain for them.

But it had been prophesied ages ago that the Messias, of the House of David, Himself, would be born in Bethlehem. However, if this were so, why had there been no shouting angels, no universal trumpets of the heavens, when that star had appeared, and why had not the world been swept up in rejoicing splendor? The Messias should surely not be born in obscurity, for His throne was on holy Sion, as the prophecies related, and He would not be born as the least of men, the Kings of Kings. Too, several years had passed, and there had been no other sign.

Still, Hillel could not forget the star, though he often wondered at the convulsion of emotion which had seized his heart on reading Hannah's letter. Even to this very evening in his garden the surge of mysterious rapture was as fresh and urgent as ever. It may all have been but a delusion, the fantasy of drunken men in a Roman tower who had observed it, or a wife's ardent desire that her first-born son be duly recorded by Heaven. But still, his stubborn and devoted heart denied all this, and he did not know why. Perhaps, he thought, an illusion which affirms joy is better than a reality which denies it, or perhaps the presence of joy attests to its verity.

As Hillel stood in his garden tonight he heard a sudden loud cry, and he started. The cry broke the smiling silence like an abrupt command, sharp and authoritative. It was not for a few moments that he realized that it was the voice of his little son, passing in the arms of a nursemaid through the colonnade. Still, he was shaken. The infant's voice had reminded him of his own father, imperious and uncompromising and firm, even didactic, impervious to doubt, scornful of hesitation. It was absurd, he thought, as the silence was resumed. A mere suckling—and the formidable old man who had ruled his household with the mere power of his appalling voice! For one moment Hillel contemplated the thought that his father had been reincarnated in infant Saul, and then he chuckled. How delightful it would be to smack the buttocks of a soul which had terrorized wife and sons and daughters in its former life! Perhaps, in a measure, that would be justice. He returned to his prayers, and now even the noisy birds were still. He repeated the words of David, with deep longing and reverent joy:

"Oh God, You are my God! Early will I seek You, my soul thirsts for You, my flesh longs for You in a dry and thirsty land, where no water is. To see Your power and Your glory, as I have seen You in the sanctuary! Because Your lovingkindness is better than life, my lips will praise You, and thus will I bless You while I live. I will lift up my hands in Your Name!"

He looked now at the fanged mountain shapes far beyond the valley, the fantastic monuments which acute imagination could distort into the likenesses of monsters, of lurking dragons, of bastions and towers and spires and temples, of pediments and columns standing alone, of twisted arches and carved walls—all hewn of scarlet stone seemingly burning in direful fire against a sky of the most intense incandescent blue. The setting sun thrust them into frightful relief so that they appeared to be marching on the rich valley land in menace and terror, striking the river Cydnus into the semblance of a wide highway of flame. Hillel had seen this a thousand times or more, but it never failed to fill him with a premonition, an amorphous fear, a heavy melancholy of soul.

Now he heard Deborah chattering with her female Greek and Roman friends, and her voice was vivacious and trilling, the voice of a happy and complacent child. He shook his head a little as if in reproof, but in some way that trivial and lighthearted sound consoled him, and he knew not why he was consoled. He looked below the mountains now and saw Tarsus on the blazing river, a city of broken golden fragments struck with crimson. He had not been born in that city, but had come to it as a child with his parents. Yet he loved it as he did not love Jerusalem, the desecrated, the alien, the lost, the land not only occupied by military conquerors but, worse still, occupied by sons who had destroyed the heart of the holy city out of wantonness and casual cynicism and faithlessness and abandon. When a city was poor it was occupied by faith and industry and hope. When it became rich and affluent evil entered, and the city was lost.

"How have I mourned thee, Jerusalem," Hillel murmured and entered his house with his head bent and his sadness on him again.

"I assured you, Deborah," a young Roman matron was saying to her hostess in the calm of the brilliant evening, "that the medal from Delphi would cause you to conceive a son."

"I wear it next to my heart," said Deborah bas Shebua. She hesitated. "Still, he could have been of a more comely countenance."

Chapter 2

HILLEL BEN BORUSH, was entertaining guests at dinner. There was his old severe and Pharisee friend, Rabbi Isaac ben Ezekiel, and his brother-in-law, brother of Deborah, the luxurious gentleman and aristocrat from Jerusalem, David ben Shebua. At the foot of the long golden-draped table sat Deborah, the modern woman who would not be confined to the women's quarters in spite of Rabbi Isaac's overt disapproval—she thought him a dull somewhat dirty old man—and young Saul's tutor, the Greek Aristo, and Saul, himself, now five years old. She knew that her presence, the pagan Greek's presence, and even the presence of the child, were resented, deplored and despised by the old rabbi, and this gave her a sensation of childish malice and amusement. As for Aristo, he was a Greek of discernment, for all he was a freedman, and he appreciated her qualities of mind and her sensibility to Greek poetry and her knowledge of the arts and sciences.

The sun was setting, the dreadful and distorted fanged mountains rearing in scarlet beyond the open doors and windows of the dining room, the peacocks were screeching, and the hot air was heavy with the scent of flowers and dust and heated stone. Deborah could hear the newly loud pattering of the fountains, the mutter of stirring trees. She could see the green of lush grass beyond the portico, the dark pointed towers of cypresses and the purple blossoms of the myrtles. She was proud and content. Her house might not be the largest in this suburb, or the most splendid, but it was a work of art and taste. The dining room was spacious and square, of splendid proportions, with a floor of yellow and black marble squares, like gold and ebony, the murals on the white walls were excellent if a little "extreme" in Hillel's conservative opinion, and the plastered ceiling was decorated in rosettes of gold and deep blue. The furniture, the chests and screens and tables and chairs, had been fashioned in the Eastern manner to be consistent with the environment, and were of lemonwood and dark ebony and teak, elaborately carved and inlaid. Here and there were scattered bright Persian rugs of intricate pattern and delicate hue. A fresh breeze moved through the pillars of the portico and brought with it a pure country aroma. Now the bells of "heathen" temples dedicated to Serapis, Juno, Aphrodite and all the gods and goddesses of the Roman, Greek and Oriental pantheon, began to ring softly over the land, striving with each other for harmonious notes, blending together to create a background of sweet and nostalgic sound. Deborah sighed happily. Her pretty face was suffused with a glow of combined innocence and complacent pride—and stupidity—and Hillel glanced down the long table at her and loved her anew, and wondered, as he often wondered, why she did not bore him to death.

Deborah's brother, David, was, in Hillel's opinion—which could be very acerbic at times—effete, ridiculous, pretentious and a parody of elegance. He was four years older than Deborah, and married to a Roman girl of a great house, and he lived more in Rome than he did in Jerusalem, and called himself "an emancipated Jew, the new Jew." He was an intimate friend of Herod, himself, and a familiar at the court, and very rich. He had fine manners and graces, and was handsome, of Deborah's auburn and blue coloring of hair and eyes, and beardless, of course, and fair of complexion with a Greek nose of which he was tediously proud, and a cleft white chin, and his figure was another source of his pride, for he was tall and slender. He was also too fastidious, in Hillel's conviction, and scented like a woman, and wore many rings on his long and delicate hands. A complicated and detailed Egyptian necklace, fringed and jeweled, hung about his neck and lay on his chest. Gemmed bracelets clasped his upper arms, and a jeweled earring sparkled in one ear, and his toga was of the whitest and most shimmering silk bordered with gold, and his sandals glittered. Hillel always tried to despise him as a decayed traitor to his race and his God, but David was so charming, so amusing, so smiling, and even so erudite, that Hillel invariably and helplessly was seduced into fondness for him on his infrequent visits to this house. David, certainly, was a Sadducee and therefore even worse than an uninformed heathen, but he was a scholar, equally at home in discussing the Torah, Philo, Euripides, Sophocles, Virgil and Homer, the latest scandals from Rome and Jerusalem and Alexandria and Athens, politics, poetry, the sciences, the stock market and banking, the state of the drachma and sesterce, the newest favorite of Caesar Augustus, the Augustales of Rome, rumors from the Palatine, architecture, archaeology, trade, commerce, and religion in all its forms, not to mention the latest fashions in living, clothing, dining and amusement.

Once or twice, in sheer exasperation at so much sweetness and light and urbanity and composure and politeness, Hillel, the mildest of men, had attempted to provoke David into a temper or a sharp reply or a contemptuous gesture, but David never defected from his pose—if it were a pose—of a totally civilized man. He would never, Hillel would think with some unkindness, impose himself on his wife if she were unwilling, or quarrel in a vulgar way with a tradesman, or dispute with a stockbroker, or pick his nose, or rub his anus, though he had no objection to a naughty story and could hint of unspeakable vilenesses of conduct of friends and acquaintances.

Reb Isaac, the old Pharisee friend, sat munching morosely at Hillel's right hand this evening, casting dark looks alternately at Deborah, who did not flinch but loftily ignored him, and darker looks at the perfumed David. He would flap his hand when David spoke in his musical and cultured accents—in Greek, of course—as if waving away a cloud of inconsequential gnats, and he would make rude sounds as he chewed, and would gurgle as he drank the wine. (A veritable pig, thought Deborah, without charity.) Only when Hillel spoke did the rabbi give any attentiveness to the table, and stop stuffing his mouth with large portions of bread or examining each dish with intense suspicion as if it were poisoned or unfit for the pure intestines of a pious Jew. He was bent and gnarled, though curiously fat and shaped like a turnip, and had a long black beard without a sign of whiteness in spite of his age, and his expression was black and fierce as were his eyes, and his nose was deplorably huge and predatory, resembling a Phoenician's. His clothing was of the coarsest linen, and of a dull dark brown, and Deborah was certain that he smelled rankly, which was not true. He was rich and learned, and feared in the Temple, and was often in Jerusalem, and spoke of himself as the poorest and humblest of men, and was arrogant, opinionated and intolerant, though very eloquent and wise when it pleased him. He was also what David called a "heresy-hunter," and devoted ferociously to the Law and the Book, and therefore an anachronism in these enlightened days. Deborah loathed him.

It enraged her to learn from her husband that Reb Isaac would not only instruct young Saul in the proper pious studies of a Pharisaical Jew—he was already instructing the lad—but would be Saul's mentor and would choose his menial trade. He was a weaver of goat's hair. Surely, Deborah would protest with tears, even a Septuagint Jew no longer believed that all Jews must not only be learned but must embrace a humble trade involving the hands and sweaty labor, no matter how rich and distinguished of family. It was ridiculous. Did Hillel, himself, now practice his trade of cabinetmaking? It was true that it pleased him to carve a small chest on occasion, or a chair for the nursery, or a little table, but did he pursue it sedulously, as the Law demanded? No, indeed. "One never knows," Hillel would say mysteriously, but he never explained what one might never know. It was infuriating.

Tonight Deborah was happy. David was her favorite brother. She was vexed that Hillel, when David was a guest, invariably invited that obnoxious old Pharisee to his table. She did not know that Hillel found both Reb Isaac and David abrasive to his temperament, and that he found himself irritably honed by them and relieved from his own amity by annoyance. (Sometimes he wondered what it would be like to be a Roman, to be filled with materialistic certitude and no doubts, and to tread the ground firmly and not to discover questions in the earth.) Between the two stones of Reb Isaac and David ben Shebua, he sometimes felt the rough grinding of an elusive answer which, he reasoned—he was always reasoning—

might not be an answer at all but only his abraded sensibilities become tender and sensitive and skinless.

He looked down the table at his son, little Saul, five years old, sitting silently beside his mother. He smiled affectionately at the child, but Saul was listening to David with that strange intentness of his, which was most unchildlike. Surely not a handsome lad, but curiously dominating for all his short stature, his breadth of chest and shoulder, his muscular arms and the strong bowed legs. His eyes had become more strenuous and alive as he grew, and they resembled cold but brilliant blue enamel over iron. His audaciously red hair was cut in the short Roman fashion, like a soldier's, and his big pink ears flared out from his round and virile skull. Deborah might deplore his Phoenician nose, and hint of wantonings in Hillel's impeccable family in the far past—which was probable, Hillel would admit—but Hillel found that nose comfortingly manly and assured and positive, and he did not know why that should comfort him. He liked the boy's hands, too, square and brown, with short square nails, and the brown sturdy throat and the deep rose on the broad cheekbones and the scattering of freckles on the low and pugnacious brow. Hillel was not sure about Saul's mouth, wide and thin and mobile. It hinted of argumentation and obstinacy. All in all, the boy had a fierce and concentrated aura about him, a fierce quick way of turning his head, a rancor of temperament, which, Hillel reflected, would procure him more enemies than friends in the future.

Hillel recalled his daughter, Sephorah—whom Deborah had wished to name Flavia or Daphne or Iris and not some offensive Jewish name. (Hillel had threatened her with Leah or Sarah or Rebecca or Miriam and so had quieted her. Sephorah was at least not unmusical.) Hillel thought of his little daughter, now almost four years, with fond passion: A beautiful golden child, with golden eyes, and affectionate manners and a humorous dimple in her cheek. She laughed at Saul and teased him. Saul, who rarely tolerated anyone, including his parents, tolerated Sephorah and played with her during the rare intervals of his leisure, and reprimanded her, but could never reduce her to tears. She mocked him. Sephorah was not at this table, but in her nursery. Deborah delighted in

her beauty, and wondered at the large golden eyes, and
curled the child's yellow hair and smeared her delicate
complexion with cosmetics against the sun, and debated
earnestly with her on the correct costumes to be worn at
certain hours of the day, and taught her to sing. It was
one of Hillel's few joys to listen to the young voices at
evening singing, first some grave song of David's, and
then the newest light song which Hillel suspected came
from the noisy gutters of Tarsus, carefully rendered innocent. Hillel did not know who was the more childish
and naïve, his wife or his daughter. At scarcely four,
Sephorah would sometimes look at her mother with sudden seriousness, her gilded eyelashes rapidly blinking, and
once Hillel was positive that the little one was pitying
Deborah.

Saul, naturally, wore the white Roman tunic of pre-
adolescence bordered with purple, on which Deborah insisted. "We are citizens of the Roman world," Deborah
said. "We are citizens of the Kingdom of God," Hillel
said. Deborah thought this absurd. There was but one
world, dreamed of by the ancients, ruled by peace and
law, and therefore secure. "Ruled by the Roman short-
sword," Hillel would say, with rare bitterness. But to
Deborah it was a safe world for her family, and that was
all that was important. It did not harm, though she did
this secretly for fear of Hillel, to make a quiet sacrifice in
the temple of Juno, the mother of the gods and men. Juno
was an exemplary mother.

Reb Isaac always insisted that he desired and could
relish "only the simplest of foods" when visiting friends,
but it was well known that his wife, Leah, was a miraculous cook and had due regard for her husband's discriminating stomach and supervised the kitchen. No one
knew what Leah thought of her husband, but she had
humor and her table was popular with Greek and Roman
and Jew alike, and so all forgave Reb Isaac's hypocrisy.
But Deborah literally believed that he was a man of
simple and austere appetite and so, when he was a guest
at her husband's table she invariably ordered the plainest
of food. This delighted Hillel, who could be guilty of a
gentle malice. So tonight there was only a broiled river
fish unadorned by herbs, a cold boiled lamb saddle, some
stewed artichokes innocent of oil and garlic and vinegar, a

lank cabbage, cold bread, wilted fruit and cheap cheese and a most ordinary wine.

As for David—the little pucker between his brows testified to his pain, and in this, too, Hillel felt some naughty satisfaction. He did not know which was the more offensive, the effeminate delicacy of David ben Shebua or the grim hypocrisy of Reb Isaac, but it pleased him that both were being punished even while he deplored his own human malevolence.

It was the conviction of Reb Isaac that Hillel ben Borush while an estimable Jew of considerable piety and faith, and a Pharisee, had not that dedication to the Book desirable in one of his birth and education in the Scriptures, and therefore not entirely without worldliness and triviality. He suspected Hillel of some timidity in this modern society of materialism and brute force and atheism and cynical expediency and the disregard of the individual, not to mention the lascivious and unspeakable Roman conquerors of the world who were at once mighty and barbaric, and the corrupt Greek and his hedonist philosophies, who had—no doubt to the wrath of the Creator, blessed be His Name—invaded the very heart of Holy Israel with his mores and his manners. He thought Hillel one of those gentle souls who preferred peace to controversy, and complaisance to struggle.

On the other hand, David ben Shebua was convinced that Hillel was, in spite of his amiability and wit and kindness, a harsh Pharisee at heart, ready to denounce and direct the stoning of any heretic, with the sure knowledge that he had the approval of his God.

David was no more correct in his assumptions concerning Hillel than was Reb Isaac.

Once he had said to his sister after one of these deplorable dinners, "Why is it that my esteemed brother-in-law invariably invites that miasmic old rabbi to my first dinner in his house?"

Deborah, who was always more vexed than pleased with her husband, said, not out of any intellectual perception but out of deep female intuitiveness and petulance, "It is to annoy you both."

As David tried to converse tonight in a civilized fashion with Reb Isaac it was like tossing pretty feathers against a battering ram. Reb Isaac despised him. David continued to converse, and watched Hillel out of the corner of his eye. Hillel was enjoying himself, as he lightly partook of the atrocious dinner.

Aristo with his pupil, Saul, at the foot of the table, was addressed by no other one, not even the disdainful slaves, for he was only a freedman, but he thought himself the superior of any at the table, for he was an Athenian and brilliantly educated. His clever black eyes, small and restless as beetles, moved from one face to another, and he listened, and he smiled in himself. Only he believed that Hillel ben Borush was the only intellectual man present, and he had the greatest respect for his master, and a sort of humorous love. In two years he would be free, Hillel had told him, according to the Jewish law which demanded that a slave be loosed after seven years of servitude. Aristo had considered this with disquiet, and had consulted with Hillel. "I am free, Master," he said, "in two years. Where, thence, shall I go?"

Hillel had reflected, with sympathy. A freed slave was open to all the vicissitudes of the free. It was evil enough to be born a freeman and to face all the wicked contingencies of life, responsible for one's actions to God and man, responsible even for one's thoughts. (But then, did that not make man almost equal to the angels?) How much worse it was to have been sheltered and fed all one's life, accountable to no other but to one master, and then to be thrown out into the icy regions where one was accountable to all! So Hillel had said, "You were purchased for my son, and according to the Law you must be free in two more years. But, will you desert us? Are you not needful, in this world of multiple peoples and philosophies, to continue to teach my son when he is of an age? Therefore, before the time is ended, we will visit the praetor together, and you shall be free as soon as possible, and henceforth you will receive a monthly payment on which we shall mutually agree, and you will be an honored member of the household."

So Aristo had become a freedman with a handsome salary, and he was, at this time, purchasing some juicy olive groves for the day when he would be old. But he never forgot that on the moment the Roman praetor had declared his freedom Hillel had looked at him with the soft sorrow of a brother, and had vaguely shaken his head. Later Hillel had said to him, "It is a fearful thing to be free before the Face of God, for the Lord, blessed be His Name, mercilessly demands all things of the free, but is merciful to the enslaved and asks nothing." He added, "God is very whimsical. But do not the Greeks declare that also?"

Aristo sometimes watched Hillel ben Borush at his prayers in the garden and he would wonder. How stern and terrible was the God of Israel! He often discussed the gods of Greece with his master, discoursing on their grace, laughter, gaiety, merriment, feasts and foibles, and their elegant adulteries, and their blithe and capricious interference in the affairs of men. Once Hillel had said, "To each people God manifests Himself in a unique form— though with this thought of mine you will not find agreement among the majority of devoted believers. He is protean. As the prophets have greatly tried to teach us, but to no avail, alas, God is a Spirit, without form and without body, omnipresent, omniscient, circumambient, in all things which live. He presents one Face to one man, and a different Face to another. We need but say, all men together, that the Lord our God, the Lord is One, though His manifestations are multitudinous and myriad, and who are we to declare, with anger and certitude, that only our pale vision is correct?"

"The Unknown God," Aristo had replied. "We Greeks speak of Him."

"Forever unknown," Hillel had answered, with a peculiar sadness. "Yet—" He hesitated, and did not continue. But suddenly his heart had lifted as a leaf lifts and he experienced, momentarily, that strange wind of ecstasy he had infrequently known from childhood. Had it come to him first when he had been told of the Messias?

"No," David ben Shebua was saying tolerantly to Reb Isaac, "I do not call myself a Stoic, but like Zeno I prefer the Cynic school, though he, certainly, formulated the Stoic philosophy. I prefer to call myself an Academic."

"Hah!" said Reb Isaac, squinting at him. He tore a piece of cold bread apart and stuffed it into his mouth and chewed noisily. (Where was the accursed baker of this house? The bread had a flat and insipid taste. The old man scowled.) He well understood that David was now baiting him as he had baited David, and he rose with some interior enjoyment to the battle. So, this smallness, this perfumed banality, thought him an ignorant man, did he? "You are not even an Academic. You are a nothingness, for you have no real opinions of your own but those you have stolen like flowers in the gardens of your masters. You have no learning of intensity and deepness, for you have denied and abandoned the roots from which you have sprung. You are like a bird with a slit tongue, which repeats all it incontinently hears and renders it again, without comprehension. You are not a Greek, with serpentine philosophies, or a Roman with brutish hubris, and you are not a Jew with a knowledge of God and of man. What are you, then?"

He shook his finger at David and leaned over the table toward him and his black eyes glittered. David flushed with humiliation.

"You are the betrayer of Israel," said Reb Isaac. "But, are you a Greek, you man who is not a Jew? Or a Roman, an Egyptian, a Briton, a Gaul, a Scythian, a Vandal, a Syrian, or any other heathen? You will tell me that you are a Roman citizen. But that does not say what a man *is,* himself, in his heart and his soul. He is more than his house, or even his name. He is, surely, more than his wealth or his learning. But, David ben Shebua, can you tell me what *you* are?"

David had turned very pale. A thin shaft of brilliant sunshine illuminated the side of his face and for the first time Hillel saw that his profile was classic Greek in the short curled upper lip, the round full chin, the marble contour of cheek, and that his coloring enhanced the resemblance. He was suddenly ashamed, and for the first time, that his brother-in-law had been so insulted in his house.

David was gazing at the old man and deep in his blue eyes something like a spark was rising. But before he could speak Reb Isaac continued in his harsh and cawing voice: "My sorrow is with you, David ben Shebua, for the sin is on your father's head and not on yours. When a man robs his son of his heritage, out of exigency or conceit or vanity or eagerness to be as others, he has done a fearful thing. He has taken certitude from his son, his identity in the nameless mob, the integrity of his soul, his joy in what he is and to what he has been born. He has taken pride from him, and without pride a man is less than a man. Do the Greeks accept you as a Greek, the Romans as a Roman? You cannot rejoice in the name of Israel, for you have spurned her, as your father taught you, for some vague citizenship you call the world. The Roman world! It belongs only to Romans, and not to you, not the Greeks or any of the other abundant races which inhabit this earth. This they know, and have their own identity, which you have not."

True, thought Aristo. I was a slave, and am now only a freedman, but I am also a Greek with a glorious heritage behind me, and therefore I am a man above all other things.

Hillel said, circumventing the very pale David, "What a man chooses is his own, and because it is his own, however we may protest it, we must respect it also. There may be a deeper allegiance than nation, or even heritage, and it may be that David possesses it."

"You speak nonsense in your beard, and you know it is nonsense!" cried Reb Isaac, turning the black glitter of his eyes on his host. He swung his heavy shoulders under their rough robes of brown linen to David. "Tell me," he said in a loud and peremptory tone, "and I will listen and will weigh your words and not scorn them. Tell me, what is your allegiance?"

Then David said, "To peace." He stopped, astonished at his own words, and then his face vividly quickened as if he had come upon some truth unknown even to himself, which he had believed and had not known he had believed. "I do not speak of supine submission, not even to the Roman, though we must recognize that he rules the world and resistance is death, or worse. We must remember Pompey, in our recent history, and our Herods. Is it not said in the Scriptures that when the storm breaks the unbending tree is broken, but the bending grass lives for another day and another storm? Let me think a moment! I am a man of peace, and peace is not to be despised. I do not speak of the peace of the slave, but of the peace a man experiences when he accepts the inevitable, which he cannot move. He must make his peace with reality. That does not bring a loss of pride. Once possessed of that tranquillity, a man can again live with dignity and even find worthiness in life. He can rediscover thought. It is civilization at its highest, and I hope I am a civilized man."

Reb Isaac had listened with all the power of his mind and spirit. A strange expression began to move his blackly bearded face, and now there was comprehension on it, and pity as well as wrath. "It is a compromise," he said. "There are men who will not compromise out of principle or love of God, and will die for their fortitude. And there are men of another nature who must compromise. They have my compassion."

Hillel had been struck by David's words, and he said, "There is nothing wrong with compromise, if the choice is between the evil of accepting reality and the evil of fantasy. Reality, however repulsive, is truth. It is far more dangerous to insist on what is not real or attainable, than to resign one's self to what is."

Then he stared at Reb Isaac with that quiet and daunting look he could use on occasion and even the old man became silent. "Let us speak of other things," Hillel said, and there was that in his voice which rang like a hard command for all its mildness.

"Permit me," said David, in a voice of pleading, "and let me have a final moment. I have not expressed my heart, I fear. What is my deepest belief is that all men are the same, and whyfore, then, should we separate ourselves into nations and tribes and cultures?"

"For the reason," said Hillel ben Borush, "that men are not the same. God forbid! If that listless day ever arrives, then all richness shall disappear from the world and all variety. Men of like mind join together and create a culture, which adds to the color and the joy of life, and is a wonder and delight to others of different cultures. God has called to Israel to remain apart so that He will not be forgotten, blessed be His Name, and that His Laws shall have a pristine source to slacken the thirst of all men."

Reb Isaac said in a rueful tone, "We need not fear the disappearance of Israel. God will forever keep her poor and afflicted, so that she will not decay and die in affluence, as other nations die."

It was evident to Aristo that Hillel, the quiet and courtly, was now dominating the table, for even Deborah, so emptily staring at first one speaker and then the other, was impressed. However, the young Saul was eying his father with no favor. He was but a child, yet his intellect, as Aristo knew, was prodigious for his age, and he had unchildlike thoughts. Now his eyes, so metallic in tint and appearance, moved to Reb Isaac with respect. Aristo shook his head slightly.

Saul had caught the climate of the conversation tonight and many of its implications, for great was his intuition. He honored his father, for that was commanded, but even as a child he did not believe in his father's intellect, for never did Hillel forcefully offer or defend his opinions. To Saul that appeared lack of courage or conviction.

Hillel was saying with a sigh, "God, blessed be His Name, speaks in centuries, but man, alas, speaks only in hours. How, then, can we be reconciled? Man is to be pitied and not always denounced. I understand Job."

These Jews! thought Aristo. They cannot give their Deity a moment's peace or let Him retreat from their voices! No wonder He smites them regularly, in exasperation, as they are always complaining. Yet gods deserve solitude, far from the exigencies of men, and some repose of mind in the blissful depths of nothingness, freed for a space from importunate prayers or even praise.

"We share, with God, blessed be His Name, our immortality," said Reb Isaac, "so we, too, speak in centuries in our soul."

Aristo wanted to laugh. He glanced at David, who was moving his spoons restlessly, for he, as well as Reb Isaac, was annoyed at this meal. David was not interested in immortality; as a Sadducee he had no belief in it. It was not even academic to him.

He said, smiling his courteous smile, "The resurrection of the body, Reb Isaac, if I may interpose in this conversation, is not unique with the Jews as a doctrine. The Egyptians have believed it from the ages, long before there was an Israel, and so have the Babylonians. It is deeply engraved in all the religions with, perhaps, the exception of the Greeks and the Romans, who, however, believe in ghosts." He laughed softly.

"No one believes it as we believe it," said Reb Isaac, in his contentious voice.

David shrugged. "No man believes as another man believes, contrary to the Pharisees and all the prophets, Reb

Isaac." Now he barely covered his yawn. "It is probable that Hillel is quite correct: If all men believed the same it would be disastrous."

Reb Isaac, in his zeal and his intention not only to rescue Hillel from what seemed to be his lukewarmness but to prevent the contamination of a holy young mind— Saul's—became urgent again. "You sophisticated men make simple things complex, out of your own elaborate confusions. God is lucent and of a boundless clarity. When He says, blessed be His Name, 'I am the Lord your God,' He has said all that there is to say, all wisdom, all that any man or angel can dream of knowing. But you invent philosophies."

"Rabbi, we did not invent your endless and wearisome commentators," said David. "They are always reinterpreting God, or revising what He has said, to suit the occasion or to make an obscure point."

Excessively true, thought Hillel. Again, between the two grinding stones of Reb Isaac and David he thought he saw a flash of the incandescent flame of the truth, which neither of them knew in full. Nor did he, Hillel. He said, "God is simple. It is only man which is an obscure darkness."

Reb Isaac threw him an approving glance. But David said, "I feel that nothing is simple, and nothing obscure. Only thought makes it so, and often I am weary of thinking."

"And so lend yourself to Greek and Roman debauchery," said Reb Isaac. "You Sadducees, who are one with the Roman, the greedy taxgatherer, the oppressor, who are destroying my people, forcing them into despair and ruin and poverty, defacing the Holy Ark, tearing the veil of the Temple, scrawling your graffiti on the walls!"

His black eyes filled with tears as he thought of the degradation and slavery and hopelessness of his people and his nation and his religion, within the sacred walls of Jerusalem. His emotion caught everyone's attention, even Deborah's. Young Saul's eyes blazed with blue fire. "You laugh," said Reb Isaac, to David who was not laughing at all. "But God will not be mocked. He will send us His Messias, blessed be His Name, and all the evil of the world will be swept away like a black fog on a swamp, and the new morning will dawn." He spoke threateningly, waving a menacing finger at David.

"Amen," murmured Hillel. Then the memory of what he had been told of the great and awesome star over Bethlehem flashed into his mind. He hesitated, but there was a powerful impulse in him to speak. He bent toward David, who was negligently smiling at Reb Isaac.

He said, "David, I have long wished to ask you a question, for you live in Jerusalem, which is near the holy city where King David was born. I have a relative in Jerusalem, who is married to a Roman, Aulus, a young centurion. He wrote me some years ago, or did his wife, that on one winter night he observed a magnificent and fearful moving star over Bethlehem—" He paused, for Reb Isaac was regarding him with an impatient eye, for it had been he who had mocked the story of Aulus.

"And the Roman thought it was an omen that his son, newly born that night, had evoked a manifestation from their heathen deities," said Reb Isaac.

But Hillel was looking at David earnestly. He expected David to smile, to wave a graceful hand. But David appeared thoughtful.

"I saw it myself," he said. "And many others also saw it." He bent his handsome head and appeared to be considering. Then he shrugged. "But a burning meteor, as the astrologists reported, or a nova. It was a glorious sight. It lit up the far and winter hills of Bethlehem like a consuming moon. It shone steadfastly, for a few nights, and then it was gone. Like all nova, it had a brief light, a brief endurance. But while it remained it was beyond description, pure and white, fervent, turning, as if on a great axis. We gathered on the rooftops to watch it. Some of the superstitious thought it an enormous comet, about to destroy us. Some said the candles and torches in the Temple flared with a vaster illumination while the star hovered over Bethlehem. Some declared they heard celestial voices—" David shrugged again. "It was beautiful. But it was nothing."

"And no one from Jerusalem went to Bethlehem—to see?" said Hillel. Reb Isaac was silently scoffing, leaning back in his chair, smiling in his beard and flapping his hand. "No one at all cared to investigate, to know?"

David considered again. "One did," he replied, and gave his light shrug.

Hillel did not know why his heart rose again as if on wings, but he cried, "Who?"

His voice, unusually vibrant and intense, drew even young Saul's eyes to him in wonderment. His face was full of passion, of hope even he could not fathom or understand, of breathlessness. David's auburn eyebrows rose in astonishment at this unprecedented display of emotion in his brother-in-law, who was always so temperate.

"A young man, Joseph of Arimathaea, whom you do not know," said David, in a soothing voice, as if fearful that all that inexplicable ardor might be dangerous. "He is my friend, of my age, an honorable councilor, who has," David coughed, "admittedly been waiting for the Kingdom of God. He is also a member of the Sanhedrin, for all his youth, for he is esteemed for his wisdom, and the wisdom of his father. He is very pious, but also sophisticated, and a student. In many eyes he has a much greater virtue: He is extremely rich." David paused and again studied Hillel with curiosity.

"And, he followed the star?" asked Hillel.

"There was no need to follow it. It was there, over Bethlehem. Joseph went with an entourage. But once in an inn—I must mention that the inn was crowded to the eaves, and even the stables, because Caesar Augustus had ordered a census and the people of Galilee were there to be counted—Joseph left his servants and proceeded a little space on foot. It was reported to one of my servants by one of Joseph's, that Joseph carried a small golden casket in his hands, a precious object, and that when he returned at midnight the casket was no longer with him and never was it seen again."

"That is all?" asked Hillel, when David remained silent.

"That is all. What more can there be? I recall that I asked Joseph what he had found in Bethlehem, but he only smiled. He is a man of few words."

"A foolish story," said Reb Isaac. "Your friend is very mysterious. Had the messenger from God been born that night, there would have been the sound of trumpets and the heavens would have blazed from zenith to zenith, calling all men to worship and to pray. The holy hill of Sion would have burned like the sun and the Roman would have been consumed instantly. Israel would have been raised up to the skies, a coronet of glory, all walls turned to gold, her battlements adorned with angels. The Messianic age of peace, joy, life and majesty would have arrived, and all men would have known it, would have known of the birth of the Holy One to a princess of Israel. Not a nation but would have heard the tidings. Not a sea but would have flamed in exultation. And He, blessed is His Name, would have been exalted and His Presence proclaimed from all the corners of the earth."

"True," said David ben Shebua. "For so it has been prophesied."

Hillel bent his head and pressed his hands together in prolonged thought. Then he said, slowly and quietly, "You have forgotten the prophecies of Isaias concerning the Messias, and His coming: 'Who has believed our report? And to whom is the arm of the Lord revealed? And He shall grow up as a tender plant before Him, and as a root out of a thirsty ground. There is no beauty in Him, nor comeliness, and we have seen Him and there was no sightliness that we should be desirous of Him. Despised and the most abject of men, a man of sorrows and acquainted with infirmity, and His look was as if it were hidden and despised, whereupon we esteemed Him not.'"

Hillel raised his eyes and looked at them. "Does that sound, from the words of Isaias, that the Messias will come in glory and splendor and all will know Him, from the ends of the earth? No! It would seem that He will come obscurely and few will know Him, and He will be rejected, the humblest of men, unproclaimed, unheralded, like a thief in the night, with no panoply, no choirs of seraphim. And who has said that He will be born of a princess of Israel?"

"The Holy One of Israel will not come unheralded!" cried Reb Isaac. "How then, would the world know, or the world heed Him? He would live as obscurely as He had been born, and I assure you, Hillel ben Borush, that He has not been born! For, has not the Lord, blessed be His Name, surely said that His Redeemer will wear government upon His shoulder, and that of His glory there would be no end? To be born as Isaias appears to you to have prophesied, would be to live and die in futility, and to be unknown to all men."

"Then, of Whom was Isaias speaking?" asked Hillel.

"I do not possess all wisdom," said Reb Isaac in a voice that disagreed with his words. "Possibly Isaias was referring to the birth of some obscure prophet. Let me speak of what he says concerning the birth of the Messias: 'For a child is born to us, and a Son is given, and the government shall be upon His shoulder, and His name shall be called Wonderful, Counselor, God the Mighty, the Father of the world to come, the Prince of Peace! His empire shall be multiplied and there shall be no end of peace. He shall sit upon the throne of David, and of His kingdom, to establish it and strengthen it with judgment and with justice, from henceforth and forever.'

"Hillel ben Borush, does that prophecy, then, not speak of the grandeur of the coming of the Messias, and that all men will know Him?"

"It is possible that they will not know Him when He first appears to them," said Hillel, and now his heart became heavy with doubt and melancholy. "I see no contradiction in the two prophecies."

Reb Isaac lifted his eyes to the ceiling of the room as if calling on the Almighty for patience. Then he said, "The sun is setting. It is time for our prayers."

Young Saul had been listening to all this and there was now a deep glow in his extraordinary eyes which Aristo deplored in his heart, for he suspected zealousness and saw that the child's whole attention had been upon Reb Isaac and not on his father. He, himself, had listened to these Hebraic controversies with boredom. Why could not the Jews be of ease and accept the birth of gods as the Greeks accepted them, and with thoughts of grace and lust and laughter, and not with proclamations of world government and castrated angels and judgments and justice and all the other dreary fantasies of gloomy men?

What the Jews needed, surely, was some of the arête of the Greeks and less of the formidable gloom of their bearded prophets and wise men. They needed lightness and joy.

Deborah had silently retired. Reb Isaac, a dark and heavy figure, was leading the way to the gardens, walking with a resounding step between the beaming white columns, and Hillel was following him and Saul in turn followed his father. Prayer shawls had appeared, apparently from the air. Aristo was alone with David ben Shebua. The Greek, as a freedman, waited for the other to speak, for David was looking at him gravely. Then David smiled and gestured slightly and went to a distant door and opened it and closed it behind him. At the final moment a daggar of sun had lit up his one jeweled earring and for some reason Aristo thought it pathetic.

Aristo went into the portico and half stood behind a pillar, to observe. The gardens were lambent with mingled gold and scarlet light, and there was an illuminated mist caught in the branches of the trees, and the palms rattled softly in the evening wind. Beyond, started those incredible red mountains, but now the sky was coldly green behind them and in that greenness stood one single star. In the east a crescent moon revealed itself faintly, like a woman's pared fingernail painted with pearl. Birds held their own colloquy, but Aristo doubted that they were singing their evening prayers as young Saul had once asserted. Yet, it was a pretty thought, and poesy should be encouraged in the young.

Saul followed the prayers of his father and Reb Isaac, raising his resolute boy's voice in response. It seemed to him that a vast crystal trumpet had lifted itself to the listening heavens, sparkling in immensity, all its facets charged with a blinding light, and from it came sonorous sound as if the earth and men had come together in one Hosannah of towering music, in salutation, in praise, in thanksgiving.

Chapter 3

"I DO NOT understand this matter of alms and charity," said Aristo the Greek to Saul. "Certainly, Socrates recommended it but it was an astonishing thought to his countrymen and was hardly taken with seriousness. We Greeks understand justice. Aristotle loved the square, for it to him represented perfect justice, equal and balanced with all other sides." Aristo chuckled. "The Romans love dice, too, but for an entirely different reason, and they are no philosophers.

"But let us consider alms. Mercy, though you Jews do not credit it, was not invented by you. We highly approve of mercy. I can quote you a dozen of our philosophers who esteemed it. But reckless alms, or even prudent ones, as a duty, is not to be understood. Yesterday, you gave your last drachma to a beggar near the gate of the synagogue, and he was repulsive to the eye and distinctly offensive to the nose. You gave it, I observed, with no open sadness and sympathy."

"I have told you before," said Saul, with all the exasperation of a youth of fourteen years. "We are commanded to give alms, and tithes. It is a holy command. It is indeed a duty. What if the object of our charity, our alms, is repulsive, perhaps even detestable? That is not to influence us."

"In short," said Aristo, "you give because it is a command of your God, and not because you feel sorrow for the object of your alms?"

Saul's red thick eyebrows drew together in a scowl. Aristo had the vexing ability to drive home a point, like a cunning nettle's sting. The youth hesitated. "I know my father gives with pity, and Reb Isaac with a blessing. If I feel no response to the beggar, it is my hardness of heart, or my youth which time will repair. In the meanwhile I obey. But that you would not comprehend, my teacher."

Aristo considered and slowly shook his head. "It has not occurred to you, of course, that charity can destroy the receiver? If a man knew he could not beg bread and a copper for wine, he would work for it, would he not?"

"That, too, is of no importance."

"You give because it endows you with a feeling of virtue?"

Saul almost shouted with his exasperation. "You refuse to understand!"

"I am only interested." Aristo grinned, his lively lips spreading almost from ear to ear. "You know, of course, that in Rome, in the middle of their abominable Tiber, there is an island with a hospital upon it, for slaves and the very poor who cannot afford a physician. You know, of course, that we Greeks have hostels for the homeless and the sick, and that our great medical university in Alexandria cares for thousands every year. But it is not guilt which inspires us to aid the infirm and the despairing." He laughed a little.

"Guilt?" cried Saul.

"Have you not told me so on many occasions, Saul ben Hillel?"

"Again you do not understand." Saul's eyes were snapping with angry blue fire. "You have the capacity to infuriate me, Aristo, and you do it with calculated deliberateness. Yet I have explained over and over. The guilt refers to our fallen race, to Adam and Eve—"

Aristo nodded. "We, too, have such a story. But it refers to the Flood, which is an historical event. One perfect couple survived. But they did not breed another race from their own bodies. The gods, taking pity on their lonely state, and listening to their prayers, told them to walk from the remaining little temple and throw stones after them. From those stones were born the Titans, and men. We, their descendants, if you believe the interesting tale, feel no guilt that we were born of stone, and that we are not of the race that perished except for that one perfect couple, whose descendants we are not."

Saul waved his hand in rough dismissal of the story. "That is only a myth. I am referring to the fact that humanity is a fallen race, without merit, through our sins, and our disobedience from the beginning. That is our guilt, and only God, blessed be His Name, can erase it and lift us from the pit of it."

"A gloomy story," said Aristo. "Why should a man feel guilt because of the sin of his ancestors, if the story be true, which I doubt? If he is fallen, who awoke him to life, and is not the Awakener guilty if the man is guilty? Does a man ask to be born into this world? Your God seems to me perverse, the Creator of evil—if man is evil —which I deny with some reservations. Your God would seem to me to curse all mankind for a sin committed by others, which would make Him less endowed with mercy than the meanest of His creatures. A vengeful Deity, and I do not approve of Him."

Saul said, " 'What is man that Thou art mindful of him, and the son of man that Thou visiteth him?' We are nothing. God has created us that we may be worthy of

His love and His salvation, which He has promised us through the ages by the merits of His Messias, and no merit of our own. We do not understand each other's semantics, Aristo, because we do not speak from the same frame of reference."

"True," said the Greek. "No man speaks with another man's semantics, and meanings, for each man's history is uniquely his alone and he endows words from his own life's experience, which can be no other man's. Yet, Socrates asked us to 'define our terms,' and much as I revere Socrates I feel he was either jesting or guilty of a stupidity. My terms are not yours, and never can they be."

"You deny absolutes."

"So does any sensible man. Yes, I know Aristotle spoke of absolutes, but he meant the only absolute, which is God. I have told you of our altars to the Unknown God, above all other Gods. But let us return to the subject of charity, of alms.

"I have heard an old story. A gentle-hearted sage of some substance was riding on his ass to the marketplace, where he would continue his study of mankind. On the road he was accosted by a beggar, who asked for a single coin to buy bread. The sage was much moved by the man's misery, and so he emptied his whole purse into the beggar's hand. Whereupon the beggar, recovering from his astonishment, remarked on the warmth of the sage's cloak. The sage removed it and placed it about the beggar's shoulders. The beggar then quickened to the subject, perceiving he had come upon either an unworldly man or a fool. He admired the girdle of the sage and its gorgeous Alexandrine dagger, and so he acquired both. Then came the sage's boots, lined with wool, and he was soon sitting in the dust avidly putting them on his bare legs and feet.

"Rising, he complained to the sage that he was far from the city and he was desirous of visiting a tavern there where he could spend the alms on food and reviving wine. The sage hesitated then, but recalling that he had a good house in an olive grove and that he was not hungry, and that he had friends in the city who would give him food, dismounted from the ass and with a noble gesture invited the beggar to mount it. The beggar avidly obeyed and sat high on the cushion and took up the whip arrogantly. Then seeing the sage standing in the road and the dust on his bare feet, without a cloak or a drachma in his purse, the beggar gazed at him with contempt. 'Begone, beggar!' he cried, and he cut his whip across the sage's face, and merrily rode away.

"Now, my Saul, could you guess at the sage's thoughts?"

Saul blinked his red lashes. He eyed Aristo suspiciously, knowing that the Greek had him in a trap of words. Then he said, "If he were a sage, then he would console himself with the thought that the beggar now had some comfort and money, and he would be content."

"If he thought that idiocy, then he was not a sage," said Aristo. "Nor was he human. Saul, were you that man, what would be your thoughts?"

Saul stared at him with his strange eyes. Then his freckled, deeply colored face broke into laughter, loud rollicking laughter. "I, myself, would have pursued the beggar, dragged him from the ass, and would have thrashed him soundly!"

"Saul, Saul, I have hopes for you," said Aristo, slapping the youth's sun-reddened bare arm. "But what would Reb Isaac have done?"

Saul laughed again. "He would have judiciously counted out an exact tithe from his purse and given it to the beggar, and so would my father."

"You have me," said the Greek. "Still, it is an interesting story, and illustrates what happens when even virtue can become excessive. A man who gives his all is as stupid as a man who gives nothing. You see, I defer to your burdened sense of guilt. I, myself, would consider I would be doing the beggar an evil by encouraging his beggary." He paused. "There is another thing which bewilders me. I have heard your father, my master, dispute with Reb Isaac as to whether, indeed, your Moses wrote ten of your David's Psalms, from the number ninety to one hundred. Of what importance is the author? Your father has recited the Psalms to me, and ·many of them are beautiful if incomprehensible in part, and beauty is all that is important. There are many who say that Homer, being blind, could not have described the burning of Ilium so magnificently, nor discoursed so tellingly of the countenances of men and women, and therefore he was only author in part of the Iliad and the Odyssey. But we do not argue so passionately on the subject as does your father, and your mentor, Reb Isaac, and of what importance is it?"

"Your Homer was merely telling tales, or the real author was, but we are concerned with the question of truth, Aristo."

"Is truth more than beauty? I dispute that. Or, in a more metaphysical way I would declare that they are one. However, is your Moses, from your uninviting heaven, calling on all Jews to defend his authorship, and David also?"

Saul pursed his wide and sensitive lips and considered. "You still do not understand. To dismiss the question casually is to belittle the Psalms, themselves."

"You Jews take nothing casually and lightly," said Aristo, "and therefore you are an irritation to other men. Tell me, do Jews ever enjoy themselves, or is their wailing about Jerusalem their secret pleasure? Must Jews be sorrowful so that they can be happy?"

"Our household is happy," said Saul, frowning again.

"Is it, truly? I have never heard much laughter in it, except in the slaves' quarters, and even there they mute their mirth in deference to the Master. I have seen no gay drinking. I have seen no real feasting, though you have many days in which you declare you are feasting, and rejoicing." Aristo rolled up his eyes dolefully. "Your father has his guests and after the meal is over they spread scrolls upon the table and pore over them and dispute until midnight and later over the most meager of obscure meanings of some commentator. Is that gaiety, laughter, joy? I have seen no musicians here or singers. I have observed no dancings. Yet, did you not once tell me that your David advocated music and singing and rejoicings in God?"

"In a spiritual fashion," said young Saul.

Aristo sighed elaborately. "I fear you do even your grim Deity an injustice. Observe the world. Is it not beautiful, intricate, majestic, harmonious? Is not the air sweet and salubrious? Are not the skies an awesome wonder at night? Is not the garden of the world green and blessed with flowers? Do not the birds sing and the animals of the field dance with glee in the spring? Do not men and women love, and is not their love the loveliest thing in creation? Does not sound of music linger entrancingly on the ear, whether it is made by man or the multitude of the voices of nature? Is not all a delight?"

"The world is but a snare for our enticing," said Saul, but he looked about the garden and a secret shadow of wild excitement ran over his face. "We are not concerned with the world, of which evil is the master, but with God."

"I still say you insult Him. Moreover, I have seen your father, at sunset, on the conclusion of his prayers, looking about him with a pleasure that is sublime in its innocence and happiness. He does not bend all his thoughts on the evil of the world. He sees deliciousness in it also. He sees brightness and glory. The world is charged with the grandeur of God."

As Hillel had often intimated such things to Saul in the past, the youth became vexed. "My father is not a man of deep spiritual dedication," he said, "and I say this without disrespect for I know he would admit it, himself."

"I think, my Saul, that he is more spiritual than you, though, frankly, I am not enchanted by the word." He put his head on one side like an impudent large bird and said, "I have observed that the Jews and the Romans seem disturbingly similar, both concerned humorlessly with the absolute law, though, of course, the Romans for the last two or three centuries have not been too meticulous about it. We Greeks call them a nation of grocers. But I think they are a nation of lawyers, and so they have esteem for the Jews who, alas, are mentally of such a breed also."

"I have not told you as yet," said Saul. "I am to go to the University of Tarsus, and among other things I will study the Roman law. I would be an advocate for my people."

"You will make an excellent lawyer. You believe you are invariably right."

It was autumn in the garden and very hot, and in the afternoon. The restless palms themselves were still, and the cypresses and the sycamores and the karob trees had taken on themselves a more shining darkness as the year waned, and the sky was a hard and brilliant turquoise against which the distant mountains, scarlet threaded with green, leaned and tumbled in their grotesque shapes. The

valley had deepened to the ripeness of the days, the grass
a heavier green, the fields bronze with harvest, and Tarsus, the city, spreading on the banks of the waters—now
a flashing purple—revealed with clarity the whiteness of its
walls, or their rose or blue or yellow, and their red roofs.
Birds were already circling like feathered wheels in the sky,
preparing for long flight. And the figs were ripe on the
trees in Hillel's gardens and there was a scent of grapes in
the humid air and golden dust and water. The year was
dying, thought Aristo, but in death, apparently, there was
a last affirmation of life. He looked at the gayly striped
awnings scattered over the garden, at the cool grottoes, at
the shining whiteness of the graceful statues, at the shimmering pond on which circled the black and white swans,
preening, and the ludicrous Chinese ducks who took themselves so seriously and were therefore belligerent. The little
bridge over the pond was reflected sharply in the motionless water below, and a young girl stood there on the arch
looking down. She was clad in a very short tunic as green
as the pond and her golden hair blazed in the sun.

The fountains were scintillating in the too vivid light,
and appeared to throw up long streamers like reaching
arms or hands, or the tossings of shaking locks. Aristo and
Saul sat beneath one of the awnings and they were sweating freely. A plate of fresh fruit stood on a rude rustic table, and Aristo picked up a plum and thoughtfully devoured it. His rough black hair was rougher with patches
of gray, now, but his Greek body was still lithe and thin,
and his narrow face was dark with the sun, and his nose
was sharp and inquisitive and his eyes ever seeking.

He looked at Saul, and recalled that Deborah bas Shebua considered her son hideous. Aristo shook his head in
silent denial. The boy might not be of impressive stature
but his body was strong and well sculptured and broad,
and even the bowed legs added to that impression of
vigorous strength. To Aristo, he was like some primitive
fire god, with that raised and crested mane of intensely
red hair, with those red eyebrows almost meeting above
his eyes, and the virile low forehead and the pointed
ears. A young Vulcan, perhaps, thought Aristo, or Hera-
cles, though certainly not a Hermes, for there was no
lightness about Saul ben Hillel, no soft grace or elegance,
but only an aura of power. Power, above all, was to be

reverenced, for it had in it a terrible beauty of its own, reflected the Greek, an appalling magnetism, something which could inspire fear but was also irresistible. Even Saul's features, the wide thin lips, the great nose, the hard firm chin, spoke of power, though the boy, at this moment, was stuffing his mouth with handfuls of grapes and licking his fingers which ran with winey juices.

When Saul spoke one listened even if not desirous of listening, for he had a deep and vigorous voice, with a curious weight and emphasis to the syllables, an emphatic pronunciation and an echoing timbre. One could not call it a musical voice, but never, even when he was excited, did it resemble a girl's. Nor had it been a girl's voice even before it had changed to the deeper sound of a man's.

Though Saul, in a very plain tunic of gray linen with no embroidery on it, sat apparently at his ease in his chair and was engrossed in devouring the fruit with gusto, he did not give the appearance of being composed or at peace. All his unruly and impetuous nature asserted itself in the ever-changing contour of his face, in the jerking of his eyebrows, in the quickness of his hands, and the tightness of his shoulder muscles. His hands were browned by the sun, and the nails pale on the short broad fingers—the fingers of a soldier—and his arms were large and muscular and sunburned. He wore the ring his father had given him when he had "become a man" according to the Jewish traditions, and it was set with a ruby as fiery as his hair, and the gold was plain and unornamented. Hillel had known his son, thought Aristo, and had chosen what best expressed him. To the Greek, Saul had a forceful and cogent beauty of his own, which in full maturity might become frightful and intimidating. He set down his strong arched feet with purpose and certainty, and he could move rapidly.

Had he height, thought Aristo—who had more affection for his pupil than anyone ever suspected except Hillel— he would be a veritable Titan. Then an odd following thought came to him: Saul of Tarsus was indeed a Titan, though but fourteen as yet, and the superstitious Greek— who denounced all superstition as unworthy of an enlightened man—seemed to glimpse the future when Saul would walk among men with authority and even with terror, hurling that voice of his into the face of multitudes.

In what obscure cataract and caves and mountains of heredity had this prodigy wrought and drunk his being? The gentle and handsome Hillel, the lovely Deborah, were very unlikely parents of this man-child, and Deborah was very petulant on the subject even before the youth, himself.

If he was violent, he was never savage or mean or vengeful. He was disputatious but he was never insulting nor did he gibe at his adversary. He took an idea and elaborated on it, or figuratively mangled and tore it apart, but always objectively, with no malice and no scorn. Ideas of others might exasperate him, but never to denunciations of the other's intelligence. He was always, he declared, being misunderstood. It seemed to him that it was not too much to ask to be comprehended, even if one disagreed with him. Saul, Saul, thought Aristo the Greek, the world will not edify you nor will it receive you kindly.

Men like Saul might evoke a holocaust, but they were usually devoured with it. Aristo hoped this would not happen to Saul, though he had his fears. Therefore, he tried to temper that vociferous disposition, to quiet the rushing assaults of speech when they became too bursting, to instill in Saul that golden mien which was the mark of a cultivated man. The world was full of timid men; they did not like boldness in others, for it seemed to threaten them. In particular they hated and feared men who demanded that they pursue an argument logically to its conclusion, and use reason.

It was into this world, thought Aristo with unusual sorrow, that this Jewish Hector had been born, all passion but no baseness, all honor but no malevolence, all duty—alas —but no frivolity. The world would not love him, therefore the gods must, and that is more dangerous.

"The figs are very ripe and sweet, Aristo," said Saul, noticing, with that sharp clarity of eye for which he was distinguished, the mournful expression on his tutor's antic face. "Eat this, which is the largest and is covered with its own honey." He put the fig into Aristo's fingers, and Aristo ate it abstractedly.

"Pigs," said a laughing voice near them as they ate under the striped awnings. They looked up to see the young girl who had stood on the bridge. She smiled at them teasingly and threw back the mass of her golden hair, in which the sunlight danced. Her eyes, almost as golden, mocked their male gorging of the fruit. Her exceedingly pretty face, fair as a lily, and as translucent, was rosy from the heat of the day, and her pert nose was burned. Her eyes were hardly less golden than her hair and her pretty mouth was always smiling, or, if a grave thought flitted across her mind, the expression of her lips might change to seriousness, which, however, appeared to be instantly about to depart. A year younger than her brother, Saul, and only thirteen, she was taller and her breasts were delicately nubile under the thin stuff of her short green tunic. While Saul was as restless as a young bull, Sephorah was as restless as a flower in a summer breeze.

She was already espoused to her cousin, Ezekiel, in Jerusalem, and would marry him on her fourteenth birthday, for she had reached puberty six months ago.

"That tunic," said Saul, "is lewd and shameless, for one of your age, an espoused woman, a modest Jewish maiden."

The girl glanced down at her long fair legs below the hem of the tunic. "Bah," she said. "Who is concerned with modesty in this garden? The day is hot, too hot even for a chiton." Her legs gleamed like marble touched by the sun. She bounced under the awning and seized a citron and tore off its skin and sank her white teeth into the pulp. Her merry eyes surveyed them. The juice of the fruit ran down her chin and she licked at it with her red tongue.

"I am thinking of not marrying Ezekiel," she said, and thrust her hand again between Aristo and Saul and took a plum. She pretended to study it. Her Greek accent was pure and sweet, for Aristo had taught her, himself, whereas her father had taught her Aramaic, and enough Hebrew as was prudent to teach a girl.

It was only when looking at Sephorah that Saul's eyes lost their metallic gleam and became almost soft. But he spoke disapprovingly. "It is not fitting for a maiden your age to display herself in a boy's tunic. Where is our mother, that she permits this?"

"It is not a boy's tunic," said Sephorah. "It is mine, of a year ago. My legs became longer." She spat out the seed of the plum. Her feet moved to inaudible music. "I think I am really a nymph," she said.

While Saul had been taught much of the Greek gods

by Aristo, during their classical studies, he did not consider it proper that his sister should know of their lascivious beauty and their adulteries, and so he gave Aristo a glance of umbrage. But Aristo was studying the pretty girl-child with pleasure.

"I think so also," he replied.

"Shameless," said Saul. "Your knees have been bitten by mosquitoes, unbecoming for a girl. They are also dirty. Have you been crawling in mud, my sister?"

"Do I ask you where you go so secretly in the mornings, when it is hardly dawn?" asked the maiden, reaching for a bunch of grapes.

Saul, to Aristo's surprise, colored deeply, and even his pink ears turned red. Sephorah laughed at him. "It must be to visit a girl, a shepherdess, perhaps, or a goose girl, or a herder of goats," she said. She shook a finger at him, a slender finger running with juices. "Shameless, indeed. You steal from the house when it is hardly light, and only I see you and put my pillow over my face to muffle my laughter. What damsel is it, sweet brother?"

Aristo studied his pupil with amusement, for Saul's coloring was deepening moment by moment and his face seemed to be swelling. The Greek took pity on him. Saul was incapable of lying, and a question would be answered by the truth and it was obvious that he was dreading such a question. So Aristo said, "It is quite common for a youth Saul's age, full of dreams and fantasies and strange longings, to go out to view the dawn alone, and to meditate."

Sephorah, herself, thought this was probably true of her brother, but she continued to tease him. "One morning I shall surely follow you," she said, "and discover the dryad in the bulrushes."

"You are thinking of Moses," said Saul, and his voice was a little thick. "And cease this talk of dryads and nymphs, and wash yourself and array yourself more modestly."

"Old man," said Sephorah and ran off, singing, her white legs flashing in the sun.

"A divine maiden," said Aristo. "A veritable Atalanta."

Saul shrugged. "She is but a chit," he said. "She has a tongue like an asp."

They sat in silence, aware of what had not been said,

and when they looked at each other again it was as if they had made a compact between them, a compact of honor. Saul smiled. "I love her dearly," he said, "though she has no mind and is only a girl."

They heard Sephorah's airy singing near the pond, a blithe light song that was no prayer of invocation but came from her child's heart and her joy in life. Nevertheless, Aristo was taken by melancholy, as if a precious interlude was coming to an end and would never be known in just this fashion again. He imagined that a beautiful statue had turned and had shown another face, and it was a more somber one.

The distant mountains were already wearing thin rings of snow and now, as the sun sank the wind freshened and the awnings bellied like sails. Saul, almost under his breath, began to chant that mournful and sorrowful song which Aristo knew presaged the coming Jewish High Holidays, and the solemn Day of Atonement when Jews repent their sins, ask for forgiveness and promise penance. Aristo thought, "Their Deity is their own, and thank the gods that they keep Him!"

Saul's faint chanting suddenly seemed ominous to the Greek. He did not speak when Saul rose and, with bent head, returned to the house. Aristo watched him go, and something dusky and premonitory but unknowable passed like a harsh wing over his mind. To him, it was an omen.

Saul had become disconcertingly aware he had truly reached manhood a few months before this autumn day in the garden, which was two months before his fifteenth birthday.

As the Jews had an earthy and realistic approach to life—though greatly employing symbols they almost never used euphemisms as men allegedly used figleaves—Saul had been duly taught the uses, meanings and duties inherent in sexuality from the earliest childhood. His father would have used a more delicate approach than did old Reb Isaac, who thought Hillel's demurrings on the subject not only ridiculous but incredible. "God made us as we are," Reb Isaac had said, staring at Hillel as if he suspected him of heresy at the very least. "We are naturally endowed with appetites, which must be controlled if we are to attain civilized manhood and walk proudly as Jews. Are we Romans or Greeks? Are we Epicureans? No, thank God, blessed be His Name! It has been said that men have been given lusts in order to conquer them, and thus become more than animals who obey all their lusts. How, then, can we know these things until we first acknowledge the lusts in honesty and understanding, and then modify and use them in the service of God and man?"

"We Pharisees," said Hillel, "know the Holy Commandments concerning all things, including adultery. We do not condone nor suffer violations. Therefore, we have taught modesty as well as restraint."

Reb Isaac's black stare had ironically widened. "You younger Pharisees, it would appear, do not know the essence of the Law! Tell me, Hillel ben Borush, would you say only to your son, 'It is not wise to caress or kiss a woman?' The boy would become confused and uncertain. But if you say to him, 'You shall not enter and lie with a woman when it is not permitted,' he will know of a certainty what you mean, for children are not so pure and innocent as you would seem to suspect. They have instincts, and some of their instincts are stronger than men's." The old man smiled what Hillel thought was a diabolical smile but in truth was only an amused one. "We do not condemn fornication, my son, though we do not advocate it! It is adultery which is the crime. Let us be men and not coy women."

Hillel, as Reb Isaac suspected, used daintier language than advocated when he spoke to Saul of "the duties of pious men." Saul had then been but six years of age. He had studied his father in dutiful and respectful silence. Only his high color became higher. He had seen the mating of swans and goats and birds and small chattering animals and had thought nothing immodest about the matter. But Hillel's hesitant approach, his open and gentle embarrassment, his pained slight smile, had not only astonished the boy but had made him embarrassed in turn, and wondering. He already knew that men mate as do the beasts, but less openly. He had not considered that his sister had been delivered by some thaumaturgy or the visitation of an angel. He was already studying the Scriptures ably.

Then the astute Reb Isaac approached the subject with bluntness. "We are warned to beware of the strange woman, in the Scriptures," he said, "for it is said that she is the gate to hell. Stolen waters are sweet and bread eaten in secret appears to be more delightful than honest bread. If a strange woman diverts a man from his duty as a man, then she has destroyed him. Hark to my words, my son: A woman is far more powerful in all ways than a man, for all she does not possess muscles of any notable size." He then became more explicit, in an effort to overcome what he discerned was the boy's shamefacedness, due to poor Hillel's stammering and circumlocution. In consequence of this determinedly brutal approach—and Saul's own barely stifled contempt for his mother's pretensions and airs and graces—and Hillel's awkward sheepishness, Saul early acquired not only a strong suspicion of women but a far more rigid attitude toward them than even Reb Isaac could have desired. He never fully recovered from his belief that there was something intrinsically vile about the relationship between a man and a woman, and that even the propagation of the race—created to praise God—did not entirely condone it. Before he was fourteen he had almost concluded that God had been in error in inventing such a process, and that one more befitting the dignity of man ought to have occurred to the King of the Universe. Reb Isaac, never a teacher who avoided the truth, admitted that the pleasure of cohabitation was the greatest of human enjoyments, and Saul, for an instant, thought the old man obscene. Understanding this at once, from his pupil's wincing expression, Reb Isaac had said, "It is said by our wise men that it is often fitting that even those pleasures which are permitted should be denied. But that is in the singular and entire service to God. My son, the Holy One has not created filth and evil. These come from the mind and soul of man, for has not Solomon said that man is wicked from his birth and evil from his youth, and that man's heart is deceitful from his childhood? God, blessed be His Name, sanctified the union between men and women, and could He have done so if it were repulsive and against our nobler instincts? It is only man who has rendered the holy unholy, the pure impure, the endearing disgusting, the joyful prurient. What God has given us must be honored, respected and enjoyed, but in moderation and in trust, and never immoderately or lewdly. When a man lies with his wife it is only one of his appetites, just as hunger and thirst are appetites. All used in excess is not to be forgiven lightly."

Saul said, "Yes, Rabbi." Then he added, "I shall devote my life to the service of God."

Reb Isaac understood immediately, and he was disquieted. He said, "You are your father's only son, and you will say Kaddish for him. A man who dies without a son to perform this holy duty is thought unfortunate."

Saul repeated, "Yes, Rabbi." But the deep and obstinate Pharisee spirit of him made its own resolution.

He was accustomed to rising before the sun now to make his way in the first pale and uncertain light to the small school of Reb Isaac, nearer the city. On reaching the bare and austere room he would be the first to greet his teacher, and they would have a brief and private prayer together. Reb Isaac had already decided that Saul had peculiar and mighty gifts of the spirit, and so while he was kind to the youth he was far sterner, more given to admonitions and censure and warnings and counsels, than he was to his other students in the Scriptures and in the life of the pious Pharisee. Saul was a rare soul; he was a vessel permitted to hold the Grace of God—if taught strenuously and led wisely. If Reb Isaac had any fears it was that he might not be wise enough and nimble enough and prayerful enough to guide this soul as it must be guided, and so Saul was often the anguished object of his deepest prayers.

Saul was not given to boyish pranks as the other pupils were given, nor did he laugh and eat with gusto, nor was there any mischief in his eyes. He studied even when it was not demanded of him, much to the hilarity and taunts of the other boys. His humor was dry and caustic, and sometimes unkind though not intentionally so, and he had a brusque way of speaking which did not endear him to his companions. Some of them were sons of Sadducees, who were not entirely worldly and Hellenistic, and a few were the sons of Pharisees. The latter youths had, several of them, already decided that indeed they would depart from the ways of their tiresome fathers when they would be far enough in distance from the lash and the angry voice and the stringencies of parental purses.

Though robust and muscular, Saul did not engage in the roistering of the other boys when relieved of the bench and the pen and the endless books. But his appearance was formidable and so he was not attacked even when considered the most provoking. However, he was derisively called "Red Hair," and his bowed legs were discussed loudly in his presence. He felt no animosity or hostility toward his mates. His attitude was of indifference, and this they could not endure, and so they taunted him. He thought them vain and weak and superficial, and often pitied Reb Isaac for being their teacher. They had no true reverence for the Word of God, no deep piety. They were careless. Therefore, he, Saul, should avoid them, lest he, too, should be drawn into the pit.

Reb Isaac often wondered if such an attitude was entirely compassionate. (It is true, he would say to himself, that compassion could become mawkish and sentimental, and therefore a disservice to God and man.) He had observed that Saul was gentle, even tender, with the old man's grandchildren, who were very young, and so Reb Isaac was frequently perplexed. He could not reconcile such gentleness with such total indifference to one's peers. Sometimes the old man thought that Saul was far deeper than even he guessed, and he humbly hoped that the Almighty knew what He was doing. Yet, he often wondered how the son of Hillel ben Borush and Deborah bas Shebua—both charming and touching in their fashions—could be so obdurate even against innocent folly and lightheartedness, and how he had acquired his mysterious character and devotion. Reb Isaac believed that environment conditioned the nature of man, as the Greeks averred, but now he sometimes doubted. What ancestral seed had sprouted his life?

Saul was of the Tribe of Benjamin. Reb Isaac pored over the history of that tribe to try to find an instance of rigidity of conscience—beyond the desiring of God—or perhaps a prophet who had met a severe execution for his expressed opinions, which had exasperated contemporaries. So far the rabbi had been unsuccessful. So Saul remained a mystery to him. Reb Isaac respected mysteries. They indicated the Finger of God. Still he said to Saul one day: "It is fitting that you devote your life to the Holy One, the Lord God of Hosts, my son, if that is your destiny and your desire. But you are young. God has not forbidden the young to enjoy simple pleasures and innocent gratifications, nor the society of friends."

This, however, did not seem to stir Saul. He said, "I often laugh, Rabbi. I find many things amusing. But there are things which do not touch my sensibilities nor arouse me to laughter. Must I, then, laugh, merely to be agreeable? Is the approbation of trivial people to be desired?" His energetic face expressed his passionate scorn.

Aristo the Greek would have been surprised to hear Reb Isaac's reply, heavily laden with depression, "You will be a wise son in Israel, Saul." The words would have been no novelty to the Greek, but the melancholy would have amazed him, for he thought the rabbi wholly contentious and fanatical.

On the morning that Saul woke to the full knowledge of his manhood the warm spring sky was still dark. He felt restless even more than his customary restlessness. He rose from his bed in his small cubiculum and then stood immobile, wondering what had aroused him so keenly. He was acutely aware of his young strong body, of the muscles in his belly and his arms and legs and shoulders. They had tensed as if about to leap. Then he put on his sandals and his tunic and threw his light cloak over his shoulders. He went outside into the dark and silent garden, feeling the dew on his feet. Nothing moved, but now he smelled the furious and urgent fragrance of grass and tree and flower. He bathed his hands and face in the fountain and he did so slowly, feeling a new voluptuousness in life. He looked to the east. A dim crown of crimson fire was brightening there but the sun was far from rising; a gray shadow outlined the crown and silently spread upwards. Saul ran his hands absently but with a kind of fierceness through his hair. The strands crackled with energy. He smiled. A thrill of intense rapture ran through his flesh and he shivered with the delight of it. He began to walk in leisure toward Tarsus, content, for once, merely to feel and not to think.

None had deprived him of joy in his youth nor treated him harshly, nor had condemned innocent joys to him, nor had darkened his days. Yet from infanthood he had been vehement and somber, passionate and uncompromising, disputatious and challenging except with Reb Isaac. However, on occasion, he had ventured an opinion or two in contradiction, but when faced with absolute Scripture and the Law and the Book he had retreated not in confusion but with dignified humility. The chidings he had received from his father who spoke so gently were not concerned with small sins or mischief, but with his firm addiction to study at the expense of surveying the world of grandeur and beauty and terrible loveliness. Deborah complained to him that he was no child, and then no youth. "You were a graybeard from your cradle," she would say with her girlish petulance. "You will regret the years of joy which you have wasted, my son."

But Saul had his secret and consuming joy. He waited for the Messias, and each day he prayed, "Though He tarries and has not come, still we shall wait for Him in faithfulness and hope and gladness." Often he prayed, "Lord God of Hosts, if it be Your will, permit these worthless eyes to gaze upon Your Salvation, promised through the ages, before they are closed in death." Sometimes, when this prayer was particularly fervent it seemed to him that his heart was seized in ecstasy and he would fall into a profound silence in which nothing lived but the Messias and himself, and he felt the awesome glory of that Presence within touch of his breath. Year by year, surety grew in him that he would not die before he beheld that Face, and had lain at the feet of the Holy One of Israel in total adoration. What joy, what pleasure, urged on him by his gentle father, and even sometimes by the disturbed Reb Isaac, could compare with that Vision? The world was nothing; it was a mere colored vessel awaiting the filling to the brim with the divine Essence. He could not speak of these things, no, not even to Reb Isaac. Once or twice he had attempted to speak but his throat closed and tears trembled under his lids, and he was forced to turn away. It was as if his very spirit would burst.

The Messias would not be born in Tarsus. It had been prophesied that He would be born in Bethlehem, as David had been born, and that He would be of the House of David also, and the rod of Jesse. Therefore, Saul ben Hillel lived for the day when he would first see Israel, and go, himself, to the little town of Bethlehem to await the Messias, Who would come in clouds of fire and with the thunder of seraphim wings and with crystal trumpets sounding from every corner of the world.

Saul left the dusky garden of his father's house and put his feet on the straight and dusty road toward Tarsus, and the house of Reb Isaac. He would be very early this morning. They would sup together on cheese and bread and goat's milk at the dawn. (Saul did not know that the old man supplemented this meager breakfast with the fine stuffs of his wife's table, and Reb Isaac never enlightened him. The rabbi already knew how stringent was the soul of this young Pharisee, and he often searched his conscience in anxiety to discover where he, himself, had sinned, in being too rigid even in the Law. He could discover no sin. Saul was Saul ben Hillel, and God, blessed be His Name, undoubtedly knew what He was doing, and why He had created one who not only implicitly obeyed the Law but insisted on more elaborate rigors in the practicing of it.)

But Saul was not praying this morning, as, in the gray darkness he passed silent houses and curtained windows on the road. He could not, as yet, see the broad river which ran through the rich wide valley, nor even the mountains, but he heard, once or twice, the faint questioning cheep of a bird and saw an occasional dim shape—heard rather than actually seen—bursting from tree to tree. It would not be long before this road would be noisy and festive and loudly quarrelsome as the peasants brought in their milk and eggs and cheese and meat and fruit and wine and vegetables to Tarsus' markets, their two-wheeled wagons creaking busily, their whips cracking, the patient asses trudging. Little half-naked boys would gambol about the animals, and be scolded by their bearded fathers, and would beg of those fathers for a copper or two to purchase some honeyed sweet or chopped spicy meat in a leaf carried in other carts. Then the dust would be bright yellow in the sun and it would be very warm, and the tamarisk trees would lift their wide green clouds to the sky and the river would be full of traffic, and the distant harbor would be crowded with sails and the sun would lie hotly on roof and wall and the stones of the road would burn through the thickest sole. Then herds of goats and sheep and cattle would fill the road on the way to market, complaining and bleating, and there would be fresh carts and wagons joining those on the roads, heaped with terrified and squawking chickens and geese, all tied together.

Sometimes a detachment of Roman soldiers on horseback would roar through the colorful throngs, who would move off the road, cursing, to escape those hoofs which struck fire from the stones. Sometimes several Roman chariots from the cool suburbs would race along the margin of the road, carrying centurions and taxgatherers and clerks and bureaucrats to their stations and their offices, and many was the bronzed and muscular fist raised in imprecation as they swept by. The Romans' faces would be set impassively, no eye glancing at the dusty peasants in their rough robes of brown and black and red and blue and at their swart faces partly concealed by head cloths to protect teeth and lips from the drying heat and dust. No Roman deigned to look down into those wild black eyes with the curse implicit in them. But a pretty slave girl standing shyly near the gate of a villa would attract their attention and a light salute, or even a whistle, and she would wave her hand in pleased answer. Cypresses would stand in stiff immutable ranks near the highway, and there would be glimpses of greening spring meadows and blossoming palms, and an occasional Roman guard tower. And everywhere would be the acrid scent of sweat and offal and animals and men on the seething road, and deafening clamor.

Saul knew of these things. He encountered the same throngs returning from Tarsus in the evening. He tried to avoid the road, walking on the stiff grass, stinging his feet with nettles, warily watching for snakes and lizards, and trying not to hear the furious uproar near at hand, trying to recite prayers, trying to step around pigeons and geese. He did not care to encounter the hordes in the morning. He was a citizen of Rome, but he did not love the Romans, who had enslaved his country. He did not love the people of Cilicia, though he had been born in their city of Tarsus. All was remote to him. Later in his life he was to say, "Never did I feel this world was my home nor my joy nor my comfort. I was an alien in the land." He would think: Truly, I always loved God alone, with all my heart and all my soul and all my mind, as I loved none other, nay, not even my parents nor my teachers. My hours were haunted by God, my years knew Him only.

Some time before he had discovered a lonely clay road branching away from the stony Roman highway, and on an impulse of curiosity he had wandered a way upon it. He never knew whose estate he then surveyed, with lush pastures and little brooks and deep trees and palms and grain and grapevines, nor did he care. But he came upon, without warning, a sudden rise of steep and jutting rock formations, tall and tawny in the early light, like a wall set in his path, or the great ruins of a temple. From an upper crevice like a mouth burst a narrow cataract of pure green water, which made a soft though thunderous sound. At the foot of the rocks, now turning to broken gold before the rising sun, was a vast pool into which the cataract poured down, and the pool was the color of lemons and curiously quiet below such turbulence. Trees of many kinds grew wild about the pool and masses of wild flowers of every imaginable color, and little poppies and daisies and ferns and yellow shrubs and emerald grasses and rosy vines. Then, as the sky awoke with morning the tumbled wall of rock stood against ardent blueness and scarlet streaks, and birds alighted on stones in the pool to drink and bathe themselves.

Aside from the sound of the falling water and the bird-song there was no other sound. It was an enchanted spot, and Saul, alone in all the world, knew of it. The young Saul forgot his first morning prayers to gaze upon such beauty with wonder and delight. He took off his sandals and stepped into the pool near the edge, and the citron-colored water was icy cold but refreshing to his dusty feet. He lifted the water in his hands to drink and bathe his face, and he saw small brilliant fish in the pond now, and saw that the pond wandered away into many little brooks and freshets on the earth, reviving the hot soil.

Many times that summer and throughout the year he came to that place, and never was it the same, but as changeful as a prism, and never did it fail to give him pleasure and peace. It was his own no matter who owned it. In the early evenings, walking home from school, he would come here also, and study his books against the background of rushing water and calling birds and murmurous trees, and then he would remove tunic and sandals and swim in the pond or stand under the argent spray of the cataract just before it plunged into ripples and small waves of light and tinted liquid.

In time, it became a hallowed place to him, where he

could not only study but could pray with renewed ardor and understanding. The months passed, and he saw no other human being near, though sometimes at a distance he could hear the faint ringing of cowbells in the evening or the far songs of slaves working in the fields beyond. Occasionally a small wild animal or a fawn or a little lamb would come shyly here to drink, staring at him with innocent eyes, and then leaving as silently as they had come.

And so he arrived at his precious sanctuary this morning, earlier than customary, and the rocks were still gray from the night and the water had a more tumultuous sound in the absolute silence. It was very cool here, almost chill, and the cataract appeared to be speaking to itself and to the pond into which it fell. Nothing had color as yet. The earth exhaled a cold but vibrant life of spring, carnal and pure and demanding. Slowly, moment by moment, as Saul sat on a dry rock near the pond and waited to watch his wall of rock turn to fiery gold, the sky turned opaline and the trees and birds awoke. Now the flowers burst into tints and hues like emerging rainbows on the land, and there was a smell of fecund ferns and almond blossoms.

Saul, delighting afresh in all this wonder and beauty of the senses, sat very still, all ears and eyes. Then he heard a slight rustle and the sound of disturbed gravel. He looked across the pond, startled. A young girl had appeared at the edge of the pond, and she did not see him. She was, perhaps, one or two years older than himself, and she was very beautiful and slender, and Jew though he was Saul suddenly thought of a dryad, or a nymph emerging from a tree. Her chiton was of white linen, coarse and spare and bound with a ribbon below young breasts, and her feet were bare and pale and so was her throat and her arms, as pale as moonlight on the snow of mountains. Her hair was long and curling and dark as night, springing about a child's face of soft amber and rose, and her eyes, he saw, in that clarified illumination of early morning, were huge and black, and her mouth resembled a new poppy.

He guessed at once, from her garment and her bare feet and her timid movements, that she was a slave girl from some house he had never seen nearby, for she cast furtive glances over her shoulder as she lifted her chiton and stepped into the still water. She lifted the cloth high and Saul caught a flash of round firm thighs, as pale and lustrous as her arms.

He had thought, in the past, that should he ever come upon another mortal in that spot it would be forever spoiled for him, and he would not come again. But he felt no outrage now at this charming vision, and he saw that the girl, too, thought she was entirely alone and unobserved. She bent as he often bent, to lift silver water in her hands, and she drank of it and then threw the rest over her face, and she laughed and shook her head and her long and heavy hair flew like a lifted mantle in the brightening air. She began to sing as she waded slowly and her voice was no more intrusive than a bird's call, and was all as musical.

Then she returned to the edge of the pond and dropped her garment and she was gone as suddenly as she had appeared, vanishing behind the trees. Saul then became aware that he had been holding his breath and that his heart's sound was louder than the song of the cataract and that his face and breast were as hot as if the sun had struck them. He was conscious of a fine trembling through his body, and he wet his lips. Now the scene seemed to him to be less beautiful for the absence of the girl, and lonely.

He was not a child. He would be fifteen years old before the deepest snows appeared on the Tarsus mountains. He was no innocent, no babe, no ignorant lad. He knew that the girl had set him afire, and he knew what he felt was the first lust he had ever known, as well as a strange tenderness never experienced before, and a mysterious urgency. He desired above all things to touch that slave girl, or that peasant's daughter, to smooth her blowing hair into quiet with his loving hands, to kiss those red lips and that pale throat, to hold those little hands in his. He wanted to hear her heart beat against his and to feel her arm about his neck, and her breath against his cheek. His loins throbbed, and sweat ran from his brow. He had seen pretty girls before on the streets of Tarsus and working in the fields and even in his father's garden, but he had looked upon them with indifference. In some astonishing way this girl was different from all others and he believed that she belonged to him as the rock and the cataract and the pond belonged to him, and no one else would ever know her but himself.

He did not think of the "strange woman" of whom Reb Isaac had told him, whose mouth was the gate to hell and all abomination. The lust he felt and the passionate tenderness, seemed to him as natural and as good and as wholesome as the morning, and not to be despised or rejected. Now he was alive as he had never been alive before, as tumultuous as a young Adam who had caught his first glimpse of his Eve, and as wild with joy. And his desire was no more evil than the desire of Adam for his newly created wife, and was as innocent.

"Of what are you dreaming, Saul ben Hillel?" asked Reb Isaac that morning. "You are absent and your eyes are far away."

Morning after morning Saul arrived silently at the rock and the cataract and the pond, but he did not see the girl again for nearly a month, and she was there when he arrived, singing childishly to herself as she waded in the water and dashed it over her face and rubbed it on her arms. He had told himself that he had dreamt her appearance or that when he encountered her again her countenance would seem less lovely and that the vision would be vanished. But, as he watched her from behind a sheltering tree trunk, she was more beautiful than ever, more desirable, and the urgency was on him more savage than before to hold her against him and taste of those poppy lips. Some water had splashed on the bosom of her chiton and the cloth clung to her young breasts and he saw the swelling outline of them and the virgin nipples. He watched her, entranced, hardly breathing, and then she stepped from the water and was gone, as she had gone that first morning, and he heard no sound of her going.

He saw her all through the summer, in the early light, and as the sun began to rise her dark hair was struck with copper and her round face glowed and her flesh was as bright as wet marble. Then she would leave, moving as light as a leaf. Despite his urgency to encounter her flesh, he did not display himself to her. For a long while it was enough to see her, to withhold delight, to dream, to desire. His thoughts did not spring beyond the first holding and caresses; he held them back as a man holds back untamed colts. And in that withholding he felt the delight of secrecy and a dizzying madness. He dared not anticipate, nor did he wish to do so.

When the summer was full and ripe and the early morning was hot, he came to his enchanted place and the girl was not there. He sat down on his favorite stone, feeling profound desolation, though often she did not appear. Then, as he was about to leave he heard a faint sound near him and turned on the stone to see her beside him, laughing silently and with shy glee. They looked at each other, not speaking, and Saul caught the scent of her, as fresh as grass and as sweet as clover and honey. He could see the veins in her child's throat and the rosy nails of her hands and feet and the half-opened red mouth and the gleam of little white teeth and the shine of large dark eyes.

Then she spoke in a trilling voice, like a small girl. "Why do you watch me in the morning?"

He felt his face swell and become hot with mingled embarrassment and joy. He replied to her in the tongue of Cilicia, in which she had spoken. "Does it vex you?"

She shook her head and her hair flew and she was delighted. "No. But it amuses me. Who are you, Master?"

He stood up. He was very close to her. She was not taller than he, and her lovely face was level with his. "My name is Saul," he said, and his voice shook.

"Saul, Saul," she repeated, and he saw her little tongue tasting the name, and he experienced fresh joy. "It is a strange name. Are you far from home?" She gazed at him curiously and he saw the welling and deepening light in her eyes and the polished whiteness around the dark iris and the thick silken lashes. He saw the smooth downy wings of her brows, and wanted to touch them as one touches the feathers of a bird.

"Yes. I am far from home," he said. "I go into the city from my father's house, to study with my teacher."

He had always experienced an awkwardness with strangers before, and a reluctance to speak until he knew them well, but it was natural and simple to talk to this girl as the high rocky wall before them turned tawny and gold and bronze and the green water danced down to the lemon-colored pool. "What is your name, and where do you live?" he asked in such a gentle voice that it would have amazed his family. He feared that a louder tone would send her running forever from him, for she appeared so light and airy and nymphlike.

"My name is Dacyl," she said, "and I am slave to my master, Centorius, the Roman captain who is praetor of Tarsus. I am the handmaid of his noble wife, Fabiola." She pointed to the top of the rock. "Their villa is beyond this, and beyond the meadow, in a grove of karob trees, and this is their estate and the noble Fabiola regards me as her daughter."

She gazed at Saul brightly and innocently, and awaited his comment. But he was fascinated by the form and scent and appearance of her. She was far more beautiful near to his sight than she had been from a distance. She seemed to vibrate and tremble with the young life in her veins and the beating of her young heart.

It seemed to him frightful that she was a slave and that she did not mourn her state or speak sorrowfully of it. Romans did not release their slaves seven years after they had acquired them, as demanded by Jewish law. They sometimes freed them, but rarely, and to a Roman, as to a Greek, a slave was not human but was called by a word meaning "thing." In short, they had no rights, as things have no rights, or humble animals.

"Are you a Greek, Dacyl?" he asked.

Her eyes widened. "That I do not know, Master," she said. "I do not know what I am, or who were my parents." She laughed with a happiness that disconcerted him, and then he discerned that she spoke as a child, for she was still a child.

"I am a Jew," said Saul. "My father is Hillel ben Borush, and we live on his estate far down the road from the city."

Jews did not despise their slaves as others did, and considered their rights as human beings and immortal souls and treated them with kindness and charity and fed them well and respected their manhood, and filled their hands with rich coins when they freed them. They taught them to reverence God and to obey and serve dutifully and with pride. But Saul knew that only Jews did so. He said, "Dacyl, does your mistress flog you?" He had heard the direst stories of Gentile cruelty.

The girl's mouth dropped open in astonishment. "No,

my noble mistress is as gentle as a dove, and her slaves adore her!"

This confused Saul. He knew only two or three Romans, and they only slightly and in passing, and he had scorned their powerful and arrogant faces and prominent noses, and would never admit, as his father admitted, that they strongly resembled Jews not only in countenance but in temperament. He said, "Is the praetor harsh to you, Dacyl?"

She laughed merrily. "No, my noble lord is very kind, though sometimes stern. So long as he is served obediently and without question or impertinence, he is just and generous. He will not permit the overseer of the hall to abuse us. We love him."

"But, you are a slave still, and may always be a slave," said Saul, more confused than ever.

The girl shrugged and stared at him with fresh curiosity. "So the gods have ordained," she said. "It is my fate. It is not an unhappy one. What more could I desire?"

Then she glanced, startled, at the newly brilliant sky, and uttered an exclamation of dismay. "It is late!" she cried. "My mistress will wonder at my absence!" She ran a little distance around the pond, then turned gayly and waved to Saul, and vanished.

She is not intelligent, thought Saul ben Hillel, the Pharisee Jew. She does not mourn her direful state. She does not conceive of it being direful. She knows no sorrow. She does not think beyond today. That seemed monstrous to him, to consider no future. A slave with no hope of freedom was tragic to him, and his heart sickened with a new grief. Men accepted the will of God, it was true, and did not question it. But such men were free. A slave like Dacyl was a slave in his spirit also, for he had no will but his human master's, and so he was never free.

Saul did not return to that spot for seven days and on each morning he told himself that never again would he return. It was too painful to see Dacyl and to ponder her ultimate fate. He had heard from Aristo that it was not unusual for some depraved and cruel Roman senators to feed recalcitrant slaves to the lampreys in their pools, or to torture them, in spite of new and languid laws passed recently in Rome. When he considered such a fate for Dacyl Saul was overwhelmed with anguish. Once he considered giving her money and urging her to flee, and then he remembered how young and unprotected she was, and he despaired. He did not know, until he experienced that despair, that he loved Dacyl not only for her beauty but for her innocence and sweetness.

"Are you afflicted by some illness of the body or spirit?" asked Reb Isaac with asperity. "Your mind wanders and your thoughts are far away, and that is blasphemous when we study the Scriptures, the Pentateuch and the Prophets and the Torah. Your countenance is less colorful than usual, Saul ben Hillel, and your manner is listless and your eye is absent."

Aristo the Greek was more shrewd. He looked at the young servant girls of the household and wondered which one had caught the eye of Saul, and for which he pined. He saw no evidence of any desire or wistfulness. He knew that no girls were present in Saul's school, and that he was always prompt in returning in the afternoon to his father's house. But Aristo knew all the signs of adolescent love, and he mused.

On the eighth day of absence Saul could no longer resist the terrible longing to see Dacyl again. He had told himself over and over that she was but an ignorant slave girl of no people and no ancestry, and therefore of no significance—for she did not even realize that she was insignificant. It was useless. He dreamed of her awake or sleeping. Her voice was the voice of the pond where it rippled; it was the voice of the spring birds. It was not forbidden Jews to love servant women. It was forbidden only to abuse them and treat them cruelly. He argued with himself endlessly.

And so he returned to the pond, not walking reluctantly but running like a hare, breathless and panting in the gray light of morning and in the first rising heat of the summer day. His red hair prickled on his scalp. His sandals slapped the silent stones of the Roman road. Birds, still sleeping, awoke to a startled questioning as he raced past. A thousand questions had tortured him over the past days, a thousand despairs, but now he thought of nothing but meeting the girl again. His heart seemed held in hands of leaping flame. The pillars of the dark and silent houses near the road were ghostly in the dim and shadowy light. Only he was alive, and he was alive with exultation.

Dacyl was in the pond, her white reflection like alabaster in the pale yellow-greenness of the water, her black hair dimly glinting with copper and her mouth very red. She saw him and gave him a blissful smile and lifted her chiton high and waded across the pond to him. Her face glittered in the first light because of the drops of water on it, and her eyes gleamed with ardent pleasure at the sight of him. He reached his hand to her and she took it and it was their first fleshly encounter and her touch ran up his arm like a bolt of lightning and struck violently at his heart. Then she was beside him, laughing, shaking out her garment and then they were face to face. It was the most natural of all things to lean suddenly toward her and give his first kiss of love on her moist poppy lips.

They were sweeter and softer and more fragrant than he had dreamed during those last tormented days. He was afraid he had startled her, but then her lips moved against his and he was startled himself, for he had not known that women responded to men in this fashion. Her breath was on his mouth, and he looked into her eyes and they were beaming and joyous. His senses literally staggered with ecstasy and his whole being seemed to burst into flame and sensations he had never imagined almost overwhelmed him. Then, laughing again, she drew away from him.

"I thought you had abandoned me," she said. "Wretch, that you made me weep!"

He was overcome. "I made you weep, Dacyl?" He could not bear the thought that he had given her pain.

Then she was laughing again at him. "Orion!" she exclaimed. "You are a mighty lover, and I am Artemis, and will set you among the stars!" She touched his bare arm and his flesh involuntarily quivered. "How strong you are! You delight my heart. Your hair and your countenance resemble Apollo's, but your shoulders are those of a Hercules. Did a Cyclops detain you, or did you forget your handmaiden?"

She was teasing him as his sister teased him when he was too serious. She could make him smile and laugh as Sephorah did, but with a wondrous and more exciting emotion. He said, and his voice shook, "I did not come because I could not."

She regarded him with sympathy. In her slave mind men had sober affairs which were exceedingly tedious, and Saul saw at once that the explanation he had ready for her question would not have been understood by her, nor did she wish any explanation. What he had implied was enough. He wished to say, "I restrained myself, for fear of what you are, but returned for the same reason." But Dacyl would not comprehend, and for the first time Saul finally knew that there were many minds, myriads of minds, which would be unable to comprehend him at all and all that he symboled. He had met incomprehension before in schoolmates and in his family, but he had thought it either malice or stupidity, or that he had been unable to express himself clearly, or that others deliberately refused to understand. Now he suddenly felt the vast isolation that every man endures, alone in his flesh, and he was aware that neither the most eloquent in speaking or writing could convey the deepness of his motives, the complexity of his thoughts. All at once he was choked by a sharp and alien compassion—though he was not a stranger to pity—both for himself and the others with whom he shared his world. It was a world in which no one truly communicated with another, and in this lay the greatest sorrow. Not even love made a common language.

"Why is your countenance so somber?" asked Dacyl. But Saul had no words. "Let us be happy, for the day is fair," said the girl and she took his hand and they entered the water together and laughed as children laugh and splashed each other.

"It is good to be happy, for that state was intended by the Father, blessed be His Name, for all men," Reb Isaac had said. But in his heart Saul had not believed that men could be happy in a world of vice and licentiousness and depravity and terror, which he had seen all about him on the burning streets of Tarsus, a world abandoned by God and abandoned by virtue, and ruled by the short-sword of Rome and taxgatherers and other fiends of oppression and lust. Yet, in a single moment, by her words, Saul knew that he had truly heard the simplest sagacity. "Let us be happy, for the day is fair."

He had thought men could be happy only in the ecstatic

contemplation of God, if they had any intelligence at all, and were not as beasts and other animals. But as he gazed with delight at Dacyl he saw indeed that the day was fair, and that she was all happiness for him.

And so it was for many days of the summer and Saul became young in heart and spirit as he had never been young before, and he hugged his secret to him, not from shame or embarrassment, but for fear that if he spoke of it the magic would fly from him, as Artemis, the favorite goddess of Dacyl, fled on the silver meadows of the moon.

The girl sharpened all his senses. She gave incandescent meanings to the Songs of Solomon, brought jeweled subtleties to the glad Psalms of David. As Dacyl never reflected on the future, not even on the morrow, so he lost his own sense of time, marveling how deep were the colors of earth and sky now to him, how precious was every flower, how exciting every tree-form, how gracious every shadow, how keen every sensation, how delicious all food, and how glorious his dreams. A cup of wine was no longer wine to him. It had the color and the taste of Dacyl's lips. It held the dance of her eyes. Now everything had a larger contour to him, a vaster meaning, an almost unbearable elation and gaiety. He found himself less attuned to Ecclesiastes and the Proverbs, and more to the bright hosannahs of the prophets, during the brief intervals when they were not mourning the human predicament and man's propensities for evil.

He was certain, in his innocence, that no man had ever experienced such ineffable joy before, and he gave thanks to God for it. Yet, never once did Dacyl utter a profound word, not even the unconscious wisdom of the unlettered and ignorant. She did not touch his mind, but she touched secret places in him, which were wiser if more primeval, with the freshness of the first morning of creation. She regarded existence as a young lamb regarded it, or a bird, or anything else as simple and natural and serene. She was a rose and she spread her fragrant petals to the sun and gave of the divine essence of her perfume. She played with Saul as a child plays, and with all the fullness of a child, though she was older than he. She kissed him as openly as a child, and fondled his hands and neck. At these times he became delirious.

Best of all, she gave him an awareness of all other human creatures, an awareness that was never to leave him.

Chapter 4

TARSUS, whom her inhabitants called "the jewel of the Cydnus River," was essentially a Phoenician city, commercial, murmurous with business and traffic both by water and highways, possessed of excellent academies and schools, mercantile establishments, factories, perfumers, weavers, forges, endless shops, remarkable museums and music halls, the freedom of Roman citizenship, cursed with a bureaucracy, gleaming with temples to many gods, Hellenistic in attitude though Oriental in emotion, famed for her craftsmen, enriched by her pirates who lived respectable and respected lives in their fine villas, wineshops, baths, bakeries, carpet manufacturers, banks, stock markets, inns where Egyptian cooks served superb meals, brothels, licentious theaters, arenas for sports and gladiatorial combats. Many were the natives who proudly called themselves "a little Rome," for a score of races lived here and the narrow streets clamored with a multitude of tongues. Here lived Syrians and Sidonians, students from Asia Minor, Nubians and Scythians, Greeks, Romans, Egyptians, Assyrians, pale-eyed barbarians from the forests of Europe, slaves, Gauls, Britons, artists, jewelers and the owners of bookshops, scribes knowing a dozen tongues, physicians, and tens of thousands of the free mobs who idled, worked when hunger threatened, scrawled graffiti on the walls at night, vociferously adored some local politician and as vociferously derided him, haunted the arenas, hunted slaves, fought with the police on occasion, gave their measure of robbers to the streets, served any master, gambled, diced, pimped, labored, sweated, cheated and behaved as the market rabble has always behaved and will invariably behave. They adored actors and acrobats and gladiators, extolled them one day and put their very lives in danger the next, harrassed unprotected young girls hurrying with messages for rich mistresses, and were emotional, passionate, dangerous, colorful, frightening, seething, amusing and lively, stinking and wildly generous, and in general heartily enjoyed their lives and hourly blasphemed the gods, and paid taxes only when pursued by a resolute publican accompanied by slaves with staves, or legionnaires carrying fasces. They were the terror and vitality of the night, the vehemence of the day, and like all who live by their wits and infrequent labor they were exceedingly clever and full of wit.

"Cities without a market rabble could not survive," Aristo would tell his pupil, Saul. "They would expire of boredom, for respectability has a certain deadness and ennui about it, a certain lack of life. It is the market rabble, dexterously turning a drachma or a sesterce or a copper here and there, which enlivens and creates trade, inspires that greed which is the mother of ambition and fortune, raises temples, gives the gods changeful faces, stimulates fashions, removes the lead from the boots of soldier and police, forms a subject against which priests and teachers and lawmakers can inveigh—what else could they do?—and, if their lustre is garish and gaudy and cheap, at least it is lustre and should not be despised. Their charlatanry, their brazen robberies, their wit and their cavortings, their heedlessness and their lewdness, their cruelty and their frequent violent compassion, are closer to the real nature of man, my Saul, than are the sober-faced philosophers and the writers of books. It is the market rabble, in truth, which inspire theses and book-writing and the best of plays, for that which is raucous and furious and even vicious has more verity before the sun than all of the old Greek virtues of continence, reflection, modesty and the Stoic imperative. This is something," added Aristo, "which you will find angrily denied by those who believe even the common man can be greater than he is, or that any man can become like the gods, but then these sad defenders of the public weal and these fantasy-weavers are far removed from knowledge and validity and reality, and one could pity them if they were not so dangerous."

Saul thought that Aristo was merely conducting an exercise in perversity and contradiction, but since he had known Dacyl he was no longer certain. The girl, though a slave and protected, was of the market rabble also. He

could not despise her. In truth, because of her, he saw
mankind as it was and not as he had hoped it would be,
and love filled him rather than repulsion. But he could
not believe, with the smiling Aristo, that evil was as
necessary as good, and that good without evil would be a
veritable hell of listlessness and dankness. He explained,
over and over, the glories and the sweetnesses of the lost
Eden, and Aristo always replied, "One should be grateful
to your Adam and Eve. Not only did they set men free
from absolute virtue, but they made them wholly human.
They bore in their loins the beauty and the madness of
cities, the great sails of commerce, the delight of theaters
and dancing girls, and all the infinite variety of life as we
know it, and without which we would live in a world of
a single color, like babes in their nurseries. They were also
very wise: they forebore to eat of the Tree of Life before
feasting on the Tree of Wisdom, for what man would
be immortal?"

On this, they had always disputed, and Aristo, Saul
would think, flourished on disputations, all cynical and full
of skepticism, all sharp and laughing. But since the youth
had known Dacyl he found himself listening more closely
to Aristo who could give a keen edge to any discourse and
fire the mind even if it disagreed with him.

"You will notice, in Tarsus, as you will notice in Rome
and Alexandria and Athens in the future, that we Greeks
have given even vice a refinement which grosser races
could never attain," said Aristo. "All men are vile, as
your Solomon has said, and is he not considered your
wisest king? But vileness should not be, among men, a
muddy animal vileness—though I wrongfully denigrate
the animals in this instance—but the vileness of the elegant and gracious gods. That which you Jews call sin
has inspired more poetry than virtue, and certainly more
temples! What would man be without danger and war and
terror and harpies and furies and even death? A sad little
languid creature munching fruit under a changeless tree in
a paradise on which terrible winds never descended nor
any wave rushed nor any thunder sounded. Without controversy there can be no wise argument; without dissension there can be no agreement; without disaster there
can be no peace, in all the meaning of the words. In a
deeper subtlety than you know, Saul, wickedness created

virtue, and all the arts, and vitality. Contrast, Saul, is the only thing which makes life interesting. And wine and love, of course."

Saul contemplated. He could never agree on a single point with Aristo, but Aristo, like Dacyl, awakened him to the many-faceted crystal of existence, and its endless colors. Hillel had attempted this, but as Saul did not respect his mind, he had not succeeded.

He was not attracted to the vice of Tarsus which he often saw. But he was less horrified and more saddened now at the sight of the tinted male whores he saw on the streets, and the cheap dissolute women in rough garments or in rich litters. He no longer averted his eyes from the incense-fuming "heathen" temples of a score of alien religions. It was true that all mankind seemed desperately, if joyously, determined to debauch the human spirit, especially in the hot streets of Tarsus, but Saul was less nauseated or made angry by this display of depravity. He pitied it, and pitied all its votaries.

Not to these had been given the Torah, the prophets, Moses and Solomon, and the promise of the Messias. Or, if the vision had been given—witness the Greek worship of the "Unknown God"—it had been nebulous and uncertain. Once Saul even entered a Greek temple and had looked at its marvelous and simple beauty and its heroic and graceful statues, and all the cloudy incense and the flowers and the charming vistas. There, too, he had found the empty altar, simple and plain and untenanted and inscribed, "To the Unknown God." It waited for That which would give it significance and truth. For those who did not know what had been precisely promised the Jews, Saul felt bitter tears in his eyes.

Hillel had often told him, "A Gentile is not less in the sight of God than a pious and reverent and devoted Jew. He, too, is a child of God the Father, blessed be His Glorious Name. He, too, according to the prophets, will partake of the salvation of the Messias. No man must be despised, nor considered lesser than another. You must honor his manhood, his brotherhood before God, you must deal with him justly and in honor, you must give him your compassion and your hand—even if he reject it. Diverse though we are—for the Father loves diversity, as He created it—in a most strange and mystical way mankind is all one. It has been said by Egyptian scientists that light, which appears to us to have a thousand hues and tints and is composed of endless colors, is truly but one light. And that light is the Spirit of God, and of man."

Saul had listened dutifully, and with the deep love he bore his father, but he had considered Hillel too simplistic and too devoid of the pride of a Jew whose fathers had been given a Covenant with God, and of whose flesh the Messias would be born. But now, as he daily walked the streets of Tarsus in the burnished autumn sunlight, he felt less pride than compassion, and he wondered why it was that other men had not been enlightened also. The Greeks had had their moral code, and so had the Romans and the Egyptians, but it had been a code rooted in some ethical principle and not in the Ancient of Days. Ethical principles devoid of a Source could be destroyed or abandoned by change, but principles established on Eternal Stone could never be moved.

Love, though he did not know it, had given him not only a sense of completely belonging to all humanity, but a tender and powerful pity for it. And, sorrowfully, in the end—because he was still very young and inexperienced and had no confidant—love brought him a terror and a wrath and disillusionment from which he was never completely to recover, and which was to haunt all his life, and cause him agony, and confound and baffle those necessary to him.

In all his short life Saul had never seen a morning so absolutely golden, so resonant with aureate tints and shades, so tawny and ebullient and life-compelling, though it was autumn and the dying year. The darkness of the cypresses emphasized the fiery yellow of other trees; tamarisks were still green but their boughs were gilded with the first topaz sun. Amber water poured smoothly with gentle thunder over the russet rocks and the pool itself was almost still and shiningly saffron. Crimson and lemon-yellow flowers bordered it and the tall grass was umbrous. The little rills and brooks which flowed from the pool quivered in bright copper over the land. The sky above was a deep purple still, pierced by shafts of bronze-like spears in the east, and beyond the very mountains appeared like lion-colored and writhing heaps of stone, pathed with the first thin snows.

Saul carried a basket of scarlet pomegranates in his hand for Dacyl, and the scent of them, mingled with the scent, rich and fruity, from the land, excited him strangely, and he felt his heart rise with promise and unknown excitement and it made him hurry along the empty and twisting road to the cataract and the pool. Once there, he surveyed it all with delight. His heart was still pacing rapidly, and he smiled exuberantly and a rejoicing in life filled him. The Psalms of adoration seemed too puny to him to express the rapture he felt, and the nameless anticipation. He looked about for Dacyl, but she was not there.

Then, suddenly, he trembled with fright. A jackal had appeared on the opposite side of the pond and the yellow creature had escaped his first notice for he blended so completely with the other natural tints about him. It was known that jackals carried rabies with them, and inflicted "the incurable wound" mentioned by Hippocrates, and Saul had watched a favorite young servant die, some years ago, choking with agony after the bite of a jackal.

Jackals were sly but cowardly creatures. Unless mad, they did not attack human beings. But once mad they were like tigers. Saul's first impulse was to run, to find Dacyl and to keep her from approaching the pond if she were on the way. Then he was again affrighted. The jackal had seen him. Instead of slinking away, as was the nature of jackals, the animal's legs stiffened, his fur bristled and his evil head appeared to engorge. His wild eyes glowed in the first light and from his throat there issued a terrible snarling. So, the creature was afflicted with the dread disease. Saul now saw the line of bloody foam along the jackal's jaw.

Stricken with terror, Saul could not look away. He dared not flee for fear of pursuit. Holding the animal with his eyes he slowly bent and lifted a heavy and jagged stone in his hand. Then he shouted menacingly. The jackal retreated a pace or two, but his snarling was like the grinding of rocks and then he uttered a howl of madness and shook from head to foot. But he retreated no more.

It was then that Dacyl appeared, laughing, calling to

Saul because she had heard his shout and she had believed that he was summoning her in impatience. There she stood, only a few paces from the jackal and on the mossy bank of the pool, looking across the water at Saul and smiling gaily, and waving.

Sweat rushed out upon Saul's flesh, and he was dumb. Then as Dacyl continued her waving and was beginning to seem a trifle perplexed, Saul found his voice. "Go into the water, Dacyl!" he called. "Swim to me! Do not hesitate! There is a jackal near you and he is mad!"

The girl turned her head and saw the beast. He had begun to crouch for the charge upon her, and she faintly screamed and fell back. "Swim!" shouted Saul, almost beside himself. "To me! Now!"

Dacyl flung herself into the water, not removing the cloak she wore against the cool morning wind. Her clothing restrained her strokes; she twisted and turned in the water too slowly, and Saul dropped the basket of pomegranates and stepped into the water, himself. He had a confused thought that as rabies brought about a fear and dread of water the jackal would turn away. But Saul was hardly a few feet from the bank when the animal hurled himself into the pool in pursuit of Dacyl. Now he was howling and choking in a frenzy and the horrid sounds echoed in the morning silence.

Saul clenched the jagged stone in his fist and began to swim toward Dacyl. He swam between her and the enraged beast, and the yellow head was like a mat of wool above the water. Saul kicked off his sandals and tore off his cloak and summoned all his strength to intercept the jackal and save Dacyl from a fatal bite. The water was chill and paralyzing, for the year was late. Saul saw Dacyl's desperate white face above the water, and the long black floating of her hair and the entangling cloak and her threshing arms. She was whimpering and straining in her flight, and her eyes implored him for rescue.

Now he was between the jackal and the girl. "Swim faster!" he shouted, resolutely facing the tormented animal. "Reach the bank!" He had heard that the power of the human eye was feared by beasts and he fixed his eyes on the jackal and did not look again at Dacyl, whose gasping he heard behind him.

The jackal, however, had apparently not known that

he was to fear the human eye, or he was too maddened. He halted briefly in the water, churning and snarling, and now his attention was fixed solely on Saul. The pool foamed about his struggling legs. Saul clearly saw the rabid glare in the jackal's eyes and for a moment or two he felt renewed and shaking terror, for his own life was at stake. His legs appeared to have a life of their own, urging him to flee and save himself. But he could not abandon Dacyl; the thought did not even occur to him. His heart was one lump of straining fire in his chest.

The jackal hesitated. Saul was swimming between him and his first pursuit, and so was nearer. He half lifted himself in the water, howling, and launched himself at the youth. And at that instant Saul's strong legs came down and encountered a rock in the water, on which he stood, and his whole sturdy body tightened itself for the attack and fear left him. His mind moved with amazing speed and order.

He waited until the jackal was almost upon him, jaws open and slavering, teeth blood-stained and snapping. Then he reached out swiftly, caught the animal by the throat with his left hand and struck him fiercely on the very top of the head with the jagged stone he still held. The sharp point sank between the wild eyes, deeply, and a hideous shriek of pain burst from the afflicted creature. He fought to release himself, as blood welled about the daggerlike point of stone. Saul shuddered with loathing at the sight and feel of him.

But he clung to the matted throat, tore out the stone and this time he plunged it directly into the right eye of the beast, turning and thrusting it with incredible strength. He felt it reach the soft and fevered brain, and now he clenched his teeth with renewed resolution, withdrew the stone again and drove it into the animal's throat, just above his own hand, and again he turned and thrust with all the power he could produce. The water about him was stained with deadly scarlet in an instant, and the rising sun glittered on the cataract and on the pool, and Saul was bloodied.

Saul felt the dying animal relax and become limp, but again he thrust the stone into the left eye, using his last strength. The jackal sank below the surface of the water, slowly, in scarlet ripples, and died, its legs and body flaccid and drifting.

Saul, watching that sinking, shuddered again. He had never killed anything before. He could hear his own breath in the stillness, raucous and groaning. He retreated from the spot where the animal had died, and he began to wash his arms and hands with clear water, for fear of the gouts of blood on them and the lethal saliva and any fleck of foam which might have been ejected onto his flesh.

Then he thought of Dacyl. He turned and began to swim to the bank. The slave girl had collapsed upon the warming earth in a huddle of wet clothing, her face stark and still as she watched Saul's approach. She could not move. Even when he was beside her she could only stare up at him, as gray as death, her black eyes great in her face.

Saul said, "The beast is dead. The pool is poisoned. Poor Dacyl. It is all over. You must not be afraid now."

Dacyl reached up dumbly for his hand and he took it and tried to warm it between his own cold and pouring hands. She was trying to speak. He bent tenderly to hear her.

"Hercules," she said, and smiled dimly. "Perseus. Odysseus."

Saul drew her quaking body to its feet and attempted to laugh. "It was nothing," he said. "Could I abandon you?" He put his soldier's arms about her body, holding it tightly against him in a sudden frenzy of joy and love. "Do I not love you, my dear one?"

Water streamed from them, but their relief and their love warmed them, and the sun began to strike hotly on their bodies. Dacyl lifted one of Saul's hands and humbly kissed it. Her wet black hair, as soft as silk, fell over his bared arm. At the touch of her lips Saul trembled again, and desire struck him like a knife. When the girl raised her head he sought her lips, not gently and pleasantly as during the months before, but with ardor and lust and passion. They were sweet against his, and moist and cool. They parted in surrender, and she wound her arms about his neck and pressed her body against his, murmuring he knew not what. He could feel her young breast against his chest, urgent and straining and taut. Instinctively he reached for her breast and held one in the cup of his immediately hot and exploring hand, and she murmured again, languidly, clinging to him.

He had never touched a woman's breast before, and the feel of it in his hand drove him almost out of his mind. Together, still clinging, they fell on the warm bank among the tall and dusty grass, and the world became one deep drum of passion and incoherent sound and heat and delicious struggle. Above them the cataract sang and the sun brightened and golden dust floated in the air, and there was a wild sweet roaring in the youth's ears.

Saul was totally lost. He obeyed the instincts of his flesh, and was caught up in inexplicable and overpowering sensation, agonizingly sweet yet terrible in its urgent intensity. He lay upon Dacyl and took her savagely, and she held him to her and gently bit his throat and moaned with delight and pleasure. Their bodies were as hot as flame, and like flame they merged together, and all about them was the scent of agitated grasses and flowers, and the singing of the water. Entwined, they were conscious of nothing but ecstasy. Saul felt the moving of Dacyl's flesh under him, and each movement intensified his sensations and he could not know if they were pain or bliss. He felt her tongue licking his ear tenderly, and heard her moaning breath and felt her quickening movements. When the culmination arrived he thought, vaguely, that he had died in one explosion of rapture and that it was a death not to be rued for it was greater than life, like the bursting of a sun or a raining of stars.

His eyes were closed. Sweating and gasping, he lay upon the girl and it was some moments before he rolled from her body and lay beside her, overwhelmed with what he had experienced. He had no immediate thoughts. He had only memory of something of immense and incredible joy and transport, beyond which was nothing comparable.

Dacyl raised herself upon one elbow and looked down at him, smiling, her lips bright red and swollen, her drying hair warm on her naked shoulders and breast. He felt her movement and sluggishly opened his eyes, and he saw her face bent over him and it was more beautiful than he had ever known. Slowly he lifted his hand and touched her cheek, and she turned that cheek and kissed the palm of his hand. He heard a deep chuckling in her white throat, of contentment and affection. One bare pale leg lay over one of his.

Then, like a cold fist hitting his heart he thought, "I have ruined and deflowered and raped and ravaged this innocent child, and I am accursed."

"What is wrong, beloved?" asked Dacyl, alarmed at the pallor and rigidity of the face below hers.

He turned his head aside. He wanted to weep with despair and regret and shame that he had taken this pure one and had defiled her, and that she had submitted to his lust out of gratitude and because she was only a slave and so could not deny an urgent man. Truly, he was anathema in the sight of God and men, and how could he atone for his sin and his crime? Who could forgive him? He deserved an ignominious death.

Dacyl began to stroke the strong red crest of his hair, and his throat. "You are a veritable hero, beloved," she said in her childish voice. "I am yours, forever. I am your slave, adorable one. Not even Venus had so puissant a protector and lover, strong beyond the strength of other men. How she must envy me, the pearl of Cyprus!" She kissed his cheek tenderly.

Above her head the sky had turned a flaming blue and the golden cataract gushed in liquid music and the pool was again the color of young lemons. The grass and moss were soft beneath them, and languor held them. But Saul suffered in his soul profoundly.

He said, "Forgive me, my dear one, forgive me if it is possible."

Dacyl's lustrous black eyes widened with astonishment above him. She bent to see him more clearly, as if incredulous that he had said these words. The metallic blue of his strange eyes were suffused with tears, and Dacyl was amazed.

"Forgive you!" she exclaimed. "It is you who should forgive me for placing you in jeopardy with my carelessness! Forgive you! I adore you, my hero, my Apollo, with hair like the sun and muscles like armor! If life holds nothing more for me than this morning, still I am grateful to all the gods that they permitted me to lie with you and comfort you and reward you."

Saul tried to smile at this innocent childishness. He stroked the soft side of her throat with a gentle hand.

"But I ravaged you, dear one. I took advantage of your distraught state. I have deflowered you, and who can restore your purity?"

Dacyl sat upright, and abruptly. She stared down at him in wonderment. Then after a long moment she began to smile, and it was a woman's humorous smile and not a girl's.

"Is that what troubles you, my foolish one?" she said with soothing affection. "Go to! I am seventeen years old, and am not a virgin. Surely, you did not believe me one!" She laughed with rich tenderness. "I have not been a virgin since I was twelve years old. I was bestowed on the overseer of my master's estate at that age, and we are to be married. I am pledged to him by my mistress, the noble Fabiola, and we will then be given our freedom and an olive grove, and we will be content! But I will love you always, even when I see you no more."

Stunned and stricken and dumb, Saul listened to that light and happy voice, and finally he understood. He had been thinking as a Jew, but this girl was a heathen and had been born and reared in an atmosphere alien to his knowledge, alien to his comprehension. To her, no sin had been committed. She had garnered pleasure as one chooses a bauble, for an hour's gratification, and then forgotten, discarded. She lived and had her being in a hedonist society where everything was permitted, honor scorned, desecration a matter for laughter, adultery a moment's mere satisfaction, fornication accepted, and lasciviousness a thing to be cultivated and pursued. She belonged to a world detested and feared by pious Jews, execrated by them, avoided by them, and she was no longer Dacyl, the innocent slave girl over whom he had wept in secret, but the "strange woman" whose lips were the portals to hell. Into the pit of her body he, Saul ben Hillel, had incontinently and precipitously fallen, and he was lost.

He was dirtied and corrupted beyond redemption. He was forsaken beyond hope, except that he devote his whole life to penance and remorse and repentance. God had averted His Face from him, and how could he atone in one short lifetime? He had lain with a harlot.

"What is it?" asked Dacyl, in consternation. She had sought to comfort and ease him. She had given herself to him in delight and love and gratitude, and he had given her the gift of enormous pleasure as she had also given it to him. Yet he lay on the grass below her with a face of bitter irony and despair.

Saul sat up, and she watched him with disbelief at his silence and his awful withdrawal. She watched him shake out his wet and wrinkled tunic. Why did he not speak, or smile? Why did he avoid her eyes? How had she offended him? Of what grossness was she guilty? Alarmed and beseeching, she touched his knee with her hand, but he started away from her as from the touch of vileness and horror. He sprang to his feet. He looked about him wildly. Tears fell from his eyes.

Then, without speaking, he fled from her and was soon lost among the trees and the puzzled and frightened girl was alone, aimlessly and distractedly pondering in her mind this peculiar behavior of one she loved and had in some way mortally offended.

She saw the basket of pomegranates which he had brought her. She began to eat one and the red juice trickled down her chin. Then she laughed softly and shrugged and shook her head. Men were not to be understood by women. One day he would return to her. She looked down at her beautiful and naked body, and was pleased.

Saul never returned to that lovely spot and never thought of it again without aversion and loathing and shame. It haunted his life. Worse still, he acquired a disgust for women which remained with him. All female flesh, thereafter, was tainted by the scent of Dacyl in warm autumn grass, and the arms of women were the arms of pale serpents, unless they were virgins or honorable wives. Even then, they were suspect and always to be feared.

Hillel ben Borush visited Aristo in the freedman's small but comfortable quarters.

"What ails my son, Aristo?" the anxious father asked. "He is silent and pallid and brooding. He loves you. Has he not confided in you, that we may help him?"

Aristo knew his pupil far better than did the youth's parents or Reb Isaac. He suspected that in some unknown spot, at some unknown hour, the rigid young

Pharisee had encountered a woman and it had shocked him to the heart. Were it not so amusing Aristo would have felt concern. He knew that Saul no longer crept away in silence too early in the morning for his school. So, it was a woman. Aristo sighed. These Jews! They regarded human pleasure with suspicion and avoided it. What a grim Deity was theirs! Aristo thanked the gods, in whom he did not believe, that such a Deity had kept His afflictions of mind and soul to Himself and His special and circumscribed votaries.

"What is it you suspect, Aristo?" asked the troubled father, who had a very keen eye.

"I voice no suspicions, lord," said Aristo with respect. "For I have none. But perhaps our Saul is coming into manhood and is disturbed by his longings and unnamed desires."

Hillel blushed, and Aristo was freshly amused. "Saul is not ready for marriage," said Hillel.

Aristo could not help saying, "Get him, then, some compliant slave girl."

Hillel regarded him sternly. "We are forbidden to abuse women, even slaves or servants."

Aristo chortled, but with respect. "That is not in accord with your teachings, of which Saul has informed me. Did not your David, the king, lust for Bathsheba, and order the murder of her husband so that he could possess her? And I have read the Song of Songs, and surely Solomon was not addressing those Songs to his wives, who were possibly very decorous and uninteresting matrons!" He smiled at Hillel. "I have always thought your hero, Joseph, a fool, or a eunuch, for refusing Potiphar's wife. Dear Master. You Jews are very rigid, and do not enjoy life. Surely your God is not a Pharisee!"

Hillel could not help smiling. "Reb Isaac thinks so, though I do not."

Aristo said, "Remember your own youth, lord, for you are a handsome man and doubtless inspired glances from maidens. It is your own counsel. Let Saul keep his."

Hillel sighed. "Life is a disease from which we do not recover, but by which we are mortally infected. I will keep my counsel, as you advise, Aristo. I will not question Saul. Questions are invariably insulting, from fathers." He paused. "It is very strange that those we beget and love are alien to us, and are understood only by others. Is that God's reminder that we do not possess our children and that we give them their flesh only, and that we must never claim them but must always let them go? Their souls belong to God, and not to us. It is sad to be a father."

One day Aristo said to his silent and stony pupil: "I do not know what it is that torments you, Saul, but nothing is disastrous, eternally, in this world. Nothing is fixed in time. We must learn, at last, to forgive ourselves."

Saul said, with sudden and startling fierceness, "There are things of which a man can never forgive himself!"

Aristo smiled faintly. "Assuredly. The betrayal of trusting friends. Dishonor where dishonor was not deserved. Malice. Returning love with hatred. Crimes against the innocent and helpless. Stupidity. Lack of tolerance. The rejection of permitted pleasure. Gloom, where there is sunshine. Abstinence, when wine is offered. Arrogance without a reason to be arrogant. Hypocrisy. Sniveling guile. Cruelty without provocation. Lies. Desertions. Malevolence. Deceit. Fasting when feasting is at hand. Denial of life and joy. Covering of the face when dancing is encountered. A harsh voice amid music. The presentation of evil when given good. Of which of these, Saul of Tarshish, are you guilty?"

"Of none," said Saul, whose bright color had faded recently.

"Then, of nothing dire are you guilty," said Aristo. But he thought, "Of some of these are you guilty, my poor pupil, but you do not know your guilt, and possibly you will never be forgiven. May your gloomy Deity eventually forgive you, though I doubt other gods will." Then he laughed to himself. "It is very probable that you do not understand your God, at all, and only malign Him!"

Chapter 5

THE family of Hillel ben Borush had intended to leave for Jerusalem, and the marriage of Sephorah after Hanukkah, the Feast of Lights, which coincided this year with the Roman Saturnalia and the celebrations of various other gods. Tarsus was very festive and never appeared to sleep in these days, and torches flared all night in their sockets on the walls and the streets resounded with music and cymbals and drums and flutes and laughter and running feet and the cries of women and the warning shouts of guards who were also drunk.

A ship from Greece came into the port of Tarsus, a small merchant vessel loaded with resinous wine which the Greeks of the city preferred to all other wines. But it did not unload though it lay at anchor for several days. Then on the fourth day it inconspicuously raised the yellow flag and put out to sea and the Roman centurions looked after it in the pallid dawn light and cursed it, and shook their fists at it, and prayed silently. Their captain warned them not to speak of this to any other, and the soldiers, feeling for the sacred medals strung about their necks on chains, saluted and fell into line and marched away, iron soles clanging on the polished black stones of the street.

But though the vessel had been guarded after doctors had examined several of the crew, and all doors had been bolted and galleys locked, the damage had been done. Several rats had swum ashore in the night and they carried with them their sickness and the fleas who had caused it. They died before morning in the gutters. The fleas found other hosts among the healthy rats of the city.

There were two sanitaria in Tarsus. Three weeks later the Greek and Egyptian physicians knew the dreadful truth: Plague was abroad in the city. They consulted together. Should the people be told of their danger and warned to leave Tarsus, thus possibly carrying the infection with them? Should the gates be closed and guarded so that none could leave and no man enter the city? In any event, the people would panic, and would mill mindlessly, attempt to escape, fight with the guards who tried to restrain them, and eventually, they would lose their minds and loot and burn and kill and commit many other crimes. The doctors decided that they would control matters as long as possible and tell no one.

Winter was upon the land and the air was sharp and clear and cold, and the fields and gardens were brown and the sun was large and pale. The grape-colored mountains blazed with snow and the river ran in dull silver through the rich valley and Tarsus smelled of baking bread and roasting meats and wine in the marketplaces and the taverns and inns. It was not for some time that it was observed that no ships put into the usually turbulent port but stood out at sea and loaded boats that came to them, casks of olives, mats of wool, carpets, silks and cottons, wines, beer, whiskeys, oil, spices, salt and other merchandise. No reason was given even when it was observed that no ships of Tarsus put out to sea. Questions were asked when expected visitors did not arrive. One by one public buildings were quietly closed. Then because there were now too many questions and too many rumors the yellow flag was hoisted over the high Roman guard-tower above the harbor, and the people were stricken with terror, and the guards walked the streets all night with naked swords in their hands.

Tarsus was by nature riotous and passionate, and for a few days the Romans were strained to their very limits of exhaustion and determination to keep the mindless mobs from too much vandalism and rioting. Terror had the people by the throat. Doors and windows were closed tightly; the streets began to be deserted except for thieves and the gatherers of the dead and the rattling of the death carts over the stones. A putrid stench rose from the gutters. Not even the Romans could force men to clean them and to wash down the streets, even at the threat of imprisonment and death, so the Roman soldiers turned to this task. No one jeered. Fright was too great. The wagons did not come into the city in the mornings but waited outside the gates and there left their wares and fled. Only hunger forced men to the gathering and the distribution. And everyone drank mightily and burned incense to the gods, but no one came to the temples. The weather grew colder.

The house of Hillel ben Borush was heated with constantly fed braziers and woolen curtains, thick and heavy, had been drawn over the windows to keep out the chill winds, and doors were barred. Deborah, for all her vanity and lightness of mind, was a sensible matron when it concerned her household, and the storehouses were full. The family was fitted to endure a siege, and all knew, now, that they were indeed besieged by something more fearful than a human foe.

It was noticed that not many Jewish funerals appeared on the blank streets. Avid and terrified eyes peered from behind curtains at the funerals of the mean and the mighty, but of few Jews. So evil rumors began to spread. It had long been believed that the Jews were acquainted with magic they would share with no others and had sorceries against illness which they kept from their neighbors so only they would survive. But the physicians in the teeming sanitaria knew that it was the Jews' insistence on absolute cleanliness and their intolerance of vermin which gave them some measure of protection against disease, even against the plague. They became alarmed at the rumors they heard and warned the Roman centurions. The Romans, the most tolerant of conquerors, the most lawabiding, the strongest despisers of tales and passions and disorders, prepared to protect the Jews if necessary, and issued warnings of their own. Those caught looting property would abide by the ancient law: Looters were to be executed immediately. Those guilty of setting fires would be thrown into their own fires, whether graybeard, child, man or woman. There was not a street, even in the harsh and brilliant sunlight of the day, which did not have its patrolling soldiers in war dress. The sun glinted on their swords, and on dropped visors and on armored chests. The resolute steps of the soldiers resounded from stone and the voices of their officers were loud in the silent city. The banners of Rome fluttered against the hard blue sky and the carriers of fasces were everywhere, demonstrating to the people that law was law above all else, and there would be no lawlessness in Tarsus so long as any Roman remained alive.

Hillel heard of these things but did not inform his household. He had no visitors and he was thankful that he lived in the suburbs. The walls and floors of his house were washed down at dawn by his servants, each and every morning, and rats and mice hunted mercilessly. All stayed within the house except for necessary excursions into the garden for last fruits and dates and citrons, and to the storehouses. Fear lived here as it lived in all other houses in the suburbs and the city, but with the fear was mingled prayers.

But the infection spread. Just when the first pale pink
blossoms were appearing on the almond trees in the garden and bare twigs were quickening and myrtle was
budding, Deborah and her son, Saul, were stricken by
the plague. As the household was small and not pretentious it did not possess a family physician in residence,
and physicians were always available from the sanitaria or
from their private practices. Hillel, for the first time in
his life, mounted a horse and rode into Tarsus. He would
not permit the family carriage to be used, for he would
then endanger a slave or a servant who would be driving
it, and he feared a chariot. The horse was the least of
his anxiety though he was accustomed to riding an ass
when he rode at all, a docile and patient ass and not like
this horse which, though gelded, moved too rapidly for
its master. The Roman soldiers laughed at his disordered
passing.

Hillel went to the largest of the sanitaria and asked for
his friend, the famed Egyptian physician, Aramis. While
he waited in the cold marble hall he could hear the
screams and groans of the dying in their wards, and he
wrapped his cloak tightly about him, closed his eyes and
prayed the prayer for departing souls. Then Aramis was
beside him, touching his arm, and he dropped the hood
of his cloak and his eyes were full of tears.

The Egyptian was very tall and dark and lean with a
thin and prominent Hebraic face. "Dear friend," he said,
and he was full of concern. "Do not tell me that your
family is stricken!"

Hillel nodded. He could not speak for a moment or
two, and then he said, "My wife, Deborah bas Shebua,
and my only son, Saul. You know them well."

"I will come at once," said Aramis, and he went for
his pouch and Hillel tried to control his despair and wait
in patience. Aramis returned, cloaked and hooded in gray
wool, carrying his pouch. His horse, a fine Arabian steed,
was waiting for him at the gate. "I cannot thank you
enough," Hillel stammered, as he struggled to rise onto
his own horse. He was not adroit; he began to fall over
the side of the animal and desperately clutched at its
mane, and Aramis' servant caught him and gravely replaced him. Hillel was hardly aware of this; his haggard
face was desolate. He stared at the physician, mounted

high and proud. "Save them," said Hillel. "Save them, and all that I have is yours."

They rode through the empty streets, Hillel tossing on his horse and hardly able to control it. Finally Aramis took the reins from his hands and led the horse. He said, "Do not despair. The plague is waning and those we now see have it in a milder form. Many survive. Before the summer comes the disease will have left the city."

But when he saw Deborah in her carved ebony and ivory bed he knew she was moribund. She had the plague in its worst form, in her lungs, and her blood dripped from her lips and she was not conscious. Aramis regarded her with sadness and pity: So beautiful a young woman, and so doomed. He could do nothing for her but relieve her last agony, and so he prepared a potion brewed of opium for her and told her servants to give spoonfuls of it to her when she could swallow. Then he threw aside the darkening wool curtains and let the wind and sun into the room so that at the last Deborah could see the sky and be comforted, and not die in dimness and seclusion. He bent over her and again touched her fiery cheek and she opened dulled and unaware blue eyes, already glazed with death. Aramis returned to Hillel, who awaited him in the atrium. The husband and father had been pacing in extreme agitation. He sprang at the physician when he saw him, and clutched his arms.

He saw, on the physician's face, what there was to see, and he let his hands and head fall and did not speak.

Aramis visited young Saul, who was delirious and tossing wildly on his bed, held there by the strength of two men servants. He had the bubonic form which, though desperate, held more hope than his mother's affliction. His buboes were leaking pus and blood and the white linen sheets were stained. But Aramis reflected that the youth was strong and sturdy and of a vital constitution and had never been ill before. He had a possibility of survival. Aramis gave his orders to the servants, and two potions in flasks, and ordered cooling baths scented with verbena. He returned to Hillel and tried to smile.

"Pray," he said. "I have hope for Saul, for youth and life are with him."

"My wife, my sweetest one, my child," said Hillel, and began to weep. He pulled his shawl over his head and addressed his God with numbed lips, asking for mercy.

Aramis remained in the household of his friend until sunset, when Deborah bas Shebua, the child in spirit, the infant in true knowledge, died with one soft and final cry. Aramis put his arm in support about the shoulders of Hillel ben Borush, who watched a servant gently close the eyes of his wife and fold her hands on her breast, and then cover her face with the sheet. Hillel began to tremble violently. He pulled his shawl over his head and cried aloud:

" 'The Lord gives. The Lord has taken away. Blessed be the Name of the Lord!' "

His voice broke and his shoulders bent, but he recited in a low and steadfast voice the Psalm of David:

"Out of the depths have I called You, O Lord!
Lord, hearken to my voice.
Let Your ears be attentive to the voice of my
*   supplications.*
If You, Lord, should mark iniquities, O Lord, who
*   could stand?*
For with You there is forgiveness
That You may be feared.
I wait for the Lord; my soul does wait,
And in His Word do I hope.
My soul waits for the Lord,
More than watchmen for the morning,
Yea, more than watchmen for the morning.
O Israel, hope in the Lord!
For with the Lord there is mercy,
And with Him is plenteous redemption—"

He paused and clasped his white hands together and said in a louder voice:

"Hear, O Israel! The Lord our God, the Lord is One!"

Then he could stand no more but fell on his face beside the bed of his wife.

Aramis shook his head in compassionate wonder. He could not understand why a man, so deeply stricken by the loss of a beloved, could recall his God and adore Him, and cry aloud to his people to remember His

Name. But then, he reflected, the Jews were an incredible people, as his own people had reason to remember. None could comprehend them. Their trust in their Deity, their meekness before His blows, offended the Egyptian's sense of civilization and pride, and manliness.

His mother had been in her tomb for a number of days before Saul awoke to consciousness, weakness and pain and drenching cold sweat. He awoke to the sight of Aramis' face, bent over him in the morning light, and the feel of his palm on his forehead.

"Saul?" said the physician gently. "Do you know me, Saul?"

The first red rays of the sun were striking on the gleaming white walls of the cubiculum, and a warm sweet wind of early spring blew out the curtains over the windows. Saul's cracked and parched lips moved in a faint whisper, and Aramis smiled contentedly. The boy would live. He ordered a cool draught for him, half wine, half water, mixed with raw eggs, and held it, himself, to Saul's mouth and bade him drink. The youth obeyed, looking fixedly at the Egyptian's face. His own was sunken; the broad and heavy bones of it were like stone over which gray skin had been stretched. The flesh was gone. Only the red hair had vitality now. The strenuous blue eyes were remote, as if remembering a far place and time.

The youth whispered, "I thought I had died."

"Not yet," said Aramis, pleased that Saul had swallowed all the draught. "You have defeated death, as you will defeat him again and again."

The neck of his tunic had fallen forward and Saul saw what hung about his throat on a golden chain, and even in his weakness and prostration he was startled. For the object was as long as his middle finger and made of gold, and it was a cross with a looped top which held to the chain. Saul felt a dim astonishment at the sight of this infamous object, this symbol of a shameful Roman death, of criminal execution. He could not take his eyes from it and Aramis, seeing this, touched it with his forefinger.

"It is the sign of man's redemption, given to my people from the ages, the sign of the resurrection of the dead," he said. "From everlasting to everlasting."

A curious thrill ran through Saul's weakened flesh but what had caused it he did not know. Yet he thought that he had discerned a flash somewhere like lightning, like the tearing of a fabric which had concealed a blazing lamp. He was still pondering on this strangeness, pain and confusion mixed with a sense of premonition, when he fell asleep, and it was a sleep undisturbed by the nightmares which had haunted him and had driven his feeble soul into dark caverns of terror.

When his father visited him at sunset he had vague memories of seeing his face bending like this over him many times during his almost mortal illness. But now he saw clearly. Hillel had aged; the brightness of his hair and beard had paled; his face was thin and filled with suffering, and his brown eyes were scored by many tears.

Then Saul recalled that he had been struck down the day after his mother. He stared at his father, and he knew. Pain took him, pain of the spirit, not for Deborah but for Hillel whom he deeply loved. He sought his father's hand weakly, and Hillel's fingers closed over his. Hillel bowed his head, and he repeated:

"The Lord gives. The Lord takes away. Blessed be the Name of the Lord."

Saul began to weep, silently, and again his grief was for his father. Hillel wiped away his tears. "I have my children," he said. "God is good, blessed be His Name."

A servant lit a lamp on the table nearby and its yellow tongue fluttered in the evening wind. Saul turned his head to look at the last light and it seemed to him that he was no longer a youth but a man. His hand tightened over his father's. His heart expanded painfully with love for this tenderest of fathers, but Saul felt that he held the hand of a child, and he did not know why he should feel so and why he desired, above all things, to protect Hillel.

It was many weeks before Saul recovered even a measure of his strength. Never again was he to feel the bodily power of the years before his illness, and the tirelessness of it. From that time henceforth he was driven less by his youth and vital energy, now much depleted, than by the strength of his spirit. He was to know weakness of the flesh and weariness to the day he died, and no more did his soul bound in him like a newborn lamb in the morning of life. He had returned from a far place and had left much behind him, never to be regained.

During the weeks of his recovery he sometimes thought of his mother, but as the days passed he found it hard to recall the beauty of her face and the sound of her voice. This grieved him. He felt himself an unnatural son that he could not mourn her as a son should mourn. He denounced himself for his lack of sorrow, and forgot that his mother had not loved him. When he stood with his father, saying Kaddish, he hated himself for what he believed was his arrant hypocrisy. He wanted to beg his father's forgiveness for lack of sensibility and hardness of heart. But he could not increase Hillel's suffering, and so he recited the prayers for the dead with him. He despised himself because he could not truly believe that his mother's soul had survived her light and trivial existence in this world; she had died as a flower dies, sinking crumpled into the earth, the petals decaying. Women, he would think, were not worthy of the grief of a man, nor his pain. He thought this even when before her tomb, watching his father lay a sheaf of summer flowers upon it.

When he thought of Dacyl involuntarily he would shiver as at an intrusion of evil, and would pray to be delivered from her memory. He considered his sister, Sephorah, less delightful to him, and he was less indulgent with her airiness and mockery and often found her laughter displeasing. When she cried for her mother he was impatient and restless.

He desired something with a great desiring and a mighty and starving hunger, but what it was that he desired in place of what he had lost he did not know.

Chapter 6

THOUGH it was the custom for a bridegroom to come to her father's house for the bride, Hillel had long ago decided that when his daughter married it would be under the light of Jerusalem, the city of her fathers and of her people, the city of Sion, the holy place of God and the Temple.

It was autumn again before Hillel ben Borush took Sephorah and Saul to Israel and to Jerusalem, and Hillel wept afresh that his beloved wife was not on this journey to take joy in her daughter but must remain behind in her tomb. He had taken Deborah from her father's house, and never had she seen it again, and he reproached himself that he had delayed. He could not endure it that Deborah would not see her daughter's wedding garments and her jewels and the gifts the bridegroom, Deborah's nephew, Ezekiel, had sent Sephorah. He would stroke the girl's shining hair, so like his own and gaze tenderly into her golden eyes, and he would sigh. Yesterday she had been but a babe. Now she was fifteen years old, and a woman. Tomorrow, she would be a mother, herself. Hillel endured the weight of time and sorrow on his shoulders and he felt old and exhausted.

They sailed from Tarsus on such a warm and golden autumn day that Saul was assaulted by emotions he could hardly control. Two unfathomable forces contended in him, both furious and contentious and denying, and he dared not examine them. He stood on the deck of the galleon and watched the fervid harbor recede and the multicolored city, as furious, noisy and busy as ever, and the traffic on the river with red and blue and green and white sails, and beyond the contorted scarlet barrier of the mountains which guarded the plains and the valley. The sun was passionate on the scene, giving it life and vitality and fervent movement, and the water was like yellow oil. Now the city became a medley of every color known to man, and the tiled roofs shimmered as if with fire, and the galleon carefully picked her way through massed ships in the harbor and her sails filled with hot wind and stood like the great white wings of birds against the ardent blue of the sky. Saul could smell warm resin and tar and hemp and heated wood and salt and the deck dipped and rose beneath his feet. It was strange to him. He had never left Tarsus before, and he tried to fix his mind on the novelty and perceive it. But the emotions that tore him like two fanged tigers would not let him go.

His father and Sephorah reclined under an awning on the deck and listlessly ate fruit, feeling sadness that Deborah was not with them, and nearby sat Sephorah's two maidens who would live with her in her husband's house and serve her. But Hillel, the simple man, had no servant with him. There was gray mingled in his golden hair and beard, for he was now nearly forty-seven, and sorrow had taken the brilliance from his eyes and had dimmed his flesh. But he smiled at his daughter and sighed. A maiden needed her mother at this time of her life, to counsel her and advise her and admonish her. But Sephorah had no mother. The family of Hillel ben Borush were to be guests in the house of David ben Shebua, and David's wife was a Roman matron who had been described to Hillel as "an old Roman," and not a licentious and worldly woman of modern society. She was so virtuous a woman, and of so distinguished and ancient a Roman house, that she was also extremely pious and had instilled in her sons and daughters not only the principles and precepts of the old stern gods but had insisted on their being given a rigid training in their father's abandoned religion. Her daughters were as discreet and modest and retiring as she had been in her girlhood, and were trained to Jewish duties and reverence—as an "old" Roman Clodia was courteous to her husband and her husband's family, for all she was of the gens Cornelius. Her sons had been circumcised; they meticulously observed the Jewish holidays because of their mother's severe insistence though they smiled at her behind her strong square back. However, Clodia was respected and more than a little feared, and of this Hillel had heard and had few doubts but that Clodia would impart to Sephorah the secrets and the exhortations necessary for a bride. Hillel had been informed by other relatives that Clodia resembled a stalwart peasant woman from the fields of the Campagne rather than a great Roman lady, whose kinsmen were honored by, rather than honoring, the new Caesar, Tiberius Claudius Nero, in that monstrous and distant city of Rome. Her father and her brothers had served in his campaigns and had been famous for valor, and her family arms and the shields of her warriors hung on the walls of David ben Shebua's house in Jerusalem.

"My wife," David ben Shebua had written, somewhat ruefully, "can at times be considered handsome, though never beautiful. She is frugal and stern, but kind and just, and would have made an excellent wife for one of the old patriarchs. She guards my purse, which I find a little onerous, but I know of her excellent investments and her large properties. Reserved and quiet though my Clodia is, rarely speaking in the presence of men, I have heard that in Rome she is the terror of bankers and stock-brokers. Her accounts would awe a moneylender, so correct are they. She visits the Court of the Gentiles on the Holy Days as sedulously as she visits and sacrifices to her favorite divinity, Juno of the harsh temper and the ever-seeing eyes—doubtless she considers me another Jupiter! Her domestic gifts are superb. My table is valued by Herod, himself, the Tetrarch, not to mention my Greek friends of the delicate palate and my Roman friends who admire her exotic cooks. Clodia is no provincial. You will notice I speak of Clodia's cooks, not mine, for she considers her domain sacred and not to be invaded by husbands. We have a cook of Greek talent, an Egyptian cook who prepares dishes to make a Syrian envious, and, most certainly, a Jewish cook. To the amusement of many, my Clodia obeys the dietary laws of the Jews!"

Hillel had always been a little incredulous about this, discovering it hard to imagine a great and noble Roman lady governing her kitchen in a strange land among strangers not of her race and religion, and deferring dutifully to what she considered to be her husband's duty, and managing her household not as a Roman but as a lady of Israel. But then, he would reflect, the Romans resemble us Jews very mysteriously. He had also heard that Clodia regarded Greeks, and Sadducees, with a disapproving eye which, Hillel would think with a smile, must cause the elegant David some disagreeable moments and some embarrassment, as well as the jests of his family and his friends.

But Hillel recalled the words of Ruth: "Thy people shall be my people, and thy God my God." Clodia had probably never heard of Ruth but she exemplified her. Clodia, therefore, was a redoubtable lady and, while the family of Shebua ben Abraham affected to find her amusing and rallied David on his wife, they respected and feared her. Even her father-in-law, the aging and urbane Shebua, deferred to her and the wives of David's brothers were timid before this righteous and determined matron. Deborah, who had first seen Clodia when she, Deborah, had been a child, had often declared that the Roman lady was "gross and with a heavy hand, more fitted to the field than to a cultivated house, and resembled a servant." So Hillel was heartened. He thought that he would find Clodia very similar to his dead and beloved grandmother, Sarah. But he wondered with some uneasiness if Sephorah who had been reared freely and lightly by her mother, could accustom herself to rarely appearing before men, never dining with them, and secluding herself in the women's quarters, over which Clodia was the rigorous queen. He had tried to tell the girl of her aunt, and Sephorah, who had heard much from her mother, was laughingly dismayed.

"A veritable Gorgon," she had said.

"Let us speak of a mother of Israel," Hillel had replied. Father and daughter had then looked at each other and had laughed a little. It was Saul who had listened with approval of Clodia, and in some way Hillel had felt this a deprecation of Deborah. Yet Hillel was relieved. In many ways Saul was more the son of a Clodia than of a Deborah and even, perhaps, of a Hillel ben Borush. During the past year he had become even more so.

Hillel now watched Saul who was leaning on the rail of the ship and looking back at Tarsus, become, in the hot noon light, a broken welter of color on the water, surmounted by those terrible mountains. The youth's chin was already faintly red with his growing beard; his crest of red hair appeared still virile and arrogant, and his ears were enormous. His profile was set and unrelenting with his thoughts, the big nose arching from his face, his chin hard and fixed, his mouth a straight and somber line. His former high color had left him; he seemed less sturdy, but taller and thinner. Yet his indomitable air had strangely increased with his decline of physical vitality, and if his body was more slender his shoulders appeared wider and more manly. His legs were still deplorable, but lately he had given up the short tunic and wore a robe to his ankles, a brown linen robe with a girdle of dull worked silver, covered by a cloak of the same unpleasant color. But for his remarkable face he would have seemed to be a son of a somewhat unprosperous merchant, simple and plain and unpretentious, bent on securing as much money as possible for goods now in the hold of the ship. He would hardly impress his aristocratic kinsmen in Jerusalem though doubtless Clodia would admire him.

There had never been much communication between Hillel and his son, though Hillel had helplessly struggled to draw closer to Saul from his childhood. He knew that Saul loved him; he also knew that Saul did not place much value on his mind and did not approve of his rare, but telling and amusing, jests about the more fanatic of the Pharisees. Saul, Hillel was afraid, was really indulging his father when he listened with silent respect to his homilies and little parables and his explanations of some obscure paragraph in the Scriptures. Saul, Hillel was sadly sure, had already reached a more subtle and learned conclusion which was possibly correct and not diffused, as in Hillel's fashion. In short, Saul was the complete and unbending Pharisee and Hillel unjustly blamed Reb Isaac for this and accused himself of not being tolerant and emphatic enough in his own teaching of his son. Hillel sighed again. There was not a fingerful of humor in Saul, except for an occasional ironic comment or some sardonic remark, and these had become more marked and frequent during the past year. The portents of his infanthood were manifesting themselves inexorably.

The old occasional tenderness, the old young impulsiveness, the old artless loud laughter of boyhood, had left Saul a year ago, not slowly, not through illness, but in a moment. He could still speak vociferously and dogmatically, but no longer did his smile offer half an apology or amusement at himself. When Saul spoke now he did not invite argument or disagreement, not even from his father. Only Aristo could make him flush when disputing with him, but now anger would light up those peculiar and compelling eyes. Surely Saul did not think himself infallible! No, thought Hillel, still watching his son, he does not believe himself infallible, but he thinks himself superior to other men in judgment and understanding of the Word of God and the precepts of the prophets and the patriarchs: A Pharisee, indeed, unrelenting, unyielding, even ruthless, in defense of the Holy One of Israel, the guardian of the Book. He talked of the Messias on every occasion dismissing all other conversation as irrelevant and time-destroying and therefore sinful and debasing. Sometimes Hillel felt weary.

Hillel, therefore, was anticipating Jerusalem, with its Romans and Greeks and many other races, its teeming cosmopolitan civilization, its many diversities and faces and manners and customs, with a relief he would have believed incredible only a year ago. Saul would be an anachronism in that lively and colorful society, and Hillel was not displeased. He felt a little guilty when he hoped that in some way Saul would not encounter numerous other Pharisees—but it was possible that even Pharisees in Jerusalem had mellowed a little. Saul was young, and the young were susceptible, and Hillel hoped that one day soon the younger Saul would return, eager with life, ready with a jest, boisterous with young laughter, teasing his sister, curious and tireless.

Saul lifted himself from the rail of the deck and slowly turned and faced his father and sister. "Come join us for wine and fruit, my son," Hillel said, and made room for Saul on the couch on which he sat. The ship creaked and heeled, and other passengers conversed loudly and there was tramping below and runnings up and down the stairs, and the mighty sails seemed to be attempting to lift the ship into the sky. A group of young Roman legionnaires stood at a distance, drinking, exchanging rollicking and obscene jests and swaggering where they stood and clanking their iron-shod feet, and furtively eying the beautiful Sephorah.

Saul saw this and he suddenly gave the soldiers a fierce and despising look. They were astonished; they were only lads and they had been admiring a delectable young lady who had not shown any displeasure. Their mouths fell open. They were insulted by this plainly clad and insignificant youth, with the flaring red hair. They clanged their feet harder on the wooden deck. One or two even touched their swords and they frowned forbiddingly. They were Romans. They were masters of the world. How dared a miserable man from Tarsus resent their conversation or their laughter and favor them with a look which consigned them to the status of the market rabble, or slaves?

Then Saul turned from them and went to his father and sister. Sephorah was half reclining on the soft divan, very conscious of the glances she had evoked from those boys. She wore a chiton of blue silk artfully embroidered in gold and silver and her smooth white arms were bare, as was her throat, and her veil was like a mist over her golden hair, and there were jewels at her neck and on her arms and hands and her feet were shod with scarlet slippers. Her golden eyes glistened and her lips were like wet rubies and her pretty nose was warm ivory and she had assumed an air of worldly languor. Perfume rose from her and Saul was suddenly reminded of the scent of crushed flowers and grass on which he and Dacyl had lain. Torment seized him.

"You resemble a harlot, my sister," he said through his teeth. "There is kohl about your eyes and a paint-pot on your mouth. Your arms are naked and shameless, and your ankles are exposed. Where is your modesty, your decorum?"

Never before had he spoken in such a tone and in such words to his once-beloved Sephorah. The girl paled and shrank. The Roman soldiers listened, even more astonished.

Then Hillel sat upright and for the first time Saul saw his father deeply angered against him, and outraged. The brown eyes became hard and daunting. "Saul," said Hillel. "Depart from us until you have prepared an apology. We will dine alone." He still stared harshly at his son. "It is said that he who insults another in public, without provocation, incurs the wrath of God. Meditate on that, while you eat your solitary meal."

For the first time in his life Saul did not bow before his father's rebuke. Instead he gazed at his father with so implacable a face and with such cold and formidable eyes that Hillel was horrified and stricken. It was a stranger who confronted him and not his son, and the stranger was not of his spirit.

Then Saul inclined his head, turned on his heel and left his father. He went down the stairs to the room he shared with Hillel. Hillel watched him go and the sorrow became desolate in his eyes.

"Father," said Sephorah, seeing this. "Saul is guiltless of offense. He spoke from some misery in his soul. I have discerned this for over a year. His illness devastated him."

Hillel touched her soft little hand. He said, "No. The change appeared before his illness, before your mother's death, may God rest her soul. He is possessed, but of what he is possessed I do not know, and I have no pathway to his mind and he bars the way."

He hesitated. He looked at the avid Roman soldiers who had listened. He thought to invite them to partake of his good wine and fruit in compensation, but by this act he would confirm Saul's unspeakable behavior in their opinion and be shamed by his own son. He sat for a little under the striped awning with his daughter, while she gently stroked his hand in sympathy, and the blinding light of water and sky dazzled their eyes. Finally he rose in silence and followed Saul, finding him in the small spare room they shared together and in which their chests had already been deposited. The sun glared through the little window. They could hear the chanting of the galley slaves below, a mournful and wordless sound. Hillel sat near his son, not speaking, and Saul sat on the edge of his narrow couch, his hands dropped between his knees, his head bent, his red hair disordered. Hillel could see nothing of his face but a clenched cheek, unusually pale, and the jutting of his pugnacious brow.

At last Hillel spoke. "Your insult to your sister, whom you once loved, is unpardonable."

Saul said, as if muttering between his teeth, "I spoke out of my conscience."

To this Hillel said, "It is remarked in Deuteronomy that that man is accursed who elevates his conscience above the divine laws of God. He is a heathen. He will have no place in the world hereafter. What crimes have been perpetrated in the name of the individual conscience, what calamities, what injustices, what errors! A man cannot trust his conscience unless it is in perfect accord with God's commands, blessed be His Name, for, what is man? A creature of dust and pride, of wanton and willful imaginings, of self-deceits, of vanity, of profound ignorance when he believes himself most wise, of illusion, of fantasy. You will recall that Moses was inspired to kill a man, and thus aroused the anger of God. Yet, what he did, of a certainty, was no doubt urged by his 'conscience.' "

Saul did not speak for a moment, then, still not lifting his head he muttered, "I spoke, then, out of the teachings of my youth, that women must not disport nor array themselves as harlots and whores, as strange women, and that always they must be of a modest demeanor with bent eyes and a quiet tongue."

Hillel studied him. He said, more gently, "My son, it was not Sephorah's raiment nor her manner which distresses you, for always was she so and I confess that I find it beautiful and innocent. If God had desired to make ugliness the mark of a good woman then He would have created no charming ones to delight the eyes of men and to array our lives with color and enchantment. Do not speak to me of temptations! God tempts no man to evil. No, it was not Sephorah, your dear sister whom you once loved. It is something else that has tormented you for over a year. I am your father. Am I unworthy to hear a son's confidence?"

Saul's hands came together in a hard wringing between his knees and Hillel suffered for him. The bent head fell lower. "I cannot tell you, my father," said the youth in so stifled a voice that Hillel could hardly hear what he said. "It is beyond forgiveness."

For an instant only Hillel was greatly alarmed and his heart gave a painful throb of fear. Saul continued: "I have violated all the precepts and teachings of my youth, have mortally offended God, have destroyed my place in Israel."

Hillel could now control the panic he had felt. He said, "What holy Commandment did you violate, Saul?"

It seemed absurd to him, and he could even smile now, that his son, hardly sixteen years of age, a student fanatically devout, an obedient son, a lover of his home, an almost immured one, could have violated a Commandment or committed any other sin of any magnitude. He saw that Saul's brow was wrinkled in concentration. He saw the side of Saul's throat move in a convulsive swallow, and he thought, "How disastrous are the thoughts of youth, of what awful and ridiculous exaggeration, and crashing thunders, and fatalities and doom!"

Saul said, "I cannot confess to you, my father, for if I should I should die of shame, and never would you forgive me."

"You are my son, and I begot you, and what you have done, and will do, will be part of my own being, Saul. If you will not confess, if you will not let me console you, remember that God pardons always a repentant sinner. The only unpardonable sin is to presume that God will find nothing unpardonable. I doubt that you are a great sinner; I doubt you have violated the Commandments. Keep your own counsel. But remember, always, that God will not despise a contrite heart."

When Saul did not answer or move, Hillel continued, "It is the way of youth to intensify, to throw itself into the depths, to climb the most incredible mountain, to rejoice as a madman rejoices, to mourn as though the end of all being had arrived. I would not have you believe that it is my opinion that youth cannot sin, and even most dreadfully. But it does take a certain amount of knowledge and experience to sin willfully and with the full consent of one's soul, and to rejoice in the sinning, and to know it was sin from the first moment of temptation. Youth has not had these—advantages." And Hillel smiled.

Saul said, and his voice was the voice of a stranger, "My father, you were always a tolerant man and not always did you adhere to the teachings of the Pharisees, and often jested at a point you considered too rigorous."

It is useless, thought Hillel. He rose, but he did not know where he should go. He was now too distressed. He only knew he must leave his son. I have lost him, he thought. And then he thought, "But I never had him and I must face this finally."

He said, "You are committing a mortal sin. You defy God to forgive you."

It was then that Saul seized the red hair of his temples in an agony and pulled his head down upon his knees. Seeing this, Hillel felt deep anguish of his own, and he pondered, his unseen hand outstretched to his son. It was not God entirely, then, which so tortured his son, nor even a misapprehension of God. This was a human guilt that beset him, a human woe. Saul was using his God as a Scapegoat, as the Receiver of his torture. When a man cried, "God will not forgive me!" he often meant "I cannot forgive myself!"

So Hillel said, "All pain passes, all loss, my son." His voice was deep and compassionate. "I thought I should die when your mother died, but it was not God's will, blessed be His Name. I had no desire to live. I longed for the sight of her face, her voice, the rustle of her garments. When I considered that no longer would I see her, no longer caress her, and that she was lost to me, I almost lost my mind. My sorrow is still almost beyond my capacity to bear. But we were born to be men, and not weak beasts, who lie in the dust and tamely give up their lives when it becomes unendurable. What tears your heart has torn the hearts of multitudes before you, and will tear them again, age after age. But hearken to this: You are young. You will survive. Your wound will heal. It will leave a scar, but it will heal."

It was as if Saul had not heard him, so Hillel slowly went from the cabin and returned to his daughter. Saul lifted his head. He said aloud, "It will not heal. No, it will never heal." He began to weep silently, in rage and love and hatred and in passion of spirit, in longing and in loathing, in yearning and in self-disgust.

Hillel said to his daughter, Sephorah, who was much concerned about his sad face and mournful eyes, "I fear it is as Aristo has said—and I dared to laugh in my ignorance when he said it!—that two giants struggle in the soul of my son: The normal young lust for life and joy in living and rejoicing in each morn, and an iron certainty that these are evil and must be smothered and murdered in order that all a man's thoughts should be centered on God. Saul, then, deprives himself of his youth and his natural young gaiety and the wonder and the beauty and the grandeur of creation, and his expectation of tomorrow and its gifts, considering these worthless and a snare for his soul. He would shroud God in crepuscular clouds and terrible lightnings and make of Him, not a loving Father, merciful and full of loving-kindness, but a Judge armed with terror and vengeance, seeking out the smallest sin or error in order to punish it most cruelly, and delighting not in His children but regarding them as an oppressive king regards his people, suspecting them of the most crimes and rebellions, and preparing for them the most hideous flagellations and death. Surely," said Hillel, as the full enormity of the thought developed in him, "that is a sin which God, blessed be His Name, must find it hard to forgive!"

He added, "In one of the Psalms David says, 'When they said, let us go into the House of the Lord, I was glad.' But Saul goes to the House of God like a chained criminal, desirous, aye desirous, not only to worship but to be chastised. What secret sin he has committed does not deserve so fearful a fate, my poor son."

Saul leaned on the rail of the ship and saw the great port of Joppa rising out of the blood-red sea and standing against a sky as scarlet and as ominous. There was the land of his fathers, the holy land, the sacred soil of the prophets, the mountain filled with fire on which God had thundered, the home of the patriarchs, the cradle of the Messias to come, the matrix in which the Messianic Age would be formed, the little land from which would speak the Voice which would reconcile the nations and bring eternal peace to the world. There rose the blessed Mount of Sion, and the golden Temple and all the wisdom which would enlighten mankind and lift the darkness in which it lay, groveling like a beast.

The thin silver thread of the new moon lifted itself over the sea and into the direful sky, and one single star, burning large and gold, stood in the zenith. Now Saul could smell the earth, acrid and spicy and lustful, as the galleon swung toward the harbor. This was an hour he had dreamed of all his life, and he had anticipated his joy and excitement. But he felt no joy, but only an anxious dread. He had no right to step on that soil, a corrupt man, except to atone, to pray that one day he might be forgiven.

He knew that among the many passengers also watching the approach of Joppa stood his father and his sister, Sephorah. He knew his father suffered for him; he knew he had given his father sorrow, and it was an awful pain in him. But how worse a pain, perhaps, if his father guessed the truth! Sometimes a small thought twisted in him that his father might not be so pained, might consider his sin small and trivial and easily forgiven, and might plead his youth and the natural temptations of youth. Perversely, for that very reason Saul could not confide in Hillel. Worse than the thought of his father's possible pain was the thought that the sin might not pain him at all! He preferred to believe in Hillel's condemnation.

As for Sephorah, Saul's love for his sister was a misery in his heart, but he could not bring himself to admit that he had been too harsh to her. If she were not restrained now in her wanton behavior, were not taught the precepts of the mothers of Israel, then she was doomed in body and in soul. Better it would be for her to die before she had been corrupted, as he had been corrupted. A virgin death was better than a harlot's life. Yet there was an intangible sickness in Saul's thoughts, as he contemplated his sister and he dared not explore the reason. She would marry Ezekiel ben David and be subject to his mother, Clodia, rumored to be a just and rigorous and virtuous woman. She would be immured from all the voluptuousness of this present evil world, and all its vices and clamors, its pollutions and its destructions. Saul sought relief in the thought, and when it did not come he was dismayed.

Hillel and Sephorah were not avoiding Saul; it was he who was avoiding them. In fact, they had begun to converse amiably with other passengers and the centurion who was the officer of the Roman legionnaires. How was it possible for them to be amiable to the enslavers of their country and their people, the despoilers and blasphemers of their land? Saul had never loved Romans. Now he despised and hated them.

He glanced sideways along the deck, full of gloom. The vast heavens, the vast sea behind and about them, still glowed as if in flames, but the ship's deck was dark, the figures on it dark also. The white sails were lashed with scarlet. Joppa rocked nearer over the burning water and Saul now saw that the famous harbor was full of ships, small and large, a forest of denuded masts like the bare branches of winter trees. A hot breath blew from the heated land, resinous, perfumed, somewhat putrid, peppery, dusty, reeking of crowded streets and humanity. Plangent sound came over the water, voices, roars, shouts, hard loud laughter, a sudden ruffle of drums. Now twinkling lights of lanterns appeared on the docks and the crimson flare of torches. And there, rising and fluttering in its hugeness, the banner of Rome, its red color almost lost against the red sky, but Saul knew what was on it: "*S.P.Q.R.*—Senatus Populusque Romanus—The Senate and People of Rome."

Blasphemous, incongruous, shameful, frightful! thought Saul ben Hillel, and he beat his fists heavily on the rail of the ship. He could have wept in his anger and hatred and outrage. Someone touched his arm. Hillel said, "We are coming into the harbor. Calm yourself, my son." Hillel's face was pale and shadowy in the light of the celestial conflagration. "It is not to be borne," said Saul through his teeth. "What must be borne must be borne," said Hillel, and returned to Sephorah and her maidens.

But the Messias, blessed be His Name, would drive the Romans into the sea as the Egyptians had been drowned, and Rome, that boastful monster of a city, that dragon of a city, foul to the heart of her, dripping with the blood of the conquered, would die in one flash of avenging lightning.

The galleon was swaying between the crowded ranks of other ships and vessels in the harbor and the crew were ready with ropes and anchors and there was much running on the deck and excited voices from the passengers, and eager laughter. The sailors darted among heaps of chests and coffers and pouches belonging to the passengers, and their hoarse and impatient cries were like the voices of foxes. Vultures, black as death and as silent, were wheeling and circling against the redness of the sky. The galleon docked. Beyond the wharfs was the tumultuous city of Joppa, full of lights and torches, clamorous. All at once darkness fell on the earth, the ominous color was gone except for one long ember on the western horizon in which the last scarlet circle of the sun still burned, a dying eye.

Amid the flickering of the lanterns and torches on the docks stood the ubiquitous Roman soldiers, helmeted, the famous short-sword fastened to their leather girdles, their legs spread, their faces apparently indifferent, their breasts armored in thick leather. Behind them seethed and fluttered welcoming relatives of the passengers, and behind them was a crowd of chariots and cars and horses and workers waiting to unload the vessel and big wagons and asses and yoked oxen. The shifting light of torches splashed them redly, illuminating a face here and there then plunging it into darkness, catching a waving hand then losing it. The noise, to Saul, was overwhelming, the heat unexpected for all it was autumn.

"We have a long journey to Jerusalem," said Hillel, coming to his son again. "We will stay the night in an inn.

It is possible that some of our kinsmen may be greeting us. I hoped we could have landed at Caesarea, but there was no ship leaving Tarsus for another three weeks and I wished to spend the High Holy Days with my people." He thought of Deborah with melancholy.

The soldiers would not permit friends and kinsmen to rush upon the ship, with the possibility of foundering it, but their captain made way for a group to embark and Hillel said with happy astonishment, "David ben Shebua, and his brother, Simon, and that is surely the young Ezekiel, bridegroom of our Sephorah, and Joseph ben Shebua also, and, no! It is! My dear cousin Hannah's husband, Aulus, the centurion!" Hillel's eyes were suddenly filled with tears. His cousin, Hannah, and her family and her husband, were his only living kinsmen for his had been a family of few children and he was the last child of his dead parents.

It was Aulus, himself, the centurion, who was, with calm and stately Roman gestures, ushering the kinsmen upon the ship and all the passengers stared to see who was so honored and so conducted, and the captain made his way to greet the Roman officer. Saul looked at him with contempt, in the light of the lanterns now lit on the galleon. Aulus was a man of some forty-five years, short but powerful, with a jovial and bearded face under his helmet, big white teeth, a huge nose and kind strong brown eyes. He was the first to embrace Hillel, seizing him in his bared arms and kissing his cheek. He smelled of sweat and hearty food and garlic and leather. "My dear Aulus," said Hillel, much moved. "Shalom."

"Shalom," said Aulus. He struck Hillel an affectionate blow on the shoulder. "I have come to conduct you to Jerusalem."

Then the family of Deborah was upon them, the elegant David scented and urbane, clad in fine wool and silk of purple and gold, the less elegant older brother, Simon, but a man evidently well-dined and prosperous and exceedingly plump and jeweled and arrayed in blue and silver with an Alexandrine dagger in his girdle, and Joseph ben Shebua, his twin brother and almost a replica, but less sleek. All, of course, wore no beards and all had their sister Deborah's marble complexion, richness of lips and her blue eyes with auburn lashes, and their uncovered heads showed their tawny hair carefully arranged, curled and perfumed in the Greek manner. However, in spite of their jewels and gold and garments Simon and Joseph exuded a certain complacent grossness, an oiled polish, which offended Saul who waited while his father was lovingly greeted. The youth Ezekiel, but little older than Saul, himself, stood apart in shy respect and deference, and Saul saw that he was thin and somewhat small and insignificant and dark and very Latin in appearance. He had his mother's Roman nose, her definite and prominent profile, but his eyes were the eyes of his father, David, lake-blue and shining. His clothing was not as elaborate and rich as his father's. He wore a long tunic of white linen bordered with gold embroidery, and a brown cowled cloak, and there was but one ring on his finger and no gemmed bracelets clasping his arms such as clasped the arms of his father and uncles.

The family did not cry "Shalom!" to their kinsmen, as Aulus, the Roman, had cried. They embraced Hillel calmly and greeted him and made him welcome. They regarded Saul with some curiosity, and were polite, and David thought that the youth had not improved in appearance but indeed has lost that bright color which had once given him an appearance of exuberance. Hillel answered them as gravely and formally. He was somewhat disturbed that the young Ezekiel was with his father, David. It was unseemly. A bridegroom did not look upon his bride until the day they were espoused, but the family of Shebua evidently thought that anachronistic and old-fashioned and unworthy of Sadducees who were civilized and cosmopolitan. Ezekiel was David's youngest son, and not handsome, but he had his mother's virtues and was very intelligent, so David had forgiven him his lack of comeliness. It was unfortunate, and a little amusing, that the Roman mother had made the youth into a reasonable image of a Pharisee and had sternly urged upon him his Jewish duties and faith.

They are not Jews, thought Saul with bitterness and disdain. They are Hellenistic heathens. He saw Aulus grinning at him amiably and turned away. He looked at his sister; she had, to his surprise and approval, dropped her veil over her face so that her features could be seen but mistily and her maidens were grouped about her discreetly. But her uncle, David, lifted the veil aside and in the mingled lantern and torchlight all saw her virgin beauty and Ezekiel, her bridegroom, turned crimson with shyness and admiration. The uncles kissed the girl's cheek and listened to her whisper of greeting, and were proud of her. "She is as lovely as our lost Deborah," said David, and he thought of the girl's rich dowry. But, after a glance at Hillel, he did not bring forward his son.

Servants of the house of Shebua carried the chests and coffers of the travelers to ornate and lavish cars, beside which waited the chariot of Aulus and the horses of his legionnaires. The cars were drawn by Arabian steeds, as black as night, as lustrous as silk, and their harness was silver and their hoofs gleamed as if shod with silver also.

Saul found himself in the car of his uncle, Simon ben Shebua, and Ezekiel, and he sat down grimly on yellow silk cushions. The other occupants were two men, servants, who were to do the driving, and they were arrayed in fine linen and were cloaked and helmeted as soldiers, to Saul's fresh scorn. Now they moved off the docks, the crowds staring, the Roman legionnaires riding about them; a few men made mocking sounds, some of them ribald. Ahead galloped Aulus and Saul was infuriated to see the banner of Rome unfurled by the soldier who rode at his side. When Ezekiel timidly asked him a question about his journey he affected not to hear him, but wrapped himself in his dull brown cloak and pulled his hood over his head. Simon saw this and thought that the son of Hillel ben Shebua resembled a peasant in his manners.

Joppa was all about them, hot, with narrow streets paved with rounded black stones which glistened in the new frail moonlight and the glare of fluttering torches, and crowded. The bazaars were still open. Saul could hear the angry voices of merchants or their wheedling tones, and he saw women with dark faces and with baskets heaped with fruit on their heads, and oxen and asses, and he could smell the vehement odors of the city. He saw Roman guard-towers and Roman soldiers and the banners of Rome, and he saw faces he recognized as Greek and Syrian and Arabian and other motley races, churning about in the bazaars or hastening through the streets, their voices hoarse, their language incomprehensible. Walls rose and disappeared; there was a scent of hidden gardens, of pine and fountains and manure and roasting meats. Camels turned corners and their riders glowered at the rich entourage that was sweeping to meet them. Once or twice there was a burst of music and women's laughter and songs from behind walls, or the crying of children. Hillel had said that Joppa resembled Tarsus, but Saul found nothing, in this pungent and sweetly fetid air, spicy and hot, of the city of his birth.

But, it was his land, his country, he told himself. He was a Roman citizen, but he was a Jew above all. This land was flesh of his flesh, blood of his blood, however alien it appeared to him in Joppa. He saw family groups on the flat roofs of some of the houses, which were pale brown in color with narrow windows, and climbed steeply. The gutters were noisome and rank and evil water ran between stones, and Saul detected a sudden stench of urine and offal. The light wind had died; the odor of salt was lost as they penetrated farther into the city toward the broad Roman road.

They stayed the night in a quiet and comfortable inn, already prepared for them by the family of Shebua. But Saul lay awake and intense until dawn, his emotions not to be known even by himself, and aware only of a heavy sadness and a solitude of spirit.

Chapter 7

THEY set out at sunrise for Jerusalem and saw the last of the sea, dark purple under a purple sky, the east, over the hills, turning lilac and gold. Hillel ben Borush rode for a pace in the rushing chariot of his friend and cousin, Aulus Platonius, his gray-gold beard flowing behind him, his hood partly covering his face, his cloak streaming in the cool morning wind. It was hardly a pleasure in which he cared to indulge, and he stood beside Aulus and gripped the rail of the chariot, much to the amusement of the charioteer who sat on the one wooden seat in the pounding vehicle. It was evident that Hillel feared for his life and did not trust the four black Arabian geldings who tore into the air and the breeze as if still puissant. They foamed at the mouth and tossed their heads and flecks of foam snapped backwards and Hillel clung as if his life depended upon it. But he wished to talk to the beloved husband of his only remaining kin. The chariot led the procession, and the standard of Rome clapped in the wind to Aulus' right, and Aulus stood sturdily, leather wristlets protecting his wrists, a red cloak flaring from his shoulders, his helmet firmly fixed on his round head, his beard lively and fluttering, and his short sturdy legs braced expertly as he drove. He loved activity, danger and rapid movement and no clash of stone against the iron-rimmed wheels of the chariot did more than sway him a little, whereas poor Hillel expected momentarily to be thrown to the road.

Deborah's brothers had always been a weariness to Hillel and the hours he had spent with them last night had been sufficient for him. God knew he would be forced to endure their company for a considerable time in Israel. He preferred this seemingly reckless charge into the morning—at least for a time—to riding with his kinsmen.

"How goes it with you, dearest of friends?" shouted Aulus over the uproar not only of his chariot but the entourage behind him and the clatter of wheels and hoofs.

Hillel shouted back, "Not too happily." Aulus sighed, thinking of the beautiful dead Deborah. He had seen her but three times in her short life and had thought her both entrancing and stupid, desirable traits in a woman. His own Hannah was the noblest of women with a sweet round face like a plate and a soft voice which assumed no contradiction, and a temperament which would not have permitted it.

The earth began to lighten as the hills lost their darkness and became of a pale copper and saffron color. Aulus glanced at his friend's face and saw his sadness. Hillel's profile was brooding and melancholy as he sought out landmarks which he had almost forgotten in his years in Tarsus. Hillel said, "What do you think of my son, Saul, my only son, whom you have never seen before, Aulus?"

"I saw him but fleetingly," said the Roman. It was not like this forthright soldier to be evasive and Hillel turned his head to him.

"Come now," he said. "We were a time on the deck, awaiting our chests and baskets and coffers and pouches, and there were many lanterns and torches, and I saw you watching my son while you directed your men and the sailors and chattered with the captain. Do not be afraid of offending me, for there is no malice or cruelty in you, Aulus, but only truth and honor."

The Roman wiped the dust from his lips with the back of his hand and stared over the heads of his raging horses. "One does not need many words to describe a man. If you say a man is weak, or effeminate, or untruthful or cowardly or a libertine, you have drawn his portrait. Your son, Hillel, has power."

"Power!" exclaimed Hillel, in wonder. "I have thought him strong and impatient and restless and determined and sometimes contentious, but I did not think of power."

"Power," repeated Aulus with a sagacious nod of his head. "The power of an 'old' Roman or perhaps of an 'old' Jew. It is implicit in his eyes, in his glance, in his movements. He also possesses authority, which is only an attribute of power. I think of him as a soldier. To say a man has power is not always flattering, for he can use that essence of soul to the destruction of others. That, Saul will never do, and I say this to you truly. He is a young man of honor, like his father."

Hillel murmured his thanks, and dared to take one of his gripping hands from the rail to touch one of his friend's. Aulus smiled at him, and now, in the growing light, Hillel could see the white shine of Aulus' great white teeth through his bearded lips. Aulus was glad that Hillel did not question him further. He had not been pleased with Saul. The youth had been too removed, seemingly too indifferent to all about him, but Aulus had seen that he saw everything and that nothing stirred him. He was like one who lived in iron, or who was tormented of soul.

"And how is our Milo?" asked Hillel, referring to Aulus' own son who was five years older than Saul.

Aulus' broad chest expanded with pride. He pushed his helmet back a little from his brown forehead. He smiled happily. "In Rome at present, with the Praetorian Guard. It is a vast honor to be chosen for the personal protection of Caesar. He is a fine soldier, my Milo! But he is of two warrior races, is he not?"

Hillel had almost forgotten that his people were indeed of an irascible and warlike breed, proud and stiffnecked, valorous and brave. The Sadducees were always vexing his thoughts and the Pharisees were too concerned with the minutest phrases of the Book, and raising an awful clamor at the slightest breech of a single paragraph of the Scriptures. When they were not expostulating and arguing they were writing commentaries which unnerved scribes. Between these two there was little space to reflect on the prowess of other Jews and the intrepid history of Israel. In an absent tone Hillel asked, "How are our Zealots and Essenes?"

Aulus grinned with wryness. "They keep us occupied," he said. "It is conducive to leanness in my men, for this climate, you must admit, is not so salubrious as Rome nor so mild, and the stony hills are endless and the caves countless. Your Zealots and Essenes still believe it is possible to defeat Rome and throw us into the sea. They must be admired for patriotism and dedication if not for extreme intelligence, and reason."

But Hillel could not smile at this. Those unfortunate and zealous young men, loving their God and their country above all else, and endlessly harassing the mighty Roman! It was useless—but it was also noble. There were some who did not ignore the Romans as did the Pharisees nor fraternize with them and admire them, as did the Sadducees. If it was folly to resist it was more heroic than not resisting. And had not God rescued the Israelites from Pharaoh and from the walls of Babylon when all seemed hopeless? Who knew the future? The dream of freedom never left the hearts of men.

Now the sun, like a golden and conquering warrior, mounted the farthest somber hill and the earth was flooded with dazzling light. It was autumn, and the harvests were in and many of the fields on each side of the road were yellow and smooth as a good cheese and sundarkened shepherds in rough robes and headcloths were moving through the last garnering with their sheep. Little villages flew past the entourage, pale saffron of brick

and stucco—narrow small houses with slitlike windows
and streets between them little more than stony slits
themselves. Here and there walls appeared, careful yellowish stone laid neatly upon stone without mortar, crowded
with climbing vines whose leaves were like blood. The
sun was hot but the air was cool and flowing, and now
the sea was lost to the left. Cypress trees, dark and stately and rigid, sometimes lined the road, then gave way to
copses of climbing pines resinous and stimulating, then to
silvery olive groves heavy with green or dark fruit, then
to rows of yellow citrons or pomegranates bending under
globes like polished fire. Gray boulders and high thistles
clustered at the roadside, surrendering to meadows suddenly green and radiant in the morning light, and vineyards whose vines were thick with opalescent grapes. The
approaching hills, and those distant on either hand, were
gray or copper and worn as huge ancient stone. The
Romans had denuded them of cypresses to build their
ships, and though many were terraced like giant steps
and carefully cultivated with vegetables and vineyards,
they had a desolate look, blasted and hungry. They were
less mountains than barriers between the crowding villages and towns of yellow or brown brick. Goats clam-
bered on those hot terraces. Now bending palms cast a
sharp shade, and rattled, and glistened with a dust as
the entourage roared by.

But little brooks and rivers shone and gamboled in the
tawny autumn light, and the whole country was exuberant
and vital with the odors of stone, floating golden dust,
fields, grapes, fruit, barley and wheat, hot green grass
and resin. Farmers were abroad, with their sons, carrying baskets in which they placed bunches of sweet syrupy
dates and figs and pomegranates and olives and citrons,
and herds of cattle moved on the meadows and girls with
geese ran across the road, laughing, their gay headcloths
streaming in the brilliant air. There would be another
crop to lay for wheat in the spring, and many farmers,
black-cloaked, with white headcloths, were plowing, the
patient asses going before, the dark earth turning and
steaming. Once or twice, as the entourage raced by, an
encroaching small hill gushed with blue or green water,
and little children splashed in the pools below and goats
came to drink, and fowl. Haystacks dotted the yellow

land, and stacks of wheat and barley, and flat-roofed little farmhouses with white walls peeped shyly from groves of palms or sycamores or karob trees. Crimson and purple flowers lay in eddies in the drying grass.

The landscape began to dance with the heat of the sun so that it hurt the eyes and there was a vast radiance everywhere. Everything swam in light. Hillel threw back his hood. He could not have enough of the seeing of his native land, and remembrance. The sky was so vivid with blue effulgence that it appeared to burn. Round tall Roman guard-towers threw shade and soldiers stood in it, young men with alert faces and searching eyes, their helmets glinting, their muscled legs polished. A few leaned against the towers and surreptitiously munched fruit, or went inside the cool interior for a refreshing drink of wine, while their officers, as young themselves, pretended not to notice.

In and out of hot villages and towns, odorous and loud even so early as this with the merchants and stalls and the market rabble and women carrying baskets and children running and shouting and the donkeys braying and the curses of hurrying men and wagons and horses and camels, the entourage roared, for they must find shelter before the full blasting heat of the autumn day. The cool wind had died. Now everyone was choking on dust and wiping lips and huddling within hoods and dashing away sweat.

"In Rome," said Aulus, "there is a refreshing wind from the sea and a coolness from the Campagna and a green breath from the Alban hills."

"Yes," said Hillel, but he thought his country more vital than Rome and its suburbs for all it was a little land, and conquered. Strange it was that men and races came and went and there were clashes of arms and change and terror and slavery, but the land and those who worked and nurtured the land remained. There was a certain eternal serenity on the earth which none could disturb. It held the dead and the living and was equally indifferent to both. It had its own being. It was a gigantic tomb, for countless nations lay buried in the earth and their flesh and bones fed it, but it was also triumphant life.

The Romans had been here when Hillel was a youth, but he saw many more rich villas now near the road than he remembered, with high stone walls and glimpses of rainbowed gardens and fountains through iron gates. This depressed him. He wondered what his son and daughter were thinking of their country, which they had never seen before. He envied them. How glorious it was to view Israel for the first time, this ancient and holy land, this land of milk and honey, from which sprang the immortal moral laws of God and which still echoes with the Voice of Sinai, and from whose flesh the Messias would be born and cast the light of His eyes! The Greeks had elaborated and cherished the glory of the mind, and philosophy, and beauty beyond imagining and reason and civilized behavior and Demos and the graceful gods, and songs, and had built radiant cities and had invented poesy and dialogue and perfect art, and the Romans had struck grandeur on the earth and had brought law above all to chaotic civilizations and barbarians and were architects and engineers and scientists beyond anything the world had ever known before, and had introduced sanitation and clean water to the remotest places, and were tolerant and just and powerful and handsome and sane, and had produced Ciceros and Catos and Virgils as well as Catilinas and Caesares, and measured representative government and order, and commerce and trade.

But neither Greece nor Rome—nor even mystic Egypt nor India—had produced the Promise of the Ages, nor had they opened the portals of men's souls to the Visage and the Law of God. Despite what the Pharisees declared, the Jews were not a people, not a race, in the full meaning of the terms. They were, at best, but the modern descendants of disparate nomadic tribes who came from no one knew where and whose destiny was still unknown but only conjectured by those who studied the Kabalah. Always they had been surrounded by the Semitic peoples: The Phoenicians, the Hittites, the Arabs, the Moabites, the Philistines, the Egyptians, Syrians, Babylonians, Persians, and a dozen others, and always they had been strangers among them, fought, cursed, reviled, enslaved, driven forth, killed, destroyed, beaten and scattered. But always they had returned to their little country, blood-stained but unconquered, to raise again the Temple to their God and to shout, as Moses had triumphantly shouted, "Proclaim liberty throughout the Land, unto all the inhabitants thereof!"

Then it seemed to Hillel that a mysterious voice sounded in his spirit:

"The Drama has just begun!" His soul lifted in a strange exultation and his eyes brightened, and he knew not why, but he was filled with both a powerful sorrow and a powerful joy. He wished to communicate these things, but his tongue felt heavy and he had no words. Alas, alas, he thought, the deepest voice of the soul cannot be uttered, except to God.

An unprepossessing youth, thought luxurious and plump Simon ben Shebua as he closely observed his nephew from the shadow of his silken hood. He is also too silent and stern of face and abrupt of manner, and his mother, my sister, was all grace and prattle and sweetness and courtesy. Hillel ben Borush is pleasing of countenance and affable of manner. How was it possible for these to produce such a son? Their daughter is charming. But this Saul resembles the less agreeable Romans. His father has written us of his intellect and the power of his mind. Yet he has the manners of a peasant. In comparison my brother David's son, Ezekiel, is a paragon of beauty and graciousness and deportment, though I had heretofore felt him the least captivating of the sons of their father. But ah! these Pharisees! (Simon had been one of the brothers who had opposed the marriage of his sister to Hillel ben Borush. He thought of his own sons with complacency. But his daughters, he reflected, were not so beautiful as Sephorah bas Hillel. However, one was already espoused to a Greek merchant, very rich and possessed of breeding and wit. Simon had considered Saul, before encountering him, as a possible husband for his daughter, Yochabel, the youngest and prettiest and only thirteen, and his favorite. Were it not for the wealth Saul would inherit Simon would have laughed at himself.)

Where Hillel had seen the eternal land—never withholding her gifts of water and fruit and grain and serenity —Saul had seen an afflicted country, forlorn and desolate. Where Hillel had observed the browned farmers faithfully plowing and seeding despite the Roman occupation (being wiser than the men of the cities) Saul had seen slaves and had wept in his heart for them, calling silently to them as brothers from his overwhelmed emotions. Hillel had heard birds and the wind, the laughter of children and women, the songs of the busy farmers, but Saul had heard only plaints and weeping and prayers for deliverance. Hillel had patience, and Saul's spirit had never known that virtue. In short, where Hillel saw a certain tranquillity, a simple wisdom, and entrancing beauty, Saul saw only turbulence, bitterness and a lightless land, stretching forth skeleton hands to the tardy Messias, pleading for rescue, invoking curses on the blasphemous Roman and longing not only to be free but to be purified.

He saw the Roman soldiers. Near Caesarea as they had passed that white and licentious city he had seen the amphitheater on the outskirts where Roman brutality and unspeakable cruelty had their being in this ravished land. Here captured Zealots and Essenes had hung on crosses for their intransigence and patriotism and devotion to the Lord their God. Hillel had averted his eyes from the amphitheater and had softly murmured the prayers for the dead and the repose of their souls in the bosom of Abraham. Men, he had thought, were hard and unjust and malicious, for that was their animal nature. If they had no victims they invariably invented them. The reflection saddened Hillel though he had never enthusiastically hoped for nor truly believed in the alleged good that lay, like a pearl, in the slimy musculature of a bestial organism. Men were men, more alike than unlike no matter their religion or race, may God, blessed be His Name, have mercy on them!

But Saul did not follow his father's thoughts. The people of Israel were unique in virtue to all other peoples and nations. Hence, their martyrdom. He forgot that they were a warrior people and that the Scriptures had lauded their less attractive disposals of captives, no matter how helpless. Or, if he thought about it at all it was with the attending thought that God had been with their ensigns and their armies and the might of their swords. (He had spoken of this to Aristo, who, after commenting that Israelites were remarkably like other conquerors, had expressed pity for the calumny against God, that He had allegedly blessed one army—as ferocious as the foe—and had shown no mercy for the helpless "enemy.")

Once Hillel had told Saul, and only recently, that when the Red Sea had drowned Pharaoh's soldiers and horsemen the angels had wished to voice their joy. But God had rebuked them, saying, "My children lie under the sea, and you would sing?" Hillel had admitted that the story was possibly only a parable, and had smiled at his son a little strangely, but Saul had been vexed. God had only one people, only one nation of sons, and all others were heathens and Gentiles. When Hillel had reminded him that it was prophesied that the Messias would be "a light unto the Gentiles" also, Saul had remained silent.

Saul could not have enough of seeing the land of his fathers, but he did not see what Hillel saw. Therefore, his agony of spirit. The blue passion of the sky was lost to him, and the green and golden earth, the orchards, the groves, the streams, the trees and the vivacity of the market crowds in the ancient towns through which they rumbled. The one fascination lay for him in their names, the birthplaces of heroes and prophets and patriarchs. He longed to see David's tomb, and the great tomb of Rachel, and other holy places. He yearned not only to be in Jerusalem, but in Bethlehem, where the Messias would be born.

His sister, Sephorah, who was fascinating her kinsmen in David's car, looked with lively interest on Israel and pondered on her shy bridegroom in the car ahead and sometimes peered at him with mischief if his eye caught hers. She had decided that he appeared kind and timid and would not be a difficult husband. Hence, she would have small trouble with him. She was a girl of much cleverness and enjoyed life and had shrewdness and wit, and possessed a naturalness of being which demanded little of others and was humorous with all, and content with her fate. If she was not a young female of intense emotions she was also incapable of hatred and gloom. She had affection for her father and had loved her mother, but above all she loved Saul and considered him afflicted, a matter time and kindness would mend. In the meantime, her wedding was approaching and it would be a joyous occasion. Saul, too, would be caught in the singing web of festivities and perhaps even he would learn to smile again and to laugh as he once had laughed, boisterously and with all his heart.

The Roman road, as the entourage clattered thunder-
ously in the sunset some hours later, climbed many steep
hills and then dashed down into valleys strewn with little
brown houses and gardens and narrow pastures and
brooks and rills. Then Aulus pointed to the empurpling
distance and said, "Jerusalem." Hillel, who had bravely
remained with him in the leaping chariot, turned his eyes
in the direction of the far city and murmured, "If I forget
thee, Jerusalem, may my hand lose its cunning, my eye
its lustre and its sight, and my heart die in dust." Aulus,
who guessed his emotion, pretended to be giving all his
attention to his horses. The Roman was a pious man who
believed deeply in his old gods, and he revered piety in
others. Nevertheless, he could not help but remember that
the Jews had twenty-four distinct sects, all of which were
vociferously proffered and declared the one true faith
and all the rest heresy. Still, he thought kindly, we Romans have adopted the Egyptian gods and have temples
in Rome to Isis and Osiris and Serapis, among others,
and give them honors and support them with taxes. We
are tolerant of all, and therefore we do not understand
the insistence of Jews, and it bewilders us. We prefer law
and order, and universal peace. He was grateful for his
Hannah, modest and sweet for all her indomitable will,
who, while living implicitly as an "old" Jewess had tolerance for her husband's belief. A remarkable matron,
thought Aulus, longing for her comforting arms. He even
permitted her to bore him with her repeated and patient
explanations that there were, in truth, two main Jewish
religions, one of prayer and synagogue, and one of the
Temple, embracing sacrifice and ceremony and learning,
one simple and without ostentation and the other of great
ritual and incense and priesthood. To Aulus, men were
men and God was God, and this seemed sufficient. But
the Jews were contentious and there was always alertness
among the Romans for any incipient rebellion or riot or
violence, for this was an abrasive people who never really
submitted, and for that he secretly admired them. There
was always at least one uproar in the surrounding provinces, alas, with resultant and ruthless carnage and executions on the cross, and flayings alive.

There upon the highest hill stood Jerusalem, yellow-
gray winding and slitted walls and battlemented guard-

towers seemingly not built by man but only an out-
cropping of regimented stones on high bulwarks yellow-
gold with autumn. Against the walls, and on the
crumbling earthy bulwarks, stood lone groups of stiff
black-green pointed cypresses and an occasional stand of
tall and dusty palms. Torches were already aflare on the
battlements and against the walls, and thus their grim and
stony yellowness was imprinted upon the dark purple
sky, and scarlet shadows fluttered over the stone and even
fingered down on the bulwarks. In the spring and summer,
thought Hillel, it is not so desolate, so forbidding, for the
bulwarks are struck with ardent green and wild flowers.
But he felt a deeper melancholy. As the Holy Days were
approaching the goat's-hair tents of some pilgrims were
already being cast on the bulwarks of the city, and the
little red fires could be seen burning here and there, and
the movement of lanterns. The city was always crowded
later at this time of the year, every inn filled to bursting,
and as the people from the provinces had neither the
money for inns nor could find room, they were forced to
bring their tents, their goats, even their geese and fowl
and asses, and an occasional milch cow. This made for
liveliness and noise a little later, as the people increased in
numbers, but now their only occasional presence on the
rising bulwarks enhanced the lonely and abandoned scene.
Hillel thought of their long hot and dusty journeys here,
with their domestic beasts and their wives and children,
and tears came to his eyes. Devotion to God still burned
in the provinces, if not in Jerusalem and Joppa and
Caesarea.

The entourage entered through the Joppa Gate but were
not challenged by the Roman soldiers on guard because all
recognized Aulus Platonius, and all saluted the standard of
Rome in the vanguard. "Greetings, lads!" called Aulus, as
the gates were opened and he pulled up his chariot in the
shadow of the arch. He spoke as if he had been absent for
months and not for days. The officer in charge, a young
man with a sun-darkened and wary face, saluted him and
came to the chariot and said, "Greetings, noble Aulus
Platonius. All is peaceful."

"That is remarkable," said Aulus, and the officer grinned
and looked curiously at the entourage. "My kinsmen," said
Aulus. "I have conducted them from Joppa."

If the officer felt some surprise that a Roman had so many Jewish kinsmen, who were apparently so very rich also, he did not reveal it. He looked with respect at the elaborate and handsome cars and the fine horses. Then he lifted his arm in salute again and the entourage swept into the city. The iron gates clanged after them.

In the smaller towns and villages and little cities there had been a certain gaiety, raucousness and ease, even under the ubiquitous eyes of the Romans. The people went about their business, farming, selling, manufacturing and negotiating. Life went on, they appeared to say with a shrug of fatality. A man must live in spite of disaster. But Jerusalem, that great and resounding city, that center of Mid-East culture and trade and commerce and wealth, and filled with many races, had a certain indescribable somberness about it, a certain darkness and heaviness of spirit. Yet, here the Hellenistic arête glowed very conspicuously among the cosmopolitan Jewish Sadducees and there were many flourishing and active Greek colonies of merchants and traders and academicians and indolent wealthy residents, and there were many Roman soldiers with their wives and families living here, not to speak of Roman bankers and businessmen and bureaucrats and administrators, many of whom had married Jewish beauties with handsome dowries. Here lived Syrians, Persians, Arabs and Phoenicians and others of the Semitic races, including Egyptians who taught in the academy of medicine or who were valued as cooks in the noblest of houses. If ever there was a heterogeneous city, as heterogeneous as Rome, herself, Jerusalem, was that city.

Therefore, the intangible darkness and heaviness which lay on the city seemed incomprehensible. Even spring exuberance and summer bloom could not lighten it, nor its multitudinous gardens, nor its fine public buildings, handsome villas, clean streets, banking and brokerage houses, and the markets and the rich mercantile establishments. A thousand different dialects and tongues could not lift its air of brooding and weighty contemplation, nor its wealth. Some said that it was because Jerusalem was so old and was bending under the history of the ages, and the devout Jews said Jerusalem mourned that she was now but a province of the Romans and could not endure Roman occupation. Hillel loved Jerusalem, but he recalled now that even as a boy he had felt the grave and subdued atmosphere of the city—and the Romans, then, were not so conspicuous as now.

The more rigid of the Pharisees declared that God, in His Temple, had wrapped Himself in His cloak, and had covered His face, because of the Romans and the defections of His people. (Apparently, said some of the more erudite Romans with wryness, He had no other affairs to supervise.) God, said the Pharisees, had thrown His Face into shadow and withdrawal, until the day when His Messias would be born and the Jews delivered forever from slavery and oppression. In the meantime, before that day arrived, God was incommunicado except to His elect, namely the Pharisees.

True it was that Jerusalem was profaned with Greek and Roman temples and theaters but Hillel doubted that this particularly enraged God. He had been wise, enough, however, to keep this heretical opinion from his fellow Pharisees. But he often pondered on the gloomy air of Jerusalem. As she was at the juncture where east met the west there should have been a certain naughty sophistication about her, a certain lightheartedness. But this was not so. Even the Greeks and the Romans found her oppressive, and they often cast troubled eyes at the mighty golden Temple, with its golden dome and spires and its golden gates and vast gardens and courts. Some of them, in a spirit of conciliation and even fear, frequently went to the Court of the Gentiles within the purlieus of the Temple, and paid for sacrifices and bought amulets. It did not harm to please and placate Eastern gods, who were noted for capriciousness. They had heard that the God of the Jews lacked humor and was famed for ferocity and was a valiant Warrior, Himself, and had a distressing way of smiting suddenly, and so the superstitious Greeks and Romans hoped to disarm Him with their tolerance. Privately, they thought Him without beauty and grace and gaiety, all civilized attributes. The music they heard distantly in the Court of the Gentiles did nothing to lift their hearts. It sounded like warning and mourning and all other ominous things. They had never heard that David had urged his people to "make a glad noise unto the Lord," for certainly the Temple in Jerusalem made the very reverse of "glad noises." Nor could the Romans truly believe—if it had ever occurred to them—that God resented their presence anywhere, for were they not the people of the Law? And was not the first command of the universe the command of order? Without law and order there was only chaos, and even the Jewish God should appreciate that.

Saul was nothing but eyes as he entered the holy city of his fathers, and he forgot the onerous and distasteful presence of his kinsmen and their jovial comments to each other. He even forgot his kinsman, the Roman Aulus, and the standard and fasces of Rome. He was but a seeing vessel and he sat stiffly in the car of Simon ben Shebua and watched everything, his heart seemingly enflamed and obviously throbbing. He could hardly breathe. The air of the city was dense and hot and dusty, with a thousand disturbing odors, and there was no breeze to lift the scent of latrines, foliage, stone, dry earth and the pervasive aromatic smell as of pepper and spice and iron, and cheese. And from every street came the clanging rattle and beat of chariots, horses and cars.

As Jerusalem was a city on a hill it rose in terraces, one above the other, a city of marble and yellow stone, of domes and porticoes and spires, of neat and narrow cobbled roads, of alleys and cypresses and palms and tamarisk and karob trees, of Roman aqueducts, of marketplaces and twisting vistas, of gardens and villas and crowded tenements and of fountains. The earth was terra-cotta; what paths could be seen were of gravel. Everywhere were walls of saffron stone, except for Roman and Greek houses which now affected the "open" appearance advocated among Roman architects.

Jerusalem was mainly a heaped rising city of flat roofs, despite the domes and spires, and so crowded that it was boasted that a man could walk for miles on those roofs without touching ground. It was on these that the multitudinous families gathered of an evening after the heat of the day. Some of the roofs bore earth, carried up in basket after basket, and here little palm trees had been planted, and flowers, and sometimes vegetables. Many had striped awnings for protection against the sun.

Saul saw it all, in the spurting red glare of torches

thrust into walls and the light of huge lanterns illuminating every street corner. He also saw the Roman patrols. He saw the crowds, emerging into what coolness might be expected after night advanced, and he heard cymbals and laughter and music and the dull roaring of any living city, magnified here. But, like Hillel, he also felt the brooding darkness and heaviness of the city though unlike Hillel he did not wonder why. He was certain he knew. He was also certain that here was the heart of Creation, the very center of God's being, and all else was irrelevant. Jerusalem would remain, though nations would vanish through the ages and be known no more. He felt this with a passionate certitude and an avenging joy.

Chapter 8

THOUGH Shebua ben Abraham had built his awesome Greco-Roman house on one of Jerusalem's more secluded and quiet streets, and though his children had been born there and his wife had been ostensible mistress, he adhered to the Roman fashion and referred to it as "the house of my son's wife, Clodia Flavius." For Shebua was now a widower, his meek wife having died just before the death of his daughter, Deborah. He had paid a literal fortune for that building of white marble and gleaming columns and colonnades and statues, and expansive gardens, the porticoes decorated with fine murals and friezes, the atrium a court in itself, and every room full of scented air like the fragrance of fern and fresh fountains. It was guarded by a wall of white stone and with gates of iron, standing in the midst of fig trees and karobs and sycamores and palms and pines, with exotic flowers in large Chinese pots scattered everywhere, and with red paths neatly bordered with square or rectangular or round beds of many-colored plants and blossoms. From its rise on the tiered city it had a view of the whole countryside and the lavender hills and the meadows and pastures and, in the distance, little crowded Bethlehem. It was a commanding house, a true "insula," and was highly admired even by the languid and amused Greeks. Herod was often an esteemed visitor, and high Roman officials, for Shebua was known for his urbanity, his elegance, his learning and his delicacy both of mind and table and taste.

The Pharisees abhorred him. He not only had a multitude of slaves but he never freed them, according to the Law. He had two concubines in fine quarters, and not even the dark cold disapproval of Clodia could force him to dismiss them. One was an Arabian beauty of serpentine charm, the other a delicious Nubian. "After all," he would say, "was not the Queen of Sheba black as night and as lovely as the moon?" The Pharisees not only disagreed that the Queen of Sheba was "black as night" but they despised Shebua as a renegade from his religion and his race, and hated him as a Sadducee and therefore an oppressor of his people. All the members of the great court, the Sanhedrin, were his friends, and he observed, humorously, two or three of the solemn Holy Days, but he believed in nothing, and especially not in the stern God of his Fathers, nor in the coming of the Messias.

He was a gentleman, an epicure, an exquisite, and in his soul—he believed—a true Greek. He had visited Athens scores of times and his true allegiance, he would often say, was to the Parthenon where beauty soared in stone and Phidias walked at midnight, and Socrates strolled amid the columns. He loved to go to the theaters in Athens and in Jerusalem, where he helped to pay for the presentations of the more glorious of the Greek plays, and was a friend and patron of actors and gladiators and athletes. His discrimination was superb, and even he often marveled at it gently. He was also deeply fond of the Romans, though he was inclined—when among Greek friends—to laugh at them softly and agree that they felt inferior to the Greeks in the matter of art and taste and nuances of thought. But he would waggle a translucent finger at his Greek visitors and say. "However, do not call them a nation of grocers, my friends! They are far more than that! Consider what they have done with the arch and all their other works of science, and the law and order they have brought to the world under the Pax Romana. These are no mean accomplishments." He had the reputation of being a very cosmopolitan man indeed. Like Plato, whom he quoted frequently, he "found no message in fields and trees."

He had many farms, many investments, many accounts

in the banks and the stock market, many interests in mercantile affairs and in ships. Once Clodia had asked him with a sour smile why he did not live in Greece, which he adored, and he had answered her as if she were a child (though he feared her Roman soul), "My dear daughter, I owe it to my people to help in their enlightenment and to wean them from the contemplation of their God and to reverse their refusal to join the world, and to make them part of Humanity. Are we not one?"

"No," Clodia had said, with firmness. "We are all human beings, but we are not one in the manner of which you speak, Shebua."

Shebua affectionately insisted, though he did not like the cold eye Clodia had fixed on him, nor her narrowed mouth, "There is no longer room in this world for insular and provincial attitudes, nor nationalistic fervors, my dear. Men are part of me, and I am part of all other men."

"So it would seem, unfortunately," said Clodia, whom Shebua deeply disliked.

He persisted, with indulgence. "We shall never have any peace nor tranquillity until we bow before a universal government, my daughter, the government of the world under one standard, under one ruler. That is the dream of ages. It was the dream of Plato."

Then Clodia astonished him. He had not thought her very erudite. She said, "I remember what Aristotle said: 'I love Plato, but I love truth more.' Plato was a fool. He never knew mankind. His Republic was not a noble dream. It was a dream of the cruel elite and the slavery of humanity. Hence, living men will always refute him, for men in their hearts love freedom."

In spite of his sweet smile of tender derision Shebua suddenly remembered the shout of Moses: "Proclaim liberty throughout the land, unto the inhabitants thereof!" Then he immediately thought, "If Plato was a fool, as this poor woman has said, then Moses was mad. Liberty—for all men. Absurd."

But among friends he seriously upheld the ideal of liberty for mankind. However, "mankind" to him was a theory, an abstraction, a poetic idea, and had nothing to do with the masses he saw in the various cities he visited. They smelled, and Shebua ben Abraham disliked smells. He scented himself, Clodia would think, like a male whore.

All his reflections were as remote from reality as his financial affairs were as strongly rooted in reality. He thought of himself as a poet, serene, tranquil, judicious, discreet and polished.

He had had no influence with his sons, except for David, and his daughter had reverenced him. The plump and sleek Simon thought his father foolish; Joseph, the hard merchant, considered him not quite intelligent. It was only David who admired and emulated him. All his sons were Sadducees, certainly, like himself. But they thought his dissertations, except for David, shallow and irrelevant. However, they held his money in the most pious regard and admitted among themselves that Shebua could make ten shekels grow where one had been planted in spite of his absurdity. And sometimes, when he gazed at them thoughtfully they became afraid of him though they did not know why. Despite his smiles and ease and manners and elegances and air of tolerance, they occasionally suspected him of implacable ruthlessness, and in this they were quite correct.

This was the man who greeted the entourage from Joppa with magnanimity, reserved affection, and solicitude, meeting them in the atrium which was lighted with many Alexandrine and Egyptian lamps, all filled with aromatic oil, some scented with jasmine and roses. He wore a white toga in the Roman fashion, his tunic underneath belted with a gold girdle, jeweled armlets on his arms, many glittering rings on his fingers, his sandals inlaid with gems. He spoke in perfect Greek, with the intonations and mellifluousness of a scholar, and statues as stately as he stood all about him in carved niches.

He embraced Hillel first, and let a tear come into his eye. "My dear Hillel," he said, "this is both a joyful and a sad occasion. But let us not repine too much. You appear well, for all your tribulations."

Hillel had always detested him, in spite of his own kind and gentle nature. He said, "My tribulations come from God and so I do not reject them, knowing, in humility that God, blessed be His Name, has His reasons, which are full of lovingkindness."

He felt this in his heart. Nevertheless, he knew it would annoy Shebua, who looked at him with sudden sharper reserve and said, "Ah, yes. We can do nothing but accept.

All else is childish." He sighed. "Deborah was my only daughter. As Rachel was to her father, so was she to me." He thought that would please or at least divert Hillel. One must concede exceptions for these pious Jews, especially Pharisees who could make themselves disconcertingly dangerous. In an odd way, he was never sure about Hillel. The family of Borush was very distinguished and many of them had been members of the Sanhedrin, and their name was notable, so Shebua could not understand the unaffected simplicity of Hillel. He had half persuaded himself it was the pretense of an assured man, and Shebua ben Abraham was not such a man.

Saul had been acutely observing his grandfather, whom he had never seen before. Shebua stood tall over Hillel, and was very lean and graceful, with long thin white hands and a long thin white face and a similar neck. He had a delicate nose, slender and attentuated, with tremulous nostrils, and his mouth was also delicate and almost invariably sweetly smiling. Friends had often informed him that he resembled one of the more patrician Greek scholars of antiquity, and this was not entirely flattery. His expression was amiable, patient, honeyed and sympathetic, conveying the message that not only was Shebua a gentleman of refinement but a man who was loving in the extreme, and full of sensibility, not to mention subtlety. One did not think of the great stern patriarchs when looking upon Shebua; one thought of scholarship and intellect and cosmopolitan worldliness. His brow was like marble, his thin hair pale and silken over his long skull.

It was only when one looked into his unusually large and almost completely colorless eyes that one saw the glaucous nature of Shebua ben Abraham, the glacial weighing and measuring of all who encountered him, the cold indifference to the spirits, sufferings, pain and torment of others, and the gigantic self-absorption and selfishness. But few discerned all this. He had an undeserved reputation for benign tenderness for every man.

He puts my teeth on edge, thought Saul, and his own teeth clenched hard together. He did not know that Clodia Flavius, wife of David, often made this remark to her husband.

Now the bright but pallid eye of Shebua fell on his grandson, Saul ben Hillel. While ostensibly greeting Hillel he had seen Saul obliquely and had said to himself, What an ugly youth, barbarian in his appearance, a veritable Vandal! He had heard from David that Saul was not similar to a beautiful statue and was not an Adonis in the eyes of his dead mother, and Deborah, in her letters to her father, had often complained that her son did not resemble his parents and was even ugly. Though she had not been intelligent she had a facile gift for words and had described Saul regularly, and minutely, so Shebua was not too startled. But he felt an immediate aversion for that flaming red hair, so puissant and leonine, that breadth of shoulder, and those metallic blue eyes, and the bowed legs discernible even under the long brown tunic. The feet, in heavy leather sandals, stood firm and stalwart on the gleaming white floor of the atrium, and to Shebua they were the feet of a wrestler or a pugilist.

Shebua had no beard to kiss, so Saul suffered the perfumed embrace of Shebua in silence. (He was scented with sandalwood.) His young body stiffened; only long training in courtesy kept him from drawing away his cheeks from Shebua's cool kisses.

Then, with his hands on Saul's shoulders, Shebua held his grandson off from him and his whole face expressed affection and pride. "My beloved Deborah's only son!" he exclaimed and again a soft tear appeared at the corner of his eyes. "Welcome to this house, Saul ben Hillel, and may you be joyful in the land of your fathers!"

Hypocrite, thought young Saul and his face was stiff. Shebua, who was very intuitive, felt the youth's repugnance and his thoughts, and the pale eyes narrowed to icy slits. But he continued to smile as with love and admiration. He patted Saul's shoulder, then turned graciously to view his granddaughter, Sephorah, and for once his smile was genuine as well as sweet. He not only thought her beautiful and nubile; he also thought she had inherited his own Grecian appearance. He embraced her, and sighed. He had loved his daughter, Deborah. Sephorah was more wonderful in appearance than Deborah had been and as Shebua cherished beauty—he admitted this, himself—he was inclined to instant appreciation and affection for the girl. His grandson, Ezekiel, was lucky; there was also a fine dowry.

He murmured in the words of Homer, as he had murmured to the dead Deborah, " 'Daughter of the gods, divinely tall and most divinely fair!' " Sephorah suppressed a chuckle. She was certain her grandfather was a mountebank but was amused rather than revolted at the thought. She considered it very discourteous of Saul to stand there and glare so straightly at Shebua as if about to challenge him.

Shebua entered genially and gently into an affable exchange of greetings with Aulus Platonius, for the Roman was not only a Roman officer but of a sturdy and wealthy family. Aulus, as an "old" Roman, thought Shebua effete and wearisome and rarely encountered him willingly, and to Aulus it was not strange that Shebua was the intimate of both Herod Antipas and the Procurator of Israel, Pontius Pilate. Both were depraved men, though Pilate was the more cruel and intelligent. He had only lately arrived in Israel, and Aulus deplored him. He was not of the fiber and the soul of Aulus' patriotic, sober and industrious fathers. Pilate hated the Jews because he had been sent here, on a matter of discipline, by Caesar Tiberius, and because the Jews were not subservient to the Romans and refused to bow before them and were incalcitrant. He was beginning to make it difficult for his officers and underlings to marry Jewish women, out of pure malice. He often rallied Aulus on his Hannah and once or twice had even tweaked the centurion's beard and said, "What! Are you becoming a Jew, my Aulus, and have you been circumcised?" Only military training kept Aulus from expressing his hatred, for to him, as to most soldiers, the decadent men of modern Rome were an affront to the gods, an insult to the history of his nation.

The overseer of the hall entered the atrium, bowed to Shebua and announced that the Lady Clodia awaited the Lady Sephorah in the quarters of the women. Shebua smiled deprecatingly at his lovely granddaughter, spread his hands in apology and resignation, and said, "My son's wife, the noble Clodia Flavius, is mistress of her house and one dares not oppose her! So you must retire, my Sephorah, my beautiful one, for refreshment and rest after your long journey."

Sephorah bowed to him, to her father, then, drawing her filmy veil over her face she bowed to her uncles, to Aulus, but pretended, as was proper, that she did not see her bridegroom who was lingering in the background, half hidden by a column, overcome with his shyness and the marvel of his fate that he was to have one so wondrous as his wife. Then Sephorah demurely winked at her brother, kissed her father's cheek in a marvelous imitation of a timid daughter, and departed with her maidens for the women's quarters.

"We live under a quaint rule," said Shebua.

He then conducted the guests into the magnificent dining room for a rich and subtly elegant feast, for he had an Egyptian cook of great talent.

The women's quarters were not luxurious nor very handsome. They had the austerity of old Rome about them and there were few ornaments and only the statues of Clodia's family gods and her lares and penates. There were no murals here and the lamps were plain and unscented and the curtains over the uncolored Alexandrine glass of the windows were of coarse wool striped in the red, black and white hues of the Tribe of Levi, to which Shebua ben Abraham belonged. Sephorah thought it amusing, but not incongruous nor discordant, to find here a mixture of both Roman and Jewish customs and furnishing, for there was a curious resemblance and harmony between them. She realized at once that they were also anachronistic in this modern age of Hellinistic Jews and opulent Romans and degenerate Greeks.

Clodia was seated within her own portico in an oaken chair with no cushions nor fringes, and she was like Demeter in her repose and dignity. About her her women were not idle; they were sewing or spinning or embroidering, though it was night and the lamps were not many. Clodia, herself, held a heap of linen on her broad knees and she was apparently mending it. She raised her calm brown eyes to Sephorah's face, scrutinized her sharply and briefly, saw all, smiled with reserve and held out her hand to the girl. Sephorah kissed it with a fine affectation of humility, and Clodia's eyes suddenly twinkled. She rose, embraced Sephorah. She smelled of fresh bread and clean strong flesh and warmth.

"Greetings, my child," she said, in Latin. "My son, Ezekiel, is greatly honored and blessed in you."

Her coarse brown hair was partly covered with the

same plain cloth as her stola, and they were both of a dull deep red. Her hands were the hands of a woman who was not ashamed to use them in labor or in the soil, and were dark and short. She was not so tall as Sephorah. She was, indeed, however, the terror of her household which she ruled in the fashion of an "old" Roman, and her sons and her daughters feared her with excellent reason. Though her daughters were married, as were all her sons but Ezekiel, her youngest, they observed the most meticulous and deferential deportment in their mother's presence. Her features were large and coarse and firm, but when she smiled her expression was truly kind and benevolent. Sephorah loved her at once, for here was all sincerity and truth.

Clodia and Sephorah dined together in Clodia's austere dining room, which was small and dimly lighted. But the curtains were drawn back for the warm night wind and Sephorah saw the mingled red and white illumination of Jerusalem and heard the dull thunder of the unsleeping city. She also heard fountains, plangent and soothing, and distant laughter and music and the rumble of chariots. She could smell rich gardens and fruit. The crescent new moon stood on tiptoe on a dark mountain. Though Sephorah was tired, she was filled with excitement and anticipation, for henceforth this would be her home.

They dined very simply on broiled fish, hot breads and stewed beans with garlic and cheese and a very ordinary wine, which Clodia favored. The gentlemen's dinner was quite different, which Sephorah suspected, but Clodia preferred a plain life for herself and her women. There was a rustic basket of fruit on the table, which was covered by a yellowish cloth, and the perfume of it mingled with the flower scents from the gardens and the pervading peppery and aromatic odor of the city.

She is dressed and gemmed finely, thought Clodia, and is of delicate structure and proud bearing, but she is one like myself and I am pleased. She inquired politely of Sephorah's journey, offered her condolences for the death of the girl's mother, and conveyed her unbending and formidable serenity to Sephorah who did not find it intimidating. In truth, the girl's weariness relaxed and she found herself confiding in Clodia as if she were her mother, and some of her remarks were so witty that Clodia laughed abruptly a few times. Sephorah's composure and ease, her charming face, her smiles, gratified the Roman lady. The girl was not impudent as were the majority of maidens in these deplorable days, and there was no impertinence in her voice, nor was she affected or brazen.

They drank wine in warm comfort together and ate of the luscious fruit. Sephorah began to speak of her brother and her anxious love for him shone in her golden eyes. She told Clodia of the strangeness which had come to him in the past year, and the fixity and gloom which nothing could shake. "Ah," said Clodia, "I saw him from my portico, in the light of the lamps at the entrance to the atrium. He stood apart. That is very unusual for a youth, for the young are always chattering. Does he love no one?"

"None but God and my father," said Sephorah with some melancholy. "Once he loved me. But no more. He repudiates me and thinks me trivial. I cannot touch him."

Clodia reflected. She held a handful of sweet ripe dates in her hand and she munched on them thoughtfully. Then she said, "I have seen a few young men like your brother, Saul ben Hillel, but very few. He recalls my own brothers to me. We, too, were stringent before our gods and loved our country with fervor. At times," and now she suddenly looked at Sephorah and the usually unrelenting brown eyes were amazingly merry, "I found it tiresome. Of a certainty, I never implied this to my father and my brothers, nor to my husband, David ben Shebua, but women have more humor than men."

Sephorah was freshly delighted by this Roman lady. The two women drew more comfortably together. "Virtue," said Clodia, "is most necessary, and discipline cannot be overpraised. We must learn this, my child, or we cannot endure in a world of men. We must be sleeplessly controlled and firm and guide them ruthlessly, or this world will surely revert to chaos. We must be veritable Penelopes on this gross, masculine earth, veritable Junos—or our men will become barbarians. It is their nature, though they pretend, in these days, to be of excessive refinements and daintiness. Alas, modern women, striving to be as corrupt as men, as vicious as men, as free as men, are hastening us all to destruction. There are few virtuous women alive in these evil times, and only they can delay the inevitable hour of death, blood and confusion."

She sighed, studied a pomegranate in its basket, then took up a red globe. She regarded Sephorah with interest. The girl's face was somewhat disturbed. Clodia said, "Do not be sad, my daughter. Civilizations come, and they go. The seed of their death lies in them at their birth. It is inexorable fate, ordained by the gods. Still," she added, "I often yearn for what I have not had." She gave a grim chortle. Sephorah gazed at her, waiting.

"Shebua ben Abraham mentioned to me, with amusement, that the Pharisee Jews believe in reincarnation," said Clodia Flavius, rubbing the pomegranate frankly on her knee. "If I were to be given a choice, in the event there is truth in that theory, I should like to be a courtesan."

"A courtesan!" exclaimed Sephorah, and her face came alight with dimples.

"Then I would not have to be virtuous," said Clodia. "I am like a weary soldier on guard."

Sephorah laughed, but for some reason unknown even to her, she felt tears in her eyes. She rose quickly to her feet and approached Clodia and fell on her neck and kissed her, and then did not know why she cried. And Clodia held her in her stout arms and soothed her as she had never soothed her own daughters, and murmured wordlessly in her ear and kissed her cheek. Sephorah sat on her knee like a child and wound her arms about Clodia, and the servant girls looked in upon them and were astonished.

It was midnight and Saul lay in sweating exhaustion in his fine bedroom in the house of Shebua ben Abraham, and his spirit was in darkness and in pain. He had recited his prayers with fervor, this first night in the land of his fathers, but they had brought him no comfort. So he rose from his heated bed, covered his head with a cloth, bent over as if in agony, and murmured aloud in the words of David:

"O Lord, rebuke me not in Your wrath, neither chasten me in Your hot displeasure! For Your arrows stick fast in me and Your hand presses me sore. There is no soundness in my flesh because of Your anger, neither is there any rest in my bones because of my sin. My iniquities are gone over my head; as a heavy burden they are too heavy for me. My wounds stink and are corrupt because of my foolishness. I am troubled; I am bowed down greatly; I go mourning all the day long. For my loins are filled with a loathsome disease, and there is no soundness in my flesh. I am feeble and sore broken; I have roared by reason of the disquietness of my heart. Lord, all my desire is before You, and my groaning is not hid from You. My heart pants, my strength fails me; as for the light of my eyes, it is also gone from me— Forsake me not, O Lord! O my God, be not far from me!"

On so many endless nights before he had prayed thus in despair and in fever, and in utter faith. Yet never had he been comforted, never had he felt forgiven, never had he felt the imminence of God as once he had felt it. Something obstinately cold and dark had fallen between him and God. He believed it was his sin, for which he could not forgive himself.

Once, during his interlude with Dacyl, he had loved all mankind, for it had reflected his love, and she was one with it and it was one with her. Now that he believed he loathed Dacyl and hated her, so those somber emotions lay on all the world of men, emanating from himself. As he had repudiated Dacyl, so he repudiated his fellows and despised them, for were they not depraved and corrupt as Dacyl—and as himself? He could not forgive himself. Therefore, he could not forgive nor endure mankind. Could not God, blessed be His Name, read his heart, know his contrition and sorrow and disgust? Why then, did silence answer in him, and long loneliness and emptiness, as if in reproach? It was said that the Lord did not reject the repentant, but hastened to meet them in loving-kindness. But though Saul had repented, the portals of communion with God had closed and he was left in barrenness and dryness among evil men, and there was muteness and despair in his soul.

In broken exhaustion, he fell on his hot bed again and was instantly asleep. He did not dream. But suddenly, as he slept and the crescent moon fell behind the mountains and a new breeze chattered amid the palms, he heard a great and tremendous voice:

"Saul! Saul of Tarshish!"

He sprang up in bed, sweat dripping from him, his eyes wild and staring in the darkness. He cried, "Yes, yes! Who is it? Who calls?"

The very walls were still ringing with the sound of that unearthly voice, that commanding voice, that terrible and masculine voice. A fierce pain ran through the young man's head, and he panted. He listened with all his power. He heard, now, only the light dry wind and the call of a lonely bird and the distant howl of a jackal, and the trumpet challenge of a guard.

I was dreaming, he told himself at last. But it was dawn before he slept again. Then he thought, "Though He reject me and will not forgive me, though His rage shall flow over me like the billows of the sea, still will I love and serve Him with all my soul, and at the last He may receive me again."

He wept and said in the words of Job, "Oh, that I but knew where I might find Him!"

Chapter 9

SAUL went with his father and his kinsmen to the Temple on the Holy Days, and Sephorah went to the Court of the Women for her religious duties.

The youth had a tremendous imagination and he had listened to his father discourse on the Temple, on its golden dome, its spires, its many courts, its gardens and walls and corridors, its vast halls where learned men walked and contemplated and conversed of sacred matters, its cypresses and palms and fountains, its quiet colonnades. He knew that the first Temple of Solomon had employed over seventy thousand men in the building of it, and that it had been destroyed by Nebuchadnezzar, king of Babylon, and that it had been restored by Zerubbabel seventy years later, and that even later it had been enhanced and enlarged by King Herod. He had heard of the marvelous yellow and white stones of its walls, its mighty bronze doors, its great columns pale and polished like marble, its huge capitals embossed with pomegranates, buds of flowers, lilies, wreaths, its arches leading to long vistas, its quiet porticoes, its wide low steps, and the cloud of incense which hovered everywhere, brightened by sun or moon. He had heard of the altar and the Holy of Holies, the Tabernacle, the veiled Torah, the scrolls wrapped around the silver rods, the hushed and solemn air, the shining floors, the silences, the dim rolling echoes. Hillel had told him of the holy maidens, widows and men who had their being in the Temple and never left it, and were seen only at a distance. There had long been a tradition that the Mother of the Messias would spend her early years in this sanctuary, in the Presence of God.

Saul had been prepared for glory and splendor and sacred precincts, but he saw now that what he had imagined was nothing compared with the awesome grandeur of the reality. Here was the heart of his people, the Tabernacle of their God, the soul of their being, their fortitude, their faith, their stubborn devotion, their pride, their honor and their dignity. Who could prevail against a people who had raised this House to the Lord their God, and who had kept it holy and immaculate and glowing, and who turned their eyes to it at dawn and at sunset? Hillel had said, "So shall it live in the spirits of the People of God, though it be thrown one stone from another, its walls shattered, its dome splintered, its columns fallen, as it has been prophesied. Let the rage of the Gentiles, as David has said, prevail against its mere being in time. But ever shall it live, loved, revered, yearned for, desired with a terrible desiring, by all Jews through the ages, though they lose their faith and are scattered. For it is our heart, and here God dwells and shall never depart from His holy place, the Invisible worshiped in invisibility—until the Messias arrive, blessed be His Name, triumphant and invincible, Father of the world to come, and He shall raise the Temple again in the twinkling of an eye for the awe of nations, to be a sanctuary for all men."

But Saul did not believe that this edifice, this worship in stone raised to God, would ever be lost to the sight of humanity, nor could he believe, though it had been prophesied, that it would be mankind's sanctuary, Jew and Gentile, heathen and barbarian. The very thought appeared blasphemous to him. And it seemed even more blasphemous that he, the defiled and the corrupt and the sinful, dared enter here, his hood over his face for fear that God

might smite him for his presumption. He found himself
numb of lip and soul as he stood with the multitude of
hooded men before the altar in the greatest of the Courts:
in the blue dimness of incense and shadow he could hear
the rustle of low voices as they repeated the prayers until
the vastness of the place seemed invaded by a deep and
unearthly wind that did not come from human throats. It
was the movement of Hosts, invisible though clothed in
white fire. Saul watched the priests and saw their upraised
hands and eyes and their long beards and their sacramen-
tal garments and heard their intonations and the echo of
their intonations and a terror seized him and a cold ecstasy, and when the crowds of men prostrated themselves
and he with them he found it impossible to rise again and
his father, with an expression of concern, helped him to
his feet.

Hillel, even in those holy moments, was appalled by
his son's face, so awful was the light of his eyes, so fixed
and stretched his features. There was a line of foam on
his white mouth. He appeared dazed, at once stricken
and lost, yet exalted. Hillel had heard of the transports of
men touched by the Finger of God, and he was frightened.
It was said that such men were frequently driven mad by
that rapture. Hillel desired that his son love God, but he
also desired that God not love him too much. There was
a terribleness in the Love of God, and wise men, though
desiring to be loved by their Almighty Father, rarely
prayed for favors and commands that could be devastating
and destroying. It was all very well for transports, provided that they did not transport men beyond the reach of
other men, and did not consume poor human flesh in the
flame. The vessel of flesh was entirely too frail to hold the
fiery essence of the Being of God, and Saul was Hillel's
only son and even for God he did not wish him to be
consumed.

Saul was trembling. His breath came hard and fast. He
stared at the Tabernacle; he shook as if in a gale. Hillel
held Saul's arm against his own body and pressed it as if
he would protect his son from God, Himself.

Saul was crying in himself, "I weep by day, my God,
and You are silent! I cry by night, and you permit me!"
The words of David rang through his soul, imploring,
worshiping, yearning. "Whither shall I go from Your Spir-

it? Or whither shall I flee from Your Presence? If I ascend up into Heaven, You are there. If I make my bed in Hell, behold! You are there! If I take the wings of the morning and dwell in the uttermost parts of the sea—Even there shall Your Hand lead me, and Your right Hand shall hold me. If I say, 'Surely the darkness shall cover me,' even the night shall be light about me—The darkness and the light are both alike to You, O my God and my Redeemer!"

The fearful estrangement he had felt for so long, the estrangement of God from him, was lifted in one flash for a brief moment, and it seemed to him that he was on the verge of some transcendent discovery and knowledge, some revelation which was most necessary to him if he should live, and without which he would surely die. His whole being urged toward that revealment; it reached like a hand for it, craving, hungry, desperate, and he did not know where he was or who upheld him.

And then it was gone. I am unworthy, he thought. I am guilty. I saw the trailing garment of Glory for one instant, and then It withdrew. Tears ran down his face and there was a groaning in his throat which only his father, mercifully, heard. Then tears came to Hillel's eyes also and he prayed, "Depart from my poor son, lest he die."

It was then that in this fragrant blue gloom, amid the echoing wind of men's prayers, Hillel saw that his kinsmen had now observed Saul and himself. He saw the bored incurious face of Shebua ben Abraham, pale under the shadow of his hood, the superb, and knowing smiles exchanged between Simon and Joseph—their cheeks were sleek—and the elegant amusement of David ben Shebua slight but discernible. And Hillel was ashamed of his own fear, remorseful to the heart that he had asked God not to touch his son, and angered, even in those holy moments, that the family of Shebua should mock the passionate communion of his son, they who knew not God, blessed be His Name, and had never desired to know Him. Hillel could have wept with his anger and his self-reproach and his desire to cover his son with his own cloak, hiding him from the eyes of these profane men who profaned the Holy of Holies by their presence, and found it a cause for silent mirth that a youth should be so transported and exalted, and should believe even to the edge of fainting or death.

The tall candles were lit along the walls, in their silver sconces; lamps brightened. There was a sound of great golden trumpets; the columns glowed with shifting incandescence. The high priest was drawing the veil that hid the Torah, the holy scrolls, and men fell on their faces in an overwhelming silence. The golden dome above was lost in vagrant shadows and the clouds of incense. But Hillel, who had put his arm over his son's shoulders even as they lay side by side, felt that this most sacred of moments had been ruined for him because he knew that close to him lay men in mockery, men faithless and impious and desecrating, obeying the letter of the Law because they considered it correct though the Spirit was far from them. For them, surely, there was no forgiveness, these abominable Sadducees! They sought men's approval even here, and blasphemed God in their hearts.

The thought that he and Saul would feast with them tonight was repugnant to Hillel ben Borush. Their bread and their meats, their succulent dishes and spicy sauces, their wines and their fruit, their laughter and their jests, seemed to Hillel more than he could endure, and his heart was hot within him and he felt a deep burning and sorrow in his breast, not only for his son but for his betrayed God, Who would not, finally, be mocked any longer.

They were standing again. The Ark of the Covenant was hidden once more, and the prayers were resumed. Hillel saw that Saul was more composed, and that his lips were moving. He entered into his own contemplations, his own prayers. The candles and the lamps flared; a soft but penetrating music of zither and flute invaded the silence, an accompaniment to devotions, and in emphasis there was an occasional clash of a muted cymbal, the murmur of harps, the somber sound of chanting.

All conscious thought was lost in Saul, whose very soul seemed drained and prostrated.

Then, all at once, he was acutely and even frightfully aware, as if a hand of flame had touched his flesh and had seared it. He swung his head about. He saw nothing but the dimmed forms of men about him; he heard their breathing, their praying, and even their faint cries. All were hooded. He could see nothing of their faces but their chins and the tips of their noses and a wisp or two of their beards. Many there were richly clad, nobly arrayed. But near Saul, as he saw for the first time, was a small group of men in the coarse garments and cloaks of countrymen, their leather sandals plain and undecorated, their folded hands rude and scarred by toil. They wore no jewels to flash in the light as did his kinsmen; their beards were not scented, neither was their flesh. They smelled of the field and the hills, of domestic animals and goat's hair, of cheese and rough dark bread and sour milk and stale oil. Not even sedulous ablutions could obliterate these odors, which now so permeated their bodies.

But Saul, newly dazed and again trembling, felt that from one among them had darted a lance of flame which had touched him. He stared at them. They prayed with quiet fervor. Nothing distinguished them from their fellows; in truth, the haughtier and richer of the men of Jerusalem had tried to put a little space between themselves and their brothers from the provinces. Before God, they often said, all men were the same. But they did not believe it. For, was it not said that the just were favored with worldly goods by a rewarding Lord, blessed be His Name, and that they were never forsaken by Him and their children never begged bread? A destitute man, a poor and humble man, a miserable toiler, then, was indubitably a sinner and deserving of his fate. The probability that they, themselves, were truly forsaken and that their children might beg in vain for the Bread of Life, did not occur to them, and had one spoken to them of this they would not only have been outraged but made wrathful and vengeful.

What? Who? thought Saul, with a kind of anxious fever. He had often heard of the poverty-stricken but holy and wandering rabbis of Israel, who frequently evoked miracles and who preached in the streets and in the dust to the heedless mobs, and who devoted their lives to the enlightenment of their fellows and to the greater glory of God. "They care not for money nor for rich meats and bread, or even for shelter and warmth or for protection against the rain and the sun," Hillel had told his son. "They sleep in barns or under arches and on thresholds, and desire nothing but service, nothing but prayer, nothing but the opportunity to extend compassion and hope to others. They are the blessed of God." ·

Was there one such among that group of countrymen? asked Saul to himself. It seemed to him that he must know, that he must approach them and lift a hood to search for a face, for a spirit which had touched him invisibly but with power. He was filled with longing, with an urgent hope. His old impulsiveness returned to him, his old recklessness to have what he desired to have. He made a movement.

It was then that he was certain that a strong and familiar voice said within the hot cave of his skull: "Be still. The time is not yet."

He thought, I am going mad! I did not hear a voice, yet I swear I heard it! I am undone. My emotions are in disarray. Wild winds disturb my soul. Suffering has distorted my perceptions. My God, my God, why have You abandoned me?

But even as he thought this a heavy peace came to him, a quietude, a surcease, as if a kind and merciful hand had been placed on his incoherent and clamorous mouth. He sank into mute prayer, into a soundlessness that was like sleep.

Though Clodia Flavius had commanded her Jewish cooks to prepare the proper feast for the Holy Days, and no rich and ritualistic dish had been excluded, and the prescribed wines had been provided, the prayers and ceremonies at the table in the magnificent dining room were languid and perfunctory. The goblets might be of gold and the platters and plates of the finest wrought silver, the spoons and the knives of artful Egyptian charm, the wreathed candlesticks and lamps scented and exquisite, the cover fashioned of cloth of gold, the Alexandrine glass and crystal vases filled with scarlet and white and purple flowers, but there was none of the sober gaiety that follows the Day of Atonement, when men believe fervently that the book of their last year's sins had been closed by the Angel of God and a new year of hope and faith lies before them.

Shebua ben Abraham and his sons and their sons did not wear the embroidered and jeweled caps befitting their situation in society. They did not wear caps at all. Hillel ben Borush and his son Saul wore them only. They had listened to Shebua's desultory and abbreviated prayers and they detected the faint and indulgent amusement in his creamy voice, and the ennui. They knew he was making a polite gesture in the direction of the faith he had abandoned, even as atheistic Romans and Greeks poured libations to the gods. It was a pretty gesture, and, Hillel suspected, even that was made only because of the presence of himself and Saul. Shebua was a man of gestures; Hillel bitterly wondered if he were anything else, for though Hillel listened keenly he never once heard Shebua make an original remark though he was very proficient in quotations from the mighty Greek philosophers and Virgil and Homer—which he delivered with a graceful wave of his hand and a soft smile that requested admiration. Even these remarks, virile and passionate often in context, exuded desultory daintiness. I am sure, thought Hillel, who was rarely moved to deep vexation—knowing the frailties of men—that even his excrement is perfumed and his urine scented. How he had brought himself to the sweat and lustiness and violent thrust of begetting these sons of his is beyond my imagination. He has two concubines. I am certain they are still virgins; no doubt he delights them with a lyre or poems or pretty little songs!

Or, thought Hillel, becoming more and more incensed, it may be that he is a practicer of Platonic love, in imitation of the Greeks. He glanced down the gleaming table at his father-in-law, and despised him. Shebua was elegantly disposed in his ebony and pearl-inlaid chair; he played with his goblet; he ate with an air of absent discrimination, every gesture excessively refined. His blue tunic, belted with an intricate web of gold and gems, was heavily embroidered; his arms were banded in armlets, glittering like stars, and on his right index finger was a fine ring which Herod Antipas had given him for favors —or friendship—unknown. He had refrained from the last enormity: Egyptian necklaces, fringed with gold and jewels, and earrings. These he had left to David ben Shebua. Again, Hillel thought that David was a parody of his father, and then he felt he was unkind. David had more intelligence than his sire, and was capable of a little originality and a little sudden imagination. Perhaps that was why Shebua disliked him more than he disliked the more pragmatic and avaricious Simon and Joseph, who made no pretense at scholarship and were frankly worldly and unashamed of their worldliness.

The dining room was finer even than the dining room of Herod Antipas, or Pontius Pilate, as they had admitted, themselves. It was, in truth, a banquet hall, of the purest white marble imported from Italy. No color touched it except for the passionately colored murals on the white walls, beautifully executed by the best of artists, the thrown Persian carpets and the high ceiling of fretted copper in a maze of entwining forms and angles. The snowy columns of Corinthian design—no Ionian simplicity for Shebua—had their capitals delicately tinted. And on pedestals, in niches, stood nude and indelicate little statuettes of white marble brought from Greece.

The evening was hot. The bronze doors stood open and the pale silken curtains had been drawn back, and Jerusalem lay below them on her hills, tier rising upon tier, sharply illuminated. They could hear the fountains outside, musically laughing to the stars, and could smell the fragrance of warm gardens under the dew. Everything that met the eye was entrancing, and Hillel appreciated it, but did not appreciate his host and the brothers of Deborah.

Hillel, forgetting the graceful conversation about the table for a moment, looked at the young man who would marry Sephorah. Certainly he was not handsome, like his father, David, but neither did he resemble his grandfather Shebua ben Abraham, thanks be to God, blessed be His Name. The youth was shy and silent, but his eyes were very blue and candid, his expression alert yet retiring. He sat next to Saul who was very gray of face tonight and whose features were set in a tense and inflexible look, as if his thoughts were far from this room and his kinsmen and were bent on seeking, yet in terror of the seeking. His coarse white linen tunic did nothing to enhance his appearance, nor did that vital flare of red hair and the deep lost blue metal of his eyes.

The prophets had often spoken of the fire that inflamed their hearts with love of God, for the fire was love given and received, and it was rapture and ecstasy. (O Love of my desiring! thought Hillel, and he felt the hot burn of tears in his eyes. But this was not the love which his son knew, for all his transports in the Temple.) Hillel sighed again, and turned with pain from his son and listened to his boring father-in-law again.

Then he spoke. "Shebua, you have been conversing of the wonderful conceptual abstractions of the Greeks, out of which rose their code of ethics—which they observe no longer. Anything based on abstractions is alien to the flesh and the life of men; abstractions are the toys of the effete mind, which will endure no suffering or the sight or sound of suffering, or any of the fevers and sores and agonies of the flesh—particularly of other men. I not only call this trivial, and insulting to the manhood of humanity, but disgusting. Words are no substitute for actualities, nor exquisite phrases a poultice for reality. Men are born; they excrete and fornicate and void; they are tortured in their flesh. They smell. They often reek. They must labor —and pay taxes. They sleep. They eat. They beget. They die. These are the earthly and immutable verities of our being, our flesh. We cannot disguise them forever in the silk and embroideries of what you choose to call Greek civilization, or any other civilization, or in cantos or pentameters, however pretty, however sublime. I do not denigrate poetry or music or any of the other decorations men can invent, for life is not lovely, not comely, for man or beast. I admire, while I pity, these desperate efforts to hide the appalling face of reality, for none can bear the vision long with tranquillity, or without the help of God. Or without softening her lineaments with the veil of art. But we must admit it is only a veil. If we do not, then we shall surely go mad."

Shebua narrowed his pale eyes upon him and began to speak, but Hillel lifted his hand. "I beg your forbearance for a moment longer," he said. He was aware that he was boring Simon and Joseph. They had fastened a look of exaggerated filial respect on their father while he had been speaking before Hillel's interruption, and he had bored them even more. They did not conceal their ennui from Hillel, and leaned back in their chairs with expressions of resignation.

"You would say," Hillel continued, "that art and the graces of the mind distinguish us from beasts. But, we are beasts with them! I do not call this degrading; I call this coming to terms with reality. From that strong base we can proceed, and we must never deny it for if we do—

again—we shall go mad. It is said that animals have no souls; I dispute this. It is of no moment. You have implied that animals have no code of ethics. Who has enlightened you on this? I have seen animals and birds with more mercy and solicitude for their kind than any man has displayed! Animals do not betray; they do not exploit; they do not oppress; they do not enslave; they do not sin. They have their being, and their being is honest, and who can say this of man? It was necessary for men to invent ethics, for, before God, blessed be His Name, man was not born with ethics, nor could he survive without them! He is the fierce devourer of his brother, a cannibal, and no other animal is such except rats, who disquietingly resemble man.

"As an exercise in grace and in handsome reason, I admire the intellectual code of ethics of the Greeks. I admire the Roman hubris, the pride of country and race. I admire the Roman law, for it is based on human reality as the ethics of the Greeks are not. But as neither the ethics of the Greeks nor the Law of the Romans is based on God and the Reality of God, they have no true verity except in the most narrow of senses. It is only the ancient laws of the Jews, set in the matrix of the Reality of God, which can survive in this world, for they are cast in mercy, in compassion, in love, in justice—all the attributes of God.

"To us, life is sacred, and this is true of no other religion, no code of merely mortal ethics, however grand the language or profound the thought. The Greeks were never urged to love their fellowman; the idea is preposterous to the Romans. So it was to the Babylonians and the Egyptians, except for one very brief period in Egyptian history far long ago. Only to Jews is human life sacred. Only to us was given the Commandment: Thou shalt not kill! I will concede that we have obeyed this Commandment no more heartily, in our past, though we knew of it, than the other peoples obeyed, and they knew it not. Yet, it is there. Thou shalt not kill!

"For uncountable generations the Greeks have practiced infanticide. They find nothing immoral in that. They say it is a way of controlling their numbers. The Romans have begun to practice it also, and feel no repugnance, no guilt. Other nations have practiced this direful crime, without horror. But Jews do not practice infanticide. They do not kill lightly, and wars are no occasion for rejoicing, though we are a warrior people. For God has warned us not to kill. He has warned us to love and revere and fear Him, and to love our fellows.

"Surely, Shebua ben Abraham, you will admit that our ethics, based on God, are superior to the ethics of the Greeks and the Romans! And that our civilization, however it amuses you, is more attuned to the nature of man and God than any other!"

Saul, stricken and mute, had begun to listen. He looked with astonishment at his father and did not know him, for the usually gentle and conciliating Hillel had a tawny flame in his eyes and his face was deeply flushed.

"You are very eloquent, Hillel ben Borush," said Shebua, whose pale face had a faint shadow of malevolence on it now. "I can hardly believe this of a rigid Pharisee, for Pharisees are notoriously devoid of both eloquence and subtlety. But I concede nothing of what you have spoken, nor do I admit the verity of it. You speak as a Jew—"

"And you are not a Jew!" exclaimed Hillel, and the hand he had laid on the table trembled with wrath.

Shebua glanced slowly at his sons and smiled faintly. "We are citizens of the world," he said. "We believe in mankind, if we do not believe in God. We believe that man has infinite possibilities and potentialities, and that he will rise to them when he has abandoned superstition and relies only on himself. We are men now, not children. We need no staff of immolating idolatry and craven fear of the Invisible to sustain us. We need no commandments but our own superior minds, and the probabilities of our minds. We no longer hear God in the thunder; we understand thunder. That is not fire on Sinai. It is natural and mindless lightning. We do not dwell in tents now, nor are we barbarians. For children there are the beliefs of children, and the little fears and terrors, for they know nothing and have no knowledge. But we are men in these days, and we know what sustains a man and what hidden strengths lie in man, and we will evoke them."

"Oh!" cried Hillel, with unusual passion. "You have embraced the folly of pride—and how dare man be proud? Of what can he be proud? His history? May God forgive us this blasphemy! You have often spoken of the future.

The future is born in the womb of the present, and I see nothing in the present, or in the past, that promises glory for man, created by himself. For he cannot rid himself of his baseness by his own effort. It is written that man cannot earn merit by himself, for he is undeserving of merit. History is our witness. Man was not born for his glorification. Scripture teaches us that man was born solely to know and to love and to serve God, and nothing else, and in that knowing and loving and serving—alone— can he transcend his nature and become more than man."

Shebua smiled at him as if at an imbecile, and shook, with a pretense of forbearing indulgence, his thin finger at Hillel. "I deny your premises, Hillel ben Borush. To me your syllogism is without validity or truth. For your premise is God. I, therefore, deny your premise. You would 'define your terms,' as Socrates has said, but you and I could never agree on the 'terms.' Therefore, the argument is futile. But I will repeat that man can transcend what you call his baseness—but which I prefer to call his piteous ignorance—by cultivating his latent powers of mind and will. This the Greeks have said. I see nothing to dispute this. We advance. We progress. Yesterday, we were savages. Today we have the Parthenon. We have the Law of the Romans. We have poetry, and a repugnance for barbarism, which, again, you would call the baseness of men. We have refinements of the mind, a love for beauty. We are inventive. One day, as the Egyptians have said, we shall stride the suns, and nothing shall be closed from us. Part of our being may be animal and we live in our flesh, as do other animals. But they do not advance. They are today what they were yesterday, but our tomorrows are filled with glorious promise."

"They are filled with death," said Hillel. "And ever will they be, until the Messias comes, blessed be His Name, and reveals the hidden to us, and gives our evil absolution in His Love, and makes of mankind—not through human law and human contriving and human conquest—truly of one blood and one flesh and one spirit, and we shall know war and hatred no more."

His voice rang with absolute authority and fervor, and his whole face was kindled and exalted, so that even the still smiling Shebua and his sons were disturbed and made uneasy, and they hated him and did not know why they hated. As for Saul, it seemed to him that he was hearing words he had forgotten and he was strangely moved, and filled with pain, and he thought, This once I knew, but now He will permit me to know it no more.

Hillel was inspired. He could no longer control his unaccustomed passion, for he saw the derision and scorn of his kinsmen, and the affront against God. He shook his fist at them, and could not refrain.

"You Sadducees!" he cried. "You have taken bread from men and have given them husks! You have taken the morning from them, and given them the darkness of hell, in which God is lost. You have based your hopes on the world, which will pass away and be known no more among the suns and the Pleiades, nor will Orion know her any longer. On this frail orb that pursues her star you think to establish the golden city of man's reason and man's aspiring alone, forever and a day. You believe that it will be by the will and design of man alone that evil will be abolished—yet evil is the very nature of man, and immutable. He is a shadow, and on the shadows you would erect eternal palaces and pleasure-ways and advance urbane conversation and peace and what you aver are ethics. You know you are mortal, and in your shallow hearts you deny mortality, and speak of the far future as if you will be there, alive and triumphant! You do not know that future, but you have deluded yourselves that you will be there! Or is your vaunted 'glory of man in the future' enough for you, who will be dust tomorrow?"

He was breathing audibly. He searched each man's coldly derisive face, and he saw the fear in them, and the terror of death. He smiled compassionately.

"How pathetic you are," he said. "Your own deaths, in this little time, has not been believed by you. You have really hoped you will be part of the future which to me appears terrible, not beautiful. You believe in pleasure, in the day's tranquillity and grace and conversation and the meeting of friends. You hold the power of the Temple now, and you have profaned it. You deny the resurrection of the dead, which has been promised, for you believe that when men are dead they are no more than the beasts of the field. It is evil enough that you have betrayed God. You have betrayed your people to the Roman, to his oppressive taxgatherers; you have betrayed their pride and their nation; you have plunged us into despair. You have consorted with the Roman to enslave the helpless; you have helped him gather his taxes for the support of an idle and polyglot Rome, where men live on the earnings of others and who will not toil as we are forced to toil. For peace in your time, and pleasure, and worthless harmonies, and prettinesses, and conversing, and pride, and dainty perversities, and music and Corybantes and dancing girls and money and handsome houses and villas and servants and laughter and strange women and theaters and baths and arenas and gambling and horses and evil little appetites and enjoyments, you have called upon your people not to resist, not to believe in the Promise of the Ages—to obey, to bow down their heads, to submit their necks to the yoke. You have taken God from them, and for that you will not be forgiven!"

Shebua's face had become thin and livid, so that it resembled the blade of an ax, and he no longer pretended to conceal his hatred. It glowed in pale fire in his eyes.

He said, "What would you have us do, we leaders of our people, Hillel ben Borush? Advise them to rise—as the Zealots and the Essenes do, those madmen!—and strike at the omnipotent Roman, and so cause our country to be put to the fire and the sword? Would you urge them not to pay taxes to the Roman? Is life not better than death? Are taxes, however onerous, not better than the grave? Is not even slavery preferable to slaughter? Obedience to a conqueror, is, to the reasonable man, less terrible than execution, or starvation. As Solomon has said, 'Better a live dog than a dead lion.' The Lion of Judah is dead—"

"And we are alive, like dogs," said Hillel, with immense bitterness.

Shebua shrugged. "We are alive," he said. "What would you have us do?"

Hillel fixed him with his brilliant eyes. "We are a conquered little country. The Roman is all-powerful. These I admit. I do not desire my people's death, for in them lives the Spirit of God, and of them will be born the Messias. I would not have them die on miles of crosses. I would not see their wives and their children slaughtered. No. But, it was your duty, you sons of Zadok—and how glorious is that memory!—to sustain your people with the hope of the Messias, to alleviate their hunger with your fortunes, to intercede for them, to nourish their faith in their God, blessed be His Name, to exalt them with patience in their tribulations, to turn their eyes to the sun and to the stars, to repeat to them the Promise that has been given to us, to strengthen their endurance. What man will not suffer in quietude if he knows his Redeemer is nigh, and that God has not abandoned him?

"But you are taking from your people the only sustenance that will save them! You have darkened their souls! You have delivered them to the Romans like chained slaves and have said to them, 'This is what is, and there is nothing more, so resign yourselves.' And why have you asked this resignation? In mercy for your people? No! Only for luxury and peace for yourselves! And you dare prate of the glorious future of mankind, you betrayers of what is noblest in man, you poisoners of wells of the water of life!"

It was unpardonable to rise before the host, but Hillel could not contain himself, so deep was his pity for his people, his anguish for their oppression, his torment for their poverty and pain and endless labor, his fury at their betrayal by their own, his torture that they had been deprived of hope—and so great was his anger. He struggled to compose himself.

His voice had become hoarse. He lifted his hands like a prophet and he was not ashamed of the tears on his cheeks, though the hate and derision of his kinsmen were like a deathly fog in the room now.

He said, in the words of David:

" *'God is our refuge and strength,*
A very present help in time of trouble.
Therefore will not we fear, though the earth be removed,
And though the mountains be carried into the midst of the sea;
Though the waters thereof roar and be troubled,
Though the mountains shake with the swelling thereof.

" *'There is a river, the streams whereof shall make glad the city of God,*

The holy place of the Tabernacles of the Most High.'"

The silence in the vast room was palpable, as though a prophet had thundered within it and no sentient thing could make sound.

Then Hillel turned and began to move from the room, and after a moment Saul followed him and they did not look back.

In the atrium Hillel, shaken to the heart, was unable to speak for weeping. He put his hands on his son's shoulders and bowed his head. And Saul put his own hands on the shoulders of his father and despised himself that he had not believed him capable of such passion and such holy anger, and such righteousness, and another woe was added to the woe he carried in his heart.

They heard a footstep and looked up, half hiding their tears, to see Clodia Flavius and three of her women moving across the atrium on a mission to be certain that the host and his kinsmen were properly served by the servants. Clodia halted and looked keenly into Hillel's face, but her own remained calm.

The Roman woman said in a voice of understanding and consolation: "Shalom."

It was Hillel, looking into her face who answered, and his voice broke:

"Shalom, Clodia Flavius."

Saul could not understand. He felt affront and bafflement and left his father and went to his bedroom.

Chapter 10

HILLEL BEN BORUSH went to visit his kinswoman, Hannah bas Judah and her beloved husband, Aulus Platonius. Saul refused to accompany him, despite Hillel's pleas. "I have no desire to converse with Romans, my father," said Saul. "What are Romans to me? The oppressors and enslavers of my people. Two nights ago you berated my grandfather for his collaboration with the Romans for a shameful peace. Last night you told me that he would not

remain unpunished, nor his sons with him, nor his sect.
Yet today you visit Aulus Platonius, a Roman oppressor!
I am astonished."

Hillel sighed. "Aulus, no more than I, loves the im-
perialism of Rome, for he is an 'old' Roman of the stern
school. Who can justly blame the Roman soldier, the
Roman proconsul, even, God forgive me, the Roman bu-
reaucrat and taxgatherer? One, if one is sensible, blames
government, not the servers of the government, not those
entangled in their governments. Was it not Samuel the
Prophet who warned the people not to set a king over
them, lest they be enslaved and live in chains and die in
chains? Government, it has been said, is a necessary evil,
but evils should be kept in weakness. If they become
strong it is the fault of ambitious men who hate their
people, and the·folly of the people that they permitted
this enormity, and their soft smiling complacence. Aulus
is not of this breed. With me, he deplores the decline of
patriotism and virtue and industry and honor in the world.
He weeps with me that the world of men have deliberately
debased themselves. He is my friend. We love each other.
I do not hate him because he is a Roman, as helpless as
I am, a Jew, in the machinations of government. We are
brothers together. Together, we honor God, blessed be
His Name."

"Nevertheless, his people have murdered Jews by the
countless thousands, have put them to the sword, have
hung them on multitudes of shameful crosses, have exiled
them, have robbed them in taxes, have imprisoned and
starved them, have slaughtered them in arenas, have taken
from them their wives and their children and their homes,
have flayed them alive. Shall I love such a son of his
people?"

Hillel wearily tried to make him understand, again.
"He, too, is a victim of his government. Aulus is no
murderer. The individual man is rarely a demon. Aulus is
no demon."

He looked at the dark and obdurate face of his son and
wondered where the old lusty and joyous and exuberantly
laughing Saul had gone, and what had caused that exile.
Then a strange revelation came to him: Men do not
change. This Saul he saw this hour was the Saul once
imbedded in the flesh of a passionate youth. The youth

had departed; the real man had risen from the discarded chrysalis. What Saul was now so he had been born, and all his boyhood and his youth had been but colorful and evanescent trappings. The man was here. Hillel remembered the loud cry of the infant Saul in his nursemaid's arms: It had been a harsh and imperative cry, proud and angry, not the cry of a child. Between the man of today and the babe of yesterday there were no barriers. They had become one.

"What are you, who are you, Saul, my son?" asked Hillel in bemusement, and passed his hand over his forehead.

Saul smiled at him grimly, as if he fully understood. "I am Saul ben Hillel, the son of my people, who are great in history and great in war and great in the love of God."

"But you know nothing of Him," said Hillel, and wondered, with fear, why these words had escaped him and from whence they had come.

Saul turned on his heel and left his father. I weep easily these days, thought Hillel ben Borush. But, do not all men weep for their children? If we feel such grief for those of our loins, how great must be the sorrow of the Lord of Hosts for His children, blessed be His Name! To pity God seemed a unique thought to Hillel. He pondered on it, as he rode in one of Shebua's gilded litters to Aulus' house. What presumption it was that man should have compassion on God, for had not David written, "Man lasts no longer than grass, no longer than a wild flower he lives, one gust of wind and he is gone, never to be seen there again?" It was as if a butterfly should feel sorrow for the sun! Yet, the thought remained of the sadness of God, and for some mystic reason Hillel felt again that powerful fire in his heart which is the love of God, and the immediate communion with the Lord of Hosts, and he was comforted and exalted. The Messias might tarry, but He, blessed be His Name, would surely come and console man.

Saul, bereft, darkly confused, lonely to his very heart, empty of spirit, went on foot to explore the city of his fathers, Jerusalem, avoiding all those whom he knew.

The day had turned chill and windy, and he pulled his hood far over his head. The feeling of desolation and oppression increased in him as he walked rapidly over the darkly glistening and rounded stones of the poorer quarters of the city. The sky had an ominous appearance, heavy with gray clouds and ridges of darkness. He saw the stony mountains, hard and barren, in the distance, growing more dismal under the somber sky. He reached one of the marketplaces, reeking with a thousand smells. Here was a walled street, arched over with stone, little booths sunken in the walls, the street itself nothing but a series, dropping down, of immensely steep broad steps of rough cobbles, on which the booths fronted. The little shops were so tiny and so crowded with goods, that only one man—or sometimes an old woman—could find space in them. But they were all noisy and clamorous and full of urgent shoutings and gestures. Here were sold meats, sizzling on braziers, rugs made of cheap goat's hair or an imitation of costly Persian carpets poorly colored, spices, nuts, globed and partly rotting fruit, pottery, pots and pans, wine, silks of a poor quality, swaths of linen and wool in gaudy tints, cheap tunics and headcloths, weapons, hot breads, rough vases, amulets, cheeses that stank, appalling imitations of Greek and Roman statues, replicas of the Temple in plaster and cement, bronze lamps, candlesticks, sandals, ivory figurines of execrable taste, garlic, onions, various limp vegetables, olives in brine, oil, violent perfumes, incense, miserable jewelry set in base metals, cloaks of poor cloth, red, black, white, gray, purple, blue, yellow, dates, pomegranates and citrons, and, occasionally, a very active booth selling Syrian whiskey guaranteed approved and sealed by the Roman customs agents but in fact truly smuggled into Israel by enterprising mountain men and heavily diluted with water. Someone had been clever enough to forge the Roman seal in lead. The Romans were not deceived, but they did not care. Their own soldiers, poorly paid, and unable to afford good whiskey, needed to be served also. Let the Jews smuggle this wretched whiskey and do a massive trade in it. The legionnaires, poor country boys, did not complain. They had no comparisons.

Some booths sold furniture of miserable taste and quality, but bedizened and painted so that they dazzled the eye.

And everywhere was the market rabble, shrieking women and shouting men, children, thieves, beggars, the blind and the halt, the hungry abandoned, the cutthroats. Roman soldiers strolled among them, eating hot meat from grape leaves, bargaining loudly for amulets and whiskey and jewelry, cursing the furiously screaming merchants, laughing, eying the girls, kicking the endless donkeys and dogs and cats, strolling lightly up and down the broad steps, exchanging jests, sucking olive pits, chewing dates, straining pomegranate seeds through their big white teeth, swaggering, laughingly quarreling and pushing each other. In short, they were like young soldiers forever and a day in an alien land, enjoying themselves, inclined to be amiable, drunken, hungry, boisterous, proud of themselves, and anxious to be friendly even with robbers of merchants. Sometimes, with utter good nature, they would reach across huge heaps of piled goods and tweak the beard of some merchant, who would pretend to wrath and shake his fist at them, cursing them in Aramaic and then swindling them a moment later. It was payday for the Roman soldiers. By nightfall they would not have a drachma left, though they would be happy and surfeited, having slept with a harlot under a bridge or among cypresses or beneath an aqueduct.

Sometimes a laden camel would appear, lumbering and complaining at the steps, tugged viciously by his owner, who delivered fresh goods to the stalls and added to the clamor with his complaints that he had been robbed by a cursed townsman.

Colored awnings fluttered in the sharp wind. Men drew their cloaks closer; women held their headcloths against their mouths in protection against the swirling dust. Animal offal strewed the steps. No one strolled, except the soldiers. The avaricious faces of the merchants and market rabble were bent on gain before the sun fell, and as the day advanced the shrill screams and bellows became louder, the pace more frenetic. It was dim under the stone arch except for the fires of the braziers, yet the gray and luminous light heightened the color of garments, the strong reds and blues and yellows and whites, and glimmered on racing feet.

The stench and noise and the press of bodies stunned Saul. Not even in Tarsus had there been this vivacity, this fury, this determined rapine, this feverish rage of sale and bargaining, this smell of rotting vegetation and dust

and vinegary wine and resin and garlic and crowding
animals and roasting meat. He forgot that the markets
close to his house in the suburbs were of superior quality
and decorum, and nothing at all like this turmoil of
buying and selling. As he had never bought anything in a
bazaar in Tarsus he thought the goods displayed here
were abominable, and he wondered who bought them
and who desired them. Merchants stretched forth hands
to grasp his cloak or his arm, imploring him to buy, and
he pulled away from them in disgust, and looked at the
Roman soldiers with umbrage and bitterness. And when
one or two, not entirely drunk as yet, paused in their
guzzling of their wine or whiskey bottles, caught his eye
they stared in astonishment at the hard blue fire of it,
and nudged each other and winked uneasily. They saw
his hatred, and it puzzled them. One or two were annoyed. They pushed back their helmets, with the crests
of horsehair, and wanted to challenge this silent but
angry young man, but their companions held them back
and whispered in their ears, and they laughed and forgot
him. They had been warned over and over by their captains and centurions that they were not to antagonize
Jews, who, on occasion, could be very formidable and
very troublesome.

Saul, wishing to escape, ran down the last steps of the
marketplace, dodging animals, men, women, children, beggars, soldiers. He emerged onto a large open place, paved
with yellow gravel and surrounded on two sides by the
yellow walls so prevalent in Jerusalem. It, too, seethed
with people, but as it was big and broad the press was
not too heavy, the animals not so ubiquitous. Here and
there stone benches were scattered, for the benefit of the
weary. Saul sank down on one of them and as he did so
the clouds parted and the golden autumn sun emerged,
warming and brilliant, bathing everything in a broad mass
of brilliance, brightening robes and gravel and wall, turning the sky to the hard luminescence of blue and polished
stone, making resonant with color every solitary thing it
touched, shining on the dusty clumps of palms and cypresses, and outlining the city in shelves of light.

Saul slowly became aware that some short distance
before him a woman was sitting wearily on a stone bench,
a spare peasant woman dressed in dull brown garments

and a blue headcloth and with bare dusty feet in thonged sandals. Her head was bent; she appeared to be meditating; her hands lay slackly on her knees, the palms turned upwards in an ancient pose of exhaustion and resignation, as if her hands had worked hard and long and could work no more for a pace, and she had come here to rest. The autumn sun was tawny on her tired thin shoulders; it glistened on her lashes which drooped; it illuminated one pale cheek and gave it a semblance of healthy color. But the lower part of her face and her hair were concealed by the headcloth which she had drawn over her mouth and nose and brow against the bright but nimble wind.

She was only a poor woman, probably from the hills of Samaria or Galilee or another of the farming provinces, but she caught Saul's unwilling attention. He did not know why he stared at her bent head and why her depleted attitude attracted him. She had come a long way for the Holy Days. A basket stood near her knee and two doves were held there, for the sacrifice, all that such a woman could offer. She seemed a member of the Amaratzim, those who labored in meager vineyards or stony fields and milked goats or tended geese or picked fruit. Her feet were partly turned, as if to rest them. Saul guessed that she was a middle-aged woman about thirty-five years of age or somewhat younger, for her figure was not shapeless, even under that shapeless brown garment, and her ankles, he saw, were delicate and very thin. She appeared to be dozing in the warm brown-gold sunlight and her breath hardly raised the cloth on her breast.

She was very insignificant in appearance and Saul was irritated by the fact that he was caught by something in her attitude. Jerusalem was filled with thousands of such women; the streets were restless with endless clusters of them. They carried baskets on their heads or their shoulders, or they came from afar to the Temple on such days. They were not extraordinary. Yet, Saul could not look away. Where were her children, her husband, that she sat in such mute abandonment and heavy drowsiness? Was she a widow, childless? The woman dozed, or brooded.

He wished he could see her face so that he could guess if she were widow or maid, young or old. The wind lifted her headcloth and she raised her hand suddenly to catch it and restore it over her nose and mouth. And so Saul saw her face, full and turned toward him, and he was incredulous at her beauty. He thought of a water-lily, waxen and pale and smooth and fresh, open to the brilliant light of the day. Her mouth was softly rose and sad, yet full in contour, the lower lip indented like the lip of a very young girl. There was something Grecian in the long shape of her white nose with the delicate nostrils, and the still and unwrinkled calm of her broad brow. Her chin was rounded and dimpled, her cheeks fragile and without tint. He saw her eyes, very large and blue, with gilt lashes, and as her headcloth fluttered he saw that her hair was a clear soft gold, straight and shining. It was a regal face, serene yet touched with sorrow, thoughtful yet living, not placid but restrained and gentle, a face from Galilee.

She is but a girl, he thought, and then it seemed to him that the light changed a little and she was old, as old as his mother would have been if she had lived, and that would be thirty-five. She was regarding him with a mild but steady interest, as if he had spoken to her and she was trying to remember him. Then her lips parted and she smiled gently and her blue eyes radiated a mournful but sympathetic recognition. He felt an almost irresistible urge to rise and go to her and tell her his name, and inquire of hers. Instantly, he was vexed. She was only a peasant woman, and she believed she knew him while he knew her not. He began to stir, readying himself for leaving before she spoke and embarrassed him by some simple boldness or impertinence.

But her beauty, as beautiful as a statue's, held him, and a kind of reluctant and angry awe touched him, for rude hills did not breed such women for all her dress. She had the aspect of a queen garbed as a peasant for her amusement. Her hands, he saw now, for all their workworn appearance, were as delicate as her face, narrow and exquisitely formed. And her radiant eyes studied him, not in crude boldness, but with maternal interest and affection. Now the light about her changed once more and she appeared as young as his sister, Sephorah, and as untouched and fresh, and even younger.

A young man approached her, as rudely clad in sand-colored garments, his feet shod as hers. He was, in appearance, some years older than Saul, a man in his first adult years, and Saul thought he must be the woman's brother for he resembled her closely. His hair was the same color as hers, and his young beard also, and he seemed as worn with work and as weary. His feet and garments were dusty; the dust in the folds of the cloth had turned golden in the sunlight, and the leather purse that hung at his rope girdle was very lean. He was moving slowly, as if he, too, had come a long distance, and his cheeks were haggard with weariness. But he smiled down at the woman and now she raised her eyes to him and suddenly her face was shimmering with love and pleasure at the sight of him. He carried a large grape leaf in his cupped hands and it was filled with smoking spiced meat, aromatic and appetizing. He laid it in the woman's hands.

"Thank you, Yeshua, my son," she said. She spoke in Aramaic and her voice was soft and ineffably sweet.

Saul was astonished. It was incredible that this girl, this very young woman, was the mother of this man of at least twenty-one years or perhaps more. The man squatted on his heels and reached into the basket which contained the doves and he brought out a leather pouch and produced a spoon for his mother. Then he sat beside her and he looked down at her with benign dignity and answering love. "You are very tired, Mother," he said. "Eat and be refreshed."

"Tinoki," she murmured, the endearing word of a mother to her beloved child. He touched one of her hands and said, "Emi." He took the spoon from her and, like a father, he dipped it into the grape leaf and lifted food in it and solicitously raised it to his mother's lips. She ate obediently, smiling, her eyes fixed on his benevolent face as if she could not have enough of the seeing.

"I thought you had—left me," she said, and now her lips quivered and she was no longer smiling.

"Not yet, Emi," he said. Saul, watching in a fascination he could not help but which he vaguely resented, was struck by the young man's voice, for it was deep and strong as a venerable rabbi's with strange and moving undertones like half-heard music. "You will know when I must go. You will not be unprepared."

Tears appeared in her eyes. She bent her head to hide

them as if ashamed. "Forgive me," she said, almost inaudibly. "But I am weak today. Forgive me, Tinoki."

He lovingly and compassionately touched the side of her cheek with his fingers, the vibrant strong fingers of a workman. She humbly took the spoon from him and ate of the food he had brought and he watched her with a deep and wistful devotion as if he were pondering on some pain he had caused her or was about to cause her. His own pain was obvious, as if his very vitals had been wounded, and yet he smiled down at his mother and urged her to eat when she faltered.

I have not been such a son to my mother, thought Saul, and it seemed to him that the pain of the strangers had reached out to him and had touched his own heart with a finger of fire. Deborah, in the light of the woman opposite him, took on a kind of radiance from her, as though she were the mother of all mothers, and women drew light from her. It was a foolish thought, Saul commented to himself, restlessly, but it held him. Deborah had been but a child who had never attained womanhood, a petulant beautiful child who had never been satisfied with her husband and her son and had complained in her pretty voice incessantly; the world had not given her her just deserts. Still, in this woman's presence the memory of Deborah became sorrowful to Saul and he felt his first real grief for his mother, and he could not understand it.

Saul thought, He is her son, and she is only a woman, yet he regards her with the respect that Greeks once gave their gods, and he is gentle with her and inexplicably tender, as if, above all women, and perhaps all men, she is the most beloved to him and the most precious and sanctified.

Respect for mothers was implicit in the religion of the Jews, but Saul had often thought it too elaborate and very often undeserved. He said Kaddish obediently for Deborah, and often wondered where that child-soul reposed and in what flowery nursery it played, or if it slept in the dust like a flower on which an iron heel had been imprinted. Yet, his mother had not been a plain woman such as this woman, and she had been born of a venerable and illustrious house, and had been a patrician and the name of her fathers was honored in the gates of the city. In her way, she had had some learning; she was no stranger to the arts of the Hellenistic culture if she were, indeed, less understanding of the religion of her fathers. Why had he not honored her as this probably unlettered workman from some scorching hill obviously honored his mother? Deborah had been almost as beautiful and certainly charming. I have been a son, thought Saul, watching the two near him, with a cold and obdurate heart. Forgive me, my mother. You did not love me and I did not love you wholly but I should have honored you. Am I less than this obscure man who regards his mother as the holiest and purest and sweetest of all creatures, and esteems her with every gesture and every glance of his eye? Alas, I am less. I am much less.

The young man reached for the basket with the doves and drew out a leather bottle of wine and a brass cup. He opened the bottle and Saul caught a scent of the wine; it was poor and cheap and acrid. The young man filled the cup and held it to his mother's lips with deference and she drank, her eyes again on his, blue and beaming. The attitude of the two, sitting in the hard and lonely sunlight, friendless and alone, was excessively touching for all its stately posture, its proud simplicity. Crowds hurried along the great courtyard; shadows were deep purple and sharp; voices and footsteps were noisy; children darted everywhere, and merchants with carts screamed and uttered imprecations. Yet these two sat in a mysterious isolation as if unseen by all but Saul, and unseeing except for each other, the one giving profoundly, the other taking with humility. Saul had seen the man's arm as it had emerged from his garments. It was brown from the sun, and muscular and masculine, familiar with labor, endowed with the ability to lift and carry with ease. His ankles and feet, too, were brown. They had known the soil of pastures and stony places, of torrid noons and bitter winds.

"We are all one, all sons before our Father, blessed be His Name," Hillel ben Borush often repeated. As that was a doctrine of the Jews Saul had believed it, but only intellectually except for one short interlude. But all at once he truly felt a oneness with these people before him and he wanted to speak in spite of his pride.

It was then, as if Saul had truly spoken, that the young

man turned his kingly head to him and looked at him fully. Their eyes met, and it seemed to Saul that his heart raised itself and shook and all his limbs were disturbed. The azure of the peasant's eyes seemed to advance on him, as if in truth he had risen and was approaching the youth, holding him powerfully with his gaze. All sound disappeared from Saul's consciousness. Now he had been drawn into the circle of remote silence and isolation with these two, and they were alone together.

To Saul there came a sensation as of deep and unearthly fear as well as of massive force drawing him to the young man. All his mind was assaulted by something mysterious and compelling, yet terrible. Part of his soul said to him, "It is absurd, for you are Saul ben Hillel, of the Tribe of Benjamin, and learned and of a noble house, and your name is not despised even among the proudest and the most royal, and this man before you is nothing but a peasant and possibly cannot even write his name! Therefore, why should he draw you to him and why is your heart inflamed and troubled and bounding like a lamb?"

But another part of his soul said to him, "Arise and go to him."

The young man was gazing at him quietly, his expression still and grave and curiously alert, and sad. Yet his lips were smiling faintly, as if he, too, had recognized Saul and knew him for what he was. The golden brows almost met above the large deep eyes; the wind ruffled the golden hair and beard. So clear was the light, so vivid the concentration of the stranger upon Saul, that Saul himself saw more intensely than usual. He saw the dim blue shadows below those pale cheekbones, as if pain dwelt there without surcease. He saw the veins in the white temples, and the throbbing of the browned throat.

The woman, too, was gazing at Saul, the brass cup near her lips. Her hand trembled a little.

They are sorcerers! thought Saul, and the terror increased in him for all a portion of his mind laughed at this superstition. So he sprang to his feet in disorder and he fled from that place and did not look back and did not cease his hurried steps until he entered the marketplace again. And the clamor and cries rose up about him and the masses of the people lurched against him, and he was free from his enchantment and the clangor of the world had never seemed so dear and safe to him as it did now, and so protecting.

I have escaped! he thought. From what he had escaped he did not know, but he was sweating violently. He felt he had been in some awesome jeopardy, but the jeopardy was unknown. He bought a handful of ripe figs and ate them greedily. Then slowly, he began to laugh at himself and to wonder at the emotions he had felt. He walked on, looking at the little shops with a friendly contempt and amusement. He looked at the pretty dark-faced slave girls and felt aversion, and then a vague pity for their state. When he came out again into sunshine he said to himself, "I am alone, and lost, and I do not know why."

It was then that he heard or thought he heard a tremendous, familiar voice calling to him: "Saul, Saul of Tarshish!"

He looked about him wildly, but only the market rabble and the merchants were about him and the asses and the camels and the screaming children as they raced up and down the broad shallow stone of the steps. I am going mad, he thought. They have laid a spell upon me, and he ran again, murmuring aloud the prayers against the evil eye. And then he stood, trembling, the figs in his hand. He had heard that voice before, in his bedroom, in the holy Temple, and he was covered with a dread confusion.

The house of Aulus Platonius and Hannah bas Judah was in an unpretentious section of the city not far, alas, from the Street of the Cheesemakers. Therefore the air was permeated at all seasons, in all days and nights, with the odor of sour, ripe or new cheese. To Hillel, remembering it, it had a reassuring scent; it was sound and earthy and full of authority and permanence, unlike the graceful and perfumed gardens of Shebua ben Abraham and his sons, which seemed—to Hillel at least—to have the odor of decay and transience and graves, not to mention decadence.

Aulus, as a rich man, and Hannah, as a rich woman, could well have lived on the heights of a mount in a fine villa with many slaves and servants, but they were frugal.

They resembled each other in temperament; their tastes were simple, not out of deliberate ostentation or because of penuriousness, but because simplicity was of their nature. They had a fine library, the heritage Hannah had received from her father, and beautiful gardens of flowers and vegetables and fruit trees and palms, though the gardens were of necessity small in that crowded area. A single fountain stood in the center of yellow graveled paths, and in the shade of a karob or sycamore tree Hannah would work with her few women.

In all this, Hannah also bore a resemblance to Clodia Flavius. Hannah, however, was of different attributes, soft of voice, deferential of manner, meek of gesture, gentle in speech, hesitant to advance an opinion, sweetly anxious to please, and of a will which made Clodia's seem to be as bending grass. The large brown eyes in the shelter of thick black lashes might appear to be the eyes of a doe, but a certain glint in them could make the burly Aulus quail and daughters tremble. As an "old" Jewish woman she kept her hair covered, but sometimes a brown strand of it, as frail as silk, would drop over her calm forehead. Her face was as round as a coin and expressed absolute innocence and womanliness, and her lips were tender and her complexion pale gold, for though, like Hillel, her forebears had come from Galilee she had the darkness of the Judean. Hillel loved her dearly; she had been like an elder sister to him from his childhood. He also remembered the weight of her hand in less loving moments. If, indeed, "all her ways are pleasantness, and all her paths are peace," Hannah bas Judah was queen of the household and, Hillel often smilingly suspected, the king also.

Aulus greeted him with pleasure and embraced him and kissed his cheek. "Shalom. This house is honored to receive you, my cousin," said Aulus. Hillel's hands lingered on Aulus' shoulders, and the Roman, who desperately at all times tried to conceal a certain sensitivity of temperament—it was unbefitting a soldier—felt that lingering and the unconscious pressure of Hillel's fingers. Ah, he thought, with commiseration, the family of Shebua ben Abraham have been too much for my poor friend. He slapped Hillel heartily on the arm and inquired of Saul and why he had not come also.

"Saul," said Hillel, "is restless and disturbed, and is cooling his fever with explorations of the city. Youth is not an agreeable state."

Aulus' eyes were kind as they studied Hillel's face. "Truly," he said. He led Hillel through the atrium into a pleasant room full of sunlight though spare of furniture, and with a stone floor on which lay a few woolen rugs of no particular value. There were no murals here, no statues, no fine vases, no lemonwood tables, no crystal or Alexandrine lamps. But it had a certain immaculate comfort and Hillel sat down. Aulus clapped his hands and a servant appeared and Aulus ordered refreshments. "How is our beloved Hannah?" asked Hillel.

Aulus as a soldier had few illusions, but he had one which could provoke Hillel's secret amusement. In spite of Hannah's absolute rule over her household Aulus was convinced that she was the most docile of women and he invariably forgot the occasions when none dared defy her will when she had collected her mind. Had he remembered he would have persuaded himself that he had capitulated out of deference to her female weakness and because he loved her and wished to humor her. He said with heartiness, leaning back expansively in his chair, "My dear Hannah is, as always, the noblest and sweetest of women." He beamed. His thick beard bristled with pride and affection. He wore a tunic of blue wool, for the day was cool, but he retained his iron-shod sandals and now he made a proud clattering with them on the floor. There was an air of suppressed excitement about him.

It was Hannah, herself, who led the servant with the refreshments, carrying white linen in her hands, her robe of gray and red, her head covered as always. She was small and plump, like a dove, with a dove's full breast. Hillel rose and went to her at once and embraced her and she kissed his cheek and then held him off to examine him acutely. She had not seen him for seventeen years or more, and her eyes were the eyes of an anxious mother. "Hillel," she said, in her gentle voice, and there was an inquiry in it.

"I am well, dear Hannah," he answered, and was horrified that he might burst into tears.

Hannah continued to smile, but she sighed. "And Sephorah, and Saul, whom I have never seen, my cousins also?"

"My children, thanks be to God, are in good health," said Hillel. "You will see them at Sephorah's wedding, which will be eight days from today."

The maternal eyes were smiling though still searching. "I have heard rumors from Aulus that Sephorah is very beautiful. My own daughters are not beautiful but have married to our satisfaction. We have grandchildren who delight us. I wish that blessing for you, Hillel, my beloved cousin."

She covered a table with the white linen and gestured to the servant who set out bowls of cheese and bread and fruit and olives and fish, and artichokes in oil and garlic and a fine bottle of wine. Hannah watched with benign attention, and arranged the pottery plates and the simple silver cutlery. She said, not looking at Hillel, "The years pass, and we see those whom we do not love and who are strangers to us, and our hearts g ow sore with longing because our kinsmen are far from us."

"There was not a year when I did not hope to return, Hannah," said Hillel.

"Ah! I am not reproaching you, my cousin. I merely observe. The years pass in duties and they are not to be despised. But still, the presence of those we love can be most dear to us."

"I will return in another year," said Hillel, accepting a goblet of wine from the servant. "And one day I will return and I will leave no more." He did not hear the sad loneliness in his voice but Hannah thought, He has two children yet he is disconsolate, my poor kinsman.

Aulus suddenly stood up and went into the atrium. His gesture was so abrupt that Hillel was surprised. But Hannah had begun to smile. "This is a joyful day for us, Hillel. I must not spoil my husband's pleasure in enlightening you." She glanced through the door. "We had hoped that the—pleasure—would be here when you arrived. There has been some delay. Aulus is becoming impatient."

There was such an air of peace and tranquillity in the house that the pain in Hillel's heart began to be assuaged. He watched Hannah's deft little hands. Hannah was some several years older than himself but calm certitude and love and happiness had preserved her as no cosmetics could preserve the youth of a Roman woman. She might have been the bride at whose wedding he had danced as a boy, except for the wisdom in her eyes.

They could hear the traffic and the noise of the street beyond the high yellow walls, and Hillel saw that Hannah was listening as if to distinguish a different sound. The air was fresh, though redolent of cheese. Hillel sipped his wine and thought that his kinsman's taste had improved. Then Hannah's face glowed with joy and a deep dimple appeared in her dusky cheek. She hurried into the atrium, and Hillel heard the hearty sound of men's voices. A moment later Aulus appeared, swaggering, holding the arm of a tall young officer in the resplendent uniform of a captain of the Praetorian Guard. Hannah trailed behind and though she smiled there were tears on her face.

"Behold whom we have with us, Hillel ben Borush!" cried Aulus, his chest swollen with fresh pride and happiness. "Our son, Titus Milo, returned from Rome to visit us! He arrived at Caesarea but today, and we had his message only a month ago!"

Hillel had never seen Hannah's son, his cousin also, until now and he rejoiced with the rejoicing parents. "Shalom aleichem!" said the Roman officer, embracing Hillel and respectfully kissing his cheek. "Greetings, my dear cousin, Hillel ben Borush, of whom I have heard much." He spoke in Aramaic.

"Shalom, Milo," said Hillel. "It is a joyful day for us all, and I mean it from my soul." He observed that Aulus stood with his hand on his son's back, his soldier's face brilliant with happiness, and again he was lonely. And then he suddenly remembered that only two nights ago Saul had embraced him, weeping, in the atrium of Shebua's house, and his sadness lifted and he thought, I, too, have a son who is heart of my heart.

Titus Milo Platonius was much taller than his father, who was of no small stature, and of a lean compact figure with a certain masculine and military grace, with broad shoulders and narrow waist and hips and fine muscular legs beneath his soldier's tunic. He wore tall boots of supple brown leather embroidered in gold, and a scarlet cloak fringed in gold and a belt of gold links, and gold epaulets, and he also wore leather armor and his arms were strong and brown with the sun. His helmet of iron, overlaid with silver, was intricately engraved and set here and there with sparkling jewels, and its crest was high and noble. And he wore the famous and terrible Roman short-sword and a dagger and there were rich rings on his fingers and his leather wristlets were inlaid with gold. He was magnificent.

But Hillel looked earnestly at his face, and saw there the shape of Hannah's, round and firm, with her dimpled chin cast in the mold of a man. He had his father's Latin nose, fierce and powerful, his father's direct eyes. But where Aulus' eyes were frequently kind, Milo's were stern and his brow had an unbending look and his cheekbones were like sun-darkened stone. Yet, his appearance and countenance were noble and proud and compelling, and Hillel thought of Roman statues of heroes he had seen, and he knew why Aulus' chest swelled at the sight of his son. This descendant of two warrior peoples betrayed no sign of baseness or hesitancy, and his voice rang deeply in the room, tender when speaking to his mother, genial when addressing his father. He put his helmet on a table and Hillel saw his round cropped head, with bristling brown hair and large ears. Hannah hovered near him, touching him softly, studying him with her maternal gaze and smiling through her tears.

"You were delayed," said Aulus, himself pouring a silver goblet of wine for his son, and Hillel knew this was an honorable and honoring gesture from a father, for "old" Roman fathers did not serve their sons except as a ritualistic gesture.

Milo, who had been smiling down at his mother, ceased to smile. "Yes," he said. He glanced quickly at Hillel, and his dark face became a little darker and it was perturbed deeply. Then he looked at his father. "You have not been on duty today, my father?"

"No. I was awaiting our kinsman."

Milo said, "There has been some trouble, near the Damascus Gate today. We will speak of it later."

"I have heard nothing," said Aulus, but his soldier's face quickened.

"I have ten of my men with me, Mother," said Milo to Hannah. "They are my lieutenants. Is there fare for them before they go to their assigned quarters in the city?"

Hannah, after one fearful glance at her son's face, hastened from the room to order food for Milo's men, and she took with her the cheese on the table for now she would serve meat for a hearty meal.

"Tell me," said Aulus, "now that you have dispatched your mother. What evil news is it, on this day I hoped to be joyful?"

"It was none of my affair, except that I am a Roman officer. But I am of the Praetorian Guard and it was a matter for the regular military, not mine. Nevertheless, I wished to intercede, or perhaps mitigate." Milo's glance again flashed to Hillel, and the strong lips became somber. "You must believe I did what I could, but the provocation was enormous."

"Tell us," said Aulus, and he sat down as if suddenly weary and Hillel's heart became sick.

"The Essenes, and the Zealots," said Milo, and he muttered a Roman oath. "Why will they not accept the immutable? They created a riot inside the Damascus Gate, and they were armed and were wild as barbarians, for they came from the desert but today, and they murdered one of your brother centurions, my father, and twenty of his men. They were then overpowered." He stared into the depths of his goblet. "There are one hundred. They have been thrown into prison. A number of others were slain on the spot, in battle."

"By Castor and by Pollux!" cried Aulus, and groaned, and seized his ears in his hands.

Milo's lips tightened. "At least two hundred Jews of this city joined the rebels," he said. "They are also in prison, those who were not slain." He stood up, put his hands on his hips and walked slowly up and down the room and would not look again at Hillel's agonized face.

"For Jews to kill Jews is reprehensible enough, according to the law," said Milo. "But for Jews to kill Roman men and their officer is intolerable."

He paused and stared down at the stone floor between his feet. "There has not been such a riot in the city for several years. In the struggle a large number of innocent women and children were injured, for the riot embraced many streets. Several shops were set afire. A Sadducee priest in his litter was dragged forth and beaten and thrown to the wall. The guard was attacked. Animals were slain. The stones ran with blood, and the gutters. I did what I could," he repeated. "I attempted to restrain—I was reviled as a Roman swine and a murderer. I spoke to the barbarians then in Aramaic and begged them to flee. If some had not listened the prisons would hold many more than they do at this hour."

He looked at his father straightly and his shoulders appeared to become broader. "I am a Roman officer, of the Praetorian Guard, and I must pay my respects to Pontius Pilate for whom I have a message from my general. My allegiance is to Rome. You must believe me that I felt as if my flesh were being torn from my bones and my vitals exposed, my father."

"Yes," said Aulus, and averted his head.

"I carry with me not only a letter from Caesar Tiberius, whom I serve, but his ring of authority in my pouch," said Milo. "It concerns Herod Antipas, who has been plotting with Agrippa."

Father and son exchanged a long dark look. Hillel whispered, "My people. My unfortunate people." His whole face trembled.

Then Milo said, "My people—also." He sat down suddenly as if overwhelmed. "An order has gone out for the arrest of known malcontents," he went on. "Though they are not concerned with this, discipline must be enforced at any cost, and potential rebels punished, as an example." He hesitated. "It is very bad. The centurion is the son of the Senator Antonius Gallio, dear friend of Caesar's."

"Octavius Gallio!" exclaimed Aulus in desperate horror. "We were subalterns together! In the name of the gods! The old Senator will exact blood and death for this!"

"He is a veritable Caligula," said Milo. "And mad as he. Did he not wish to murder all the Jews in the Trans Tiber only two years ago? Yes."

"My God, my God," said Hillel, in anguish. "What have they done, my reckless people, those wild youths burning with patriotism and love of God and country? They have destroyed themselves, and others. They have set themselves as frail battering rams of flesh against a wall of stone, but they will not desist, though they die of it. What have they accomplished, but torment and death for themselves and their brothers? Yet, I cannot find it in my soul to upbraid them, to denounce them, for if a man has no country of his own, no land which is free and his own, what has he? He is less than a beast who does not know that he has nothing."

Aulus and Milo looked at him in compassionate silence. He said to them, "If Rome were seized by an alien force and subjugated and enslaved and robbed and oppressed, would you not rise to deliver her, though you knew it was hopeless?"

"Yes," said Aulus. "I would give my life for my country though it were futile."

"And I," said Milo, "would give my life both for Rome and for Israel. Is not my state a wretched one?"

It was then that Hannah came back into the room, pushing aside a curtain to do so and they saw by her pale countenance and her shaking lips that she had heard. She carried a silver platter of cold meats in her hands. She laid it on the table, and then her gaze wandered from Hillel to her husband and then to her son.

"Is there naught we can do?" she asked.

"I did what I could," said Milo. "In a pretense of cutting the rebels down I dispersed them and urged them to disband and flee. A number looked into my face, and then obeyed and fled."

"But now?" said Aulus.

Milo lifted his hands then let them fall on his bare knees, and the gesture was both Jewish and eloquent.

Aulus turned suddenly to Hillel. "Shebua ben Abraham is the father of your dead wife, Deborah, and his grandson is to marry your daughter. He has a powerful influence with Pontius Pilate."

"Shebua ben Abraham," said Hillel in a voice heavy with loathing, and like a curse in its intonation. "When has he ever interceded for his people? Would he jeopardize his security and his luxurious life and the favor of Romans? Forgive me, Aulus, but my heart feels as if it is draining away my blood. Shebua ben Abraham!"

"Nevertheless," said Aulus Platonius, "you must appeal to him. Desperate causes demand desperate men. Ah! I have remembered! There is an influential Jew here whom Shebua honors and courts, Joseph of Arimathaea, who, it is said, is very mysterious but more important: very rich. He is honored by Pontius Pilate, the Procurator. Pilate is superstitious; it is said that Joseph has told him he will participate in an event which will shake the world forever, and so Pilate believes that one day he will be named emperor of Rome. He, too, courts Joseph. Joseph is of a great family, and a pious Jew, and a Pharisee, and a member of the Sanhedrin."

Hillel, in his agony of confusion and grief, pondered. He had heard the name before, but could not immediately remember. But he had learned enough from his wife's kinsmen to doubt that such a powerful Jew—who had not been beggared nor persecuted by the Romans—would assist his miserable fellow Jews whom he would stigmatize as "the market rabble," or insurrectionists or troublemakers or rioters for the mere sake of rioting. Too, the Essenes and the Zealots had no reputation but that of violence and excessive zeal among the more powerful Jews and especially the priesthood. He began to shake his head dolorously, then paused. It would do no harm.

He said, "Aulus Platonius, and Milo, I understand why you, yourselves, as Romans, cannot appeal to any puissant man, and particularly not to Romans, in this matter. But I shall appeal both to Shebua ben Abraham and Joseph of Arimathaea. I fear that it will bring no succor to my unfortunate people. Nevertheless, I will try."

He rose. It was then that Hannah said, "You have not dined, Hillel, and men need sustenance. Therefore, compose yourself. Is not my dear son here, who is of your blood? To leave now would be a discourtesy to him and a harm to yourself. Food can give a man courage." Thus spoke Hannah bas Judah, the mother of children, and Hillel remained.

Chapter 11

AULUS PLATONIUS sent a messenger to Joseph of Arimathaea to ask for an audience for Hillel ben Borush, and in that message he conveyed the information given him by his son, Titus Milo. In the meantime Hillel set forth for his father-in-law's house to seek help which he more than feared would not be forthcoming.

The air had turned nimble again and became, as sunset approached, wine-gold and scarlet. An amber light lay on the crowded and mounting levels of Jerusalem, and gilded the tops of pine, palm and cypress, and a trumpet sounded from the heights of the Temple, warning the people that sunset and prayer were almost at hand. The sound, to Hillel in his despair, was both triumphant and lost. The gilded litter of Shebua ben Abraham, carried by six Nubian slaves magnificently garbed, climbed and descended through the teeming streets and past high walls. Hillel had drawn the curtains of the litter so that he could survey the throngs of his people and pray for them in silence.

On entering the atrium of Shebua's house Hillel encountered his son, Saul, who was wrapped closely in his dingy cloak, as if cold. Hillel put his hand on Saul's arm and looked into his face and saw the pale bemused expression. He said to him, "My son, it is my desire that you accompany me into the presence of your grandfather, for I have direful news to relate and I need the comfort of you at my hand."

Saul said, as if he had not heard, "I fear I am becoming mad. One night, in this house, while in my cubiculum, I heard a man's great voice call me, and today, in the marketplace, I heard the same commanding voice."

Hillel considered him acutely. "And it frightened you?"

Saul hesitated. He drew his cloak closer about him. "I do not know," he pondered. "I am filled with both fear and exaltation. But it was only a delusion."

Hillel shook his head. "Who can say?" he murmured. Then he took firmer hold on his son's arm. "Come with me." The overseer of the hall entered the atrium and Hillel requested him to ask Shebua to see his son-in-law and grandson. While they waited the atrium became darker, and they stood in silence.

The overseer returned to inform them that his lord, Shebua ben Abraham, had just emerged from the baths and was now in his chamber, preparing to dine with the noble Procurator, Pontius Pilate, and King Herod Antipas. He could grant Hillel but a few moments. Hillel's pale mouth trembled with renewed wrath. He kept his hold on

Saul and followed the overseer to Shebua's chambers, which were luxurious and warmly scented. Shebua was seated in an ebony chair near a small lemonwood table, and his concubine, Asa, the beautiful and serpentine Nubian girl, was polishing his finger- and toenails and perfuming his hands. He wore his usual air of negligent elegance and lay back in his chair as if exhausted. He was arrayed in a tunic of fine silvery cloth and his toga lay on a chair, shimmering as if dipped in moonlight, and his sandals, enlaid with gems, awaited him. His ambiguous glance warned Hillel that he was still unpardoned for his past words, and discreetly disliked.

"Ah, Hillel, and my grandson, Saul," he said in his mellifluous voice. "I regret that I must leave you soon, and can give you but a little time." His pale eyes surveyed them with glacial indifference. His light hair was polished with unguents. Hillel's nose distended with dim disgust. Shebua did not urge him and Saul to seat themselves, and so they stood, though Saul first went to his grandfather and gave him a dutiful kiss on the cheek, at which Shebua smiled graciously. As twilight was now rapidly approaching Asa drew the silken draperies across the window and lighted two tinted lamps, whose bases were of rosy alabaster. Hillel hid his mortification at being forced to stand like a servant before his lord.

Hillel began to speak, and as he did so he watched both Shebua and Saul. He spoke concisely, trying to conceal his agony, and as he spoke Shebua's face subtly changed, became rigid and distant and haughty. But Saul showed his overwhelming distress and anguish. Finally Hillel had done, but he and Saul gazed intently at Shebua.

Shebua held out his slender arms to Asa, and she reverently clasped the gemmed armlets on them, and put rings upon his fingers. Then she stood beside the chair which held the toga, the ivory instrument of arrangement in her black hand. Her eyes were limpid and without interest. She might have been a statue, obediently waiting.

Shebua examined one of his rings. "A dolorous affair," he said. He shook his head. "Why will they not learn? Or, do they delight in violence and disturbance?"

He turned his head and regarded Hillel with calm and

amused malignance. "I assume that you have come to me with this sorry tale to ask my intervention with Pilate and Herod?"

"True," said Hillel. He added, "In behalf of your people."

Shebua said, "All people are my people, Hillel ben Borush. I am not a provincial, as I have observed to you before. I am one with all men, and there is no division. If criminals resort to illegal violence and murder, then I am against them, for I believe in law and order and rightful obedience, and resignation to what is."

"Resignation to intolerable oppression and exploitation and taxation and cruel tyranny?"

"Ah, you use the words of violence yourself, Hillel, and I deplore this. I thought you a more temperate man. What is it you wish me to do? Debase myself before Pilate and Herod like a mean little rabbi from the Provinces, whimpering for mercy? These men are my friends; they know my temper; they understand that I regret and denounce useless rebellion as much as they do. They know I am a civilized man. They know these wretches are nothing to me, though they call themselves Jews."

Hillel thought he would die on the spot with his suffering and his anger and hatred. He put his trembling hand to his throat. "Shebua ben Abraham," he said, "deceive yourself though you will: These are your people, your kinsmen. You have none else. Would a Roman be indifferent to the torments of Romans, or even a Greek? No! Aulus Platonius has told me that he would die for Rome and his people, however useless the struggle. He is a man of honor and pride and loves his country."

"And I do not?" said Shebua ben Abraham. "I am not a man of honor and pride? That is your opinion. Our values, our premises, differ, Hillel ben Borush. We have argued this before, and have come to no conclusion, no agreement. I tell you, these criminals are nothing to me. They endanger their whole people, put all of Israel in jeopardy, threaten Israel with the Roman short-sword and total annihilation. Is it not better that a few die for their country than all Israel be destroyed? A Jew who loves his country will ponder on that."

Hillel was stricken. Then he said, "Do you think Pilate

will honor you as a civilized man, that you do not ask for mercy for your people? Herod is partly Jew, partly Greek. Will he honor you for silence, for a pretense that your people are nothing to you? They will laugh at you secretly, as a pusillanimous man!"

Shebua's pale and slender cheeks flushed. "We shall avoid the subject tonight!" he said. "They know my opinions."

"You have not answered my questions," said Hillel. "No matter. You are an adept at sophistries and evasions, Shebua ben Abraham, and I am no match for you. My cousin, the Praetorian captain, Titus Milo Platonius, suffers for Israel. Aulus Platonius, the Roman, is struck to the heart for those who are not his people. Is a Roman less, or more, than you, Shebua?"

Shebua stood up and indicated to the Nubian girl that he wished his toga. She flung it over his shoulders. He stood tall and glimmering in the lamplight. The girl knelt before him and began to arrange the toga artfully and he became absorbed in the fall of every fold. He spoke a word or two, pettishly, to her, as if nothing was more important. He arranged the sleeve of his left arm with meticulous irritation.

Saul regarded him with a fixed and peculiar expression, as if his young face had become stone, and his blue eyes glittered with contempt and bitterness. His hands clenched and unclenched at his sides. He felt, above his pain, the humiliation cast on his father and himself, as if they were importunate beggars which only kindness prevented from being dismissed and driven away with whips.

Shebua then turned glaucous remote eyes on his kinsmen. "I can do nothing. I am a realist, and I know when I can do nothing. As a civilized man I cannot extend mercy to the merciless, tolerance to the intolerant. What else but mercilessness and intolerance have the violent extended to those they murdered? Were the Roman soldiers not doing their duty, in protecting themselves, the law, and even all of Israel? Did the violent consider their people, and the consequences to their people? They have brought disaster to many who are innocent, and caused innocent deaths. Shall I, then, plead their cause?"

"I have told you," said Hillel, with renewed despair.

"Many of those arrested and now facing shameful deaths were not engaged in violence, as you choose to call it. They were taken from their households."

"They are known malcontents," said Shebua. "They are potential assassins, though many come of noble houses. They have not tried to support law and order, to restrain the violent. To be tacit is to agree."

"There are children, and maidens, and youths, among them," said Hillel, trying to suppress his weeping. "There are wives."

Shebua shrugged. "It must be brought forcibly to the attention of potential inflamers that this is a warning, an act of discipline." He flushed again. "Do you think me a man of marble and malevolence, who loves bloodshed and death? No! Do I rejoice in the thought of agony and grief and misery? No! But I know what must be done, if Israel is to survive."

"You care nothing for Israel," said Hillel. "All your words are but sophistries. You care for nothing but your own household, your wealth, your position. I knew this before. I knew in my heart that I could not move you. If I had not given my word, if my dear wife had not agreed, the marriage of my daughter to your grandson would not take place, for I would not wish her allied to the house of Shebua ben Abraham, nor would I desire her to give birth to one of your blood. I have wasted my time, and time grows short. I will have recourse to worthier men, men of valor and honor and justice."

He turned and Saul accompanied him from the chambers. The youth gazed at his father and thought again how he had misjudged him, though with love, and woe came again to his heart.

"Come with me," said Hillel. "We go to the house of Joseph of Arimathaea."

"To the man who declared he saw the Star over Bethlehem?" asked Saul, with faint scorn.

Hillel stopped suddenly. His face changed, became full of emotion and a light shone behind the tears in his eyes. "To Joseph of Arimathaea!" he said.

Father and son lay in the gilded litter as it wound its way through streets glaring with red torchlight, and lamps, and through throngs of hurrying people and soldiers and mounted cavalry and camels and asses.

Saul said, "It is wicked to denounce those of your blood, according to the Scriptures, but Shebua ben Abraham is an evil man."

Hillel said, "No, he is not evil. There are occasions when the evil can be touched. Shebua is a frightened man, and none can appeal to a man of fear. He is distracted. He is beyond reason. I saw fright in his eyes. I spoke to him harshly, yet I pitied him. God may forgive the evil, if they repent, but how can even angels make their voices known to a man filled with panic?"

But Saul said, "He is an evil man."

Hillel sighed. "I wish he were only that. I can forgive all but cowardice."

"And expediency," said Saul.

"Are they not, at the last, the same?"

The house of Joseph of Arimathaea was on a wide and level street, below the Mount of Olives. Behind the wrought iron gates the house stood in tranquillity and calm, the portico filled with lamps, the gardens aromatic, heavy with pine and palm and the spires of the dark cypresses. The gatekeeper opened the gates and the litter entered the red gravel path to the bronze doors. The doors opened, and Joseph of Arimathaea stood on the threshold, and then he stepped into the portico, with its white and shining columns, to welcome his guests.

He was a tall and massive man, in his long blue tunic belted with gold, his arms bare. He was in his middle years, and beardless, and he was nearly bald. His head was large and heavy and oval, larger than the head of the average man, and the first impression of strangers was that he was ugly and without comeliness. His features were too big, his mouth too ponderous, his chin corpulent, his fat ears protruding from his skull, which was polished like stone. But his eyes were dark and radiant, mystical and kind, under black brows which met totally over the bridge of his aquiline nose.

He said, in a very sonorous voice which aroused echoes in the gardens, "Greetings to Hillel ben Borush, and his son, Saul. Welcome to this house, which knows your illustrious name!" He extended enormous and muscular hands to Hillel, then embraced and kissed his cheek. He smiled at Saul, and his smile made his face beautiful. "Shalom," he said.

Hillel struggled to control himself in the face of this tender and gracious greeting, and returned the embrace of his host. Joseph led them into a wide and illuminated atrium, where the overseer stood at attention, and then into another room tastefully furnished and permeated with the scent of fresh fern. Joseph clapped his hands and servants entered laden with linen and plates and cutlery.

"I have dined," said Hillel, "though my son has not."

"Come," said Joseph, with another of his luminous smiles. "When can a man not enjoy food?" He studied the young Saul, and then a curious glimmer touched his eyes. For some unknown reason Saul was disturbed at that frank gaze with its overtone of mystery. Saul did not love luxury, and this house was at least as luxurious as his grandfather's. But it seemed to him that the luxury here was not so studied, not so pervasive. He sat in silence near his father while the servants prepared the table.

Hillel said, "You know why I have come, Joseph of Arimathaea?"

"Yes," said his host. "I received the letter from my dear friend, Aulus Platonius, who is your kinsman. But, you are weary. Let us first refresh ourselves."

"How is it possible, when I am so distraught?"

Joseph said, "All things are possible with God, and He is not without mercy, blessed be His Name."

Hillel's eyes filled again with tears. He said in a broken voice, "Forgive me, but my heart is afflicted. I am not usually so womanish."

Joseph said in a gentle voice, "When are a just man's tears womanish? If we did not weep on occasion our hearts would be only as dead earth. And do we not have reason to grieve? Enough. Let us dine in peace, trustful in the promise of hope."

"What hope?" thought Saul with renewed bitterness. "What hope is there for man?"

He slowly became aware of the peacefulness about him, in this house. Even Hillel, in his terrible distress, was soothed and partook of some wine, cold meats, vegetables in oil and vinegar, fruits and pastries. Saul, hot of heart and afflicted of mind, could not be insensible to the quietude of this house, the harmonious repose, the placid beauty. He thought to himself that Joseph's house reflected his taste, that everything in it and about him was an extension of himself. But Shebua ben Abraham's house did not reflect him, for there was no substance in him to reflect. His house was the creation of others' tastes and others' values; he, himself, could create nothing. The very soft light on the white walls of this room appeared but an emanation of Joseph of Arimathaea's own spirit. Saul felt certitude, not the certitude that comes from faith in men but in faith beyond men, and his young cramped soul shook its crumpled leaves and reluctantly began to expand. But he remained suspicious, wary of platitudes.

Joseph's voice did not break the silence; it rode upon it easily. He said at last, "I have seen Pontius Pilate, who owes me much, and I have seen Herod, who owes me more. I knew of the tragedy at the Damascus Gate almost as it happened, for shall one of my people suffer without my knowing or my caring? Alas, it was a sorrowful tragedy, and I grieve for both Roman and Jew, and for all who clash arms anywhere in a conflict which is never resolved. For so long as men exist there will be war and hatred and oppression and rebellion, until—" He paused, and he gazed into space as if seeing some heroic vision yet unfulfilled.

He resumed. "Is it better to die in a just cause which may never succeed, or to live and work in hope of its final success? This has always been the enigma which has faced man, especially in his youth. The Greeks say it more brutally: 'It is better to die on your feet as a man than to live on your knees as a slave.' But merely to die, however nobly, is to remove a warrior. We cannot spare warriors." He gave Hillel his gentle smile again but this time it was a little cryptic.

Hillel was regarding him with painful attention.

"Let me comfort you in a small way," said Joseph in a compassionate tone. "There have been killings today, and Romans do not look upon killings of their soldiers with equanimity. Nor do we regard the killing of Jews with uninterest. The Romans call themselves the men of law and reason. They can understand the anger of the Jews, for they would feel as we do if Rome were occupied by an alien power and its laws enforced on her. Romans are also pragmatists—when it concerns other men's patriotism and spirit. Who is stronger? Rome. Who, therefore, has the major right to rule, engage in trade, regulate commerce, build, change? Rome. This is not a new manner of regarding the conquered, but Rome has made of it a virtue. It is not hypocrisy. The Romans are honestly convinced that they are the civilizing and welding force in the world, and they have always dreamed of a world-government, which they believe they have brought about under the Pax Romana. Competing nations, rival empires, appear disorderly to the Romans, trivial, duplicating, self-indulgent, extravagant, expensive, without efficiency, and dangerous. If the Roman spirit could be described in one word it would be Economy, economy in thought, deed, philosophy, action.

"Forgive me if I seem to be astray, and tardy. I wished you to understand that I comprehend the Roman, and comprehension is half the battle when engaging in controversy. For, who can hate the man he understands? He can only approach the adversary, or the friend—and it is strange how often they are the same!—with kindness and reason, and even with sympathy. This is not subtle wiliness. It comes from the heart, if it is genuine. Therefore, though I know Pilate well, and know him for a cruel and superstitious and ambitious man, I also know him as a man, of my human flesh and my human spirit, and I know he is not happier than I, not more content, not alien to my being. He shares with me all the afflictions and all the hopes and avarice of mankind, and he knows that I know this of him. As for Herod, he is a man to be pitied, the man who cannot reconcile his Jewish nature with his Greek instincts.

"To them both today I brought my understanding, and my importunities."

He peeled a large ripe plum for Hillel and put it on the small golden plate, and did not wait for the servant to serve Hillel more wine. He poured it himself. Saul watched him and thought with disgust, "He is but another player on words, another deft pleader for the Roman, another compromiser, another agile man who can release himself from a trap. Such men have sold their souls for comfort, for riches, for security, and do not know the sorry bargain."

As if he had heard the young man's thoughts Joseph rested his bright dark eyes on him for a moment and a shadow of sadness touched them. Hillel had listened acutely, and had not felt dismay nor repulsion. It was as if a strong cool hand had been laid on a feverish cheek, and so he waited and a faint calm came to him.

Joseph said, "I have persuaded Pilate to release those seized in the city as potential malcontents, who have opposed the Roman obdurately but not with violence. They have been returned to their homes with stern warnings, but they are now in the bosoms of their family. 'Shall the lamb be sacrificed with the lion?' I asked Pilate." Joseph smiled. "He also owes me considerable money, for he is a reckless gambler, and Tiberius Caesar, that harsh and rigid man, does not like gamblers. He has also compromised himself, in company with Herod, with Agrippa in Rome. Fortunately, I have friends whom Tiberius trusts, and so Pilate is not to be recalled." Joseph paused. He looked at the wine in his goblet. "He has a role to play, and I have seen it in my visions. I am a visionary man."

Hillel's face had become tremulous with hope. Joseph lifted his hand.

"I did not use my money nor my influence in Rome to sway Pilate, for that would be more degrading to me than to him. I used Roman reason on him, and the Romans do not like disarray or emotionalism. Nor do I. The emotional man is a man who has lost control of himself. Therefore, how can he rule others or give a judicious opinion? That I said to Pilate, and he knew I spoke in truth. Emotion should have no part of justice, I assured him. Was it just to punish the innocent for the fault of others? Only the Greeks believe that, I told him, and he nodded his head." Again Joseph smiled. "The Romans, in their hearts, believe themselves inferior to the Greeks. They always welcome one who assures them of their superiority."

He is a wily hypocrite! thought Saul, with increasing rage.

But Hillel said, "Thanks be to God, Joseph of Arimathaea, that you have saved the innocent! But what of those hundred or more of the Zealots and Essenes who await a monstrous death, in the prisons of the Romans?"

Joseph said with sadness, "They I cannot save. Nor do I believe that they desire to be saved. They are rash and dedicated young men, and it is the young who believe in heroic causes and court death as older men court mistresses. They believe they set a standard for others to follow, that they carry a banner which will strike fire in the hearts of other men. It is beautiful. But not very sensible."

"So, they will die," said Hillel.

"Not without glory in their souls, not without exultation," said Joseph. He poured fresh wine. "To that they have always aspired. I do not deny their love, their patriotism, their devotion to God. But on the altar of these they are more than willing to be sacrificed."

Saul could not restrain himself. "I, too, am willing!" he cried.

Hillel, even in his agony of spirit, wished to rebuke his son. But Joseph again lifted his hand and said, "And so you are, my child, and so it will be."

Dread filled Hillel's heart, for he was a father. He had heard that Joseph had mysterious gifts of prophecy and penetration.

"I would rather my son lived for his people," he said.

"And so he shall," said Joseph, with his kind smile. This seemed enigmatic to Hillel. Saul's eyes were like polished metal, reflecting his deep passions and anger. Joseph went on, "I know when I have a possibility of succeeding, even a faint one, which I will press. I know when I cannot succeed, when it is useless to try. So the children of the desert must die. Pilate said to me, 'Do you Jews not have a law saying "an eye for an eye, a tooth for a tooth?" And, a life for a life.' I knew he was adamant on the subject of the deaths of his soldiers and officers. Who can blame him? I was grateful enough that he spared the innocent, though we know they are as inflamed as those men, if more discreet. They are also more pious. They await the Messias, and His deliverance of all men from their sins and their sufferings, blessed be His Name."

Hillel's face again became tremulous but before he

could speak Saul said, "And you pleaded with Herod,
Joseph of Arimathaea?"

"I did. I have persuaded him to give a painless poison
to those of the young heroes who showed even the slightest fear of death and suffering. A man should go to his
self-evoked death with pride and rejoicing, and even with
gratitude. Those of feebler and gentler spirit should be
preserved from the agonies of inexorable execution."

Hillel dropped his head and clasped his hands on his
knee. Joseph looked at him with compassion. "Hillel ben
Borush, death is not the supreme terror, nor the most
monstrous of calamities, nor is life greatly to be desired
by wise men. We know this, as Jews. And it was Aristotle
who said, 'There are circumstances and occasions when
the reasonable man will prefer to die and not to live.'
You suffer for our young countrymen, for you are a Jew,
and I suffer with you. But man's life at its best is brief
and full of trouble and pain and despair, and there is not
a man alive today who will not be dead in less than one
hundred years. A century from now, and few among us
will be remembered, no matter if they were evil or
just, saints or demons, traitors or patriots." He paused.
"Only One will be remembered, blessed be His Name."

But Saul said in youthful agitation which overcame
his taught respect for those older than himself: "You
believe that no cause is worth fighting for, no banner
worth following, and that men should be complaisant before evil?"

"I did not say that," said Joseph. "I wished to imply
that a giant is not overcome by a flea, and however
determined and devoted the flea he cannot slay the giant."

"Goliath was killed by a stone, flung by David," said
Saul. He was almost panting in his defiance and his scorn.

Joseph meditated for a moment. He said, "God has
His reasons, and we know them not. We can only look
knowingly on events when they have become past history. It is my belief that God now has a different role
for Israel, a spiritual conquest of men, a conquest of love
and joy and salvation, and not a conquest by death and
blood. Except—" He stopped again, and Hillel looked up
from his brooding misery.

"What is it that you wished to say, dear friend?" he
asked.

Joseph hesitated. "I have had visions," he replied. "I may not speak of them, for the time has not yet come."

"You believe that the coming of the Messias is at hand?" cried Hillel.

Joseph took a pomegranate in his hand and studied its scarlet surface. "What if He has already come?" he asked in a distant tone, as if proffering a theory.

"He has not come!" said young Saul, more scornful than ever. "If He had come, the whole world would now be proclaiming His blessed Name and rejoicing, and the Roman would lie in the depths of the sea as did the Egyptians!"

"You believe, Saul ben Hillel, that God hates the Roman, who is His child also, and that He will send Messias only to the Jews? 'A Light unto the Gentiles,' it has been prophesied." A sternness appeared on Joseph's face, a rebuke.

Hillel's sad eyes had become ardent as they fixed themselves on Joseph. He whispered, "You believe He has come?"

But Joseph was silent. Hillel's heart began to beat with strong urgency. "I have heard of the Star over Bethlehem, and I have heard that you went to the city of David—"

But Joseph still did not speak. Saul laughed in himself. These old men loved mysteries; they loved to appear elusive and wise. He looked at his father, Hillel, with the light on his drawn features, and was ashamed for him that he could lend himself to this folly, this blasphemy against God, Who would send His Messias with legions of angels, with golden trumpets which would shatter the highest battlements and with a glory that would daze the earth, and not obscurely, not in the night, not with equivocation.

"I have prayed that I would see His salvation," said Hillel, humbly.

Joseph gazed at him with a strange long look. "So shall all the just," he said. He sighed. "Ask me not of the Star, or what I saw in Bethlehem, for the hour has not yet come." He directed his gaze upon Saul, and though it was intent it was also far, as if seeing what others could not see. Saul was suddenly and dreadfully struck with the thought that such a gaze had been directed on him by the poor peasant in the marketplace. He was filled with a chill fear.

Joseph conducted his guests through the atrium and the portico, and he kept his arm over Hillel's shoulders in a tender embrace. At the door he kissed Hillel on the cheek, in comfort and said, "Do not grieve. All is in God's Hands, blessed be His Name."

"I do not know why, but I am comforted," said Hillel, and he smiled through fresh tears. He hardly heard Saul's infuriated denunciations of Joseph as they sat in the litter.

Later, as he prayed in his cubiculum, he heard the return of Shebua ben Abraham, and a loud commotion and men's disordered voices. He rose and drew his bed-robe about him, and opened the door and peered out beyond the hall into the atrium. It was lighted brilliantly. Shebua was there, struggling in the arms of his servants, who were apparently attempting to restrain him, and he was uttering the most incredible blasphemies and oaths and rages. Hillel's first impulse was to go to him. Shebua's toga was covered with the stains of wine and meats and fruits, his hair was disheveled, his face pale and sweating and distorted. He is drunk, thought Hillel, and remembered that one is not to disgrace another by observing his drunkenness, and he prepared to shut his door.

But there had been something in Shebua's manner and voice and struggles which was not solely of drunkenness, though he had drunk mightily that night in contradiction with his usual restraint. Hillel paused, watching through his half-shut door, as Shebua fought with his servants and cursed them.

Then, to Hillel's bewildered pity, Shebua burst into tears, and collapsed in his servants' arms and they bore him away, and one remained behind to blow out the lamps. Hillel closed his door, and pondered on what he had seen, and he was filled with sadness. What had caused Shebua's unusual orgy of emotion and chaotic derangement could not be known to him, Hillel, but he remembered that Joseph of Arimathaea had spoken of the oneness of men in spite of their apparent differences. May God have mercy on us, prayed Hillel ben Borush, and went to his bed. May God have mercy on all men, for we are afflicted.

May God avenge us, prayed Saul ben Hillel, and he

wept in his rage and sorrow and hatred. And then he found, to his horror, that he could not resume his prayers. There was a deep numbness within him like an awful absence.

Chapter 12

"DO NOT go to the place of execution. I implore you," said Hillel to his son. "You are young. It will break your heart. Accompany me to the Temple, where we will pray for the souls of those valiant young men."

"No," said young Saul. He seemed to his father to be growing more emaciated each day, and there was a cold austerity now on his freckled forehead and a burning look in his eyes. "I would be less than they if I did not suffer in my heart with them."

"You torment yourself; you bite at your flank as a beast tears at his sores," said Hillel. "Have you forgotten when we were carried into exile by the king of Babylon, Nebuchadnezzar? Those of us who were not, gathered together to form a rebellion against our oppressors. The Prophet Jeremias saw that this would bring upon our people a greater calamity, and he put about his neck a wooden yoke to symbolize to us our ebullient and reckless hopes before the reality of catastrophe. But the false prophet, Hananiah, tore the yoke from the neck and shoulders of Jeremias and broke it into fragments, saying, 'Even so will I break the yoke of Nebuchadnezzar, within two years!' "

Saul stared at his father in mute bitterness, his lips pressed together.

Hillel sighed. "Jeremias left the false prophet but God, blessed be His Name, commanded him to rebuke Hananiah, saying, 'You have broken wooden bars, but I will make in their place bars of iron.' And Hananiah died within two years. For the hour of His deliverance had not come, and it was not the season. Be certain that God will deliver us, for have we not His promise? The young men who die today are impatient."

"You speak, my father," said Saul, "almost with the

tongue of Shebua ben Abraham, whom I despise for all
he is my grandfather. I do not understand you. It was
but two days ago when you sought help for the heroes
who die today, yet today you are as ambiguous as
Joseph of Arimathaea, whom I despise also."

"I would not have you suffer," said Hillel, the father,
and could not help himself. But Saul made a faint and
tortured sound and left him, swinging his cloak about
his shoulders.

It was a day of coolness and the sky was curiously
brazen and against it stood the bald mountains, the color
of grapes in the still air. Saul went on foot to the Damascus Gate, for beyond, in the barrenness and desolation outside the walls, the ardent young youths were to
be crucified by the Romans. Jerusalem was strangely silent, as if all had drawn a deep breath and was holding it, and the shops were shut and no children ran on
the stony streets. The atmosphere, quiet though it was,
seemed to be half inaudibly filled with mourning, and
only the soldiers were visible, clanging in their battle
array, and watchful. All the light appeared to have gone
from the city, so it was dull and yellow and abandoned,
and everywhere were echoes, faintly crying or distantly
booming. The Roman banners hung lifelessly above the
gates of the city, the bronze eagles among them, as it
were, brooding. The soldiers did not prevent any man
from leaving the city, and as Saul walked to the Damascus Gate he was joined by speechless men in black, and
hooded, with cloths drawn over their faces. And now at
the gate the crowd was many, and their footsteps raised
the only sound and the sound was doomful.

The gates made a harsh grinding as the grim-faced
soldiers swung them open and the crowd poured through,
not speaking, not weeping. One could see only their eyes,
dark and glittering and passionate. Saul walked among
them and thought, I alone of that household come to this
direful place! Not even my father deigned to be here
with his prayers! And the bitterness increased in him
and his head ached savagely and his eyes were dry as
dust and as hot.

The land beyond the gate was bare and lifeless, the
yellow earth crumbling and full of rubble and stones,
and here it was suddenly hot as if the doors of a furnace

had opened. Beyond lay the wilderness of Syria, and the hard mountains purple and somber, and the sky that was too close and jaundiced. And there, on a flat open place fifty crosses lay on the ground, waiting, and at the side of each stood a ragged youth, bearded and wild but silent, his eyes fixed on the unanswering sky, the unresponding heavens.

Saul and those who had come with him joined those already there, in motionless and ominous ranks, shoulder to shoulder. There were many young Roman soldiers with cold and angry eyes, unusually silent, for these men they were to execute had murdered their comrades and their officers, had violated law and order, had lifted their hands in violence against those the gods had ordained to rule them in the name of justice and peace.

Saul looked upon the faces of the condemned, the remote faces, the praying lips. Some were younger than he; not many were of mature years. He wanted to weep, but could not. He wanted to curse, but his lips were numb. He wanted to beat his breast. He slowly became aware of the lowest of chanting, hardly to be heard, and knew it to be the prayers for the dying. But Saul could not pray. He could only gaze on the faces of the condemned, who appeared already dead, so motionless were they, so indifferent, so far. It was as if nothing that was of them stood in this place, and that they had already departed.

Then against that terrible silence a man's voice rang out, pure and strong and certain:

" 'My help comes from the Lord, Who made heaven and earth! He will not suffer your foot to be moved. He that keeps you will not slumber. Behold! He who keeps Israel does neither slumber nor sleep!

" 'The Lord is your Guardian. The Lord is your shade upon your right hand. The sun shall not smite you by day, nor the moon by night. The Lord shall keep you from all evil. He shall keep your soul. The Lord shall guard your going out and your coming in, from this time forth and forever!' "

The condemned started as one man, the rags and skins of their garments moving in a place where nothing moved, and they turned their young sun-darkened faces eagerly in search and now their faces were the faces of children who had heard the voice of their father.

I have heard that voice before! thought Saul, and the thunder of his heart was in his ears, and he turned with all the crowd and searched for the speaker. But a confusion seemed on all as all eyes denied that their tongue had spoken the solemn promise of the Lord. A dim muttering rose, then died.

The soldiers had turned to statues and they, too, as one man, searched for he who had cried out with such loud faith and even exultation and comfort. But they could not find him. A dull shadow ran over the earth and raised a dry yellowish dust and a hotter breath, and now the brassy sky darkened a little, and a Roman officer looked at it uneasily, for Romans were superstitious and they had heard tales of the vengeance of the Jewish God. Let it be done, he thought, and gestured with his mailed hand, and the soldiers seized the nearest youth and flung him on a cross. Immediately there was the dolorous and awful sound of hammering as nails bit into young hands and feet, and there was nothing else, not even a cry.

The valiant die valiantly, thought Saul, listening to the iron hammering which seemed too close, too dreadful, too imminent, in that silence. When the soldiers raised the cross with the youth upon it, and forced it into a hole in the brittle yellow ground, the shock of its falling into the socket appeared to be a shock on Saul's heart, so awful, so dolorous, it was, so final, so hopeless. The youth sagged with his own weight but did not groan.

One by one the youths were crucified, and not a cry or a protest or a shriek of agony came from a single heroic throat. Some were proud and disdainful; some were set of lip and eye. Some appeared to have fallen into a dream and looked only at the sky. But not one whimpered. Their rags and wild skins were the garments of sacrificed children.

It was the watchers who began to weep, to beat their breasts, to beat their temples. But soldiers and the dying seemed not to hear, to be aware. The soldiers worked very fast, sweating and speechless, not looking at the faces of their victims. There was an extraordinary hurry about most of them, for this was the first crucifixions the majority had ever engaged in before, and they were very young and their hearts were not of stone. They had hated these youths, many of whom were their own ages, but now they did not hate. Not one jeered or taunted. This was an evil task, and it could not be avoided, and they wished it to be over and forgotten.

"Vengeance, vengeance!" whispered Saul fiercely, and thought he would die with his own agony. "Where is the God of Israel, that He permits this?"

Then that hidden voice, so passionate, so strong and musical, rang out against the brazen quiet:

"Be strong and let your heart take courage, all you that wait for the Lord!"

For the first time the crowd of black-robed men responded:

"I have waited for the Lord, blessed be His Name, and He comes on the wings of the morning, my Succor and my Hope, my Lord and my God!"

The voices broke into weeping, but did not falter. The young men on those crosses, so close together, listened and a rapt smile of touching joy passed over many of their faces. Now all could see how emaciated they were, how poor and hungry, for their ribs arched starkly under the tight brown skins, the arms were all dark bone, the legs the legs of children. And the scarlet blood, in that brassy light, began to stream from hands and feet, and sweat, the color of quicksilver, ran down each drawn cheek and lay in the corners of pallid mouths. Here and there, urine and feces released by agony, dripped down the crosses and a stench arose.

The shadow ran over the sky; it ran over the earth. The soldiers retreated a distance, and stood about their red standards and did not speak, nor did they look at each other. There was only the sound of lamentation as the mourners prayed. There was no sun, yet the armor on the soldiers glistened, and so did their swords, and every face appeared illuminated with a ghastly and searching light, and too distinct.

Saul, sunken in his grief and despair, heard a disturbed and wondering sound, and felt a quickened movement about him. He raised his head, to see the young peasant he had encountered in the marketplace moving from the ranks of the mourners, and he wore a rude brown robe and his feet were dusty in his sandals. But he moved with slow majesty to the crowd of the crosses, walking without sound, his uncovered golden hair and beard shining cloudily in the increasing gloom. His face was very quiet and serene, his profile lifted. He was tall and slender and muscular, and he left deep footsteps in the dust, which swirled about his ankles. A radiance, shifting and nebulous, seemed to lie on his shoulders and throat.

Saul watched. The mourners forgot their weeping. The soldiers looked at him alertly, but none made a motion to stop him. He began to walk among the ranks of the fainting and dying and tortured. He stopped before each cross. He lifted his blue eyes to the faces of the youths. He smiled gently. He moved on, slowly, pausing, smiling. He spoke no word.

Yet the eyes of the dying followed him, and the contorted faces became quiet, and mouths opened as if to reply to something only they heard and which had consoled them. It was as if he had given a potion to each, which had taken away pain and fear and despair, and had left peace behind it.

There was not one he neglected, not one he ignored. His air was tender and valorous, sorrowful yet comforting. Every man watched, including the soldiers, and all were as still as the men on the crosses, and only eyes moved.

He was approaching the final rank and now he was close to the Roman soldiers who looked at him from under their young and uneasy brows and made bold faces. He stopped for a moment to consider them, and to Saul's astonishment no anger touched his peaceful brow nor did his lips curl in an imprecation nor did his face pale with stern wrath. In truth, his expression became exceedingly compassionate and even more gentle than before, and Saul suddenly remembered the words of Amos, repeating the words of God:

"Are you not like the Ethiopians to Me, O people of Israel? Did I not bring up Israel from the land of Egypt, and the Philistines from Caphtor and the Syrians from Kir?"

They were the loving words of the Father of all men, tender and merciful, and Saul was struck by them, and he trembled. It seemed that the nameless peasant who gazed at the Roman soldiers was repeating this inwardly, too, and remembering, and directing it at the soldiers.

No, no! cried Saul in himself, fearful that his rage and pity would leave him, and in their leaving he would lose his strength and his hatred which gave him that strength. If one believed that the worst of men were also the children of God then one could not fight evil, could right no wrongs, could deliver no oppressed, could not, in truth, defend the Name of God. He looked at the peasant and told himself that he was presumptuous, and he thought again that the stranger was a sorcerer who was numbing the victims with his mind and deceiving their heroic spirits.

The stranger still gazed at the Romans, and they gazed back at him, and they were more uneasy than before, and oddly discomfited. They shifted their iron-shod sandals; they shrugged their shoulders. Some even put hands on swords, the gesture of frightened men. But they did not speak. And some there were who looked at the stranger and their faces were moved. When he went on as before, they watched him, then exchanged disquieted glances.

He had done. Now he stood before the first rank of crosses and looked at the dying upon them. He lifted his hand to all and he said in a voice that had the soft sound of distant thunder in it, the words of the Shema:

"Hear, O Israel! The Lord our God, the Lord is One!"

Now, for the first time, the dying spoke in unison, and their voices were triumphant and exultant and prayerful, and they cried also:

"Hear, O Israel! The Lord our God, the Lord is One!"

The raptness of their straining faces increased. They saw only the stranger and he smiled at them, a smile of infinite love and kindness, like a father, and they drank in that love and kindness, that sorrowful yet reassuring sweetness, as those dying of thirst drink the living waters of life.

The stranger bowed his head, and he covered the golden crown with his hood, and he prayed, and one by one the weakest among the dying passed into that faintness before death and their heads fell on their chests. The blood poured in dark ripples from their hands and feet; their bodies sagged. But all was silence again.

The stranger turned, and Saul saw his face, white and motionless as a statue's, with eyes that appeared to see no one any longer. He approached the crowd of watchers, and melted among them, and Saul, against his will, wished to be among those near him. But when he came to the thickest of the crowd he heard only bewildered and hushed voices:

"Where is he? He was here, but he has gone. He was among us, and is no longer with us!" And they craned and searched, and pushed comrades aside, and peered and questioned and exclaimed and shook their heads and shrugged and lifted their hands in bafflement. "He was here, but he is not here!"

It was then that a roar of enormous thunder shook the brassy sky and the purple mountains and a great wind rose and a long booming assaulted the earth. Then the sky turned very dark and black clawing clouds rushed across it and a sudden torrent began to fall.

Saul felt someone take his arm and he started wildly, and he saw that the man who had accosted him was Joseph of Arimathaea, his hood pulled over his head.

"Come with me," said Joseph, and he led Saul away and Saul, though he would have resisted could not. They passed through the Damascus Gate and there was Joseph's litter, waiting, and he pushed Saul through the curtains onto the cushions and sat down beside him. The bearers lifted the litter and hurried away through the sudden crimson lightning and the screaming wind that flung the curtains about and the bursting violence of the thunder.

Saul felt weak and undone, shattered in body and mind. What he had seen, what he had endured, flooded over him. He was horrified to the heart, but he began to weep. Joseph watched him compassionately in the mingled flaring and dimming of the lightning.

Saul found his kerchief in his pouch and wiped his eyes and blew his nose. He did not wish to speak to Joseph of Arimathaea, but he said, "Who was that man, with the presumption of a prophet, who attempted to console the condemned?"

"He is not a prophet," said Joseph in a peculiar tone. "And he comforted them."

Saul tried to see Joseph's face, but the darkness increased. "Who is he?"

Joseph did not speak for a moment. Finally, in a very kind voice he replied, "One day you will know, Saul ben Hillel. Ah, yes, you will know!"

Hillel decided that he would ask for his daughter, Sephorah, to come to him despite Clodia Flavius' rigid dictum that women should not appear in the men's quarters nor in the main house, and especially not virgins, unless the occasion was imperious. But Hillel's misery was too acute and he was desperately lonely and full of grief and a sense of abandonment.

But before he could clap for a servant his wife's brother, David ben Shebua, appeared in the atrium. He looked at Hillel and it was a moment before he responded to his greeting. He appeared sober and a little stern, most unusual for the graceful and courteous David. His mouth was set and he seemed coldly displeased. He indicated a carved chair and asked Hillel to seat himself, and then he regarded Hillel under his light brows and his blue eyes were hard. Now the earring did not look absurd to Hillel, who was vaguely disquieted, but even a little sinister.

"Were you desirous of visiting my father?" asked David.

"No. My daughter."

David continued to contemplate him as one contemplates an unpleasant stranger. He said, "You have gravely disturbed my father, Hillel ben Borush."

"He has gravely disturbed me," said Hillel, coloring with humiliation, for was he not a guest in this house, though unwilling? "I assume you are referring to the night I implored his intervention with Pilate, the Roman Procurator, and King Herod, in behalf of his people?"

David raised a slender and impatient hand. "Not only that. You have perturbed him since your arrival."

"For that, I am indeed sorry," said Hillel. "We are in conflict in our characters. We are armed against each other, in our beliefs. I fear your father considers me uncouth and provincial and uncultured. I consider him superficial and effete and an alien to me." He tried to smile in spite of his distress, and David's expression changed in a peculiar way and he regarded the rings on his fingers pensively.

"I believe," said David, "that it is the teaching of the 'old' Jews that one must give respect under all circumstances to one's elders, and particularly those in a patriarchal position." The faintest smile passed over his beautiful lips. "I should ask my father's forgiveness for even suggesting that he is a patriarch. The very idea would revolt him."

Hillel could not help smiling in the very face of his wretchedness. "True," he said. "It may be that I was amiss recently, but you know I spoke truth, David ben Shebua, and so did your brothers. They hated me and that is proof enough. Is it now an evil thing to plead for the condemned? That disturbed your father more than our previous conversations."

David sighed. He fixed his eyes now on a distant wall, and considered. "My father," he said, "is not what you think he is. He is the creation of the style and postures of others. He is a mirror of what he believes is admirable. You shattered that mirror. He is now confined to his bed, under sedatives."

Hillel was astonished. He said, "Is it possible I made an impression on him? That I discomfited him? I thought him an armored man, armored in his disdain for such as I."

"You do not understand," said David. "My father cannot live without the esteem of others. He cannot endure it that a single man might despise or criticize him. He is not a man. He is an image, easily scratched, easily stained; he is colored plaster."

Hillel was even more astonished, but he was also incredulous. He said, "I have heard that of all the traders in Israel, and the merchants, and the bankers, and the stockbrokers, and the investors, he is the most astute! I have heard that in these pursuits he is a man of iron, and cannot be moved."

"That, too, is true," said David. "But those he deals with in those matters are men like himself, of sweat and iron and bronze and hard fists. However, only in the reek of the marketplace. It is a different Shebua ben Abraham who returns to this house and goes to his baths and his concubines and his perfumes and his togas. He no longer remembers those grimy adversaries and allies, those adroit dealers. He is the great gentleman of culture and fineness and sophistication, in this house, and in those houses he visits—which are not the houses of his companions of the day. The Shebua ben Abraham who is raucous and adamant in the marketplace is not the Shebua ben Abraham who visits Pilate and King Herod and dines with the philosophers and the elegant Greeks. This Shebua is a cosmopolitan, another posture, another appearance, another countenance, another aim, another desire, another aspiration. And that dainty man is easily shattered, easily injured, if others look upon him, even for a moment, as if he is still a man of the marketplace."

"Or a man of flesh and blood," said Hillel, with bitterness. "You are implying that I made that delicate man tremble in his plaster and rattled his rings and bracelets? Are you not saying that he is very fragile? Shebua is not one, even in his postures, to care for the opinions of a man like me, who has no pretensions."

"He is fearful of the bad opinion even of a slave," said David. "Ah, I meant no offense. This is the house of my father. In this house he stands in imperial dignity and beauty and refinement. It is all his borrowed creation. You thundered ruthlessly among the silks and the perfumes and did it on a number of occasions, like a wild man from the desert roaring into a lady's bedroom."

"The analogy is, perhaps, very apt," said Hillel. "And so your father is annoyed?"

"He is overcome," said David. He was smiling handsomely now. "I know you have considered me an imitator of him. Let me suggest that he imitates me, instead."

Hillel exclaimed, "I had not thought of that! But it may be true."

"It is most true, and that is why he dislikes me," said David.

Hillel felt a little regret. "One must admire him for his aspirations above the reek of the market place."

"I trust you will remember that," said David, and he was stern again. "There is another matter. My father dearly loved my sweet sister, Deborah, and he cannot forgive you that you made her sorely unhappy."

Hillel's tired brown eyes widened in utter stupefaction. "Deborah! I loved her with all my heart! I thought of little but her happiness! I cherished her, protected, sheltered her! She was as a daughter to me, a precious one. I would have given my life for her!"

David was studying him keenly. "That is not what she wrote to my father. She wrote of your lack of interest in her, her loneliness, of avoidance of her, of neglect, of your devotion to more spiritual things, of your relegation of her to the level of a concubine, or the meek mistress of the kitchen."

"Before God, it is not true," said Hillel, and felt the anguish of betrayal, the sad gall of it, the unbearable acridness. He could not believe that his adorable Deborah, his charming child, for whom his heart was so broken, could have betrayed him in such a fashion, and in such cruel false words, could have craftily written letters unknown to him, accusing him of things of which he was not guilty. Deborah's face subtly changed before his agonized inner eye. It became the face of an ugly malicious stranger, who hated him, who leered at him, slyly.

"Did you think I loved such as you?" she seemed to be saying with contempt.

This was worse than her death to him, the knowing that she had despised his love for her, that she had lain in his arms detesting him, plotting evil letters to her father, deceiving him, that he had embraced a woman he had not known at all and had given her all his heart—which she had mocked. Even one so unendowed with true intelligence—even a dog—knew when love was given. But a dog returned that love. Hillel could have wept with his overpowering grief and degradation, considering the treachery which had been done to him. He mourned for one who had never existed except in his mind and his soul, and he mourned that Deborah had been what she was. Light though she had been, he would have trusted her with his life.

David, watching him, felt compunction. "Women are very trivial and not to be trusted," he said. "And Deborah was more trivial even than the majority of women. Not all have wives like my Clodia, who can make life very stringent, but is a shield and a sword in the house. I would tell my father that Deborah was only a pampered child, and that she complained like a child, but he chose to believe her and take her most seriously."

But Hillel hardly heard him. He had been prostrated by

Deborah's death. He was now more prostrated. He had been lonely. The loneliness he had felt, the bereavement, was nothing to the loneliness, the hollowness, of what he felt now.

"My father chose to believe Deborah because he has never liked you," said David, with kind candor.

"But he arranged our marriage," said Hillel in a muffled voice. "He sought me out."

David laughed a little. "That was because you were of a truly noble house, and a pious Pharisee Jew, and though he does not know it, my poor father, he has a Jewish soul and has lurking fears that the God of Israel is a very jealous God—though he does not believe in God, naturally. Let us be charitable and admit that he did not seek riches for Deborah, and many there were here in Jerusalem, and Romans of great houses, too, who desired her in marriage, and were notable for wealth. Who can penetrate the secret caverns of a man's heart?"

"Not I," said Hillel. "I confess I do not understand even myself."

"I did not tell you about Deborah to sadden you," said David. "It was merely in explanation of my father's antagonism to you, which has many reasons. I wished you to think of him more kindly. He deserves your pity."

"That I know," said Hillel. He rose. "I wish to see my daughter, Sephorah."

"Ah," said David. "She is ministering to my father. He dotes on her now. If you were to deny her in marriage to my son, to take her away, he would bear her away as did the Romans with the Sabine women."

"He will turn my child against me!" cried Hillel.

"No," said David. "She is a wise child, your Sephorah. You are heart of her heart, my poor kinsman."

But I have nothing at all now, thought Hillel, neither wife nor child, for my daughter will marry a stranger and forget me, and my son is obsessed with God and belongs to no one, not himself, and perhaps not even to God, blessed be His Name. In truth, he has never been my son. Though he comes from my loins his soul is far from me. I am abandoned, and there is none who loves me, and at the last that is the most unbearable thought of all—that one may die and never be mourned or remembered by those he loved.

The thought of the everlasting love of God could not console Hillel now. He needed the love of a human creature. It was then that he thought of suicide for the first time. "In the grave there is no remembrance."

The overseer of the hall entered and said one Rabban Gamaliel desired an audience with the lord, Hillel ben Borush. He had opened the bronze doors of the atrium and the sudden storm, dark and scarlet and blazing, seemed to explode into the still whiteness of the hall.

"Rabban Gamaliel!" exclaimed Hillel, his pain overcome for a moment by his joy. He turned to David and his worn face was transformed. "I was named for his grandfather, Hillel, may he rest in peace! The Rabban is Nasi* of the Sanhedrin. What an honor it is to receive him, though I knew him in school in Jerusalem and we were lads together! I did not seek him out, fearing presumption."

"I know the Rabban well," said David, in a dry voice. "But let us invite him into this house lest he drown in that rain and smother in that wind. That would be a sad fate for the illustrious Teacher of the Law."

But his tone, his condescension, could not impair Hillel's joy, and he hastened to the doors of the atrium and stood in the portico. A sturdy curtained litter stood outside held by four dripping youths who winced at every crash of thunder. The sky had steadily darkened. Though it was but midafternoon it seemed on the verge of night, lit only by the inflamed lightning. Impatiently, hands extended, Hillel awaited the guest, who pushed aside the curtains, alighted, then ran like a youth for the portico. Hillel fell upon his neck, embracing him, kissing his cheek, uttering incoherent exclamations of affection and happiness.

"Greetings, and welcome to this house, Rabban," said David, who waited near the fine bronze doors.

"Shalom," said Gamaliel. "Shalom to this house, and all within it." He held out his hand to David, for he could not release himself from Hillel's frantic embrace. It was as if his coming had heralded rescue to the suffering and distraught man, who was almost beside himself, and Gamaliel gently patted his back, for he was extremely perceptive and felt the emotions of others in his own flesh.

*The president, or chief presiding officer.

The great Gamaliel, one of the most noble of Jews, was a very small man, with a slight figure and minute hands and feet, the latter shod in fine soft leather boots laced with gold cords and reaching almost to his knees. His garments were excellent but sober in color, gray and dark red, and fringed with the deep blue fringe of the pious Pharisee Jew. His cloak was black, but spangled with gold dots, and his hood was lined with cloth of gold. Despite his height, hardly that of a young girl, he exuded authority and dignity and power and a certain restraint of the spirit. Hillel finally released him, but he held his hand as a child holds the hand of his father, though they were nearly of the same age, and looked upon his face with a touching raptness.

At first glance it was not a notable face, nor a patrician one, nor comely. It, too, was small, and bony, and dark in color and of a hard texture, like a peasant's. There were those who were unkind enough to refer to it as a simian face, particularly the judges in the Sanhedrin who did not like his wise and merciful judgments, and resented his authority and his antecedents and wealth. Certainly, the area between small and tilted nose and wide thin mouth was overly long, the chin small and receding, the lips slightly protruding, the little skull crowned with rough black hair which no brushing and combing could tame. He had been unable to grow an impressive beard; what hair grew on his chin was sparse and tufted, like the hair on his head. His ears flared out largely; his brow was not lofty, but low and narrow.

It was in his eyes that his greatness glowed, large gray eyes, diamantine in their fire and brilliance, flashing like a knife at one moment, gentle as a woman's the next, leaping with humor at an apt phrase, fixed as marble before folly and malice, radiant at the thought of God, and seeing all things even when he appeared not to see them. His eyes gave him a beauty which was not of his flesh but of his spirit, so that those who knew him well said that never before had a man been endowed with so wonderful an aspect before which the loveliness of a woman was as nothing.

He gave the impression of enormous vitality, of constant and restless movement, of energetic gesture, of quick response, of imperishable endurance. He was potent in all things, and his voice was like a trumpet, emphatic and clear and penetrating, so that those who heard it for the first time were startled and thought it harsh, and later thought it most eloquent.

A servant took his cloak and he stood in his gray and crimson robe clasped at his tiny waist with a rope of silver. He wore a magnificent opal on the index finger of his right hand but no other jewels. The elegant David, beside him, was a Hermes, with his fair hair and Grecian features and curly lips and blue eyes, but the effect was only momentarily. David diminished, and there was only Rabban Gamaliel, vividly beaming at Hillel and still patting his back gently and uttering soft sounds of wordless consolation.

Hillel, always scrupulous, always aware of the amenities to be extended to visitors, could only say in a broken voice, "I am beset. God has sent you to me."

David's delicate nostrils quivered as if surprised and he raised one fair eyebrow, indulgently.

"Ah, but you were here before Rosh Hoshonah and Yom ha-Kippurim, innah nefesh," said Gamaliel, but he said it tenderly. "You did not come to me nor invite me to you, Hillel ben Borush."

Hillel said, as he had said before, "I am beset."

David, the diplomatic, said, "He is loath to lose his daughter to my son. Too, he is a man of humility and modesty." And David smiled with charm.

"I have heard of that wedding. Am I not to be a wedding guest at the marriage of the daughter of the man who was named for my grandfather, may he rest in peace?"

Shebua ben Abraham had invited the grandest of guests to that wedding, but he had not invited the Nasi of the Sanhedrin for fear of a rebuff, for Gamaliel had never deigned to enter this house before nor had he greeted Shebua at meeting places with overwhelming cordiality. He was a man of a great house, and though Shebua often referred to him as to an intimate, they were less than friends. Inferior members of the Sanhedrin, however, had been invited. David's handsome face quickened with pleasure and he thought how delighted his father would be to receive Rabban Gamaliel, whom Pilate deeply honored and consulted, and whom Herod was proud to embrace.

"Knowing your tremendous burdens," said David, "we did not wish to be presumptuous."

"Ah, then I am invited," said Gamaliel, with an air of gratitude, as if David ben Shebua had been excessively gracious. But the gray eyes were amused. Gamaliel was humble enough before his God, prostrating himself in ecstasy and rapture and with a fire in his heart, but he was not humble before man, knowing his fellows, unfortunately, too well. However, his knowledge did not decrease his pity for them, nor his lust that they be given justice.

They repaired to an inner chamber where the tinted windows had been shut against violent storm and the noise was dimmed. Gamaliel moved like a young child, active and lively, and he perched on the edge of an ebony chair with a gold velvet cushion and looked at Hillel with a smiling and expectant expression. He had seen more than Hillel could guess. The continuous lightning dashed its sharp black shadows on the white walls, where they appeared to dance and sway, and David kept wincing at particularly noisy crashes. But it might have been a summer morn for all the notice Gamaliel gave of it. He leaned forward in his chair, his hands clasped before him.

Before that affectionate presence and those kind and searching eyes Hillel began to speak of the years since he had last seen his friend, and Gamaliel did not interrupt and made but slight gestures to emphasize his interest. Only once or twice did he murmur, "Ah," and then was intent again. He did not speak of himself, and when Hillel had done Hillel said, with shame and embarrassment, "I have spoken only of what concerns me and the years that have passed, and my children, and have asked nothing of your family and their health, and yours. Forgive me."

"I am one of those fortunate men," said Gamaliel, "whom God seems to have forgotten, blessed be His Name!" He laughed, and the sound was endearing. "It is enough that I remember Him. I do not wish to be another Job, nor one of the Children in the Fiery Furnace, whom God tests and tempers. It is possible that He considers it would be useless."

"My Greek friends tell me that it is well if the gods are unaware of your existence," said David. "Good luck, then, is not impeded, and evil is averted. I have heard that when they believe that the gods have noticed them they hastily sacrifice to Fear."

Gamaliel chuckled. "The Greeks are very subtle, and their gods are admirable symbols of philosophy and phenomena but are not to be taken literally as the unlettered insist on doing. But the God of the Jews must be taken very literally, for has He not said He is a jealous God?" He looked at Hillel again, who had fallen into another sad revery.

"Tell me of your son, at more length," he said. Hillel did not answer, and Gamaliel calmly waited, and David, the very sensitive, understood that they wished him to leave. He clapped his hands for a servant and ordered refreshments for his guest and Hillel, then charmingly excused himself and departed.

"I find David ben Shebua a man of much sensibility and true aristocracy," said Gamaliel, in his candid fashion. "He is a far superior man to his father."

Hillel cried, with a sudden exacerbation of his despair, "I do not know my son! I never knew him!"

"So all fathers say, as do I," said Gamaliel, and his smile did not lessen though his eyes sparkled with understanding. "It is not a matter of the generations, and the few years between father and son, nor experience, nor wisdom, nor obstinacy, nor youthful stubbornness and blindness, and rebellion. It is a human matter. No man knows another. It is unfortunate that men believe that because a son is of their loins they have a closer intimacy, a dearer comprehension, as if they were one being! Yet a man's friend, older or younger than himself, often has deeper loving insight into his heart and his thoughts than does a son, for kindred is not a matter of blood but a matter of spirit. Blessed is that rare man who discovers in his son a friend! He is celebrated in story. One must not forget that King David's son attempted to kill him, and David mourned, 'Absalom, my son, my son, would that I had died instead of you.' But that was the delusion of a father who thought his son of his heart. It was Jonathan who was truly David's son, brother, father, kinsman, for they were kindred in spirit."

"Then, our children are strangers to us?" said Hillel in the exhausted voice of grief.

"Almost invariably," said Gamaliel. "Wise is that father

who knows that from the beginning. He clothed his son in his flesh, but he is not the father of his soul. Let him cultivate his son's friendship, as he would cultivate the friendship of a stranger, and if friendship is repudiated friendship should not be demanded, for what man can be a friend to another if the sympathy is not there, and cannot be forced? I do not deny a father's love. But a son's love is a vagrant thing, and may be given or not be given without reason, and it is not a jewel in the marketplace which gold, or even devotion, can buy. A man must not seek to compel his son to love him, for it may be impossible for a thousand illogical impulses. He must only demand respect and honor, and in the end they may be of more value."

"Your words increase my sense of loss, dear friend, and my bereavement, for how can a man who loves his son accept them with equanimity?"

"You have forgotten," said Gamaliel with a sardonic smile. "The Commandment is that we honor our father and our mother, but it does not demand that we love them."

In spite of his despair Hillel laughed with his friend. "Your commentary is very pertinent," he said. He felt suddenly relieved, as if Gamaliel had touched his inner wounds with sweet-smelling ointment, and he began to speak of Saul with less emotion though with no less urgency. In the meantime servants had entered with refreshments and were serving them, and the wine brightened Hillel's sunken eyes and the gray in his beard and hair no longer gave him the appearance of years beyond his own. For in the presence of Gamaliel, who listened with all his attention and concern, Hillel felt himself in the presence of a friend who knew all and understood all, and the brittle pain in his heart began to shatter and melt as ice under the sun.

Gamaliel said, "I have met others—but not many—like your son, Saul, young men. The ranks of the Essenes and Zealots are filled with them. They have no doubts. They are full of an absolute certitude, which may offend God, blessed be His Name. For how can a man be certain of the Will of God, or the desires of God? These are found only by humble seeking and never by too much egotistic fervency, by self-surety, by ruthless assumptions, and emphatic convictions. It would be useless for you to tell Saul that those crucified today, in pain and blood and agony, sought death with exaltation, in service to God (though, my friend, I often wonder if God desires such passion and if it would not be better if they would first consult Him). Their devotion, their fire, their sacrificing of self, must be acknowledged as noble, and I trust the angels who conducted them from the crosses were merciful and patient. God does not ask us to die for Him. He asks us to live for Him. If death is inadvertently our fate for our faith, and is imposed on us rather than sought by us, that is a holy thing. But your son Saul would not understand that. Do not lay that to his youth. I have seen graybeards of his opinion."

His tone was calm and soothing, and temperate, but his eyes had a shadow of sadness in them.

All at once the bitterness of his pain surged over Hillel again, and he said, "If I had my youthful years again I would commit the sin of Onan and spill my seed on the ground, and have no children! For what does it avail a man that he give another life and have that other scorn him and think him a fool, and his words mere prattling, and he become his enemy? A man has enemies enough; he need not beget them!"

It was then that he glanced up to see his son, Saul, in the doorway. Hillel turned in his chair. He would have spoken but Saul's appearance appalled him. It was as if the youth were walking in a dream, a fever, and was not conscious of those in the lightning-lit room before him, and that he was wandering. His face was drawn and ghastly, his eyes like blue coals, his cloak wet. He was shivering.

Then Hillel cried out, forgetting his own words and said, "Saul, Saul, my son, what is it?" and rose and went to his son and took his arm.

"I saw them die," said Saul in a loud and grating voice. "I saw their blood. I heard the nails bite into their flesh. And one was there, a rude peasant, who comforted them, and there was none else to give them such comfort but only a craven congregation, of which I was one! Anathema, anathema!"

Hillel began to tremble with his grief for his son and

his own pain. He did not know what to say. Then he saw that Saul was staring at Rabban Gamaliel fixedly.

"Saul, my son," said Hillel and he could barely speak. "We have an illustrious guest, whose fame is great in Israel, and of whom I have told you often in the past. Rabban Gamaliel, my dear old friend, my most honored and reverend friend, Nasi of the Sanhedrin, priest of the Temple, Teacher of the Law, to whom nothing is hidden and who will lie close in the bosom of Abraham."

Saul left his father's arm and took a step toward the Rabban who sat and looked at him in intense silence. Saul made a disordered gesture. "But you were not there, Rabban Gamaliel!"

Hillel was horrified at such desperate insolence, which came as close to blasphemy as was possible before a human being.

But Rabban Gamaliel's eyes shone with a light of their own upon the youth, and he said in the gentlest voice, "I was in the Temple, and I saw their souls as I prayed for them. What is life? Of what moment is it how we die, or when we die, for is it not the fate of man to perish? I tell you, Saul ben Hillel, that those zealous young men will never know the sorrow and loss and loneliness of age, the sad yearning for vanished faces, the lost love, the silence, the emptiness, the abandoned rooms, the voiceless halls, the mirrors which do not reflect the smile of the beloved, the floors which do not echo to the step of the beloved. They will not know betrayal, treachery, despair, disillusionment, vanity, frustration, grief. We all endure pain before we die, and some of us endure more of it, but the pain of living is far worse than the pain of death, and all pain is inevitable."

Saul gazed at him with the blank and unblinking eyes of a statue, and so Hillel thought he had not heard until he said in that same rough and stammering voice, "It was that they died for nothing that is frightful, and that no one cared that they died nor for what they died!"

Rabban Gamaliel's face changed at once and became as stern iron.

"And who informed you of that, Saul ben Hillel? Who whispered things in your ears? Has God confided to you in secret the reason a babe dies in his mother's arms or a child is torn in the jaws of a wild beast or a woman is bereft of her husband or a man of his wife? Has He also imparted to you the knowledge that they died for nothing, that no one cared that they died? Is the soul of man so valueless to God that He is unaware of its passing? He who created it? You have made of God a Being less worthy than the lowest man, a Being as mindless as a beast, and as uncaring!"

Hillel drew in his breath, for these were terrible words from the lips of Rabban Gamaliel and it seemed to the father that the echo of Sinai was in them, and the rebuke, and Hillel could hardly refrain from falling on his face before his friend in abject shame and contrition.

"No man," said Gamaliel, "dies in vain for any just cause, though his name may be forgotten, and he is lowly and despised. God keeps accounts of a man's intentions."

He smiled ruefully. "Even if those intentions are not God's. It is enough for Him that they were done in His Holy Name, and in love for Him, and so I say that those youths are happier than we."

It was then, to Hillel's crushing pity, that Saul burst into tears and covered his face with his hands and shook from head to foot. Saul cried aloud, as he had cried before, in the words of Job, " 'Oh, that I might know where to find Him!' "

He turned and fled, despite Hillel's attempt to restrain him. Gamaliel rose, and came to his friend and embraced him tenderly.

"Weep not, Hillel ben Borush. Saul weeps for himself, and it is a sacred weeping, for I heard his words, and he is the first youth I have known who cried out in them in such anguish. My heart is exalted with a mysterious joy. I have taught thousands of youths. God has spoken to my soul. I will teach your son. Send him to me in two years, in Jerusalem. There is the sign of God on his forehead, given to few to see, but I have seen it, and though his destiny is obscure to me as yet I know it will be for the greater glory of God, blessed be His Name. His name is on the holy scrolls of Israel." The Rabban's voice was like a trumpet, raising echoes.

Hillel was comforted. He dropped his head to his friend's shoulder and was not ashamed of his tears. He had been bereft and someone had filled his hands with gifts.

Chapter 13

SAUL went to his bedroom as to a refuge, a tomb. The sharp lines of the rain at the window reflected themselves on the pale gleaming walls and the air was alive with thunderous sound. It was cold in the cubiculum and drafty and Saul shivered and looked about him vaguely. He went to the window and stared out, and he saw the yellow stone of the courtyard below his window, wet and running with water and vaguely polished, and the turtle doves which were bustling upon it, and he could hear the dolorous dripping and slashing of the rain. Beyond the courtyard was a clump of dark cypresses, bending in the wind, and beyond them a wall of the same yellow stone of the courtyard on which fluttered the last tattered purple flowers of the dead summer. The dull gray sky boiled and rushed as if pursued, or as if caught in a whirlpool.

Desolation overcame Saul. His mind remained empty of thoughts for his emotions were too dolorous and anguished. His shivering became stronger. He sat on the bed and pulled a fur rug about his shoulders and his red head bent until his chin touched his chest. A powerful longing for death shook him. It seemed to him that he did not possess organs within the flesh of his body any longer. He was one stony and churning pain, too deep for tears or sound, and he did not know the full reason for his suffering.

Then he was asleep on the bed and the evening came and the window turned black and the bedroom sank into deep shadow and it was night.

He began to dream. He was once again on the yellow rubble and sand and dust of the fearful spot beyond the Damascus Gate, and he was there to mourn and weep. But only one cross stood there, and it was taller and wider than the others he had seen and it loomed against a murky sky as red as blood and trembling with flame. There were men there, Roman soldiers, and the sound of lamenting, but Saul did not heed them. His whole attention was fixed on the man who hung on the cross, with the dull blood streaming from his hands and feet. The light, though crimson, was not strong enough to see all details, but it came to Saul that the man's brow was bleeding also in many small places, yet Saul could not see what was causing this phenomenon.

Then Saul perceived that the man on this gigantic cross was the unknown poor workman or peasant from the provinces who had looked at him with such intense penetration in the marketplace, and who had walked among the dying victims in this very spot, comforting them, only a few hours before.

An awesome silence lay on this desolate place which was, and yet was not, the familiar place of execution. There was no sound of chanting, no voice lifted in consolation and hope and promise, no comforter. The Roman soldiers were like a graven mass of dark stone huddled together, and they did not move, and it was as if they were amorphous statues dwindled and attenuated against that doomful and bloody sky. But the cross and the crucified appeared to fill all the heavens, to rise from the four corners of the earth, human yet enormous, portentous and majestic, yet appalling. It came to Saul that something of direful portent had been done in this place, and yet something greatly holy and that the earth had moved from her place and had been lifted up.

Saul could not stir an arm or move a leg. He could not turn away his gaze from the man on the cross. It was as if he had been turned to iron. He was only sight and hearing, and not flesh.

The crucified had large limbs as white as moonlight, on which the red shadow of the sky shook and moved in ripples. His golden beard and hair were dappled with blood. He appeared to sweat blood. There was a wound in his side, and that, too, bled slowly and steadily. But his face was calm and most beautiful and reflective, as if he were alone and in some ineffable peace beyond the understanding of men. His ribs arched against his pale skin, and he sagged upon his cross, yet he uttered no word at all.

Saul thought that his heart, encased in the paralyzed metal that had replaced his flesh, would burst with grief and terror, and he did not know why, for this man was a stranger, no more important or valuable or tortured than those who had died before him in this place. Saul asked in himself, Why has he been executed? And there was no answer.

It was then that the man lifted his fallen head and looked fully at Saul, who seemed not to be standing on the earth but some little distance above it, so that his and the man's face were level with each other's, yet at a considerable space. The man's face was illuminated, but the light seemed to come from within and not from that calamitous sky. Its radiance increased, and the blue eyes enlarged so that at last Saul saw nothing but those eyes and the immense depths of them, as if they had looked upon endless ages and would look on endless more, and had known eternity.

Then there was a great sound as if the sky had cracked, and the cross and the man were enfolded, as it were, in a shell, the carapace of a tremendous seed, and the ground opened and the cross and the crucified descended into the black tomb. To the very last, until the earth closed over them, the eyes looked upon Saul in recognition and in love. Then there was nothing but that place, and even the soldiers had vanished and the dim lamentation had ceased.

The bloody light of the sky had faded. A soft gray darkness lay over all things. Suddenly birds were singing, and in the east the sky turned aureate and streamers of scarlet raced toward the zenith, and there was a rustling like a mighty wind on the earth. Saul saw, with incredulity, that boundless sprouts of green grain were rising from the earth, rushing to fulfillment, to fruition as the world became light with a new dawn. From moment to moment the grain sprang exuberantly from the ground, whispering, murmuring, ripening, until a vast and horizonless plain spread before Saul covered with wheat, and it rippled like a glittering gilded sea under the sun and the scent of it was rich and swooning.

Saul, all at once, lost his grief and despair and he looked at the infinitude of grain with exultation and rejoicing, as if from death and sorrow life had been resurrected to feed all men—from the giant seed which had fallen into the earth and had been buried within it.

He heard a tumult of voices and young men appeared, bare of foot and humble of station, with their robes lifted about their sundarkened legs and the hems pushed into their rope girdles. Their heads were covered with coarse cloth, which protected their necks, but their beards blew in the warm and shining wind. They carried scythes in their hands.

They stood below Saul and contemplated the sea of grain, and then Saul saw that they were few in number, and their bodies and their arms and scythes were puny before that vastness awaiting them.

Saul was seized with a passion of impatience. He called out to the men, "Give me a scythe, also, that I may cut the grain with you before it is night and the winter is on the land!"

But the men did not turn their heads nor appear to hear him. They conferred together. They looked at the grain, swollen with life and promise, and they were only little men and this was a task for giants.

Then Saul heard that powerful and familiar voice he had heard before: "The harvest is great, but the laborers are few!"

Saul, in a frenzy and fever of impatience and desire cried out again, "Give me a scythe, also!"

The men had heard him and they turned and looked up at him with troubled expressions and he saw their dark and distressful eyes. Then one came to him and reached up and put a scythe in his hand, and they suddenly smiled upon him and said, "Come!"

But he could not move. He struggled in the iron which was his flesh and could not stir a single finger. He cried out, over and over, his spirit in torment, and the iron burned him as the sun rose higher and heated it and he felt his sweat like a torrent flowing internally, and his blood seemed to bubble and boil in his paralyzed veins.

Suddenly a darkness like death itself fell over him, and he dropped down into a lightless abyss where it was colder than snow and he saw the looming of spectral ice mountains about him as he sank deeper, and the glint of an unearthly moon on the frozen pinnacles that fled upwards from his descent. He heard the winds of eternity beating against his ears and the bitterness of frost against his lips.

"You ask the impossible, Hillel ben Borush," said Shebua to his son-in-law, in a reasonable voice. "We cannot delay the wedding. The doctors have assured us that my grandson will survive and that he will recover consciousness soon, though he has lain in his fevered swoon for three days and three nights. He has no disease. He has an affliction of the brain, mysterious but not contagious. He has excellent nurses who leave him not for an instant, and though he does not open his eyes he drinks wine with water and spiced potions and medicines. He will live! It is an evil thing, say the superstitious," and here Shebua smiled, "to delay a wedding. I am not superstitious, but my many guests—including the illustrious Rabban Gamaliel, who has been here with you and Saul daily—have been invited and it would be beyond forgiveness if I were to send messages to them that the wedding was not to take place."

"Sephorah is his sister, and he loves her," said Hillel.

Shebua smiled again, superbly. "Hillel, he would not have the wedding delayed because of his illness. He would be mortified, embarrassed that he had caused inconvenience and disarray."

Hillel, considering his son's temperament, was forced to agree. He left Shebua and returned to Saul's chamber, where a brazier burned against the autumn chill and the woolen curtains were drawn and where Saul lay under thick fur rugs in his baffling and unwakening swoon. Hillel had slept in a chair near him for three nights, since the night Saul had been discovered fainting on his bed. The doctors had come and gone, day and night, frowning, puzzling over the symptoms, discussing the intense fever, the fulminating sweats, the tremblings, the quiverings and shakings and strange discordant cries, of the stricken patient. The head of the Roman health department had appeared with his best physicians, for all sudden diseases had to be reported, for fear of the plague endemic among the accursed Parthians beyond the frontiers of Israel and Syria. The Parthians were many and turbulent, and an affliction to the Romans who knew that the Parthians had sworn to overthrow them and drive them from the east, and though the thought was absurd—to the Romans —the threat remained, also the diseases of the Parthians. (In truth, the discipline and occasional harshnesses the irritated Romans inflicted upon the Jews were due partly to the huge menace of the Parthians beyond the borders, who could not make up their minds whom they hated more: the Romans or the Jews, and were equally enthusiastic about killing both.)

The Roman official and his physicians had duly examined Saul, had questioned his doctors, had gravely examined the other members of the household, and had come to the correct conclusion that no plague existed or any of the other diseases of the unspeakable Parthians. So the seal of quarantine was not affixed to the doors of Shebua ben Abraham's house, and the official and his physicians graciously accepted Shebua's invitation to dine with him that evening—and, later, his lavish gifts given in mighty relief that nothing threatened his house.

Clodia Flavius assisted the nurses and ministered to Saul also, and told the father, "There is a fever in his soul, and that is worse than a fever of the body, but not fatal. He will recover, Hillel ben Borush, though it is possible that he does not; deep in the depths of his afflicted spirit, wish to do so." She regarded him kindly as she would a child.

She was like tireless strength in that chamber. She permitted Sephorah to enter her brother's chamber, and Sephorah wept over him and put cool wet cloths on his burning cheeks and brow and called to him in her soft and fluting voice. But beyond his sudden wild cries and threshings, his sudden struggles as if he were trying to escape from his flesh, he did not answer nor open his eyes, and his face became smaller and grayer as the hours passed, and sunken.

Aulus Platonius and his son, the captain of the Praetorians, visited the anxious father and consoled and cheered him, and so did Joseph of Arimathaea who stood for a long time in silence beside the bed, gazing down on the unconscious youth and listening to his incoherent groans and exclamations.

On the day before Sephorah married Ezekiel ben David Saul regained consciousness. His fever had subsided. The sweat following it had been washed away and he had been clothed in fresh white linen. He opened his eyes to see the face of his father bent over him. But one of the eyes did not open fully open, though Hillel was not aware of that in his joy that his son had regained his senses.

"It is well, my son," said Hillel, with tenderness, and

he kissed his son's cheek and rejoiced that once again it was cool. "You have been ill, but God, blessed be His Name, has spared you to me. You will soon recover your strength."

Saul whispered, and tears appeared on his eyelids, "I would that I had died."

Rabban Gamaliel was in the chamber also, and he came to the bedside and said gravely, "It is God's will that you live, and you must not dispute Him. You must rest and become strong, for He has wonders for you to accomplish." His face was suddenly exalted, and Hillel gazed at him mutely and with a far fear.

"I fell into the darkness, and it was death," said Saul, still in that faint whisper, and it was as if he had not heard the Rabban. "I was not afraid, though it was only nothingness."

He suddenly fell asleep, but his left eye remained partly open and they could see the white of it and the lower edge of the blue iris as it was upturned.

It was not for some days that the physicians regretfully informed Hillel that the fever had partially paralyzed that eye and while it was not blind it would never be as the other again. And it was still later before they knew that the fever had permanently affected a part of the brain, which would leave Saul a victim of occasional seizures. "The epilepsy is not serious," they told the grieving father. "It is possible that it was latent before his illness and has only been somewhat intensified. Is he a youth of passions and strong urges and vehement emotions?"

"Yes," said Hillel, sadly. "But he has had no seizures."

He lifted his hands and said, "Why has God afflicted my child? Why did He not afflict me in his place? If He had stricken Job's children, then God and Job would not have triumphed over Satan! For what man can witness the suffering of his children and not turn from God?"

Rabban Gamaliel said, "It is written that we must not question God, for His ways are not our ways, and we trust in Him, that in His wisdom He has a reason for all."

But Hillel could not be comforted. He sat for hours beside Saul's bed and looked upon him and his heart was as bleeding fragments. There were times when he knew that Saul was not sleeping and was aware of his presence. But Saul did not speak.

Chapter 14

SPRING was on the land and the almond blossoms were like pink butterflies and the sycamores took on a liquid green and even the dark cypresses had a bloom. Captain Titus Milo Platonius was recalled to Rome, for his leave had expired. He was departing, with his men, for the Joppa Gate, in the radiance of the early morning, and his father, Aulus, accompanied him in a last farewell.

I am a soldier, thought Aulus, but I am also a father, and my years are increasing and it may be long before I am permitted to return to my beloved country, and in the meantime I shall not see my beloved son. I must remember that I am a soldier and am born of soldiers and I would have nothing else for my son, but still I have a human heart and it is sad.

The market places were already in great ferment, and wagons were being unloaded from the country and the merchants and farmers were haggling with blasphemies and oaths and threats and shaken fists and wild and furious eyes. One market place was a replica of another; the awnings were blue or red or green, and the narrow streets were weltering with hurrying men and women and children, all vociferous. But many of the houses still slept quietly behind their yellow walls, while slaves cleaned the gates and washed down the courtyards and tended the new gardens. The early sun was already warm and the breeze fresh from the distant sea.

Milo soberly discussed the condition of modern Rome with his father, and their faces became increasingly somber as they rode steadily to the Joppa Gate. "We have talked of this before, my father," said Milo, "and have come to no conclusion save that Rome as she is now cannot continue unless the good citizens are more and more oppressed and finally enslaved in the service of the inferior. We know that new-born infants can no longer be supported by parents once called the 'new men,' the middle-class, and are being exposed so that they must die. Each day that passes sees more onerous taxes inflicted on the industrious and reverent and productive men, for the enhancement of a lavish court, subsidies to farmers, the looting of politicians, the free housing built for the idle, slothful, stupid and degenerate mobs, the free entertainment provided for those self-same mobs, the erection of grand government buildings to shelter the ever-growing and lustful armies of the bureaucrats and other petty officials, the granaries which dispense free food to the rabble, and the ambitious dreams of the sons of freedmen to remake the streets, the alleys, the roads, the houses and the villas and the countryside of Rome into a grandiose 'city of alabaster!' Then, there are the wars to nourish the manufactories which make war materials and blankets for the mercenaries, and which drain the public purse—now almost empty. Tiberius Caesar began with a noble thought: To restore the Treasury, to pay the public debt, to encourage the thrifty and to punish the idle. But he, too, succumbed under the evil pressures first established by Julius Caesar, who paid the mobs to support him."

"No nation," said Aulus, who was a student of history, "took that path without perishing. So, Rome must perish." His face darkened with pain.

Milo said, "In our lifetime we can live virtuously and with strength, scorning the weak and the depraved, detesting the luxurious, honoring our gods, paying our debts." He smiled. "And our taxes—when the murderous tax-gatherers catch us."

"If all good citizens of Rome refused to pay taxes, what then could a tyrannous government do?" asked Aulus, with an eager glance at his son, compounded of humor and wryness.

Milo laughed, reining back his tall black horse to prevent the treading down of a scurrying child. Then he no longer laughed. "Do you think the lustful mobs, the luxurious, the decadent, the abandoned, the slothful and the contemptible, would not fight for their sustenance from the purses of the proud? I tell you, Caesar would turn the mobs on good Romans and let them loot and burn and destroy as they would, and kill, until Rome was one river of blood and the fruitful men reduced to beggary and slavery. You will recall that Catilina attempted that, but he had Cicero to oppose him and finally to destroy him. But we have no Cicero now, no loud patriotic voice, alas, and few Romans remain to fight for their country, for the honor of their gods, the ashes of their fathers, and for their heroic pride."

"Despair," said Aulus, "is not an evil. It is a virtue, and can inspire men to restore grandeur to their nation and virtue and industry and pride. But the swine have taken even despair from the hearts of men and have left worms behind and Circe seducers who say that all is in vain, that sufficient it is to the day to endure and survive and let tomorrow fend for itself. So men who should man the battlements and guard the gates look upon their wives and children and shrug helplessly, and do not despair. Despair left them long ago, when liars told them it was useless to oppose tyrannical government which professed to love the mobs and had infused those mobs with envy and greed and lusts and had informed them that those who worked for their bread were their 'natural enemies,' and should be looted through taxes. If I dared," said Aulus, "I would erect a temple to the goddess of Despair and clothe her in flaming armor and give her a terrible bright sword, and would implore her to destroy the festering creatures who are eating my country alive and devouring her bowels and drinking her golden blood!"

"As my mother would say, 'Amen,'" said Titus Milo Platonius. "Do not the Jews say, 'He who does not work, neither shall he eat?' Amen. Amen. Once Rome had such admonitions, but it is so no longer. However, as Cicero said, do not a people deserve their government, their fate? It is true."

They had reached a converging of streets. Milo and his father drew in their horses abruptly, and their entourage halted also. A wild and roaring crowd had drawn together, and they were raising sticks and bringing them down furiously on the heads and bodies of half a dozen men in their center, and cursing and reviling them. The men had fallen on their knees, protecting their heads with their arms and wailing for mercy. About them were strewn books and papers and pens, and the mobs stamped upon them and dispersed them and spat upon them.

Milo lifted his mailed hand and a soldier trotted his horse to his side. "Inquire, if possible, as to what is causing this unseemly disturbance," he said.

Aulus frowned. "It is my duty, as a centurion, to keep order."

"True," said Milo, and he was faintly smiling again. "But I think, in this matter, that you would prefer to turn aside your eyes."

The soldier trotted back, saluting. "Lord," he said, "the men are beating the taxgatherers, and it would seem that they not only desire their blood but their lives."

Aulus prepared to dash forward, but Milo put a restraining hand on his father's horse's neck. He lifted his eyes serenely to the broad blue sky.

"It is a pleasant day, and I am enjoying the first part of my journey," he said. "Let us enter this street, which is peaceful." And he turned his horse sharply aside.

Aulus gaped at him, frowning deeper. "We employ the taxgatherers," he said. "They are doing but their duty."

"And with pleasure," said Milo. "They oppress their own people, because they are mean and evil little men, who enjoy the sight of pain and distress. Therefore, let them have a taste of what they bring upon others. In a small way it is our own revenge on the taxgatherers of Rome, herself, and would that Romans had the spirit of these poor and distracted Jews! For once, let the goddess, Justice, be satisfied."

Aulus smiled in his beard, and the entourage turned down the quiet street and left the shouting and tumult and screams behind them, until they could hear the sound no more.

I have been remiss, thought Aulus. My duty was plain. But, is it not a fearful thing when one's duty is tyranny and the rescue of the abominable and the punishment of those who are justified in their despair and anger? When does the maintenance of law and order descend into the offal-pit of oppression?

Behind him, he heard the chuckling of Milo's men and he hoped that they were chuckling with the same thoughts that were passing through his own mind.

Twenty-five Jewish taxgatherers were attacked in the streets of Jerusalem that day by the despairing people, and ten died of their injuries. For a time, thereafter, the taxgatherers, though protected by the Romans, walked carefully and did not rob nor extort nor torture nor seize property nor call upon the guards to arrest. They knew the hatred their own people bore them, and the desire for vengeance in their hearts, and so for a time they did not provoke them, and moved with circumspection. Romans were not always present.

This was partly due to the intervention of Aulus Platonius who issued a proclamation to the effect that any taxgatherer caught in a venal act would be executed. He would collect scrupulously and fairly, and without threats and implications of punishment, and would not extort any longer nor take the bread from the mouths of children nor the roof over a man's head. Otherwise, he would die, and publicly, as an example to other criminals.

A general "arrest and seize" had been issued by Aulus against those desperate men who had maimed and killed the taxgatherers, but for some strange reason none were ever arrested. "After all," said Aulus virtuously, to fellow officers, "it is truly none of our affair. We employ the taxgatherers. That is true. But if they are criminals, themselves, let their own people administer their rude justice. Have we not said that of all nations we have brought into the Pax Romana? Above all, we wish peace."

With less irony but with even more virtue Shebua ben Abraham, the Sadducee, said, "It is a monstrous thing that government agents and officials cannot pursue their office and duties without being threatened by rebellious creatures, who have no respect for law and order." But then, Shebua, through his friendship with Herod and Pontius Pilate, paid little in taxes, and much of his profits was discreetly banked in Rome and Athens in the care of even more discreet bankers, who professed not to know the true names of their clients. The friends of Caesar bore no burdens nor suffered hardships, and preened themselves on their safety and their devotion to law, and no one menaced their households nor seized their property nor inflamed their crafty hearts with wrath, nor diminished their fortunes. Nor did they look upon the conquerers of their nation with anger and hate, for they had no pride, and love of God and country was dead in them, or had never lived.

Hillel ben Borush, weary with winter and afflictions, looked upon the spring gardens of the house of Shebua ben Abraham and stood in the dew, and he said aloud, and softly, in the words of Solomon:

"For, lo, the winter is past, the rain is over and gone! The flowers appear on the earth, the time of the singing of birds is come, and the voice of the turtle is heard in the land. The fig tree puts forth her green figs, and the vines with the tender grape give a sweet fragrance."

He went down the red gravel paths, winding his way around fountains brightly twinkling as if they, too, rejoiced, and he saw the buds of the white lilies rising through the leaves and the red cases of roses within their thorns, and the purple and yellow banners of blossoms opening on the walls, and the fig trees and the palms painted with bright green, and he smelled the pungent scent of the cypresses and the karobs, and the whole earth to him appeared freshly created, bright with the first dews, arched by the first peacock sky, and when he heard the birdsong he wanted to weep with pure joy.

He found his son, Saul, sitting alone on a marble bench beneath a spreading sycamore tree, and he knew at once that Saul saw nothing of the blue wings of the morning nor the black swans on their pond nor the water lilies nor the beautiful marble statues or fountains, nor the soft shadows on the paths nor the roses and the lilies. And Hillel said to himself, as an old father had said before, "My son, my son, would that I had died for you!"

Saul sat huddled in a heavy fur cloak, though it was warm, for his heart was like black frost, and he was no longer young in his soul, and he appeared ill and exhausted and emaciated, for his recovery had been slow. He heard his father approaching and he lifted a dull face without expression. The half-paralyzed blue eye gave him an arcane appearance, and his freckled face was very sallow under the gingery spots. Hillel sat next to him and said, "You can travel, my son. We leave in three days." He paused, and sighed and smiled. "Your sister is with child, and this is an occasion for rejoicing."

Saul did not speak. Hillel cried out in his sudden sharp pain, "Do you not see the earth about you, Saul, and its pristine glory as on the first morning of creation, and the benign sun? Do you not smell the sweetness of life, the frail fragrance of hope? Are you blind? Are you insensible? To be blind is to be pitied. To be insensible is to be blind of the spirit, and that is man's sin and God's affliction through man."

He saw it was useless. Saul saw nothing. Hillel thought he was remembering only the day of those dread crucifixions. In this Hillel was wrong. Saul was pondering with a strange intensity on the feverish dream he had suffered before his collapse, and he could not shake it from his mind, nor its dread and terror, nor his own passion to reap the corn and join the laborers. He could not forget the swelling of his heart, his hopeless struggle, and, at the last, his enormous unease for the unknown man he had seen crucified, then dropped into the earth. Wherever he glanced, even this morning, he saw that man's eyes, compelling, commanding, filled with love and recognition. But what they had compelled, what they had commanded, he did not know, and his whole spirit was wracked with the longing to know.

"I understand," said Hillel, laying his fingers on his son's knee, "that you have endured much, but the sorrow should not be kept before you, nor should you remember your illness. You are young. Your eye may have some deformity, the lid half fallen, but still it is not blind. Saul! The world lies before you, and you can do what you will for Israel, and for God!"

Then Saul, who rarely spoke these days, replied to his father in the words of Job, dolorous and slow and heavy:

" 'Oh, that I might know where I might find Him, that I might come even to His seal! I would order my cause before Him and fill my mouth with arguments. I would know the words which He would answer me, and understand what He would say to me. —Behold, I go forward, and He is not there, and backward, but I cannot perceive Him! On the left hand, where He does work, but I cannot behold Him. He hides Himself on the right hand, that I cannot see Him.' "

Hillel's mouth opened in compassion and kindred suffering, and he did not know that his tears touched his cheek. He pressed his son's cold and unresponsive fingers. He said, "You have not completed what Job said:

" 'But He knows the way that I take. When He has tried me, I shall come forth as gold! —For He performs the thing He has appointed for me.' "

Saul looked at him fully and fiercely for the first time.

He tried to speak, but only a mournful sound came from him. He seized his father's shoulders in his hands and pushed his intensely agitated face close to his, and Hillel was afraid, for Saul's passion seemed to presage a seizure or a return of his illness.

"Do you believe what you have said, my father?" cried the youth.

"I believe. Before God, I believe."

Saul still stared at him while he slowly dropped his hands from his father's shoulders. He still searched his face, for a kind falsehood, for false compassion. Then when he saw that Hillel believed, that he had spoken what he felt was the truth, the youth burst into silent tears and bent his head. And he shook that head over and over, and at last he whispered, "He has hidden Himself from me, for I am not worthy."

Before Hillel could answer, Saul continued: "I do not know who that man is, though I have seen him three times, twice in reality, once in a dream. He haunts my soul. I do not know his name. I cannot flee from him in my thoughts; he pursues me like one on the heels of a deer, and would have me. When I sleep, I hear his voice. He would have me do—but I do not know what it is he would have me do!"

"Who?" asked Hillel, in consternation, and thought of the physician, for Saul was distraught.

Saul said, "I do not know. But I must leave this place, for it was only in my dream that he died, and he walks this earth and I am afraid that I may encounter him again. He is an enigma. There are times when I do not believe he exists, that he is a chimera of the Greeks, a fantasy, a nightmare, a threat."

Hillel put his arms about his son and drew that tormented face to his breast and he thought of angels—or of demons. From both, thought the wretched father, may mere poor mortal man be delivered!

"Hush, hush, my dear one," said Hillel, with tenderness. "We shall go home. We shall not remember enigmas nor fantasies nor chimeras, in the safety of our house, in the peace of our gardens. You shall recover your health and grow into full manhood, and then God will reveal His will to you, blessed be His Name."

Saul said in his broken voice, "I would know God's

infinitude, for nothing else will satisfy me, and I have been denied."

"Listen to me!" said Hillel, "for this is a story I heard in my boyhood, and it was vouched for that it was true.

"Three holy men went into the Temple to pray and contemplate and reflect, and they were pious and good men of much learning and wisdom. They sat in silence in the shadow of the great columns, near the High Altar and gazed upon the veil that hid the Holy of Holies, and they thought of infinity.

"They let their minds roam over God's endless universes of which the Greeks speak, and of the constellations and the galaxies, and one wheeled beyond another, and another beyond that one, and they extended into eternity, and of eternity there was no end.

"The human minds of those men pursued the universe and the constellations and the galaxies into the farthest of space and time, and roamed on and on, and there was no end and no beginning. And their minds reeled with the thought and could not understand nor comprehend nor enfold it, for surely, their human intellects told them, and their knowledge of reality, there is a beginning, there is a border beyond which there is nothing—and at the thought of nothingness, at the thought of endlessness, and even beyond that the abysses of other endlessnesses, and more universes and constellations and more nothingness and no borders, their minds were stricken, and they shrank, and they were filled with the awful cold horror of the thought of infinitude—for what man can grasp it?

"Now one of the men rose up and drove a dagger into his heart, for he could not endure infinity, for it became of unearthly horror to him. And the second man went mad, and ran roaring and raving into the street. And the third man—" Hillel hesitated. "The third man lost all his faith and he returned to his companions and said, 'There is no God.'"

Saul lifted his head and again stared at his father's face. Hillel smiled sadly.

"I have told you, and the Scriptures have told you, that no man can comprehend God nor His creation, for what He sees in immediacy and in eternal noon, and near, can be conjectured by man only in terms of our feeble world reality of time and space, which is a delusion."

He said, taking Saul's hand again, "He who seeks God will surely find Him—and let him beware when that happens, for it is a gift which can either kill or save or drive mad! Surely it is best only to love Him and let Him reveal Himself gently, as He wills, and not to demand all. For Moses alone saw the Face of God, and of that Vision, it is said, he expired."

"But we have been told of the Messias, and that we shall see Him with our mortal eyes, and we shall not die of it," said Saul.

"You have forgotten," said Hillel, and he was much cheered, for a glow had appeared on Saul's haggard cheek, and even the sunken eye had a light in it. "The Messias will be clothed in our flesh. 'Unto us a child is born, unto us a Son is given.' "

Part Two

MAN AND GOD

—For I am God and not man, the Holy One in your midst, and I will not come to destroy.

Chapter 15

HILLEL BEN BORUSH said to Reb Isaac, in Tarsus: "My son is of an age to marry, and even beyond it, for he is twenty years old. He has completed his studies with you. He has learned the art of a tentmaker, and he will earn what he will, as befits a teacher, who cannot accept payment. He has distinguished himself in the University of Tarsus, in Roman law and other studies. He has learned sedulously from his Greek teacher, Aristo."

Reb Isaac nodded his white head reflectively. "He is, then, a man of the world."

"A man of the Book," said Hillel.

"A man must be many men these days," said Reb Isaac. "It is not enough, any longer, that he be learned in the Scriptures and the holy disciplines of our people. He must be a Roman, a Greek, an Egyptian, and others. He must move freely about the world, discovering new textures of humanity, new smells, new ideas, new thoughts, and, probably, new depravities. That is the modern world. Bah," said Reb Isaac. "Better it is that a man in these evil days becomes an Essene or a Zealot and removes himself from the world and walks with bare feet in the wilderness and eats wild locusts and honey and the uncultivated grains of the field, and strange fruit, and lives in caves or in the mountains and does not shave his beard, and wears outlandish garments and, when he ventures into the stinking cities, shouts in the streets in contempt and condemnation and utters execrable oaths."

"And is beaten or arrested by Roman soldiers, or the guard," said Hillel. "Come. You would not have Saul an Essene or a Zealot, Reb Isaac?"

The old man replied gloomily, "Who knows what a young man should be these evil days? Should he withdraw totally from the world and despise it—and it is worthy to be despised—or should he become part of it, mouthing meaningless words, giving meaningless smiles, because it is not only expected of him but demanded of him? Shall he do what his parents, his teachers, his kinsmen, his neighbor, think desirable for him, or shall he say, 'I am a man in my own right and I will do what I will, and please none but myself'?"

"You are not serious," said Hillel, smiling. "Are you discussing chaos?"

Reb Isaac shook a gnarled finger at him. "Let that nation beware that becomes fat and complacent and the men of her cannot be distinguished by their faces or their words from their neighbors! Are we ants, beetles, flies, worms, which cannot be told apart? No. We are men. I, for one, do not denounce chaos, which is man's last desperate rebellion against conformity in habit and in living, a last desperate striving to be himself, unique, individual— though he make a monstrous fool of himself in the process. I prefer such a fool to a man who, like a coin of the same minting, cannot be told from another coin."

"I thought," said Hillel, "that we were discussing a possible marriage for my son, who is not stamped, like a coin, with the self-same image on other coins, and who is individual, so individual at times that I fear for him." He was surprised at the old man's strange diatribe.

"I am speaking of others, and in particular some of my present students," said Reb Isaac. "Do they want holiness? Do they want the mystery of the Scriptures? Do they wish to divine the occult words, the profound meanings, the labyrinthine thoughts? No. No. They wish to be men of this world, and woe to Israel—again—when she goes whoring after strange gods, such as the Sadducees do."

"You know my son has always wished to be what you would have him be, not to please you, Reb Isaac, but to be a learned Jew, and to please God."

"True," said Reb Isaac, in a surly tone. "But I am not so certain he is pleasing God, blessed be His Name. He is sedulous and fervent enough in his prayers, but I have the thought frequently that he is like Jacob wrestling with the angels, but this time the angels are not only triumphant and will not reveal secrets to him, as they did to Jacob, but they depart. What would you know of this, Hillel?"

"Nothing," said Hillel, with sadness. "I have discussed it with you many times. I have a stranger for a son."

"So do we all," said the old man, shrugging.

It seemed to Hillel that Reb Isaac had changed enormously in the past years and that he was doubtful of his former surety and certitude, and so was irascible.

As if he had divined Hillel's thoughts Reb Isaac said, "I am an old man now, and I admit that the years, instead of enlightening me, have confused me. A man comes to me now in grief but not in repentance, and says to me, 'I have lain with a good woman, whom I love and cherish, for the wife chosen for me against my will is a woman evil in her nature if not in her deeds and of a foul tongue and is a curse to my household and a terror to my children, who flee from her. I would divorce her save that I cannot return her dowry—which she has spent in her extravagance—and I would not have a divided household and leave my children to her vile humors. So I have violated the Commandment that I must not commit adultery and I find no sorrow in my heart, for she I love is like warm milk and pomegranates and the sweet dates of life, and enfolds me and comforts me. Condemn me if you will.'

"What shall I say to such as this man? Thirty years ago I should have thundered at him and mentioned the wrath of God and sent him from my threshold with anathema. I should have felt righteous, and justified. But, should a man be condemned all his mortal life to loneliness and despair? It is said that a man must accept the life ordained for him, with meekness and try to discover some meaning in it for him alone." Reb Isaac shook his head. "I tell you, I no longer know. It is said that we must not murder. But if a thief enters our household and threatens our lives and the lives of our family and our servants, is not the householder justified in killing him, if possible? God has not condemned the wars we have waged, yet often He has spoken that to Him the Egyptian, the Ethiopian, the Syrian, the Philistine, and others, are also beloved of Him, and that He has intervened in their distress. Who are we to interpret the Almighty? Shall we say, 'He has spoken thus, and therefore He means thus?' We know only that He is full of lovingkindness, and that the sinner, to Him, is often more to be cherished than the man who spends much of his time in the Temple, offering sacrifices."

Hillel said, "God sent bears to devour the children who mocked Jeremias." And he smiled again.

"So it is written," grumbled Reb Isaac. "We shall never know the meaning of God until He sends us His Messias, blessed be His Name, and He shall make all things clear. It is said," added the old man, sourly.

"We were speaking of Saul, and his marriage," said Hillel.

They were sitting in the hot gardens of Reb Isaac's house, in the shade of a striped awning, and were drinking cool spiced wine and eating honeycomb and fresh wheaten bread and refreshing fruits and a cold broiled fish. The date palms were heavy with fruit. Grapes, ripening, climbed the burning walls which enclosed the garden and scented the air deliriously.

"Ah, yes. Saul," said Reb Isaac. "He will go to Jerusalem soon, to study under Rabban Gamaliel. A mighty Teacher, Nasi of the Temple. I know him. Saul will also pursue the trade of the tentmaker." The old man chuckled. "When his hands are sore he will become more humble. No matter. Have you a maiden in mind?"

"Yes," said Hillel. Reb Isaac waited. He eyed Hillel shrewdly. The younger man had aged beyond his years; his once golden beard and hair were almost white, and his figure was bowed and there was sorrow in his brown eyes and secret grief. Was it possible he was still mourning for his Deborah, who had had the mind of a child, and was that the reason he had not taken another wife? Hillel said, "I would that he were safe as soon as it is possible."

"Safe? And why?"

But Hillel did not answer. He only looked down at the hands clasped on his knee. Reb Isaac frowned. He had great intuition. It appeared to him that he was moving in the lonely darkness of Hillel's mind, in which there was no light and no flowering, and only muteness of soul.

"No man is ever safe," said Reb Isaac. "This is a most terrible and dangerous world, and always was it so and always will it be. It is the delusion of parents that they can protect their children and assure their happiness, so they vainly lay up treasures and properties, thinking—though they know it is not true—that a rich man's wealth is his strong city, and his happiness also. I tell you, no man born of woman is happy, and if he say so, then he is a liar or a fool. Nor is there ever safety, for the world constantly changes and new governments arise, and new taxes, and often a man's wealth is like water."

Then Hillel spoke in a very low voice. "I would that my son be safe. In love. In the care and comfort of a good woman, who will cherish and soothe him and wipe away his tears, who will bear him children who will bring him a little joy in this dolorous world, and console his age and give him the gift of peace."

Reb Isaac was about to say, with sarcasm, "Such as the one you possessed?" But the very cruelty of the words appalled him. He had not thought that he had the capacity for such derisive heartlessness. He prayed internally for forgiveness, marveling, as always, at the intricate chambers of a man's mind, and the fearful inhabitants thereof, of which the man, himself, often has no knowledge until such an occasion as this occurred. *Now I understand why a man can kill, and without regret, or commit any other crime,* he thought, *for the demons are forever lurking and waiting in the dark chambers, and the man inadvertently opens the door for them. Of such fearful stuff are we made! The larvae in our souls are deadly, and they eat away our virtues, until we are poisoned and hollow.*

The old man repeated what he had said before: "Have you a maiden in mind?"

Hillel looked at him straightly, and said, "Yes. Your granddaughter, Elisheba."

Reb Isaac gaped, amazed. He stared at Hillel and his old eyes became very wide and startled. "Elisheba? She is but a child!"

"Fourteen, is she not? Of an age to marry, according to the Law, and even above the age."

Reb Isaac swallowed visibly, and Hillel thought of an old shepherd with a favorite ewe-lamb, for Elisheba was to her grandfather that lamb, and very comely and beautiful, slight and delicately formed, with hair like smooth black silk flowing down her slender back, large dark eyes with thick lashes, a pale but luminous small face, a soft little nose and wondrously pink mouth like an almond blossom. She was young, but she was nubile, and her voice was the voice of a tender woman when she was cajoling her grandfather, and she possessed a deep long dimple in each cheek.

It was obvious that Reb Isaac was profoundly aghast at the thought that his Elisheba was of an age to marry and that she ought now to be espoused.

"It is ridiculous!" he exclaimed, making a gesture with his hands as if rejecting something preposterous. He forgot Hillel, and brooded. He loved all his grandchildren and thanked God that he was not their father, but Elisheba was like the child of his own loins and a perpetual babe who would never grow old, but would remain at his side forever a child until he died. He could not conceive of a day without Elisheba. He had quickly married off his daughters, and his two older granddaughters and had expressed his pious gratitude that they were no longer in his house but securely in the houses of their husbands. He had not thought this of Elisheba, who was uniquely and only his own. Now his anger was rising. He winced at the vision of his Elisheba in the profane arms of a sweaty man, and he not there to rescue and defend her, she who would be weeping for her grandfather.

"You are mad," he told Hillel.

"Why?"

Reb Isaac fumed. His stare at Hillel was inimical. His wrath became stronger.

"It is true," said Hillel, "that Saul will have no great fortune, for I returned to Sephorah her mother's dowry—and one can be certain that Shebua ben Abraham counted every shekel of it! But I had had it wisely invested and lost not a copper of it, and I have kept the interest, and that, too, is growing. Saul will not want, nor will his wife."

"Ha!" said the old man, and his withered face became crimson. "You know I am not without resources, nor is Elisheba's father, and that she will have a handsome dowry! That is what lures you, Hillel ben Borush."

Hillel sighed. "You know that money has never been of importance to me, Rabbi. I am not rich, nor am I poor, according to my bankers and my brokers. What I have will be Saul's. I have even returned Deborah's jewels and Sephorah has them." A pallid darkness began to flow over his face, and Reb Isaac forgot his outrage for a moment to wonder at the shadow, and to feel compassion for the thought that had caused it. Hillel continued: "My family is not without note and has an honored name in Israel, and Deborah's mother had an illustrious family.

Let us consider my son. You have said it yourself, that he is of enormous intellect and power of mind, and once you remarked that the Finger of God had touched him—"

"Ahah!" cried the old man, joyous that he had discovered an excuse to reject Saul. "I wish no grim prophets in my family, especially not for Elisheba, who is a blossom! The Finger of God! It is wise not only for men to avoid the company of a man who has been so touched— but it is even wiser for women! It is not well to be in such a man's proximity. There are dangerous lightnings."

Hillel could not help smiling broadly. "Does so pious a Jew as Reb Isaac speak this? Have you not bewailed the fact that we have no Jeremiases nor Aarons nor Hoseas to marry our daughters in these debased days? Not even Joels. But my son—"

"I know all about your son!" shouted Reb Isaac. "He is possessed! He is entranced! I sometimes gaze at him with fear, for all my affection for him. He shall not have my Elisheba!"

"Then, being so fair and her grandfather so adamant against men of God, she will doubtless marry a Roman or a Greek, or worse still, a Sadducee. Alas."

Reb Isaac could have struck him. He sat in his chair, his rheumatic knees asprawl, and he trembled with rage. His white beard shook as if in a gale and his black eyes glinted and sparkled. He tried to speak and could not and so he impotently beat his thighs with his clenched fists.

"Or possibly a gross rich merchant of Tarsus, or even an Egyptian," said Hillel.

The eye fixed on him brightened with ferocity.

"There are few learned and pious Jews remaining in the world, alas," Hillel continued. "Regard the youths whom you teach, and their worldliness, and their ennui with your exhortations. Have you not frequently said that you would wish no damsel to suffer marriage with them? I tell you, Reb Isaac, Jerusalem now seethes with such, if not worse. I could speak of abominations—"

Reb Isaac lifted his hand and shook it furiously. "Halt! You have said enough!"

As he sat in his chair he gathered his robes about him and gnawed his lip and the corner of his beard and stared at the ground. Occasionally he glanced up at Hillel with a look that avowed his hatred, but Hillel was not disturbed nor startled.

Then the old man said, "Your son is not of a handsome countenance. What florid appearance he once had has diminished. Moreover, his right eye droops. His constitution, it would appear, is not of the best. His disposition, once inclined to be merry and expansive and generous, has become leonine and cold and distant, though I see passions not of this earth sometimes flash across his face. Is such a one fit for my gay Elisheba, who is like a lamb in the springtime, or a nightingale? He would break her heart."

"It is true," said Hillel, with new sadness, "that Saul would appear to have changed, but in truth he is the same as always. I experienced premonitions when he was but a babe. But I tell you, Reb Isaac, that something has whispered in my heart at night that he is destined for many things! Ah, you smile darkly, but it is true, and have you not hinted so, yourself? As for his appearance, he is not handsome, but he is not revolting, and there is a strange charm about him, brought to my attention by his tutor, Aristo. He has a most eloquent voice. He will be heard in the Temple. He will move men's hearts. He is devoted to the service of God. He is virtuous. These are a few of his attributes. At the last, Shebua ben Abraham offered me his favorite granddaughter as a wife for Saul, and Shebua is no fool." He paused. "The damsel could make a meaner marriage."

"Tell me this!" shouted the old man. "If you were Elisheba's father and I the father of Saul, would you agree to such a marriage?"

Hillel was taken aback. He thought. He tugged at his beard. Then he said, for he was an honest man, "I do not know. But my daughter, Sephorah has married one less distinguished, and with fewer of the attributes we value, and she was the flower of my heart." He paused again. "I do not know if Saul would bring happiness to Elisheba, but we do not count happiness in this world the highest good. But of a surety he would never betray her nor treat her lightly nor darken her heart with accusations of pettinesses nor tempers nor humors. Saul is not trivial, not petulant. She will have pride in him. As for Saul, I should like to know that Elisheba is his wife, for her sweetness would lighten his life and her kindness would enfold him. I have been candid. I can do no more."

"Elisheba has seen him," said Reb Isaac in a sour voice.

Hillel was startled. "Was that seemly?"

Reb Isaac grinned at him savagely, and shrugged. "He fell over her several times when she was a very young child and romping at my feet. I did not confine Elisheba. She has seen your son very often, but at a distance these past two years. She declares he resembles a young Moses."

Hillel stared. Then he began to laugh, and there were tears in his eyes, and he held out his hand to Reb Isaac who at first ignored it, then accepted it.

Aristo considered, looking up into Hillel's face, for he was squatting and teaching a young servant how to weave a tender basket for ripe olives. Then he said, "Master, I am afraid you have false hopes. Saul will never marry."

They were in Hillel's garden and the pond was as green as grass and the curious bridge was black against the blue autumn sky.

"That is nonsense," said Hillel. "I thought that you might prepare him. For my suggestion," he added lamely.

Aristo stood up and shook shreds of reeds from his garments.

"There is nothing—wrong—with my son," said Hillel, remembering that Aristo was a Greek and the Greeks had lewd minds.

"No," said Aristo. "But there is One, apparently, who has the power to suppress a man's potency." He smiled his sardonic smile. "I am happy that our gods are not so powerful, so castrating."

"I do not understand you."

"Master, let us go apace." They walked together to a distance, and when Aristo spoke again his antic face was grave and the restless black eyes were quiet. "I know Saul," he said. "What he has not told me of his thoughts I have divined. There have been some, even among us Greeks, who were like him, retiring to forests and to caves to contemplate divinity, but not of the human kind, such as women. We called them madmen. But Zeus frequently set them in the constellations for men to marvel, at night."

Hillel could not speak. Aristo continued: "Some years ago I guessed that Saul had encountered a young female who taught him the arts of love against all his convictions. No, he did not tell me. It was sufficient for me when he informed me that he had committed what he called a 'vile sin,' against all the Commandments. Now," said Aristo, and he could not help smiling, "Saul is no thief, no coveter, no breaker of the Shabbas, nor does he envy, nor does he blaspheme his God, nor does he worship graven images, nor does he dishonor his parents, and he loves his God with all his mind and all his heart and all his soul. You will see I am now well-versed in your religion, for Saul would have converted me, in his zeal. So, what is left that he could consider a sin, in your Commandments?"

"Adultery," said Hillel. He found himself smiling. "I doubt the—lady—was married. Or, was she?"

"I doubt that also. So, let us say a young female from one of the farms near these suburbs."

"But, that would only be fornication," said Hillel. "Consider us gloomy, if you will, but we do not consider fornication an unpardonable sin, and we know human nature. Unless," he went on, "the girl was a harlot from the town. We are forbidden to patronize harlots, for many reasons."

"Saul rarely went to Tarsus," said Aristo. "But I do know that on many dawns on the way to Reb Isaac he encountered a damsel. I have lived long, even longer than you, Master, and I know the aspects of young love, and those aspects were on Saul in those days. He was ecstatic, glorified, handsome as Phoebus, exalted, and there was a certain trembling in his voice. Suddenly, it was gone, and he became what he is now."

Hillel also recalled Saul's frequent and passionate assertions that he was "not worthy" to worship God. He had thought them the exaggerated transports of a deeply religious youth. Now he said, "Saul has not spoken like this for several years. He has not mentioned any 'sin.' He speaks only of entire Service to God." In spite of his distress his smile became broader. "We have a saying that when King David became old he wrote the Psalms, and King Solomon wrote the proverbs in his great age. Before that, they were lusty men."

"In short," said Aristo, "when a man's testes wither his wisdom flowers. It is an old story. Unfortunately for the wise old, youth now understands the reason, and that is

unfortunate for youth, also, for it would be an improve-
ment if youth would accept the wisdom without suspecting
impotence."

"But Saul is young, and he has juices," said Hillel.

"He suppresses them. He believes that pleases his God,
or he is making some amends to his God, or adores his
God and there is no room in the temple of his heart
for any other inhabitant."

"My son is no Zealot, no Essene!"

Aristo gave an eloquent shrug. "Master, I have told
you what I have surmised. Saul has not confided in me.
But I am not his father. I can look upon him with an
objective eye. I can only say that he will reject any
marriage."

"I would have him marry a good woman, and I know
such a woman, and she is beautiful and virtuous and sweet
as honey," said Hillel. "I would have him safe."

Aristo stared at him with the same incredulity that
Reb Isaac had shown. "Master, there is no safety in this
world, no security, and men who seek such are less than
men. They are women in their souls. Or eunuchs. Man is
a very dangerous animal, and always will he be. I know
this about Saul: He is of a nature to court danger, and to
despise safety, for he is a man and not a girl in a man's
body. Let him be, I implore you. We are all called to
different destinies. Let Saul seek and find his."

Hillel was silent. Aristo regarded him with sharp pity.
Some perpetual sorrow now lay upon his master, some
grief that haunted his days. Hillel turned away without
speaking again. But that night he accosted Saul.

"I would have you beget a son to say Kaddish for you,
my son," he said. "It is a terrible grief to a Jew if he has
no son to do that for him."

Saul had listened without speaking to his father, but
his somber face had expressed nothing, not even outrage.
Then, as he heard Hillel's final words that somberness
softened.

"It is said, my father, that some men are called to the
field and the forest and some to the hearth and marriage,
and some to labor in the vineyards, and some to tend the
flocks. Each man to his season and his life. And some
there are who are called to the service of God only."

Hillel, in his grief and despair, flew into anger. "How

do you know that?" he cried. "Has God told you that in the darkness of the night? Has He whispered that in your ear? Are you not presumptuous, even perhaps blasphemous?"

Saul half-turned away and in a low voice he answered, "I only know that it is so. Where He will lead me I do not know, but where He leads me, there shall I go. I can only speak with the surety of my inner knowledge. I have asked myself a thousand questions, doubting, and the answer is always the same, stronger and more insistent. How did the prophets know, before they heard the voice of God? How did Moses know, until he saw the burning bush? I await the call. I can only wait, certain that I will hear it."

"I have lost my son, my only son," said Hillel, and struggled with his tears. "What crime have I done to merit this? Have I been an unnatural father, stern and cruel and unjust? Have I turned from my children with harsh words and rejecting gestures? I have tried to walk humbly with my God—and I have lost my son."

"Father," said Saul, and there were tears in his own eyes. But Hillel silenced him with a frantic gesture.

"Reb Isaac is an old man, and wise, and a Teacher, and your teacher, and he has agreed to this marriage with one as fair as Bathsheba, herself, and of the tenderest soul! Is he not wiser than you, older than you, with knowledge far beyond yours? Yet, you despise his wisdom, you repudiate his dearest treasure! Must I tell him, 'My son claims superior knowledge to yours, Reb Isaac, and a deeper wisdom, therefore he declines Elisheba'?"

"Father," said Saul, and for the first time Hillel heard a moving sorrow in his son's voice, and a grief for him, himself, "I will tell Reb Isaac myself."

"Do so! And then let him despise me as a feeble father whose son will not obey him and looks lightly upon him as a fool! Let him hold me in contempt that I have such a son, who looks for visions and not for life! Let him suspect the most unspeakable! It is all I deserve. Let him spurn me with his foot as an ingrate and a low creature, for I persuaded him to agree to this marriage, and now he will know my full degradation as a man and a father!"

He hurried away to the house, and Saul, at first taking a step after him and then halting, looked about the bright autumn of the gardens and shivered. He put his hand to his forehead. It felt numb and chill. He was shaken to the heart and full of sorrow for his father. He wanted to weep, and could not. He had no words to tell his father of the love he bore him, and his helplessness before the fact that he must hurt him. He only knew that in some moment he could not remember, long ago, he had heard a call and knew that he dared not refuse it and that if he refused it his life would mean nothing, but in answering it he would have the only joy he would ever know. Oh, sublime and terrible joy, Oh, fire that consumed and thereby increased, Oh, bliss that tortured and replenished and healed, Oh, death to life that was the only life, Oh, love of man's desiring and man's hope and man's peace and ecstasy! The grandeur and glory of the landscape he sometimes glimpsed seemed to him too ineffable and rapturous to be borne for more than an instant of time.

The young man raised his eyes to the sky and it seemed to him that he saw a great and powerful flash, more brilliant than the sun, more terrifying than lightning. If it consume me, he thought with a rush at his heart like wings, and reduce me to ashes—so even my ashes shall praise Him and adore Him!

He picked up his cloak and made his way to the house of Reb Isaac.

Father and son did not speak for two days and then Reb Isaac visited Hillel ben Borush and they retired to Hillel's chamber. The old rabbi put his hands on his friend's shoulders and looked deeply into his eyes, and his own were no longer irascible and glinting but soft and compassionate as a woman's.

"Saul has come to me," he said. "Do not grieve, my dear friend. Saul has spoken to me. I listened not to his words but that which was behind them."

Hillel groaned, and turned away. "I only know that God, Himself, has said that it is not good for man to live alone, without a helpmate. For Adam He created Eve. Moses had a wife. The prophets had wives. How dare, then, my son say that he will not marry, that he will only devote his life to God? Has he not violated the very Words of God in his decision? A man who serves God is also human, and God has not only provided for his needs but has commanded them as a duty."

"There are some," Reb Isaac reminded him, "who can only serve God, and cannot be distracted even by a loving wife and children. There are not many, but they are known to us, and we revere not denounce them. Are they weaker than us? Or are they stronger? That we do not know. We rabbis marry; we do not serve God the less because we have wives and children. Often, our wives hearten us, for it is a lonely road that a man travels without a woman, and a bleak and bitter and silent one. A good woman often brings us closer to God.

"But there are some whose souls are so filled with God that there is no place for a human love. They are rare. But they are also known. We dare not reproach them."

"And you believe Saul is such?" said the distracted and disbelieving father, who now looked at Reb Isaac as at an enemy.

"I believe so. Yes, I believe so. Send him to Rabban Gamaliel, the wisest of the wise. The time has come. Rejoice, Hillel ben Borush, for it is possible that you have been greatly blessed in having this son."

But Hillel could not be comforted. However, he resumed conversation with his son and he was so kind that he did not wish Saul to detect, any longer, his profound disappointment and despair. If Saul saw them, and he did, he knew he was helpless.

On the day of his departure for Israel he wrote to Reb Isaac:

"I must go. But I fear for when I go. I have heard my father's wandering in the night, and I do not believe that it is only I who has caused him such misery. There is a grief of which he never speaks, but which has been with him a long time. Comfort him, dear teacher, for I have no comfort to give him. I go, but I know not where. I only know I must go."

Chapter 16

"SHALOM. Greetings to my father, Hillel ben Borush, from his son, Saul ben Hillel:

"I trust that your silence, dear father, has not been due

to illness but from mere care and the preparation for the High Holy Days. I have not heard from you since early in the spring, though Aristo writes me that he visits you often from his olive and pomegranate and date groves and that he finds you well, thanks be to God, blessed be His Name. However, his last letter troubled me, for he hinted that you appeared melancholy and that he heard from the gossiping servants that you spend more and more time at my mother's tomb, though she has been dead some ten years! (I still remember her in my prayers.)

"I have heeded your admonitions, given frequently, to betray less impatience in my manner and speech, and to quell it in my thoughts. But my temper is a thorn in my flesh, and I fear, alas, that it will always be so. We have not seen each other for two years, when you last visited Jerusalem, and, as I have written you, matters do not improve here but rather deteriorate. I have visited the provinces recently, notably Galilee, and the lot of the peasants and farmers and artisans becomes daily more onerous. It is bad enough in the cities, where at least one-third of a man's labor is devoured by the taxgatherers— those evil and detestable and accursed men!—but it is far worse in the provinces. I am told that if a man earns the worth of two loaves of bread a day he is permitted to keep but the worth of half a loaf! The people of the provinces, therefore, live in the most appalling poverty, squalid and desperate, yet the taxgatherers, with their Roman guards, constantly seize their small belongings, even their copper Menorahs and their little store of holy oil, or even take their children from them to be sold into slavery, if the amount of taxes does not meet with the approval of the taxgatherer and does not match his books. It is quite customary for a hungry and hopeless man to be thrown into the filthiest of prisons for 'failing to meet his legal and proper taxes,' as defined by the taxgatherer, and who can gainsay the word of these vilenesses that walk in the shape of a man? Truly, it has been said that God holds the taxgatherer as more debased and less worthy of forgiveness than a murderer or a harlot, a thief or a pederast, a liar and an adulterer, for does he not combine in his one person the traits and despicable qualities of all of these? It is incredible to me that any Jew, however he has sunken below the standard of humanity, can agree to be a publican.

"Our cousin's husband, Aulus Platonius, informs me that the great Marcus Tullius Cicero frequently warned the Roman Republic that when one-third of a nation's income is devoured in taxes that nation is at the edge of the abyss. Today, Aulus tells me, over half a man's sustenance in Rome, herself, is taken by taxes, and the Empire groans in bankruptcy, venality, crime, despair, the luxury of politicians and their schemes and wars, the hopelessness of the dying Roman middle-class, the power of wicked men fattened by the people's labor, and the licentiousness of the Augustales and Tiberius' court. If Rome suffers, despite the purloined wealth of her conquered nations, think of the sufferings of Israel, where the people are taxed by the Romans for more than two-thirds of their labor! Jews do not even have the government alms of free housing, bread, beans, meat, clothing and circuses, as do the Roman mobs. But, would we not spurn them in our pride, as unworthy of men? Truly. We are not to be bought through our stomachs nor through our senses, nor by depravities and gifts.

"There is something fervid transpiring in the deserts and the barrens and the desolate places beyond the cities, and Joseph of Arimathaea has promised to conduct me to one of the lairs of the Essenes in the lost caves beyond Jerusalem. In my heart I have often begged for forgiveness for my earlier scornful judgment of him as a wordsayer and a compliant man, fearful of the Roman and one willing to compromise with evil. I see, in this large and gentle man something mysterious, such as you discovered, for he does not speak all he knows and his kindness to me is baffling, for I have done nothing to deserve it. But what it is that is transpiring in the hot and lonely spots, haunted only by goats and their herdsmen, is known only to Joseph and he will take me there within a few days. I remember the condemnations freely heaped upon the Zealots and the Essenes by the men of the cities, the accusations that they will bring destruction upon Israel by inciting the Romans against us, but when I consider the state of Israel today I believe nothing can be more evil, more crushing.

"If the Messias, blessed be His Name, tarry much longer

there will be no Israel for Him to rescue, no stone left upon the holy hill of Sion, no voice to speak His Name, no eye to rejoice and behold Him, no Temple, but only abandoned stones and lifeless arches and empty market places, and rubble, and fallen houses and buildings, for my people can endure no more. He will find but a desert, burning in the sun, and marked only by dead groves and fruitless terraces. When a nation totally despairs she must die, for her heart and soul have suspired. Let the Roman and his loathsome taxgatherers rejoice then in a universal desert!

"But, alas. The Sadducees wax fat and contented still and serenely engage in their various pursuits and speak Greek and visit Rome and Athens and Alexandria and dress elegantly in silks from the Orient and begem themselves and live in corrupt fashion with concubines and are entertained in the arenas the Romans have built beyond the gates, and gamble, and join the Romans in Pompeii and Herculaneum and Caprae during the fashionable seasons, and live luxuriously in the Roman style, and are as depraved. If one complains to them—as I do in my grandfather's house—of taxes and the despair of the people, one is regarded sternly and contemptuously as a barbarian who does not understand, as they say, 'the responsibilities of modern governments to gather taxes for the general welfare of all.' It is useless to remind them that empires and nations have died in dust and ashes in the past because of taxation and the profligacy of governments who buy the people with their own money. They merely reply, with superb smiles, that this is another age and that what is past is past. Too, they remind me, a certain portion of the revenues collected by the taxgatherers goes to the support of the Temple, and, they ask, is that not a worthy cause? I think of the High Priest and his cohorts in their gold and purple and gilded litters surrounded by slaves, and I know the Temple is profaned by their presence and that God is outraged by their very existence. These too, the venal priests, oppress our people. Many of them smile when one speaks of the Messias, and they murmur a faint word concerning 'myths' and 'ancient tales,' and the need of modern man to deal with his certain reality and not with fantasies. Are *these* priests, the shepherds of the people, the conservers of vulnerable flocks, the tender guardians of ewes and lambs, the lifter of hearts, the sustainers of souls? No! They have betrayed both God and man. They have made desolate the holy places, have removed sanctity from the Ark of the Covenant, have smeared the flaming words of the Torah, have subverted the natural laws of God, have dismissed, with an arched eyebrow, the Statutes and Judgments and Ordinances, have defamed, with soft amusement, the meaning of the Commandments, saying that they were valid for an earlier age but not for today.

"Because of the priests who have betrayed God and man the Temple is no longer a sanctuary, a dwelling place for the Most High. It is now but a marketplace where strange philosophies are discussed in the shadow of colonnades and in the dusky passages and in the quiet gardens, and men gather there under umbrellas held by slaves to exchange sophisticated conversation and news of banking, merchandising and brokerage. The priests are no more virtuous than these, no more pious. They are content that the Romans pay their stipends and make luxurious their houses. It is nothing to them that the people despise and mistrust them, that they avert their heads from them, that they regard them as their enemies and not their guardians. They give their flocks stones to eat and dry dust to drink, and instead of hope they bed them in the sheds of despair.

"I often remember what God has said of these: 'My people are destroyed for lack of knowledge; because you have rejected knowledge I will also reject you. You have forgotten the Law of your God, and I will also forget your children.' The priests lead us now, as God said, 'into a way that seems right to a man, but the end thereof are the ways of death.' Ah, let the evil priests, who have betrayed their God and their flocks, beware of the judgment of the Lord, Who neither slumbers nor sleeps!

"The priests offer their sacrifices, bought with the sweat-stained coppers of their oppressed people, and I recall again the words of the Lord concerning the false shepherds who have led their flocks to destructions: 'I hate, I despise your feasts, and I take no delight in your solemn assemblies.'

" 'Even though you offer Me your burnt offerings and cereal offerings, I will not accept them, and the peace offerings of your fatted beasts I will not look upon! Take away from Me the noise of your songs! To the melody of your harps I will not listen! —But let justice roll down like waters, and righteousness like an ever-flowing stream.'

"But they heed neither the Words of God nor the admonitions of such as Rabban Gamaliel, at whose feet I sit daily. Each morning he prays with increasing fervor that the Messias show His Face and deliver His people, Israel. Sometimes he weeps, and his tears come hard, for he is by nature, as you know, a lively and learned man of much patience and remembers, as once you told me, that God speaks in centuries and not in days.

"I do not understand what he means when he implores the Messias to 'show His Face,' for the Messias has not yet come, for He has not been born to us according to the prophecies.

"Though you have urged me to visit my grandfather, Shebua ben Abraham often, because he is ailing and of a sore mind—I have not detected this!—I cannot bring myself to do so but on far occasions. I avoid him. I also offend him. When last I dined with him he was entertaining a number of Scribes, those men of mind who do nothing worthy to be called labor or accomplishment, but only write books and advise politicians and dispose themselves elegantly and speak longingly of serving 'kings' and a 'superior government.' They consider themselves of enormous intellect! I often wonder if they have bowels. I recall seeing some of the murals extant in Mesopotamia of these Scribes, who are always depicted with book and pen in hand by the side of an overseer with a whip and reverently in the rear of the man on horseback, the despot. How they long to rule, themselves, these little feeble men who call themselves philosophers and intellectuals! For their hatred of the people is manifest in every urbane word they utter, and they have contempt for the common virtues and the simple faith. They have nothing but words, and the words may be eloquent but they have no verity, no texture except sound, no profundity. Many of them are pederasts, as my grandfather once remarked in my hearing, but he laughed rather than displayed disgust, as if this were some endearing little eccentricity instead of a repulsive depravity. Some of them write poetry, and have it copied by lesser scribes and sold in the bookshops, and the poetry is like the breaking of wind. Who is the more contemptible, the Sadducees, the priests or the Scribes, is debatable, or who is more of an abomination.

"At least my grandfather, and my uncles, Simon and Joseph, though Sadducees, work in their fashion and are producers and not mere devourers of other men's work as are the Scribes. I thought to compliment my grandfather on this, jesting at the Scribes I have met in his house, but to my surprise he was offended. He spoke of the Scribes as the creators of the culture of a nation! If what I have observed of them, and in my listening and in my studies, is 'culture,' then I repudiate it with revulsion and want nothing of it. The company of a rude peasant, smelling of manure and black bread and cheese and vinegar is far preferable, for his words deal with honest realities and the things of the honest and holy earth, and his hands do needful tasks, and bring food to the market place. But what do the Scribes bring to any man's table? Delicate noise which signifies nothing. They are only postures without import.

"Once the Scribes were worthy of respect: They kept records for their lords and their masters, and counted the wares on ships and in granaries, and made reports. They made for a certain order. But these modern Scribes consider themselves Gentlemen and feel they should be prized simply because of their facility with words and writings, and their grave and empty chatterings! Aulus Platonius speaks of them in Rome, and calls them 'deadly,' but also remarks that Tiberius Caesar dislikes and mocks them—which tends my mind in approval to the Roman for that at least! Aulus calls them 'maggots in the other men's meat,' and I confess when I heard this I laughed as I have not laughed in many months. —I asked a Scribe, in my grandfather's presence, 'Whose books do you keep of household matters, and who is your master'—I was only referring to the ancient occupation of the Scribes!—and my grandfather was much incensed and implied that I had insulted his guest, a dainty creature with Hyacinthine curls and rouged cheeks and reddened lips, and perfumed like a whore. I was informed that this particular Scribe had written a play to compare with one of Aristophanes', and which would soon be produced in a Greek theater. I am afraid I made a sound of which you would not approve, but I can see you smile.

"To happier matters: My sister Sephorah's last child, a maid, is delightful beyond description, and Sephorah and her husband are pleased, for they have three sons and Ezekiel had desired a daughter. Sephorah grows in beauty and Clodia Flavius declares she is a young Juno, which I doubt will please you. Clodia then added, 'And possibly a young Rachel.' Sephorah still has a certain lightness of deportment and a certain jocular manner and a tendency to jest overmuch, which are unbecoming a matron of some twenty-four years. But she does keep her hair covered and has a grave demeanor at times and conducts herself circumspectly, thanks to that revered lady, Clodia Flavius, but then her eyes will glow like gold with the sun upon it and she laughs without a reason I can discern, and teases me that once I was not so serious and so solemn. Immediately afterwards, those same mocking eyes will fill with tears and she will embrace me. I find women incomprehensible.

"The pouch of gold sesterces you sent me was received with gratitude and affection. But I assure you that my earnings as a tentmaker are sufficient for my slight needs. I sleep in the rear of my shop. I am content with simple foods and the plainest of wine and a handful of fruit. I do not dress extravagantly. Rabban Gamaliel once told me, 'Had your childhood and youth been spent in penury you would not be so easily satisfied now,' a remark which seems too subtle to me. Was he implying that one reared in comfort and even in luxury finds later poverty less onerous and unbearable? And that poverty is endured best by those accustomed to excellent food—as if this were an adventure and not a hardship? It is possible, then, that the Rabban was not only correct but wise. I dine sometimes at his house, and I must confess that I enjoy his table, though it is simpler than that of Joseph of Arimathaea's, even if Joseph is not half so rich.

"Do not upbraid me. I gave the sesterces for the relief of the poor. Joseph of Arimathaea distributes grain and meat and wine and cloth to the destitute—and they are legion in Jerusalem in spite of the wealth of the city and of thousands of its inhabitants—just before the Sabbath. What these unfortunate ones now receive in the Temple purlieus is a disgrace to the name of charity, for charity, too, has fallen on cynical days. Few are concerned with the poor and wretched any longer, and yet charity is one of the virtues demanded by God of the Jews.

"I implore you, my dearest of fathers, to write to me frequently. There are things in my heart of which I cannot speak, for always that which was closest to me was the most inarticulate for my tongue. Words cannot encompass the soul. I am happy. I never knew happiness before as I know it now. I have not fulfilled myself; I have not reached the promise. It is still behind the distant hills, but I strive toward it on all days. Sometimes I am weary with work and study, and there is a numbness in my hands and in my brain, and I long for my home in Tarsus and the sight of familiar faces and gardens. These are but passing weaknesses. I would not change my fate for aught in the world! I have young students who listen to me reverently.

"I feel I am approaching some Revelation that is flowering in the darkness and the silence of my nights, but what it is I do not know. I only know that it is there, and my soul bounds with a joy that is close to agony. What is my afflicted eye to all this, or the fact that I have lost the strength of my boyhood, and must drive myself as a man drives oxen? God has given me the sinews and sturdiness of the spirit, and that is more than sufficient. Therefore, do not grieve for me. Concern yourself not for me, nor have anxieties in my behalf. I am doing only as I must, and so I implore you to rejoice with me and know that if I had not had such a father I would not possess my present courage, and my patience.

"I send greetings to Aristo, my old teacher. I pray he is not robbing you when he sells you the produce of his vineyards and his groves. Keep me in the treasure of your prayers, and know that I keep you in mine. When you next visit my mother's grave, take a rose for me.

Your son,
Saul"

The handsome car with its fine four black stallions rode out of Jerusalem at dawn, and Saul ben Hillel and Joseph of Arimathaea sat on red velvet cushions tasseled and fringed with gold. The driver was a great Nubian with a splendid face and arrayed like a barbaric king, for Joseph indulged his servants with love and respect for their foibles and desires. Another servant held a wide umbrella of silk over the heads of the passengers, though it was not yet dawn and the dew lay on grasses and gardens in the city and the sky was as black as the Nubian's face and struck with throbbing stars. The Roman soldiers at the Damascus Gate knew Joseph well and honored him, and were grateful for the small pouches of sesterces which he always brought for them.

"They are good and simple and childlike boys, these young soldiers," he said to Saul. "They are proud of Rome. Once Rome was to be deeply honored, when she was a Republic, and worthy of any civilized man's respect, for never had so great a nation been founded on so great and noble principles—though admittedly built on a fratricide. Her Bill of Man's Rights, propounded by her Founding Fathers, notably Cincinnatus, has never been equaled, no, not even by the Code of Hammurabi, and not even by our Moses. But her Constitution was inevitably eroded by ambitious and wicked and lustful men, in whom patriotism had long died, and who saw their nation not as a Colossus of freedom in the world and a light to the nations, but an arena in which they could gain prizes and eventually crown themselves. It is true as Aristotle has said, alas: 'Republics decline into democracies, and democracies degenerate into despotisms.' Yet, Republics have the potentialities for immortality, if they retain their masculinity and do not become feminine democracies. Forgive me. I love the vision of the Roman Republic, ruled by just and honorable men. I weep that she has become a female Empire, lascivious, cruel, bloodthirsty, terrible, powerful with evil, an oppressor and an enslaver. But that is the history of nations who first forget God, then honor and virtue."

He sighed. "Those boys at the gates are not to be held accountable. They believe the lies they are told by their government. When will people not believe the lies of their government? If that day arrives, surely the Messianic Age is at hand, and a Theocracy emerges!"

A few years before Saul would have expressed his loathing for Rome in execrations, but now he listened, even with still some dubiousness. He knew his cousin's husband well, the noble Aulus Platonius, and Aulus' son, Titus

Milo Platonius, and he loved and respected them and visited their house and dined with Aulus and Hannah bas Judah. His rage remained for Rome, but not for the individual Roman who was as helpless as he in the golden fist of Empire. But more even than Rome herself he hated the traitors and collaborators among his own people, who pressed their heels on the prostrate necks of their kinsmen. Empires lived for loot and conquest, but the betrayers of Israel lived only for their pleasure. True it was that little Israel could never have resisted Rome, but it was not necessary that the suave Sadducees and the Scribes and the merchants should eagerly fawn on the conqueror and assist him in degrading a helpless little people and robbing them of their sustenance and torturing them with despair.

Joseph was reflecting: "Our young Saul has advanced into manhood these ten years since first he came to Jerusalem, and he understands now that man's evil is ubiquitous and that there are no good nations as opposed to evil nations, just as there are few if any good men. Ah, what a marvelous world this would be if any nation were righteous, even if she boasted only ten thousand inhabitants! But wickedness is endemic in man; it is the hidden plague in his soul, awaiting the implosion of infection. A little kingdom is no more righteous than a great Empire, nor are her rulers more virtuous. We of Israel have been a singular nation, admonished and led by God through the centuries. We have eaten out of His Hand as lambs eat from the hands of shepherds. We have been given guides and prophets. We were given Moses. We have been given the Messias. As the householder tends his children and teaches them and loves them and cherishes them, and protects and guards them, so has God guarded Israel and loved her. Yet, we are not now more honorable than Rome, more worthy of mercy. His judgment has fallen upon us, just as it will fall upon Rome, for God is no Respecter of persons, and all men are His own and one is no dearer than another, nor one more deserving of punishment than another. May God have mercy on the souls of all men."

The earth was dark and silent, lit only by the huge and wandering light of the stars, and it was very still out in the desolate places. It was also chill, and Saul wrapped himself in his dull warm cloak of goat's hair, which he had woven himself, and it was stiff and unyielding. The iron-shod wheels of the car rumbled over thin rubble and gravel and sand and dust, and the horses' hoofs struck fire on stone and a fresh sharp wind lashed the face. It was an arid wind, smelling only of rock and desolation and a few acrid desert plants, and it also smelled of the ages, for this was an ancient land and the dead earth was the tomb of vanished nations.

Dawn comes with sudden swiftness and a kind of silent and enormous tumult in the lands of the east. At one moment the earth was blank and dark, the hills invisible, and at the next the whole eastern sky was a blazing amber conflagration and the hills started against it and then they poured with a glittering coppery light like water that had been set aflame. That light rushed down mountainside and terrace, engulfing them in burning radiance, and cypresses and sycamores and groves seemed to leap into existence where there had been nothing before, and little white houses turned red as if their façades were on fire. Then the sun stood shouting on a mountaintop and the earth awoke with a murmurous echo.

Saul, always sensitive to the sights of the earth and beauty—though he frequently and sternly said that these were distractions from the contemplation of God—was awed as always. He glanced at Joseph of Arimathaea but Joseph's large bald head and part of his long oval face was still hidden by his hood, and now he leaned forward and murmured something to the Nubian driver who touched his whip hand obediently to his forehead. The car turned on the dry yellow earth; the stallions' hides were flecked with foam. They reached a spring and the horses drank. Joseph said to Saul, "We have far, still, to go, into the desolate places, so refresh yourself." So Joseph and Saul left the car and bathed their faces and dusty hands in the spring and drank of it, and Joseph produced cool fruit and wine and bread and excellent cheese. He shared this with his servants, courteously, and he and Saul ate and drank, and the sun became excessively hot and Saul threw off his cloak, revealing his dark gray linen tunic. His red hair caught a vivid blaze from the sun and Joseph said, re-garding his fair and freckled face, "It is not well to expose yourself in these places, Saul, so draw your hood to give shelter to your complexion and to protect your eyes."

His own eyes, so big and dark and liquid, beamed on Saul with affection, and again Saul was baffled at the kindness to him of this good and renowned man. Saul could not see himself as Joseph saw him—a young man of ardent if somber passions, with an ascetic face strong with square and angular bones, and with eyes that appeared to glow with visions.

There were many who considered Saul formidable, and ruthless with slow men, and arrogant with knowledge, and impatient beyond toleration, but Joseph knew him as a young man with destiny large in his blue eyes, even in the eye that drooped and reddened at too much light. Saul had many imperfections; he was unable to endure fools gladly, as Solomon had suggested, and he had no patience for weakness and fragility of character and compliance and that effeminate gentleness which many of the Sadducees and the Scribes cultivated, as part of their civilized lives. ("We are kind," they appeared to be insisting on all occasions, in rebuke to others they considered ungentle. But Joseph remembered what a sage had said: "Strange it is that those who wish all men to be kind are themselves incapable of kindness.")

In Joseph's estimation—and he was a man who knew men—Saul's manifest virtues, some of them extreme, overlaid his imperfections as a fine and brilliant glaze overlaid the base coarseness of pottery. They were not virtues which would endear him to many but rather aroused their contempt, their hatred, their uneasiness and their hostility. He was incapable of the gentlest of hypocrisies or the slightest of deviousnesses, and he spoke bluntly and roughly and offended many—often to his own bewilderment for he still retained some of his younger delusion that men preferred truth to lies and candor to guile.

They drove away in the cauldron of yellow light which was now full morning, and the heat beat at them like heated rods through their garments.

Saul was not a stranger to deserts and lifeless places, but now, as the wheels turned rapidly farther in the direction of Damascus he was stunned, not only by the heat but by the complete and barren desolation which lay all about him, empty of all life even the most hardy, except for thistles, treeless, raging with incredible and blinding light, the hills beyond a pure stony brass, the ground below saffron and thick with dust and boulders and gravel and flat as a man's palm, the sky a stark and staring blue too intense for more than a quick glance, and cloudless, the sun an enormous hole of flame approaching the zenith, and here and there, where little spring rills had run, straggles of dry amber crawling over the stricken earth. Vultures, black and silent and sharp as ink, soared against the sky, seeking and bending and wheeling. Occasionally, scattered caves appeared, trembling in waves of heat, their openings like great dry mouths dead of thirst, and gaping. There was no waterhole visible anywhere, no green oasis in this landscape of Gehenna. Once Saul thought he saw the lurking shape of a jackal casting a clear shadow on the parched and blighted ground, but as jackals were the color of the landscape, itself, it was impossible to be certain.

Saul had often pondered on the thought that he would like to retreat to the desert for a space, to this immense and lifeless silence, this incandescent light. But as he looked about him now he confessed that he could not understand why even the most dedicated and fervid Essene or Zealot should choose a place which could only resemble hell. It was said that these man could find locusts and wild honey when necessary, and water, but Saul saw no spot where these could be obtained. They were far from the city, and yet they penetrated more and more into the wilderness, and Saul guessed, by the sureness of the Nubian's driving of the black stallions, that this was no new territory to him and that he was familiar with it. His massive earrings cast golden shadows on his polished ebony cheeks, and he was gazing about him with indifferent pride. Saul began to be more than grateful for the umbrella raised over his and Joseph's head by the servant who sat between them.

Joseph lifted his hand and pointed toward the hills and Saul saw below them, dancing in heat-waves, a cluster of low caves, just beginning to climb the lower flank of the nearest hill. "Our destination," said Joseph.

In that air, as clear as molten glass, the caves appeared to be much nearer than they truly were, and Saul was beginning to suffer from heat and thirst long before the yellowish stone of the caves reluctantly approached them across the barrens. Suddenly the tiny figure of a man appeared on the top of the lowest cave—or cavern— and he seemed as black and intensely sharp as a vulture against the sky. He waved an infinitesimal hand in greeting, then stood there, a wild and bearded little figure, watching them. After a while he was joined by similar figures, and there was a shagginess about them which suggested fur garments about their loins. They wore no cloaks nor hoods to shelter them from the sun and the heat, and as the car raced closer to the caves Saul could see their faces, almost as black as the Nubian's, and thick with beards. Their arms and hands and legs were dark and thin but muscular, and now they leaped as lightly as goats to the ground and their voices could be heard, vivid yet fragile as flutes: "Shalom! Shalom!"

Joseph was smiling in the shadow of his hood. He made a trumpet of his hands and called a greeting in return to those who awaited him. They were growing in number. Now there were at least fifty, then more, then more, and then more than one hundred. They seemed to leap not only from the caves but from the earth itself, and the sun struck gleams from their eyes and from their teeth. From their actions, their gestures, their movements, Saul could see that they were young, and that some were hardly more than boys who had just reached early youth, for these had small or no beards. He felt his own sweating chin. He wore no beard, himself, for his skin was so fair that a beard irritated it beyond sufferance, and induced sores, and Rabban Gamaliel had said: "God desires us to love and to serve Him, but not to endure unnecessary pain in that service, for that is vainglorious. And did not Lucian, the Greek, say that if beards were necessary for wisdom a goat would be a veritable Plato?"

Some of the younger of the desert dwellers could not restrain their joy and enthusiasm at seeing their friend, Joseph of Arimathaea, and came running toward the car, raising fiery clouds of yellow dust in their wake. Saul glanced at the provisions Joseph had brought: Leather bottles of wine, wheels of cheese, wheaten and oaten bread, fruit, and vessels of artichokes in vinegar and garlic, and kegs of beer and closely wrapped bottles of sound Syrian whiskey. There were baskets of onions, also, and citrons, very pungent in the heat, and heaps of dates and figs and boxes of pastries and jars of rendered fat and dried meats. There were small leather pouches which Saul more than suspected contained respectable amounts of Roman gold sesterces and drachmas. There were also many books, tied with rope, and blankets and pottery and cutlery. In truth, the huge car was so provisioned that there was barely room for the four riders in it.

The young men had now reached the car and were shouting and laughing and calling like children, and grinning at Joseph and casting curious looks at Saul. They leaped and they danced, and clapped their hands, and Saul, who had expected gloomy recluses with stern and remote faces, thought that he had never seen so merry a gathering, and so joyous. They shouted inquiries of Joseph. They asked of his family and his and their friends. They uttered laughing oaths at the mention of the priests in the Temple. Some, in their exuberance, engaged in little running wrestling matches. Their feet were bare and sinewy and almost black, or, at the most, they wore rope sandals. They might be as lean as bone and their flesh like hard strings and sinews, but their eyes shone with clear delight in living, and glowing passion.

The Nubian watched all this with the indulgence of a man several years older than these dark and dusty youths and even deigned to smile occasionally and flicked elegantly at his silken turban of many colors and shrugged his golden necklace about his long and serpentine neck. He was a barbarian emperor in the midst of his wild and almost naked servants, and he bestowed a very white smile upon them and urged them to watch the horses' hoofs, which only made them dance the merrier into dangerous proximity. The air was clamorous with their young voices. They sang. They guided the Nubian to a place behind the nearest caves, and here, to Saul's amazement, the shadow cast by the caves was almost cool, and purplish, and in its midst was a bubbling spring. He thought: "The shadow of a great Rock in a weary land," and understood completely, for the first time, the full meaning of the phrase in the Scriptures.

Now a man rounded the side of the sheltering cave, an older man of some thirty years, broad of shoulder and tall and incredibly emaciated, but giving the impression of immense vitality and indomitable strength and authority. His beard was black and thick and curly, his nose sharply and thinly beaked and predatory, his mouth faintly smiling, his black eyes large and shining under shaggy black brows. When the youths saw him they fell back in respect, and he held up his arms to Joseph and almost lifted him from the car. The two then embraced and kissed each other. Joseph, as usual, was finely clad, but the man he held so tenderly was nearly nude with a goat-skin about his loins, and his burned skin glistened with sweat. They held each other off and gazed into each other's eyes, and smiled, and embraced again, and murmured the holiest of greetings, concluding with a passionate, "Hear, O Israel! The Lord our God, the Lord is One!"

Then holding his friend's hand tightly, Joseph turned to Saul who had stiffly alighted from the car and had thrown back his hood to catch the coolness of this place.

"Jochanan, my brother, my friend, I have brought him of whom I have written, Saul of Tarshish, who chooses, like us, rather to obey God than man, and to serve Him."

Saul looked directly into the countenance of Jochanan, who had been greeted as a brother by Joseph of Arimathaea, and as the dearest of friends, and he discerned, with a kind of shrinking awe, the pure and terrible holiness of those great black eyes, which seemed to force their gaze into his heart to discover all that lay there, and to pass inexorable judgment. It was like facing the blaze of the sun, from which nothing can escape. Saul felt himself mute and small and miserable and uncomely and without significance, and an intruder.

Then Jochanan set his long hands on Saul's shoulders and smiled down at him with a fearful scrutiny, and then his brows drew together, then relaxed, and he said in a most gentle, almost compassionate voice, "Shalom. Greetings to the friend of my friend, Joseph of Arimathaea, and may Our Father, blessed be His Name, grant to you all that He desires to grant. Welcome, Saul of Tarshish!"

As if some intense moment and climactic had arrived and then had passed in safety and peace, the youths, at a distance, raised a happy cry of jubilation, and Joseph smiled as though in relief. And Saul, who was bemused and bewildered, felt a loosening in him and the banishment of the fear he had momentarily experienced, and which could not be explained.

Some of the younger and chattering boys were capering away with the provisions, which they carried to the cave where they stored their few goods and their meager possessions. Jochanan put one arm about Saul's shoulders and the other about Joseph's, and led them to another cave where the dimness was welcome after the conflagration outside, and where there was a coolness as if the earth were breathing through some crevice. In truth, Saul felt the light chill breath and sighed with pleasure. The cave was large and furnished with a pallet on the earthen floor, a low wooden table, and two benches. The floor bore scattered black and white hides of goats, and in one corner was a heap of scrolls. There was nothing else. The two guests sat down and Jochanan said—and Saul heard the deep and rapid timbre of his manly voice—"Thanks to you again, Joseph, we shall have a feast!"

"You have but to say the word, Jochanan, and every seven days such 'feasts' will arrive without fail."

Jochanan shook his powerful head. But he smiled. "My young friends would then grow fat and long for the fleshpots, and there would be few else to praise His Name and keep pure His Commandments, and speak of the Messias." His mighty knees gleamed darkly in the spectral light of the cave and his chest was like leather armor, and black with thick hair. He looked with kindness at Saul and said, "Though you do not know me, I know you, Saul of Tarshish." He paused. "Joseph has written often of you." But Saul felt that he was speaking with constraint and not saying all he could say.

Two youths with lively faces brought in plain pottery plates and a platter heaped with the cheese and bread and fruit and meat which Joseph had brought, and earthen goblets foaming with beer and a bottle of wine. Saul discovered that he was hungry, but Jochanan ate sparely as did Joseph, and the two friends spoke together in quiet grave voices of things mysterious to Saul. Nevertheless, they were words of import.

"I leave, before the full moon," said Jochanan. "Therefore, we do not meet again, Joseph, for some time."

"You have received the summons?"

"True."

Even in the dimness Saul could see the sudden sadness of Joseph's face. He heard him sigh.

"The drama, then, begins," said Joseph. He clasped his hands together on the table and contemplated them.

"And never ends," said Jochanan. "Come, dear friend. Would you have it otherwise?"

Joseph was silent for a space. Finally he spoke, still contemplating his hands: "We cannot avoid, even by prayer, what has been ordained from eternity. Of a certainty, we should rejoice that we have been permitted to know this hour. Still, as mortal man, I am filled with sorrow and with pain. I would die one thousand times, ten thousand times over, to spare him one pang. I would lay my body before his feet, for the trampling, and call myself blessed. I would be flayed alive, for his sake, and rejoice. But that is not my destiny."

Jochanan touched the clasped hands quickly. "No, it is not your destiny. You have another. But rejoice with me that I have finally received the summons, and must go."

To Saul's amazement, Joseph's eyes filled with tears and he bowed his head. Of what man were they speaking? What prophet unknown to him, what holy man? If they knew of such, why was not he, Saul ben Hillel, permitted to sit at his feet?

As if Joseph had heard these questions, he lifted his bent head and strove to smile at Saul. "Forgive us, that we seemingly speak in riddles, my Saul. We cannot tell you as yet, but in His time God will enlighten you. That, Jochanan has told me."

Saul's red brows drew together and he could not refrain from saying, "We have met but today! He knows me not!"

"Ah," said Jochanan, "God, blessed be His Name, has told me many things. Do not be impatient, my son." His puissant face darkened for a moment. "How He will call you I do not know, though I know He will. Do not turn aside when you hear His voice."

Saul frowned again. He felt himself diminished to the state of a schoolboy, for all he was twenty-five years of age and this wild man—with the rude accent of the province of Galilee—was hardly more than five years older.

He said, "I am not without friends. My cousin's husband is the Roman officer, Aulus Platonius, and his son is Titus Milo a Praetorian captain in Rome, and I am a Roman citizen versed in Roman law, and my grandfather is the friend of Herod Antipas and Pontius Pilate, and if there is some Jew who is in danger or pursued or under sentence of death, it is possible that I could plead for him."

He had no sooner said these words than he colored with shame of himself, though his boasting had been innocent and he had felt himself offended.

The older men regarded him gently. Then Jochanan said, "There is none who can save him, for he has chosen this for himself."

Saul remembered how Joseph of Arimathaea had saved many from the dreadful death on the cross nearly ten years before, and had preserved others from suffering. So his harsh anger—at both himself and the others—disappeared. But it was replaced by discomfiture. He drank more wine. Suddenly, he remembered the dream of the nameless peasant who had perished on the cross also, and whose dying body had become encased as if in the shell of a seed and had dropped into the earth, and had given birth to a limitless harvest. Saul's face changed.

"Yes?" said Jochanan, in a quick and urgent voice.

Saul stared at him in open surprise. "I was but remembering a dream," he said. "It was a dream that preceded an almost mortal illness of mine, and which left me with this half-closed and sunken eye."

"Tell me," said Jochanan.

Saul told himself that this was absurd. Why should Jochanan, and Joseph, also, be so intent on him now, demanding that he speak of a dream he had had so long ago, and which was only the precursor of a fever? Or the result of it? He smiled in embarrassment, but the two men kept their gaze upon him, commanding.

Thereupon he told them, watching for amused smiles, for shrugs, for answering embarrassment, even for a laugh. But their faces became more intent and grave, and they began to exchange glances and leaned closer to him, and they seemed hardly to breathe.

"I was sickening," said Saul. "I had seen the execution of fifty young Jews by the Romans. There was death and agony in my heart. I was also chilled by the storm and

wetted by the rain that followed. I could not free myself
from the memory of the poor workingman—though he
was none of importance—who had walked among the
crosses and had appeared to lighten the suffering of the
dying. Joseph saw him, also." He glanced at Joseph who
nodded speechlessly.

Saul continued: "I had seen him once before, during the
High Holy Days, with one he addressed as his mother.
She called him Yeshua. His face haunted me. I do not
know why. He was poor and humble. Why I should dream
that he, too, had been executed, had fallen into the
earth—" Saul became silent.

There was silence all about him. He looked up to see the
moved faces of the older men and now even Jochanan's
eyes were wet with tears. Joseph made an impulsive gesture, but Jochanan laid his hand on his wrist, as if in
warning.

"It was but a dream," said Saul, in a lame voice, and he
was ashamed again that he had been indiscreet.

"All life is but a dreaming, though a frightful one,"
said Jochanan. "But one day you will understand the
significance of that dream, my Saul. Come. The sun is
declining and you must soon leave us, and I wish to speak
to my boys, for soon, I too, must go."

They went outside. The sun was falling to the west and
though the earth and mountains still glowed as if from a
furnace the air was slightly cooler. The youths had gathered together, crouching on the ground, sitting, squatting,
and waiting for Jochanan. Jochanan, with the dignity of
a king, climbed the top of one cave, and then another,
until he stood over them like a dark statue imbued with
wildness and authority, and all faces were turned to him.

His voice sounded among them like a gigantic trumpet.

"I go because I have been summoned and the hour is
come! I go to prepare the way! This you know, this you
have been told, my children, my little ones. I go with rejoicing and in triumph.

"You must not grieve that I leave you, for you will
see me again. I ask but your prayers. I ask but that you
wait, for the last hour draws near."

He looked down at those silent faces and his own great
one became tender, as the face of a father is tender, and
he spoke in the words of Isaias:

" 'The people who walked in darkness have seen a great light! Those who dwelt in a land of deep darkness, on them has light shined. For the yoke of His burden, and the staff for His shoulder, the rod of His oppressor, God has broken as on the day of Midian! For every boot of the tramping warrior in battle tumult, and every garment rolled in blood, will be burned as fuel for the fire.' "

A deep awe appeared to spread over all the desolate land and invade the very sky. Jochanan's face became lustrous, exalted, filled with a mighty light of its own, and he raised his eyes to the sky.

" 'It shall come to pass in the latter days that the mountain of the House of the Lord shall be established as the highest of the mountains, and shall be raised above the hills! All the nations shall flow to it, and many peoples shall come and say, "Come, let us go up to the mountain of the Lord, in the House of the God of Jacob, that He may teach us His ways and that we walk in His paths!" For out of Sion shall go forth the Law, and the Word of the Lord from Jerusalem. He shall judge between the nations and shall decide for many peoples. And they shall beat their swords into plowshares, and their spears into pruning hooks. Nation shall not lift up sword against nation, neither shall they learn war any more!' "

It was as if fire and flame had touched his cheek, and the sun his eyes, and Jochanan came forward on the roof of the cave and lifted his hand in exultation, and cried:

" 'For unto us a child has been born, and to us a Son has been given!' "

All wept, even Joseph of Arimathaea, but Saul stared up at the brilliantly illuminated figure of Jochanan with overpowering bewilderment, for the change of tense in the latter words was astounding and incomprehensible to him. He said to himself, It is but the rude pronunciation of the Galilee dialect, with which I am not familiar in all its nuances.

Jochanan stood, a tall image of burnished bronze against the suddenly empurpling sky, and he lifted his face and he was lost in contemplation and prayer and did not speak again.

Joseph touched Saul's arm and said, "It is time that we go, for it will soon be dark and the desert lurks at night with robbers."

While they prepared to depart Jochanan still stood as if caught in timeless ecstasy, his face transfigured, and his youths stood and gazed up at him and did not move, nor were they aware of the departing guests. At the last Saul heard them raise a tremendous shout:

"Hear, O Israel! The Lord our God, the Lord is One!"

The car rolled rapidly toward Jerusalem and the desert air became chill. Saul was silent for a long time. Then he said, "I do not understand that peculiar man. I do not know whereof he speaks. He repeated the words of Isaias. Nevertheless—"

Joseph said, and Saul could hardly believe that he had heard the words:

"He knew of this hour in his mother's womb. Like Sarah, Elizabeth was of a great age when she bore him, long after her years of fecundity. His father, Zachary, had been an old priest and in the Sanctum of the Temple he had been told by an angel that his wife would bear a son, and he had not believed. Elizabeth was bent and wrinkled and her hair was as white as a dove. Because he had not believed, he was stricken dumb. But it indeed came to pass that Elizabeth gave birth, and the lusty child was called Jochanan, and when the men came to kiss the beard of Zachary his speech was restored and he praised God. But of his words of rejoicing I cannot speak, though I know them.

"I implore you, Saul, do not question me. The time has not yet come." He covered his face with his hood and the astonished Saul knew that he was weeping, but why he wept he did not know. Saul pondered with increasing incredulity on what he had heard and seen this day and finally it appeared all a dream in a blasted desert, and Jochanan a madman, and the cultivated Joseph of Arimathaea one deluded by a wild creature of the desert who was probably capable of casting spells, and had a devil.

Chapter 17

"WE have a story," said Hillel ben Borush to his old and now decrepit friend, Reb Isaac.

"When did a Jew not have a story?" asked the ancient rabbi, and shrugged. But his glance was kinder than his words. He was much alarmed at Hillel's appearance, for though Hillel was but fifty-seven he appeared very aged, and bowed, and gaunt, and there was a silvery cast in his white beard so that he resembled a prophet. They were sitting in the rabbi's library and a cold wind was rushing down from the scarlet mountains and the garden was withering and winter was advancing on the land. Here it was very warm, for the rabbi's old bones demanded heat now, and there were two braziers burning on the stone floor and there was a fur rug over his knees. Woolen curtains protected the windows from drafts, and a harsh wind was blowing.

"We have a story," said Hillel, as if the rabbi had not spoken. "Four men went to a great feast to which they had been invited. One had come reluctantly, but he had been summoned by the king and could not refuse. He had little appetite for the rich and spicy dishes and the wine, and he would have been satisfied with mere bread and cheese and milk. For he was a man in whom the juices of life did not run strong. The second man ate heartily, but his appetites were more gross, and as he was not very intelligent he did not enjoy the erudite conversation about him. He was filled with ennui. He thought of his absent dancing girls with longing. So he was dissatisfied and felt himself offended, and yawned, and found nothing of interest surrounding him. The third man enjoyed himself and hoped that the feast would continue until morn, for the dishes were delicious and the wine heady, and he regretted that this must eventually end, and at moments he was sad at the thought of the swift passing of delight.

"And the fourth man was pleased to have been invited to the feast and was grateful to his kingly host, for all about him was beauty and music and stately vistas, which moved his soul. The meats and the fruits and the breads and the wine lay lovingly on his tongue. His reflections moved with the conversation and his mind was afire and he participated in the speaking with an exquisite pleasure. He did not regret that this must end. He knew it must, but it was sufficient for him that he now possessed it for the hour. And his gratitude to his host increased. He felt himself surrounded by the most solicitous of friends, and his heart was full.

"Now," said Hillel, watching the old rabbi with a hidden look, "the first man who had little appetite for the good food, and did not recognize it as such, decided to beg leave to depart. The king was sad, but gave his permission. The second man was surfeited, for he had eaten and drunk too much, and was yawning with boredom, and he had not heard the music nor cared for it, and he wished to sleep. He, too, asked permission to leave, and the king, growing more sorrowful, gave his consent. The third man lingered, still hoping the feast would not end, still gazing after new delights on the platters in the hands of the servants, though his face was showing fatigue and his hands trembled with weariness. He kept glancing through the columns, dreading to see the morning. The king, observing this, sighed, and said to him, 'My guest, the hour is late. You must leave.' The guest tried to protest, but the king gently indicated that he must rise and depart, and he did so, weeping, exhausted though he was.

"But the fourth man," said Hillel, "had suddenly been stricken with a sense of sorrow and emptiness, and he no longer cared for the music, nor for the smiles of his friends, and he wished only to lie down in some dark and silent place and know no more. The food and wine had become repugnant to him. His lust for them had gone, and he did not know why. A vast loneliness overcame him, a sensation that he had been abandoned and that he desired nothing more, no, nothing more in all the world, and no pleasure, and he was bereft. A pain had come to his heart. He found it more than his strength could bear to sit on the divan; his speech left him. 'I am surfeited. I have had enough,' he said to himself. 'The feast has become intolerable to me.' The wine lay like vinegar on his tongue. The voices of his friends were painful in his ears. 'I desire nothing more,' he thought, and wondered if the king would think him discourteous if he should ask for dismissal. And everything had lost color and beauty and meaning.

"It was then that the king gazed upon him and said, 'Your three friends have gone. Do you desire to leave also?' "

Hillel fell silent, and his haggard face was the color of ashes and his cheekbones showed through his beard.

The rabbi contemplated him. "I think I comprehend," he said. "The king had invited his servants to a feast, rejoicing in their company. But one had nothing in his soul with which to respond, or he had dulled his response with dull living and a refusal to look at the beauty about him in life so that he had lost his ability to see it. So, he left the feast early. The second one had surfeited himself too soon, had devoured too much too greedily, and so when he could not eat more he did not sit in quiet and contemplate the loveliness about him, for all his appetites had been gross in his life and he believed that once surfeited there was nothing left but departure, and pleasure only of the body and not of the mind, and therefore he heard no conversation and no wit. So, why remain?

"And the third man feared the ending of pleasure, for he had relished his life heedlessly and he enjoyed the kingly feast, and he could not have enough of living and clung to existence, though he was palsied and needed rest. He feared the morning, for the morning was the end of the feast and he believed that the morning held nothing for him. So he wept when the king was compassionate and suggested that he depart, for where would he go now and to what bed and what quietude, he a man who had hated quietude and repose?"

"Yes," said Hillel, in a very low voice.

The rabbi fixed his old but still keen eyes upon him. "And the fourth man, grateful to the king for the invitation to the feast, and rejoicing in it, and enraptured with taste and smell and touch and sound and sight, at first thought the feast was delightful, and his gratitude increased, and he adored the king for his lovingkindness. But, there came a shadow over him and an anguish, and all faded from his sight. Yet, he was loath to beg the king to dismiss him, for he would not be ungrateful though all had become shadowy to him and a burden and a weariness. But the king only asked him, 'Do you desire to leave also?'"

"Yes," said Hillel, and bent his head as if to hide tears.

The rabbi ruminated. "What do you think should be the guest's answer to the king?"

"I do not know," whispered Hillel. "But the guest believed that he could remain no longer, and prayed in his heart that his king would say to him, 'Go, and rest.' "

"Let us assume," said the rabbi, with deep compassion in his heart, "that the king said to the guest, 'Your company pleases me, and I would have you with me longer at this feast, so bear with me, and do not ask me to dismiss you. I know you are weary to death. I know of the sorrow in your soul, and I am the only one who knows it. But I have bidden you here, and I know why I have bidden you, so remain.' "

Hillel was silent. The rabbi stroked his beard.

"The great King," said the rabbi, "knows why He has bidden His children to the feast, and He was saddened when the first did not enjoy it, by reason of the guest's own fault, and He was grieved that the second could only devour and then in ingratitude desire no more, no, not even His company. And the third incontinently lingered too long, for he was afraid, and had lived only for pleasure and the gratification of self, yet his pleasure had been the pleasure only of a beast and not of a man. So, in pity the King dismissed him.

"As for the fourth man," said the rabbi in a grave low voice, "the King wishes him to remain and keep Him company for a while longer. The King does not compel. He only asks, Is it too much to grant His request, until He is pleased to ask you to depart?"

Hillel started. "It is only a story," he said, and his eyes seemed pits of dull suffering. "I was speaking in a parable, a fantasy."

The rabbi shook his head. "I know all the stories, all the parables, men have already spoken. I do not know this one."

"Why does not the King, in mercy, dismiss the last man?" asked Hillel, and now his gaze was a burning in the hollows of his cheeks.

"Perhaps because He is merciful. He is the King. He knows His feast. He has His reasons."

"Which I do not understand," said Hillel.

The rabbi sighed. "Have you lived this long and not discovered that it is impossible for man to understand God?"

"I have none at home," said Hillel, as if he had not heard the rabbi's question. "There is none awaiting me.

Do not speak to me," he said in sudden passion, "of men who have less and suffer more, of the homeless and the agonized with disease, and the lost, and all the sufferers whose name is Legion! They have their own pain, and why they still linger at the feast is nothing to me any longer! I only know that I wish to leave, that I can no longer await the dismissal!" He clenched his hands together. "I can no longer wait!"

"For no one desires you nor loves you the most dearly nor holds you first in his heart?"

Hillel averted his head. "It is not that, perhaps. Do not ask me more, my friend. But I will tell you this: I never gave my heart lightly, and when I gave it it was despised. It was a betrayal of the soul." He stood up. "God has abandoned me. I feel it in my very flesh, though you speak of feasts and the request of the King that I remain. He has not asked it. He has already departed and I see at the table only cold sauces and dead wine and bread eaten by mice. I can linger no longer."

The rabbi understood that this was an old story, for he was an old man, but the intricacies of human suffering never failed to move him. Always, however, he had assumed a stern visage and an admonishing attitude, and these were usually sufficient. He said, "A man who leaves —the feast—before the King grants him departure casts degradation and despair on those who love him, for they reproach themselves thereafter, asking themselves if there was aught they had done, or not done, or what sin they had committed, or what love they had not given in full measure, or what seeming indifference they had displayed, or what neglect, which had impelled the afflicted one to turn from them in silence and enter into the everlasting darkness. What soul of compassion can endure the misery of those it has left behind it? It would be monstrous, indeed."

"You still do not comprehend, Reb Isaac," said Hillel, standing at a distance and half-averted. His posture was that of a man too feeble to bear a burden any longer. "I am unable to exert myself to feel anything now, or to experience any emotion. I only know that to see another day, another noon, another night, is an insufferable weariness and anguish to me. To bathe, to breathe, to dine, to drink, to assume garments and shoes, to speak, to give commands, to decide on the merest matter, to smile when a smile is expected, and even to sleep knowing that I will awake, have become too oppressive to me. Habit is no longer done without thought; each accustomed task, however trivial, demands an onerous attention I can give no more."

He turned now and his gaunt and tormented face was horrifying to the old rabbi.

"Do not speak to me of forfeiting my seat in the world hereafter, of being cast into the darkness, of insulting the King! I have lost my faith. I have lost what illumined my life, and it left many years ago. I blame no one but my own weakness, that I trusted in love. It is possible it is not even that, which now afflicts me. Once I had hope."

"Yes?" said Reb Isaac.

Hillel spread out his hands mutely. After a moment or two he said, "I have no hope. It was a dream from the beginning. I have told you of the Star my cousin, Hannah bas Judah's husband, saw on a certain winter night over Bethlehem, some years before my own son was born. I had dreams. I dreamed the Star signaled the birth of the Messias, but it was not true. At this time He would be some thirty years in the flesh, and some there would be in that little land who would know Him, and He would surely visit His city, Jerusalem. But my son, Saul, writes me nothing of this and seems bewildered at my written questions. My friends, Rabban Gamaliel and Joseph of Arimathaea, would certainly know if He were here. They tell me nothing, but only have smiled at me strangely when I have seen them in Jerusalem. I fear they consider me a fool, and I am in agreement. The thought of the Messias sustained me through much sorrow and loneliness, but the sustenance was false and I have eaten of bread filled with wind and have drunk of briny waters which could not quench my thirst."

"You are not the only one whose soul yearns for the tardy Messias, blessed be His Name," said the rabbi, frowning. "When I was younger I was certain that I would live when He lived on this earth. I am disappointed. I only know that He will come, if not tomorrow, then another tomorrow. He will surely come!"

"Is it not written that hope deferred makes the heart

sick?" asked Hillel, in the fainting voice of a dying man. "But now I no longer desire even to hope. I care no more."

Without even a farewell he left his old friend. The rabbi sat in a turmoil of distressed thoughts for a considerable time. All men despair, he told himself. All men of intelligence sometimes curse the day they were born, as did Job, and long for death. Yet they endured. It is possible that Hillel ben Borush has some physical affliction which is draining his hope, unknown to himself. I must consult his friends.

Then the rabbi suddenly remembered that Hillel's friends had frequently complained to him that they saw Hillel with less and less frequency, and that when encountering him they were struck by his air of remoteness and uninterest. He had not been seen in the synagogue for a long time. He accepted no invitations. The leaders of the Jewish community remarked that his tithes were as prompt and as generous as always. But they did not see the man, himself, but only his messengers. "Dear Father!" said Reb Isaac aloud, in consternation. "A man dies of his longing and his despair before one's very eyes, and one does not see! How blind we are! It should have been plain to me, when I visited Hillel, that none was present in his house—though once his friends thronged there—and his only company was that rascally Greek former slave of his—Aristo? Aristo. He is a rich man now, I have heard, and his produce moves in caravans afar, thanks to Hillel who freed and recompensed him according to the Law. I must write to him and ask his assistance."

It galled the proud old man that he must write to a former slave, and a Gentile, to implore his help to save a noble member of a Jewish family. But he wrote the letter at once and dispatched it by a servant, and sat and ruminated and prayed and reproached himself, then poured a goblet of wine and made grimaces as he drank it—though it was excellent—and assured himself over and over that Hillel was at heart too pious a Jew to cause his own death, and that some ill of the body was responsible, or the time of his life. By sunset some tranquillity returned to him, for he believed that men at heart were sensible and shrank from death, even the most desperate, and he enjoyed his dinner.

Aristo was in his flourishing and far-flung olive groves when a slave—he owned fourteen now—brought him Reb Isaac's letter. He read it with incredulity, standing there in the chill thin autumn light of early evening. It was a very mysterious letter. The rabbi wrote with stiff formality and obscurity. Hillel ben Borush was in sad spirits; his mind was dark with melancholy. Some affliction had been cast over his soul.

As if I did not know that! thought Aristo.

The rabbi continued that it would please him—"Hah!" said Aristo aloud, with a wry smile—if Aristo would go to the house of the noble Hillel ben Borush that evening and converse with him and give him cheer.

The letter was the first indication that Reb Isaac had even been aware of Aristo's existence, for never had they exchanged a single word or greeting, or even met eye to eye or had acknowledged the other's presence. How he must have writhed to bring himself to this pass! thought Aristo with considerable amusement. He contemplated the proud old man painfully writing the letter to a former slave—thus acknowledging that he had been conscious of him occasionally—and he was more amused. Then he stopped smiling. He sat down on the dry grass and stared at the sheep which wandered through the groves in their eternal symbiosis with the olive trees, and reflected.

A Greek did not consider death at one's desiring and by one's will either shameful or criminal. Nor did Romans, nor Egyptians, nor other sensible people. When a man decided he had had enough of living, or living had become unbearable or dishonorable, his friends and family understood his act and while they were saddened they considered his departure a release from what had been afflicting him beyond endurance. Only unthinking animals suffered life at its worst, and clung to it. And Jews, of a certainty. Aristo shook his head. Jews were beyond comprehension. They considered life sacred, even their own and even when they were afflicted beyond bearing. But life was not sacred unless it had a purpose and a meaning and was as placid and enjoyable as possible. Aristotle, himself, had set the limits on what a man of intellect should be called upon to tolerate in life.

Hillel ben Borush had set his limits. Why should anyone, even a friend who dearly loved him for his virtues, contradict him? It was an impertinence, a vulgar insult, an intrusion, an outrage. A man knew his own heart, his own capacity for suffering, his own reasons, and only a base barbarian would argue from his ignorance of another man.

Then Aristo thought of his loved pupil, Saul, and he pursed his lips, frowning. Saul was a Jew, and the thoughts of Jews were strange and not to be understood. Saul would not agree with either Aristotle or his old teacher, and he had the deepest affection for his father—whom he had never comprehended in the least. "Why can they not let him go in peace and wish him a safe harbor?" Aristo asked himself, and ran his lean hands over his bristling hair, which was now as gray as ashes. Then he rubbed his palms over his bony knees, shook grass from his garments and rose, a tall and agile man as lithe as a youth still, though he was older than Hillel ben Borush. His restless black eyes were still as polished and clear as a young man's, and now they were narrowed with thought. He put his cloak over his shoulders and set out on foot for the house of Hillel ben Borush.

The sun was setting in deep golden light and the scarlet and tumbled mountains threatened the wide and fertile valley as always, and the river ran in brilliant gilt. Aristo moved rapidly and surely along the road, thinking deeply. He had known that Hillel was suffering some ill of the soul or the body in silence, and this had been for many years, but Aristo had a certain restraint which kept him from inquisitiveness. However, he had visited Hillel often, bringing him some fresh fruit from his own gardens, or some Greek sweetmeats which Hillel had appeared to enjoy, or olives steeped in oil and flavored with garlic and peppers, and other Greek delicacies. Of what had they conversed in the evenings and in the early nights? Hillel's children, or the weather, or some newly discovered work of Philo's, or they had argued obscure philosophic thoughts. But of late Hillel would fall into heavy silences and often Aristo would take his departure and Hillel would not be aware of it.

Aristo reached Hillel's house, and was informed by the overseer of the hall that the Master had not returned as yet from his gardens. He led Aristo through the house and Aristo went into the gardens alone. Here the light was suffused with faint rose and gold, and there was a pungent scent of autumn in the air, blowing from the trees, and the leaves rattled dryly. But the red gravel paths were neat as always, and the fountains sang their frail little songs, and the white statues postured among late flowering bushes and the black ornate bridge arched over the pond, writhing with its dragons and serpents, and stood against a deep aureate sky.

Aristo squinted and looked about him, at the marble benches, which were empty, at the bridge reflecting itself in the green stillness of the wide pool, at the black swans and the absurd Chinese ducks and the white swans and the peacocks who were ruffling their Argus-eyed feathers. Aristo saw no one. He had the thought that Hillel was not here at all, for there was no rustle, no movement, no hail. The Greek waited. He called once or twice, "Master! Master?" His voice echoed emptily in the silence.

There was no answer. Aristo hesitated. He advanced further into the garden. There was no sign of Hillel. He came to the bridge, pondering. He walked up its arch, and leaned on its low wall. He looked down into the green water, which was without a ripple. Even the swans did not disturb it.

Aristo gave the slightest start. Then he continued to gaze down into the water, which was much higher than a man's head here, and faintly glittering with the last light. Aristo stood there a long time, seeing, and did not move.

Then he said, gently, "Go in peace, dear Master, and may your God look upon you more kindly than I suspect He will, and may He remember that there was no man more virtuous than you, nor more loving, nor more tender, nor more just. May you find, in the Isles of Bliss, which you merit, what you did not find in life. Farewell."

Chapter 18

"No, lord, you cannot send this letter," said Aristo to Reb Isaac, to whose house he had been called. "Saul ben Hillel is a man of deep sensibilities. Your letter could possibly destroy him, and he is a man who must not be destroyed."

For Reb Isaac, in his grief and his own self-reproach and his own fear for Hillel ben Borush's eternal fate when called before a stern God to account for his deathly act, had written a letter he would have inconsistently deplored in another. He had reproached Saul for apparent disregard and indifference to the kindest and sweetest of fathers, so that that father had taken his life—it was a judgment on his heedless and selfish children. Children who loved their parents and had shown those parents their love never had to endure this sorrow. But parents left lonely and abandoned in an empty house were often driven, in their torment of mind and in their longing and yearning, to the unpardonable act, and the unpardonable portion of it lay forever on the souls of the neglectful children. Who, asked Reb Isaac in a letter reeking with bitterness, had possessed a more worthy father than Saul ben Hillel? That father had never complained of his children's indifference to him. No, he was too tender for that. He had only suffered. Reb Isaac did not exactly call down pious imprecations on the head of Saul but the impression was there. The parchment was stained with his own ancient tears.

"It is an unjust letter," said Aristo, to the old rabbi, whose eyes were reddened and swollen. "Saul loved his father, and so did Sephorah, that beautiful young matron. I knew them well. I knew Hillel ben Borush well also, far more than did many of his—friends. I guessed his intentions long ago."

Reb Isaac regarded him fiercely, his black eyes blazing. "And you did not attempt to persuade him that he must live, you who have more reason than most to revere him and be grateful to him?"

"It was for that reason that I did not so attempt," said Aristo. "Lord, we cannot come to a meeting of minds in this matter, for our philosophies differ. What I understand you cannot understand. What to you is a crime against your God is not a crime to me. Nor to millions of others. We did not ask to be born. But we can choose when to die, for surely a man has dignity! You believe in a life beyond this. I do not, though I wish my dear former Master an existence of bliss. As Socrates said, one should not fear death, for if it is only an endless sleep, is not sleep sweet?

And if there is life after death, it cannot be worse than this life. Have mercy. Do not send this letter to Saul, nor to Sephorah bas Hillel. I will go to Saul, myself, and I will tell him—"

"What?" exclaimed the rabbi, and now he frankly wiped away fresh tears.

"That his father had been ill of an old sickness for a long time. That, you will agree, is true. He had not wished to cause his children anxiety for him, and fear, and so had refrained from enlightening them. That is true, also, though now I see you shaking your head. So, when in his gardens, calmly standing on the bridge, he had been taken with a last chill, a last vertigo, a last fainting, and had fallen into the water. His face, when taken from the pond, was peaceful and quiet—and so it was—and therefore he had not known that he was dying and had not struggled. We can believe, I will tell Saul, that it is possible that he was dead before he fell into the water. I implore you, do not continue to shake your head. For it is true that Hillel ben Borush died long ago, long before that final evening, in the stillness of his gardens."

"Sophistries," said the rabbi. "You Greeks are full of sophistries."

"A sophistry is preferable to the cruel truth," said Aristo, faintly smiling. "And, do we know the truth of this? No. It lay in the heart of Hillel ben Borush, and was not open to the eyes of others."

"Why cannot you tell Saul, then—you so fond of sophistries—that Hillel died tranquilly in his bed, and not in the pond?"

"For the reason that the world is filled with men with wagging tongues, and we can be certain that on some day a visitor to Jerusalem, who knew both Hillel and Saul, will tell Saul that his father was found in the water. We—have been discreet. We implied to no one what we knew, and so Hillel sleeps beside his wife, unreproached. But Saul is a man of imagination. If I lie to him, and say his father died in his bed and he later hears I lied to him, then he will know, of a surety, that his father took his life and I had desired only to spare him. He will not be grateful, but his life thereafter will be one agony. Do you wish that, you, his old mentor?"

The rabbi was silent, and the tears fell from his eyes

and dripped into his white beard. Then he said, in a hoarse voice, "I can understand now how you Greeks have seduced our people in Israel, with your sophistries and your clever arguments."

Aristo laughed softly. "Do you wish that I regret that? No. I am pleased. Your prophets were grim men, I have heard, with no joy in life, and only doom and admonitions on their tongues, and threats of punishment, and other unfortunate things. I have been told that these matters so prophesied did come true. But why should men suffer apprehension in advance? Do not all men err and covet the naughty joys of the world? It is our nature. Lord, I beg of you—I see the words on your tongue—not to tell me the meaning of the prophets and the lowering Countenance of your God. I heard them to weariness from Saul, who lusted to convert me. You and I have two different frames of reference, and never shall they meet. But on one thing we can agree: The gods love a merciful man."

"He is full of mercy," said Reb Isaac, and his voice broke.

"Then I will admire Him," said Aristo. "Write another letter to Saul, and I will take it with me. I have never been in Israel though some of my produce passes through that nation in the caravans. And I wish to see Saul again."

"It is a horror to me," said Reb Isaac, "that Hillel informed me, the evening he died, that he had lost his faith in God."

"Then, perhaps, that faith has been re-established," said Aristo, and smiled. "That will give him happiness."

"In Gehenna?"

Aristo rolled his eyes upwards. "Are you drawing the boundaries of your God's mercy, and making Him less compassionate than a man? Is that not what you would call presumption?"

Reb Isaac reached across his table and drew parchment and ink to him. "I will write Saul a letter more pleasing to you." He gave the Greek a bitter look, and a surly one, but Aristo was pleased.

Aristo took passage on the next and swiftest ship to Israel, carrying with him a consoling letter from Reb Isaac and letters from Hillel's lawyers, for the dead man had left a considerable estate, which must be settled.

On the ship he met a fellow Greek, one Telis, expansive, wise and cynical, who had a house in Jerusalem and estates in Cilicia. He was an amusing companion, and informed Aristo that he had spent over a year in Tarsus and in Rome. The antics of politicians, he said to Aristo, were an endless amusement. He was uproarious over the quandaries of Rome, faced with national bankruptcy, an unsurmountable national debt, wars, insurrections in the streets, riots, and an enormously increasing demand from Roman mobs for new and excessive amusements, housing, food and gifts. "Greece decayed also, from similar maladies," he observed to Aristo, "and the Roman Republic virtuously commented on this, notably one historian, Sallust, and their Cicero, whom I admire. Never, said Cicero, must Rome decline to this depravity—ours—nor this bankruptcy, and the government be a meek slave to the howling mobs of the marketplaces. Nor would Rome, Cicero hoped, ever become so venal, lascivious, corrupt and luxurious." Telis laughed heartily. "But it has all come to Rome, on a much vaster scale than in Greece, and I, for one, am happy over the condition of that nation of grocers!"

"If Rome falls, she will bring down the world with her," said Aristo, thankful that he had land as well as money.

"What a world!" mused Telis, his wily and humorous face puckering with a thousand wrinkles of cynical mirth. "I am over sixty years old, and I find this world endlessly amusing, so craven it is, so weak, so whimpering, so greedy, so exigent, so fearful of government, so heedless of history and its warnings, so brutal and sentimental and filthy with an infinitude of crimes of body and soul!"

"It was always so," said Aristo. "And always will it be."

"My friend, I agree with you." Telis was as tall as Aristo and as dark, but under the darkness of his complexion there was a peculiar pallor. "I am a skeptic," he said, scratching his cheek thoughtfully, as they both leaned over the railing of the bowing ship and looked at the sea and the sky. "I am also not superstitious, as are the Romans. Is it not amusing how they garland their necks with amulets from Delphi and other shrines, both Greek and Roman, and even Egyptian, and the gods know where else? If an oracle at a shrine informed them that they must wear a horseshoe on their heads they would un-shoe every horse in the world, and a horseshoe would be worth its weight in gold. The Romans have already de-based their currency to meet their debts—another sign of imminent collapse—and are using copper. Someone should, of a certainty, start the rumor that horseshoes guarantee the wearer a lifetime of luck and the hand-somest women and feasts and success at the gaming tables, and the Romans could then use iron in their currency, which is cheaper than copper, and lo! most of their problems would be solved."

"Why do we not finance such a shrine and hire the best priests as oracles?" asked Aristo, smiling.

But Telis had fallen into thought. He said, "I have re-marked that I am not superstitious. More than a year ago I acquired a strange pain in my right side, and I began to spit blood occasionally. The episode passed. I ignored the pain, which grew stronger over the months, and went on my journeys. While in Rome I consulted a physician who informed me that I have a cancer in my lungs, and that my days are numbered."

Aristo made a sound of commiseration and sympathy, but Telis raised a hand. "I am returning to my house in Jerusalem," he said, "because Israel teems with holy rabbis who cure the sick in the twinkling of an eye, I have heard, though I never saw such a miracle for myself. Again, I am not superstitious, and most miracles are superstition. But I have heard a strange rumor, out of Israel, from a traveling friend. Another holy rabbi has appeared, it is said, out of Galilee, and on a visit to Jerusalem, on one of their High Holy Days, he cured a blind man, a man in extremis, a woman with a cancer, a crippled child, and, it is said, he raised a youth from the dead, whose body was being conveyed to a cemetery. He has aroused much enmity, and much love. I hear he has returned to his province for a space. It is my intention to seek him out. I will fill his hands with honest gold, and not debased Roman currency. Now, why should not such a man es-tablish a shrine—for us—in Israel, and make a fortune for us?"

"An excellent thought," said Aristo.

They debarked at the beautiful port of Caesarea, and Aristo saw that Telis was growing weaker and paler in spite of his natural liveliness and humor. "I have friends in Caesarea," he told Aristo, "and I have promised to visit them. Herod Antipas built a fine house for Pontius Pilate here, and they know him well. I hear he is a man of some refinement, for all his alleged excesses and brutalities—before I left Israel he had ordered the crucifixion of some hundreds of youths in Galilee for defying the taxgatherers and urging the overthrow of the Roman garrison, and even attacking it, and tearing down its standards and spitting on it. Tut, tut, that grieves me!" He gave a dark smile. "The Romans have their troubles everywhere, in spite of their Pax Romana and their leadership of the world. Do I wish them well?" He made an obscene sign and Aristo laughed.

"One should pity them for doing exactly as Greece did, and empires before her throughout history," said Aristo. "For her end will be the same."

They parted at Caesarea but not before Telis had arranged, magnanimously, for Aristo to be conveyed in lavish style to Jerusalem. "What is money?" asked Telis, with a wink.

Aristo surveyed the country luxuriously as he was driven in a fine gilded car with four white horses to Jerusalem. He did not find it entrancing, for it was winter, and the air was chill and the bare mountains were gray and the fields blasted. The towns appeared dismal to him, and the valleys unfruitful, for he was accustomed to the lushness of the valley of Tarsus, even in winter. As a Greek, he felt superior to all other men, and these poor Jews in the fields and the crowded little towns appeared to him to be a miserable and hopeless people, their faces sullen and reserved and abstracted. He saw the round and square brick Roman fortresses, and the ubiquitous soldiers and the snapping standards of Rome. In Greece there were these also, but the people accepted them with droll smiles and witty tauntings and did a fine cheating business with the Romans, and mocked them merrily so that the Romans had to laugh in spite of themselves, and were friendly. They were also awed at the fabled glory and majesty of an ancient Greece, and desired to be known as cultured also. This was hilarious to the Greeks, who humored them for gain.

But the Jews were a stiff-necked people who thought

their pride and myths would sustain them, and eventually would free them from the Romans. In the meantime they despised them openly and fought with them vainly—a mouse challenging a tiger. Of course, there were the Sadducees of whom Hillel had told him. To Aristo, they appeared wiser men than their fellow Jews, more realistic and therefore more civilized. To do rich business with the conqueror, and rob him in the process—over a goblet or two of wine—was sensible, and a subtle revenge. The majority of Jews did not understand this, or would not accept it. Therefore they were neither clever nor astute, and had no humor.

Aristo was not impressed by Jerusalem, though this was the teeming commercial center of trade between the east and the west, and always full of caravans. But he did admire the delicate austerity of some Greek temples he saw, and smiled at the large ornate Roman ones. He thought the air of Jerusalem dreary and somber, and too crowded. At sunset, he entered the fine inn recommended by Telis, and was pleased both by his bedroom and the fare of the kitchen. The food was a strange mixture of Jewish, Greek, Roman and Egyptian cooking, and exotic, and the wine was excellent, and Aristo thought that he could endure a week or two in this city, and retired to a soft bed and listened awhile to the howling of the jackals outside the gates. He would find Saul tomorrow. As a wise man he refused to dwell on the meeting and the news he must convey. Tonight he would sleep.

The next day Aristo hired a chariot and a driver from his host, who directed him to the Street of the Tentmakers. It was in a very poor quarter, near the walls, and next to the Street of the Cheesemakers, and as goat's hair and cheese are pungent in odor Aristo did not find the air delightful. Again, he was appalled at the queer habits and beliefs of the Jews. The sons of rich men, who chose to be rabbis or teachers, learned a humble trade, for they could not accept either money from their fathers or from those they taught. They had a revolting belief in the sanctity of bare labor and endless work, and despised the idle and the malingerer, though they freely gave alms to the unfortunate.

The narrow little Street of the Tentmakers was very

steep and roughly cobbled, though clean and barren, and each side was filled with tiny shops where the harsh goods could be purchased. Aristo saw the glow of small reddish lamps within, for little winter light reached this street, and he saw the bearded old men and youths in their shops, or saw them bustling about in the rear. They had an air of dedication, such as men who labor strenuously wear, and it depressed Aristo. What a people to believe in work for its own sake, as if hard labor was not to be despised but to be cherished!

Some came to the entry of their miserable little shops to stare at the expensive chariot that came rocking over the stones, for it was evident that few such came here to purchase this humblest of wares. They stared at Aristo in his rich cloak and hood and his embroidered boots and raised their eyebrows. When he halted at one shop and asked for the shop of Saul of Tarsus astonishment overcame the bearded old proprietor. "Saul, Saul, Saul of Tarshish?" he muttered, with incredulity. "You wish Saul of Tarshish?" The old man pointed at the lower end of the steep street. "His shop is the smallest and the poorest, Master, if you desire better goods, I have them."

So, thought Aristo with wryness, our Saul has not told these poor creatures that he is the son of one of the noblest families in Jerusalem. It is certainly like him, unfortunately.

"He has an afflicted eye, and his work is clumsy," wheedled the old man, hopefully. "Now, Master, if you will honor me, I will show you splendid goods."

"I am not buying," said Aristo, with courtesy. "I have come with news of the family of Saul of Tarsus." He gestured to the contemptuous driver, and they rolled down the street. The old man watched his passage in new amazement. What family could that impatient and ill-favored and stricken and lonely young man possess, that one dressed like a king and in a gilded chariot should visit him with news of that family? The old man ran inside to his grandsons to convey the gossip, and to shake his head. "I have heard," said a grandson, "that he studies with the great Rabban Gamaliel." But the old man could not believe it.

The last shop was indeed the meanest, smallest and darkest of all, and Aristo looked into the recesses to see the tall loom and a busy figure seated before it. The Greek stood for a moment or two, observing, and shaking his head. He had seen Saul but once in eleven years, on the occasion of Saul's visit to Tarsus five years before, and the change in the twenty-seven-year-old man appalled Aristo. He was thin to gauntness, and bowed, and his red hair was long on his neck and shaggy, his strong profile like an eagle, his cheeks hollow, his mouth much sterner than before. He was very pale, from lack of sun, and too much work and study. Rolls of goat's-hair cloth lay all about him, and the odor was repelling. His hands flew. His thoughts seemed far away. His garments were those of the poorest of men and his sandals, in this chill, could not have warmed his feet, for they were made of rope. It was apparent that he disdained boots, such as Aristo wore. One tiny lamp, flickering and smoking, lighted the recess, and Aristo, knowing of Saul's afflicted eye, was alarmed.

Saul, feeling himself observed, glanced up impatiently, and the two men stared at each other across the wooden counter that stood between them, also heaped with rolls of cloth. Saul blinked. He did not immediately recognize his old tutor, but he rose courteously and approached the counter. "May I serve you?" he asked, and it was the old powerful voice, full of hauteur and command, which Aristo remembered.

The Greek was so moved and so dismayed that he could not answer, and Saul came nearer, blinking, and now the feeble light shone on those metallic blue eyes and red lashes and the virile nostrils. Then Saul stopped abruptly, and a look of intense astonishment and disbelief rushed over his face, and he cried, "Aristo? Aristo!"

"Yes, it is I, Saul," said Aristo, and he pushed himself between the counter and the wall and entered the dreadful little shop. Saul watched him approach, and then with an odd and muffled cry he flung himself into Aristo's extended arms and embraced him, and clung to him, and tried to laugh but the laugh was more of a dry sobbing. He rested his head on Aristo's shoulder, and Aristo held him close to his own body, and hated himself for the news he must convey.

"Aristo, Aristo," Saul said in a choking voice. "How happy I am to see you!"

"And I to see you, my dear pupil," said Aristo. He was

not an emotional man, but he struggled to prevent himself from weeping.

Saul slowly lifted his head from Aristo's shoulder and stared up at his face, and was silent, his brilliant and intelligent eyes searching. Then he said, very quietly, "It is evil news you bring me." He had always had great intuition, and it was keener now. A spasm raced down his thin throat. "Tell me," he said. "You would not have come to Israel on a mere pleasant journey, or to visit me. It is my father."

Aristo held him tightly by the arms. "It is so," he said.

Saul released himself and went toward the rear of the shop, slowly. He said, without turning, "Come into my bedroom, where I live, and let us sit down."

He picked up a sharp knife and Aristo was freshly alarmed, but he followed Saul to the rear, which was concealed by a length of goat's-hair cloth. The room was tiny, and contained only a low pallet, two chairs, a table heaped with books, a small chest on which a lamp stood, and a tiny unlit brazier filled with ashes.

Saul sat down on the floor. He slashed his poor garments in silence. He reached into the brazier, removed a handful of ashes and strewed them on his head. Then without sound, though his lips moved, he rocked back and forth in the ancient movement of mourning. Aristo sat down in that gloom and misery and now he could not refrain from tears, not for Hillel ben Borush but for his son. He took his perfumed handkerchief from his sleeve and the room was immediately filled with the scent of roses as Aristo wiped his eyes and cheeks and could not stop his tears.

"He was the noblest of men," said Aristo, "the kindest, the gentlest, the most tender. Rejoice that he was your father."

But Saul continued to rock back and forth on his buttocks, and the slit places in his long gray tunic showed his thin arms and breasts and thighs, and the ashes ran down his cheeks to mingle with his tears. And now the faintest wailing came from his lips, in Hebrew, and though Aristo did not know the language well he recognized the sound of grief and prayer.

The room became darker and darker, and Saul was but a shadowy figure, and Aristo sat and waited and shivered in the chill for all his leather boots, his embroidered wool tunic and cloak. He looked about for wine, but there was none. The wailing rose and fell in measured cadences, mournful, even majestic, but terrible to the Greek's ear.

Finally the Greek could endure it no longer. He knew that Saul had forgotten him, and that he could leave this place and his going would not be observed or noted. But Aristo could not bring himself, in spite of his own pain, to depart. Too, he had letters for the younger man.

He said, with sadness, "Saul. Saul, I am here, your friend and your tutor, and you know my love for you, and I know your love for me. We are men. There are letters for you and things you must do, in spite of sorrow. You have a sister, and kinsmen, and they must be told."

It was dark now in the room. Saul stood up, bent and slow as an old man, and he went into the workshop and brought a taper mutely to Aristo, and Aristo understood that he must light it at the lamp in the workshop and then light this lamp on the chest. Sighing, he did so, in silence. Saul had resumed his seat on the floor, and was again rocking back and forth.

The wretched little lamp hardly lightened the room. But now Saul was looking up at Aristo, and he said in a hoarse voice, "Tell me."

However, Aristo himself could not speak, so he gave Saul Reb Isaac's letter, which he had written at Aristo's dictation. Saul bent forward and read it slowly. His father had been ill a long time but had not desired his children to know or to be alarmed. He had died peacefully in the pond, into which he had fallen during giddiness. He lay in the tomb beside his wife, Deborah. He had not suffered, except from weakness. It was possible that he had fallen into the water because he had expired on the bridge. His son would say Kaddish for him on the Sabbath, of course, for a year. Reb Isaac spoke eloquently of Hillel's character and his nobility of soul. The old man sorrowed, not for Hillel, who now lay in the bosom of Abraham, but for his children. He was certain that he would not wish his children to grieve, but to rejoice that the long travail of living had ended for him and had delivered him to bliss and the Vision of God, blessed be His Name.

"Truly, my son," the old man had written, "your beloved father could all his life say with David: 'How amiable are Your Tabernacles, O Lord of Hosts! My soul longs, even faints, for the courts of the Lord. My heart and my flesh cry out for the living God! Yes, the sparrow has found a house and the swallow a nest—Blessed are they that dwell in Your House. They will still be praising You!'

"So your father lived, longing for his King and his God all the days of his loving life, and now he will sorrow and long no more, but rest in peace. The Lord gives, the Lord takes away. Blessed be the Name of the Lord!"

Saul muttered, "The Lord gives, the Lord takes away. Blessed be the Name of the Lord! Hear, O Israel! The Lord our God, the Lord is One!"

Aristo compressed his lips. He would never understand these Jews! The gods afflicted: wherefore should they be praised? Prometheus was a nobler Titan than this. He defied the gods—and who should not, for was not the lot of man dark and desperate and ordained to suffering, his soul flickering out at the last like a little lamp in the eternal night? For this fate then, this fate that moved poets to tears, should a man rejoice? He should rejoice only at the moment when he dies, for he is finally delivered from life, the evil Fates having cut the cord of his existence and returned him to the nothingness from which he came.

He said, "Saul, you have duties, as I have remarked before. I have letters from your father's lawyers. You are a man of property and much wealth, my Saul, and you must consider what you must do."

Saul rose. "I go to the Temple," he said, "where I will pray for the repose of my father's soul." He stopped and looked at Aristo, and now his whole countenance appeared to shatter. "Why did he not write me and call me to him? Why did not you tell me? I would have flown to him at once! O, I am indeed afflicted, that I never looked upon my father's dying face and begged his blessing!"

Aristo sighed. "My chariot stands without," he said.

Saul bent his head and wept. "No, I must walk," and he left the shop in his slashed garments and with the ashes on his head, and that low wailing began again.

Chapter 19

ARISTO did not see Saul again for four weeks, for those were days of family mourning. So the Greek remained in his inn. He had no taste for Roman arenas and gladiators and pugilists. He had lost his lust for women, except on rare occasions. He was alone in Jerusalem, which he strongly disliked for its air of brooding and ominous destiny and pent and silent violence of spirit. Even the Roman soldiers were less hearty here, and went about with gloomy faces. Aristo struck up a few conversations with their officers, and was invited to a few dinners, and entertained at his inn in return. "This Israel," said one officer, shaking his head. "It is more than I can endure. No one can ever comprehend the Jews. Pontius Pilate, once moved to generosity and expansiveness, offered to put a statue of the Jewish God in the temple of Jupiter, so He could be honored, also, and had to withdraw the offer hastily, for all Israel vowed insurrection even if the last man among them died! How can a reasonable man understand such a people? And what a Deity they possess! He is a veritable Pluto! Without an entrancing Proserpine, of course. In truth, there is no beauty in their God, nor in His Heaven, and who would desire to go there?" He shuddered.

"They love Him. One conjectures why," Aristo said. "Nevertheless, you must admit that their Temple is grand and lovely, so it is possible that their God does not despise beauty."

Aristo attended a few Greek theaters and gloried in the spectacles. But he was growing bored when he received a letter from his friend, Telis, asking him to visit him at his house, he having returned from a mysterious journey to a small, and possibly barbarous, little Jewish town called Capharnaum. Telis mentioned that it was a poor market town of no significance. But he, Telis, had a tale to tell! Aristo must dine with him that night.

Aristo was only too happy. He arrayed himself magnificently, as befitted a man of much land and many groves and considerable money, and he remembered that Telis had promised to introduce him to his stockbroker who was a man of enormous talent, in Jerusalem. So he hired a fine litter with silken curtains and rich cushions and was carried in state to Telis' house. He understood that though the majority of men deplored the panoply of wealth—especially if they were wealthy themselves and indulged themselves in that panoply—they had a low opinion of men who dressed and lived simply. Aristo had put his most fiery large opal, surrounded by diamonds, on his right index finger, a chain of emeralds about his neck, gemmed armlets on his arms, a golden girdle about his waist, and jeweled sandals on his feet. His cloak was of cloth of gold. "I am a veritable Zeus, blazing," he said to himself with satisfaction. He would remind Telis that he knew stockbrokers of great gifts in Tarsus, which was a seat of culture. He also had Roman stockbrokers and was invested in a ship. He had not, certainly, mentioned to Telis that he had once been a slave, and from some gestures and intonations Telis had unwittingly displayed at times Aristo suspected that Telis had himself once endured that state. Gentlemen do not recall unpleasant matters to each other. Aristo had hinted that a dear friend of his, the noble Hillel ben Borush, had left him a considerable legacy—which was quite true—and had also hinted that the legacy had been given in gratitude, which Aristo hoped was true.

The house of Telis was on the lower flank of a mount which was unusually green with trees and groups of cypresses, and it was a large and impressive building of white stone and gardens and gates, and Aristo was duly impressed. It was sunset, and the house beamed with rose. Telis met Aristo in the portico and embraced him and his voice was full and round as if greeting a friend one has known for life but has not seen for a long time. His manner was high and exuberant, his walk swift, his gestures vivid. He conducted Aristo into the atrium, which was colorful with Persian rugs, lively with bright murals on the walls, and large and stately and excellently furnished with tables of lemonwood and ebony and carved chairs inlaid with ivory and mother of pearl and gorgeous with velvet cushions of every hue. There was a fountain in the center, of alabaster, somewhat indecent and depraved, but beautifully carved, and the leaping waters were scented with the odor of lilies. Aristo was careful not to display undue admiration, for this incited contempt as for a base fellow who had never seen luxury before.

However, it was also evident that Telis expected some comment, discreet, as from a connoisseur, and from one who knew the worth of treasures. So Aristo kindly remarked that this bronze or alabaster statuette on a golden or black onyx pedestal was surely worthy of a Zeno, or even a Phidias, and those Alexandrine lamps in purple or crimson glass were among the most delicate and graceful he had ever seen. Even his friend, the noble Hillel ben Borush, of Tarsus, noted for his magnificent house and treasures, had no better than these, and everyone knew that Hillel was a discriminating collector of art. He had had emissaries not only in Greece but in Alexandria, also, being somewhat of an Egyptologist (and may gods overlook the lie, thought Aristo, if there are gods, for was not my Master a man of better taste?).

These amenities now concluded, Telis clapped his hands and the overseer of the hall entered and Telis ordered him to tell his mistress, the Lady Ianthe, that his master and his noble guest, Aristo, were prepared to dine. While waiting for the summons from the Lady Ianthe they would enjoy a goblet of wine in the atrium, which was pleasantly warm.

"The Lady Ianthe is your wife, Telis?" asked Aristo with some surprise, for Telis had never spoken of a wife before.

"No. My daughter. A childless widow, alas, who now dwells with me. She cossets me like a devoted wife, and I do not reject the cosseting, for she is my only child."

Aristo preferred the company of young women, and girls, and he was somewhat distressed at the thought of a middle-aged widow, for Telis was at least sixty for all his newly virile appearance and the color in cheeks and on lips which had not been there on the ship. Aristo hoped that Telis observed the "old" Greek order, and that Ianthe would not be present at dinner, and then he remembered how Telis had jested over the "old" Jewish women who kept hidden in the houses of their husbands. "What is more charming than a fair face at a feast?" he had asked. "Women are not intelligent, but they are enchanting to gaze upon."

Chilled wine was brought, and the goblets, wreathed in vine leaves were of carved silver and the wine was marvelously colored and the flavor delightful. Aristo made a judicious face on tasting it, and knowing his host was watching, gave a slight nod, the cultured accolade, again, of the connoisseur. He wondered, not without amusement, if Telis knew he was attempting to deceive him, and so the air between them took on a mirthful sparkle. He glanced at Telis and wondered anew at the new animation of his host, his vivacity, his color, the vitality of his hair and his look of absolute health. Was it possible that this man was the pale and tenuous shadow he had met on the ship from Tarsus, the shadow who had a cancer and had but a short time to live?

"You are looking much improved in health, Telis," he said.

Telis' face took on a light of ardor and his dark eyes glistened. "Ah!" he said. "That is a miraculous tale, which I intend to tell you tonight!"

"You have met one of those holy Jewish rabbis who cure in a twinkling?" asked Aristo, with incredulity.

The overseer returned to announce that the dinner was waiting, and Telis rose and said, "Let us dine, if it please you, my friend. Then, we will converse."

They entered the dining hall and Aristo was again deeply impressed by the large beauty of the room, which was far handsomer than the dining hall of Hillel's house, and crowded with treasures, and here large Chinese vases stood in corners filled with gilded sheaves of wheat and exotic flowers and huge green leaves, and the air was scented. The white marble floor gleamed where it was not hidden by beautiful Persian carpets, and the table was covered with cloth of silver and five slaves were waiting, beautiful boys finely clad, to serve the lord and his guest.

Also waiting was a lovely woman, apparently not yet thirty, and in her ripest and sleekest years. She was tall but slight, and she was clad in a blue silken chiton with a jeweled circlet about her slender waist, and her sandals were jeweled also, and her white arms were bare and smooth and exquisitely formed, as was her neck. She had the true Grecian face, with the round full chin, the daintily curled red lips, the long nose that tapered from her white brow, without an indentation at the bridge, and the calm smooth brow. Her eyes were like silver coins and very bright and sparkling and her lashes were autumn colored, as were her brows, and her auburn hair was dressed in the Grecian manner and bound with silver ribbons. Brilliant earrings clung to her rosy ears and cast their reflection on a cheek like pink alabaster. Aristo had not seen so enthralling a woman since the delightful Deborah bas Shebua, and he silently, with his eyes, gave her the worship of a Greek due a woman like a goddess. She saw this, and smiled demurely, and dropped her eyes.

Her father took her hand tenderly and again she smiled, this time with deep affection, and Telis said, "Is not my Ianthe a veritable naiad?"

Ianthe blushed, and Aristo was delighted, for he could not remember seeing a woman blush before, and this was no virgin but a widow. She sat beside her father and it was evident that she intended to give all her attention to his comfort and to help him to the most tasty morsels, and Aristo marveled at such devotion and envied Telis. The woman, of course, was a fool, but an adorable fool, and Aristo approved of beautiful women who were fools.

Alas, that his next thought was that all this luxury, all these jewels, were not the result, of a certainty, of honest dealing and virtuous affairs. Aristo suspected that his host was engaged in some nefarious business, such as smuggling under the noses of the Romans, if not worse, as well as open pursuits. So, Aristo envied him, and wondered if his friend, Telis, could not give him a confidential word or two when they were alone.

Aristo was confirmed in his suspicions when he saw the silver platters, and the silver and enameled plates and the golden spoons and knives and the gilded goblets. The napkins were of the silkiest of Egyptian linen and scented with rose. The repast was not like Roman repasts, of which Aristo had recently sadly learned from his new Roman friends. It was Greek—though, thank the gods, the wine was not resinous. But it was of a Greek style that could only have been inspired from Olympus, which cultivated Jews now favored above their own fashion in food. There were tiny brown fish broiled in butter and smoked British oysters, and butter as sweet as honey, bread as white as snow and hot as Hades, roasted lamb in a divine sauce with mushrooms and touches of rosemary and bay and ginger root from China, artichokes in sour wine and garlic—a mere suggestion of the latter, unlike the Romans —a roasted pig so small that it was evident it had not even had time to suck, and russet and crackling and luscious and stuffed with herbs on a gleaming platter with a pomegranate in its mouth, and rolled cabbage leaves filled with spicy hot meat and grapes steeped in wine and honey, and gilt bowls heaped with a medley of fruits and nuts and a carved board bearing many choice cheeses, and pastries so delicate that they appeared fashioned of clouds, enclosing sweetmeats that oozed a thick red jelly. And wine whose bottles were so dusty that they attested to age and mellowness.

Ianthe never ceased a soft and gentle murmuring as she selected morsels for her father to eat, but that murmuring did not annoy Aristo. It merely added to his enjoyment. He watched Ianthe's white hands deftly moving, deftly serving. She had little time to eat, herself, though the boys expertly served her and Aristo, gliding like beautiful statues about the table. Somewhere, there was the benign and musical stirring of zithers and the threnody of a harp, and all was harmony, and the lamps glowed and the wine was beyond compare.

Aristo noticed that his host, so tenderly coddled by his daughter, ate magnificently and with gusto, and his plate was constantly refilled, and he drank like a Roman centurion. Moment by moment he was a man rejoicing, who could not have enough of the rejoicing, and sometimes, when she gazed at him, Ianthe's charming lower lip trembled even though she smiled. There was something very mysterious here, Aristo reflected. Moment by moment Telis became younger and more vibrant and heartier, and his lips gleamed with oils. The man was transformed almost into a youth. Aristo began to feel like Tantalus, and his impatience grew.

The Bacchian feast drew to a close and Ianthe retired after bestowing so sweet a smile on Aristo that he was stunned for several moments. When Telis began to speak Aristo was forced to make a strong effort to hear and understand him. But finally his astonishment grew and his disbelief.

"When you left me at Caesarea, dear friend," said Telis, "so that I could visit my old acquaintances there, I became extremely ill. I woke, one morning, after distressing dreams, to discover my bed soaked with my blood, which had flowed from my mouth. My friends called their best physicians, including one who waits upon Pontius Pilate, himself, and they announced, with shakings of the head, that I was in extremis from my cancer. I could not lift my head from the pillows, nor could I swallow aught but a little wine, and I prepared to die.

"This was sorrowful to me, for I have lived a life of excitement, if not actual joy, and I still consider life, as we Greeks say, the Great Games. I have property and extensive lands in several countries, and my bankers and brokers are comparatively honest men—as much as it is possible for bankers and brokers to be, which is not extraordinary, alas—but I still wished to engage in the Great Games, and I have a daughter, who is the light of my soul." Telis sighed. "You will have observed that women of intelligence are not devoted nor greatly tender, for they have sharp eyes for men's deficiencies of character and are not averse to conversing about them on all occasions, even before guests. If a man ails, they are wont to regard him coldly and suggest that he rise and go to his countinghouse or his business or other affairs, as the household needs money and the bankers are pressing, or a daughter requires a dowry or a son is entering adolescence and there are celebrations to be arranged. Moreover, the gods need sacrifices, and God help the household which neglects them! I will admit," added Telis, "that under such prodding and pressure we do rise from our sick beds and before sundown arrives our malady has mysteriously disappeared. Nevertheless, a little tenderness and commiseration—while they will delay our recovery—soothe a man's soul and are balm to his flesh. Often a man's ailments are not of the flesh at all, but of the spirit, something a woman of intelligence will not tolerate in the least. I fear such women suspect men do not possess spirits.

"On the other hand, the stupid woman is sweetly servant to her husband, or father, and she will indulge him with tenderness, and not urge him to rise and put on his garments and leave the house and apply himself to his affairs. She will persuade him to rest in his bed, and will bring him delicious morsels and feed him with her own hands, and order the best wine for him, and will sing, if she has a pleasant voice, and stroke and cool his brow, and keep the household quiet about him while he contemplates his illnesses and listens intently to the grumbling of his body, and indulges himself with grave thoughts concerning life and death and the meaning of it all. As I have said, this is not conducive to the quick restoration of health—illness under these circumstances can become delightful and lingering—but does a man live for money alone, or even good health?" At this Telis winked and Aristo laughed.

"So," said Telis, "I grieved over my daughter, Ianthe, who will inherit my entire estate. As she is beautiful as well as wealthy, she would be a prey to evil and exigent men. A thought comes to me: Is Ianthe stupid at all, or is she one of those rare women of intelligence who pretend to be stupid in order to please men? There are moments, when I come upon her diligently working over the household accounts, and swiftly writing in books and summing up, and scrutinizing the reports of bankers and my investments, that I am impelled to believe that she is a genius of a woman, in that she pretends to stupidity but is, in truth, a woman of mind. But so long as she does not claim to be an Aspasia and insist upon the recognition, I will not complain. However, I feared for my Ianthe, for even an intelligent woman is no match for taxgatherers and ruthless lawyers and bankers and brokers, who regard a woman without male protection as their natural prey, to be devoured.

"I also did not wish to die for I do not cherish the thought of extinction, nor do I believe in the gods nor in the Elysian Fields—a dreary country if one is to believe the priests. I also have a charming mistress, and I love good food and excellent wine, and though my life until I was thirty years old was dire in the extreme, I now live pleasantly. So, I did not reflect on death with equanimity.

"While struggling with the blood that constantly welled up into my throat, and I fought to breathe, I remembered the story I had recently heard from Jerusalem of the mysterious young rabbi who cured so many with one word or one gesture. He had a few dingy followers from his poor province of Galilee. Nevertheless, he was acclaimed as being far more proficient in the matter of instant healing than other Jewish rabbis of whom I had heard.

I had also been told that his followers, and even himself, claimed some mysterious direct contact with the Godhead, which is unusual among these holy Jewish healers. I do recall, before I left a year ago or more on my travels, that one wild man from the desert roared into Jerusalem, prophesying this rabbi, saying he came to 'prepare the way.' All laughed at him. Now, this is strange. It is said that Herod did not laugh at him at all, and asked him if he was the reincarnation of one of their prophets—a peculiar name. I believe it was Elias. Who knows about these Jewish gods? At any rate, King Herod Antipas appeared to be impressed by this stormy man from the desert, one of their screaming Essenes or Zealots, or the gods know what they call themselves, though they are a poisoned thorn in the side of the Romans, and for that they have my gratitude."

Telis motioned to a boy and the goblets were refilled. Three of the boys were listening closely, their eyes large and intent, but Telis and Aristo were unaware of this.

"Herod," said Telis, "is half a Jew and half a Greek, as are most of the cultivated men of Israel. It was amazing, therefore, that such a man, the Tetrarch of Israel, and powerful, and a friend of Pontius Pilate, and a sacrificer to the Roman gods as well as an observer of Jewish laws, and brother-in-law to Agrippa in Rome, and a man of no small mind and of much learning, should even condescend to listen to the ravings of a bearded and sweaty and unwashed denizen of the desert. However, incredible though it seems, Herod did listen. He was even prepared to honor that wild man! Is that not astonishing? But even the most distinguished men are sometimes superstitious. How did that wild man repay such unbelievable kindness and condescension from a king? He reviled him, he accused him of the most monstrous of crimes, he shouted before him that he was an adulterer and a murderer, and perhaps even worse!"

"No!" exclaimed Aristo. "That is beyond belief. A beggar—and a king. But, in truth, nothing surprises me very much concerning these Jews. I have even observed in Tarsus, on their High Holy Days, the most noble among them scouring the streets for the most degraded and abandoned, inviting them to feasts and filling their hands with drachmas. I often believe they are mad. But continue."

"Thank you. I believe Herod's patience was finally exhausted. He had the madman beheaded because of his insulting prophecies and his revilements. And then Herod brooded. No one knows why. Even his brother's wife, whom he took from his brother and married, a lovely woman named Herodias, could not console him, and she is a veritable Aphrodite, I have heard. I tell you all this because the wild man from the desert spoke of that unknown holy rabbi to whom were accredited the most astounding of miracles. Such rabbis love their God, but this particular rabbi—" Telis shook his head wonderingly.

"Go on," said Aristo, after a few moments.

"Yes. You know that we Greeks have an altar to the Unknown God. It is related that one distant day He will establish Himself on that altar for our ultimate worship, for it is said that He is greater than Zeus, himself. The Egyptians and the Babylonians and the Persians have this tale, also—and await Him. It is an old story. He will rule the world of men, when He comes, forever. The Jews call Him their Messias, but He belongs to all."

"So I have heard, from my noble friend, Hillel ben Borush."

"Ah, yes. To be concise about it, it is rumored that that holy rabbi, lately appeared, is the Unknown God."

Aristo burst out laughing, and laughed until there were tears in his eyes, and one of the boys, seeing his crimson face and hearing his gasping, refilled his goblet hastily. Aristo drank the wine in one gulp, and it appeared that he was about to choke. Merrily, he looked at his host with a mist over his eyes, and waited for companion laughter. But, to his surprise, Telis was very grave and completely silent, and he was looking down at his clasped hands and appeared not to have heard Aristo's mirth. The newly ruddy cheek swelled and contracted, and to Aristo's stupefaction a tear dropped upon it.

"I saw the Unknown God," said Telis.

Has he gone mad, himself? asked Aristo inwardly, with dismay.

"Please bear with me," said Telis, and now he looked at Aristo with such passion, such emotion, such urgency, that Aristo was freshly astounded, for he had considered

Telis a realistic and pragmatic man, whose reason controlled him at all times and who had nothing but disgust for the man of vehement and disorderly mind.

"I have lived in Israel a long time," said Telis. "I know that very often rabbis appear whose followers claim that they are the Messias of the Jews, for they perform miracles and are blameless men. So there is a law in the Sanhedrin that such rabbis, or teachers, or dwellers in the desert, must be brought before the Court for questioning, and examination, for even the wise and learned men of the Sanhedrin are eager for their Messias. But at no time did the rabbis claim to be the Anointed One, and were sad that their followers so shouted. They wished only to serve their God in peace, they said, and then the Sanhedrin dismissed them. They did not blaspheme, these meek and gentle men. As you know, a blasphemer, among the Jews, deserves death and he usually is visited with it.

"But, I heard in Caesarea, this new rabbi was not denying that he was the Messias, among the poor people of his province, nor was he rebuking his followers for so claiming. It was nothing to me. It was enough that he was a miracle-worker. I lay in my bed in the house of my friends, and contemplated. I made inquiries. The miracle-worker was in his province of Galilee, in the miserable little town of Capharnaum, on the shores of the Sea of Galilee. My friends, who are superstitious, offered to send a retinue for the Jewish rabbi, and escort him to their house—they are excessively kind. It is a long distance to Capharnaum.

"But that night I had a most mysterious dream. I dreamt that a large white hand, like marble, extended itself to me and a voice—a most beautiful voice—said to me, 'Come. I await you in Capharnaum.' So in the morning, though I was still too weak to raise my head, I told my hosts that I would leave for that wretched little town in the blasted hills. They are Greeks, and they were aghast. They called to me a Jewish elder, of much renown in Caesarea, who told me that though the majority of the Jews believe that the Messias will appear in heavenly splendor, so that all nations will know Him instantly, it was also prophesied that few or none would know Him.

"The elder repeated the words of one of their prophets from the Holy Books:

" 'He was despised and rejected by men, a Man of sorrows and acquainted with grief. And, as one from whom men hide their faces, he was despised, and we esteemed him not. Surely, he has borne our griefs and carried our sorrows! Yet, we esteemed him stricken, smitten by God, and afflicted. But he was wounded for our transgressions, he was bruised for our iniquities. Upon him was the chastisement that made us whole, and with his stripes we are healed.'

"I confess," said Telis, "that I did not understand these words, which meant nothing to me. But the elder did not urge me to desist from going to Capharnaum. I had told him my dream. He covered his head, in the way of Jews, and appeared to pray, and then he raised up his hands upon me and blessed me and asked that I be given strength. After he left me I was indeed given some strength and I prepared for my journey, in accordance with my dream."

Aristo could say nothing. It was as if he had suddenly been seized by a spell. He looked at the full and ruddy face of his host, and at the sparkling youthful eyes, and was silent.

"My friends were kind," said Telis. "I left the next morning in their most luxurious car, and covered with fur rugs, and attended by their most solicitous servants. It was a long journey to that area of black basalt hills and earth and desolate mountains and starved little valleys. But it passed like a dream. I slept and rested. I was taken by the most ardent desire to look upon the face of that holy rabbi. My blood still oozed from my mouth. At times I was delirious and fevered and we halted often at various inns. There were even other times when I believed I was already dead, for all was a haze before me in which glittered brilliant threads of light. Often I was not aware at all. Death was at my throat. A heavy languor had my limbs, and I rejected food.

"You do not know these little Jewish towns, so poor, so driven by the taxgatherer, so despairing, so dejected, so shabby and sad and crowded with wretchedness. They are full of woe and hopelessness. They live in fear, yet they are proud. Capharnaum was typical of them. I was now beyond speech, and the days had heat and the nights were cold, and death grew closer. We found a desolate little inn of much rudeness, and there we spent the night.

"The next day the kind servants asked about the holy rabbi, and they were told that he could be found in the streets and addressing the sorrowful people and bringing them a message of hope in their anguish. They loved him. They thronged about him, touching his garments, beseeching him with tears, and he smiled upon them gently and spoke of the mercy of their God. It was said that his words moved them less than his countenance and his manner, for he appeared all love and strength and fortitude and consolation.

"So the next day I ordered the servants to convey me in a litter through the dreadful little streets of Capharnaum, searching for the holy rabbi. I thought to find a venerable old man with a white beard and a halting step, for there are few young holy men! But we came on him suddenly, as he was speaking near a fountain, and the women and the children and the aged men and the youths and the maidens were crowded about him, in their miserable clothing and with their scarred hands, and they could only gaze upon him, weeping, seeking to touch him. The women carried baskets on their heads, filled with a few wilting vegetables, and some had jugs on their shoulders for water, and their children were almost naked in their poverty, and the old men, too weak with age and hunger, sat on the stones near the rabbi's feet. It was enough for them that he was there.

"I raised myself in the litter with an enormous effort and saw him."

Telis paused. He could no longer restrain his tears. The slave boys, listening, were moved to tears also. Aristo frowned. All this seemed unworthy of his friend.

"I tell you," said Telis, in a hoarse and breaking voice, "that never have I seen a man like this! Ah, he was poor and clad in the roughest garments and he wore sandals with wooden soles and ropes about his ankles, and his cloak was poor and patched. But, he was as a king! He was fair, as are the people of Galilee, who have not mingled with us, and as fair as the Macedonians and the people of Cos, and his hair and beard were golden and he had blue eyes like an Athenian sky. He was young. But he was tall and muscular and virile, and his cheeks and hands were brown with the sun, and he had power and majesty. He was a king in rags.

"I knew him at once. Do not laugh, my dear friend. I knew him instantly as the Unknown God, and do not ask me how I knew. I do not know it, myself! But a surety came to me, and a joy beyond imagining.

"About his broad shoulders was the inevitable prayer shawl of the Jews, and he moved the tassels as he spoke to the people in the gentlest accents. I do not know what he said. I was filled with gazing and exultation. I watched him touch cripples, and fondle the little babes in their mothers' arms, and it was as if a god had condescended to these poor wretches, and their faces glowed with joy.

"Who was I, I asked myself, that the Unknown God should glance at me, or care for me? It was enough that I had seen Him, had known Him. I was prepared to depart, for a deep peace came to me, a surcease of anxiety and pain, and death no longer was of importance to me. I had been blessed, by the mere gazing upon Him. I wanted to sing, to embrace, to laugh, to love, for it was as if I had been renewed, and the blind given sight. What was my illness to me?

"It was then that He turned His heroic face to my litter, and we gazed at each other across a long space, in silence. Then He smiled. He lifted His hand to me in salutation, as if recognizing a friend who had come a long distance to see Him. I immediately fell into a deep long sleep. I did not awaken for some time, and then we were far from Capharnaum.

"But, my friend! Strength and health were flowing in me! The oozing of blood had halted. I was furiously hungry. I demanded sustenance. When we reached an inn I bounded from the litter and the servants stared after me in amazement. I ate as a starving man eats."

Impossible, thought Aristo. Or, he had encountered a sorcerer with spells.

"Look upon me!" cried Telis. "I am in the most perfect health! The physicians are baffled. They can find no fault in my flesh, no cancer! It did not happen day by day. It came in a twinkling, in an instant. The Unknown God cured me by the simple glancing of His compassionate Eye!"

Aristo cleared his throat. He said, "Then you will become a Jew, in gratitude?"

Telis looked at him strangely. "We know that Jews proselytize, and seek to bring all men into their own knowledge of God. But He upon Whom I gazed said no word to me. He gave me His holy compassion, as brother to brother. I await His call."

"His call!" exclaimed Aristo, with more and more incredulity.

"Surely it will come," said Telis. "In the meantime, I will be a more honest man."

Aristo reflected. It was said the Jews could cast the most amazing spells. It was obvious that such a spell had been cast upon Telis by a poor and nameless Jewish rabbi. Aristo was happy that his friend had recovered his health. But if he were about to become an honest man that boded ill for Aristo's own ambitions to learn new secrets of acquiring riches.

"You will know!" said Telis, in a buoyant voice of absolute conviction. "You also will know!"

Aristo thought that a depressing prospect. He wished to enjoy life, and one knew that Jews did not enjoy life. The nameless rabbi had been ragged and poor. He could have made his fortune in Greece, and in Rome, where all men are superstitious.

Telis gleamed with happiness and vitality, and this Aristo could not deny, for the dying had been given strength and youth again. Aristo shook his head in dubious denial.

Telis said, "You have looked upon my daughter, Ianthe, and she looked upon you with interest and pleasure. Consider her as a wife, Aristo. Let me tell you. I was once a slave, but I had a good Roman master, and he educated me, and left me a legacy and freed me in his will. Therefore, I do not hate all Romans. But—I have been a slave."

Aristo was greatly moved. He said, "I, too, Telis. But consider what you have offered me! Your daughter, who shines like the moon. She could have a worthier man."

Telis held out his hand to him at the table, and Aristo took it, and it was as if a shock of great power passed from him to Aristo, and Aristo's heart became light. His head blazed with radiant phantoms, and he knew the first joy since his youth, and the first love for a woman. In this mood he could even overlook the delusions of his dear friend.

Chapter 20

SAUL BEN HILLEL said with gloomy contempt, "I am amazed that you give even a semblance of belief to the story of your Greek friend, Telis, who has a lurid reputation in Israel. Not," added Saul, with a shadow of a smile, "that this is too nefarious, considering that he swindles the Romans, and smuggles richly and has been known to sell the Roman ladies marvelous rare gems which later are revealed as worthless pebbles or polished glass. He has friends among Roman and Jewish officials whom he bribes lavishly to overlook or conceal these rascally things, but I believe there was an interdiction against him for three years in Rome. It appears he sold a Roman lady, alas, a magnificent Egyptian necklace which he alleged was of the purest gold, exquisitely enameled and set with the finest gems. Unfortunately, the Roman lady had a brother who was a Senator, and he had a friend who was a jeweler, and it was discovered, after Telis had neatly taken himself off to lands unknown, that the necklace was not only not worth the twenty-five thousand gold sesterces the lady had paid for it but that it was of gilded brass, the 'ancient' enamel was merely cheap paint, and the gems were flawed or imitation. I believe the price was finally determined as being worth five drachmas, or less. And that is the man who told you the strange story about an alleged Messias out of the burning hills and meager valleys of Galilee, and Nazareth!"

"He says," said Aristo, "that he has now become an honest man. Or, to quote him directly, 'a more honest man.' "

Even the grieving Saul laughed reluctantly. "I see he has not wholly committed himself, which is truly Greek. I am willing to admit that his precious Galilean rabbi may have some healing powers. Many of our poor wandering rabbis do, for they are selfless and truly holy men, in that they serve God rather than man and keep all the Commandments and Judgments and sacred admonitions. You say he had told you that he had a cancer. Did you consult his physicians? Did they swear that he had that disease, and that now he is mystically cured? No. It is possible that he had no cancer, or the physicians were deceived, and it is also possible that he was merely afraid that some of his crimes had been discovered and he was about to be arrested. That would be enough to give such an awesome thief pains and chills and fevers, and perhaps a bloody cough. But when the danger was passed, he recovered. I am giving you the choice of explanations, my Aristo."

"I only know that he appeared to be a man on the verge of death," said Aristo. "I have seen many dying men in my lifetime; I am rarely deceived. He had all the aspects. Telis is no fool. He is a cynical man and not superstitious. Yet, he is convinced that a miracle was performed for him."

"A miracle performed for a lighthearted and unrepentant and unbelieving infidel?" asked Saul, shrugging. "A thief? A famous criminal? God does not grant miracles for men who are sinners, unless they repent and say, 'God, forgive me, a sinner.' But what did your friend do? He merely had a rumor; he merely had a dream. So he hies himself to the miserable rabbi of Nazareth and he is instantly cured of his malady. He is not even a Jew!"

Aristo bent his head with mock humility. "Yes, I comprehend. Your God disdains all but Jews, and therefore we are presumptuous in hoping, or believing, that He may glance at us kindly at times."

Saul laughed again, a little less reluctantly than before. "I am always speaking rudely and roughly, though that it is not my intention. I am no diplomat, alas. You know I did not intend to insult you. I was only exposing your story to the light of day, my dear Aristo, my dear friend and tutor."

Aristo was touched, remembering the younger Saul who could blurt and then remorsefully apologize, as this older Saul had done now. "Still," he said, "the man was dying. I often heard his racking coughs on the ship. I saw him furtively wiping away blood from his mouth. Even if he had not had a cancer, but the consumption of the lungs, it would not have been cured in a twinkling. Verily, the man was dying. And now he lives, and is well and like a youth and full of the joy of life, and health. Why this was done for him I do not know, but have you not always said that God moves in ways that men cannot understand?"

Saul smiled. "I have given you my own sword, have I not? Well. You also spoke of your thief's story of the wild man of the desert, who was executed by King Herod. I met him once, in the wilderness. One Jochanan, son of two old Galileans, a lowly priest named Zachary, and his wife, Elizabeth. I was convinced that he was a madman, but he had a wizard's voice and eloquence, and could deceive even my friend, Joseph of Arimathaea, who took me to see him. I admit he had an appearance of a young prophet, a manner of speaking which was overpowering, and that he was not an ignorant man, though a Galilean, and had learning and was familiar with the Pentateuch and all the other Scriptures, and could quote from them.

"He dazzled me, as he did others, and then he offended me. Or perhaps I misunderstood his rude accent, though Joseph did not speak of that. He implied that the Messias had already been born! 'Unto us a Child has been born, unto us a Son has been given!' Now, that is blasphemy. If the Messias had been born Jerusalem would have been lifted to the very heights in a ring of glory and light, and would glitter in the sun. Holiness would abound on the earth; truth, justice, love and immortal life and peace would have established their reign in the instant of a breath. The gates of Jerusalem would have suddenly been set with scintillating jewels, blinding in their intensity. Labor would be no more; the winds and the rains would set the seed and harvest it, and cities would be built in a second, at the mere command of a voice. The Messias would have built His new Temple between one breath and another, and there would have been restored to it, at once, the Ark, heavenly fire on the altars, the Golden Candlestick, and there would have been in that temple the Shechinah, and the Seraphim, for all to see. The nations of the world, hearing of these wonders, having been informed of them, and of the resurrection of the dead—in accordance with the prophecies—would have poured from the four corners of the world into Jerusalem, heralded by angel voices. And Israel would have absorbed the world in one boundless beatitude of love, and there would be no other nations.

"Has this come to pass?"

"No," said Aristo. "And, candidly, it does not appeal to me. I am one who prefers this world, with all its injustice and vagaries and uncertainties. At least, because it is capricious and unpredictable, it is interesting, whereas the world of which you speak would bore me to a longing for death—which you have said would then be unobtainable."

"You prefer, then, the yetser hara, the impulse to evil. Ah, my Aristo! You will never change. But let us return to that Jochanan, the Essene of the desert, the barbarian and madman. I do not condemn the Essenes and the Zealots. My heart is with them, for do they not love God and their country and uphold the Law and despise the oppressor, and refuse to obey him? But that Jochanan was a deceiver, a believer in his own phantoms. He believed that the Messias is already amongst us, and that is not only folly it is blasphemy. We punish blasphemy, adultery and murder with death. He fled to escape it.

"Last year he appeared in Jerusalem, heralding, he said, the coming of the Messias, and said that he was preparing the way. He influenced many unlettered and simple men, including a goodly number of Greeks. He baptized them in water, and told them that he had already baptized the Messias, Who is sinless and needs no cleansing, blessed be His Name! You see how absurd all this is? As you know, we Jews have the ritual of washing to be freed of sin. Is the Messias sinful? It is a blasphemy even to ask the foolish question. Yet that Jochanan, whom the Greeks now call John the Baptist, had the unpardonable effrontery to say he had performed the ritual for the Messias! For that alone he deserved death, and he received it."

Aristo yawned. "You Jews," he said, with a fond smile at his former pupil. "You speak of your Messias as the Anointed, presumably of your God, the Christus, as the Romans would call Him. You think that a miracle of miracles. But as you know our gods and our goddesses mated regularly with mortals and had a multitude of sons and daughters, and we do not marvel and contemplate the thought in ecstasy. Gods are gods, and they have the attributes of mortals as well as their venalities, and I think the thought charming and beautiful. In any event, my friend, who is a man of considerable learning, swore that the rabbi who cured him was the Unknown God Whom we await."

"Blasphemy," said Saul. "Do not smile. Was not your Socrates given the hemlock cup because he blasphemed?"

"I believe the real reason was because he urged young men to think, and not meekly accept the beliefs of their fathers and their government as sacred, but to reflect for themselves. Who knows what turmoil he would have created had he been permitted to live? Good and wise men surely deserve to die, for they are alien to this world."

"You are not serious, of course," said Saul, with a flash of his usual deep impatience before jesting. "Ah, I wish that mountebank, of which your friend has spoken, as did Jochanan, the Essene, that pretender who permits the ignorant to believe he is the Messias, would come to Jerusalem, and I would denounce him to his face and expose him to punishment!"

"But, I heard he has already visited this city, many times. Do not you Jews have a command that those able to walk or ride appear in this city on your High Holy Days? Yes. You have told me. So that poor Nazarene, from the misery and dejection of Galilee, must have been here very often in his lifetime. I also heard he performed miracles here."

"I have heard of no such miracles!" cried Saul. Then he halted. He stared at Aristo with his eyes which were so like the blue glaze on a sword. "Did your friend note his appearance?" He had turned somewhat pale and the freckles on his gaunt face were prominent.

Aristo thought, then described the rabbi as his friend had told him, and as he did so Saul's red eyebrows became a knot over his eyes and his long wide mouth whitened.

"What is wrong?" asked Aristo, finally noting all this.

"Nothing," said Saul. "I think I have seen that Nazarene, twice in reality, once in a feverish dream. I knew him for what he was, immediately. A sorcerer. Therefore, he stands condemned, for such have a devil." He shivered, and then, to his own amazement, he felt a deep pang of a grief which had no name, but seemed connected with a betrayal.

Aristo was growing more bored with the conversation. They were seated in Saul's appalling little bedroom, with its earthen floor and all its pungent smells. Aristo had brought wine and cakes with him, which Saul had absently shared. The dull little lamp flickered; the day was drawing to sunset.

Aristo said, "My friend told me, later, that the rabbi, holy or not, was not alone, that he was accompanied by disciples, or followers. Among them was the son of your great and powerful Annas, himself, of whom even King Herod is terrified and whom Pilate honors above all else. Who truly rules the Temple, but Annas, as the Jewish elder told my friend, and who can ruin or raise men up, and who controls the treasures of the Temple, but Annas? Is he not also a high priest, father-in-law of the High Priest in Jerusalem, one Caiphas? Yes. You see, I inquired of these things, for then they interested me, though I confess they no longer do. Annas has a son, one Judas Iscariot, a rich young man, and he is a follower of your ragged holy rabbi."

"Nonsense," said Saul. "I have heard of that son, an Essene, whom his father disinherited, though his mother dotes on him and sends him rich gifts of money. Nonsense."

Aristo yawned very widely now. He had stayed long over his time in Israel, because of the Lady Ianthe, to whom he was betrothed, and whom he adored. There was still the matter of the dowry to settle, and though Telis now proclaimed himself a completely honorable man he was not above shrewd dealing. Men, even with a vision, are still men, Aristo thought, smiling. He would return for his bride in six months, for her period of mourning for her dead husband had not yet been completed. Aristo was also certain that Telis, that careful trader and rascal, was doing some investigating, very quietly, of his prospective son-in-law. Aristo was not offended. He would have done the same, and in fact, he had already done so.

He said to Saul now, "You have matters of estate to settle in Tarsus. Are you not returning with me?"

"I have lawyers there, and agents," said Saul. "What does property matter to me? I will arrange to have it given to the temple in Tarsus, and a certain tithe for the Temple in Jerusalem."

Aristo stared at him as if he was mad. "It is riches!" he cried. "You are a rich man, a man of power! And you would give it all away! Come, my Saul. You are not demented, are you? You are not serious?"

"I am not demented, and I am serious," said Saul.

"O gods," Aristo groaned, rolling up his eyes. He had another thought. "What of your beautiful sister, Sephorah, and her children? Do you not wish to leave them a fat legacy?"

"Sephorah has her own dowry and she is married to riches," said Saul. Then he fell into thought. "I should like to see my dear father's tomb," he said in a sad deep voice. "I should like to say Kaddish for him in his own temple in Tarsus. Yes. I know my sorrow will grow greater in Tarsus, but it cannot be avoided."

"At least, keep your house, which your father loved," said Aristo. "It will be a refuge for you, in Tarsus, when the world grows too much for you."

"Perhaps," said Saul, with indifference. But at heart he was not indifferent. He thought of the house in which he had been born, and which was filled with loved memories. He would keep that house, for it was Sephorah's home also, and she spoke of it wistfully.

He said, "There is one thing of which I cannot forgive myself: I never understood my father."

Aristo sighed. "Saul, Saul. Do you understand me, or your sister, or your friends? Do you even understand yourself? No. Therefore, do not reproach yourself for not understanding your father. It is more than possible that he did not understand you, either."

"I do not know why," said Saul, smiling his pale and reluctant smile, "but in some way you comfort me, as none other can, no, not even Rabban Gamaliel nor Joseph of Arimathaea."

"It is, probably, because I speak sensibly," said Aristo, "and not in mysteries and in symbols."

He took his leave of Saul with affection. Saul sat alone after his friend had gone, and absently drank some of the good wine, which he really did not taste, and he pondered, and there was more than sorrow in his heart. There was a dread and shadowy uneasiness which he could not name, but which was like the haunting of great wings over his soul.

Chapter 21

RABBAN GAMALIEL was discussing philosophies with his pupils, among them Saul of Tarshish.

"The Greeks," he said, "have declared that there is a great similarity between their Ascetics and our ancient Faith, and have pointed out that God, blessed be His Name, has commanded us not to be obsessed with the secular world—for fear of losing our eternal spirits and the world hereafter—and their Ascetics have declared that the world of men is extraneous to the spirit, ordered by arcane and demonic divinities and inspirations.

"But there is a difference of tremendous proportions between us and the Ascetics. The world is not irrelevant to us; it is part of our being, as our body is of the earth and the dust thereof, and our physical manifestation is as animal as that of the bull and the horse and the bird. In that manifestation we must deal with the material part of the world, and if we fail in this, our duty, we have failed the Almighty Father, also, for has He not told us that His Messias will take on our flesh, and would He take on our flesh if it were despicable and unworthy of Him —He who created it? To despise the world, therefore, and the creatures of the world, is, in a measure, to despise God, Himself. Why do you frown, Saul of Tarshish?"

"Forgive me," said Saul. "I am afraid my mind wandered somewhat, for a moment."

The famous Rabban's lively face puckered slightly. He knew that Saul had not been entirely candid in his reply, for the young man was flushing. The Rabban resumed:

"We Jews acknowledge that there is a spirit of Evil in this world, Lucifer, the fallen archangel, for in the Book of Job it is related that God and Lucifer contended for the soul of that faithful man. Whether symbolic or not, we know, each man of us, that good is always warring with evil in our own hearts, and that is not mystical but actual. As God has His Legions of the Blessed to assist Him, so Lucifer must have his legions of the Damned to assist him, and so we acknowledge the actuality of demons, though the Sadducees smile superbly at the idea and speak only of a man's 'conscience,' which they allege is the creation of the superstitions of the man's parents or his own response to living, or his particular religion or of no religion. But the Sadducees do not explain why a man has a conscience at all, whether fantasy or reality! Only man possesses such. Why? No matter. That is not part of this argument, though the Sadducees do aver that man is good, is inclined to good, and therefore has the inner voice of Goodness.

"But we do not believe that the spirits of evil, however malign, are more powerful or as powerful as the Spirit of Good, which is God. The Greeks believe that in their realm they are as powerful, and that is why they often sacrifice to them to propitiate them. The more pious among us exorcise them, if manifesting externally, though we know that the internal manifestation is more formidable. We should, therefore, perhaps," and the Rabban smiled his genial smile, "exorcise ourselves!"

The pupils gave him the expected chuckle. He became serious again. "We know that some unfortunate men are possessed by demons. However, these are rare. The true evil lives in the heart of men. But that is not the argument. The Ascetics of the Greeks believe that as the world is alien to men, under the reign of demonic divinities and therefore inhospitable to the spirit of man, it is necessary to destroy the world and all its manifestations, including our learning, our art and our law. In short, anarchy. The Ascetics may believe this desirable—but can man live in chaos? No, he would perish. I believe that is the malicious desire of the Ascetics. They appear to believe that if the world is destroyed and the physical manifestation of man is destroyed thereby, the spirit of man is released. To what they do not specify. Can spirit live without manifestation in some form? God, Himself, manifests Himself in His Creation.

"The Ascetics and the Jews, accordingly, are far apart in explaining the world and evil. But we do acknowledge the Golden Mean of the Greeks. A man should not be entirely of the world, lest he lose his soul, nor must he be entirely of the spirit, lest he lose his common humanity —which is a manifestation of the Lord, blessed be His Name. We have understood this for a long time, and that is why we fear and suspect the man of absolute mind who does not know how to labor and to deal with the things of the earth. Absolute mind can be evil as well as good. Moreover, it has a tendency to madness and excess. Man stands with a foot on materialism and with the other foot in the realm of spirit. That is why, knowing this, we have said that the world is truly our home, and that the Messias will transfigure it, and our flesh, and make it a house worthy of the spirit. We cannot encompass the thought as yet, for we think of the world as of boundaries and limitations, but to the spirit there are no boundaries and no limitations. It is a great mystery. It is Truth, but it is always a mystery to our finite minds.

"In conclusion, we should remember this: If God did not love this world of ours, but only despised it, He would not send His Messias to us. Rather, He would lift the souls of men above the world, and destroy the earth beneath—this lovely green garden of God. Let us, then, love the world of men, not with maudlin sentimentality or with delicate tears of insincere compassion, but because the world of men is a manifestation of the Almighty. Man must be judged justly but never with lenience. His sins must never be explained away, lest God is mocked. As he pays for his errors of spirit in the world hereafter, so he must pay for his errors of flesh in this world. He is responsible for his actions, which the chaotic Ascetics would deny. Whether weak or strong, foolish or wise, slothful or industrious, beggarly or proud—man must answer solely for himself, judged wisely and impartially among his fellows. He is not a slave to circumstance, as the Ascetics imply. He is master of all he thinks and does. Other men may oppress him, but in his soul he is free. How he responds to that freedom is answerable to God.

"In short, we Jews declare that man is born free and remains free, no matter his environment, whereas the Greeks talk of Fate, especially the Ascetics, who would prefer to blame Fate for their own sins and evils and not themselves, and wail that it is the world of their fellows which is responsible for their immediate state—and not their own weakness and indifference and apathy, and inferiority of will. I have my own theory about the Ascetics: They hate and loath themselves, for they know what is in their hearts, and therefore, for all their protestations of love for man and sorrow for his fate, they truly hate man, as an extension of themselves."

He sighed. "It is an old aphorism: We hate and condemn in others what is really in the secret places of ourselves. But rather than condemn ourselves—for man is conceited without reason—we prefer to chastise and denounce our brother, and accuse him of the vileness that lives in us. And, to conceal that vileness, we will eagerly sacrifice the reputation, the happiness and even the life of our neighbor."

"Then," said Saul, "man is truly contemptible?"

The Rabban studied him intently for a few moments. "I did not say that, Saul of Tarshish. Have you not been listening to me?"

He seldom rebuked his pupils, and this was the first time he had rebuked Saul. The young man flushed with mortification, and his harsh blue eyes hardened. The other pupils, who did not love him, bent their heads demurely and smiled in their young beards. This further mortified him, and his lips became tight.

Later he said to the Rabban, "I am leaving tomorrow for Tarsus, for there are matters of estate to settle, the legacy of my father. I intend to sell all, and to give all to the temple in Tarsus and to the Temple in Jerusalem."

Rabban Gamaliel considered him with secret thoughts. He said, "That is an exemplary thought, but God, blessed be His Name, has also exhorted us to provide for ourselves in this world, so that we will never be a burden to our neighbors and our communities. Our religion is a very sensible one, and practical."

This was not the reply Saul had expected, and then he remembered that the Rabban, though famous for his charities, did not neglect the well-being and the luxuries of his household. Nor did Joseph of Arimathaea. "As I have explained," said the Rabban, "we live in two worlds. We should despise neither. So, I advise you to keep some part of your fortune, lest you come on evil days and can no longer labor. You will then be an imposition on your people, and that is manifestly unjust."

"But God has commanded us to charity and the building of His Temples."

"He has also commanded us to use the common sense He has given us," said Rabban Gamaliel.

He looked at the back of the young man as the latter retreated from him, and he shook his head. There was one, it appeared, who believed that in despising and retreating from the world he served God, and that it was necessary to reject man in order to accept the Almighty! How unfortunate that he had been born a Jew! He should have been an Ascetic, of the Greeks. Then the Rabbān fell into deeper thought concerning Saul of Tarshish, and his spirit pondered and was troubled.

The early summer day shimmered with light and every street of Jerusalem appeared to sparkle and quiver with it, even the Street of the Goat's-Hair Weavers and the Street of the Cheesemakers, and the crowded bazaars and the narrow alleys. The cypresses and the myrtles, the karobs and the palms, the sycamores and the pines, were encased in light, so that they seemed to be exuding it, themselves. The dust was golden and dancing, as it rose in the air under a footstep, or the hoof of a camel or an ass or a horse, and the far mounts were the bright color of copper. Every wall poured with red and purple flowers and vines, and the people were exuberant, for the day was so brilliant and yet not too hot, and enlivened by sound and bustle. The fields beyond Jerusalem were at their most vivid and fertile green with rising grain, and the young grapevines displayed, secretively, the fattening green fruit on their stems, which would later be large and opalescent. The olive groves on their terraces were a shining silver in the light, and sometimes they resembled glowing forests of mercury. The citrons bore yellowing globes.

Even the somber Saul was not indifferent, however he tried, to the wide generosity of the day and of living. He sat in a large car with four black horses, the loan of Joseph of Arimathaea, who was accompanying him to the Joppa Gate. There, Joseph would leave him in the car, for the journey to Caesarea, where his ship awaited to bear him to Tarsus.

Joseph, these days, appeared filled with the spirit of excitement and expectation, which mystified Saul. Joseph did not explain. But there was a vast perceptible joy in him, and a brightness of countenance, as though he had heard wondrous news. He did not confide in Saul. He saw Saul rarely now, for the younger man gave the impression of constant retreat, even from his few friends.

As they approached the walls of the Temple—which shone like a huge golden mirage in the sun, domes and spires and towers aflame—they saw a large crowd in the street. Roman soldiers stood idly on the periphery, indolent in the summer warmth, their thumbs tucked in their leather girdles, their bare legs spread far apart. The crowd was unusually quiet, not vehement and laughing as usual as when something out of the ordinary attracted them. Joseph held up his hand to the driver of the car and the man drew in the horses. Joseph said to Saul with quiet command, "Come, and hear."

Wondering, Saul alighted with him, drawing about his shoulders his plain woolen cloak and walking in his rough sandals. Joseph gently touched a shoulder, and the owner turned—to stare at the rich gentleman in his fine clothing and the slave who followed him, red of hair and hard of lip and angular of jaw. Then the man moved respectfully aside, and another and another and another, until Joseph and Saul, unchallenged, reached the inner edge of the crowd.

In the very center of the broad Roman street stood the stranger Saul remembered, the rude Nazarene with his fair locks and fair beard, broad muscular shoulders and large blue eyes. He wore no cloak. His robe was of coarse gray cloth, his feet as humbly shod as Saul's. His arms were bare and strong, and so was his sun-burned throat. Saul winced at the sight of this blasphemer, the man Aristo had claimed had cured his friend, Telis, nearly a year ago, through some dark sorcery—if indeed Telis had been cured at all. This was the man whom the wild Jochanan had heralded, it was rumored—the Essene the Greeks now called John the Baptist, newly dead, having rid the world of reason of his incoherent presence. (Saul could not, himself, understand his own burning aversion and inexplicable rage at the memory of that day in the desert when Jochanan had so misinterpreted the prophecies, nor the fact that these emotions increased on every recall.)

There was a small gathering of Pharisees at the edge of the inner crowd, conspicuous by their blue fringes, and a few litters containing—it was evident—some delicate Scribes, the men of "pure mind" whom Rabban Gamaliel so excoriated. They were listening to the Nazarene intently, the Pharisees with vexed faces, the Scribes with faintly amused smiles. They held kerchiefs to their thin noses and inhaled the perfume, as if the Nazarene had an offensive odor. What interested Saul for a second or two was not the Nazarene but the tolerance of the Pharisees, those pious and learned men, and the Scribes, who considered themselves learned. Why should they listen to this unlettered peasant from the provinces, even for a single moment?

Then Saul was caught by the Nazarene's expression. It was not gentle now, nor compassionate and mysterious, as it had been on that dreadful day of the crucifixion of the Essenes and the Zealots, nor was his countenance as sadly benign as it had appeared when Saul had first seen him, so many years ago. Saul was struck by the fact that though this man must be well within his fourth decade he appeared as young as he had appeared over twelve years ago.

His face, strong and manly, expressed at this time both anger and contempt and disgust, and the hands that swung at his sides were clenched. His blue eyes sparked and glowed. He was gazing at the Pharisees and the exquisite Scribes, and the crowd was listening with silent pleasure. It was evident that the Nazarene had been addressing the Pharisees and the Scribes in undisciplined language.

The Nazarene had begun to speak again and his pale cheeks suddenly flushed and his voice was loud and passionate in the sunny quiet, in that clarity of morning light. It was also—as Saul suddenly remembered from before—like muted thunder, and no one stirred, not even the affronted Pharisees nor the sneering Scribes.

"Woe unto you, Pharisees, for you love the uppermost seats in the synagogues, and greetings in the markets! You tithe mint and rue and all manner of herbs, and pass over judgment and the love of God!"

"Not to be endured!" said Saul to Joseph, who did not turn to him and who seemed fascinated by the Nazarene. But Joseph laid a quelling hand on his arm and Saul fumed, and listened again. The crowd had begun to chuckle with approval, and was glancing slyly at the Pharisees and the Scribes.

It was incredible to Saul that the Pharisees did not turn away with contempt and why the Scribes did not order their litter-bearers to run down this man who threw such remarks into their faces.

The Nazarene captured the Pharisees' eyes—as it were —within the rims of his own fervent eyes, condemning them—they the pious who held only to the Book and the Law, and the Scribes—who honored only men who thought and did not regard those who labored worthy of civilized consideration. It was strange to Saul that the Pharisees, who despised the Scribes, as the Scribes despised them in turn, should stand shoulder to shoulder together, as if they were friends and allies, while this man hurled epithets against them both. But what was that rude Aramaic saying: "When you need a thief to catch a thief, you cut the rope." It was apparent that the Pharisees and the Scribes had this in mind in some form.

The Nazarene spoke in Aramaic and Saul reluctantly had to admit that he gave the "language of the people" both eloquence and power, and his look was authority and there was a curious gleaming on his brow.

"Woe unto you, Scribes and Pharisees, hypocrites! For you are as graves which do not appear to be graves, and men walk over them not aware of them! Woe unto you also, you lawyers, for you put burdens on men too grievous to be borne, and you, yourselves touch not the burdens with one of your fingers!" His eye now fell on a group of taxgatherers among the lawyers present, and his chest swelled and his throat enlarged, and Saul felt his first approval. For the lawyers were the friends and supporters of the taxgatherers and invariably, in the courts, stood with them against the despairing petitioners, and were often taxgatherers, themselves.

"You build the sepulchers of the prophets, and your fathers killed them! —Woe unto you, lawyers, for you have taken away the key of knowledge. You did not enter in, yourselves, and you hindered those who desired to enter!"

He turned to the people now and cried, "And I say to you, my friends: Be not afraid of them that kill the body! They can do no more but that! But fear him, who, after killing the body has power to cast into hell. Yes, I say to you: Fear him."

A veil of lighted mist floated before Saul's eyes and he heard the sudden rising and furious beat of his heart, and he was afraid, fearing one of his infrequent seizures. But he did not tremble, as before a seizure, nor did sweat break out upon his forehead nor did his tongue cleave to the roof of his mouth. Rather, he experienced as one experiences in a dream, remote yet imminent, strange yet familiar. He heard the Nazarene speaking, in that haze of illumination, yet he did not hear the actual words until the last roared in upon him:

"When they bring you into the synagogues and before magistrates and powers, take you no thought how or what thing you shall answer, nor what you shall say! For the Holy Spirit shall teach you in the same hour what you ought to say."

The Nazarene had spoken in plain Aramaic, and there was no language plainer. Yet, of a sudden, it came to Saul that he spoke in mysteries, which needed a key, and which could not be understood in a single moment or even after pondering. Saul knew that Jews had such a way of speaking, especially these poor, sore-footed street rabbis, so it was not new to him. But it was obvious that this Nazarene meant that only the Spirit of God could solve mysteries and not a learned man of great repute—no, not even Rabban Gamaliel, one of the Pharisees this peasant spoke of with such huge scorn.

The silent Pharisees and Scribes still had not moved. Then a man in modest garb, and young, and bitter of face, approached the Nazarene, who turned at once and waited in courteous silence. The Nazarene was still breathing as one breathes who has been consumed by anger, but he was visibly controlling himself, and he bent his head to listen.

The Pharisees exchanged a glance with each other, and moved closer to overhear the conversation. The young man gave them a murderous but servile glance, then turned solely to the Nazarene. He had begun to tremble; he made several efforts to speak, choked, then resumed:

"Master, I know whereof you speak, for I have been rejected in a court presided over by a Pharisee magistrate. My older brother and I were the sole heirs of our father, may he rest in peace in the bosom of Abraham. My brother stole my portion. But my brother, who is a rascal and a thief, has a friend who is both a Pharisee and a magistrate, and my plea was brought before him. Master,

I was robbed, my case was thrown out of court, and the Pharisee rebuked me, and my brother laughed in my face and spat at me! A great wrong has been done to me— under the law, which is corrupt. I pray of you, Rabbi, that you speak to my brother and persuade him to do me justice and restore that part of the inheritance which belongs to me."

The Nazarene regarded him and a mysterious look of both impatience and sorrow passed over his countenance. It was as if he had spoken long and eloquently and clearly, yet had not been understood. Yet, it was with gentleness that he spoke:

"Man, who made me a judge or a divider over you? I have said it before and I say it again: My Kingdom is not of this world. Take heed and beware of covetousness, for a man's life does not consist in the abundance of the things which he possesses."

When the man stared at him, uncomprehending, the Nazarene continued. "I am no divider of men."

The man is ambiguous and elusive and equivocal, thought Saul. At one moment he upbraids the lawyers and their taxgatherers, and calls them frightful epithets for their oppression of the people and their injustice. And then, on the other hand, he dismisses a poor man who has been dealt unjustly with in the courts and robbed of his inheritance! Are they not, in a measure, greatly the same?

The Nazarene touched the young man affectionately on the shoulder and looked in his eyes and said, very softly, "For where your treasure is, there will your heart be also."

Saul glanced at Joseph, expecting amused speculation, but Joseph was gazing at the Nazarene as men gaze at the Veil in the Temple, which conceals the Holy of Holies, and his lips were quivering. Saul's mouth fell open in astonishment. Surely Joseph of Arimathaea had discerned the specious fallacy in that Nazarene's remarks, and his adroit moving away from the subject of justice?

But Joseph was as one who had heard a Prophet and an angel of God, and Saul wondered if he had lost his wits.

Then a Pharisee spoke, with a mockery of respect: "Rabbi, I am of poor intellect and you have baffled me. You have accused the lawyers of injustice and of burdens laid upon the oppressed—yet here, at hand, is a poor man so oppressed by his brother and a magistrate, and you tell him, 'I am no divider of men!' If there is a difference, I implore you to enlighten me."

The Nazarene understood instantly that he was being mocked, and the crowd eagerly awaited his response. He said, and he looked deeply into the Pharisee's eye, "You have not understood because in your mind is only confusion, and you will not understand. I say to you, The life is more than meat, and the body is more than raiment."

Swift comprehension came to Saul as he heard this, and for an instant it was plain to him what this dusty Nazarene had meant, in the most subtle of fashions, and yet not subtle and even with a plainness. There was no ambiguity at all! Then, like a fog passing over a clear landscape full of light, comprehension departed from Saul and he was contemptuous and disgusted again, and in dimness.

Several miserably clad men now gathered about the Nazarene, and Saul knew them for his disciples. All the poor street rabbis had such disciples, vagrant, hopeless yet hopeful men, pious, ignorant and meek, who longed for justice and the Messias. The Nazarene prepared to leave, then all at once he turned his great august head and looked directly at Saul, and something deeply blue and radiant shone in his eyes and he smiled. Then he was gone with his friends.

Joseph said, "He knows you."

"Not at all!" exclaimed Saul. "I have seen him rarely, once in a market place when I was a youth, with one he called his mother, once more at the crucifixion of the Essenes, where you were also, and then in a dream. I have told you." He was enraged again, as he had been before, and yet again he felt loss and sadness. He looked after the Nazarene, but he had disappeared in the surging crowds. "I have never exchanged a word with him. And why should such a word be exchanged? Who is *he*?"

"You will know," said Joseph of Arimathaea, as he had said so many years ago, and he would say no more. The Pharisees turned now to their friends, and the Scribes to theirs, and again they ignored the existence of the others.

Saul looked about for the young man who had been dismissed by mere words, and he was astonished, for the young man was gazing after the Nazarene and his shaking lips were curved in a smile and it was as if he had seen a vision, and had heard celestial words, and he was strengthened and comforted. He, too, is mad, thought Saul.

The hasty-tempered Saul had learned one hard lesson: When another man, arguing with you, speaks objectively and with temperance and coolness, and also with dispassionate reason, you can then both define acceptable terms and frames of reference, and the argument can proceed without animosity or heat or disorder, to mutual satisfaction and pleasure. But when a man argues solely from his inmost and emotional tempers, and is entangled, like the Laocoon, with his own passions from which he cannot extricate himself, you argue with him at your peril, for even if you lose the argument in a cauldron of steaming incoherences your opponent will hate you forever afterwards. The Scriptural father did not so resent the rape and seizure of his daughter and the flight with her as he did the theft of his household pieties, for had he not said, "You have taken away my gods?" Take all from a man and he will forgive you. Take from him his sentimentalities and his unreasonable convictions and you have an enemy for life.

To call man a rational being is to arouse the ironic laughter of Heaven, thought Saul. So, as he had a deep respect and love for Joseph of Arimathaea he curbed his usually acerbic tongue and made no comment on the Nazarene, the thought of whom made him more and more irritable. (Joseph of Arimathaea was a Pharisee. How, then, could he have smiled so fatuously on the Nazarene's attack on the Pharisees? What a fine example of irrationality!)

The journey to Caesarea was uneventful and pleasant and Saul was careful to speak only of unimportant matters. He did not see Joseph's half-hidden smile, nor did he know that Joseph understood. Joseph said, "It is unfortunate that your ship will not take you directly to Tarsus but will have to stop at one of the most easterly Greek islands. But the weather is fair and the sea is soft and gentle at this time of the year, and you will rest."

I never rest, thought Saul. Even in my sleep, I never rest. But he forced a difficult smile in order to please his friend. Rabban Gamaliel had also recommended serenity and rest, and Saul had wondered at this, for the Rabban talked continually of the duty of man to live each day in the Presence of God and not to waste a precious hour or moment in wanton idleness and thoughtlessness—for did man not have to account for that hour and that moment?

They were in Samaria, the province of those Jews who laughed at the Judeans and teased them on the holy days by lighting fires on their hills so that the Judean priests would be deceived, and observing those fires would believe that the sun was rising. The Samarians were lighthearted Jews, who enjoyed the hard life in their stony hills and narrow little valleys, and sinned with gusto and airiness and committed adultery with joy, and were hardly better than heathen or infidels. So, when Joseph and Saul halted at a large inn at night it was no surprise—though a vexation—to Saul, to hear the sound of music and the stamp of dancing feet within, and much revelry. "It is not a crime before the Face of God to laugh and dance and sing," said Joseph, whose few hairs were now white. "It is also a delight to gaze at the countenances of the young, when they cavort like new lambs."

Saul would not join Joseph in the common dining room where all this unseemly merriment was taking place. He begged that he be given goat's milk, cheese, some fruit and bread in his own room over the inn, and Joseph gave him a sad look and nodded. But he substituted a bottle of fine wine for the goat's milk Saul had requested, and Saul smiled a little grimly. However, not to offend his friend, he drank the wine and it refreshed and eased him, and as the cheese was excellent and of different varieties and well aged and plentiful, and the bread white and soft and the fruit fresh and full-flavored, and there was also a broiled fish, Saul found himself relishing his dinner. He loved solitude. He could reflect. Once Rabban Gamaliel, gazing at him over the heads of the other pupils, had said, "There are men who can be happy only when enjoying their own misery," and Saul had colored with resentment. The eminent Rabban, he thought, had not understood. Saul found the company of others tedious, especially when those others were not engaged in learned discussions but talked of inconsequential matters, in which he was not interested. What misery, therefore, was there in this?

He was asleep when Joseph of Arimathaea somewhat unsteadily came into their chamber, smiling in memory of a joyous evening. One small lamp sent its flittering light over the yellow plaster of the wall and the low ceiling. By its illumination Joseph could see the sleeping face of the younger man on its flat pillow. It was the face, alas, thought Joseph, of one of the Greek Ascetics, who believed the world was evil and alien to man. (Joseph did not know that Rabban Gamaliel had expounded on this but recently.) Saul's profile was stern, even harsh, the big predatory nose like the beak of an eagle, the jaw angular and firmly set, the mouth speaking only of self-repression and the discipline of self, the large ears combative, the eyelids quivering even in slumber as if restless and discontented, and the mass of thick red hair emphasizing the whole. To Joseph, there was something greatly tragic in Saul's appearance, and he remembered to pray, most earnestly, for joy to enter again into that dark and dedicated and passionate spirit, which believed the way to God was a dolorous way, set with stone and danger and terror and struggles—but never with peace, though occasionally with ecstasy. Joseph blew out the lamp and fell asleep, his mouth still sweet with the taste of wine and roasted fowl and pastries.

The next day they reached the wind-struck and scintillating port of Caesarea. Several of the Roman galleon's sails were already set, and she bobbed and danced on the blinding waters like an enormous dove. Saul's belongings, his chests and his one pouch, were taken below to his small cabin. He took affectionate leave—somewhat stiffly—of Joseph, and said, "I will return within two months."

"Rest," said Joseph. "Reflect. Meditate. It has been years since you have visited your home."

An expression of intense pain passed over Saul's countenance. "Do I not know that? Do I not condemn myself? If I had returned earlier I should have seen my father's face and have received his blessing before he died."

"It is my hope that tranquillity will come to you," said Joseph of Arimathaea. Saul stared at him, incredulously. "I am always tranquil!" he exclaimed. "What passions of this world disturb me?"

But that is not what I mean, thought Joseph. He kissed

Saul on the cheek, like a father, his long oval face tender and melancholy, his large dark eyes liquid and soft. He stood on the dock for a long time thereafter, watching until the last high white sail sank below the blue and watery horizon.

Saul had brought books of commentaries with him to study, but he found a sort of languor, compounded of sea wind and sun, overcoming him. He tried to reprove himself. He fought against a desire to sleep, to yawn, to gaze only on the sky and the sea. It was sinful not to think; it was an offense to God not to meditate upon Him constantly. Man had no reason for being except to study about God and to adore Him, and to endeavor to learn of His Will. For the world of men was but an evil dream which would pass away; it had no substance, no reality. Saul had wandered far away—though he did not know it— from the teachings of his own Pharisee sect. He had absorbed the stringencies, but never the lightnesses, and during those days on shipboard it did not occur to him that this was what the Nazarene, Yeshua, had meant, on the hot street in Jerusalem. Piety without joy, faith without gladness, duty without innocent pleasure, worship without delight—these did not please God, the Nazarene had intimated.

Despite his most formidable efforts—and they were indeed formidable—Saul found himself daily becoming more enervated, more languid. His mind was no longer the sharp knife cutting through irrelevant phrases down to the bare and uncompromising fruit. It wavered away from books, from subtleties. Saul was sometimes surprised to discover himself leaning over the ship's rail, staring down into the fascinating colors of the sea, the changeful colors which were purple and turquoise and limpid blue, transformed at sunset into one endless plain of deep gold. Then the conflagration of the skies awed him, the terrible and silent manifestation of God made him quail. He could only mutter to himself, "When I gaze upon the Heavens, the work of Your Fingers— What is man?" And then, "The Heavens declare His Glory, and the firmament shows His Handiwork!"

Even Saul could not resist this majesty, though only a little before he would have reproached himself that by admiring the world he was forgetting God. I wonder, he thought once, if we have not overlooked many things concerning the Psalms of David, and have concentrated only on his cries of despair and piety? It was, to him, a blasphemous thought and he tried to put it aside.

The name of the small Greek island at which the ship stopped on its long and dreamlike journey escaped Saul, for it was of no consequence and its port was rude and noisy. It had little cargo to be taken aboard except for crude statuettes destined for heathen houses in Tarsus. There was also but one passenger, who was surrounded, on the dock, by men and women who vehemently kissed his hands, his cloak, the hem of his garment, and even his feet, and called him "Divinity!" Children raced about him, pausing to touch him and grin delightedly upon him. Baskets of fresh fruit were laid at his feet as offerings. He was a tall man, obviously a Greek, and of a slender but muscular appearance, and his light hair was mixed with gray and he was a man at least of some forty years. His garments were poor, his cloak patched, his feet in rude sandals, and a big pouch lay near him. He wore but one ornament, a large ring on his right index finger, a knightly ring of singular beauty and fire and of enormous value, and it was this that captured Saul's interest.

He looked at the Greek's face, and saw its pale and sculptured planes and outlines, and its large and steadfast blue eyes. The man had a stern yet gentle appearance. It was obvious that he was not pleased by the adulation poured upon him by these poor worshipers—did they consider him a god?—but he would not rebuke them nor repulse them, out of his kindness. He was a handsome man, yet in some way forbidding, and Saul noticed this with meager approval, and there was a somber level to his fair brows.

"Apollo!" cried some of the people, adoring him. "Asculapius! Chilon!" The children screamed and embraced his knees, and their parents looked upon him as at the sun.

Saul noticed that he carried a staff with the two serpents of Mercury winding upwards upon it, and then he saw that the pouch was really the pouch of a physician. Saul felt some disgust. The man, then, had been born a slave and educated as a physician, and then freed by some benevolent master—otherwise he would not be wandering about the sea islands in such wretched garb and with such

liberty. Like most Greeks, he was probably also a mountebank. Then the thought came to Saul that mountebanks
did not travel like this, in obvious poverty, and there was
also that knightly ring on his long index finger. A gift
from some superstitious rich man? Or, had it been stolen?
Greek physicians, who had been born slaves, were not
above thievery.

Saul had not mingled with the other passengers on the
ship nor had he deigned to give even the captain, Gallo,
more than a curt word. He suddenly found Gallo standing
beside him at the rail of the ship, and Gallo, a big bluff
man, was staring at the miserable Greek slave-physician
with a lighted countenance. "Yonder," he said, "is the
famous physician, Lucanus, adopted son of the greatly
noble Roman, Diodorus Cyranus, whose name all Romans honor. For he was a man of the true Roman spirit
and patriotism and pride, a tribune and the procurator
of Syria, and a favorite soldier of Augustus Caesar. Alas,
there are few left like Diodorus. Lucanus does his adoptive father's memory an honor, for he is celebrated along
the Great Sea, and is a man of considerable fortune, and
one cherished by Tiberius Caesar, himself. He accepts no
fees, no gifts. It is enough for him to minister to the poor.
He will accept no rich patients, except those abandoned
by their own physicians as hopeless, and then he will
demand that they give to help the wretched." Gallo smiled
and shook his large cropped head.

Saul's interest, reluctant though it was, was held. It
was not like a Greek to reject money! "He wears a magnificent ring," he remarked.

The captain threw back his head and shoulders. "It is
the ring his adoptive father, Diodorus Cyranus, bequeathed
to him, and it is of the family!" He hesitated, and looked
sideways at Saul, and then he coughed. "Once he was on
this ship, of which I am captain. It was feared that plague
had broken out among the galley slaves. Many of their
bodies were thrown overboard at midnight, when the passengers were asleep." The captain coughed again. "We
were flying the yellow flag; we were not permitted to land
at the ports. Yet—this Lucanus cured the sick and dying
of the plague in one night!"

"How?" demanded Saul, with some derision. (These
wily Greeks!)

"How? I do not know," said Gallo. "I, myself, laughed at the thought, and gaily reproached Lucanus for affirming that it was the plague. Plague is not cured in a few hours and the victims restored to complete health! My own physician, whom I later punished, also asserted it was the plague."

"So. It was not the plague," said Saul, shrugging.

The captain scratched a thick eyebrow. "I thought not," he said, and his heavy voice was suddenly quiet. "But later I knew it was."

Saul swung to him, his face disbelieving and almost grinning. "Impossible!"

"Ah," said Gallo, very serious now. "So it was said: Impossible. But it was also true. I am not superstitious. I do not believe in the gods. But Lucanus did, of a certainty, cure the dying and restored them to health in a twinkling. It is strange, also, that he, too, denied later that it was the plague, though he had asserted it was the plague in the beginning."

"I see," said Saul. "If a physician denies it was the plague, then it was not the plague."

"But, it was," said Captain Gallo. "I saw some cases of the plague later, and I recognized them. They all died."

Lucanus, the Greek physician, had finally disentangled himself from his adorers, and was coming aboard, carrying his staff and his pouch. Gallo went to greet him at once, and embraced him with fervor and respect and affection. He led Lucanus below to do him honor in his own quarters, with fine food and wine, and as they passed Saul at the rail Lucanus gave him an absent smile and a faint nod. He had hardly seen Saul, nor was it evident that, in truth, he had noticed him at all.

The crowd on the dock had knelt to receive his blessing, before he went below, and he had given that blessing, Saul saw, with a faint frown of impatience and yet with love. When he had disappeared with the captain the throng rose and threw kisses at the vessel, and flowers, and the baskets of the fruit were brought aboard, the only gift the people could bestow out of their poverty.

Saul mused. A rich man who refused more riches, who would minister only to those who could not pay him: It was not like a Greek, nor like other men either! Men, in the majority, are not moved to live in mercy and for mercy. At the very least, they desire fame. But what fame did this Lucanus possess? Only the miserable and the starving, the peasants and insignificant, acclaimed him. There had been no guard of honor to conduct him to this port, no finely clothed man to embrace him, no litter at his disposal.

For some reason, which exasperated Saul, Lucanus suddenly reminded him of Yeshua the Nazarene, when it was obvious there was no similarity at all between a rich Greek who had been adopted by a noble Roman family, and a sun-burned humble son of Galilee.

Chapter 22

THERE is one, thought Lucanus, the Greek physician, on the third day from the little port, who is at war with man —as I am at war with God.

He was reticent, himself, yet the reticence of the young man he had learned was called Saul of Tarshish, of a noble and distinguished Jewish house, was not of his own kind. Lucanus' reticence rose out of his distaste for adulation and fawning, but Saul's rose—it was evident—out of an enormous dislike for humanity. Gallo had said to Lucanus, pointing out Saul to him at a distance on the deck, "There is one who is returning to his home to dispose of his fortune, for he now lives in Jerusalem, and I had been commissioned by a famous Jew, and very rich, named Joseph of Arimathaea, to give him every courtesy and consideration. I was also," the captain grinned, "given a substantial gift. These Jews can be generous. I attempted to make a friend of Saul, of the gloomy countenance, but was repulsed. This ship carries renowned passengers, but Saul will have none of them. If they approach him, he goes to his cabin. I have sent special dainties to him, but he has rejected them, with politeness but also with disdain. A number of bottles of exceptional wine were brought aboard for him, the gift of Joseph, but he gave them to me, not graciously but with contempt. It is said," the captain resumed, "that he despises all mankind. Of a certainty, his glance is cold and censorious and aloof, and he will not respond to any courtesy."

Lucanus was not a man who approached others without encouragement, except if they were ill. Like Saul, he was restrained. But he found himself curious about this young Jew with the fiery red hair, the fierce profile, the afflicted eye, the harsh mouth, and the bowed legs which he tried to conceal under a long tunic. Saul also had a pallor, and freckles, and the sun burned his fair skin. He walked with a rolling motion. His air was abstracted and crepuscular. He frowned. Lucanus had never seen him smile. He wore no ornament at all. He had strong freckled hands, the hands of a man who knew labor. Lucanus also knew much about the Jews, so he understood. More and more Saul incited his curiosity, and this baffled the reserved Greek. Was it the Jew's obvious look of proud misery which attracted him, the icy hauteur, the resolute step, the embittered countenance he revealed to others? The expression of removal, of condemnation, of rejection?

As I have removed myself from God, and condemned Him and rejected Him, so this unfortunate young Jew has removed himself, has condemned and rejected man, thought Lucanus the physician.

The Greek was troubled. It was well to reject God, for He was merciless to His creation, and had, Himself, repudiated the tortured little animal called man, who could only suffer and die without hope or recompense. But, it was not well to reject humanity, which was not responsible for its predicament nor its agonies. If man was evil—as he so monotonously was—then he had been created so. Should he, then, be condemned by the One who had ordained his evil? No, only compassion and tenderness should be extended to him, and his pain alleviated when at all possible—for did he not live in a pain he could neither understand nor conquer? Prometheus, the immortal Titan, who had not been truly man, had been so moved by the anguish of humanity that he had defied the gods, themselves, and had brought light and warmth to the world, out of his tremendous pity. Lucanus could understand Prometheus, but he could not understand Saul of Tarshish, who did not have the look of a stupid man.

One day Lucanus brought himself to approach Saul as the younger man leaned over the rail and stared broodingly at the sea. Lucanus forced himself to smile, and it came to him with amusement that he had as much difficulty in being affable as did Saul. His amusement, therefore, gave him a confidential and merry expression and Saul, turning, was somewhat disarmed. Lucanus said, "Forgive me, but I am interested in your eye. Is it blind?"

Saul was immediately affronted. He said, "No."

The single word was daunting, but Lucanus, who was older, was not easily daunted. "I am a physician," he said. "You must pardon my professional curiosity."

"Why?" asked Saul.

The query was so quick and so telling that Lucanus' inner merriment broke into mild laughter. Saul began to smile, his unwilling smile. Lucanus said, "Will you join me in a goblet of wine? I confess that I am not a judge of wines, though it is possible that you are, Saul of Tarshish."

Saul's red eyebrows rose. "You know my name? I also know yours. Like yourself, I am no judge of wine."

"I thought all Jews were Epicureans," said Lucanus, artfully. He saw at once that his remark had amused Saul. "No," said the younger man. "Many of us prefer Syrian whiskey."

"A bottle of which I possess," said Lucanus. "I, too, prefer it. Wine, to me, however wonderfully perfumed, tastes like vinegar on the tongue. Moreover, it is impossible to drink enough of it—to forget. One only sleeps heavily, a sad sleep, and awakens unrefreshed and sluggish and with a nausea. Whereas whiskey is very rapid and leaves no residue, unless it is drunk like wine. Will you join me?"

Before Saul could reply Lucanus had motioned to a servant dawdling on the deck and had spoken to him. Very soon the servant returned with two small silver goblets and a bottle of whiskey. Lucanus and Saul sat down under a striped awning, out of the steaming sun, and Lucanus poured the golden liquid into the goblets. Saul tasted, made a grimace, then drank a little. He said, "It is possible that you, too, wish to forget, Lucanus?"

"I would I could drink of the waters of Lethe," said the Greek, and his face became a subtle mask of pain. "There are times I cannot endure the agony of mankind."

Saul regarded him in a long silence. Finally he said,

"The agony of mankind is deserved. Have we not brought it upon ourselves?"

Lucanus was acquainted with the religion of the Jews, so did not stare in surprise. He looked into the depths of his goblet. Saul said, "It is, perhaps, not the agony of all mankind which disturbs you, Lucanus, but the agony of one or two or three whom you have loved."

"True," said Lucanus, and lifted his large blue eyes to Saul's face. "But do we Greeks not say that argument should be from the general to the particular, if it is to have verity, and meaning? Yes. The general argument touches all—and none completely. You are correct. I have loved, and I have lost, and now I love no more, except in the general sense, which I have admitted is not valid at all."

Saul did not comment.

"I have heard," said Lucanus, full of pity, "that there is, in Israel, a man of miracles. Is it true?"

Saul visibly started, and his face changed and became ugly. But his voice was temperate and controlled when he said, "We have many wandering rabbis in Israel, and many of them are miracle-workers, for they are simple and God-fearing and God-loving men, and they believe they can heal. It is not unusual when they do. Faith is not incredible." His lip curled.

"But," said Lucanus, who saw that in some manner he had struck a tender spot in Saul, "I am speaking of one man in particular, a man who has caused much excitement in these days in your country. You will recall that we Greeks build altars to the Unknown God in our temples, and we await His arrival. I have heard that the countryman of yours, of whom I speak, is the Unknown God." He watched Saul keenly.

A look of fury spread over Saul's face, and of disgust mixed with horror. Yet, there was no surprise in that expression. "You must remember," said Saul, "that there are many superstitious Greeks and Romans and Egyptians and others in Israel in these calamitous days, and they are always gazing after the preternatural and are urgent for miracles. For they find that the world of present materialism does not satisfy the soul of man, however comfortable and easy materialism is. Man does not live by bread alone. It is disastrous that modern man has discarded his belief in the supernatural, in the Being beyond mere Manifestation—as if manifestation can occur without a cause—!"

Lucanus nodded. "Yes. I recall the words of Aristole: 'Life belongs to God, for the activity of the mind is life, and He is that Activity. Pure self-activity of reason is God's most blessed and everlasting life. We say that God is living, eternal and perfect, and that continuous and everlasting life is God's, for God is eternal life.'"

Again Saul's face changed, became eloquent and moved. He nodded.

"But we were speaking of the new miracle-worker, the rabbi, in Israel," said Lucanus. "Have you heard of him?"

"Yes. He is a blasphemer and a fraud, and a calumniator of better men."

Lucanus pursed his lips thoughtfully. "So I believe," he said. "I do not know about the blasphemy, of a certainty, but I suspect the man is a fraud. I lost my dear friend and servant to him, a black man from Africa, who, having heard an unlikely tale of your miracle-worker left me in the silence of the night and went seeking for him. Ramus was mute. I suspected from the beginning that it was hysteria, though Ramus was a learned man, and healthy of body and mind in other respects. He believed," and now Lucanus looked at Saul closely, "that your Invisible God would not only restore his speech but would deliver his people from the curse inflicted on Ham. So, he sought your countryman, and wandered for a long time."

Saul was staring at him fixedly. "And Ramus died, or was lost."

Lucanus drew a deep breath. "I have had a letter from him," he said. "He swears that he looked upon your countryman and prayed to him in his heart, and his speech was restored and he returned to the land of his fathers, rejoicing." Lucanus hesitated. "My Ramus was not a fool or a peasant. He was acquainted with many languages. He said he had witnessed a youth being raised from the dead —by your countryman—in a little town named Capharnaum."

"It is a lie!" said Saul so quickly that Lucanus was startled. "The man is a mountebank! I have seen him on several occasions, and I tell you he is nothing—nothing at all but a poor workingman, of no learning, from the stony province of Galilee! I, myself, believe he is a cunning sorcerer, that he has a devil."

Lucanus said seriously, "Your Devil, then, has begun to perform good and merciful works?"

Saul's mouth tightened and his eyes flared. "You are mocking me, Lucanus. Evil cannot perform good. That man is deceiving the people, and the Romans will not look on the deception with favor, for he is an inciter and desires to destroy that law and order which is so precarious in Israel." Now Saul was averting his face. "Do not misunderstand me. I am no conciliator and traitor like the Sadducees, who look with indulgence on the Romans. My heart is with the Essenes and the Zealots. But I fear, now, for my people's safety, though I have thought of becoming an Essene or Zealot myself. Above all, I fear for my people's uncorrupted faith—which this man would destroy in confusion and controversy."

He passed his hand over his face. "I am not an articulate man, though my teachers have told me I have eloquence. No matter. It is the faith of the Chosen People which has restored them from exile and calamity and has enabled them to establish a nation and a Temple, and has brought them the Promise of God of a Messias. If that faith is destroyed then God, in His wrath, will smite us again. We cannot permit blasphemy! We cannot allow that God be mocked! To do so is to destroy all that we have so painfully built through the ages, and to cast us again into the wilderness, for millennia upon millennia. Have we not suffered enough? Yes. But the Nazarene has come into the heart of our country and he has permitted it to be said that he is the Messias! Can we allow this blasphemy? No!"

"The Unknown God," said Lucanus.

Saul winced. "I beg of you, Lucanus, to forgive me, but you do not know what you are saying!"

Lucanus said, "It is evident that you love your God. Therefore, you will not pardon me when I say I challenge Him and possibly even hate Him, for what He has done to mankind, for the afflictions He has heaped upon it, and the darkness and the silence and the agony. So little a beast for so mighty a Force to expend Itself upon!"

This was a novel argument to Saul, who looked at Lucanus with amazement. He stammered when he exclaimed rapidly, "You do not understand! It is man who is the affliction, the outrage against God, the contemptible being who stands on his hind legs and dares to gaze upon the Ineffable and to question It!"

Lucanus saw that he had not been mistaken in his judgment of Saul, whose face was contorted with umbrage and anger. So he said pacifically, "I see we can never come to an agreement, to the defining of terms. I am enraged against God. You are enraged against man. It would take a lifetime to conciliate us, to reach an understanding, and, I am afraid, we do not have that lifetime." He smiled. "We can only argue, after all, from our own intimate experiences, and not from the experiences of others, for who knows what lies in the heart of the individual?"

When Saul did not answer but only sat there, fuming, Lucanus said, "I leave this ship tomorrow for another little island—where I will attempt to alleviate the suffering of the victims of your God. We shall not meet again, Saul of Tarshish, so let us part friends."

Saul reluctantly took the Greek's hand and he looked for an instant into those grave and compassionate blue eyes and he thought involuntarily: I should like to have this man as a friend, for all he is a Greek, and a blasphemer against God, blessed be His Name. But I will never see him again.

When Lucanus stood up from his chair under the awning his long tunic gaped at the top and Saul saw that he wore a thin golden chain and that from that chain was suspended a slender golden cross, looped at the top so that it held the chain. Lucanus saw Saul's gaze fixed upon it and he said, "It was the last gift to me of a girl I loved, who had received it from the physician of her father's household. He had told her it was the sign of the Unknown God, beloved of all peoples, and the sign of the resurrection of men's bodies into perpetual life." Lucanus smiled slightly, but Saul, he observed, was not smiling.

"It fell from Rubria's hand into mine, as she died," said Lucanus. "To me, it is a sacred thing." But Saul said nothing. He was suddenly dazed, for he was remembering his dream of the great Seed which had fallen into the earth and had begotten a harvest.

Chapter 23

"YOUR friend and your pupil, Saul, recalls to me the story of Ixion, in Hades, the accursed one who whirls about with soundless howls, following and fleeing from himself," said Ianthe to her husband, Aristo.

Aristo regarded her with admiration. He adored his wife more than ever. To him, she was both Artemis and Aphrodite, elusive like a nymph, and as sturdy as Heres. She was a constant delight. He never knew if she was stupid or very wise, and he dearly hoped he would never find out. Her comment on Saul was profound and subtle, but she had spoken it with the blandness of a child and the delectable sweetness of a witless woman. She was truly delicious and he thanked the gods—in whom he did not believe—that he had discovered such a treasure—with a large dowry.

He said, "Ixion. Yes. My unfortunate Saul. He does not know that he dwells in Hades, and walks the fields of asphodels and inhabits the twilight and sleeps with Despair. Like many Jews, he is haunted by his God. Yet his father was once gay and light of heart and had a humor and his conversation was fascinating, and his sister is a veritable minor deity of much beauty and charm. His mother was not a woman of mind, and she was trivial and frivolous, but she laughed happily and resembled a statue and had graces and could sing. From whence this stormy young man came is a great mystery. Still, when a child and a youth he had a boisterous laugh and a wry wit and much impulsive kindness, and simmered with life and his countenance would dance like wine in the sun. If he lives in Hades, he has ventured there of his own will and was not driven there by circumstance, and if he has espoused Despair he sought her out, preferring her groans to love's embraces."

"He is not handsome," said Ianthe. "Perhaps the girls avoid him. Why does he not marry?"

"He has dedicated himself to his God, like the King of Nemi," said Aristo. Ianthe gave him an amused glance then repaired to her kitchens to oversee her husband's afternoon meal. He had discovered another joy in her. She was an excellent matron and it was her hand which seasoned the dishes at the last moment so that they made the tongue ecstatic. He went out for a moment to contemplate his land with contentment, his wide groves and orchards, his cattle and his sheep, his horses and his asses, his outer buildings which surrounded his pleasant house, and then the wide river running in gold below the scarlet mountains of Tarsus. He thought about Saul with a certain melancholy. Saul had delayed his return to Jerusalem, and lived alone in his father's house with the servants who had been freed, according to the Law, on Hillel's death. But though Aristo invited him often to his own house—he had lured him here but twice—and others also invited him, Saul was more solitary than ever. He had told Aristo that it was his intention to return to Jerusalem before the High Holy Days in the autumn, but it was autumn now and he still lingered. There was a certain silence and lassitude about him which no kindness or affection could penetrate.

Indeed, a kind of apathy had seized on the lonely young man. Each morning he told himself that the next day he must return to Israel, and the days passed and he remained. He felt as if he were one who had been banished from the theater, in which drama was being enacted and great choruses were speaking, and the gates had been closed to him and he did not know why. When the thought occurred to him he laughed at himself for his notions. He spent many hours in his father's library and many hours in the garden, standing on the black arched bridge over the pond on the very spot, he had been told, his father had stood and had there been taken by vertigo and had fallen into the water. Saul gazed down for long periods into that water and a few times he had been deluded that he saw Hillel's body lying there, the garments rippling gently, the white face closed and peaceful.

Saul went to his parents' tomb, but he felt that Hillel did not lie there but lay in the water of the pond. He tried to visualize his father in his seat in the world hereafter, praising God with the seraphim and the cherubim, his radiant face reflected in the bright sea of glass. But he could only see his father sleeping, as if waiting.

His sister Sephorah wrote him in her usual merry

fashion, and he did not discern her anxiety for him, and her love, in the richness of her phrases. She wrote of her family, her husband, Ezekiel ben David, her beloved mother-in-law, Clodia Flavius, her uncles—who were eminently prosperous—and her grandfather, Shebua ben Abraham, whose health was declining and who had lost his old placidity and ease of countenance and urbanity. "But he is a very old man now," wrote the young Sephorah, "and he often wanders in his mind and appears distressed. Sometimes he speaks of our father, testily, as if he were still alive, and a disagreeable thought to him. Yet he often asks when our father will visit him again. It is very strange."

In her last letter she had written, after the usual prolonged news of the family, which was tedious to Saul who rarely thought of his mother's relatives: "We have had much turmoil in Jerusalem lately and much excited discussion, and there is much contempt and laughter. A young rabbi from Galilee has been disturbing the people, and the priests and the Sanhedrin are very anxious, for the Romans are scrutinizing him. We are very frightened that if this Galilean causes riots and rebellions—it is rumored he is an Essene, and we know how fervid such are—the Romans will destroy us once and for all. They have been lenient to Israel, as they have been lenient with none others, exempting us from military service, respecting our Sabbath, refraining from using the image of Caesar on their banners, and even minting special coins for us which do not bear the heads of their tyrants. Nor will they bring a Jew before a magistrate on the Sabbath, nor do they profane the Temple but stand in the Court of the Gentiles with respect and listen to our holy men. It is true that they tax us beyond bearing, but not more than they tax other peoples and their Empire is tremendous. They have shown much tolerance, under provocation, for our wild young men of the desert, who have abandoned the ordered world and have disdained it. But we fear that if this Galilean, who is alleged to perform prodigies of miracles, incites the people the Romans will lose their patience and put us to the sword and burn the Temple. —For the last month we have drawn easier breaths. The wandering rabbi has removed himself from our midst and returned to his hills, and we deeply hope he will remain there. We who have children are always fearful, and look for threats when there are possibly none."

Even Saul, that scrupulous inspector of his own conscience, his own motives, his own thoughts and their sources, could not understand why the very mention of the Nazarene should immediately inflame him with anger and disgust. He took Sephorah's letter to the old rabbi, Reb Isaac, who was now bent and his beard and hair thin and white.

"Once," said Saul, "my sister despised the Romans as I despise them still, and once she admired the Essenes and the Zealots as I admire them—though I am sometimes alarmed by their excesses. One understands that she is the mother of children, and so is distressed for their possible fate, but she is not to be derided for this but rather respected. So if Sephorah, who was well-taught by our father, and loves Israel as he loved it, is made uneasy by this—Nazarene—and fears, then surely we all have reason to fear."

The old man ruminated, not moving his filmed yet still irascible eyes from Saul's flushed face. Then he said, "You have lived for a long while in Jerusalem. Tell me. Have you heard of this Galilean before, and have you seen him? Not once have you mentioned him to me."

The ugly flush on Saul's freckled face deepened. "I have seen him," he said in a pent voice. "I have heard him."

The rabbi waited. But Saul said nothing more. The rabbi said, "And what was your opinion?"

"He is an unlettered man," said Saul. "He is an ignorant Galilean, though I admit that he has eloquence. He speaks in riddles—"

"A common Jewish characteristic," said the rabbi.

Saul made an impatient sound. "But these riddles appear to incite the people. As for his appearance, he is fair like most Galileans. Am I not of Galilee, myself, through my family's blood on my father's side? He is not—uncomely, yet not beautiful. At times he appears most ordinary. At other times—I have heard—he appears transfigured."

"You do not hold him in high repute," said the rabbi.

"No. He is a blasphemer, a mountebank. Surely, Reb Isaac, you have heard from your own friends in Jerusalem, concerning him! He is permitting it to be said that he is the Messias!" Saul's breath came fast and his eyes gleamed with rage. "I have heard that he consorts with harlots and depraved women, and even with taxgatherers! If that is true, then he is the most degraded of men."

A curious expression passed over Reb Isaac's face. "Perhaps he hopes to lead these degenerate wretches to repentance?"

Saul stared at him. "Then you know much of him?"

The old rabbi, seated in his library, turned his ancient head and gazed through the window at the golden countryside. "I know of him. Israel seethes with these wandering rabbis, who sometimes perform miracles. He is one, in these respects, with the others. Yet, we do not hear of the others. Therefore, he is extraordinary, not in fame, not in the world's awareness of him, but in person. Obscure, apparently unlearned, speaking only in Aramaic, without house or household or money or possessions—like the other poor rabbis—he yet seizes on the imagination of those who encounter him. Why? Is he a prophet?"

Saul felt something enigmatic in the manner and the words of the old man. He became wild with impatience. "A prophet! Never was there so bedraggled a prophet! Nor one less honored. Prophets do not blaspheme—"

The old man smiled wryly. "They were accused, very often, of blasphemy, and were not held in respect, if I remember the Scriptures correctly. So, if the Nazarene is reviled by many, as I have heard, then it is possible that he is a prophet. People never change. If I were to be asked to give one description of an authentic prophet I would say, 'He was hated and despised, he was held in ridicule, he aroused the deepest hostility, he was the object of shy malice and derision and contempt, the darkest motives were assigned to him, he was rumored to have a devil.' "

Saul's face became transparent with pallor but the rage increased in his eyes. "He is not a prophet," he said, and his voice was somewhat hoarse. "He is nothing."

"Nothing," said the rabbi, now staring at him frankly, "never arouses emotion. I discern that this Nazarene disturbs you profoundly. I will not ask why. You have given me a reason: blasphemy. I do not think it is that. I think that not even you know."

"I know!" cried Saul, clenching his strong hands on the

rough linen that covered his knee. "He is permitting it to be said that he is the Messias! We know that is blasphemy. I am dedicated to God and His revealed Truth, and I am outraged that this Nazarene presumes—"

"What does he presume?" asked the rabbi, when Saul paused. Saul did not answer. There was a light sweat on his forehead, an indication of intense agitation. The rabbi said, "When you speak of him, you are almost beside yourself. You are a young man of great passions, which you discipline. Why, then, do you become disheveled in manner and speech, and almost incoherent, when the Nazarene is mentioned?"

Saul exclaimed, "I hate him!"

The rabbi did not speak but only gazed at him.

"He will destroy Israel!" cried Saul in a louder voice.

"What? A miserable, beggarly Galilean, however inflammatory? Do we not have guards and magistrates and courts to subdue and suppress him, if he becomes dangerous? Are you not," suggested the old rabbi, "giving him too much importance in your mind?"

"He is of no importance at all!"

The rabbi shrugged. "Then, why do we discuss him? At one moment you show me the letter from your sister, obviously as alarmed as she, and at the next moment you say 'He is of no importance at all.' My son, you have not been candid with me. You say you hate the man, and that I believe, but something stirs in you at the very thought of him."

"He is a sorcerer," said Saul, and then found himself, in spite of his own will, speaking of the Nazarene, of the times he had encountered him, and even of his dream. His voice rose and fell in that great agitation; his hands clenched and unclenched. The rabbi listened and did not move.

Finally Saul said, "He is a sorcerer, and we are commanded to put sorcerers to death. He looked at me and I became faint and for a little I had no resistance and I would have followed him—I would have sought him, as if at a command—I would have given—" He looked at the rabbi in mingled fright, understanding and horror. "Therefore, he seduced my soul, and is a sorcerer!"

Reb Isaac looked at that pale and square and implacable countenance with a strange fixity. Then he rose and went to his window, walking lame and slow, and looked out upon the countryside. He said, "It was your father's prayer, all his life, that he live when the Messias arrives. I believe his—illness—which caused his death came from his disappointment."

Saul frowned. He thought to himself, The old man wanders. He has forgotten our conversation. Reb Isaac said, as if musing to himself, "Your father was told a peculiar tale a few years before you were born, that his cousin's husband had seen a great Star over Bethlehem, from his guard-tower in Jerusalem, during the feast of the Roman Saturnalia, and that it hung in the sky for a number of nights, and then disappeared as abruptly as it had come."

"I recall that story, from my childhood," said Saul. "It was a comet, or a wandering star."

Reb Isaac tottered back to his chair and slowly stroked his beard, his eyes contemplating the floor. "I laughed at the story. I suggested to Hillel that it was a Roman soldier's drunken illusion. I saddened your father's heart. I would that I could recall my words. He believed, or hoped, the Star was the signal of the birth of the Messias."

"I know," said Saul, with freshly rising impatience. "But, it was not. I know that others saw it, including Joseph of Arimathaea, and my uncle, David ben Shebua. However, they were not deluded."

The rabbi sat in thought, pushing his lips in and out through his beard. "I am an old man. You will recall that we say 'The old men dream dreams, and the young men have visions.' I have dreams, and they are mysterious ones." Now he looked straightly at Saul. "I am not certain, any longer, of anything, except God, blessed be His Name." He pondered. "When you were younger, and were in Jerusalem the first time, you were broken and savage with grief that none came to the rescue of the Essenes and Zealots, who were crucified by the Romans outside the gates of Jerusalem. You accused your grandfather of being a pusillanimous man. Your heart was smitten. Yet now you express your fear that this Nazarene will incite the people, this rumored Essene, and cause the wrath of the Romans to fall upon our people. You speak as your grandfather spoke, and as all the temperate men spoke, whom you despised in your youth."

Saul pressed his lips together in vexation. "No, I do not speak like them. My heart is still with the Essenes and the Zealots. I would that my people could drive the Romans from the sacred soil of our country. I would have them die, if necessary, but in a heroic cause, the freeing of Israel, or even in an attempt to free her. But not for a wretched carpenter from Galilee, who is a blasphemer!"

Reb Isaac sighed. "You believe him a sorcerer, and you have expressed your hatred for him. Yet you have also said that you were drawn to him, that it was as if he were about to give you a command."

"Thaumaturgy," said Saul. "An attribute of evil."

"You believe him evil?"

Saul felt a vague confusion. He let his mind wander over his memory of the Nazarene. Thrice he had seen him in reality. He recalled the Nazarene's countenance, his manner, the muted thunder of his voice, his glowing gestures and again that unknown sick pain assaulted him. He said, "We know that evil can come in the guise of an angel of light."

"But evil does not perform good. That would destroy its nature."

Saul looked at him incredulously. "Reb Isaac! You, too, have not been deceived by tales of this man?"

The rabbi lifted his bent shoulders and then let them fall and spread out his hands. "I have told you. I am not certain of anything any longer. I am an old man. It is only the young who are emphatic and vehement and see visions and scream down what is not pleasing to them, and attack that which they cannot understand. I have seen too much in my life to deny anything, however preposterous it sounds, however amazing it appears. If I were younger I would go to Jerusalem and discover this man."

Saul stood up and spat between his teeth, "I will soon return to Israel, and I will see this man again, and I will denounce him to his face!"

When Saul had gone Reb Isaac stood up painfully, settled the red velvet gold-trimmed cap on his head, folded his hands together and prayed aloud. "Lord, let us know the truth of this matter, for my heart is disturbed and my dreams are strange, and there is not the tranquillity of age upon me but the strong disquiet of youth." He thought of what the people had said to Moses, "Let not God speak to us lest we die." The old rabbi shook his head and pondered, knowing it was a terrible thing to hear the Voice of the Lord.

But Saul did not return to Jerusalem as he again planned. He castigated himself, reproached himself that he was wasting time, that God was vexed with him. He had not reached the knowledge of the immediacy of God's presence, of which Rabban Gamaliel had spoken, nor had the divine silence been shattered, nor was the way shown to him yet. He could only serve doggedly, as a faithful but neglected servant serves, out of love and devotion. He had periods of ecstasy, flashes of sudden intuition in which all seemed explained, and his spirit glowed with rapture. But the next moment he could not even recall the sensation of the experience, or what he had understood. He had heard nothing. He had actually seen nothing. Yet the very memory of something he could not remember was a burning in his soul, and he lived for those rare episodes. He no longer cried, "Oh, that I might know where to find Him!" He only prayed that he would be given enlightenment. Often he waited, in his prayers, his heart beating, but there was no answer. He felt no bitterness, no angry impatience. He believed himself still unworthy, that he must undergo more purification of the spirit. At times it occurred to him that God wished him to destroy the Galilean, the blasphemer who permitted his ragged and humble followers to call him the Messias, the man born in obscurity, the man without heavenly splendor, without a crown on his head.

He applied himself to study. He wrote letters. Once, on the plea of a friend of his father's he took the case of a man falsely accused of murder and appeared in the court in Tarsus, as the defender after he had become convinced of the man's innocence. This exalted him, especially when the man was acquitted and the magistrate had complimented Saul on his lawyer's eloquence and his dramatic defense of the accused. Saul thought, Does God intend me to be a practicing advocate, defending the innocent and upholding justice?

He was not content, as he waited. He was like a restive horse. But still he did not return to Jerusalem. It was as if he had been forbidden to return until a certain hour. That thought offended his reason. He accused himself of laziness, of loving, too much, the quiet and peace and modest luxury of his father's house, of taking too much pleasure in the gardens and of spending too much time on the black carved bridge that arched over the pond. Something in him was in abeyance, but it was beyond his capacity to know why, though his mind urged him back to Israel.

He took to wandering on the roads to the city, when it was quiet and the sun was high and the returning throngs did not fill the roads. He could think little; his thoughts seemed too ponderous for the warm serenity of the autumn weather. They wearied him.

One day he saw a young boy about thirteen or fourteen playing in the long and dusty grass near the road, with a small dog which barked shrilly. Saul heard the boy's laughter before he actually saw him and it came to him that there was something familiar in that laughter, as if he had heard it before. Then, out of the golden dry grass and weeds a head arose, shouting at the dog, and then there were youthful shoulders, then flailing arms. The hair was furiously red in color, and the face was strong and square and the eyes were deeply and flashingly blue and the nose was big though well-formed. The color of the countenance was ruddy and sprinkled with ginger freckles.

Saul found himself, to his stupefaction, looking on his own young appearance. He stood in a trance, staring. The little dog bounded to him, and snapped at his ankles, but he was unaware. The boy rushed out of the bright dust and grass to the road, and Saul saw his own bowed legs, as sturdy as young saplings. Saul also saw enthusiasm and exuberance and humor on the lad's face, and the wide thin lips parted in mirth to reveal teeth like his own, broad and square and very white.

The boy halted, abruptly, at the sight of this man who had seemingly appeared to have dropped from the sky. His smile went away. He stood in silence and looked at Saul. His tunic was scarlet, almost the color of his hair, and his belt was of silver and his sandals, though simple, were artfully crafted of good leather. He wore a boss about his neck, and it sparkled in the tawny sun of the season.

Saul's mouth and throat had turned to stone and he could not swallow or speak. The boy stared at him frankly, as no peasant or slave dared to stare, and his look was bold yet pleasant and inquisitive. Saul saw that his throat and neck and legs were sunburned, for the skin was fair, as his own was fair. And he knew at once and his heart plunged and then quickened and he was both affrighted and strangely exultant, though ashamed beyond any shame he had known before.

The boy waited courteously. The little dog ran to his master and the boy picked him up and nestled the head under his firm chin. He looked inquiringly at Saul.

Then Saul could speak. "Who are you, child?" he asked. His voice was muted and constricted.

"I am called Boreas," said the boy, and he began to grin. "Because I am noisy, it is said, and windy, and stir up tempests."

He seemed all movement, though he stood still with the dog in his arms, and he gave the impression of thrilling with energy.

"And who is your father—Boreas?" asked Saul.

Boreas pointed swiftly down the road in the direction of the pool which Saul had never been able to forget. "My father is overseer of the lands of the noble Roman, Centorius, and is a scribe and keeps the accounts. He is a freedman," added the boy, and lifted his proud head. "But I was born free."

Saul felt his own face tremble all over. "And your mother—Boreas?"

The boy shrugged. "I do not remember her. She died when I was born."

Dacyl, thought Saul. And now his tormented soul, always ready to accuse him of all sins and all laxnesses and indolence, stirred sternly. It was not enough, thought Saul, that I lay with Dacyl, whom I loved and hated, though neither was her fault. But on her I begot this child who does not know me as his father, and must never know.

"Is your father a man of kindness?" he asked.

The boy was astonished at this strange question. Saul noticed that his manner was free and unafraid, and he rejoiced while he waited the boy's answer. He saw the boy's eyes widen and stare. Boreas said, "My father, Peleus, is a good and worthy man, Master. He married another woman, after my mother died, and I have three sisters."

Do not call me "Master," thought Saul in his heart. He had noticed that the boy's voice was his childhood's own, somewhat loud and dominant and assertive, and quick. Boreas was speaking again. "I have a tutor, from the very house of Flavius, the tribune," he said, and smiled gleefully at this stranger, as if his words were amusing. "My father wishes me to be a scribe also, keeping accounts and held in respect."

Saul wanted to take Boreas in his arms and hold him to his chest and embrace him, and only then did he realize how lonely he was, lonely beyond any loneliness he had ever imagined. He was filled with love, and with pain.

"It is well that your father is so esteemed," he said, and his voice was gentle.

"He is also rich," said Boreas, with the extreme candor Saul had once known, himself. "A man of much wealth gave him a fortune in Roman sesterces when I was but four years old."

Saul's pulses jumped. "And who was this benevolent lord?" he asked.

The boy's red eyebrows rose, and he shrugged. "I do not know, Master. No one knows. It was given through a bank, and lawyers. It is said that once he saw me and liked my appearance, and gave my father large purses in order to nurture me."

My father, thought Saul, my father who had no grandson from my loins but this, my father who never told me. And this is my son who will never say Kaddish for me, nor stand beside me in the synagogue, nor look upon my face and call me "Father," and never rise at my entrance into his house. Nor will his children know me, nor cluster at my knees when I am old. He calls another his sire, and that man has my own and I have nothing.

"You are a Greek, Boreas?"

Again the lad shrugged. Now his smile was not so ready. His brows drew together a little, and he studied Saul more acutely, Saul in his plain long tunic bound with leather, his cloak of rough cloth, his coarse sandals. Saul was not dressed as finely as himself. So, with a touch of hauteur he said, "My father is a Greek—Master. He was born in Athens and has an education."

For the first time he observed that he resembled Saul and again he stared. "Who are you—Master?"

"My name—my name—" Saul halted. Did Peleus know this youth was not of his own loins? Dacyl had spoken of him. For the boy's sake he must not be recognized by any of the house of the tribune, Flavius, and for his own sake, also. He said, in a voice that spoke farewell, "I am of no consequence, Boreas. I am a stranger, an alien in the land, and I go to the city, and will not pass this way again."

Boreas nodded condescendingly. The dog was struggling in his arms, and Boreas shouted with Saul's own laughing impatience, and the dog fell to the ground and ran. When Boreas had caught him again the stranger had disappeared. There was no sign of him on the narrow and winding road. Boreas considered a moment. He had been attracted to Saul, whose voice had been very kind and gentle, and whose face had shone upon him. But he had also been poor and footsore, and he had no chariot, no horse, not even an ass. It was possible that he was a fleeing slave from one of the great houses along the road. Yet his voice had not been the voice of a slave. Boreas shook his head in bafflement. Then he heard the distant voice of his father calling him, and he ran and forgot Saul at once.

Saul, who had plunged into a thicket when the boy had turned his back, later made his way back to the road, and his house. He thought of his father again, his father who had not spoken but had recognized his grandson, and out of the greatness of his heart, and his love and his knowledge, had assured the future of Boreas. What pain had he suffered in his nights, what longings to embrace Boreas and claim him? The boy was not even circumcised. He was a Jew, and none knew it now but Saul alone, and the boy would never know. He would never know the God of his Fathers, nor would he hear of Sinai and Moses and all the prophets. He worshiped the gods of the heathens; he would marry a woman of his mother's blood and Saul's seed would be lost forever, dwindled away in bodies which would not exist but for that anonymous seed.

When Saul reached his house he went at once to his chamber and threw himself face down on his bed and gave

himself up to grief and remorse and longing for the son
he could never acknowledge, who would never stand at
his tomb and sorrow and pray.

I will return at once to Jerusalem, he thought with
resolution. But he did not. He lived near Boreas, of his
flesh and his blood, and there was a weary reluctance in
him to leave this place as yet.

Chapter 24

SOMETIMES Saul permitted himself the agonizing pleasure
of seeing Boreas at a far distance, in the direction of the
pond which he, Saul, never had visited since that last day
with Dacyl. On those days he fasted as a punishment for
his weakness, and for the danger he had brought near the
youth. The fasting was not very onerous, as his tastes
were simple and austere, so he sought a way to increase
his punishment. He worked in the gardens with his servants, ignoring the cold winds that rushed down from the
fiery mountains, and he gathered the grapes and the dates
and the pomegranates and raked the leaves and scythed
down the grass. When he discovered that he was enjoying
this he abandoned it, only to discover that his health had
been improved by the labor, and God had sternly warned
men to regard their health so that they might better serve
Him and be no burden on their family and neighbors.
So he returned to the labor. By nature a man of action
as well as a man of mind, his flesh hardened in the work
and he slept more peacefully at night.

He even cut wood for the baths and the fires and the
stoves. The servants shook their heads, but admired his
skill and endurance. He was like one, they said among
themselves, who was training for the Great Games. He
even learned to ride a horse and would often gallop down
a lonely Roman road with a cry of exuberance. For a
brief while his youth returned to him, his early youth. He
discovered appetite and the comfort one could take in cold
goat's milk and cheese and fresh chill water and good
warm bread and fruit and fish and roasted lamb. He even
began to like wine and enjoy it. But he visited friends

of his family very rarely, though invited, and entertained none. However, he would greet Aristo with real affection and feel an emptiness when the prospering Greek—who had now entered two fine horses for the races and had his own charioteer, and was investing in ships returned to his house.

"Saul ben Hillel pursues his God as Cadmus sought his sister, Europa," Aristo said to his wife, and she replied, with that bland and lovely stupid smile of hers, "And with as little success," thus again delighting her husband. "He will never build a Thebes," said Ianthe.

The High Holy Days came and went and the Day of Atonement had much significance for Saul, even greater than usual. Overcome with emotion in the synagogue he beat his forehead on the stone floor and prayed, "Harken to my anguish, Lord, that I may know Your Will for me and may follow it, rejoicing, without sin, without repining, and only with joy." For the first time in his life, as he rose, the tears on his cheeks, he felt that God had not only heard him but that He had opened His lips and was about to speak, and that His countenance had become faintly benign. It was a matter, now, only of the hour.

Then the snow wreathed the scarlet and distorted shapes of the mountains, and the wind was icy and the rain came to the valley in long gray spears of slashing water, and there was a howling in the porticoes and fistlike sounds on the windows and the strong bronze doors vibrated. The river turned to tumultuous lead, tossing wild spray to the dark heavens, and great ships rocked in the harbor and did not raise their sails. Sometimes, in the mornings, there would be hoar frost on the ground, in the stalks of the dead grass and on the branches of the trees, and the orange rising sun would make it sparkle and dazzle the eye. Then it would lift in a mist and be gone and the air would have a clear resonance so that the voices of far distant shepherds could be heard sharply across field and meadow and the atmosphere seemed permeated with tiny points of whirling light.

The red-legged storks flew over Tarsus and there were noisy clouds of other birds, migrating, and the winter was on the land.

A mysterious dreamlike peace came to Saul. He knew he must wait, that the hour was almost at hand. He was not forgotten. He had never attended any of the Roman games, but he had heard of them from Aristo, who had once told him that in every chariot race there was another charioteer waiting, so that when the first was thrown from the vehicle the other could take his place. He felt like that waiting charioteer, impatient for the race, for the victory, for the prize. Somewhere the first charioteer had fallen, or was about to fall, and Saul would be called.

Then the first pink almond blossoms appeared and Saul, like one amazed, saw that the spring was on the earth again and "the sound of the turtle was heard in the land." The weeks had gone and he had not noticed their passing. He received a letter from his sister, Sephorah, pleading with him to return to Jerusalem for the Passover, for the Seder, which was almost at hand. If he hastened, she wrote, he would be in time. Why did he linger in Tarsus? His business was concluded. His family in Jerusalem yearned to embrace him.

He walked in his gardens and saw the deepening blue sky, the blue pond, the freshening grass, the brightening and flowering trees and the smell of the holy and fecund earth. His heart lifted like that of a warrior who hears a trumpet note, and he cried aloud, with joyful impatience, "Yes, yes, Lord, speak!" Sometimes he found himself trembling. Life flushed into his veins, passion made his spirit soar. He said to Reb Isaac, "I will soon hear the call." And Reb Isaac said to him, with his tired seamed smile, "Recall what the people said to Moses, 'Let not God speak to us lest we die!' "

"But you, Rabbi, have heard Him speak often in your soul."

The rabbi gazed at him a moment and then muttered, "But not as He will speak to you, unfortunate—or blessed —man!"

Saul accepted Reb Isaac's invitation to dine at his house on the occasion of the First Seder. And one morning Saul awakened to the knowledge that at sunset the feast of the Passover would be held, that most holy day commemorating the "passing over" by the angels of wrath who had preserved the Children of Israel in their captivity in Egypt.

Before the feast they would go to the synagogue, and then the Jewish families of Tarsus would gather at their own tables in their houses and solemnly recount the awe-some occasion of the first Passover, and the grandfathers would look at their grandsons and would retell the won-drous tale, and there would be rejoicing and the finest fruits of the season and wine and laughter and lighted candles, and fathers would give thanks that they had fine sons and beautiful daughters and gracious wives.

It was warm now in the gardens, and Saul wandered in them exhilarated, as he had never been exhilarated before, at the wide loveliness of the earth which appeared to be rejoicing with men. Birds were chorusing in the passionate green of the trees. The myrtles were blossoming. The sweetest wind frolicked among new flowers and there were small white clouds in the vivid blue of the sky. The buds of the lilies were like long bulbs of alabaster, glistening and translucent, and their leaves were thin green spears. It was noon, and it was unusually hot, and Saul sat down on a marble bench and looked at the whispering and singing life all about him and laughed to see a jeweled little lizard race near his feet then race away. The black and white swans and the foolish Chinese ducks swam in their re-flections, and the water of the pond was like a liquid sapphire.

The heat increased, and Saul felt drowsy and re-entered his house and slept for a while. When he awakened he ordered milk and bread and cheese for himself, and his heart was like a ready cymbal waiting to be struck. The overseer of the hall came to him and said, "Lord, there will be a storm."

The doors of the atrium were open and from his seat in the dining hall Saul could look through the atrium into the garden. The light outside was now so incandescent that it hurt the eye. There was no sound of bird or wind, only that iridescent silence. The trees stood in it, quiver-ing with brilliance, and the pillars of the portico seemed to have a core of fire within them, so intensely were they glowing. But Saul saw that the sky had become of a more radiant and fervid a blue, utterly cloudless.

After he had finished his small meal he went into the gardens again, and admitted to himself that never had he seen such awesome light nor felt a greater heat, no, not even on the desert. He panted, and beads of sweat ap-peared on his fair and freckled face. His afflicted eye smarted in the benumbing effulgence, and began to water, as did his good eye. His blue tunic clung to his body and stung him with moisture. Every object, every tree and flower, every wall—now rippling with scarlet and purple flowers—the white walls of the house, the very pond itself, burned with a blinding radiance as if each were being consumed by the sun. A very holocaust of flaming scintillation hovered over all things, appeared to emanate even from the pebbles of the paths. And the heat mounted.

But there was no cloud, no rushing wind, no sign of any storm. Saul looked at the red mountains. Surely they were raging as if being devoured by internal furnaces! Saul could not look at them long. He walked to the road where he could see the valley and the river. The hurrying water was so bright that he had to shut his eyes, and when he did so it was as if he saw, on the darkness of his eyelids, the river again, and now it was the color of blood. A curious oppression fell on Saul, a deep foreboding, a pale terror, a wan agony. He sat down on the marble bench, and panted in the heat, and yet his sweat had turned cold.

He kept his eyes closed, wondering at his sensations which almost prostrated him. He was bemused. Then, all at once, he felt a vast coldness and heard the sudden howl of a wind and it struck his flesh with savage blows. He opened his eyes.

He could not believe it. Black night was on the land, and there was only the most absolute darkness upon him.

I have gone blind, he thought with renewed terror. My sight was taken from me in that fearful light! His hands became wet, and he clasped them together, and again was conscious of the cold. I cannot live if I am blind, he thought. Of what use to God is a blind man? He groaned aloud. And then—horror of horrors—his groan was echoed from the very vitals of the earth in one low vast thunder, and the ground under his feet moved and swayed and the wind howled louder and the chill was shuddering.

Again and again the earth moved and groaned in torment and the wind screamed to the black and empty sky, and there came sudden human voices, bursting out in confused fright and stunned alarm and the sound of women's screams, all coming from the alarmed house.

The earth rumbled and slid and tilted like a vessel, and thundered in her heart as if dying.*

Saul, unable to move, now understood that he had not gone blind, for he heard the cries for "Light! Light! Light the lamps!" from his house, and he let his pent breath leave his lips slowly and held to the bench lest he be thrown from it in the heaving of the earth.

He thought to himself, "This is the terrible Day of the Lord, which Joel prophesied," and he was exultant, then terrified again, for had not the prophet Amos rebuked the people, saying, "Woe to you, who desire the Day of the Lord! Why would you have the Day of the Lord? It is darkness, and not light; as if a man fled from a lion, and a bear met him. Or went into the house and leaned with his hand against the wall, and a serpent bit him. Is not the Day of the Lord darkness and not light, and gloom with no brightness in it?"

Despite his terror Saul was convinced that this, indeed, was the dreadful Day of the Lord, when God's wrath would sweep with the whirlwind and the thunder over the face of the earth and all things and all cities and all men would fall before it, and the earth would rush apart in earthquakes and devour all the works of men forever.

His breath came with shallowness and constriction. The earth subsided, but the deep growling remained for some time, as immense stone slipped over stone in the unfathomable abyss below, and chaos was created and chasms disappeared in the endless night. The cold black air quivered like curtains against Saul's cheek and arms and throat and feet. He did not know if the earth was still trembling or if it was now only his flesh.

Staring into the darkness he waited for what was next to come, hardly aware of the cries and shrieks coming

*An enormous earthquake occurred at this hour in Nicaea. In the fourth year of the two hundred and second Olympiad, Phlegon wrote that "a great darkness occurred all over Europe which was inexplicable to the astronomers," and that it engulfed Asia also. The records of Rome, according to Tertullian, made note of a complete and universal darkness, which frightened the Senate, then convening, and threw the city into an anxious turmoil, for there was no storm, and no clouds. The records of Grecian and Egyptian astronomers show that this darkness was so intense for a while that even they, skeptical men of science, were alarmed. People streamed in panic through the streets of every city, and birds went to rest and cattle returned to their paddocks. But there is no note of an eclipse of the sun; no eclipse was expected. It was as if the sun had retreated through space and had been lost. Many earthquakes, some of them very destructive, occurred widely. Mayan and Inca records also show this phenomenon, allowing for the difference in solar time.

from his house. The wind began to fall; it was becoming less furious. The bitter chill was moderating. A breath of warmth touched Saul's body. Then moment by moment the night receded, and a pale shine began to lighten the zenith. All at once the sun rushed into being again, as effulgent as ever, and as warm, and the growling in the earth subsided, and all was calm and sweet and placid and birds began to chirp and question and a strong and passionate fragrance rose from the blooming ground.

"Thank God," said Saul aloud, and rose up. He tottered for an instant, like an old man with the palsy and understood that he had felt the deepest fear of his life, more awful than the fear of death.

He went to his house. His servants were prostrate on the floors, their arms covering their heads. They were weeping, but whether with fright or with relief Saul did not know. They raised their heads and showed him their tears.

"It was an eclipse of the sun," he said to them, kindly. "All is well now."

It was a compassionate lie, and he knew it, but he did not know the cause of the phenomenon. He had studied both astrology and astronomy, in Tarsus and in Jerusalem. No eclipse had been predicted for this Eve of the Passover. Had there been a strange storm over Tarsus? He had never heard of such a one before, but then his life had not been long. Still, his father had not spoken of a storm like this, nor was there any record pertaining to any like it. Earthquakes were not uncommon in this part of the world, but quite frequent. Still, it was very odd that the sun had disappeared and night had descended —the deepest night he had ever known—and the earthquakes had accompanied the disappearance.

He went to his chamber and sat down and pondered. Had the phenomenon been observed all over the world? He would write to Jerusalem at once.

Then it came to him that something fearful, something dire, perhaps, had happened in the world, something inexplicable, something of calamity and terribleness, and God had uttered a Word and the firmament had been shaken and the foundations of eternity had trembled and the world had been convulsed. Saul pressed the palms of his hands together and shivered.

He decided not to delay in going to Reb Isaac's house, and then to the synagogue, though it was far from sunset. It was still only the middle of the afternoon. He dressed himself in a white tunic, the best he possessed, with an embroidery of gold at the throat, the gift of his sister who deplored his usual raiment. Over this he threw a brown toga, of not so fine a material as the tunic, and put on his new sandals. He called a quaking servant for the small chariot and drove away to the house of Reb Isaac. The fields and the streams of the valley basked in the gentlest light, but Saul saw disturbed groups gathered in the porticoes of the houses he passed, and standing on the grass, discussing vehemently. He passed a temple to Isis. It was crowded, the people swarming in the portico and he could smell sudden incense and could hear the incantations and prayers of the priests within, and the rising wails of flutes and the cry of harps and zithers.

The house of Reb Isaac was calm, but the old rabbi was very pale and his hands had a tremor. He said at once to Saul, "I thought it was the fearsome Day of the Lord."

"And so did I," Saul answered. Then seeing the old man's suppressed agitation he impulsively embraced him. "It will be explained," he said, as if to a child.

"Will it? Will it?" muttered Reb Isaac. "I wonder, with all my heart."

Two days later when Saul again walked in his garden he saw that the lilies were wide open to the sun, their golden stamens shining, and that from them rose a perfume of such intensity that it was like a prayer.

Chapter 52

SAUL wrote to Jerusalem to his sister, Joseph of Arimathaea, and to Rabban Gamaliel, asking them if they had observed "a remarkable and uncommon phenomenon," which had occurred on the Eve of the Passover in Cilicia. He, Saul, considered it a local occurrence, not significant, but "interesting." He sealed the letter and sent it to Jerusalem, not without some sheepishness. In the meantime he rationally explained the event over and over to himself and particularly to Aristo, who merely cocked an eyebrow over one of his black and restless eyes and smiled. He made but one observation: "My Saul, I believe it a most ominous event. If I believed in the gods—which thankfully I do not—I would say that Olympus had been convulsed to its very heart, and that Zeus had decided to destroy this world out of some divine wrath but had been restrained at the last moment, probably because it came to him that if the world were destroyed so would be thousands of lovely maidens. That is a thought not to be borne lightly."

Saul did not care for this levity nor did he speak of his own terror on that day. A black storm cloud, he suggested, had gathered over Tarsus for a space and then had withdrawn. "So black a storm cloud," said Aristo, "not only the sun had gone but the stars peeped out. I saw them myself. No, Saul, I am inclined to believe that the event was preternatural." And he laughed, seeing that he had vexed Saul.

The spring, golden as dawn, melted into the green and abundant summer and a luminous haze softened the mountains. Saul became more and more impatient, as he was more and more convinced that he was awaiting a call and yet was not receiving it. Again, each day he resolved to return the next to Israel. Then early one morning his overseer came to him in great excitement to inform him that he had a noble visitor, a Roman, a captain of the Praetorian Guards. "Titus Milo Platonius!" exclaimed Saul, hurrying in from the gardens, his hands brown and damp with soil, and he was delighted; and amazed to see his handsome cousin awaiting him in the atrium. The men embraced affectionately. Milo removed his helmet and loosened his belt, and looked about him with pleasure. "And all this, for a man without wife or child!" he said. "Not even I, in Rome, have such a villa." His strong brown face was heavily furrowed with weather and his cropped brown hair revealed streaks of gray, but his old spare elegance was with him still, and his manner of military grace, and as always he was stately.

Saul showed him to one of the guest chambers and clapped for servants to attend the noble soldier and refresh him. Saul had not known such pleasure for a long time, so long a time that he could not remember. He realized how lonely he had been in his father's house for nearly a year, and now the house was warm with love and friendship again, and he eagerly awaited Milo's joining him in the summer portico, where colorful flowers bloomed tall in Chinese vases and pots and a fountain cooled the hot bright air. He clapped for wine and light refreshments, and threw his kitchen into wild dismay, as "light refreshments" were usually not encouraged in this house. But by the time Milo came out into the portico the cooks had contrived some delicacies and had unearthed some good wine from the cellar and had brought in a salver of young green onions, radishes and some hot artichokes swimming in oil with a touch of rosemary. From some mysterious hiding-place—not so mysterious to Saul who lightly frowned—they had "discovered" some marvelous cheeses. (They pamper their stomachs, the servants! he thought, but was reluctantly pleased.)

Milo had removed his leather armor and wristlets and cloak and military garb and had dressed himself in a short yellow tunic bordered in red Grecian keys, and his tanned legs were still the legs of a sturdy youth and his feet arched in their fine sandals. He even wore an armlet of wide plain gold.

"I suppose, dear cousin," he said to Saul, "that you wonder at my appearance here in Tarsus."

Saul was astonished. He considered. "No," he confessed. "I did not think of that at all, and that is very peculiar. I was only glad to see you."

Milo smiled, showing almost all his white teeth, and he studied Saul shrewdly. He sampled the refreshments, sipped the wine, and revealed his pleasure. Even his big protruding ears were brown, and his hands were bronzed. He looked at Saul with his father's kind eyes, and appeared to think and turn his thoughts about.

"I am returning to Rome from Jerusalem," he said, as if he were examining each word. "My parents are old. My father also wishes to return to Rome, where he hopes to be elected a tribune. He is old now. So is my mother. I had not seen them for four years, nor had I seen my sisters and their children for that time, and I have some leave. Do not concern yourself about my men; they are ensconced in an inn in Tarsus, and they are young lads who have never been in this city before and are, without doubt, now investigating the feminine possibilities here."

His smiling face became suddenly very serious, and he ate some bread and cheese as if lost in his own thoughts. Seeing this, a vague uneasiness came to Saul. But Milo said, "My ship stopped in Tarsus, and I decided to visit you."

"Otherwise, you would not have done so," said Saul, and was surprised by his own disappointment, for he thought affection had brought Milo here.

"You are wrong," said Milo, and gave his cousin his quick if somewhat saturnine smile. "I chose that ship because I wished to visit you."

"Ah," said Saul, and with his old impulsiveness he stretched out his hand to his cousin and they grasped each other's fingers in a brief firm clasp. Then Saul said, "You have something grave to tell me. In the Name of God, blessed be His Name, tell me at once, if it is bad news!"

"It is not bad news," said Milo. "It is most portentous news."

"Of my family?"

"In a manner of speaking. But it concerns—" Milo paused, and did not look directly at Saul now but out upon the shimmering gardens. It was as if he feared, as customary, any extravagant language, for was he not a Roman? Yet, what but extravagant words could convey what he must convey? "It concerns," Milo continued, his brown cheekbones coloring as if with embarrassment, "the whole world."

Instantly Saul's thoughts flew to the phenomenon of the Eve of Passover, and the letters he had recently written. But he did not speak. He only looked at Milo with the bright blue metal of his eyes, and waited, and a sensation of extreme tenseness came to him.

"I am Jew, as well as Roman," said Milo, and expertly fished out an artichoke with his fingers and slowly savored and chewed and swallowed it. He contemplatively, then, licked his fingers, ignored the luxury of the warm water in a silver bowl, floating with rose leaves, and wiped his hands on a napkin. The fastidiousness of the savoring was familiar to Saul, the Jew, but the roughness of the Roman manners would have, under other circumstances, annoyed him. Then Milo, as if wishing to escape Saul's penetrating eyes, bent over the cheese salver and made a delicate choice in long deliberation. After he had removed his selection to his silver plate and buttered some bread, he went on, lifting his eyes for only an instant to Saul's, and Saul was freshly amazed at the stern yet thoughtful light in them, for never had he seen it before.

"I sacrifice to Mars, my patron, in his temple," said Milo. "I give the deepest devotion to Jupiter, though I cannot, in all truth, consider Julius Caesar and Gaius Octavius Caesar divinities. But I honor them also, in their temples, though I laugh in my heart. Do I believe in the gods of Greece and Rome, and several of the Egyptian gods? I do not know. They are full of splendor and beauty and are understandable by men. They partake of our nature. And they are subtle as well as gross. On the other hand, I am my mother's son, and so I have been circumcised and was presented in the Temple—I believe a slight sum passed from my father to the priests—and I was Bar Mitzvah, though the other boys taunted me as a 'bloodthirsty Roman,' and as a child and a lad I learned the Five Books of Moses, and all the prophets, and Jewish customs and the things forbidden, the Torah, the Psalms—and all that you have studied, Saul. In those days I was called Titus Milo ben Aulus." He smiled again, and Saul thought the smile wry.

"Now when I go to the Temple or the synagogue I stand in the Court of the Gentiles, but what I hear from within the Temple stirs my blood with ancient cries and movements. But when I stand before the altar of Mars I am also so stirred, and I believe in my patron with absolute faith—just as I believe in the God of Abraham and Jacob."

Saul said, "The Greeks believe that all religions contain a measure of the truth, but not the whole truth, Milo."

Milo caught the reserve in his cousin's vibrant voice, and he said, quickly, "But you do not?"

Saul hesitated. "I would be lying if I said I believe the Greeks. I believe that there is but one Truth, blessed be His Name, and I await His Messias." Again he hesitated. "Forgive me if I have offended you, but I cannot lie."

"I am, at times, in a very contradictory situation,"

said Milo. "Sometimes it is an untenable state. At other times it is as if I see a broad landscape, not narrowed to one little vista, but embracing the world. No matter. It is my nature to be direct, and I fear I am not being so now, for I have been witness to astounding events."

Saul's thoughts again flew to the Eve of the Passover, and he said nothing.

"I was fortunate," said Milo, "to arrive this time in Jerusalem to celebrate the Passover with my parents. You know that two of my sisters are married to Jews. They gather in my father's house for the Holy Days. Does it seem amazing to you that my old Roman father wears a skullcap on those occasions and exhorts his grandchildren on the history and the glories of Israel, and the Covenant God made with her?"

"I have heard of it," said Saul, and could not help smiling. "And Hannah, in gratitude and love, has the Roman lares and penates in her house."

"My father, like myself, honors all the gods, though he honors the Jewish God more. What Rome will make of this, when he returns, I do not know. But Romans are tolerant of all religions, so long as those religions do not teach rebellion against Rome. They even erect temples to strange gods and honor them, as you know. I am very proud of both my people."

"You have something to tell me," said Saul.

"Yes." Milo refilled his goblet and looked at the winey contents and swished it around and sniffed at the bouquet. Saul saw that he was bidding for time, and his uneasiness sharpened.

"You have heard of the Galilean, Yeshua of Nazareth, or Jesus, as we Romans have interpreted the name?"

A cold stiffness made Saul sit upright. He nodded without speech, but his face tightened.

"Your sister, my cousin Sephorah, has written you concerning Him, this Jesus, and I bring her letter to you, and letters from Joseph of Arimathaea, and my own parents." Now it was Milo who hesitated, then lifted his brown gaze and looked at Saul steadily. "Was Tarsus darkened also, on the Eve of the Passover?"

A tremendous excitement seized Saul and he cried, "Yes, yes! I have written to my friends of this, and my sister! Did it darken Israel? Impossible! It was but a storm cloud over Tarsus!"

"A very strange cloud," said Milo, in a musing voice. "I have received letters from my compatriots in Rome, my fellow soldiers. That 'cloud' covered Rome also, for a considerable time, and at the hour it covered Cilicia and Israel. And, I have heard, Egypt and Asia Minor and the Isles of Greece. A very strange cloud."

Saul's nostrils drew in with the sharply drawn breath. "It—can be explained," he said. "Surely the astronomers are now explaining it."

"But, to no one's satisfaction, not even their own. There is prattling of comets and their sudden disintegration which hid the sun. This argument fails before scientific examination, as the scientists understand, themselves. The darkness did not last long enough, and when it lifted it lifted suddenly, and all was as it was before. Except for one thing—"

"Yes?" cried Saul, leaning toward him.

But Milo said, "You have not heard from Sephorah since some time before the Passover? No. I must tell you why. Her son, Amos, was about to be Bar Mitzvah, and as he is the favorite of all the family, a boy of great wisdom and learning and tenderness and virtue and strength, and beautiful, the family intended to make of it a great celebration. This was some short weeks before the Passover. But on the three days before Passover the boy fell gravely ill of some mysterious disease, and he was given up for dying by his physicians."

Saul uttered an exclamation of grief and great anxiety. "But the boy recovered?"

"No," said Milo, and again he looked at the gardens. "He died."

"Oh, God!" cried Saul, overcome with anguish. "Oh, it is not possible! I knew the boy. He had the face of an angel. He resembled my father!"

He covered his face with his hands and groaned, "You swore to me that you did not bring me evil news! But now you have broken my heart."

"Let it be healed," said Milo, gently, and Saul, blank with astonishment, dropped his hands. His face ran with tears.

"The boy died at dawn," said Milo, and he looked

straightly at Saul's pallid face. "The three physicians were there, one the renowned Egyptian, whom the Greeks call Horus, though that is not his name. In two hours the child was of an icy coldness. They had closed his eyes and his white lips. The house had been gayly decorated for the Bar Mitzvah. The decorations were taken down, and the brothers and parents and grandfather of Amos, and the uncles and grandsons and nephews, sat down in ashes and tore their clothing. Sephorah was taken to her bed, overcome. The house was filled with mourning. Burial clothes and oils and spices were prepared. A tomb was chosen. The dead boy lay on the floor, hourly becoming more livid and ghastly, so that it was an agony to look upon him. The sunset was approaching, when he must be entombed."

Saul closed his eyes quickly as he saw what Milo had seen, and his heart began a slow sick drumming.

"It seems," said Milo's voice, as if at an immense distance, "that there was a servant in the house who had looked upon Yeshua of Nazareth and had fallen at his feet. He was an old and devoted servant. He had loved the boy, Amos. So, knowing that Yeshua was newly arrived, again, in Jerusalem, doubtless to celebrate the Passover in Jerusalem according to the Law, he ran out, seeking him. And he found him."

Saul's face so changed that Milo could hardly recognize it. It had become fierce. This disturbed Milo. But he went on:

"While the women washed the dead child the Nazarene came to the door of the house with several of his miserable disciples, the old servant leading the way. And the Nazarene entered that beautiful house of your grandfather's and looked sadly at the mourners. He did not speak to them. He approached the dead boy, who was now being wrapped in his grave clothes. He contemplated him. It seemed that Yeshua, or Jesus, as we Romans call him, was about to weep, not because the boy was dead—"

"He profaned my grandfather's house," whispered Saul in furious soft horror.

"Listen to me!" cried Milo, losing his military composure for the first time. "You have not been listening to me, Saul ben Hillel! You have been listening only to your own thoughts, you obdurate man! But were you not always so, alas?

"Listen to me! Jesus stretched forth his hand and he said, 'I say to you, arise, Amos ben Ezekiel!' And the boy stirred in his grave clothes and he opened cloudy eyes and he looked about him strangely and raised his head, and the mourners sprang to their feet with terrible loud cries and then flung themselves about him, to feel his warming flesh and to see the color returning to his white cheeks and lips. None but the adoring servant saw the Nazarene leave, this Jesus, and none thought of giving him so much as a goblet of wine, or offering him a shekel!"

Saul jumped to his feet and moved rapidly to a column of the portico and he stretched out his hand against it to support himself, and his back was to his cousin.

"Do you not understand?" said Milo, rising also, but standing by his chair. "He who was dead was given life. He who was dead was restored in a twinkling to health and to his family's arms. He, ready for the grave, was Bar Mitzvah, before Passover. Your nephew lives, Saul of Tarshish, your nephew lives!"

"You are mistaken," said Saul, in a muffled voice. "He was never dead."

"I was there," said Milo. "I swear to you, by the God of Abraham and Jacob, that I was there, and I saw it for myself, and so did many more. I am a soldier. I have seen death countless times. I know the sight and the smell of death, even new death. Your nephew was dead, as dead as any man slain on the battlefield."

"Then," said Saul, not turning, "it was by some evil incantation, and better it would have been that my nephew had remained dead. Who knows what has been done to his soul?"

Milo was profoundly shaken. He said, "You do not believe that. No, you do not believe it. Therefore, you have implied I am a fool and a liar, and a deluded wretch."

Saul turned now and his eyes were a terrible blue blaze. But his voice was quiet. "If I have offended you, Milo, my cousin, I crave your pardon. I do not believe my nephew was dead. I believe he was in a state of suspended animation, that even the physicians were deceived, and that the boy would have awakened as he did even if— This state is not unknown, and there is always much fear that the 'dead' will awaken in the tomb and die there."

Milo sighed, a big gusty sigh. He sat down heavily in his chair, bent his head and clasped his knees in his hands. He shook his head over and over. Saul returned to his own chair. He felt weak and dazed. He said, "And that is another portentous piece of news." He could not keep the satire from his voice.

"Saul, Saul," said Milo. He refilled his goblet. "You have forgotten the darkness. For, you see, Jesus of Nazareth was arrested for blasphemy, at the instigation of the High Priest, who is a friend of Pilate's, just before Passover. He was brought hastily, at night, before a few members of the Sanhedrin, a very few, for he was not considered important, but only a poor workman, not worthy of the meeting of the whole Court, and he was found guilty of blasphemy. And worse, though it was not mentioned by the Court, of inciting the people of Israel to riot against the Romans, and so destroying law and order. It was told me that the High Priest said, fearing the Romans, 'Better it is for one man to perish than his whole nation.' "

Saul could hardly speak, but a kind of ferocious joy filled his eyes. "And so he was crucified!"

"Yes," said Milo, looking at him with a formidable stare. "He was crucified. At noon, on the Eve of the Passover. He died, three hours later, on the cross, in the Place of Skulls, called Calvary, and on the instant of his death there was a great thundering and the earth shook and the world fell into darkness. And—the Veil in the Temple, which concealed the Holy of Holies, was rent in an instant."

He still gazed at Saul. "I was there. At the Place of Skulls."

And then, to Saul's absolute stupefaction, Milo related a story which resembled, in every particular, even to the murky sky and the fear of the Roman soldiers, Saul's own dream of the crucifixion when he, himself, in his illness, had almost died. Nothing moved on his face; his eyes did not blink. He appeared hardly to breathe. At moments Milo believed he was in the midst of a seizure, and that he was unconscious. Only those blazing eyes gave any sign that he heard, and even of this Milo was not very sure.

"I was not in charge of the crucifixion," said Milo. "I was there because of what I had seen in your grandfather's house, the raising from the dead of your nephew, Amos. I was there to witness the death of a good man whose very look was mercy, whose very glance was beauty and power, a poor man whom no one cherished but a few—and even those deserted him except for his mother and one or two others of his followers. Alas. He had done no evil. Many loved him, and thousands were there, on the mounts, grieving and afraid. But nearer still was the market rabble, the lustful, the base, hating, ignorant and eternally envious and malicious market rabble, who love to witness suffering and death, who did not know this man except that he had been accused of blasphemy—and what did they care about blasphemy, these screaming and grinning and taunting mobs? It was enough that this was a spectacle of agony which they could enjoy, and make of it a holiday. Do we, in Rome, not know this thieving rabble, and fear it? We have tried to placate these fat wretches, these wretches with enormous buttocks, sweaty, dependent, unwashed, indolent, greedy, demanding, howling, savage, lightless but filled with malevolence, boiling with lying rumors, worshiping the tawdry and despising the heroes and the just and the merciful—do they know that they do not deserve mercy? Yes, we know them, in Rome, too, and we have been appeasing them for a whole century, with free housing within the very sight of the Palatine, within sight of Caesar's palace, with free food and beans and wheat and bread and meat and swine, with free entertainment. For we know them, now, to be the menace of empires, to be the real Vandals within the gates, the destroyers. Woe to that nation who gives them votes and voice, and listens to their howling! This we have done, and inevitably Rome must fall."

The controlled and military voice had risen into passion. The soldier's hands were beating his bare knees. "The curse of nations!" he almost shouted. "There is not a nation that has not been destroyed by their vilest, and there will be nations in the future who will be destroyed by them! Ah, they were there at the Place of Skulls, though this Jesus had been but a rumor to them before, a man of Galilee of little consequence, blood of their blood. But that was of no importance to them, that a Jew was to be crucified by the Romans on a Roman charge that he had been inciting his people to rebellion against Rome. *It was enough that he was hated by the very authority they hated!* But like all rabble—hysterical, craven, maudlin and restless—they were a fawning rabble, eager to appear and to denounce, for a smile from the oppressors. If I had my way, if I were Caesar," said Milo, clenching his fists and striking his breast with them, "I would put such rabble to the sword, in any nation in the world, for they eat away the vitals of the people and devour their substance!"

"Go on," said Saul, when Milo, from excess of rage and emotion, fell silent. His own voice was faint, but cold. "I do not love the market rabble, the mobs, more than you."

Milo wiped his sweating brow with the back of his hand, and shook his head.

"While the people mourned the death of this Jesus, standing and weeping on the other mounts, holding up their children for a last glance of the Man, and perhaps for His blessing, the market rabble howled, as they had howled the night before, when Pontius Pilate had presented Him to them, and they screamed, 'Crucify Him! Give us Barabbas!' For Barabbas was a thief, and it was fitting that a thief be released to them, thieves themselves! Enough. I have told you that He was crucified between two thieves, and one adored Him and was given a promise of Paradise, but the other shrieked, 'If you be the Messias, save Yourself and us!' But, I have told you. The Roman soldiers were disturbed both by the aspect of Jesus and by the furious screaming mobs demanding His death, and one sought to assuage His pain but He would have it not. When the darkness fell and the earth quaked and the terrible wind arose and the cold, the Roman soldiers said, 'Surely, this was a just Man!' I was there."

He looked at Saul's white and unreadable face. "At the last He said, 'It is finished,' and delivered up His spirit. Saul, was that not prophesied by David?"

Saul averted his head and stared at the floor.

Milo sighed. "I know Pilate well, and do not honor him, for he often tried to incite the Jews by inflicting random punishments for nothing, and having his banners lately inscribed with the heads of gods and Caesars and animals and other pictured things, and taunting the pious, and conducting mass crucifixions for no real reason at all, but 'as a warning.' He wished to so oppress the people that they would all, in truth, rise in one rebellion, and then he would have his excuse to massacre them. Is he a wicked man? As Joseph of Arimathaea has said, he is a bored man, and he is under private exile—for Tiberias dislikes him—and he hates Israel for it does not possess the pleasures of Rome and licentious Roman companionship. A cruel man is less to be feared than a man suffering from ennui. It was because of what Pilate has done to Israel that I was sent there by Caesar, and not only because I had my leave. I was sent to warn him, that he must not provoke the Jews any longer. Even his friend, King Herod Antipas, that red fox, that uneasy dweller between two worlds, was aghast at him, and wrote his brother-in-law Agrippa who brought the matter before Caesar.

"I, as a guest, remained in Pilate's house for a few days, before going to my parents' house, and Pilate complained that he was expiring of nothingness in Israel and begged me to use my influence with Caesar to recall him. Then he spoke of this Jesus, and said it had been reported to him by Roman centurion and priests alike that He was an Essene or a Zealot, and was inspiring rebellion against Rome. I was at Pilate's side when Jesus was brought before him for questioning. It gave Pilate pleasure, in the face of the frightened priests, to balk them. He said, 'I find no fault in this man,' and washed his hands in public, as is customary. But still he said to me, 'The man must die, for He is creating confusion and unrest in Israel, as did his cousin and friend, one John the Baptist, whom Herod had executed.' Therefore Pilate gave the order for His crucifixion. Are you listening to me, Saul?"

"I am listening," replied Saul. It was very hot, but he found himself unaccountably shivering.

"Pilate also told me, with a peculiar smile, that his wife had had a dream, that he must not order the execution of Jesus of Nazareth, or Yeshua, as you call him. She told him that dire events would follow, and he, Pilate, must not have this blood on his hands. Pilate, though a superstitious Roman, still ordered the execution, and after that he sacrificed to Castor and Pollux, as a precaution against the wrath of the gods, though, as he told me, he did not believe that our Roman gods were concerned with the death of this Jew. Then, suspicious of the followers of this Jesus, Pilate asked me, as a favor to him, to conduct the command of Temple guards and Roman legionnaires, at the tomb of Jesus, so that His followers could not steal away His body and proclaim, according to what He had prophesied, that He had risen from the dead on the third day."

"Ah," said Saul, and it was as if his body, enclosed in icy iron, had been released, and he raised his head and almost smiled. "That was the end of it."

"It was the beginning," said Milo, and again poured himself wine as if he were greatly overcome and must have refreshment. Saul watched him in bemused astonishment, and even then he uttered a passionate and tremendous denial in himself. His cousin, after all, was half a Roman, and superstition is inherent in Roman nature, and a willingness to believe in miracles from any source whatsoever. The Egyptian Serapis was now in vogue, and all Romans sacrificed in the Egyptian temples in honor of the god. Tomorrow, it would be another god, alleged to be as strong as Zeus. It could even be this Yeshua! Saul uttered a derisive sound.

"It was the second Passover, and it was night," said Milo, "and after I feasted with my parents I went to the tomb of Jesus. He was very poor, and so was His Mother, and His followers. They had no money for tombs. But Joseph of Arimathaea gave them a tomb, a very lavish one, outside the gates. Did you speak? No. So the women had anointed Him with oils and spices and wrapped Him in grave-clothes, and had laid him within the tomb, the day before. The soldiers and the Temple guards had then rolled a mighty stone before the mouth of the tomb, so heavy and ponderous that it took several gasping men all their strength to move it. Jesus was entombed, and we were the guards. It was a warm and quiet night, aromatic and dry. The soldiers had built bonfires around the tomb and were eating and jesting and casting dice, but I would not permit them to drink much wine for fear they would fall asleep. It was not a night for sleeping. As Pilate had said, when Jesus remained within the tomb and decomposed, then that would be the end of His followers and their faith, and peace would come again to that disturbed land. As for myself," said Milo, dropping his head meditatively, "I had witnessed the crucifixion and the events when He died, and I wished to prove the truth to myself. Therefore, I did not relax for an instant. I ate the food the soldiers prepared for me, and stood while eating, and patrolled with them around the tomb—which is in a desert place near a wild garden—and gave the homesick boys the news of Rome. I had seen the interior of the tomb before the Man was laid there. It consisted of a shelf within of light yellow marble, and nothing else, but it was large for a tomb. I even examined every outside spot on it, looking for another entrance or exit. There was none. It was solid stone.

"The moon was yellow and low when we started our vigil. It became brighter and clear as it rose. We heard the rejoicing sounds from without the gates, and saw the reflection of fires on the mount on which the city is built, and heard cymbal and flute and harp and zither and laughter and the coming and going of people who were hurrying to other feasts, and we heard the occasional sound of trumpets from the Temple, and marching feet and challenges and drums, and tumults of happy voices and the cries of animals. But here where we guarded—without the gates—was silent and deserted, with not even the sound of a night owl, and only our lanterns and our fires to keep us from the darkness. Not even a follower of the dead man, not even a grieving woman, came near the tomb. I had heard that all His followers had fled the city, for fear of vengeance.

"The guards were alert. They had slept the day, for this very vigil, so they would not be overcome by sleep, for tomorrow, it had been said, the alleged Arising from the dead would take place. The guards laughed. Some of them tried to move the stone, but it had become fixed, by its weight, into the ground. Some of them rapped on the tomb, calling, 'Are you awake, Jesus of Nazareth? With the help of Sisyphus, will you move this stone, and have you called him from Hades to assist you?' 'No, he has called on Hercules!' another soldier laughed, and others then uttered loud and threatening growls and waved their swords. Yes, it was very merry—and the merriment was tiny in that silent and desolate place—and I could see, that in spite of their laughter, the guard was uneasy. That pleased me. Uneasy men do not let down their alertness nor do they sleep.

"The hours went on. It was past midnight. The soldiers began to sing, to add new meats to their pots, to renew the fires, to begin new games, to relate preposterous stories in the way of military men. The moon rose higher, and now it seemed to concentrate its luminous whiteness on the tomb, so that it was another moon in itself, warmly white and brilliant. And the desert place lay all about us, blanched and wan as death under the pale light, and full of rubble. Over and over I circled the tomb, with a lantern in my hand, looking for intruders. But, there were none.

"I had not slept the day as the other soldiers had slept," continued Milo, and he fixed his brown eyes on Saul's pale and skeptical and waiting face. "But I knew my duty. I drank a little wine. I am accustomed to long vigils without sleep. They are nothing for a soldier. I was there, not only on duty, but—for myself. Again and again I tested the enormous stone before the entrance to the tomb. I am a strong man but I could not stir it a fraction. And the others watched me, and jested at me under their breaths. Then one said, 'Captain, only the gods could command that to be moved without a dozen men.'

"The night was wearisome, and now I began to think this guard absurd, for what crucified man within, whether or not He had truly died, could remove this stone Himself and emerge? Besides, I had seen them testing Him for His death. A spear had been plunged into His side, and water and blood had emerged, sluggishly. They had not broken His legs, as was customary. He was let down into His Mother's arms and she cradled him to her breast as one would cradle a beloved babe. I swear to you, Saul, that I could have wept, though she did not weep. She tenderly removed the thorns they had thrust on His brow, and she stroked His blood-soaked hair and kissed His cheek and held Him to her. Only two or three of His followers had remained, even in their fear, and one said to her, 'He gave you to us as our Mother, and we must take Him away to the tomb prepared for Him, where with the other women you will anoint and wrap Him.' And so they bore Him away and I swear that I could not bear the sight, for He who had raised Amos ben Ezekiel from the dead was dead, Himself, and speechless, and deaf and blind. I saw His glazed eyes, partly open. He was truly dead."

"What other did you expect, Milo, of this blasphemer and mountebank, and sorcerer!" cried Saul, and now his pallor was gone and he was exultant and smiling. He spread out his hands. "And that was all." A boundless relief came to him, a slackening of tension. He even laughed a little.

But Milo did not laugh. The brown eyes regarded Saul darkly.

"It was the beginning," said Milo, as he had said before. After a moment's brooding thought he continued, but it was as if he spoke to himself, in dull amazement and wonder, and chilling fear.

"We heard the jackals howling in the wilderness. We saw the moon grow more luminescent against the black sky. The night began to slope to dawn. We awaited it as men await deliverance, for now my men were showing increasing uneasiness. The tomb glowed in white light. It appeared to me to shimmer, to wax and wane. Once I thought I heard the sound of gigantic wings. The men built their fires higher, and raised their voices against the silence, for now there was no sound, not even from the city. They stuffed bread and meat in their mouths, to warn off fright, and played games more feverishly. Some cursed the Jews for this stupid vigil, and the temple guards glowered. Some, imbued with the religion of the Egyptians, spoke of Osiris rising from the dead, and still others coarsely laughed at them. Many rose and began to wander, scanning the opaque countryside and desert, frowning. We all looked at the sky, for the dawn."

For the anxious and uneasy men it appeared the dawn would never come, but at last there was a hazy rose-colored flush over the eastern mounts, the hem of Aurora's robe trailing and blowing silently into the dark sky, and before that hem the nearer stars began to flee. Then the top of the mounts was rimmed with sudden bright gold, a brilliant tracing against the rose. The soldiers and the guards looked at it happily. Within the hour they would be at home, and free. The moon, a mere wan skull, declined and fell behind a mountain and was lost.

Titus Milo, relieved, himself, yet strangely depressed, glanced at the tomb. Then he uttered a faint cry. For it was as if the sun itself had fallen upon that tomb of death, and it blazed in an awful whiteness. The soldiers and the guards, alarmed at Milo's cry, turned and saw what he was seeing, and they also saw the blinding radiance that shot in rays from the tomb and illuminated the nearby desolation, so that every pebble and every stone was ignited. Those who had remained near the tomb had fallen into a swooning sleep near their fires, and their faces quivered with scarlet, and there was no sound at all now but the crackling of burning wood and no movement but the rising of thin dark smoke. Breastplate, scabbard, helmet—they reflected the trembling of the fire, and did not stir on the ground, and the scattered pots glimmered.

The men with Milo uttered one fierce yell of terror, then, as if struck by lightning, they fell one by one on the earth, into a profound trancelike slumber.

Milo stood and could not move, and he saw, through streaming eyes dazzled by the blazing of the tomb, that in that light moved tall masculine figures of even brighter light, and they were rolling the stone at the entrance as easily as children roll a ball. He saw their giant limbs, their Titan faces—beautiful as gods—their bare arms and manly shoulders, their flowing hair. And all about them the radiance palpitated, blowing with what appeared to be multitudes of white fireflies, bright and restless as stars.

Titus Milo Platonius had never known panic or terror in his life before like this, no, not even when he had fought the Germanni and the Parthions, in his early youth, before he was a Praetorian Guard. It seemed to him, as he tried to shield his eyes from the unearthly light, that he possessed no heart any longer, that it had flowed away leaving only the most frightful fear in its place, and that his bowels had melted. The big muscles in his legs and arms shook like a palsy; there was a choking and a burning in his throat. It was as if he were being consumed by flames.

The great figures, several of them, moving the stone, appeared to become aware of him and they turned their majestic faces to him and he saw their lambent eyes and their remote expressions—and he knew them for what they were. Though they possessed the bodies and limbs of men and the contour of men's faces, they were not men and there was about them that aloof splendor and impassive neutrality toward him which announced their apartness from his flesh. They did not glance at the soldiers and guards on the ground. Even as they looked at Milo it was as if Olympian deities regarded him, and with as much uninterest. It was this, more even than their presence, and the tremendous light on the tomb, which made Milo's spirit quail and sink, for his humanity was wounded and he felt reduced to less than a beast.

He saw that the stone, moving away, had begun to reveal the black aperture to the tomb, and the terror he had felt before was as nothing to this. He turned and let himself fall headlong on the ground, and he covered his helmeted head with his arms and waited for death, expecting he knew not what.

He closed his eyes for very dread, but the shadow of the light wavered over his lids, even though he tried to protect them with his arms. He did not know how long a time passed, but at length, as he lay shivering and quaking, he heard a slow and monumental footstep. It came toward him, seeming to bend the dry and dusty earth under him, and then it paused beside him. He closed his eyes tighter. He feared to look, for now he remembered, from his Jewish teachings, that those who look upon things not permitted to men must die.

But that which was near him did not go on, as he prayed incoherently in his heart. It remained. So he parted his lashes a little and saw beside him two feet of light, sandaled with gold, and sparkling like alabaster fired from the sun. Against all the screaming of his will, his desire to rise and flee, his urge to shout and roll away, he opened his eyes wider, as if forced, and they rose slowly over a robe brighter than the moon, glowing in every fold, glittering with rushing points of light that flaked and fell and blew away, and they rose to a girdle of gold, then over a breast throbbing with lucency, to a column of pale marble which was a throat.

And then to the Face, the powerful, gentle, stern yet tender Countenance, the Face of a Man such as had never been seen before, implicit with grace, puissant and kingly.

"He," said Titus Milo to his cousin, Saul, "wished me to

see Him. And I saw. It is enough to last me to the very end of my life. It is more than enough."

Saul's face had dwindled, became absolutely white and strained and as tight as if it had been dried and parched for days in the sun and had no juices remaining.

He said, and he tried to smile indulgently, "Did you recognize that—Face?"

Milo looked at him long and somberly. "I did. It was the Face of Jesus of Nazareth. I knew Him at once." He paused. "He had died, and He had risen. He had been entombed, and angels had rolled away the stone. He had risen—from the dead."

Saul was silent.

"I must have fainted," said Milo. "For when I awakened all the soldiers and the guards were still asleep, fallen into a trance like death. And I—I rose and I went away. I went," said Milo, "to the Temple and I prayed there all the day and told no man."

"And the tomb?"

"It was empty. The light had receded as the light of the sun falls behind the curve of the world. It was nothing but a tomb. I looked within, by the first light of the morning. The grave-clothes were there, discarded, and their pungent perfume floated in the dense air of the tomb. I thought, for a little, that I saw the bright outlines of two of those Titantic forms, but I remembered their celestial indifference, and so I fled. The tomb was empty."

Chapter 26

IT WAS very hot in the shade of the summer portico now and the gardens were humming with multitudes of insects and the fountains splashed and scintillated languidly in the sun. The massed cypresses and karobs and sycamores panted in the bright heat, and the pool had turned to a vivid silver and the water fowl had retreated from it.

The two men in the portico were not aware of their own sweat and discomfort. Their eyes held each other's. Then Saul rose and went to the edge of the portico and seemed to be regarding the garden. He said, without turning, "There is an explanation. The wine was drugged, or the food, which your men and you consumed."

Milo uttered an oath in exasperation. "Who would do this? Pilate? Herod? For what purpose? It was the will of Pilate and Herod that He be executed, this Jesus of Nazareth, and that He be entombed, and that He rot, and so kill the faith of His wretched followers and restore, as they said, peace to Israel. Or are you implying that in some fashion His poor disciples drugged our meat and the wine, to which they had had no access? They had fled to the desert, to little hidden towns, all but a very few, among whom was His Mother, as poor as they and as helpless. The soldiers and guards were struck swooning to the ground. I had eaten and drunk as they had eaten and drunk. I was not affected—"

"Still," said Saul, his strong back still to his cousin, "you had delusions, hallucinations, which can come only from administered drugs. Who did this I do not know, nor do I know the reason, unless that it was someone's purpose to steal the body and then so declare that he had —risen. Or, you were hypnotized, and your men with you."

Again Milo swore, incredulously. "There were no drugs! I have been wounded in my campaigns and was given nepenthe and opium for the pain, and I know the sensations. I did not have them that night. I was awake as I had never been awake before, disturbed and uneasy. As for being hypnotized—who did that to me? My parents, by Jupiter! I saw no one that day but the members of their household. And how is it possible for a large number of men to be hypnotized simultaneously, in the darkness, by an unseen person? I have watched hypnotists, physicians. They gaze into the eyes of those they desire to influence. There was none there that night but the legionnaires and the guards, and myself! Who hypnotized whom?"

"Perhaps you all expected—him—to rise, or some preternatural event to take place. And so you dreamed, or imagined."

"You are straining wildly, Saul. None expected Him to rise. I had seen Him die. The men were simple soldiers, jesting, eating, gaming, laughing, looking for the dawn. They have testified they saw nothing, and only that they fell like trees to the ground before the lightning. But I—I did not fall. And I saw. I saw Him. With these eyes I saw Him, and none other."

"Sorcery," said Saul.

Milo groaned in his vexation. "With a word—which is mysterious in itself—you dismiss the event. Men give a mystery a name and then believe it is solved! I am not hysterical. I am not a woman. I am a soldier, and not a dreamer of dreams, nor do I believe easily. I have told you of the immense radiance that fell on the tomb, which almost blinded me, and blinded my men. How do you explain that, you man of facile words?"

"The moon was exceptionally bright."

"The moon had fallen before."

"Then the rising sun struck it."

"The sun had not yet appeared over the mountains. It was still dark."

Saul turned suddenly and his freckled face was tense with fury. "What is it you believe? That this Yeshua of Nazareth, this Jesus, as you call him, is the Messias of the Jews, this unknown carpenter from the hills of Galilee? If you believe so, then you are blasphemous, for we know that when He comes, blessed be His Name, the whole world will know in a twinkling, and He will come in clouds of glory for all men to see. He will not creep from obscurity like a thief in the night, with only a miserable handful of the inconsequential to herald Him! Titus Milo, you are a Roman, and you are a man of hard realism. How is it possible for you to believe that—he—is the Messias?"

"I believe He is the Messias," said Milo. "I believe the testimony of my own senses, my sight and my hearing. I was in your grandfather's house and I saw the child restored to life. I saw the death of Jesus of Nazareth, and I saw Him rise from the dead. This was not done by the artful magic of unknown deceivers, by Castor and by Pollux! If there are such deceivers, then they know thaumaturgy unknown to other men, and men of such gifts do not move slyly in darkness when they could make their fortune."

"Listen to me," said Saul. "I have seen Indu magicians, here in Tarsus. I have seen them toss a long rope into the air which immediately became rigid like a pole, and very high, higher than the height of four men put together. And I have seen several men swarm up that rope—and disappear instantly before my eyes! I do not attempt to explain it, except that I know it is not supernatural. And did not Pharaoh's magicians perform wonders before Moses, and was he not given the magic to surpass them? This is not unknown."

Milo sighed despondently. "You will not believe."

"I do not trust, always, the evidence of my senses. Our senses are frail and easily deceived and distorted. There are a thousand rational explanations for what you believe happened."

"And each of them is more incredible than the other," said Milo. "I have brought you letters. Read them."

With a face full of dark suspicion Saul read the letter from his sister, Sephorah, in which she related what had occurred in her grandfather's house, as Milo had related it. "He is surely the Messias!" she wrote, in words of joy. "We know it, in our hearts and our souls, all of our household. The house is blessed, that He entered it and restored our son to us. We wept when we heard He had been condemned for inciting riots and rebellions against Rome, and for blasphemy. But we remembered the prophecies. We waited in patience—and He rose from the dead, as He had raised our son from the dead. Blessed is Israel that she has known this day, and blessed are we that we lived in His years. Now with greater happiness and dearer peace we can say, 'Hear, O Israel! The Lord our God, the Lord is One!'"

Saul shuddered. How was it possible that his sister, gently reared like a princess in her father's house, fastidious, cosseted and loved, a daughter of a noble name, could believe that this Galilean was the Messias? The very thought horrified the young Pharisee, and shamed him, and he feared for her soul for this blasphemy. His enormous pride was wounded, and it smarted with rage, for had not Sephorah complained of this Yeshua a few months before? Now she adored him!

There was a brief letter from Joseph of Arimathaea who had written:

"Your cousin, Titus Milo Platonius, will tell you what he saw with his own eyes and what he heard with his own ears. But I knew Him from the beginning. I gave

Him the tomb in which His mortal Body reposed for a brief space, and I knew it would be brief. I had seen Him die, but I knew it would be so, as it was prophesied. I wished to see Him rise from the dead, as He had foretold, but I was given a silent message that I must not be there. I was sorrowful in my heart, but now I know that if I had been present it would be rumored that I had stolen Him away and had secreted Him in my own house! Such is the infamy of the human mind, and the soul's rejection of truth. I rejoice! For God has not forgotten His people, and has given to us our Messias, and the world has been moved from her place and has been absolved of her sins. For the Messias had said, and I heard Him, that He came not to destroy the Law but to fullfil it."

Saul put aside the letter in gloomy silence, then stared down at it where it lay on the table. He felt he hated Joseph of Arimathaea for this appalling folly; he felt personally betrayed, for had he not come to love Joseph as a second father? He remembered that day on the desert, and Jochanan the Essene, whom the Greeks called John the Baptist. Was it on such that men of great houses and culture and nobility, and of education and intellect and pride, built their immortal hopes? And their faith? Had these cultivated men lost their reason, their wits, that they could descend to worship and to hail vagabonds and mountebanks? Had they, unaware of it, themselves, absorbed the Greek mythologies of gods disguising themselves as men and performing wonders and rising from the dead? Or the Egyptian myths? Adonis and Osiris: They were fantasies as surely this Yeshua of Nazareth was a fantasy of fevered and hopeful minds. They, too, Adonis and Osiris, had risen from the dead! It was an old, and pretty, story, but it was only a tale for children.

Saul turned to Titus Milo and the Praetorian captain saw, with considerable grief, the great distaste and even dislike his cousin revealed for him, and the umbrage.

"I will return at once to Jerusalem," said Saul. "I will do what I can, with what influence I own, and with what money, and what knowledge, to destroy this myth of Yeshua of Nazareth, for if it is not destroyed then must all Israel perish in heresy and blasphemy. The wrath of God must be appeased."

Milo said, "Seek, rather, that you, yourself, do not provoke it, Saul of Tarshish."

Chapter 27

SAUL, in his young manhood, had become mistrustful of his own subjective apprehensions, emotions and observations, for, as Rabban Gamaliel had often told him, "It is a fallacy, and often a dangerous one, to expect others to accept our subjective conclusions and experiences as objective fact. Therein lies peril, as the history of good men has often illustrated, for good men, convinced that their subjective convictions have verity, have sought to impose them on others—with considerable violence and enthusiasm—and this has frequently led to massacres, cruel and oppressive laws, coercions, despotisms, and universal madness."

Saul, who tended in his own nature to excess and positive affirmations—or negative ones equally intense and violent—reluctantly had to admit that the Rabban had been quite correct. He practiced self-discipline at all times, sometimes successfully and sometimes with no success at all. He now had a wary mistrust of his subjective impressions, suspecting that he threw the shadow of his mind on reality and called it a fact which should, surely, be obvious to other men!

Yet, when he entered Jerusalem his senses, or his intuitions, or his imagination, led him to believe that the city had changed in some indescribable and subtle way. As he was driven through the streets in a car he had engaged at Joppa, he saw, or thought he saw, a certain stillness that permeated all things, even the market rabble, and that the light had altered. He told himself that this was absurd. He had expected some change and his imagination had obliged him. But—was that not a different aspect on faces now, a thoughtfulness? Were the markets and the narrow rising and winding streets less noisy? Was it possible that a city had a life of its own, secret from men, and that its vast and hidden thoughts metamorphosed the very air, the angles of light, the cast of shadows, and made men vaguely aware of them?

It was late summer and the hills and fields were golden with the coming harvest, and the distant mountains were a deep pulsing purple, and the twisting walls of Jerusalem had had, to Saul's eye, a deeper and brighter yellow than he had ever seen before. Still, he remembered, no day or night or even hour was the same as the one preceding it, and in nearly a year Jerusalem must have inexorably altered. That was what the traveler discerned; the inhabitant did not observe.

He went first to his shop on the Street of the Tentmakers. Had it always been so narrow, so dark, so ill-smelling—and so subdued? The rattle and clang of the looms was louder, now, than the voices in the shops. Had it been that way before? He dropped his few pouches and his one small chest, and looked about the dusty gloom of his own shop with a sense, not of homecoming, but of exile. He shook out his blankets and they smelled musty. He pushed open shutters. The mice had been busy here and there, and he cursed them. He went to the nearest market and, standing on the black cobblestones, he drank some poor wine and ate some cheese and bought a grape leaf heaped with hot and steaming spiced meat. A merchant was arguing nearby with another miserable merchant, and though they were hidden from Saul by the wall of their little shop he could hear them clearly.

"I tell you, He was truly the Messias!"

"Quiet. You will be accused, like Him, of blasphemy and heresy. Or of incitement against Rome. If the priests don't seize you by the neck the Romans will!"

"You are laughing at me. But I say to you again, that I saw Him send light and sight into the clouded eyes of a blind man, who had his station at the wall of the Temple, begging!"

"I have heard of this from many of our penniless rabbis in the past. Is that all the proof you have?" The merchant chuckled.

"No. It was something else. I saw His Face, and I knew Him for the Messias. My heart told me; my soul quivered—"

"If you do not tend that fire your meat will quiver into cinders!"

There was a muttered cursing, a wave of smoke that bellied out into the street, a stench of overcooked meat. Saul was frowning, and eating without awareness. Titus Milo Platonius had said the same thing: "I saw His Face, and I knew Him for the Messias." The merchant said, panting and choking somewhat, "Laugh if you will, Amos, but it is true, and one day you will know it is true."

Saul walked slowly past the shop and with pretended unconcern he glanced within it, to see two burly men with white and black headcloths and garments chopping meat and seasoning it on a plank of wood not too clean, and mixing it with onions, and stirring it in pots. Their hands were soiled and their nails grimy. Saul dropped his grape leaf on the stones. He still idled. He caught the odor of the men, rank and tinged with garlic, and he saw their heat-flushed coarse faces and their big red mouths. He smiled darkly to himself. From among these, Yeshua of Nazareth had drawn his followers! He was welcome to them, and to their base, vulgar acceptance of Him. There were only a few men of family, like Joseph of Arimathaea and his cousin, Milo, who had been so deceived.

He returned to his shop, bathed and put on his better clothing and went to the house of his grandfather, Shebua ben Abraham. He had bought, in Tarsus, gifts for his sister and her five children and in spite of his frugality he had spent considerable money. He had also brought a tithe for the Temple in Jerusalem, as was customary. The gift for his sister was a flexible golden serpent with ruby eyes and a glittering tongue, to be worn on the arm, a silly Egyptian trifle in his estimation but one sure to please Sephorah. For her children he had bought golden small replicas of the Ark of the Covenant, piously inscribed, and excellently wrought. It came to him, as he placed them in a pouch, that he had bought nothing for Sephorah's husband, that silent gentle young man with the lake-blue eyes. Saul was annoyed. But one easily overlooked Ezekiel, who never had anything to say for himself.

For his favorite of Sephorah's children, Amos ben Eze-kiel, he had made a special gift, an ornate cap of black, red and white, signifying the Tribe of Benjamin, elaborately bordered with gold embroidery and heavily inset with precious jewels. At the top was a round fringed circle of blue, the sign of the Pharisee. The expensive thing was not to Saul's taste, but immediately he saw his sister's face he knew that he had delighted her. She put it on Amos' fair curls and stood off to admire it. The boy smiled at her indulgently. Though he was now a man, according to Jewish tradition, he still wore the purple-bordered tunic of adolescence.

Saul, at his request, made in a letter to Clodia Flavius, was admitted to the women's quarters of his grandfather's house. He knew that the Roman lady had granted him a rare privilege: Men were rarely admitted to the women's quarters by ladies of propriety, and only on specific invitation, though women, if they desired, could invade the rest of the house. Clodia had told Sephorah, "Men are very tedious and vain and childish, and a woman of sense can endure them only infrequently. Hence, the ladies of my generation, and all true ladies even in these degenerate times, adhere to the old ways of a woman's sanctuary." Sephorah's two older sons, Amos and his brother of fourteen years, were received in these plain but pleasant quarters only for certain hours of the afternoon. Within a short time they could not enter except on special occasions, and on invitation. The younger boys, still children, and the little maid, lived in the women's quarters with their mother and grandmother.

Clodia Flavius had become plump and even more sedate over the years, though her eyes were still clear and observant and mildly severe, and she sat in an ebony chair near Sephorah, who everyone believed was now a most decorous young matron. But her golden eyes were still dancing and merry and eloquent as she looked at her beloved brother, though her hair, bright as gilt, was concealed by a headcloth. Her clothing was modest and demure. She sat with her hands folded patiently in her lap. Saul, for the first time in his life, approved of her, though he had never ceased to love her.

He had come here for a definite purpose, and Clodia sensed it within a few moments and she looked at him openly and waited.

Saul drew Amos to him with a gentle but peremptory hand, and the boy stood at his knee and looked at him with Hillel's soft brown eyes, which had an inner radiance of intelligence. Amos was tall and slender, with a beautiful strong mouth and a complexion of rose. So Hillel must have looked in his youth, thought Saul, with the familiar pain at his heart.

"I should like to ask you a few questions, my nephew," he said, and glanced at Sephorah. "With your grandmother's and mother's permission."

Clodia's thick eyebrows twitched and Sephorah bent her head serenely.

"I was told of your illness, before the Passover," said Saul and now he looked steadily into the boy's eyes. "Tell me. Did you eat anything—peculiar—or drink it before your illness? Anything that your brothers and your sister did not eat?"

The boy shook his head, puzzled. But suddenly Clodia and Sephorah exchanged a quick look, and leaned forward in their chairs.

Still fixing the boy with his fierce and commanding blue eyes, Saul said, "The servant, the old man, Cephalus, the Greek, did he not give you a sweetmeat or a pastry—before your illness, or a cup of wine, which your brothers and your sister did not share?"

"No, my uncle," said Amos. "Cephalus does not come to these quarters, and I did not leave them before my Bar Mitzvah, though sometimes I saw Cephalus from a distance. I have spoken to him but three times in my life."

"When?" The word was as sharp as the crack of the whip.

"Once, when I was very young," said Amos, the puzzled frown still between his eyes, "and I had strayed into the garden of my grandfather's father, Shebua ben Abraham. He returned me. He carried me over his shoulder, like a lamb. And I saw him after that a year ago, when he delivered a message to my grandmother from my grandfather, David ben Shebua." Amos paused.

"And the third time?"

The boy moved uneasily at this intent questioning. He was afraid of Saul, who could be very intimidating. "After my illness, Saul ben Hillel."

Saul clasped his hands over his knees and studied the youth grimly, as if doubting his every word, and Amos looked back at him with increasing uneasiness. Once he glanced at his mother who had become pale and still.

"Tell me," said Saul. "Did you ever accept any dainty or wine, or even a cup of water, or a fruit, from any other member of my grandfather's house, from any servant, who came to you secretly and quietly and offered it to you, and you ate or drank apart from your brothers and your sister?"

"No," said Amos. He was now clearly alarmed at this interrogation, the lawyer's intensive interrogation which had frightened others older than he in the past. His under lip quivered, and he caught it quickly between his teeth, remembering that he was no longer a child.

Saul sat back in his chair but his daunting eyes did not leave the boy's face. He studied him even more grimly. "Perhaps you forget," he said. The boy shook his head.

"Are you implying, Saul ben Hillel, that my grandson was deliberately poisoned or drugged?" asked Clodia Flavius. "If so, you are in error."

Saul did not look at her. He still gazed at his nephew.

"Amos," he said, "how long did you feel languid or indisposed before you fell into that great illness?"

The boy suddenly looked sheepish, and Saul leaned toward him, waiting. "For two weeks, perhaps," confessed Amos. "But I told no one, fearing that the festivities attending my Bar Mitzvah would be delayed, and I would pass the occasion in my bed. I did not desire that. But I was stricken at last, three days before, and from that day I remembered nothing."

"Nothing?" The word was relentless.

The boy's white lids fell over his eyes. "I remember nothing of my illness, except for an hour before I became unconscious. I believed I was dying. My fever consumed me like flames. My head was like cracking stone. I could not even drink water. Then all became dark."

"Ah," said Saul. "Remember Amos, remember. During those weeks before did you eat or drink anything strange, and alone? A berry in the garden, perhaps, which not even birds eat, or a root, or a fruit you found, or an enticing sweetmeat left idly on a seat in the garden?"

Now Saul's own quick temper suffused the boy's cheeks and his eyes sparked, and not with alarm. "Saul ben Hillel," he said in a firm voice, "I am not an infant. I do not put chance articles into my mouth. Nor am I an idiot, who thrusts oddments between his lips!"

Clodia smiled tightly and Sephorah, looking at her again, also smiled.

"You are disrespectful," said Saul. "Your deportment has been neglected. I am your uncle, and I have a serious reason for questioning you, for do I not love you, and is it not my wish to protect you from evil superstitions and delusions and the enticements of dark spirits? Therefore, answer me without impudence or quickness, and be temperate.

"Tell me. You fell into a stupor of illness and fever, and do not remember your illness which lasted three days. What is your next memory?"

But, to Saul's own surprise, the boy became silent and an undescribable expression appeared on his fair face and a melancholy and a curious sadness. Saul took his hand. It had become cold and faintly tremulous. "Tell me, Amos ben Ezekiel," he said, "for I hold you dear and would not have you harmed. Has anyone asked you this question before?"

"No," whispered the boy, and now his lips were trembling.

"So it is that I ask you," said Saul.

"I—dreamed," said Amos, and tried to take away his hand, but Saul held it strongly.

"Of what did you dream?"

"Is it lawful," asked Clodia Flavius in her sturdy Roman voice, "to question of these things, Saul ben Hillel?"

"It is," said Saul, still not looking at her. "For the sake of the boy's soul. I am not inquisitive. I know the Kabalah. I know why I question. Amos, of what did you dream?"

The boy uttered a deep sigh, which was almost a moan. "I awoke in a beautiful country, more beautiful than any vista in Israel." His voice was hushed and low. "There were mighty ivory and gold mountains in the distance, shining, though I did not see the sun. The sky was very blue. And between me and the mountains there were vast valleys and gardens and many quiet trees and flowers, and the air was full of singing, but I saw no singers. I stood on the bank of a river as green as grass and swiftly flowing. It seemed very deep and wide. And on the farther shore—"

"Yes?" said Saul. The room was completely silent now.

"My grandfather stood there, Hillel ben Borush, in white garments that were like light. I knew him at once, for I had seen him before he died." Now the boy looked directly into Saul's eyes, not defiantly, but with a demand that he be believed. It was a man's imperative gaze, stern and reserved.

Saul was much moved, despite his growing anger and his conviction that the boy had been secretly drugged by a servant, a follower of Yeshua of Nazareth, in order to create just this occasion.

"I believe that you dreamed you saw my father, Amos."

But the boy's voice rose clear and decisive. "I did not dream, my uncle. I saw him. And he smiled at me and beckoned to me, but the river lay between us. And then he lifted his hand and the river narrowed to the width of a brook and he reached his hand to me, and I took it and I stepped over the brook and we laughed together, and watched the river widen again." His words were now loud and tumultuous. "The singing in the air increased and I wanted to weep with joy, and my grandfather said to me, 'Blessed is that man who dies in his youth and has not sinned, and who awaits here the return of the Messias, Who sits at the right Hand of His Father, blessed be His Name!' "

"What blasphemy is this?" cried Saul, truly appalled. "What is the meaning of your words, Amos ben Ezekiel?"

"I do not know!" said the boy, with emphasis. "I only know what my grandfather said."

"But the words mean nothing, they are nonsense, for the Messias has not yet left Heaven, and He has not yet come unto man. Do you not understand this, Amos? Do you not understand the absurdity of your dream?"

The boy repeated, "I only know what my grandfather said."

"All dreams but the dreams of holy men and the prophets are ridiculous," said Saul. But the boy did not look away from him and the soft contours of his cheeks had hardened and he reflected his appearance of when he would be a man in truth. His brown eyes were no longer soft or dreaming. They were resolute and courageous.

Saul sighed and shook his head slowly, and the boy waited. Finally he said, "And what is your next memory, Amos?"

The boy did not answer for a moment or two. He was watching Saul with an incomprehensible expression. Then in a slow and deliberate tone, as if expecting ridicule and preparing to combat it, he said, "I heard a voice. I had never heard that voice before. It was the voice of a man, and it filled the whole transparent air and it was as if the mountains and the valleys and the river listened. And it said to me, 'I say unto you, Amos ben Ezekiel, arise!'"

A chill unexpectedly seized Saul, and he fought it. He said, "I believe you, Amos, that you are not lying when you tell me of this dream. But you must tell me: What did your grandfather say—when he heard that voice?"

"He wept."

"He wept?"

"Yes. And he released my hand and walked with me to the river again, and again it narrowed and he indicated to me that I must cross over and be on the other side, and I wept also, for I did not want to leave that place of peace and singing joy and my grandfather. But I knew I must obey that voice, but why I should obey it I do not know. The voice had not commanded me to cross the river once more, but I knew that I had been commanded. So I leaped over the brook, and immediately it widened and was wide and running and my grandfather waved farewell to me and turned and descended into the valley and I saw him no more. I called him, but there was no answer and no singing, and where I stood it was dark. It became darker, and it was like night before my eyes, and my heart was filled with sorrow, and I had never known sorrow before. And then it was light again, but not the light I had seen. It was a dimmer light, and paler, and I saw that I lay on the floor of my bedroom—" He looked over his shoulder at his mother and grandmother, who were hiding their tearful faces in their hands now. "And my parents and my kinsmen and my brothers were on the floor with me, shedding tears and clasping my hand and kissing my cheek, and they were crying aloud, calling my name."

His eyes fell away. A deep silence filled the room.

Saul was moved again, but his anger was growing. He put his hand on the boy's shoulder. "And that was all, Amos? You saw no more?"

"I saw—Him," said Amos. "I saw Him before I looked at the faces of those who love me. He smiled at me, and He was sad and, it seemed, regretful. His face was most beautiful, and He turned and left the room and two or three strangers left with Him, and I saw Him no more, though I wished to implore Him to remain."

"Why did you wish him to remain?"

The boy's face visibly darkened with pain. "I felt He was my—life, and my desiring, and it was a glory to gaze upon Him, and when He left it was as if the sun had retreated and everything was diminished."

Saul now caught the boy's shoulders in both his hands and he drew him abruptly to him. "Amos ben Ezekiel, you must listen to me, for your soul may depend upon it! The man you saw in your bedroom, that miserable Nazarene, is not unknown to me! He is a sorcerer, a fraud, a mountebank, a blasphemer, and he was executed for his crimes, justly, and he had bewitched you in some arcane way before he even entered this house! I do not know the reason. I am only certain that is what happened—perhaps to delude this house, which is an influential one, great in Israel. You must listen to my counsel! You must forget him. You never died, Amos. You were drugged, or in a state of catalepsy, induced by sly enemies, or servants of the Nazarene, who wished to reveal 'wonders' and cause awe, and to deceive. Had he never entered this house you would have recovered. You must believe me, Amos."

But Amos, to Saul's rising wrath and excitement, only shook his head from side to side in quiet denial. Now the sound of the women's soft weeping could be heard.

Amos said, "I believe, my uncle, that you believe in your own words, and you fear for me. Do not be afraid. I know who He is."

"Who?" exclaimed Saul, but he knew, with dread, what the boy would say.

"I know He is the Messias, and I know He rose from the dead, and I know He sits at the right Hand of our Father, as my grandfather told me. How I know I do not know, but I know."

The awful and familiar words were like hard fists beating on Saul's heart.

"You dreamed," said Saul.

The boy sighed. "Then, I wish I had never awakened from my dream."

The broken words, spoken in a man's voice, made Saul, himself, want to weep. He touched the boy's arm and put him away from him, and rose. He looked with coldly furious eyes upon his sister.

"You have let him believe monstrous lies, which threaten his soul," he said. "May God forgive you, though I cannot, Sephorah bas Hillel."

He turned and left the room.

The atmosphere of the house had mysteriously changed. Saul knew it at once, as he advanced to the atrium. It was an atmosphere of serenity, of peace, of composure. It was—and the very thought to him was absurd—like the air of a quiet enclosure of a garden in the Temple.

His kinsmen were awaiting him, Shebua ben Abraham, David ben Shebua and Sephorah's blue-eyed husband, Ezekiel, who rarely spoke but whose very eyes always seemed to be listening gently but surely. The two younger men rose and embraced Saul, who accepted their greetings impatiently. Over their shoulders he looked at his grandfather, who appeared much older, not suave any longer, not urbane and superbly smiling, but calm and untroubled. He was like a prophet and he wore, for the first time Saul could remember, the ritual hat of the Tribe of Benjamin but not an elaborate one. It was simple and austere. He was a veritable patriarch. He accepted Saul's brief kiss on his cheek and pressed the younger man's shoulder with his long white hand.

"Welcome to this house, my grandson," he said. "We have longed for your return."

Saul's mouth curled somewhat wryly. Shebua's voice was not the voice he remembered, arrogant and smooth. Shebua clapped his hands and when a servant appeared Shebua asked that the Greek servant, Cephalus, be sent to the atrium at once, as Saul had requested.

"You have come to doubt, and to express your doubt, Saul ben Hillel," said Shebua in a mild tone. "I do not censor you, nor complain, for had I not seen with my own eyes what had occurred in this house I should doubt also, and probably with more contempt. For I had never believed, no, not in the God of our Fathers, the God of Abraham and Jacob, not once in my life, not even in my youth. But now I believe." His pale eyes dwelt on Saul without rancor or challenge. They were kindly, and steadfast. He said, almost in a whisper, "Hear, O Israel! The Lord our God, the Lord is One."

To Saul's angry and amused amazement David and Ezekiel repeated the words, their heads bent, their hands clasped, as they stood near Shebua.

"The sorcerer, the necromancer, is more powerful than I thought," Saul said.

As if he had not heard Shebua said, "Blessed is this house, that He entered here, for there was no holiness amongst us, no faith, no piety, no humility, no trust. Blasphemy had dwelt here and all the trappings of a meaningless and secular world, whose name is confusion and whose voices are like those of beasts raving in the wilderness. Yet, He came to us and raised our child from the dead, and delivered him once more to our arms, and I saw His face—and I do not know why, but I knew Who He was."

"I also know," said Saul, and his teeth clenched together. The old servant entered and came to stand before his master who touched his arm with the affection of a brother.

"Cephalus," said Shebua, "this is a son of our house, Saul ben Hillel, of whom I have spoken. He would like to put some questions to you."

Saul regarded the old man with detestation. He was not even an apostate Jew, not even a member of the Amaratzim—the peasantry, the market rabble. He had been a slave, bought in his youth by Shebua ben Abraham and later freed, and his tasks were humble, as he carried wood for baths, emptied the kitchen refuse, swept floors, weeded the gardens, picked fruit, washed walls, and carried burdens. He was unlettered. He was thin and bent with labor, and had a long but meager white beard and thin white hair and a crooked nose, and his countenance bore the stigmata of generations of laborers in the dust and the fields.

But his eyes were great and bright and brown, like the eyes of a youth, and they radiated joy.

Saul had been prepared for a lip-sucking, sly, sniveling old slave, full of the arts of the malicious poor, fawning, nodding, eager to please and just as eager to do mischief. But as Cephalus looked at him respectfully and with interest Saul could not detect any falseness in the old man's face. He had a curious dignity in spite of his obviously undistinguished origin. He folded his hands and waited for Saul's questions, and there was no apprehension about him.

It was plain to Saul that Cephalus was simple and that he believed what he had decided to believe, without hypocrisy and falseness or a desire to be singular.

Before he could speak Shebua said, "Cephalus, show my grandson your right hand."

Cephalus immediately extended his right hand, wrinkled and worn, to Saul, showed him the back of it, and then the palm. Saul frowned. Shebua said, "Cephalus came to us as a young man with a withered hand, twisted and gnarled and bent like a claw. He had had an evil master who, when Cephalus had been a child, punished him for some small crime by forcing his hand into a fire. I bought him out of pity, when we were youths together, and he has been in this house ever since. You will observe, Saul, that the hand, though worn and veined and discolored like my own, is not maimed but healthy and clean. His withered hand had been restored to its present condition in the winking of an eye—by Him the Romans call Jesus of Nazareth, but Whom we know as Yeshua."

Saul's face expressed his cold disbelief and distaste. He said, "This is a minor miracle, my grandfather, but it is well-known that our wandering and holy rabbis frequently heal when implored for healing."

"Speak, Cephalus," said Shebua. The old man gave him a timid look, then faced Saul again.

"Lord," he said to the young man, "I am not a Jew, but a Greek, and I knew nothing of these rabbis of whom you have spoken. I am not young. I have had reason to fear my fellows, and my health has been failing for many years. I rarely left this house, where I had known the only kindness in my life. I feared to leave it." He spoke in a trembling and feeble voice, and his Greek was unlettered and unrefined, the accents of a slave. "But one day one of the maidens in the servants' hall spoke of Jesu the Nazarene, and she is Greek, also, and she related that it was said that He was the Unknown God, worshiped by my people, who await His coming.

"My hand, through all these years, had never ceased to pain me, and as my years advanced the pain became stronger and there were nights that I moaned, for I could not sleep. It was useless to me. I tottered through my days in weariness and agony, longing for death. Then I heard that Jesu the Nazarene was in Jerusalem again, before the Jewish Passover, and I said in my heart, I will follow Him and if He is the Unknown God I will summon courage to touch His garment, without His knowing, so that I should not offend His majesty by speaking to Him."

The old man paused, and a quick trembling ran over his face like the ripples of sunlit water and his joys widened to a blazing of joy.

"There was a great crowd about Him, shouting, 'Blessed is He who comes in the Name of the Lord! Hosannah!' And they were throwing palm branches before Him and flowers, and the women were holding up their infants for Him to gaze upon and bless, and He rode slowly among them on an ass, a Man in rude dress but with the aspect of a King, of a Zeus, armed with lightnings. And His Face was beautiful, and yet it was not the beauty we call by that name, for I have seen many such as He from Galilee, and of His complexion. I crept behind Him, at a distance, insinuating myself through the ranks of His followers and the shouting and laughing and adoring crowds of men and women and children, who were tossing blossoms in His path. Many rushed to kiss His hands, His feet, to look up into His Face, and there were moments when that Face became that of a Father, loving, serious, grieved.

"And then I was behind Him, in the footsteps of the little ass He rode, and I crept closer to Him and stretched out my withered hand and touched His sleeve. A mere touch, a brushing, of my crippled fingers. The sleeve was of rough brown linen, such as slaves and workmen and field laborers wear."

The old man sighed and now his eyes were tearful, though he was smiling in his rapture.

"Jesu did not see me nor heed me, nor did He turn. But I believe that He knew that I had touched His garment, though the beast He rode carried Him on through the throngs. I halted, gazing after Him. Then I became aware that the awful pain in my hand had ceased as if it had never been, and when I looked down at it I saw the fingers uncurling like petals, the wrist straightening, the scars slowly disappearing, the skin becoming smooth and clean. And I raised my arms in the air and I gave thanks to the Unknown God, unknown no longer, but among us in His mercy and compassion, and I wept and others around me looked at me with wondering smiles and doubtless thought that I was mad."

"Hysteria," said Saul, and his expression was colder and full of aversion.

"Lord?" said the old man. But Saul did not answer. After a moment the servant continued:

"I blessed His Name and adored Him and prayed to Him, though He had vanished and then I returned to this house and showed the hand to the servants and they marveled. One of the cooks is a Jew, and a skeptical man, and he has known me for many years. When he heard my story he said, 'Truly, this is the Holy One of Israel, blessed be His Name,' and the cook told me of the Messias of the Jews, and I knew it was He.

"Then," said Cephalus, his voice dropping, "the child Amos ben Ezekiel became ill to the point of death, and there was lamentation in the house. Soon it was said that he was dying, and then we heard, in the hall, that he was dead, the lovely child to whom I had spoken but once or twice and had seen only from a distance since he was an infant. But we knew him to be fair and kind and virtuous, and we mourned.

"Then I bethought myself of Jesu of Nazareth. I do not know what seized my mind! It was like a sure madness, a vehemence, a passion, and I could not explain it. But I ran from the house and sought Him, and He was entering the Temple with His followers, and I rushed upon Him, crying, 'Lord, Holy One of Israel, a child is dead in my master's house, and only You can restore Him!' "

Cephalus shook his head in dazed wonder. "I am not a man of courage, of impulse, of exuberant youth, a man of enthusiasm. Had I been told a few days before that I would have thrown myself from this house, racing like a boy, for a stranger, to implore Him, I should have said that the very thought was madness! Yet, I did this.

"He—He halted. His followers rebuked me, saying, 'Why do you disturb and halt the Master, slave? Begone, lest we drive you away!' But He looked down at my face and my shaking hands, and He said, 'Let no man turn from Me any who seek Me,' and He gestured that He would follow me." Cephalus bowed his head. "And He entered the house with me, and I led Him to the chamber of the child, and though He had not asked the name of the boy He gazed upon him, as he lay on his coverlet on the floor with the mourners weeping about him, and He said, 'I say to you, Amos ben Ezekiel, arise!'"

Cephalus raised his head and his hands in an attitude of awe and absolute adoration. "And the child opened his eyes, and they were still filmed with death, and he murmured—and he lived! But there was no happiness on his face, that he had been restored, and I turned to Jesu the Nazarene, and His own Face was sad and full of repining. Then, with no word more He left the chamber and the house.

"Lord," said Cephalus, "that is all."

During this recital Saul had kept glancing at his kinsmen, and to his disgust he saw their moved faces and the tears in their eyes. Then he turned implacably to Cephalus.

"Fear no punishment, but I abjure you in the Name of God to tell the truth, slave. I will grant that your hand was healed, for I know my kinsmen do not lie. But you were healed through the belief in your own mind, that you would be healed, and by no miracle of Yeshua of Nazareth. He did not even know you had touched him! Yet, what you believed was some miracle from a holy one transported your mind, making it a prey to fantasies and ecstasies. This is not uncommon for those in the throes of religious ecstasy—especially among the simple and unlearned.

"You yearned to make your hero celebrated, to have him perform some marvel, some wonder, in order to justify your adoration. This, too, is not uncommon. Zeal is very powerful. So, you reflected. And then you gave my nephew, all trusting in you, a servant of this house, a potion, a sweetmeat, or a fruit, or a little wine, which contained a drug which induces a trance, or a somnolent state, a dormant condition closely resembling death. The child fell ill. He appeared to die. It even deceived his physicians. When he was laid upon the floor to receive the anointing and the spices and the oils and his grave-clothes, you ran from this house and sought him you call Jesu of Nazareth, and finding him you brought him here, where he apparently arrived just as my nephew was awakening. He saw the boy's condition, and seized his opportunity."

Saul smiled a most ugly smile, and his eyes glinted. He spread out his hands. "That is the story, the true one. Cephalus, if you have any gratitude to your lord, Shebua ben Abraham, who rescued you and freed you and gave you shelter and kindness in his house, tell the truth. You will not be punished. We shall feel affection for you that you so loved that man, though he is nothing but a vagabond. Devotion is very moving. But it must not becloud truth. For a lie is a dishonor even in a servant."

Cephalus had listened to this in absolute bewilderment, staring at Saul as at a basilisk. Then he stammered, "Lord, I gave the child no drug, for whence would I receive it? I have not spoken to him nor approached him since he was an infant, for I am a humble man, and not pleasing of countenance, and I shrank from speech with others. Nor, lord, did I ask another to give the child any harmful potion, for who in this house would do such a thing? Lord, I swear to this with all my soul, and by the love I bear Jesu of Nazareth."

Saul exclaimed, in his sudden frightening fury, "I do not believe you! You are lying, and you seek to deceive, for that is the way of the base-born, the low, the degraded, the slave! You would make yourself important in this house, and honored as the recipient of some divine mercy, as a man apart, for your slave's heart longs to be distinguished! Get from my sight, rascal, lest I kick you for the dog you are!"

But Cephalus looked at Shebua ben Abraham, not in terror, but in beseeching, and Shebua said, "Go, Cephalus, and we thank you."

These words made Saul gasp, even in his stupendous rage, for Shebua had spoke to the old servant as one speaks to a brother. Incredulous, he saw the Greek bow and leave the atrium, and he was alone again with his kinsmen.

He looked at their greatly moved and strangely tranquil faces, and he shouted, "Is it possible that you believe this foul nonsense, this insult to the rational intelligence of a man, this affront to decency, this outrage against God, Himself?"

"We believe," said Shebua for his son and his grandson. And David said, the elegant Sadducee, "We believe." For the first time Ezekiel spoke, in his modest and uncertain voice, "I believe."

And again Saul heard the loathed words, "Why it is that we believe we do not know, but we know that He is the Messias, the Holy One of Israel, blessed be His Name."

"He is dead!" Saul almost roared. "His body was stolen away, to make a lie a verity!"

"He was dead, and the darkness came and the Veil in the Temple, over the Holy of Holies, was rent, and the earth thundered and shook and terror was on the earth. And in three days He rose from the dead, and there are those who have seen Him."

Saul groaned in his anguish of rage and revulsion, and without speaking again he turned and left his grandfather's house. They called to him, but he refused to hear them. They implored, but he ran from them.

And he was filled with an overpowering hatred.

Chapter 28

SAUL sat before Joseph of Arimathaea in a condition of wild and frustrated passion and wrath, so fierce that it was almost malignancy. When he could speak he said in a voice that was unusually deep and hoarse with repugnance and suppressed violence:

"Forgive me. You have been my friend, Joseph of Arimathaea, and I have been grateful, for I know I do not possess the graciousness and ease of other men and you have shown me patience and kindness and, often, peace. Why this was I do not know. I was content and happy that you accepted me for what I was, for others do not, alas. I trusted you above all other men except Rabban Gamaliel—I trusted you above my father, may he rest in peace.

"I thought that not only were you a pious Jew and a Pharisee but above self-deception, though I had detected a certain—trustfulness—toward him whom the Greeks call John the Baptist, though we know him as Jochanan

ben Zachary. I believed you loved his removal from and
rebellion against the Roman oppressor of our country,
and therefore were indulgent in the face of his excesses
and zeal. It is true that you spoke of the Messias as imminent, but do we not all hope that? You frequently
spoke in mysterious riddles, but that is the way of older
Jews, and I could bear with it, though I am a pragmatic
man. I knew you loved and adored the Lord our God as
deeply as any man could, and would defend His honor
and His Name to the very death.

"Yet now, in this house, today, you tell me to my face
that Yeshua of Nazareth, vagabond, wandering ragged
rabbi, deceiver, vainglorious madman, fraud, liar and
blasphemer, an unlearned Galilean, whom none knew until three years ago, is the Messias, the Holy One of Israel! You tell me that you have 'known it from the beginning!' You tell me that you gave him a fine tomb 'for
what I knew would be only three short days!' You tell
me that not only did he rise from the dead—but you
have seen him since his execution!

"If another man but you, Joseph of Arimathaea, had
told me of this I would have said, 'You lie, or you are
mad.' "

They sat in Joseph's small library to which the bronze
door had been closed. Joseph regarded Saul gently and
silently and his large dark eyes seemed to wax and wane
with an inner lambency. He was not angered. He was
very calm and in repose.

He said, "Yes? And what do you say of me, Saul of
Tarshish?"

The lid of Saul's half-shut and afflicted eye visibly
quivered, and there was a tight tremor about his mouth.
"I do not know what to say," he replied, "except that I
know you do not lie. What then, is the answer? That
you, a man of a great house in Israel, a gentleman, a
man of culture and taste and learning, have been frightfully deceived and betrayed by scoundrels and mountebanks and necromancers of the basest sort. What is their
object? To destroy Israel, to bring down the wrath of
God upon us. Who pays them? The Romans? Infidels,
heathens, Parthians? We do not know, but I am certain
there is someone! They are our enemies. It could be they
are enemies of all men. At the very least they are mad."

Joseph took Saul's goblet to refill it but with a savage gesture Saul refused more wine. He leaned forward to stare at Joseph with a bitter look.

Joseph said, "I saw Him in His first resting place, with shepherds from the hills about Him, in a manger, in a cave, in Bethlehem. I had awaited Him, as I told you, when I saw the glorious Star. I had had dreams. I saw Him with His young Mother; she was not past fourteen, a young girl in the full of her innocence and virginity. I saw Him with His young adoptive father, Joseph, a carpenter. The shepherds knew Him, for they had heard the good news from God's own angels in the wintry hills over Bethlehem, and they had come at once, without doubt and without scorn and without fear, as all simple men approach God. It is a divine simplicity. I found them kneeling and praying about the child-Mother and her Infant, and I brought a gift, though He who made all gifts has need of none. I gazed at the Child. There was but a lantern glow in the dark of the cave, and the night was cold and black outside. He was but a child as all the sons of man are children, and yet—" Joseph paused, for the memory moved him almost beyond bearing. "I knew at once Who He was. I had no doubt, no misgiving, no second thought, no hesitation. And I prostrated myself before Him, the Holy One of Sion, the Holy One of Israel."

Joseph gazed as at some far distance and his eyes filled with tears. He murmured, "As He has said, Himself, 'Blessed are those who see and believe, but more blessed are those who do not see yet believe.' Before I had seen Him I had believed. When I saw Him the belief was confirmed instantly. I knew where He was during His childhood. I saw Him before He was Bar Mitzvah, in the Temple, a boy questioning the wise men, and answering them. I know where He was for the years wrapped in mystery, but I am not permitted to say. I know where He went after His Ascension, a place as yet unknown to men, for He has said, 'I have sheep you know not of.' I knew when He resumed His trade as a carpenter to support Himself and His Mother. There was not an hour that I was not conscious of him. Saul of Tarshish, that is all I dare tell you. But the Promise of the ages has been fulfilled. The Lamb of God has saved His people from their sins and has turned death into eternal life, blessed be His Name."

Saul was so horrified, so enraged at this—which he considered the foulest of blasphemies—and so afraid before Joseph's words for fear of God's instant punishment —that he sprang to his feet abruptly, and the chair fell back from him and crashed to the marble floor. He put his hands over his ears. "My God, my God!" he cried, "that these ears have heard so monstrous a story, even from you, Joseph of Arimathaea! May God forgive me that I have listened, but may God not forgive those who have so evilly deceived and confused you! I shall avenge you, my nephew, Amos ben Ezekiel, my sister, my unfortunate kinsmen, and all those of my countrymen who have been so wronged by a dead dissembler and hypocrite and madman and rogue! I shall destroy his followers, as they have sought to destroy us and to defame God, and invite His vengeance upon us."

Saul lifted his hand and swore the most solemn and terrible oath he had ever uttered, and then he said, "From this day hence he, the dead malefactor, has no greater enemy than I, nor have his wretched disciples!"

Joseph waited in silence, and then in a voice both mournful and gentle he said, "Saul ben Hillel, I know this: One day He will have no greater friend than you."

With a cry of smothered agony and despair Saul flung himself out of that house into the warm late summer wind and sea-burdened rain. He pulled his hood over his head and wrapped himself tightly in his plain cloak. He hurried through the streets but had no destination. He had thought a thousand times of going to see Rabban Gamaliel but for some reason even he could not understand he shrank from the thought. The celebrated Nasi of the Temple—would he not confirm Saul's horror and rage against the blasphemers? Would he not denounce that miserable man, Yeshua ben Joseph of Nazareth? Why, then, this almost cringing reluctance to go to the Rabban, who could offer him consolation and a glimpse of sanity, and soothe his pain and fury? He did not know.

Instead, Saul went to the house of the High Priest, Caiphas, who had induced Pontius Pilate, after much argumentative exhaustion and imploring, to order the execution of Yeshua the Nazarene on the charge of inciting the people to rebellion against Rome. It was a long distance to that house, through the gray rain and wind and the throngs hurrying into shelters and to their homes. Camels were squealing as they were tugged vigorously in the narrow streets; asses complained, and boys whipped. Saul dodged through the market places, through the growing darkness. He reached the house of the High Priest. It was in truth a palace, surrounded by high walls and guards, and it shone in the twilight—wet and white—like alabaster. The gardens were pungent with freshly aroused fragrances and the trees lashed and clattered in the wind.

The guards were instantly suspicious and contemptuous of this wild man at the gates, with his wet red hair clinging to his brow and cheeks and neck, his unprepossessing if powerful face, and his workman's clothing. But he said to them imperiously, "Tell your lord that Saul of Tarshish, grandson of his friend, Shebua ben Abraham, desires to see him on a matter of much importance!"

Saul waited while one of the sneering guards went to the house with the message. His heart was tumultuous; he kept drawing great audible breaths, and the other guards looked at him curiously, their helmeted heads cocked. Saul was thinking. In all the world there was none he despised more than Caiphas, the son-in-law of the legendary and ruthless Annas, who was mightier than Herod Antipas, himself. Saul considered the High Priest the most despicable of traitors to his people, the sycophant of Rome—the vestments of the High Priest reposed, at the will of the Romans, in the Fortress of Antonius, next to the Temple. He was High Priest so long as the Romans permitted him to be so. He was their servant. He was hostage for the obedience and docility and submission of all Israel. He was paid by the Romans. To offend the Romans would be to be cast out of this beautiful palace, to become a beggar, to be divested of all monies and glory and power, to be shamed forever. (But was that not preferable to treason against his people, to infamy against God?) Nevertheless he, Saul ben Hillel, needed this detestable man in order to protect his country and keep the Name of God from blasphemy.

Caiphas, a sepulchral but stately man of about forty-five years, and with a carefully shaped gray beard and fine, apparently artless, blue eyes, received Saul with unexpected courtesy. He conducted Saul from the atrium—a magnificent room—into a secluded chamber bright with silk and velvet and murals and Persian rugs, and a guard obsequiously closed the door. "I know of your illustrious house, Saul ben Hillel," he said, in a very rich and unctuous voice. "Your grandfather has no dearer friend than I." Wine was brought in jeweled goblets, but Saul, struggling to conceal his hatred and scorn, motioned it aside with impatience. He sat in a beautiful chair, dripping with rain, and offered no apologies. Caiphas was a shrewd man, and very subtle, and he only lifted his eyebrows and smiled affectionately. He recognized Saul for what he was and was not deceived by the rude garments and the rough gestures and voice. Caiphas adjusted his tall oval and pointed Pharisee hat—of white silk embroidered in gold—and waited with a paternal expression. He had no doubt at all that Saul had something of immense importance to tell him.

He was not disappointed. He listened acutely, not only to Saul's words but to his inflections, and he thought, Here is the one for whom I have been seeking!

When Saul had concluded, and the brightening lamplight was glittering in his eyes, Caiphas sighed and affected to be overcome with weariness and bent his head and rubbed his forehead. A beautiful ring sparkled and shone on his right index finger.

"Alas," he said, and there was a deep throb in his voice, "the dangerous days have not departed from our afflicted and holy land, Saul ben Hillel. In truth, I am afraid the danger is increasing. Pilate angrily accused me of knowing that his followers had removed the body of Yeshua of Nazareth from the tomb, though later he apologized. But he was distraught. His accusations, he knew, were both unjust and hysterical, for had not I delivered the malefactor into his hands? Why, then, should I plot to make it seem that he had risen from the dead, as he had 'prophesied'? Ah, those were sad hours! Yeshua's wretched followers fled Jerusalem, but now my spies say they are returning, and that they are seen worshiping in the Temple again, with their fellow Jews on whom they have brought disaster. They engage in soft harangues, trying to convince their brothers that Yeshua ben Joseph was, indeed, the Holy One of Sion. To reject him, they plead, is to reject God, Himself, blessed be His Name. Unfortunately, and to my terror, hundreds are being convinced! They had seen Yeshua, himself, and had listened to his uncouth utterances in the streets and in the Temple. Did you know that he had the effrontery and outrageous impudence to drive the currency-changers from the Temple, and the sellers of sacrifices, and the bankers? He shrieked that they were making his Father's house 'a den of thieves!' "

"I have heard," said Saul.

Caiphas peeped at him from under his hand. "And have you heard, Saul of Tarshish, that my dearest friend, your grandfather, and your grandfather's family, have been seduced into the madness of believing that Yeshua of Nazareth is the Messias?"

Saul flushed darkly. "I know," he said. "That is why I am here. They must be convinced that they are the victims of a low necromancer, in collusion with a thief of a servant in their own house."

Caiphas sighed as if with pain, and dropped his hand and gazed mournfully at the frescoed ceiling. "There are others, even of equally distinguished family," he said. "Who shall deliver us from this madness?"

"I have told you, lord. I," said Saul.

"Ah, yes. You are a Roman citizen, an officer of the Roman Law and Roman courts." He looked at Saul. "Did you know that my brother-in-law, Judas Iscariot, hanged himself after the arrest of Yeshua? Rash young man! An Essene, he had left his father's house, his father, Annas, and his mother's devotion, to live in the desert with other savage creatures like himself. He became one of Yeshua's disciples. He believed this Yeshua was the Messias. Judas was a proud and haughty young man. How he had convinced himself of that appalling blasphemy I do not know! But he was always hasty and uncontrollable, and pampered. To 'force' Yeshua to reveal himself as the Messias Judas contrived to deliver him into my hands. He thought that if Yeshua were seized and arrested, the very angels would descend to rescue him! Ah, ah.

"And when Yeshua was flogged by the Romans, and a crown of thorns thrust on his head, then Judas—tragic young man—knew that there was no Messias, no Holy One of Sion, but only a cheap magician, a spinner of foolish tales, a deceiver, a man of delusions and conceit. According to the Law, I had to give Judas the prescribed thirty pieces of silver which is the reward for the exposure of a blasphemer, and Judas burst into the most awful tears and flung the money into my face, and ran from me with great howls of despair and torment. When I think of my wife's brother, Judas Iscariot, so distraught over his own betrayal by Yeshua, my heart bleeds with sorrow."

For the first time there was a genuine distress in his voice. He seemed surprised at this, himself. He smiled faintly at Saul.

"Tomorrow I will have the letter from the procurator, Pontius Pilate, in my hands, with your staff of authority and a parchment proclaiming that you are the Roman prosecutor of troublemakers and rebels in all of Israel, Saul of Tarshish. May God, blessed be His Name, strengthen you in your holy task, in your firm determination to rid our afflicted land of blasphemers who would destroy her."

He embraced Saul with secret elation. Saul of Tarshish, Roman citizen and lawyer, Saul ben Hillel, grandson of the noble Shebua ben Abraham—what more formidable man than this could be on the side of the angels, and on the side, of course, of the High Priest Caiphas?

But it was Pontius Pilate, himself, who graciously summoned Saul to him, invested him—with his own hands—in the robe of office, gave him the rod of authority and had him repeat the oath of fealty to Rome. (The latter made Saul turn very white, but he forced himself to remember it was only the price he must pay to defend his God. He would pray, on the next Day of Atonement, to be loosed from the oath demanded of him.) Then Pilate informed him that as an officer openly in the service of Rome he would have an entourage of legionnaires who would seize and arrest at his will, and Saul, therefore, would live in a suitable house in Jerusalem, kindly bestowed on him by the procurator.

"I do not believe, lord," said Saul, "that the matter will consume much time. A few weeks, perhaps, a month or so—"

Pilate was a dark thin man, somewhat tall, with a bald head and an elusive expression and a large Roman nose and a tight wide smile. He smiled at Saul's words, then shook his head. "Alas, Saul of Tarshish, I am not so sanguine. News of Jesus of Nazareth and his death and alleged arising from the dead, has spread far and wide and converts among the Jews increase in number daily. I have also heard that they have left Israel in many numbers, to proselytize among their fellow Jews in other countries also. It is as if reports of him have been borne on the wind, and the wind is becoming a hurricane."

His palace was stately and magnificent, and the hall where he had received Saul was the grandest the young man had ever seen. Pilate walked from him, meditatively, pacing up and down the vast room. He said, "I have just returned from Caesarea, and have seen and heard remarkable things there—from a Greek physician who was a guest in my house. But it is of no moment. The peace and tranquillity of Israel is our purpose, yours and mine, Saul ben Hillel. I entrust the matter in your hands for so long as you desire it."

He turned to Saul and seemed about to ask a question, then refrained. Saul bade him farewell. Pilate watched his going, and he pursed his lips then made a wry expression. How these Jews adored and defended their God! How they hated blasphemy! It was absurd; it was laughable. Certainly, Marcus Tullius Cicero, a century before, had been accused of blasphemy in Rome and had almost been tried on the charge. But Rome had thrown off that stupidity, had become fully enlightened, in these past one hundred years or less. No nation coveting the name of civilization would endure such childish abominations any longer—except for these Jews. Long before Rome, they related, they had been a nation and a people, and had possessed their God—yet they had not progressed in the arts of urbanity and tolerance. Had they done so the word "blasphemy" would be a jest now, and not the gravest of charges. A murderer, a true malefactor, the worst of thieves and degenerates, were not regarded by them as so loathsome as a "heretic" and could often receive mercy. But heretics were stoned to death in public places! Incredible.

If I remain here longer, thought Pilate, I shall lose my wits also. Suddenly he recalled again the man who had been a guest in his house, and he sat down to think and to frown and to pull his lip and to fear, as he had feared then.

That night Saul prayed with the greatest ardor of his life, and with all-consuming power and exultation and conviction. "God of my fathers, God of Abraham and Jacob and David, God of Sinai and Moses, King of Kings, Creator of the Universe, Redeemer of Israel, my Lord and my God: I now know Your Will for me, that I rid Your holy land of blasphemers and idolators, of Your wickedest enemies, of Your defamers, as You have commanded in the past and as You command this day! Oh, joy of joys, that I have known this hour, when You have spoken Your will to me! I shall hunt out this Yeshua ben Joseph of Nazareth who was conveyed, still alive, from his tomb, and hidden in order to deceive the simple, and I shall expose him to the light of Your ineffable day, so that all may see. I shall bring all to justice, so that Your land will be cleansed and worthy again of Your blessing, my Lord and my God!"

It seemed to him that there was a profound tenderness near him, a profound sweetness which thrilled through his flesh and his bones and almost consumed him with delight, and that a divine gravity had been turned toward him—and a waiting. He fell to the floor of his chamber and lay in utter peace, a peace he had not known for a long time, a peace he could not remember. Somewhere, something imminent had moved in his direction and was gazing upon him, and he buried his face in his arms both afraid and desiring to see the vision.

Chapter 29

THE people of Israel remembered that it had been said that a man's most desperate and relentless enemy was of his own flesh, his own blood, his own house, his own name, his own city and his own country. And that that desperate and relentless enemy often rode and lashed and killed in the Name of God, and was justified in his own sight and in the sight of many of his followers, and was exalted in his heart. It was a frightful mystery. "Surely," many whispered, "one who violates the Laws of God in the Name of the Lord has committed the most unpardonable of sins, and let us leave him to judgment if not to mercy."

To the people of Israel Pontius Pilate was the present terror, aided by Herod Antipas and the Roman legions, and tolerated by the Sadducees in the name of peace, and by some more exigent Pharisees in the name of the Law. But now another terror had risen whom the Romans called Paul of Tarsus, a pious Jew, an erudite Pharisee, a pupil of the great Rabban Gamaliel, a man of position and family, a Roman citizen, an executor of Roman law, a lawyer of a notable house in Israel. Even those of immense piety who believed in the punishment of blasphemers and heretics were alarmed, and spoke with pity of their fellow Jews, who, though deluded that one Yeshua ben Joseph, of Nazareth, was the Messias, and who, though they proclaimed his name in the Temple openly, were gentle people of mild mien, harmless as doves, poor and unassuming, without violence or insistence. They adhered to the Laws of the prophets and the Commandments with even more devotion than did their fellow Jews who laughed at the name of Yeshua, and visited the Temple more frequently and were more assiduous in their pious duties, and were certainly more charitable and patient.

Many of the disturbed people said, "Have we not many sects in Israel, all quarreling with each other and determined that each should prevail? Do we not live in peace with these emphatic men of our blood and our bone? Why, then, should those of us who believe that the Messias has already been born to us not be visited with the same tolerance, even if we laugh at them? Why this unbridled fury, this persecution, this perfidious alliance of Saul of Tarshish with the Roman oppressor? What excesses he has been commiting in every Province and every town, and in the countryside, dragging the wives and children of those whom the priests call heretics from their homes and imprisoning them, and holding them hostage until fathers and husbands swear not to spread the erroneous message any longer! Never has Israel seen this before! Our fellow Jews are beaten in the streets, until they flee for their lives from the hands of the market rabble, who are incited by this Saul of Tarshish. Not even the wildest of the screaming Essenes and Zealots, howling in the market places for an open rebellion against Rome, have been so hunted down and so terribly, as these poor harmless Jews are being hunted! Saul of Tarshish sets the Roman legionnaires upon the defenseless creatures, who beat and cripple them on their own thresholds, and have thrown them into noxious prisons at Saul's command."

The bearded and dusty rabbis were more than alarmed at what appeared to them incredible cruelty and madness. It was one thing to dispute with fellow Jews in the streets and the market places and even in the purlieus of the Temple, and warn against heresy, and quite another to deliver brother Jews to the cruelty and punishment of Romans. The priests could deal with heresy and blasphemy, and gently lead the deluded from their errors, or impose punishments. For truly awesome heretics who were a danger to Israel there was the Sanhedrin. But these "heretics," though in error, were hardly more in error than the members of the other decayed sects, who in their turn had been denounced as blasphemers.

Some said, in argument, "It is not unpardonable to dispute a doctrine or reinterpret the words of Moses and the prophets and the scholars—for this is a matter of opinion and humans err. But it is another thing to assert vehemently, or mildly, that the Messias, blessed be His Name, was in the person of a poor wandering rabbi from Nazareth whom even his own neighbors despised, and who died at the hands of the Romans. Who was he? A carpenter from a little miserable village, seized with a desire for grandeur! He caused riots and aroused dangerous Roman anger against all Jews, and for this he was executed, and laid in the tomb. Do not speak to me of the strange events that occurred when he died! The priests and our wise men have explained it to our satisfaction, for it was all coincidence, even the disappearance of the sun and the earthquakes. Yeshua ben Joseph did not rise from the dead, as his disciples claim. It is well-known that Joseph of Arimathaea was among his followers, and that he bribed the Roman soldiers and the temple guards to permit him to take the still living man from the tomb, and then, after he recovered from his injuries he was seen among his followers who proclaimed that he had risen from the dead. Joseph, though a kind and famous man, has some reason for the misleading of his people, perhaps a secret reason of his own which we will one day know. But it is hardly fair to the people of Israel at this time, for the Romans make no distinctions between us and the heretics, and are only too pleased to beat us on the streets without discrimination or provocation, when it serves to amuse them. Is this just to us, who desire only peace, and who await the Messias? Let us be calm, and understand why Saul of Tarshish does as he does, and not condemn him as an enemy of his people. He is concerned with our safety and our lives."

Multitudes agreed, expressing their horror of this monumental heresy, that the glorious Messias had been among them, had wandered in the meanest places footsore and beggarly and without a roof over his head, consorting with taxgatherers and harlots and the base, and that God, blessed be His Name, had permitted His Anointed to be so shamefully murdered by the Romans without the appearance of a single avenging angel with a sword of fire or a single proclamation from Heaven! The very thought was outrageous, offensive to God! But even these who were incensed by the "heretics" and whose piety and faith were insulted, and who feared the vengeance of God, were even more incensed that their fellow Jews were hunted down like diseased rats in the Holy City, itself, and were hounded from their homes and driven into exile. Persecution had an evil way, too, of passing from the guilty to the innocent, for men were notoriously inflamed by bloodletting and finally killed and hunted for mere sport and wicked gratification.

And there were thousands who muttered uneasily to themselves: "If it were indeed a blasphemous hoax that Yeshua ben Joseph of Nazareth did not die on the cross, but was taken alive to his tomb, and later restored to scores who swear they saw him and talked with him, what is the meaning of the hoax? As the Romans say, 'Who gains?' Yeshua of Nazareth? It is said that he has already disappeared, that none see him any longer, and none hears from him. His miserable poor followers? They do not appear to be men who desire to be honored and exalted and granted fame and fortune or treated as prophets! They do not even defend themselves against the Romans and fight with them, as do the Zealots and the Essenes! They submit, like sheep, praising God. If hoax this is, then who has benefited? Are they mad that they court prison and suffering and infamy and derision and hatred? Not even the mad do that! They behave like men of the deepest conviction, the deepest surety, the deepest faith and devotion. What is the meaning of this? Men do not submit to prison or humiliation or beatings in public places for something they know is a lie, or a cheap jest. Therefore, they believe. Therefore, even if deluded they do not believe they are deluded, and declare openly that they have seen the risen Yeshua with their own eyes, and have seen him ascend to Heaven, or they believe others who declare they have witnessed these marvels."

Accordingly, in fearful secret and in quakings, even many of the priests of the Temple, and thousands of the Jews in Jerusalem, listened to the stories of those called Apostles and disciples, and hundreds were baptized in the dark of the night in the narrow golden river near the city. In their turn they sought out others to whom to tell the "good news." But with discreet terror they attempted to remain obscure, and as so many were poor and humble this was not too difficult a task. Still, the news traveled, and invariably it reached the ears of Saul ben Hillel whose dismay and rage increased daily.

He consulted frequently with Pilate and with the High Priest. Pilate was beginning to find the whole matter amusing. He had always hated the Jews. It pleased him that a vigorous Jew, in the person of Paul of Tarsus, was persecuting, denouncing, imprisoning and punishing his own people. It lightened his days of ennui. He kept his own sense of uneasiness to himself, and attempted to forget the Greek physician, Lucanus, and what had occurred in Caesarea. Too, Herod Antipas was behaving like a man beset and was muttering in his red beard, which he regularly sacrificed to Jupiter in the latter's temple, and then regularly regrew for the Day of Atonement and the Passover. Pilate found life becoming interesting.

Saul heard that the new and blasphemous Jewish sect had spread like the wings of the morning beyond Israel, was in Syria now, and in his own land of Cilicia, and, incredibly, had shown indications of reaching Greece! It was now another Passover, another Pentecostal Feast of the Jews, and the dreadful sect—so insulting to God—appeared to flourish like the plagues of Egypt and to appear in the most unlikely spots. There were rumors that many Roman soldiers had adopted this faith, as well as humbler priests of the Temple, itself, and Saul thought of his cousin, Titus Milo Platonius, in Rome with his aged parents, and his rage rose to frenzy. He felt himself friendless. He knew himself unwelcome in the house of his kinsmen in Jerusalem, and an enemy to them though they made no overt acts to gain converts, and remained in seclusion. (But he suspected, out of his great intuition, that they gave aid and comfort to the persecuted.) He believed that he hated them, and more than all else he hated his sister, Sephorah, who had so deeply betrayed the faith of her fathers, and the faith of Hillel ben Borush, who mercifully had not lived to see this infamy, degradation and blasphemy for himself.

Why did all his efforts, in the service of God, blessed be His Name, appear to bear no fruit? He no sooner eradicated a source of infection than it sprang up, like the phoenix, in another spot, larger and more vigorous than ever. He stamped out a little fire, and a conflagration blazed at a distance, like a mystery out of Gehenna. Was God testing his determination in His service? Was He trying him, as He had tried the prophets and all the saints, to make him more worthy to carry His sword of vengeance and purity? Was He tempering His servant, as He had tempered Job? "I am afflicted!" Saul would cry to himself in his chamber in the house Pilate had assigned to him in Jerusalem, and he would bow his head in exhaustion and frustration, and try to discover where and how he had failed God that the blasphemous sect should still flourish and even spread. He feared the anger of God for his failure. He strove with the Almighty.

"I am but a man!" he would exclaim in his prayers. "I have but human endurance! It is true I have stamina, which You have given me, Lord, but it is not without a breaking point, and I am approaching that. None assists me but Pilate and the High Priest and a few of his creatures, and the lickspittle informers who look for the thirty pieces of silver—the market rabble I have always despised! Can You not deign to give me worthier allies? Better none than these!"

There were times when he was convinced that he was indeed being tested, that the task was greater than he had believed and therefore he needed more tempering, more resolution, that the enemy from hell was more powerful than he could know and demanded more strength than he had shown heretofore, that God was preparing him, as the Greeks would say, for the Great Games, for the amphitheater, for the circus, when alone he would be forced to fight the leagues of evil single-handed—for the open glorification of God. At these times he felt an enormous and intoxicating pride, and an overwhelming exultation that he had been so chosen for so mighty a task. He would then smite his knees with his strong fists and laugh aloud, and then he would praise God in so loud and passionate a voice that his servants in the house would listen in wonder, shrugging, for they were Greeks. But some would shudder, and would touch a tiny little object of metal which lay over their hearts, and some would pray for this violent and desperate man out of the touching charity of their souls.

But there were other times when despair overcame him and he would groan on his bed, "I have failed, and God will not forgive me, though I have striven to fulfill His Will, and have fought with all my strength and have wearied my brain with thought and plans. What, then, will be my end, that I have been defeated by creeping wretches who can hardly be considered men, and who still live and spread their pollution and lies and errors among my people? But—no, no! I shall not be defeated! I shall not endure this mortification! I shall not let worms halt my footsteps with their slime, and fill up my path! This is the one task the King of Kings has set me. May I die in disgrace, forever forgotten by men, if I do not succeed! Moses accomplished a far more formidable task. I am no Moses—but I can do what I can do, and even God can ask a man no more than that."

And then were other times when he thought of the Nasi of the Temple, Rabban Gamaliel, who neither sought him nor wrote to him nor sent him messages of consolation and encouragement, he, who above all, should inspire him. At these moments Saul was filled with a passionate anger and umbrage and even fury. But he tried to remember, to believe, that the Rabban desired him to struggle and fall or win by his own efforts, for had he not always said that each man, in his turn, must face God alone and create his own fate? That confrontation, fearful and inevitable, came to all men. Others dared not interfere in the final hours of struggle and darkness and wrestling with the angels of God. The victory must be each man's, and not the victory of others, lest it be weak and not sustaining. Saul tried to be grateful for the silence of the great Rabban, who knew best. Still—a single letter, a single word of encouragement—I am betraying weakness, Saul told himself sternly.

Once or twice it came to him that he heard nothing from Aristo in Tarsus, though he had written his old teacher several times. Finally he wrote to Reb Isaac, to receive a short letter from his granddaughter, the widow Elisheba, who had once desired to marry him, to the effect that Reb Isaac now lay in the bosom of Abraham since the last Day of Atonement. She did not speak of Aristo, though Saul had inquired of him. Saul was overcome by the news of his old mentor's death in his deep age, and it seemed to him that he heard another snapping of a link of a chain which bound him to those he loved and had loved.

I am all alone, he said to God, in his sorrow. I have been abandoned, except by You, my Lord and my God. It must suffice. I am hated by my own people for my deeds in their behalf and for the sake of their souls, except for a few I despise and would not have about me. Even those who deplore blasphemy almost as vehemently as I do avoid me. I have no friends, no kinsmen. But, are You not enough for man's desiring, for man's passion, for man's surfeit of joy? For, there is none else but You, and if I am deserted by man, surely You, King of Kings, have not deserted me, for I have desired no other save You, my Bread of Life, my Source of living waters.

It seemed to Saul that he heard the words of God which had been spoken to Job, "Gird up your loins now, like a man! I will demand of you, and declare you unto Me! Deck yourself now with majesty and excellency, and array yourself with glory and beauty. Tread down the wicked in their place. Hide them in the dust together, and bind their faces in secret. Then I will also confess unto You that My own right Hand can save you!"

"Lord, Lord!" cried Saul, overcome with humility and remorse that he had been so human as to grieve and to voice his plaint that none helped him. Had he not God as his Advocate and his General, and did he not carry His immortal banner? He, Saul ben Hillel, should rejoice at his trials as a singular manifestation of grace, and never doubt of the victory. But, for some awful and terrifying reason, he was not comforted, and he sorrowed that God had rejected his repentance, and was offended at his weakness. It was, however, all he deserved.

One day in the heat of late summer Saul heard a report that stupefied and dazed him, and struck at his soul so violently that he feared for his sanity, and his bewilderment was crushing.

He knew that the apostles of Yeshua ben Joseph of Nazareth, and his disciples, were rumored to be causing great miracles in Jerusalem and the Provinces, notably one Simon Peter, a poor fisherman from Galilee. Saul had sent out many spies and soldiers to apprehend this dangerous man, who deceived many and corrupted the faith of Israel, but always Peter escaped as if melting into mist, and his followers with him. It was reported that many of the rich and illustrious were helping these criminals, these blasphemers, not only hiding them in their houses when pursued but sending them to country estates for safety.

Worse still, many members of the Sanhedrin, it was reported to Saul by Pilate with enjoyment, were secretly questioning those of Peter's followers who were apprehended, and a number of them had been enormously moved and impressed by Peter's eloquent dissertations, and some, it was rumored, were being baptized in the name of the Nazarene and so becoming heretics. Though the law was plain, that the heretics were enemies of the Romans and of Israel, and were inciting mobs to rebellion and to bloody riots, and so must therefore be delivered up to the justice and discipline and punishment of Roman law, and that they were blasphemers, tales were being whispered that the Sanhedrin were not obeying the law, except for a few members, and that they were advising the criminals not be overt in their proselyting but to employ discretion, and then dismissing them with mild admonitions. It was said that after one such confrontation Peter, famous for his effrontery and rebelliousness and lack of respect, had actually exclaimed to the merciful Sanhedrin: "Whether it is right in the sight of God to listen to you rather than to God, decide for yourselves! For we cannot but speak of what we have seen and heard." Apparently the members had decided that he had spoken from what he believed was the truth, or his courage had aroused their admiration and his piety had moved them, so they had not held him for justice.

Saul sought out confirmation of this, for he was incredulous, but everywhere he met only raised eyebrows and silent smiles and shrugs. This, intended to allay his suspicions, only increased them and his anguish of mind and his bafflement. It was as if hell had opened and had disgorged demons who were driving even the most erudite and pious insane, and inspiring them with heresy and treason. He thought of Israel as under siege by internal enemies who had become demented and lustful of death. He would hear that the blasphemers were preaching and exhorting in the Portico of Solomon in the Temple, and he would hasten there with his soldiers to arrest them. But when he arrived he discovered that they had fled, as if mysteriously warned, and only confusion and shouting and emphatic voices remained among those who had listened, and those of the sick of whom it was reported that the Apostles had healed in the last hour. He would disperse the clamoring and insistent mobs, the Romans using the flat of their swords against the most recalcitrant, and he would seek out some of the priests to demand their explanation as to why they had permitted these fools to gather in the Portico and had not driven them out.

The priests would smile at him helplessly and respectfully and remind him that Jews had access to the holy Temple at any time, and that disputations among sects were quite common not only in the Portico but among the columns and the gardens and in the halls and the courts, and it was not forbidden. It was even encouraged by the elders, who believed that disputations and argumentations and searchings for truth were salubrious and enlightening, and a guard against error and heresy. If this were forbidden, said the priests, then commentators on the Torah and all the Scriptures—the holy commentators —should be forbidden also, for did they not often offer novel interpretations and comments? To this argument, which seemed to Saul enragingly meretricious, he would reply: "But the commentators and the elders did not advance blasphemy, nor did they encourage the proscribed and permit them to spread heresy and confusion and disorder." The priests would then remind him of many wandering rabbis, even of the near past, who had inflamed the people also in the Temple purlieus for a short time, but later their teachings were shown to be manifestly false and the people quieted. This would, doubtless, happen to the followers of Yeshua ben Joseph of Nazareth, if patience were expended. After all, were not these men Jews also, and were they not extremely charitable and kind, and mild of speech, and did they not exhort the love of God and obedience to the Law and the Commandments? They lifted their hands against no man. They were not wild like the Essenes and the Zealots and other denizens of the desert. They obeyed established laws meticulously, and flouted none, save the one that they must not spread their error—which, it was admitted, they did not obey. But time would cure them, and what was false would be winnowed from the wheat and that would be the end of it.

Saul saw that the humbler priests and many of the elders despised and distrusted him as an arm of the hated Roman, and that they took some malicious pleasure in thwarting and maddening him, for all their elaborately respectful manner and their reasonable voices. He could have gladly murdered several when they said to him, making large and innocent eyes at him, "Naught occurs without the Will of God, blessed be His Name, and let us trust in His wisdom, for always He has smitten His enemies and rescued His faithful. To believe He will not do it again is to flout and question His power and His love for His people."

Saul seethed with rage at this mockery disguised as respect for himself and his authority, but he, always ready with flaming words, could find no adequate words in answer, except threats. The law was plain: The heretics were proscribed both by the High Priest, Caiphas, his father-in-law, Annas, and Pontius Pilate. To permit them to speak in the Temple was not only blasphemous but seditious, and an affront to God. The priests smiled humbly and bowed, and were silent.

"These rebels breed like locusts," said Pontius Pilate with manifest pleasure at Saul's frustration and fury. "One day there are ten and the next day there are thousands! What are we to do with them?"

Saul suspected what Pontius Pilate would like to do to all Jews, including the heretics, and he inwardly shrank. Sometimes he pondered as to whether or not he was endangering all of his people by his pursuit of the heretics, but he would immediately put this appalling thought aside as a temptation of Lucifer. He could only go on, daily becoming more despairing yet more resolute, in the service of God. Before multitudes in the Temple he would shout, "By protecting the blasphemers and hiding them, or keeping silent about them, you are invoking the wrath of God, blessed be His Name, for He will not much longer endure the heresy of so many of His people! Therefore, deliver the malefactors to me, that they be punished and silenced, and peace return to us, and the delight of God in His holy land! To do aught else is to invite ruin and death for all of us, and the destruction of Israel."

They would listen in silence, some with dark and assenting faces, some mutely and blankly, and Saul would leave, groaning in his soul.

There was a rumor that several of the disciples and preachers, being imprisoned on orders of Saul, were miraculously delivered one night and were again at large, preaching what they called the Gospel, the Good News. Saul ordered the guards seized for drunkenness and carelessness, despite their protestations that the prisoners had disappeared from their cells though the doors remained locked. To this absurdity Saul replied with a spate of his rare obscenities and anger. He delivered the guards to Pilate for proper punishment. Pilate said, watching Saul with open amusement, "My men swear that divine creatures clothed in light opened the gates of the prison and delivered the malefactors, and that my soldiers could not lift a hand." He laughed at Saul's enflamed expression, and shook his head. Verily, he was not so bored these days, and for that he thanked the gods, in whom he did not believe. He would say to Herod Antipas, that capricious and gloomy man, "Your Paul of Tarsus is very redoubtable. It is sad that he does not accept your invitations to dine with you." Herod would bite his lip and his pale eyes would glow, but he would not reply. His dreams these days were frightful.

Then Pilate summoned Saul to him one evening, and his clever face expressed vexation and displeasure. He did not offer Saul wine, which was an ominous signal, and one not overlooked by the young Jew.

"You have spoken to me often of your famous teacher, the Nasi of the Temple, Rabban Gamaliel," said Pilate. "I know him well. I have entertained him in this house and have been entertained in his. He is a man of wisdom, wit and erudition and I have enjoyed his company, and have rejoiced in it, for this is a tedious country and not to be understood by a worldly man. So few men of cosmopolitan tastes and understanding!

"Have you not wondered, yourself, Paul of Tarsus, why you have not seen him nor have heard from him?"

"Yes, lord," said Saul, and immediately an icy chill enveloped his spirit and he felt ill with premonition.

"It is suspected that he is a new heretic," said Pilate. Saul sprang to his feet, trembling, swollen and scarlet of face. "Lord!" he cried, "that rumor is not to be borne, to be suffered! You know Rabban Gamaliel; you know that he is chief of the Sanhedrin, the Nasi of the Temple, a man famous in Israel and even in the world beyond for his piety and his wisdom, his devotion to God, his writings, his lectures, his dissertations, his influence!" Saul began to shudder. He had thought that he had endured all he could endure, yet now he was faced with this horror, this blasphemy, this terror and shamefulness. "Lord," he stammered, sweating in his extremity though the autumn evening was cool, "those who spread such evil tidings should be mercilessly punished—and destroyed, for the Rabban is a holy man before the Face of God, and God should not be so flagrantly insulted in the powerful person of His Rabban! It is a plot to crush the very foundations of our Temple, our holy land, our belief, our very survival! If this can be said of Rabban Gamaliel then none is safe in Israel, all are exposed to lies and blasphemies and traducers, all are suborned!" He stopped. His voice choked in his throat. His eyes had reddened with blood. He feared that he would have a seizure, that he would die on the spot of his agony and his abhorrence and dread. It was as if, before his very sight and presence, that the Veil of the Temple had been torn away and the Torah seized and desecrated and befouled by beasts, and that animals had defecated in the Sanctuary. He pressed his hands convulsively to his temples, holding there the roaring cataract that swelled within, threatening to break loose and smash him to fragments. His heart screamed with pain; he could not breathe. His tongue clove to the roof of his mouth; he saw fire and sparks before him and felt a heaving beneath his feet.

Pilate watched him with curious interest and reflection, then seeing that Saul was indeed in extremity he finally called for wine and himself stood and pressed the goblet into one of Saul's rigid and shaking hands. "Drink," he commanded, "or you will surely die! Gods! What exaggerations, what extravagances, you Jews display, out of proportion to the cause! I have said it is a rumor, only a rumor. But you sprang to your feet like one who has been seized by the furies, by Hecate, herself, or as if Charon had appeared before you! Let us be calm. Drink. I command you."

Convulsed with tremors, hardly aware of Pilate, Saul obeyed. He could not speak. Tears like burning acid rushed into his eyes. He feared that he would burst into violent weeping and be undone before this Roman, who would only laugh at his agony. For how could Pilate comprehend the awfulness of the lie against the Rabban, the holiest man in Israel, the most learned? Saul was taken by a direful fear. He had not striven hard enough. He had failed his Lord, his God, that such a shameful rumor dared to be started in Jerusalem. He felt himself pushed into a chair by Pilate, and he sat there in a state of collapse.

He whispered finally, and in a hoarse voice, "You do not comprehend the monstrousness of this accusation!"

Pilate shrugged. He said, "I can believe anything of the Jews, my Paul. You are an incredible people. But, be calm, I implore you. I dislike excesses of emotion. They are uncivilized. I thought you a cultivated man, a man of restraint." He put his tongue in his cheek.

A little control came to Saul. He stared at Pilate with

hatred. "What if I gave utterance to a rumor that your Emperor, your Caesar Tiberius, was a pederast?" he asked.

To his amazement Pilate laughed. "I would put nothing past the Caesares," he said. "I have heard worse." He regarded Saul with smiling derision. Then he said, "Let me tell you what I have heard of Gamaliel, but, in the name of the gods, discipline yourself."

Chapter 30

"IT IS well known," said Pontius Pilate to Saul ben Hillel, "that the High Priest, Caiphas, and Rabban Gamaliel are not the most affectionate of friends, for the Rabban has little respect for Caiphas and Caiphas is embarrassed before the Nasi. Annas, the father-in-law of Caiphas, is a subtle and malicious man and delights in the discomfiture of his son-in-law, and therefore cultivates the Rabban who has regard for neither.

"In the matter of your heretics Caiphas has been relentless for many important reasons, as you know, my Paul, and not only out of fear of me and Rome. He had taken it upon himself to hear their trials in the Temple, and before the Sanhedrin, even in the case of the least of them, including simple old women. He is the High Priest. He is concerned with the consideration of heresy, he proclaims, and would keep the faith of his people pure and unshaken. He appears, however, to have an almost demented hatred for the Nazarene which he cannot fully explain himself. No matter.

"As Nasi of the Temple the Rabban is concerned with the immutability of the Law and all learned matters, and teachings, connected with that Law. As chief of the Sanhedrin he is rarely called to listen to accusations against those who infringe the Law, for that is the concern of lower judges. He was not, for instance, present when Jesus of Nazareth was brought before a handful of the judges, for, who was this man? A mere traveling teacher, who spoke only Aramaic, an unlearned man, a carpenter, penniless and homeless, with followers as undistinguished as himself. Such as Rabban Gamaliel would not be called to judge so poor a creature, so humble and without consequence."

"I know of these things!" said Saul, with impatience. He was still trembling with shock. Pilate again regarded him thoughtfully. He did not like strong and emphatic men; he considered them barbarians.

"Ah, yes," he murmured, playing with the stem of his goblet and leaning backwards in his cushioned lemonwood chair. "Do you not know of these things! But my spies have been informing me of late that Rabban Gamaliel, who has matters of grave moment on his mind every hour, has taken to appearing silently and quietly in the Sanhedrin when the followers of Jesus of Nazareth are brought before the Court, and he has listened to them acutely though never intruding a question or uttering a reprimand, he the chief of the Court. He has neither affirmed nor set aside the opinion of those meeting in the Court, though it is more than his privilege. He has merely listened, and then has departed, without a word. So the High Priest has told me. He finds the presence of the Rabban disconcerting."

"That is understandable," said Saul, with contempt. "Caiphas is a fool, for all his erudition, and a traitor to his people."

Pilate arched his brows coquettishly at Saul, but Saul was beyond noticing small matters.

Pilate continued. It was but yesterday that the fisherman of Galilee, Simon Peter, spoken of as the leading Apostle of Jesus of Nazareth, was brought before the Sanhedrin with a number of his followers. He was one of those who had been loosed from prison by drunken or bribed guards, who were now in prison, themselves. He was found preaching, again, with his idle followers, in the market place, and was arrested at once by some of Saul's own soldiers, while he, Saul, was busy pursuing another investigation. Some members of the Sanhedrin were always meeting hastily in these perturbed days, and so a few were summoned to try this Simon Peter again and this time to assure themselves that he would not escape.

Again they questioned him, seeking to have him boldly proclaim his blasphemy as he had done often before, that

Jesus of Nazareth was the Redeemer of Israel, as the prophecies had foretold. It was a weary subject, and the Sanhedrin, though incensed, yawned. They had now decided on this wretch's fate: He would suffer the punishment of blasphemy. He would be stoned to death. The Sanhedrin gave their verdict, and rose to leave as the guards seized Simon Peter.

It was then that Rabban Gamaliel rose, small of stature but heroic of mien and radiating authority and personal grandeur. He commanded that Simon Peter and his followers be taken to a room near the Court and there detained until he had spoken. He was an old man, but his gray eyes were sparkling like ice and his glance was powerful.

Then he addressed the other judges, who were far inferior in station to him, standing before them as if an advocate and not the chief of the Court, itself.

He said, "Of what are these men accused? They are accused of blasphemy. They are accused of adding another sect to the many now plaguing Israel. They are not accused of crimes against man, but of a crime against God, by pleading that the Messias has already been born to Israel and was executed by the Romans for sedition and inciting riots among the people.

"Let us examine the alleged crime against God. We know He will not tolerate blasphemy, blessed be His Name. But these fellow Jews of ours, whom we call heretics, exalt God, do not blaspheme Him, contrary to the opinion of many of this Court. They are more passionate in their pious duties, as Jews, than many of the members I see about me now. If they believe that the Messias has already been among us, that he has fulfilled the Law and the Prophecies, is this aberration so heinous? We have had many such rabbis as this Yeshua of Nazareth who were thought to be the Messias, and we, remembering the prophecies that he would arrive obscurely and be wounded for our sins and that we would esteem him not and know him not, had these rabbis brought before us to question them, more in hope than in ridicule and outrage.

"The only difference between Yeshua ben Joseph and the other poor rabbis of the past is that he did not deny that he was the Messias. Let us consider. We know these poor provincial countrymen of ours, and their devotion to the God of their fathers. Some rave and prophesy. Some wander abroad to teach, in their little learning. And some, we have learned, are poor unfortunate madmen, obsessed and haunted by God or their imaginings about God, and disappear into the desert, to be heard of no more except by the stones and the jackals and the vultures. Some, we know well, performed miracles out of the purity and innocence and faith of their souls, for the Almighty looks with gentle tenderness on these children of His who adore Him and live only to serve Him."

Rabban Gamaliel permitted himself the smallest of smiles. "We have a legend that the Messias, in Heaven, is continually wounded by our sins and suffers enormous pain and agony, and that the angels bind up His wounds and comfort Him. We have legends that He has even been seen by men, wandering the earth in His bandages, and mourning, and that none knew Him except infants at their mother's breast and little ones who gazed at Him in compassion. Other legends assert that He had been driven from villages by those who knew Him not, this bloodstained wanderer Who would have men know Him and accept His love and His redemption.

"So be it. The followers of Yeshua ben Joseph of Nazareth believe fervently, with all their minds and all their souls and all their hearts that the Nazarene was and is the Messias, that He was scourged for our sins and died for our redemption, the Lamb of God. Their belief is not unique. It was believed before, according to the words of Isaias, and was not accounted too horrific.

"Men of Israel!" said the Rabban, lifting a portentous hand. "Take care what you are about to do to these men, who await your judgment in the adjoining room. For some time ago there rose up Theodas, claiming to be somebody, and a number of men in Jerusalem, about four hundred, joined him. But he was slain, and all his followers were dispersed. And he was brought to nothing. After him rose up Judas the Galilean in the days of the Census, and drew some people after him. He, too, perished, and all his followers were scattered abroad. So now I say to you, keep away from these men and let them alone. For if this plan or work is of men it will be overthrown. But if it is of God, you will not be able to overthrow it. Else, perhaps, you may find yourselves fighting even against God!"*

He then turned on his heel and left the Court and the Court and the judges sat in stupefaction and amazement, and pondered, and then argued and discussed vehemently. Many disputed. But the Rabban was illustrious and loved of the people and honored by them, and by themselves, and they did not criticize him even by a word, but only by doubtful frowns. In the end they ordered Simon Peter and the followers with him to be scourged, but not too severely, and commanded them to preach no more in the Temple and the streets and to cry no more that Yeshua ben Joseph of Nazareth was the Messias.

Concluding his recital, Pilate smiled questioningly at Saul. "Would you, then, consider Rabban Gamaliel to be a heretic, in that he protected these blasphemers and counseled that they not be made to suffer the punishment for blasphemy?"

Saul had listened, all his instincts and passions protesting and denying what he was hearing. It was not possible! He said, "Lord, who is your informer?"

Pilate sighed. "The High Priest, himself. You may consider him a traitor and a liar, but that is unfair. He is at heart a timorous man, and wishes only peace for his country and his people. Fearful that I would not believe his story he brought with him members of the Sanhedrin, who confirmed his words, and they are men of truth and dignity."

Saul stood up and began to pace the hall in almost uncontrollable agitation, groaning in himself. He said at last, "Why did they not come to me, instead of to you, lord?"

Pilate plucked at his smiling lips. "I am distressed to admit that they now fear you, even the High Priest who brought you to my attention. Perhaps they consider you too—zealous?" His face changed, became dark and vicious and he stood up and faced Saul in his path. "Perhaps they have already heard that I had two thousand rebels executed in Tiberias, in Galilee, but four days ago! Could that be the answer to your question, Paul of Tarsus?"

Saul recoiled from him with tremendous loathing and burning hatred. Seeing this Pilate said, "What is the difference between us, my dear friend? Do we not persecute,

*Actual words of Rabban Gamaliel, Acts of the Apostles, 5:34-39.

or prosecute, equally? For the same reason, the same purpose?"

Pilate laughed in his face. "What? You start back? But have you not harassed, yourself, Paul of Tarsus, those of your own blood and your own bone? Have you not condemned, ordered lashings and imprisonment? I do not look upon you with disgust and repudiation. I understand you. If," said Pilate softly, "your friend Gamaliel does not."

Saul turned and left him and there was as the roaring of tumultuous wings in his ears. But he had no thoughts, only terrible emotions and tears of blood seemed to seethe against his eyelids, though he could not weep. He returned to his house and fell on his bed like a stone and lay for hours staring sightlessly at the walls until it was midnight.

He dared not think. He could only adhere to his purpose though he died of grief from it. His heart was torn and throbbing. But he could not retreat. When he slept a little he saw a forest of crosses, and the crucified, and he moaned in his slumber and his pillow was wet with the tears he could not shed when he was awake.

Chapter 31

THE DREAD news of Pilate's execution of two thousand men and women of Galilee reached Jerusalem, and there was hardly a soul but was stricken with anguish and horror. Multitudes asked each other in the street: "Of what were these peasants and humble laborers guilty? That they believed the Messias had come, even though we believe He is still tarrying? It has been called blasphemy, but now confusion is upon us, and sorrow for our kinsmen. Woe unto us, that we have seen this day!"

In their despair and anguish the people set upon Roman soldiers who arrested "heretics" in Jerusalem, and injured them in their numbers and drove them off and rescued their fellow Jews and hid them and smuggled them from the city at night. It was nothing now to the rescuers that their brethren had been denounced as blasphemers from the Temper purlieus themselves, and had been proscribed. Angrily the people said, "These are of our blood, and they are our neighbors, and if they be in error let God judge them and not the Romans, and not the venal priests who have oppressed us in all these years! Are we market rabble that we should hoot and encourage the soldiers in their cruelties, and yell like hyenas? No! Our people are our people, and no stranger shall murder them any longer!"

Caiphas sent for Saul and said, wringing his long white hands, "We have lost control. The issue is in darkness and confusion. Once it was as clear as spring water. Now it is muddled, and roiling. Once it was the matter of blasphemy and God's command that blasphemers be put to death. Now it is pious Jew protecting heretical Jew, and crying aloud, 'We are of one blood and one nation and one God!' The people are aroused, since the news from Galilee. They stone the Romans in the streets; they attack them in the dark; they shout imprecations upon them. They flock to listen to the heretics who preach to them in spite of rigorous punishments. They fill the river at night, to be baptized. They are like men seized by madness and they know not what they do. We were in danger before Yeshua ben Joseph was executed. We are in more peril now than then, and Pilate waits like a wolf, licking chops and slavering. He needs but a little more prodding—"

Saul said, "We must not only continue our efforts and our struggle, but we must increase them in intensity and dedication." He was very lean and haggard now, and his red hair was startling against his pallid flesh and over the hot metal of his blue eyes. "What other choice have we? We, or the heretics, must perish. In truth, we shall all perish unless this heresy is destroyed, Jew and heretic alike. Why did God permit this affliction to come upon us? It is my belief it is His punishment that we tolerated the Sadducees and let them rule us and collaborated with the Roman, who has desecrated the holy earth of Israel. We are being punished by the wrath of the Almighty. We can but accept the flagellation and strive to atone for our sins, and drive the blasphemers into the sea." He put his weary hands over his tormented face for a moment. "Indeed, once it was clear to the people, and now it is no longer clear. Hell has clouded their minds. But we must persevere, and attain victory. Lord, give me a letter to the elders of Damascus, for I hear the heresy has broken out there in enormous fury and is raging like a disease. For the moment, let the people of Jerusalem be at peace, so that they can regain their wits and understand, again, that we fight not only for their souls but for their very lives."

In his extremity he believed that Caiphas was truly one with him at last, and as alarmed as he, and in this belief there was considerable truth.

He felt betrayed and beset, abandoned by every man, and that he was struggling alone against a legion of the damned, who did not faint or fail. He dared not think of Rabban Gamaliel lest he lose his mind, nor did he think of Joseph of Arimathaea. But they thought of him and spoke often of him, quietly between themselves.

Caiphas summoned Saul to him one chill winter evening and said, with a heavy and tragic face, "We have a problem of exceeding delicacy."

Saul sat down weightily, for his weariness grew day by day. "Another one?" he asked, and accepted a goblet of wine.

Caiphas sat near him and folded his hands in his lap. "You have heard of the house of Tobias, elegant Hellenistic Jews, patrons of art and the theater, Sadducees, whose sons are Scribes and officials of Roman government, and possessing fine houses in Athens and in Rome and Jerusalem and Alexander, and learned, and esteemed, noted for their taste and discrimination, and as sophisticated as the Greeks, themselves?"

"I have heard of them," said Saul. "They are friends of my grandfather. I, for one, do not esteem them." His face grew hard, that haggard face with the new deep lines plowed into it, and its thinness so that the harsh large nose protruded more than ever.

"They are celebrated for the men they have contributed to the Sanhedrin and to the sciences, particularly medicine, and to the professions, particularly law."

"They are also celebrated for their atheisms," said Saul, "and for the amusing poems and books they have written deriding the Pharisees and the more stringent aspects of the Mosaic laws, and have gracefully approached the very edge of heresy." He regarded Caiphas with impatience. "What have these exquisites, these arbiters of elegance, to do with me, and my mission before God?"

"It is very delicate," said Caiphas. "There is a youngest son in the house, still unmarried, of great beauty it is said, and strength and charm, Stephen ben Tobias. He has studied in Athens, Rome and Alexander. He is a man who has directed his gifts and his talents, God-given, nowhere in the service of Israel, preferring to be a great gentleman in the Greek and Roman manner, strolling the world and observing it voluptuously, and enjoying himself. He not only appears to have a Greek soul, he resembles a Greek amazingly. That, of course, is not of importance. His family has never been supporters of the Temple except for the most meager of tithes, nor have they had respect for the priesthood. In short, they have been heathens in attitude, and Stephen ben Tobias is a true son of his fathers."

"I am not concerned with Sadducees and their admiration for the Greeks, nor even their atheism," said Saul. "Worthless Jews are of no moment to me. Let God be their judge, not I."

Caiphas coughed and studied the priestly ring on his finger. "It is known that Stephen ben Tobias has embraced the new heresy of the followers of Yeshua ben Joseph of Nazareth."

"I do not believe it!" cried Saul. "A man of the useless house of Tobias, overcivilized, posturing, perfumed, dainty, rich, garmented in silk and gold and jewels—and the poor and starving heretics, unlearned, debased, craven!"

Caiphas coughed again and fixed his light gray eyes significantly on Saul. "It is not harder to believe than that your grandfather and brethren have also embraced the heresy."

Now Saul heard the soft threat under the High Priest's quiet words and a cold sweat broke out upon his flesh, a sweat of fear and dread. He said, "If my kinsmen believe there is some merit in Yeshua ben Joseph's blasphemous teachings, they have not sought to proselytize, nor have made overt acts, nor have they refrained from their devotion to the Temple. In truth, they are now showing more devotion to the Law and the prophets and the Temple than ever they revealed before! So I have heard. I do not seek out," Saul resumed, his terror brightening the exhausted dullness of his eyes, "those who are suspected of error, but those who advance it, insist upon it, harangue about it, and declare blasphemy in public. We do not enter a man's house and demand evidences of his adherence to our faith, for his house is his own and so sacred. We do not demand even that he believe! We command only that he keep his own counsel discreetly, not create public disturbances, not openly beard priests in the Temple and call them 'keepers of the word of the law but murderers of the spirit,' and not insist, publicly and openly, that Yeshua ben Joseph was the Messias. What a man believes is between him and God, blessed be His Name, for faith is a gift of God and cannot be forced or willed. But public blasphemy is another matter, and incitement to riot against the peace of Israel, and open treason against our nation and our God."

Caiphas sighed. "Calm yourself, my Saul. I heard no word against your family. It is as you have said. But I have heard word of Stephen ben Tobias. I hear that he has been named one of the Seven among the heretics, that is, a leader, a privileged and influential man, a man appointed with authority by them to teach, to harangue, to destroy our faith and our security. How the infection reached him is a mystery. One less attuned to any faith, however esoteric, than Stephen ben Tobias could not have been found in all of Israel, or one less careless of holy matters. Yet, I am assured, he has placed his private fortune at the feet of those they call apostles and disciples, has taken to living openly among them, dressing himself humbly, and is full of fanatical fervor. It is as if a peacock had turned himself into a crow, a noisy insistent crow, preaching heresy. Now, my Saul, what shall we do about this man?"

"It is incredible," said Saul. Caiphas murmured, "Stephen has a rich villa of his own at Caesarea, where he has entertained Pilate and Herod. He has delivered this fine property to the heretics, for a shelter, for living quarters, for a meeting place of other heretics. When among them there he labors in the fields he owns, with the basest of them, plowing, speaking, preaching, exhórting, and eats at the common table with them. He is like a man possessed."

"He is doubtless possessed," said Saul. "No man of his kind could descend to that unless he is mad. Have none of his kinsmen requested a priest to exorcise the evil spirit that is now residing in him? Surely, they are perturbed!"

Caiphas spread out his hands. "That, I do not know. That house has always been an aristocratic one, patrician, scornful, haughty, cold—and corrupt. What they think of Stephen is not known, and woe to any man who would be impertinent enough to question them concerning a member of their house! They are remote and dignified— and very rich. It is possible they think it a young and lively man's temporary aberration, and so probably smile a bit indulgently, just as they have smiled at the iniquities of other members of the family who have embraced Greek and Roman lewdnesses. Their conduct has often approached the scandalous and there have been murmurings among the priests in the past. But they clothed it all with a graceful discretion, if indeed it was shameful."

The High Priest looked at the silent young man whose lips were compressed and white and whose look was bent on the marble floor.

"Had Stephen shown the discretion of his family we should not now be faced with a dilemma," said Caiphas. "But, he is not discreet. He is now in Jerusalem, and I have reports that he is exhorting large audiences in the Temple purlieus and proclaiming with passion that Yeshua ben Joseph is the Messias, and making new heretics by the score. For he is a man not only of consequence and one of cultivated and authoritative speech, and a gentleman, but he has been trained in rhetoric and dialectics in Athens and speaks with eloquence and passion, moving even the most devout, it is said, to tears and acceptance. He is a veritable Demosthenes of heresy. He has convinced many priests and has lured them into blasphemy. Amazingly, he is persuasive even among the very learned."

When Saul did not speak Caiphas continued: "He also has a restless mind, and is curious and inquisitive. I am certain he is well informed of the beliefs of the heathen, for, as I have said, he is a Hellenist and has spent more time in Greece than in Israel. Speak, Saul. What shall we do, for Stephen ben Tobias is dangerous, more dangerous, perhaps, than any other living heretic."

"Do you advise me to arrest him and throw him into prison?" Saul fixed his fiery eyes on the High Priest almost in contempt, for he knew Caiphas' reverence for his own caste and his protection of them.

"His kinsmen would be at my throat," said Caiphas, and Saul, even in his anger, could not keep from smiling.

"Report him to Pilate as a seditionist against Rome," said Saul. "Let Pilate then choose his fate."

"His family is influential, and, as I have told you, they know Pilate well. This situation would only amuse Pilate; he is endlessly amused at us. He would only say, 'I have left this in your hands, my dear Caiphas, as you requested, yourself.' He is a very capricious man, and a murderous one. He enjoys punishing Jews, but not such Jews as the house of Tobias. He would not lift his hand. He would jeer at the thought of Stephen inciting our people to sedition against Rome, for several of the family are Roman citizens and married to Romans and reside in Rome, and are friends of Caesar's. When I have mentioned heresy to Pilate he has almost laughed in my face. He thinks our devotion to God is ridiculous. He cares nothing about that, as you know."

"Yet he executed two thousand miserable heretics in Galilee," said Saul, and grimaced with an anguish he could not control. "Our fellow Jews."

"You are a very ambiguous man," said Caiphas. "You hunt down heretics and imprison them and order them to be lashed and admonished, yet when Pilate punishes them with death—and is not death ordered for blasphemers?—you quail. No matter. It is probable even you could not explain it. It is possible that you draw a distinction between your threats of massacre and the actual massacre! Or is it heinous for a Gentile to do what a Jew would do? In matters of justice and law we can make no distinctions. Pilate ordered those executions because the heretics were advocating open revolt against Rome."

Saul stood up, with a vehement gesture. "With what weapons? Do they possess arms and armor, swords and fortresses, legions and centurions and generals and ships of battle and fortunes and mercenaries and chariots and horses trained in war, and banners?"

Caiphas shook his head in wonder. "You are one who speaks from the bowels in this, and not from the mind. Let us return to Stephen ben Tobias. He must be silenced."

Saul's pale face was suffused with scarlet, for the High Priest had touched him sorely with his words. He exclaimed, "Have you no eloquent priests, no devoted priests, no men of stature and faith, who could arouse the people against this heretic? Have we no fanatics, no zealots, amongst us, to protect the Temple and the Book and the Law? Have we not even the army of Gideon?"

Caiphas was silent.

"What is the task of the priests but sustaining and protecting our holy faith against all enemies, and advancing and strengthening it? But the priests have now become mere discoursers of obscure commentaries; they delight in random philosophies and the inconsequential things of this evanescent world! They do not shout of the prophets and the law. They speak no more of Sinai, except on the High Holy Days, and then listlessly. They have become as secular as the people, themselves! They are ritualistic—but faithless. They have hidden God from the people in languid ceremonies and in clouds of incense, and are more concerned with tithes and their privileges than they are with the souls of their people. They urge more aqueducts and public buildings and roads upon the Romans, and speak of these things as necessities, but the immanence and glory of God are far from them. They believe the luxuries of their living, and their political influence with the Romans, are more than the souls of our people.

"This heresy would not have arisen among the people of Israel had not their souls been languishing for the exaltation of faith, the renewal of faith, the devotion to faith, which the priests have not been offering them!" Saul went on, becoming fired with his rage and indignation. "Yeshua ben Joseph brought to them an ardor and a power and a transcending passion again, and even if he permitted it to be said that he was the Messias, and so was a blasphemer, at least he stirred their fainting hearts and their souls! But our priests have taken our people into the desert of faithless despair and have turned their minds only to this world, and have deprived them of living waters. On your head, Caiphas, and on the heads of your priests, lies the reason for this heresy!"

Caiphas stared at him in sudden and uncontrollable terror, for it seemed to him that Saul had suddenly become clothed in flame and prophecy, had enlarged mightily in stature, had been infused and magnified, and so expanded beyond human flesh that he appeared to fill the chamber and to make it blaze with lightning and resound with thunder. The eyes flashed blue rays, the face was transformed like the face of the prophets, and his voice was terrible.

Saul flung his cloak about him, and though he wore no sword it was as if he were arrayed for battle.

"As for this Stephen ben Tobias, I will pray how I must deal with him; Caiphas. In the meanwhile, search for a fervent priest or two to counteract this heretic's blasphemies—if you can." Saul went from the chamber and the sound of his leaving was, to Caiphas, the footsteps of an avenging man, clangorous and echoing.

Chapter 32

HE HAS the face of an angel, thought Rabban Gamaliel as he looked at young Stephen ben Tobias who had dined with him in company with Joseph of Arimathaea. Alas, we see this splendor of countenance among the young seldom now in these drab and restless days of discontent and lack of certitude. If one asked of him, "Who are you?" he would not sit down to ponder and contemplate uneasily and with despair as so many of his generation now do. He would reply with smiling pride, "I am Stephen ben Tobias, a Jew of a great house, a servant of God, blessed be His Name," and in saying that he would say all that could be said, and beyond that there is nothing more.

Stephen was young and he had a sprightliness of spirit and a passionate warmth that was as full of humor as it was intense. Always, he had had such a temperament, but now it was richer and deeper and gave a bright glow to his face. He was tall and handsome and athletic, and

indeed, as Caiphas had said, he was the embodiment of
Grecian masculine beauty such as was seen only in
Macedonia and not among the dark and agile Athenians.
His curly hair was like amber and glittered with health
and life over a full face with a strong and rounded chin,
the classic Greek nose, the open lustrous eye, the sensitive
and animated red lips so extolled by Greek poets, and a
grace of movement that was like a poem, itself. For this
visit to Rabban Gamaliel he had dressed as he had always dressed before, in fine raiment, a long tunic of thick
yellow silk bordered in red embroidered flowers, a golden
girdle and Alexandrine dagger, jeweled sandals and armlets, and many rings, and even an earring in one ear. But
his hands, once so delicate and perfumed, now revealed
the marks of rugged labor, and were as brown as a nut, as
was his complexion. His expression rushed in one moment from the most absolute seriousness to such gentle
and hearty merriment that the old men who sat with him
felt their hearts move with affection, and with sighing
memories of their own youth and assurance and vigor.

"Nevertheless," said Joseph of Arimathaea with anxiety,
"I beg of you to be discreet, Stephen. We have spoken
of Saul ben Hillel, may God have mercy upon him, and
he is a ruthless man now, a relentless one, full of dedication and fanaticism, a veritable lion of God. We await
the blessed day when he will see the glory of that which
he now attacks, for always we have known, in some
measure, his destiny. But until that day and hour it is
well to step lightly about him. I am certain he has heard
of your proselyting, for nothing escapes him for long, nor
is he a respecter of persons. I pray you will not encounter him."

"I thank you for your concern, Joseph," said Stephen,
and though his face had become grave there was still a
twinkling upon it. "I am sorry that he was not invited to
this house tonight, so that we could debate. I have seen
him at a distance, and indeed he does resemble a lion,
with that red mane of his, the fierce eyes, the commanding
manner, the nervous impatience and the lithe movements,
and his regal gestures. I feel that our conversation would
be, at the very least, furious and interesting, and intelligent, and not weighty with the stones of ritual doctrine.
The men I usually encounter are either hostile and dull,

or docile and dull, rejecting or accepting with equal lack of positive reason. In truth, the docile and blandly accepting disturb my spirit, for they are no warriors of God."

He flung out his hands. "What He has spoken of among us is not womanish nor resigned nor meek nor flaccid. It is a call to battle, as the prophets called, and Moses. Our faith is not a faith for the eccentric and timorous and unthinking and placid and shy. It is muscular and powerful; it calls for banners and trumpets and drums and battlements and all the strength a man can give it, and not soft words and hesitant manners and mild preachments. It is strong drink, not milk. While it is tender and merciful toward the weak and the unsheltered lambs and ewes, and for those oppressed by man and hopeless, it demands that even those must gird up their loins after their wounds are healed and stand fearlessly before enemies and lies and Godlessness. It demands an 'Aye!' to the face of God, regardless of persecution or death or exile, and a joyful noise before the Lord. Let not those who fear, come to us, nor those who would dilute the power of our certitude, nor those who would say, 'This may be so, but on the other hand that may be so, and should we not be men of kindly reason who not only can give answers but can listen tolerantly to questions and weigh them judiciously, remembering that perhaps those questions pose a truth of their own?'

"The truth is of one piece," said Stephen, and now his face glowed with that unearthly light which so many found fascinating and exultant. "It is true in all things or it is false entirely. It must command all that a man is, or it can command nothing. That is what the prophets have told us, and which our Redeemer and our Savior has told us: *'He who is a friend of this world is an enemy of God.'* In short, the world is black error and you cannot serve error in the morning and serve Him at night." He smiled at his friends. " 'He who is not with Me is against Me.' "

Rabban Gamaliel plucked at his bearded lips and regarded Stephen with thoughtful concern. "Still," he said, "the ages will be plagued by commentators who will interpret in a novel fashion or reinterpret, leading to the confusion of the faithful and causing them to fall away, or to dilution and the uproar of many tongues and many opinions. Every man is a mirror unto himself and reflects himself even in his faith."

"Truth is so pure and so simple," said the young Stephen. "The angels have no difficulty accepting it. Only man casts his own shadow upon it."

"If I remember correctly," said Joseph, smiling, "there were quite a multitude of angels who did not find truth so simple. You are asking almost too much of man to find it so."

Stephen laughed. He applied himself with hearty appreciation to the fine viands before him in Rabban Gamaliel's luxurious hall, and the old men watched him fondly. The young man said, "When I say that truth is simple and pure I do not mean that it is always obvious, for there is nothing so mysterious and sublime as simplicity. A man must indeed be born again of water and the Holy Spirit to comprehend truth, for then his eyes are without film, he hears but one Voice and not disputatious comments, all irrelevant and contentious. He sees things wholly and he sees them clear and in their oneness. It is only error that is intricate and forever open to change. A man who knows the truth is not dogmatic as we know the word, not sealed like one of Solomon's vessels. He is merely aware of error, but he is far from it, and he advances the truth he knows with dedication of soul and gentleness of mien but with stern resolution. He sees the mountain, rooted in granite and immovable, while those in error say, 'You declare it to be a mountain, but it may be a mirage or a wall or an illusion. It is a matter of opinion.'"

"Your path, I fear, will not be a sunny one," said Joseph.

"It has all the brightness of eternity," said Stephen. His face changed again and he sank into thought. Finally he continued:

"There are some among us, even those who walked with Him, who say that we need no ritualism. But ritual is necessary, desirable, in that it is the visible symbol of the holy invisible Thing it symbolizes. However, when it exists as a formal and complete entity in itself, the Thing it symbolizes and explains forgotten or unheeded, then it is an empty form. With that, I agree. Such ritual can even be dangerous, for the people come to believe that ritual alone is worship. But it is valuable only when, like the shell of a nut, it reminds of and intimates the delectable and life-sustaining Kernel within. The Kernel forgotten or lost, the shell is worthless, however gilded. It contains no life. That is what the Lord meant when He attacked the ritualistic Pharisees who thought form, itself, was enough."

He drank the fine wine with appreciation, and examined the beautiful and jeweled crystal of the Alexandrine goblet with admiring attentiveness. The Rabban said, "I think I detect a Hellenistic shine upon your words, Stephen."

"That may be true," said Stephen, "but then, have not Greece and Greek philosophy always had a deep influence on our faith since the first Greek entered Israel? What is beautiful has verity. And variety. To reject the verity of beauty is to reject a profound mysticism, for God, blessed be His Name, is all beauty and all glory and all joy. I am immediately suspicious and repelled by a man who finds our faith grim and joyless and life-denying, instead of a song of rapture sung in the morning in the sun."

"Do you encounter these?" asked Joseph with surprise.

"Too many," said Stephen. "I also encounter the weak who see in the Savior of His people a refuge from their petty adversities, from which they seek to flee, instead of a Temple in whose sacred precincts they can find the strength to endure the world and take up their burden without quailing or complaint. The weak have brought down more temples, and more nations, than we can know, and their self-serving voices have drowned out the very Voice of the Almighty. Life is not a purse from which prayers can draw treasures. It is, as the Greeks say, truly the Great Games, where only courage and strength and faith can win the prize, and fortitude crown the victor."

"As you have said," remarked Rabban Gamaliel, "the new Covenant is not for men of timidity and demands and uncertainty. I recall the words of the Prophet: 'Trust in the Lord with all your heart, *and lean not to your own understanding*. In all your ways acknowledge Him and He shall direct your paths.' "*

"But, there will be arguments," said Joseph of Arimathaea.

*Proverbs 3:5–6.

Stephen laughed gently. "There already are," he said. "They began even before He was crucified."

He was so brimming with vitality and youthful certitude that the old men sighed and silently prayed for him, and he guessed this for he regarded them with respectful affection. He said, before he took his leave of them, "I will encounter your Saul of Tarshish yet, and then we shall have our argument, and it will be a marvelous day!"

It was only, thought Joseph of Arimathaea, a sharp autumn night wind on old bones that made him suddenly shiver as at an awful portent.

One day a centurion came to Saul and said, "Lord, there is a Hellenist among the people of great repute whom we have not taken because he is of a notable and wealthy house, and a man of nobility, and his family are friends of the High Priest, Caiphas, and even of the procurator, Pontius Pilate. We have overlooked his inflammatory speeches in the Temple of the Jews, and the synagogues, but now an uproar is among the Jews, and they fight each other and shout and even smite each other, in the purlieus of the Temple, itself."

"Stephen ben Tobias," said Saul, and his face took on the expression of dark flame. "I have heard of him."

The centurion nodded, and said, "I have news that at this moment he is in the synagogue of what is called the Libertines, and Cyrenians, and Alexandrians, and of Cilicians and of Asia, and the people are listening to this Stephen and are disputing furiously with him, or listening and hailing him. There is a crowd without the synagogue, which cannot enter as it is overflowing, and struggles and blows and bloodletting is rife among it. Two of my legionnaires attempted to bring order, and they are now bleeding and wounded in our hostel. What shall I do?"

Saul rose from his desk in the fine house which Pilate had given him, and he took up his woolen cloak and fastened, for the first time, the sword which he had been given about his waist, and his manner was quietly grim and resolute. His thick red hair flowed unkempt to his shoulders and his eyes glittered in his pale and freckled face. "Bring with us ten legionnaires," he said to the centurion. "We go to the synagogue." He paused a moment and his red thick brows wrinkled like the brows of the lion he was growing more and more to resemble. "Send a messenger to the Little Sanhedrin and ask, in my name, that they meet at the house of the High Priest, Caiphas, immediately, to judge a heretic, a blasphemer."

"And not in the great Court of the Hewn Stones in the Temple?" asked the centurion, who had lived long in Israel and knew that powerful and wealthy malefactors and criminals and celebrated men were usually brought to the Court of Hewn Stones, before the full Sanhedrin, as befitted their station in life, for even judges must defer to rank.

Saul looked at him with his haughty contempt. "Is not that Stephen a Nazarene, a follower of Yeshua ben Joseph of Nazareth, who was himself brought before the Little Sanhedrin in the house of the High Priest? Shall a servant be greater than his master? What was judged sufficient for Yeshua ben Joseph is sufficient for this Stephen ben Tobias, who has lost the respect of praiseworthy and distinguished men, and is not higher than the carpenter he serves."

The centurion went to seek a messenger and order the extra soldiers and then Saul joined him and his men, who had come to fear him in spite of lewd jests behind his back. It was known that he sought no women, therefore, it was hinted, he sought men, though there was no evidence to support this.

The distance to the synagogue was not far. The centurion rode in his chariot, and Saul stood beside him, his eyes fixed murderously ahead, his white lips a mere line between his flat cheeks. He had endured enough! Thinking of his own aristocratic kinsmen—and fearing for them— he had refrained from confronting this Stephen ben Tobias, as there was nothing more fatal than a precedent in law, as he knew. And Stephen was the only aristocrat among those now called the Nazarenes who mingled openly and incitingly among the common people, or harangued in the Temple or created disturbances. Still, once touch the proud patrician wall and none was safe, and even in his present mood of desperate determination and wild hatred Saul understood this, and he sweated under his cloak for his sister and her husband and their children. Lord, he addressed God in his agony, I am only of human flesh, and I love those of my house, though recalcitrant and blasphemers. Protect them, Lord, and bring them to repentance, lest they die, and I die of grief, for always You must be obeyed!

He thought particularly of his beloved nephew, Amos, so foully deceived and betrayed by those appointed as his natural guardians, and Amos' brothers, and the beautiful young maid, their sister, who was like a carving in ivory. He thought of his sister, Sephorah, of his twin blood, whom he loved dearly, and his eyes closed on a spasm of anguish.

But above all God must be obeyed and served, even if a man died from it of a broken heart and a tormented spirit. And then in a twinkling Saul's gorge and hatred reached a height that made him sway and stagger in the chariot: Stephen ben Tobias was the true threat against the house of Shebua ben Abraham, and the children of Sephorah bas Hillel! He, and he alone, had put them in this awful jeopardy, had broken down the gates between the market rabble and the patricians, and had placed the patricians at the mercy of rascals and thieves and yelling and mindless slavers! Stephen ben Tobias was the enemy of those of Saul's flesh. He had called down the vengeance upon them. Therefore, he must die.

Those of power and influence and blood had a Godly imperative: They must uphold law and courtesy and order against the lustful rage of those who were hardly more than animals. They must lead judiciously and with temperate sanity and reason, for what were the people? Only wild and roaring beasts, such as the Romans confined in cages for the circuses, fang-toothed and milling, red of claw.

Now Saul cast his eyes on the people, who filled the streets, with overpowering detestation and felt an almost uncontrollable desire to ride them down and crush them under the wheels of the chariot. For, were they not destroyers of the holy places, the barbarians, the shriekers and blood-lusters, the hyena-laughers, the jackals, of every city under the sun? Why had God created these? Or, was man solely responsible for their being, or hell, itself? He suddenly thought of what his cousin, Titus Milo Platonius, had said of the rabble who had done Yeshua ben Joseph to death, and a cold finger, as of iron, touched Saul's inflamed heart, and a cloudy confusion momentarily passed over his eyes. He thought, And Stephen ben Tobias consorts with these!

Jerusalem lay under the late winter sky in a strong but pale light, like silver struck by the sun. The air was clean and fresh and faintly chill, but exhilarating. The winding umber walls were almost colorless in the frank radiance. Many looked after the racing chariot and many there were who recognized the cloaked figure in it, and some faces darkened or glanced away in sorrow, and some merely smiled and raised eyebrows. These Pharisee heresy-hunters! Now they were in full cry after the members of that new cult founded by the Nazarene! Tomorrow they would discover another heresy and go roaring through the city, threatening scourgings and prisons and exile. But some, scenting excitement, halted their business to pursue the clanging vehicle and the men marching fast behind it. When Romans moved like this it was not to attend a dinner.

The chariot reached the synagogue, or rather it forced its horses through gesticulating and shouting mobs, and faces eloquent either with outrage or despair turned upon Saul. Some men sat on the stones, holding broken heads or noses, and here and there scufflings were under way, accompanied by roars and curses. Some vilified the exhorter within; some implored as passionately that he be heard, for who knew through whose lips God, blessed be His Name, would choose to speak? The centurion had to use his whip lavishly to disperse from his path some of the more engrossed in raging controversy, and they screamed imprecations upon him and shook fists in his direction. He laughed. His soldiers made a circle about the chariot and threatened the surging men with their drawn swords.

Not looking at the people Saul jumped from the chariot and went inside the synagogue. It was a large rough building of gray stone, almost circular, and it was smoky from the fire on the altar where several dismayed and bearded priests stood aghast and helpless. The air in the synagogue was hot both from the fire and the thickly crowded men, who stood shoulder to shoulder and elbow to elbow. Here it was quieter, for only one man spoke and he stood before the altar and his fine sonorous voice could be clearly heard in its pure Greek intonations, its wonderful inflections and musical cadences.

Saul halted and looked at the man he now so malignantly hated, the handsome young man who looked like a Greek indeed, though he was a Jew. He wore his prayer shawl. His head was covered with the hat of the Tribe of Dan. But his garments were of coarse gray linen and his cloak was of brown wool and his feet were bare except for plain leather sandals. But nothing could remove from him his aura of authority, sweetness and power, nor dim the sparkle of his open eyes nor diminish his native elegance and patrician surety.

The light was uncertain and dull, for the windows were high and narrow, and the floor floated in semi-shadow. Only the crimson light on the altar illuminated the interior, and it flickered on listening faces and on the shut expressions of the priests. They could not silence him. It was Jewish law that any man could enter a synagogue if moved to speak and there be heard in courtesy.

Saul felt that his heart would burst with his mighty rage at this man, this heretic, this blasphemer, this betrayer of his people, this man who threatened the house of Shebua ben Abraham. He moved closer, despite grumbling, to hear what Stephen was saying and the hand that never knew the lust of a sword before knew it now.

"It has been said by the Messias," Stephen was saying, "that though the Temple be destroyed, and even the holy city, the truth will not pass away, but will endure forever through the ages and even to the end of the world."

Saul halted, shaken to the soul, for to a Jew the very thought that the Temple might not endure, and that the holy city of Jerusalem might be known no more, was a mortal blasphemy in itself, for did not God dwell on Sion and in His Temple and in His city, and was it not said that He would never desert them? Numbed, he could not believe that this fellow could speak so and not be thrown to the stones and stamped upon. But the men were listening.

"For the faith is more than stones, more, aye, than the gold that lies in the vaults of the Temple. It is more than a city. What is mortal, what is made with human hands, dies in its time as do all things, but truth is eternal. Moses was given the dimensions of the first Temple, and the elaborations thereof, to the last detail, for it is a good thing that men build the House of the Lord, not only with the best they can bring, but with the treasures they have earned and gathered in their lives, and the best of their own houses. For, who will deny the Lord and keep from Him which is justly His own and which He has only lent to men? All that a man is, in wealth and in blood and in heart and in soul, is a small sacrifice and even a mean one, and it is only the lovingkindness of God which prevents Him from spurning that sacrifice. But He accepts what we bring, as a father accepts the pretty little stones and dying worthless flowers which his children bring to him, and with tenderness and love. It is not the valuable which is truly the valuable, but only that given with humility and faith, however valueless, if it is all a man has to offer his God. Did not the Messias say that a widow's mite—which was all she possessed—was of greater worth than the gold of a rich man?"

The listeners murmured and moved restlessly. So, thought Saul, this wretch deprecates sacrifice, insults Moses, and scorns the gold which lies in the Temple vaults, which assures our precarious security and supports our faith.

"To teach us these things, that the works of men will not endure, nor the cities he builds, nor his pride nor his science and his art and his strength and his power and his glory, but only the things of the spirit, the Messias chose to be born in a stable, of a poor Maiden of the House of David, and to live obscurely and to learn the trade of a carpenter and to labor at His trade. Is not a man's soul more than his habitation, the piety of his thoughts more than silken raiment, his eternal destiny more than his treasures? His soul will survive though the earth itself be forgotten and lost in her orbit and changed into dust. This world is not our abiding place, no, not the world we see with our eyes. It has no verity and value in itself, despite its Rome and its Jerusalem and Damascus and Alexandria and Athens, its buildings and temples and thoroughfares, its cities of the sea. Our world is but a charnal house, the cemetery of countless civilizations which waxed and waned and died and left but a heap of stones, forgotten of name, forgotten of heritage and all their pride. And so it shall be in the ages to come. Man boasts to the wind and the wind carries away his voice and it is as if he had never spoken!

"But that which is of the spirit never changes nor dies. It is immutable. Therefore, is not that man a fool who puts his faith in masonry, however sacrosanct it is declared, and in his powers as a mortal, and in his treasures of banks and mind and learning? His destiny is not with them, as the Messias has told us over and over. His destiny is in eternity; his flesh is that of a beast and no more. He lives his life as beasts live their lives, and who can mark the distinction, for man as an animal only is less than a beast, for he does not possess a beast's loyalty and purity of being and simplicity, nor its singleness of purpose, nor even its value.

"Only that in man which dies not possesses verity, for it is given of God, blessed be His Name, and the sinful soul is redeemed from death and hell by its great Lover, its Savior, who died on the cross for the forgiveness of our sins, our absolution, our reconciliation with God, the Father, and our eternal life beyond these little, dark and broken shores we call our home."

Stephen raised his long and aristocratic hands and his look kindled with love and passion and fervor on the listening men, and he said, "His peace I bring unto you, as He brought it to us, the Warrior of Israel, the Holy One of Israel, Who from the ages was promised to us who awaited Him, the Redeemer of His people, our Lord and our God!"

Saul could contain himself no longer. His whole body, his very flesh, appeared to him to gather to itself enormous strength and fury, and he advanced through the throng as if he walked alone and there was none in his path. He reached Stephen ben Tobias who looked at him with a sudden and flashing smile of recognition, and Stephen made as if to speak and he half lifted his hand, desirous of touching the other man. But Saul seized a burning brand on the altar, and he shook it in the face of the priests then struck the altar with it in one violent movement. Sparks flew. The priests recoiled. The crowd craned and murmured, knowing this intruder.

Saul raised his roaring voice and he shouted to the priests, "Do you dare stand there and not protest the words of this blasphemer who has told you that our Temple will be destroyed and our holy city? Who would destroy them? This fellow and his followers, these so-called Nazarenes, these cultists, these heretics! It is not enough that they have brought contention and bitterness and hatred between brethren in this sacred city and in our holy land. No! They have brought fear to us, the hard attention of the Roman. They have divided us, confused us, caused us to commit the sin of blasphemy and doubt, to look with derision on all that we hold holy, to flout the prophets, to weaken our resolution, to dissipate our strength through controversy and quarreling. They have brought us far from our God with lying preachments. They have set house against house, until there is not an hour but what anger erupts and men strive with each other. They have imitated through Satan miracles and prodigies, for the confusion of simple minds and the desecration of all that is holy.

"And, what are they?" cried Saul, turning from the priests now and facing the people, who were murmuring loudly and pushing against each other. "Base creatures, degraded creatures, superstitious and ignorant creatures, who question the Law and the Book!"

He paused and Stephen's voice rang out clear and firm. "This is not true, Saul of Tarshish, and you speak falsehood whether you know it or not! We do not destroy the Law nor seek to change it, but to proclaim its fulfillment in the Person of the Redeemer of Israel, the Messias of God. He has made a new Covenant with us—"

Saul struck him fiercely on the cheek, and when Stephen involuntarily stepped back a pace Saul advanced on him and struck him again. The synagogue was immediately filled with shouting and imprecations and the altar fire caught wild and glittering eyes.

Saul looked at them. His breast rose and fell with his uncontrolled emotions and his despair and hatred. "Who will testify now against this fellow, this traitor, this apostate Jew, this Hellenist imbued with the paganism of the Greek and all their heathen philosophies? Who will go with me to the house of the High Priest, where the Little Sanhedrin is now called, and witness against this man, our enemy, the enemy of God, Himself, blessed be His Name?"

His eyes were blue lightnings; froth appeared at the corners of his mouth. He visibly shook with his wrath. "Men of Israel!" he cried. "Do you wish the anger of

God to descend on us again, that we go whoring after strange cults and blasphemous lies and the idolatry of a miserable Nazarene? What good can come out of Nazareth? Woe unto you, men of Israel, men of the holy city, that you have listened to this heretic! Should the very stones you stand on rise and smite you to your death, it would be little enough punishment. For, in this place, dedicated to God and His worship, you have permitted a rascal, a thief of your souls, to speak to you without protest. Woe unto you!"

It seemed to his now affrighted listeners that he was as large as a statue, filled at the core with fire, that he possessed strange attributes, and was a prophet, for he stood in the light of the altar like a red-haired Moses prepared to destroy the Tablets of the Law because of their sins. His countenance was terrible. His eyes, they thought, were frightful in their power and intensity, as they roamed their faces.

Then a man shouted, "We have heard him speak blasphemous words against Moses and against God! And against this holy place and the Law! For we have heard him say that Yeshua of Nazareth will destroy this place and shall change the customs which Moses delivered us!"*

The man turned to those near him and exclaimed, "Who will stand with Saul of Tarshish and witness against this Stephen ben Tobias, that he may be punished for his crimes against us, and against God?"

Hands flung themselves into the air and a great shout rose, and Saul looked upon the congregation, then looked with a malignant smile at Stephen ben Tobias who had folded his hands under his prayer shawl and whose lips were moving in silence.

"Seize him, then, men of Israel, the faithful of God!" said Saul, "and we will take him to the house of the High Priest, Caiphas, and before the Little Sanhedrin, for a judgment."

The crowd erupted into the street, tossing those who awaited outside as a sea tosses sticks, and they were led by Saul ben Hillel who was like a raging storm. The centurion looked upon him and said in a low voice to his

*Acts 6:13–14.

men. "That is not our affair. Nevertheless, let us follow where they go."

Still, he glanced with some compassion on the torn and bleeding Stephen ben Tobias, the patrician, who was being half carried and half dragged, away from the synagogue, followed by the screaming and cursing mob. The centurion thought of the mobs of Rome of whom even Caesar Tiberias lived in fear, and who now really ruled the city and distorted the voice of law and reason with their howls and their demands, and who devoured the flesh of the industrious and the manly to satisfy their base appetites and who shrieked for bread and circuses, for beans and for housing and benefits they had not earned, and dared to call themselves Romans! The centurion shook his head, and with a melancholy countenance he motioned to his men, and stepped into his chariot and followed Saul and Stephen and the wrestling and sweating mob. He obeyed his orders, given to him by Pontius Pilate.

The High Priest awaited the arrival of Saul and his prisoner, and so did the few members of the Little Sanhedrin, hastily summoned. Caiphas said, "This will surely be the end of Stephen ben Tobias, for I know this Saul of Tarshish, and he is a man of vengeance and will of a certainty deliver us of the blasphemers."

"I know the house of Tobias," said one judge, his eyes resolutely on the marble floor of the hall and his expression inscrutable. "Let us hope that house does not exert its own vengeance."

"I have heard that they have secretly denounced their son, Stephen," said another judge. The others sighed with relief. The judge said, "They would not lift a hand either to help or avenge him, for he impudently exhorts them to give their riches to the poor that they might have salvation!"

The others laughed faintly. One said, "If only there were an end to this foolish cult!"

They heard a discordant sound of huge tumult approaching the palace and the High Priest said with distaste, "The mob, once more. How I detest them!" He sat on his gilded chair and brooded and waited, and he thought of Stephen ben Tobias in the hands of that savage rabble and shuddered.

The captain of Caiphas' guard rushed into the hall, his sword drawn, and crying, "Lord, there is a huge mob outside the gates, clamoring to be received by you, and with them is one Saul of Tarshish, who demands admittance with his prisoner, Stephen ben Tobias! And with them also is a Roman officer and some legionnaires!"

Caiphas said, "Admit Saul of Tarshish and his prisoner, and the witnesses against the prisoner, but none else, no, not even the Romans, for this must be a seemly trial and not a heathen circus."

"Unlike the trial of Yeshua ben Joseph," added a judge, and Caiphas turned to him sharply but the judge's face was bland. Nevertheless, Caiphas fumed, thinking of Rabban Gamaliel and Joseph of Arimathaea and the defected priests of the Temple. A few moments later there was a scuffling and a howling in the portico and muffled shrieks, and then Saul hurled himself rather than ran into the hall, and he was like a tempest crowned with fire, and behind him rushed a dozen men beating one in their midst and kicking and reviling him. Their garments blew with their vehemence and their feet slapped the marble like brutish applause.

Caiphas rose and lifted his voice in anger, gazing at Saul who had paused before him, "Are these animals or are they men, Saul ben Hillel, that they swarm before me like swine? Where is their decorum in this company of the Sanhedrin?"

"Lord," said Saul, answering him in the deliberate Latin he spoke, "forgive them, for they are inflamed by their fury that this blasphemer dared exhort them in their very synagogue, where they were peacefully at prayer, and offer up blasphemies to offend their ears." But he turned and spoke in a loud hard voice to the witnesses and they stared once at him with restlessly gleaming eyes, breathed heavily, then flung their prisoner at the feet of Caiphas.

Stephen ben Tobias was hardly conscious and bleeding from several small wounds in his face and on his arms. His amber head, so crisply curled and shining, lay on the marble floor, dabbled with blood, and his arms and his long and elegant hands were stretched before him. Now a deep silence suddenly filled the chamber and the judges in their chairs craned to look upon this scion of a celebrated house, and some knew him and bit their lips and looked aside, and some were curious. Caiphas closed his eyes briefly. He opened them to regard the disheveled witnesses in their many-colored garments and he saw the lust to kill on their dark and bearded faces and he thought, It matters not to them what this man has done or not done, or whether he blasphemed or not, for what do cattle know of blasphemy? They only wish to kill him. When will this horror end? Why has Israel been cursed with another new and militant sect?

He said to Saul, "Is the prisoner dead or only fainted, and can he be aroused to answer to the charges?"

"Request wine for him, lord," said Saul, still speaking in Latin. "He is not dead."

Caiphas clapped his hands and when a slave appeared he ordered wine. Then he hesitated. He loathed Saul as he loathed all contumacious and turbulent men for they not only vexed his mind but disturbed his digestion. In some manner, deftly and with all too human a dexterity, he had shifted the blame for the origin of the persecution of the blasphemers and cultists from himself to Saul, and at times considered himself a sorely distraught man who desired only peace. So, to ease the spasm within him and to annoy Saul and perhaps even to insult him, he said to the servant, "Bring also a chair for this prisoner and some water and towels for his wounds, and serve the wine in one of the suitable goblets, for this is Stephen ben Tobias of a distinguished house in Israel, and not a workman from the Street of the Tentmakers nor a peasant from the vineyards."

Some of the judges, with pardonable pleasure, saw that Saul's face swelled and that he bit his lip until a bead of blood appeared upon it. But he stood rigidly in silence, like an image of himself, and stared over the High Priest's head at one of the high windows through which fell the strong pale sunlight. His countenance had turned gray, his mouth was livid.

The servant helped assist Stephen to his feet and into a chair drawn before the judges and the High Priest and Stephen fell against the back, his pallid face the face of a dead man, his eyes closed, his cheeks bleeding. Great bruises were already appearing on his flesh and on his throat. But even these, and his poor garb, could not diminish his patrician aura. When the wine, in a superb Alexandrine goblet, was pressed gently against his lips he swallowed it slowly, drop by drop, and a faint color returned to his handsome face. Then he looked at the High Priest and said, "Caiphas."

"Yes, it is I," said the High Priest. "It is an evil day when a scion of a noble house is caught in blasphemy, Stephen ben Tobias, and arrested like a common felon and brought before members of the Sanhedrin. Speak, Stephen, what have you to say for yourself, what denials do you wish to make?"

Stephen appeared to ponder, not moving those open lustrous eyes of his from the High Priest. At last he said, "So He was brought, like a common felon and judged, and I feel no shame. I am overjoyed that I can imitate Him." His cultured voice grew stronger instant by instant, and then, incredibly, he smiled. He turned in his chair and looked at Saul, who moved his head stiffly in his direction and returned his gaze.

"Long have I wished to dispute with you, Saul of Tarshish," he said, "for we are men of the same breed, and I have prayed to reason with you."

"Reason with me now," said Saul in his loud and bitter voice, "for you have betrayed what is best in Israel, the obligation of a man of an illustrious house to set an example to his people. You have behaved indeed as a common felon, as a cheap and rowdy blasphemer, a low fellow creating unrest out of mere mischief, and exposing our people to danger, and to the wrath of God."

Before Stephen could answer him Saul raised his hand peremptorily, and said, "But what are you, Stephen ben Tobias, but a Hellenist, an apostate Jew, who cannot honor the faith that has guarded Israel through the centuries because he knows little or nothing about it, its history and its saints and its prophets! No, rather, you have idly embraced false gods and evil philosophies, and have been easily led into error and blasphemy. I am prepared," said Saul, for his heart was filled with an unfathomable pain, "to have you confess that you have sinned out of ignorance, and out of lack of knowledge, and not out of conviction, and perhaps only to amuse an effete self."

The judges glanced at each other in amazement, and the mouths of the heaving witnesses fell open, for the formidable Saul of Tarshish had offered the prisoner an escape so that he would suffer, perhaps, only a few lashings and then be released.

Saul did not understand even himself, and all the complex emotions, wound one within another like many threads rolled together, which had impulsively moved him to suggest to Stephen how he could avoid the punishment of a true blasphemer, and so receive only a flogging and short imprisonment. Perhaps it had been Stephen's name and house, or perhaps the beauty of his face and the openness of his look, and his youth, for he was younger than Saul and only on the threshold of full manhood, and in some manner he reminded Saul of the boy, Amos, his nephew. He had seen that at the very altar in the synagogue, even in his rage.

It was possible that Stephen, with that keen insight which had come to him lately, understood all this, and his eyes welled and darkened with compassion, as if he, not Saul, was the accuser and the judge, and Saul the victim.

Caiphas said quickly, "Confess, Stephen ben Tobias, that you have been in error, not out of conviction but out of ignorance, as Saul of Tarshish has—accused."

But Stephen did not turn to him. He continued to contemplate Saul, and now a deep excitement filled his eyes and the sweetest of smiles curled his Grecian lips. He rose slowly and feebly from his chair, then stood beside it, his hand upon it to support himself. Then it was that he looked at the judges and began to speak in his seductive and enchanting voice.

"I have been accused of being an apostate Jew, with little knowledge of our sacred history and the saints and the prophets, and therefore inclined to misinterpretation and error. But, lords, this is not true."

He glanced strongly at Saul and said, "There is a worse betrayal even than that of a friend or a kinsmen, or a people, and that is betrayal of God, blessed be His Name, and the betrayal of His truth."

He turned to the judges and said, "Lords, hearken unto me and tell me then in all justice if I am a Jew ignorant of the history of our people."

He embarked then on a long and eloquent dissertation on the history of his people and the saints and the prophets, and now there was no sound in the chamber at all but his compelling voice and no gesture but his moving and graceful gesticulations, and even the witnesses did not shuffle their feet and Caiphas and the judges listened in astonishment, and Saul, himself, in spite of his efforts, could not glance away from that glowing face near him.

There was not an event, however obscure, how far away in the clouds of time, that Stephen did not relate, and it was as if he were telling an absorbing story which none had heard before. He spoke of Abraham and Jacob, and Joseph and Moses and Aaron and Solomon and David, with precision and deep knowledge. He had the cultured man's genius for assembling facts and presenting them logically, with no vague hesitations or uncertainties, but with absolute order and incisiveness. Moment ran into moment, and time into time, and all were held by his voice as if held by his hands.*

He came to a halt. It was understood that he had not finished, but he looked smilingly at the bemused judges and waited. Saul, too, seemed to be under a spell, and his face was wrinkled and drawn.

Then Saul said, "A witness against you, one of those present, has declared that you have said, of the Temple, 'Yeshua ben Joseph of Nazareth will destroy this place and shall change the customs which Moses delivered us.' What have you to say in answer?"

Stephen, again only addressing him, replied: "It is written in the Scriptures: 'Solomon built Him a House. "Howbeit the most High dwells not in temples made with hands—saith the prophet." "Heaven is My Throne and earth my footstool. What house will you build Me?" said the Lord, or what is the place of My rest? Has not My hand built all these things?' The Messias has told us," said Stephen, his voice deepening, "of these things again, reminding us that gilded houses made for God may be pleasing to man's reverence, and therefore to God, but men can pray and be heard in the open fields at their labor, and in their secret places and not only in the synagogues and the Temples, and in their beds, and alone.

*Acts 6 and 7.

These He said, and I have repeated them, and like Him, I have repeated the words of Solomon, for we have forgotten them, as men always forget the words of God and prefer to listen to their own desires.

"In quoting Solomon, lords, was the Messias a blasphemer, and am I, too, a blasphemer?"

Now Saul was freshly infuriated. He exclaimed, "You are a quibbler! We are astonished at your knowledge of your people and their sacred history, as you intended us to be astonished. I praise you for your erudition! But you have been accused of saying that Yeshua ben Joseph will destroy the Temple—"

"I never said that, nor did the Messias, blessed be His Name. He prophesied that our Temple will be destroyed, our nation dispersed, and Jerusalem laid low and the walls of her be broken down. But He repeated what prophets before Him had said, and He again prophesied that Israel will once more bloom as the rose, after the days of tribulation."

The witness against Stephen raised a shrilling cry: "He lies! He lies! I have with me men who will testify to his lies!" And he turned violently on his companions and shouted. "Is it not so, men, and will you not swear by your fathers' beards that it is so?" He stamped his feet like a madman, and glared like a beast.

For the briefest instant the men with him hesitated, then swept by his passion and believing what he had said, they raised their voices in a thunderous affirmation, and it seemed to them that Stephen had indeed said that his Master had declared he would destroy the Temple and the Law. "Aye, Aye, it is so, it is so!" they howled.

Stephen, still standing by the chair, still oozing from his many small wounds, gazed at the men and sighed, not with impatience or disgust, but with pity. Then, as if he had heard a commanding voice he started and lifted his eyes to one of the windows and an ineffable smile broke out upon his face and he raised his hands in awe and worship.

He said, and his voice shook, "Behold! The Heavens open and I see the Son of Man standing on the right Hand of God!"

He is demented, thought Saul, and now his pain left

him and he said to himself, He has a devil, and blasphemes.

He said to the High Priest and the judges. "You have heard his lame falsehoods, and now his open blasphemy, declaring that Yeshua of Nazareth stands at the right Hand of God!"

Still Caiphas hesitated. He turned to the judges. He saw them pondering. If they dismissed the charges against Stephen ben Tobias then these witnesses would cast it abroad that the Sanhedrin feared to rebuke and punish a rich man of an illustrious house, though they had not hesitated to deliver Yeshua of Nazareth up to death at the hands of the Romans, for was not Yeshua only a poor man and a carpenter? They would howl: "One law for the mighty and another for the weak!" Worse still, they would proclaim that the Sanhedrin had upheld a blasphemer. Chaos would result.

So one of the judges said, "Let him be delivered to the ultimate punishment."

The witnesses yelled with joy, and losing all restraint and respect now they rushed upon Stephen and seized him, and they hurled him with them out of the chamber and the tumult died behind them.

Caiphas looked at Saul and said, "What? Are you not accompanying them to give a semblance of the order of law to the proceedings?" He smiled richly, and with malice, and his jewels flashed on his hands.

Saul said not a word but went from the chamber and Caiphas thought, I have repaid you, my arrogant friend of the audacious red hair and the leonine countenance, for the insults you have heaped on me since I have known you, and the proud glances, and the condemnations.

The turbulent procession of vociferous and bellowing death, led by Saul ben Hillel, and followed resignedly by the Roman centurion and his men, clamored through the streets of Jerusalem, adding to itself other throngs as a river on the way to the sea gathers brooks and rivulets unto it. The late winter sun was dropping in the west, and it was a hole of red fire in the whitish heavens, for a cloudy mist was rising. And now a dusty wind rose that swirled through the narrow streets and billowed under the many feet of the hurrying crowd. The mounts were a lilac-bronze, not yet taking upon themselves the green of spring, though islands of dark cypresses lifted their spires here and there.

Merchants closed little shops to run at the rear of the procession, and to ask questions, and now some men joined that procession on little asses, and from side streets camels and their riders stared, and women peeped from small windows, and little boys ran shrieking, stuffing sweetmeats into their mouths and opening wide their dark and shining eyes in excitement. "They are taking a blasphemer to the Field of the Stoning!" they shouted. It was a festival, for the children were too young to know of death and death by so horrible a method, and they laughed gleefully among themselves until men in the running cavalcade drove them off. It would be no sight for children.

The centurion, being an "old" Roman, did not love the Gracchi nor their memory, but he recalled that the Gracchi had been stoned to death by such a rabble as this, mindless and jeering and delighting in agony. Of what had the Gracchi been guilty, though, deluded men? Of an effort to raise these creatures to manhood; they had declared that such had "rights." Of what was this Stephen accused? Of blasphemy. Of a certainty the gods did not like to be insulted, but this Stephen had not insulted them except by proclaiming that one of them had deigned to take on the flesh of man and lead mankind into light and truth. Did a man deserve death for that? Well, Prometheus had brought fire to man, and the gods had been vengeful and had punished him for eternity. That was their prerogative. It was not man's.

The Roman could not see Saul at the head of the increasing mobs. Then it came to him that it was not fitting for a Roman to follow the rabble. Nor was it fitting to lead it! However, there would be a challenge at the gate by Roman soldiers, and there would be confusion and probably violence if these wretches were delayed in their madness, so the centurion whipped up his chariot, forced a way through the press of bodies, and his men followed. When he came to the head of the tumult he glanced to his left and saw Stephen ben Tobias being dragged by and pushed by a dozen arms. He appeared hardly conscious. His eyes were closed. The blood was streaming from him again. His face was like that of a fallen statue, dyed red with his life's fluid, and his pale garments were bloody. For an instant the centurion had a thought to drive his sword mercifully through the condemned man's heart. Then he remembered that Pilate had ordered him to obey Saul of Tarshish, that terrible and beset man marching with incredible speed before all of them. The centurion passed him. But Saul saw nothing; his eyes were fixed ahead and he appeared to be in a trance. The centurion thought: He is not a man any longer. He is only a force.

The soldiers at the gates came to the road to stare and to point, their helmets gleaming in the colorless light, and above them folded and unfolded the standards of Rome and the great bronze eagles over the gates seemed alive, poised for the death-swoop. Seeing the centurion whipping his horses they ran to the gates and opened them, and saluted, and disbelievingly watched the mob as it sailed out onto the bare and saffron plain, which was strewn with boulders and stones and gravel. To the soldiers it seemed that half of Jerusalem was streaming and thundering onto the plain, braying like asses, howling like jackals, ululating like hyenas, a many-colored apparition of flapping robes and galloping feet. There was something in their midst being dragged, something white and limp and stained with red, something which bobbed up and down flaccidly, something which they could not believe was human except that the brightness of disordered amber hair caught their eyes.

After the streets of the city the desolation outside was too wide and open and silent for the mobs, and they suddenly halted, those in the front, and those behind them collided with their bodies, and there was a vast confusion. Now Saul took command. He did not glance at the Romans who had moved apart beside their officer. He lifted his hand and his voice was loud and resonant as he shouted in that awesome silence:

"Let those who have testified against this man, before the High Priest and the Little Sanhedrin, stand forth, for it is the law—'the hand of the witnesses shall be the first against him.' Those who are not witnesses must stand back, in quiet and in order, or I will command that you be driven back within the gates and dispersed! This is not a celebration. It is a solemn occasion of righting a fearful wrong against God, blessed be His Name."

So tremendous was the power of his personality and his superhuman authority, and so awful were his expression and his eyes, that the mobs became instantly quiet, breathing audibly like gusts of wind in the silence. They turned their savage and impatient eyes on the witnesses, who dragged their limp burden before Saul and threw him at the young Pharisee's feet.

Stephen lay there, broken and dazed, his white cheek resting on the yellow gravel, his legs sprawled helplessly, his arms spread as if nailed to a cross. He did not open his eyes; his golden lashes lay on his cheeks and his gray lips were parted in a feeble breathing. The scion of the House of Tobias was already close to death, his beauty shattered in the dust, his body without movement.

It was Saul who took a brief and almost groaning breath, for this blasphemer was young, almost a youth, just recently glowing of countenance and brilliant of eye, stretching forth a hand in friendship, debating, standing proudly before the High Priest—that detestable man!—and not defending himself but defending One he loved beyond his own life. What power had that carpenter, that miserable wandering rabbi, possessed that men like Stephen should follow him and lay down their lives for him and raise his name as triumphant soldiers raise a banner on conquered soil? There had been others before him, claiming mighty powers and doing miracles, and they had had their followers, and they had died and been forgotten and their followers had disappeared on their deaths. But the Nazarene, even in death, had the power to raise up men from stones to proclaim his name, and to call forth a hundred disciples where only one had stood before!

Saul looked down at the head of the condemned man, lying so near his dusty sandals, and the pang that struck him was like a sword in his flesh, a burning in his throat. I would have spared him, he thought, but he was mad, and now he must die, for God must not be mocked lest we all perish.

The young Pharisee raised his hands and the witnesses pounced upon Stephen and tore the long tunic and cloak

and prayer shawl and cap from him, and his girdle, leaving
him only his loincloth. And there were some among the
avid watchers who were amazed at the marble symmetry
of his young body, the perfect carving of the muscles
under the white and silken skin, the cunning loveliness
where joint joined socket without flaw. And a few, who
had seen Greek temples and had even entered them,
thought that Stephen resembled a statue of Hermes. It
was these who began to retreat uneasily and to wonder
how they had come to this place, and they hid themselves
in the throng at the rear and some even returned silently
through the gates, and some were horrified that they had
been part of the rabble, and began to flee.

As always, it was hotter here than within the city, for
the breath of the desert was near and as the sun fell the
mountains, reflecting this light, sprang into hard and
vivid copper. The witnesses, feeling the sudden heat, took
off their cloaks and looked at Saul, and he stepped back
and motioned, and they threw their garments before him
in a heap.

Then, like scorpions in their dark tunics they raced
about, bent, searching, in a wide circle, and they seized
stones and weighed them in their hands and their eyes
sparkled with anticipation and delight. From them, in the
curiously pent silence, issued sounds heard usually only
when men were in the extremities of copulation, and
Saul's face, now so strained and convulsed, shivered with
disgust and even hatred. Each took two stones, the heavi-
est and sharpest they could hold, and they returned and
stood about Stephen.

Saul again raised his hand. It was his impulse, almost
uncontrollable, to turn and flee, but he had commanded
this and he would remain if he died for it.

The first stone thudded between Stephen's shoulders,
and a long tremor ran down his body but there was no
expression on his quiet countenance. Saul thought, I pray
that he is unconscious, that he will know nothing. The
sound of the thud had been horrible to all except the
witnesses, for it was flesh on which the stone had fallen.
Now an enormous wound appeared between Stephen's
shoulders, like a ragged gaping red mouth, spewing
blood.

The witnesses, seeing the blood, appeared to go mad.

Several danced, a parody on sacred dancing, their knees bent stiffly, their movements insect-like and awkward, as though made of wood. As they circled they hurled their stones on the beaten body in the yellow dust and gravel, and screamed like women. One found its heavy mark on the back of Stephen's head and the last of the amber locks disappeared in a torrent of scarlet. The thudding became unbearable, and echoed back from the waste places.

I must not faint, I must not fall, thought Saul ben Hillel, and the ominous sparks he knew too well began to rage behind his closed lids, and there was a trembling in his flesh and his mouth dried and his tongue rose to stick on the roof of his mouth. He felt the little bubbles of foam at the corners of his lips. And then he thought, Yes, let me fall and see no more!

But something opened his eyes, and even he forgot the screams of the murderers and the pounding on white defenseless flesh, for between the dancing and hurling witnesses he saw a form and a tall figure he had seen long ago, a carved pale face and large somber blue eyes beneath a mass of gilt hair tumbled with silver. The man stood a distance in front of the watching mob, wrapped in a blue wool cloak, his hood hanging about his neck. He was not gazing at the murder transpiring near him. His whole attention, his brooding glance, his strong fixed look, dwelled on Saul only.

Was that accusation in his look or hate or condemnation? And who was he, this stranger, this man obviously not a Jew? A blazing ring captured the light of the dying sun and it was like a star on his right index finger.

Saul, trembling violently, returned his eyes to the stoning. Stephen was now a pulp of bleeding and lacerated flesh and purple bruises and wounds. Lord, said Saul in his heart, let him be dead and let it be the end.

The stoners were gasping for breath now, for their exertions had been strenuous and they still picked up the bloody stones that had bounced from the prostrate body and hurled them, though not with such force now, for they were spent. Little rivulets of scarlet were mingling with the dust and crawling away like wounded snakes over the dried umber earth and gravel, and they caught the light and glinted. He is dead, thought Saul, and again the pain came to him, and again the seizure struck him.

But at that instant the crushed body of Stephen stirred, and to the amazement and affrightedness of many he raised himself on his hands, those long elegant hands bleeding and shattered now, and his young face was suddenly the face again of an angel, lighted and blazing with an inner transport and an inner joy. He had lifted his distended eyes to the sky; he was in rapture, enthralled, full of visions. His body arched. He was like one rising precipitately to answer the summons of a recognized and beloved commander. The blood ran from his head and forehead and down his face and even from his eyes and his nose, but he was radiant, shining like the moon.

He cried out, in a great voice, "Lord, Lord Yeshua, receive my spirit!"

He was shaken over and over by his exultation. He smiled with exquisite love and awe, and a glory seemed to fall upon him so that he was transfigured.

Then, though he still smiled in his rapture tears dripped from his bleeding eyes, and he said in a beseeching and tender voice, "Lord, hold not this sin to their charge."

Again he was shaken as by an invisible force. His arms bent. He fell on his face, murmured once, shivered, and expired. Now he lay in peace, and none could hurt him any longer.

The first martyr had died in the Name of Yeshua of Nazareth, whom the Romans called Jesus and the Greeks, Jesu. His open dead mouth appeared to drink the dust of the desert, and his gentle palms lay upturned as though in merciful prayer.

Saul put his hands over his face. His seizure had passed. He felt mortally cold though the winds of the desert were still hot. He felt ill as he had never felt ill since he had almost died in his early youth. He was one hollowness of pain.

Then he drew his strength together. What was done was done. Where, then, was the sense of duty fulfilled, of a task accomplished which must be accomplished? Where was the experience of feeling that he had obeyed God? Stephen ben Tobias, the deluded, the enchanted, the blasphemer, had died like a joyful hero and a prophet beloved of God, and he, Saul ben Hillel, was centered with agony.

When he could look at Stephen again he saw that some one in compassion had thrown the dead man's cloak over his crushed body, and a mighty feeling of gratitude swept over Saul so intense that he could hardly restrain his tears. The witnesses, haggard and still half demented, were taking up their cloaks with an air or righteousness and almost with a swagger, but the crowd had retreated far from them, nearer the gates, their passion spent and confusion upon them.

Then it was that the stranger whom Saul had observed, and whom he had seen before, advanced to the silent body sprawled in the dust. He knelt slowly beside Stephen. He gently drew back the cloak from the battered head. Then he lifted the head to his breast like a father and held it there, and the features of the dead man were the features of a sleeping child against the heart of a living man. And over that head the cold and thoughtful blue eyes dwelt again on Saul, and he could not read them.

Suddenly Saul remembered. This was the Greek physician, Lucanus, adopted son of Diodorus Cyranus, the Roman legate of Syria, the tribune of wealth and power in Rome. This was the famed physician of the seas, the merciful defender of man against God!

It was then that Lucanus addressed Saul over the body of the dead man, and the head held to his breast, and his voice was clear and passionless in the quiet:

"Is it permitted that I carry this boy to a place of burial which his kinsmen will designate, among his people?"

Saul was taken by such an anguish that he thought he would die, and it maddened him, and he flung evil words at the physician in his extremity of suffering:

"We are not heathen Romans nor Greeks! We do not take vengeance on the dead!"

He turned to the centurion, whose Roman face was stern and averted, and he summoned the soldier to him. He came, his armor clanking.

"Do not accompany me to my house," said Saul. "Place the body of the condemned in your chariot—" He paused. He looked at the kneeling physician. "And permit this —this physician—to accompany the dead man wheresoever he desires to go, and take your men with you."

The centurion called to his soldiers, and Lucanus relinquished the body after he had again covered it with the

cloak, and the soldiers laid the body in the chariot and
Lucanus climbed up into the vehicle and sat down near
Stephen ben Tobias. Without a glance at Saul they drove
away and the soldiers left with them. The chariot rum-
bled and churned its way over the stones and gravel and
Saul watched them go, that somber entourage of death.
To the last he saw Lucanus' fair head bent over the
mangled wreckage at his feet.

Saul stood for a long time as if in a trance, until he
became aware that he was as cold as death and quaking
with pain. He also became aware that the desert was
swiftly darkening and that a dull moon was rising like a
skull from the west, and that none was near him at all,
not a single man, not one of the rabble, not even one of
the witnesses, and that he was alone, abandoned. He saw
the tall distant gates of his city, open for him. With a bent
head he turned toward them and, with the step of an old
and broken man, he began to walk. Stephen ben Tobias'
blood was a black pool on the desert floor, shimmering
feebly under the moon.

Chapter 33

*"—And at that time there was a great persecution
against the Church which was at Jerusalem, and they were
all scattered abroad through the regions of Juda and
Samaria, except the apostles. As for Saul, he made havoc
of the Church, entering into every house and haling men
and women committed them to prison. Therefore, they
that were scattered abroad went everywhere preaching
the word."**

RABBAN GAMALIEL and Joseph of Arimathaea stood before the smooth white tomb of Stephen ben Tobias and
contemplated the flowers laid upon it, as fresh as dew. The
tomb stood in the quiet cemetery and in the section devoted
to the house of Tobias. Others were there, sad-faced men
and women in humble raiment. But one or two were clothed

*Acts 8:1-4.

richly. A man of some forty years, short and broad and of a great round belly, stood there with his hand on the tomb. He was fat, but did not appear gross; rather, he had an immense air of contained dignity and self-control. He wore a white toga bordered with gold and scarlet, and scarlet shoes like a Senator, and when he breathed the toga fell apart somewhat to reveal a white tunic of the finest silk. He also wore a gilt embroidered cap of the tribe of Dan, and there were marvelous rings on every finger of his fat white hands—the latter carefully plucked of hair—and armlets heavily jeweled, and a golden chain inset with rubies about his neck. Two servants stood respectfully at a little distance from him. He appeared to notice no one. His round pink face, with its several chins, had a disciplined expression, though from all other evidences he had led a lascivious and luxurious life. He had no beard; he exuded an odor of verbena and mint, and his square fingernails were as polished as opals. All proclaimed him to be a satyr or at least a man who enjoyed life and had denied himself nothing, yet his face revealed hearty health and reflection.

His perfumed hand stroked the tomb, but his expression did not change. He did not even sigh. At length he turned from the tomb and saw the Rabban and Joseph.

"Greetings," he said in a rich and assured voice. "Rabban, Joseph."

"Shalom," said Rabban Gamaliel, and his famed voice was deep with pity, "Tobias ben Samuel."

The cold hazel eyes dwelt on them as if in examination. Tobias said, " 'Shalom.' Peace. To whom, my friends? My son who lies in this tomb, murdered by evil men, of whom Saul of Tarshish is the most evil? To my house, to my wife, to my daughters? Who shall restore to me my only son?"

They could not reply out of their deep emotion. "It is said that I had cut him off from me, his father, and his family. It is true that we laughed at his folly. But he was a very young man, of much ardor and given to quick passions and enthusiastic attachments, and we hoped that he would recover, as he had recovered before. That would, without doubt, have come to pass. Gentlemen, of what heinous crime was my son guilty? You would say 'blasphemy,' and is not blasphemy a dreadful crime?"

Tobias ben Samuel suddenly smiled and it was a smile of bitter and ironical disgust. "Have we progressed no more than this, in our boasted age of great civilization, that a youth can be murdered for blasphemy—if indeed he committed blasphemy? If those who killed him loved their God so much, why did they not leave my son in his hands —if he exists? Are they fearful either that he has no verity or is too weak to defend himself—their God? Or, were they fighting their own disbelief and shouting down their own denial?"

He clasped his plump pink hands before him and continued to regard the others with that cold and derisive smile. "My son. Stoned to death like a murderer, a harlot, a monstrous criminal. What harm had he done in his short life? He had loved girls and wine and song and bacchantes and feasting and laughter and music. He had loved his family and his friends. Never once did he speak evilly or maliciously of another. Never did he do any man an injustice or injury. Foolish he may have been, but he was like sunlight in my house since the day he was born. Alms was not a word to him; it was a vocation. Kindness was not a mere pretension to him, for he was no Scribe! I spoke sternly to him often, to conceal my love for him, and because his jests and his tender gibes sometimes annoyed me. But, in all ways, in his father's house, he was a joy, and to his friends he was a delight, and to his mother, who lies sleepless and speechless in her bed, now, he was the whole world.

"Who will restore my son to me?"

Joseph's eyes filled with tears, and the old Rabban's face was much moved. He said, "Tobias ben Samuel, there is an old story: A man wept unceasingly for his son and his friends said to him in pity, 'Why do you weep? Nothing will restore your son to you.' And he replied, 'That is why I weep.' We have no pietistic words to comfort you, for there are times when men are beyond comforting and their tears lie in their hearts like frozen rain. So, I will not exhort you as Job's comforters exhorted him, for that would make me a superficial and petty man of no understanding." He hesitated.

" 'Who will restore' your son to you? God. You smile. But I know it to be truth. I do not say 'I believe it to be truth.' I repeat that I know it to be truth, for I, myself, have seen the dead restored to life—"

"Aha," said Tobias ben Samuel with a brilliant and mocking look. "Restore my son to me, not in some fabulous and mythical future beyond this tomb of his, but to my arms today."

"Your son lives, and lives as he never lived in this iniquitous world," said the Rabban. "You will consider this the illusion and fantasy and childish faith of an old man. But, hearken to me. I dreamed last night of your son. I have seen him but five times in his short lifetime. I have been in your house but thrice, and always when your beloved wife sent for me in an extremity, the illness of one of your children. I have never been in your chamber nor," said the Rabban, with a sorrowful smile, "have I examined your coffers nor your chests, nor do I have spies in your household." He paused.

Tobias ben Samuel became intent on him, though his thick pink lips were still curved in a contemptuous smile. "What is this you are telling me, Rabban?"

"I have told you. Your son came to me in a dream. His face was like the sun but there were tears on his cheeks. He said to me, 'My beloved father has no belief and I would know him when he departs his world, and I do not wish him to sorrow that he denied our God, blessed be His Name. But if you tell him that you dreamt that I live, and more gloriously than ever I could have imagined, he will laugh at you, for all his sadness. Therefore, I give you a message for him, a message only he will understand, so he will know I live.' "

The face of Tobias became as rosy marble and obdurate and resistant with outrage. But Joseph saw the trembling of his eyelids. Tobias said, "And the message, Rabban Gamaliel, which only I will understand?"

They seemed to be surrounded by a sunny silence and isolation, and the mourners stared at them from a shy distance.

The Rabban said, "I did not understand your son, which was what he intended, and that I swear by the beard of my father, may he rest in peace. Therefore, I cannot throw my own interpretation on the words of your son. He said to me, 'Tell my father to take from the gilded chest which he keeps under his bed that which he showed me on my Bar Mitzvah, and ask him to remember the light things he said, at which we laughed together. And beg of him, in my name, if he loves me, that he will place what is in the bottom of that chest where it belongs, and that he lay in my hand the pretty thing he gave me on my tenth birthday on which is inlaid, in emeralds, the words: "Thou hast the dew of thy youth." For the pretty thing belonged to his father, then to him, and he gave it to me as a child and said to me, "Keep it for your own son." The treasure lies in what belongs to me, as both belong to me.' "

While the Rabban had been speaking the face of the bereaved and cynical father had begun to change violently. The color left his cheeks and his lips; his mouth fell open, his cold hazel eyes widened and stretched as at a vision, and there was a trembling through all his flesh. But he gazed at the Rabban with enormous intensity, and his gaze did not leave the old man for several moments after he had ceased to speak. And it seemed to Joseph that the unfortunate father was pleading, most desperately, in his silence, that he was not being deceived out of mercy.

"Do these words of your living son mean aught to you, Tobias ben Samuel," asked the ancient Rabban with gentleness, "or have I merely dreamed?"

Tobias said, the bitter skeptic and cynic, "Do they mean aught to you, Rabban Gamaliel?"

"Nothing, and again I swear to this by the beard of my father, and even if we stood before the Holy of Holies I would repeat these words to you, Tobias ben Samuel."

Tobias cast his eyes on the ground. He was as pale as death. The Rabban said, "This is the second visit you have paid to this tomb, Tobias ben Samuel, and those lilies there are from your garden, and you came on an impulse but an hour ago, saying to yourself, 'He is not there, and it is vain to visit the dead, for they are deaf and blind and my son is no more.' "

Tobias lifted his eyes and now his whole face was shivering. Suddenly he put out his hand and caught the gray sleeve of the Rabban in his fingers and he pulled himself closer to the old man. His eyes were glittering; there was a throbbing in one of his cheeks.

"Do you wish to know what my son desired to convey, and what it means?" His voice was hoarse.

"Not unless you desire me to know, Tobias."

Tobias bent his head. "In that chest, at the bottom, forgotten until this moment, lies the prayer shawl given to my father by your father, Rabban Gamaliel, before I was born. He treasured it, for all he was a skeptic like all my house. There is also a blue sash embroidered with gold. My father respected tradition, though he had no faith, and on the High Holy Days he would place that shawl over his shoulders and tie that sash about his waist. I did, indeed, show both to my son, Stephen, when he made Bar Mitzvah, and asked him if he desired to wear them, and he—he looked in my face and saw my mirth and out of his love for me he shook his head, and we laughed together, speaking of superstition."

Tobias gave a groaning sigh. "And wrapped in them, put away with childish other things, is a ball of shining gold, a lovely plaything and inscribed as you have repeated. I—I had forgotten it, but when I laid it away I thought, 'His son will possess it and love it, as I did, and my father before me, and as Stephen did.' I have not opened that chest for many years."

"Blessed be the Name of the Lord, the Holy One of Israel," said the Rabban, "for He will forsake not those who love Him, and He will wipe away all tears."

"My son," said Tobias ben Samuel, and he turned and looked at the tomb and there were sudden hard tears of both anguish and relief on his face. "I will have the prayer shawl of your grandfather placed about your neck, as you desired, and your plaything laid in your hand, and I know you live."

He turned again and regarded the Rabban as a distraught man gazes at a rescuing angel. He said, when he could control the heaving of his breast, "My son was not given to delusions, though to enthusiasms, and if he was willing to die for that—for Yeshua of Nazareth—then surely that Yeshua had embraced his soul. I do not know what you believe, Rabban Gamaliel, nor you, Joseph of Arimathaea, but I pray that you send to me one who can tell me something concerning Yeshua ben Joseph, and I will listen, for I know that my son desires this."

"I will," said the Rabban.

Tobias ben Samuel was not a man to be lost in emotions. He brought control again to himself, as it was before, though his eyes were limpid with tears.

"I will, however, bring to justice those wicked men who helped to destroy my son, for all they have dined in my house. I have written to my dear friend, Vitellius, Legate of Syria, and have asked him to punish Pontius Pilate and the High Priest, Caiphas, for they did my son to death with their proclamations. Before this season has passed Pilate will be recalled and Caiphas will lose his power."

He raised a clenched fist briefly. "As for Saul ben Hillel, whose family I honor, I swear I will bring him down, as I have brought down the others."

"Your son does not desire vengeance, for there is no room in his heart for it," said the Rabban, with considerable alarm. "I do not plead for either Pilate nor Caiphas, for they are evil men, though I would not lift a hand to punish them. As for Saul ben Hillel—he has a destiny which none can disturb, for it is in the Hands of God, and I have known this for many years."

The ironical smile returned to Tobias' mouth. "You say this, and he destroys those who believe as my son believes?"

"He is destroying himself. But God will hold his hand," said the Rabban.

Tobias considered. His emotions seethed in him. He sighed shortly. "You speak in riddles, dear friend. But now I hasten to my wife to console her with your words."

He turned away. Then he hesitated. Slowly he faced the two men again. He touched his brow, his lips then his breast, and now there was no mockery in him. "Shalom," he said. He went on, in a lower voice, "Hear, O Israel! The Lord our God, the Lord is One! The Lord gives and the Lord takes away. Blessed be the Name of the Lord!"

"—Saul, yet breathing out threatenings and slaughter against the disciples of the Lord, went to the High Priest and desired of him letters to Damascus to the synagogues, that if he found any of this way, whether they were men

*or women, he might bring them bound to Jerusalem. And,
as he journeyed, he came near Damascus—"**

"He sickens," said a Roman legionnaire, leaning from
his horse to speak in a whisper to his nearest companion.

"He is mad," said the companion. "They say he has
the divine disease."

"The Jews say he has a devil," said the first rider, and
laughed.

But the second soldier said, "The Furies have him by
the hair, and Medusa has turned his face to stone."

"I would that I were in Rome," said the first, wiping
his sweltering face with the back of his hand, and cursing. "What a wilderness is this! It is as if Phaeton were
driving his father's chariot too close to the earth, and it
has seared up all life and water and plant and man and
beast. Regard those black vultures swinging against the
sky! They are waiting to pick our bones."

"If not the vultures, then the Jews," said the other
Roman sourly. "Nowhere are we hated as we are here."

"Even their God hates us," said the first soldier, and
they both laughed though their eyes were uneasy, for the
hatred of gods is a fearful thing. As they were very young
and superstitious, they both furtively touched the region
of their amulets under their armor.

They had left Jerusalem six days before, crossing the
green Jordan, narrow but full and in spate in the early
season of the spring, her banks bursting with almond
flowers and rue and mint and thyme and wild blossoms
and the feathery gold of young trees, the fresh leaves on
the oaks shimmering in rising light, the infant vines,
gnarled and small but sturdy, and black, grasping the
steaming soil, and all about them the intense emerald of
fecund meadows and bright water leaping from stone and
distant mounts growing round and soft with verdure and
olive trees thrusting forth new silver and grazing cattle
and little lambs bounding about their mothers. They saw
little white houses standing shyly among sycamores and
pomegranate trees, and flowering palms, and geese running indignantly before their horses, and children wading
in pools and women milking goats.

The young soldiers were delighted by all this laughter

*Acts 9:1–3.

and joy of the earth, as they passed through the Damascus Gate and crossed the river. They saw distant Jericho, her tall brown houses sullenly meshed together. But on the second day the earth was no longer exuberant with life and greenness. The wilderness was about them, stark and terrible and blasted, the sky white with heat, the desert floor gray and olive and rough with gravel, dust and stones and boulders, the far mounts like brass. Here lived silence and thorns and brambles and jackals and vultures, and springs were far and scarce, and strange mirages palpitated on the horizon—unearthly cities and oases and lakes and trembling purple shadows and columned temples and even the shores of a nameless sea.

They camped at night under monster stars both vivid and icy cold, and the desert wind bit through their leather armor and even their blankets, and they slept armed for fear of the robbers who roamed the wilderness searching for caravans. They slept about fires to keep away the beasts of the desert and often they saw yellow eyes glaring at them in the red light, and fearsome howls tore the appalling stillness of this abandoned land. They ate together, the young soldiers and their subaltern, but one sat apart, wrapped in his brown cloak, his eyes fixed on the fire, seeming never to sleep, rarely eating, drinking but a little, his face hidden in the shadow of his hood, his chin on his bent knees. And the soldiers would whisper together and shrug and wonder at his strength by day on his horse, and his sleeplessness at night, for never did he lie down and when he spoke they were startled, forgetting the infrequent sound of his authoritative voice.

"A direful man is this Paul of Tarsus," the young officer would mutter, gazing at the man apart over his shoulder. "One cannot understand these Jews; one is particularly unable to understand this Jew. What are we about? To arrest his people in Damascus for blasphemy! If it were not so mysterious it would be absurd."

"Still," said one of his men, "I have heard tales that their God rises easily to wrath and vengeance and flies in a storm of fire, and has an outrageous temper, and levels mountains with the glance of His eyes and demolishes cities by the mere raising of His hand and can, if He wishes, divide the earth like an apple with His sword. One does not trifle with such a Deity."

"I have heard," said another soldier, "that His God is also tender and merciful and loves man. But that is manifestly ridiculous! What god can love men? Unless it is maidens and nymphs and dryads of much beauty."

"It is possible that he is an oracle," said still another, "or a soothsayer, and a wise man does not enrage such for fear of death."

"Hah!" said the subaltern, lifting his big young shoulders, "I have been in this land of the Jews for longer than any of you, and I have seen one they call Yeshua but whom we call Jesus of Nazareth, and I saw him die, and many called him their God, but he died only as a man. They say he rose from the dead, but that is a tale of women. Nevertheless, I have also heard that the Jews are often sorcerers, so let us keep our peace and obey our orders."

The soldiers were accustomed to campaigns and austerities and denials and adversity and hardship, and though these were not to be desired they could endure them. But they marveled that a civilian, a man reputed to be a scholar and a rabbi, and a man of the cities, and not a soldier, could endure what they endured without complaint, and be the first on his horse in the morning. One or two of the soldiers were convinced that he was either demented—and therefore had superhuman strength—or that he was semi-divine—and therefore had superhuman strength. No ordinary man, they thought, could live as he lived and not die of it, days ago.

Sometimes they found a cave in which to sleep, for which they were thankful.

And sometimes they heard Saul of Tarshish murmuring under the vast loneliness of the moon and the stars, and they made signs against portents and Furies and Hecate and Hecuba and the evil eye before they slept. It did not come to them that they accompanied a man in torment and agony and deep in the dark night of the soul. They rode behind him, seeing his powerful shoulders under his poor cloak, and they caught glimpses of his pallid set face and nose and leonine expressions and afflicted eye and tortured mouth, and to them he was an enigma and often an object of fear.

"I have served You all my life, Lord, King of the Universe," he would pray. "I have dreamt that You had turned Your Face to me, knowing that I have obeyed all Your Commandments except for one evil day in my youth; I have believed You listening. I would rejoice to die at Your Hand! My Lord and my God—how I adore You! But there is suffering in my heart now, a greater suffering than I have ever known before. There is only silence where I thought there was a Voice. How have I offended You? If I have offended by a single breath— destroy me, for I cannot live in such pain! What is my sin? I do not know. I have imprisoned and flogged Your enemies, those who dared to blaspheme You. I am on my way, my heart one enormous burning, to right the wrongs committed against You. Gaze upon me, Lord, a beggar, a worm at Your blessed Feet, a sparrow beating against the prison of Your Fingers, a dry mouth open in weeping. What am I, that You should notice me? Nevertheless, I have served You with all my spirit and all my heart's longing. Deign to give me but one radiant flash of Your approval, lest I die in my yearning for You and for Your Word."

Out of his exhaustion and his pain and inexplicable sorrow, he would fall briefly asleep near the fire, his face on his bent knees. Sometimes he dreamed of Stephen ben Tobias, and he would cry out to the shining whiteness of that dead face: "I would have saved you, but you refused the saving, and I mourn for you, you youth of beauty and resignation!" On awakening he would say to himself, "Can it be I am being beguiled by a demon? Is that the reason for the blackness and melancholy of my spirit, for surely he was a sinner before the Lord!" But the depression and misery remained.

On the ninth day they knew they were approaching the fabulous city of Damascus for sometimes at noon, sometimes at sunset, they would see distant caravans on the horizon which were not mirages, and the awful desert air would bring to them faint voices and the petulant complaints of camels. Once at an oasis they saw that only the night before an entourage had been there, for the spring was muddied and the pungent herbs trampled. The hot sky was becoming hotter; the young men suffered from rashes and their heads were wet under their helmets, and they wondered anew at the stamina and fortitude of the man of the cities who led them, tireless and silent.

The desert floor yellowed, the sky became a flame; shadows were sharp and black. The soldiers yearned for the nearing city and thought of girls and water and perfumes and something more to eat than dried beef and cheese and stale bread and more to drink than the common wine of the country, and fruit on sun-cracked lips and unguents on sun-blackened skin. They had compassion for their horses, whose eyes were staring and reddened and whose hides frothed, and they cared for them at oases before they cared for themselves. They did not observe Saul of Tarshish watching their boyish ministrations. He would think: I did not know that Romans had pity in their hearts for man or beast! And he was ashamed, and he remembered that the Messias would be a Light unto the Gentiles and he marveled that once he had rejected that prophecy, and he was humbled. They are only boys, he commented to himself. They are younger than myself, and I am young also.

On the morning of the tenth day he said to the officer, "I have been preoccupied with many thoughts of my mission, and so have given thought to nothing else. But in my pouch there are salves, and bottles of good wine I have not drunk, and excellent cheese and dates wrapped in silk. Tonight, you shall have them, for I need them not."

The young officer stared at him, incredulous, then exclaimed, "Lord, you are a veritable divinity, in your kindness!" His boyish face was so burned that he was almost as black as a Nubian, and he went off to boast to his men that he had persuaded the rich and incomprehensible Jew to share his wealth with them. Saul overheard this. He had not smiled for a long time, perhaps for years, but now he smiled and the smile was youthful and even gentle. And, as he smiled, some of his anguish lifted.

On the tenth day he said to the subaltern: "Let us press on, even into the night, for then at dawn we shall be in Damascus, and can rest, weary though we shall be. As you know, Lucius, I am to be the guest of a man named Judas on the large street called Straight. But you will go to your military quarters and remain there until I send for you."

Lucius saluted and agreed that they should press on, even into the night, for now the endurance of his young soldiers was lagging and fatigue was heavy on their limbs. But he again marveled that Paul of Tarsus, as they called him, betrayed little weariness and that his iron-blue eyes were not cloudy nor reddened.

The soldiers received fresh strength, knowing they were approaching the end of their wretched journey, and that night they celebrated with Saul's wine and refreshments, then neatly put out their fire and gathered up their belongings and leaped upon their horses again.

The night was peculiarly lucent, the moon full and huge and burning in white fire, the desert floor streaked with black shadows. The sound of the horses, the voices of the men, the occasional laugh or snatch of ribald song, awoke gigantic echoes in the crushing silence, but now the young men did not glance superstitiously over their shoulders nor search for their many amulets. They would sleep in Damascus.

The moon rose higher. Midnight came and departed. The harness on the horses tinkled like little bells. The soldiers were quiet now. Sometimes they dozed in their creaking saddles, weary again. The hoofs of the horses struck fire on stones.

It was not possible, thought Saul, that the silence can become even more silent! He looked about him. The desert floor was like a still sea of white milk, scarred only by their shadows, and it had an odd shimmering on it, flashing and shifting and sparkling. The moon appeared to enlarge, to advance on the earth. The stars were one shaking mantle of light. Saul gazed about him with a quick sharpening of awe, and he searched his mind for a fitting Psalm to repeat. But nothing came to him. It was as if his mind had been emptied like a cup, a vessel, and naught was within now but a thin and unbearable thrilling. He put his hand to his brow, afraid of fever, but the sweat of the day had dried and his skin was cool. His heart, as if affrighted, began to beat in his throat and ears, and his flesh started.

It was then that fear struck him, a fear so profound that he became cold as death. It was an enigmatic fear, beyond mortality, overwhelming and nameless. Am I about to have a seizure? he thought with terror, remembering his mission. Am I about to fall from my horse, perhaps even to die on this desert? Lord, have mercy upon Your servant, Lord, have mercy—

But his mouth did not dry. His tongue did not cleave to his lips. His sight was clear and not distorted by rainbow scintillatings. There was no severe and sudden pain in his head, no tremblings nor preliminary jerking of his limbs. In truth, his sight was keener than ever before, and all his senses were alert like soldiers awakened by a shout. He looked about him at the desert and then at the moon and the quaking stars, and his fear deepened until he was afraid he would die of it and his blood chilled. But what he feared he did not know. He glanced behind him at the soldiers. They were quiet now, some yawning, some drowsing. There was no fear in them.

But the fearsome terror mounted in him. His hand fell to the shoulder of his horse and to his increasing alarm he felt the animal quivering as if it, too, was startled into fear. It shivered, faltered, stared before it. But there was nothing there but the silent milky sea of the desert. Saul searched frantically for a prayer. His mind was as blank as a babe's, and this affrighted him more, for never had his thoughts betrayed or fled from him. I am weary, weary, he thought in his terror. It is only that, and the enormity of this desert moon, and the lonely places and the ghostly silence, and the suffering I have endured. It will pass.

He was a tenacious man, and he touched the shoulder of his horse peremptorily. He looked before him, hoping for a glimpse of the city, praying that it would rise like a silver mirage on the endless white desert, that he could see the glinting of its gates. There was nothing there.

"What is that?" exclaimed the subaltern in a loud and tense voice which shattered the silence, and he reined in his horse and his men halted with him. "I heard a stranger speaking, the sound of a man! Lord," he said to Saul who was still going on, "did you not hear something, a voice, a command, a question which did not come from one of us?"

"No," said Saul, and now he was almost beside himself with his fear, convinced at last that he was enduring an objective and not imagined horror. He abruptly reined in his horse.

And then before his eyes there was a vast explosion of

ineffable light, palpitating, a boundless cloud of light, filled with drifting sparks of white fire, glowing at its heart with blinding gold, more vivid than the sun.

And then he saw Him, standing in the center of that golden core, on the desert level.

He was as Saul remembered Him, in the market place, with His Mother, on the street, in his dream, and walking among the dolorous crosses, yet He was glorified, transfigured. He was the mighty Man, the heroic and beautiful Man, with all His monumental grandeur of divinity, majestic of face, possessing the blue power of imperial eyes, stately of kingly beard and head, radiating a stern white purity of brow; an effulgent whiteness of robe, the prayer shawl about His shoulders seemingly inlaid with stripes of rainbow color and fringed with jewels. Still, He was as Saul remembered Him in mortal flesh. Or, had he only dreamed of Him? Had he known Him always, from birth, from the instant of being?

Saul lifted his hands and his mouth opened and he knew, at last, for Whom he had been searching, with longing and despair and hope and love—and with vehement denial. His eyes, though filled with that splendor which shone upon him did not blink, did not turn away, did not scorch. A quietude, as immense as the ocean, fell upon him. His heart bulged in his breast, shaking. His flesh quailed. But the ecstasy increased moment by moment, and he tried to speak, to whisper, and finally it was enough for him to see.

Then He spoke in that great masculine voice which he, Saul, had heard before:

"Saul! Saul of Tarshish!"

It rang over the desert, that Voice, and it seemed to Saul that the mountains started and listened and the earth caught her breath. He saw only the vision before him, yet he also seemed to see the whole world, nation upon nation, city upon city, battlement upon battlement, and sea upon sea, and then constellation after constellation and glittering universe after universe, prostrate, adoring.

The voice, commanding, not to be denied by anything that lived, called again: "Saul, Saul! Saul of Tarshish!"

Saul did not know that he had slipped harmlessly to the desert floor, and that he now lay there, only a seeing vessel. What he saw was all life and all knowledge and all-encompassing certitude and fulfillment, explanation of mysteries, revelations. He forgot where he was, and even who he was. He forgot the soldiers about him, who were huddled together in fear, hearing a voice but seeing nothing.

Saul thought he would expire in his transports. His hands moved before him on the rough gravel, groping. He could not look away from the powerful Figure in that dazzling core of gold, a Figure much greater in stature than a man, a Colossus of brilliance, imposing, armed with the authority of divine might, beautiful beyond dreaming, and yet terrible, implicit with virility and with the fire of creative force.

Again the voice spoke, like approaching thunder: "Saul, Saul of Tarshish! Why do you persecute Me?"

O overpowering love and bliss to hear that remembered voice, the voice which commanded angels and worlds and suns and all men!

"Lord," Saul whispered, creeping closer to Him Who was the center of his life, "Who are you, Lord?" His exaltation heightened. He desired only to touch that divine foot, to lay his tired cheek upon it, to rest in the blessedness of knowing. Oh, joy of man's desiring!

Did the voice gentle, as if in pity, lose something of its resolution and severity? It said, "I am Yeshua of Nazareth, Whom you persecute. It is hard for you to kick against the pricks, is it not, Saul of Tarshish?"

Even if He destroy me in punishment and kill me forever, yet shall I rejoice that He has spoken to me! thought Saul. Let all the world roll over me and crush me into nothing—and I will cry out in my delight, shouting Hosannah! that He remembered me! It is enough that I have known Him, have seen Him with these eyes, as I have yearned all my life.

"Lord," Saul murmured, "what is it You would have me do?"

"Arise," said the Lord, "and go into the city and it shall be told you what you must do, Saul of Tarshish." And now He smiled as a father smiles, or a brother, or the dearest friend any man can know, and bliss assailed Saul again and he was transported again and ecstasy again seized him, and eternity was his own.

The incredible light remained, golden at its heart, storming with flecks of radiance, but the Figure had departed. Saul gazed at the light, longed to hurl himself into it, to suspire in its holy depths, to lave in it, to sleep in it, at rest forever. He dreaded to return to the world of dim shadows and pain and the flesh, to mundane things, to men and wearisome roads and the hungers of the body, and the mirage of cities and the meaninglessness of tongues, and dull breath and humiliations and stone and dust. How could he endure the world, after that vision and that glory? Better to die in the remembrance than to resume life again. All longing that he had ever known was nothing to this craving of the soul, this urgent passion, this anguished yet delighting love.

The soldiers, almost beside themselves with fear, having heard but a voice though not the words, and having seen nothing, dismounted and ran to the prostrate man. They saw his face, his staring eyes, his parted lips. His countenance was brighter than the moon. It was as if he had beheld a divinity, for he was transfigured. This so frightened them that they started back from him, shivering, for it was dangerous to touch one stricken by the sight of the divine. "Has he seen Jupiter or Apollo or Mercury?" whispered one soldier to his officer. "He has the appearance of one who has approached the gods."

The subaltern overcame his fear after a few moments. He had his honor as a Roman to maintain. He touched Saul on his rough woolen shoulder and Saul arose, not wearily, not with a swaying motion, but like a boy. His eyes were still filled with a glory, a reflection of something not of this earth, and again the soldier recoiled and touched his amulets. Saul's face had become preternaturally elated, changed, drawn like gold, exultant.

Then he said, as if announcing a wondrous message of such great import that he could hardly speak: "I do not see. Yet I see. Let me not see with these eyes again lest the delight be taken from me!"

The soldiers glanced at each other in trepidation. Then the officer said timidly, "You have been blinded, lord?"

Saul clasped his hands together in a convulsion of rapture and exquisite adoration.

"What does it matter to me, now that I have seen the Messias?" He paused. He was like a man who had gazed too long at the sun and now saw its aureole, its timeless image, printed on his retina, and yet was not afraid. "I have seen my Life," he said, and did not see the soldiers. "I have seen the Truth, the Everlasting! I have beheld the Holy One of Israel, and it is enough for me. My long search is over. I have found Him, at last! O, my Lord and my God—at last!"

He struck his breast with his fists. He cried aloud in his indescribable joy.

Then, though he could not see he became aware of the disordered breathing of the men about him, and felt their fear, and a deep tenderness touched his heart. He said, "I am blind, but take me to the house of Judas, on the street called Straight, in Damascus."

They put him on his horse, shrinking to touch one who had seen what must not be seen, and his flesh was like a vibrating harp. They led him through the rest of the night to the city, in silence.

Chapter 34

"There was a certain disciple at Damascus, named Ananias, and to him said the Lord in a vision: 'Ananias!' And he said, 'Behold, I am here, Lord.'

"And the Lord said to him, 'Arise, and go into the street which is called Straight, and enquire in the house of Judas for one called Saul of Tarshish, for behold, he prays, and he has seen in a vision a man named Ananias coming in and putting his hand on him, that he might receive his sight.'

"Then Ananias answered, 'Lord, I have heard by many of this man, how much evil he has done to Your saints at Jerusalem, and here he has authority from the chief priests to bind all that call on Your Name.'

"But the Lord said unto him, 'Go your way, for he is a chosen vessel unto Me, to bear My Name before the Gentiles and kings and the Children of Israel, for I will

show him how great things he must suffer for My Name's sake.

"And Ananias went his way—"*

JUDAS BEN JONAH was in a dilemma.

He was a rich and respected resident of the ancient city of Damascus, a man of some forty-eight years, grave, circumspect, dignified and courteous, a banker and a merchant. His family was old and revered, he had married a lady of distinction and piety, and his sons had married similar women. His daughters had not disgraced him in their marriages. He would say, with modesty, that there was not a city of note in the world in which he did not have a devoted friend, and he had round innocent brown eyes that saw everything and underestimated no enemy nor overestimated any acquaintance or even a member of his own house. His beard was rich and brown and carefully tended and only slightly fragrant, and he moved sedately. This was partly a matter of flesh and partly a matter of temperament. His large house on the street called Straight was most comfortable though not luxurious, nor were its appointments ostentatious. He would often say in his soft deep voice that God had been good to him, blessed be His Name, and he was heralded for his alms and the tithes he paid to the Temple and his journeys to Jerusalem on the High Holy Days, and his devotion.

His whole life had always been in accordance with the Law and the Commandments, and he found no tediousness in it. His counsel was invariably wise, if dull. He would say that a man who considered life precarious and capricious was a man who had not ordered his own life well, and he suspected excitement, enthusiasms and wonder.

He was a friend not only of Pontius Pilate and Caiphas, the High Priest, but of Shebua ben Abraham. Shebua valued his friendship, and Saul ben Hillel had met him on a few occasions in his grandfather's house, and if the young man had discovered him to be a man of formal and uninspired convictions he had also come to respect him. So, Saul had announced to Pilate that he would live at the house of Judas ben Jonah while on his mission to

*Acts 9:10–17.

Damascus, and Judas had extended him a cordial if prudent invitation, not at first understanding to the full.

Now he understood. Hence, his dilemma. For Judas ben Jonah had become a follower of Yeshúa ben Joseph of Nazareth, not with instant interior acclamation and joy and revelation and delight but only after prolonged and judicious study. It was evident, to his pedestrian mind, that the crucified Nazarene was the Messias, but how he, a discreet and cautious man who took much time to reach even an insignificant conviction, had arrived at his belief was not known even to his wife. "I believe," he had told her with his usual gravity, and that was sufficient. He was willing to grant that less blessed men did not believe, and he pitied them.

He had noticed recently that many of his fellow Jews were entering Damascus from the provinces of Israel with stories of persecutions inflicted on them by the High Priest, Caiphas, and Pontius Pilate, because they were adherents of the new cult. He assisted them with his usual quiet prudence, and in secrecy, not out of fear—for he lacked the imagination to fear much—but out of charity. "This, too, will pass," he said, quoting Solomon. A man needed only to have patience. When some mentioned Saul ben Hillel as one of the most ferocious persecutors he was mildly incredulous, and he welcomed the visit of the young man for he liked visitors and gossip, and he respected Shebua ben Abraham who had been of service to him in the past.

Two days before Saul had arrived at his large walled house on the street called Straight he had heard the full story, and for the first time in his ordered life he knew acute distress. Then it came to him that God, blessed be His Name, had arranged this in order that he, Judas ben Jonah, could bring the young man to reason and deflect him from his intransigent ways. As a man of good will, himself, he was convinced that most men had instincts of good will; it was only necessary to inspire them. Evil was banal and trivial; good was powerful and invariably triumphant. This was the conviction of Judas ben Jonah, though he did not carry this belief too far in the market place, and so enhanced his reputation for astute prudence.

The street called Straight was not straight, but was

even more winding and serpentine than the other fervid streets of Damascus. However, it had a certain decorum and quietude, for all the houses were the houses of rich men who did not flaunt their wealth. Judas had ordered apartments for Saul, whom he remembered as a pugnacious young man with fiery red hair and impatient eyes and an abrupt manner, and a man who was not as respectful to his elders as was seemly.

He awaited the arrival of Saul as his guest with superbly concealed anxiety and apprehension. But Saul had arrived long after midnight last night, though not expected until the morrow, and he had come in blind mute disarray with Roman soldiers, who had led his horse into the courtyard, and, after delivering Saul to his host, had departed to their barracks. They had told Judas, in their blunt and artless military fashion, that Saul had apparently seen a god on the desert, for he had been instantly deprived of sight and his face had glowed like the moon. Judas observed this, himself and he was filled with the first wild conjectures of his staid and serene life. Had Saul ben Hillel become mad? Judas ordered servants to conduct Saul to his quarters, and commanded water and scented towels and fine soap to wash away the soil of the desert, and unguents, and a nourishing supper. Saul, without protest, and seemingly unaware of all that transpired about him, departed with the servants and Judas sat down in the atrium to consider the matter.

He did not like the unexpected, the strange. He sat and frowned and stroked his beard and ruminated, and turned the fine rings on his plump fingers. He let some time pass and then went to the chambers he had assigned to Saul, and there he had sat before the young man with his staring blue eyes and the clean coarse garments in which the servants had dressed him. Judas noted that the supper had barely been touched. He became uneasy. There was no sign of injury to the eyes opposite him, which hardly blinked in the light of the pleasant lamps. Saul appeared wrapped in some vision, some profound meditation, which made him unconscious not only of himself and his surroundings but of his host.

Judas hesitated. It would soon be dawn and he was weary and he was a man who believed it almost sinful not to retire to his bed at the usual hour. But he was not only anxious; he was curious. He said, in a kind voice, "Are you ill, Saul ben Hillel, and why do you not see?"

"I have seen all of Life," said Saul, and these were the first words he had uttered. Suddenly his face shone like lightning and a quickness as of unbearable exaltation flashed into his eyes. "But I must wait." He paused. He turned his blind eyes in Judas' direction and said in a less passionate voice, "Forgive me, Judas ben Jonah, for not greeting you and thanking you for your hospitality before this hour, but I am assailed by celestial revelations and must meditate on them all."

A pucker appeared between Judas' big brown eyes. He again considered if Saul had suddenly become mad.

"I have seen the Messias!" said Saul, and his voice thrilled like a trumpet and he smiled exultantly and pressed his sun-darkened hands convulsively to his breast as if to restrain a leaping heart.

Judas was more confused. Was this Saul ben Hillel who had been reported to be the most relentless foe of the Nazarene? "When?" he asked, with his usual caution.

"But a few hours ago," replied Saul. "In the desert, before we approached the gates of Damascus." He spoke simply and with a childlike candor, and Judas could not remember such candor in the young man before.

"The Messias," said Judas, as if reflecting.

"I saw Him!" cried Saul, and he stood up and looked about him with a great and rapturous smile, though he could not see. "You must believe me, Judas ben Jonah! I saw Him, He Whom I have been persecuting, and He did not reproach me nor strike me dead! He has given me a mission, and I am filled with revelations which He is bestowing on me, moment after moment! He has chosen me—the most base, the most contemptible, the most loathsome, the one most worthy of the fires of hell and utter destruction. Why do I not expire at the very thought of such magnanimity, such mercy, such love?"

"I do not know," mumured Judas, more confused than ever. He had heard of the inspired disciples and Apostles of Yeshua ben Joseph, though he had encountered but one of them, and he convinced and elated if not extravagant. Saul was like a red sun, a red lion, in this pleasant chamber with the flickering lamplight and with the warm wind stirring the damask curtains and bringing into the room a scent of heated stone and flowers. No one more alien to the house of Judas ben Jonah had ever entered here before, and Judas was disturbed by this wildness and vehement joy and unearthly certitude.

"Why do you not see, then?" asked Judas, in a reasonable tone, as if attempting to bring matters to a rational level. "God does not strike men blind out of love."

Saul paced a few steps, then retraced them. His strange excitement was growing. "I have been blinded in order that I may see, fully, for the first time in my existence!" he cried.

Judas could not comprehend this. It was not sensible. "Perhaps," he suggested, in a paternal tone, "the sun was too strong on the desert." He glanced at the carved ivory and ebony bed, with its fragrant linen and silken covers. "Rest, Saul ben Hillel, and if your sight is not restored by morning I will call my physician."

Saul's eloquent face expressed his tremendous impatience, and then he controlled himself and smiled with a gentleness Judas found startling. "I have been told that one will come to me within a few days, and he will baptize me and my sight will be restored, and then I shall embark on the way He has ordained for me, blessed be His Name."

It was evident that he believed that he was speaking reasonably and that Judas would understand these plain words without further explanation.

"Who will come to you, Saul?" he asked.

"A man named Ananias." The impatience was returning to Saul's face.

Judas knew Ananias, a poor and saintly scholar, who had been instrumental in bringing Judas into the company of the Messias. Before he could ask Saul how he knew this man Saul said, "I have been told of him since I was struck blind, and he will come."

Judas rose. He said, "Let me conduct you to your bed, dear friend, for you are exhausted and need your rest."

For a moment it appeared that Saul would resist, that he did not desire sleep, and that he wished only to sit and to meditate on the ecstatic, incomprehensible thing which had come to him. Then he permitted Judas to lead him to the bed, and he lay down and Judas covered him. The older man then contemplated the strong sunburned face and thick red hair on the silken cushion. "Shalom," he said at last, and blew out the lamps and went to his own chamber, his thoughts most chaotic.

Though Judas was a banker as well as a merchant he respected scholarship and wisdom and preferred to be known as a wise man rather than a wealthy one. Therefore, he greeted Ananias with grave courtesy when the elderly man came to his door, and welcomed him to his house and ordered refreshments for him. He pretended not to observe the poor clothing of his guest and the patched leather boots and the thin meagerness of his cloak and his lean pouch. Ananias had come a long way through the streets on foot, and his pale and slender face and gray beard wore a patina of golden dust threaded with sweat. Yet, in spite of his quiet manner and evident weariness his expression was bright and youthful and his eyes were the eyes of a boy, lustrous and polished.

"This house is honored by your presence, Ananias," said Judas ben Jonah, and himself poured the wine the servant had brought, and as he was a man who appreciated the refinements of life he was pleased by the golden ewer traced with Indu enamel in various colors. But Ananias drank sparingly and with an apparent absence of mind, and there was a troubled line across his forehead. He declined the sweetmeats, though Judas informed him that they had been prepared by the hand of his talented wife.

"I have a peculiar mission," said Ananias at last, in the sweetest of voices. "You have a guest, one Saul of Tarshish." He hesitated. "Judas, we both adore the Messias. We know He sends us commands which we dare not disobey, for has He not given His blessed life for us, and does He not love us? Do not, therefore, ask me questions I cannot answer. I have been sent to your guest."

"He awaits you," said Judas. "I confess I understand little of this. His words frighten me, when he deigns to answer my questions. His manner has about it something of madness. He has sat these three days in my house wrapped in a dream, and he murmurs under his breath and prays without ceasing, and he is as another Jacob, absorbed in visions, or a young Moses, gazing with blind eyes upon the Promised Land. Sometimes, though he cannot see, he paces his chamber, uttering great cries and sobs and clapping his hands together, and sometimes he weeps aloud or laughs in exultation as if a teacher had taught him an absorbing lesson and he had come to a mighty conclusion of his own. He does not eat. He drinks little. If he sleeps, I do not know it. He is like one consumed. He appears like one in a fever, restless, transfigured, staring, burning of eye, dry of lip. I have offered to conduct him into my gardens for the sun and the air, but he refuses to leave his chamber. Insistence brings on a fit of terrible impatience, for which he immediately apologizes and begs forgiveness. He has said to me, 'I must be alone, so that I may learn and observe that what I saw in obscurity and murk, and as through a glass darkly, has been shining in color and light from all eternity—and I was blind! I once said with Job, "Oh, that I might know where to find Him!" and behold, He was at my right hand always and I did not see Him, for I refused to see! But now I see, and cannot have enough of the seeing, and I await His call.' "

Ananias looked with compassion on his troubled host and said, "I comprehend his words, Judas ben Jonah. At first I was dismayed, for is this not Saul of Tarshish, whom the Romans call Paul of Tarsus, the fearful enemy of our people? There is an old Lybian saying, 'That once an eagle, stricken with an arrow, said, when he saw the fashion of the shaft, "With our own feathers, not by others' hands, are we now smitten." ' The people of Saul ben Hillel have been smitten by him, but not in malice, not in deliberate cruelty or rage, but in ignorance."

"No matter the reason for smiting," said Judas, with a wry expression, "the wound is just as painful."

"True," said Ananias, rising. "But now I pray you to lead me to your guest."

They went in silence to the chamber of Saul. They found him sitting on his rich bed, his hands clasped on his knees, straining to hear. Ananias paused on the threshold to contemplate this man of terror, who had come to destroy the faithful, and who had had a vision on the road to Damascus. He was a young man with hair like the sun at sunset, disheveled and uncombed, and his face was ghastly with sleeplessness, yet trembling with exaltation, and his eyes, one drooping in affliction, shone with an unusual blue light like metal, and he had the powerful aspect of a young lion held by a chain, and straining, and overcome with eagerness for the arena. He leaned forward, craning toward the door, for beyond it he had heard footsteps, and so vivid were his eyes that Ananias could hardly believe that he did not see.

The old man said softly, "Shalom. May the joy of Abraham, Isaac and Jacob be with you, my son, Saul ben Hillel, and may the peace of God, blessed be His Name, attend you always."

Saul sprang to his feet. He moved two steps in the direction of Ananias. He cried, "Ananias!"

"It is I," said Ananias. "I know all that you would tell me for I, too, have seen a vision." Now for the first time he felt pity for this young man, this passionate man, this most vehement and resolute man, and saw much in an instant of time. He sighed. At the sound Saul came forward again, wildly smiling, and now there were tears on his darkened cheeks. He fell to his knees before Ananias and clasped his hands and bowed his head.

Ananias glanced beseechingly at Judas, and the other man, who was agape with curiosity, left the chamber and closed the door behind him. Ananias laid his hands on Saul's rough head, and sighed again. He knew, without knowing how he knew, that all Saul's life had been one agonized search, in suffering, in despair, in occasional rapture, in confusion, in hope and in yearning. He had found what he had sought, but Ananias knew with a preternatural knowing what fate lay before this young man. Saul would not fall aside. He would never falter. He would know pain as he had never known it before, but he would accept it, not meekly as quieter and more composed men accepted it, but with a furious joy. Yet, he had far to go, and the light would not always lie on his path, and he would grope and struggle and fight in a far vaster wilderness than any he had experienced in his short lifetime. He was a warrior, one of God's heroes, and he would not lay down his sword and his armor until his last breath.

Ananias raised his head and prayed almost inaudibly, that Saul's sight might be restored to him, if it were the will of God, and that God would always comfort and uphold him in the direful way ahead. He bent and pressed his palms against the young man's feverish cheeks and kissed his forehead like a father, and there were tears in his own eyes. No more was he troubled, and no more did he remember the letters from the High Priest, Caiphas, to the leaders of the synagogues in Damascus.

Sunlight filled the chamber. A great peace inhabited it and flowed like bright water over the kneeling man and the old scholar who bent over him so tenderly. Light reflected back from the white marble floor, struck on the walls, and then it turned the hair of Saul to fire. It was like a brilliant aureole about his head, and for an instant Ananias knew fear. Yet the breeze from the opened windows was soft as silk and scented with fountains and flowers, and there was the shadow of trees wavering in the radiance, and the cry of birds.

Saul lifted his head. He smiled up into the face of the old man, and with joy.

"I see," he said. "No more am I blind, but behold the world in glory as I never saw it before! I see!"

"Yes, my son," said Ananias. "For the first time in your life, you see. Shalom."

Part Three

APOSTLE TO THE GENTILES

Stand fast therefore in the liberty wherewith Christ hath made us free, and be not entangled again with the yoke of bondage.

Chapter 35

IT SEEMED incredible to Joseph of Arimathaea that the sun-darkened man before him was Saul of Tarshish, and he peered at Saul with age-dimmed eyes and his mouth moved soundlessly in the way of very old men, as if chewing, and his white beard fluttered on his chin. It was hot and still in Jerusalem today, and the sky was white with heat and the cypresses were dusted with golden particles and not even the fountains in the gardens could cool the burning air. Yet Joseph was wrapped in woolen shawls and his feet were covered with high boots lined with sheep-wool, and he rubbed his hands as if they were chill.

If he was aghast at Saul's appearance, Saul was even more aghast at the ruin of the splendid man he had last seen only five years ago. But, thought Saul, did I believe that time stood still here while centuries rose and fell in my mind, and nations appeared and vanished, and the revelations of Heaven shafted down on me in fire, in the deserts of Arabia? Joseph was aging when I last saw him, but I did not perceive it. Now the years have revealed themselves. Have I changed also so stringently? I am thirty-three years old, no youth, eheu! but neither am I old with a beard. He looked at his hands and they were almost as black as a Nubian's, and he knew that his countenance was blackened also, in spite of his once-fair complexion, and that he must appear as an African lion with his great mane of red rough hair and rough brown clothing and his dark feet and the deep tawny color of his arms and throat. Only his blue eyes were the same, glistening with the powerful force of his spirit and the passions that had always lived with him.

"And what did you do in the Nabataean kingdom?" asked Joseph.

"I pursued my trade as a goat's-hair weaver and tentmaker," said Saul, in that deep melodious voice that Joseph remembered. "I spoke to the peasants and the farmers of the Messias. I lived and ate with them." He faintly smiled and his large white teeth flashed. "I was never a man for luxuries, nor was I ever a voluptuary, but I had been taught, as a Jew, to cleanse myself frequently. Those with whom I have been dwelling were not so fastidious."

"So I observe—through my nose," said Joseph, and chuckled. "All the perfumes of Persia could not wash away the redolence that attends you, Saul, though I am certain that you have bathed much recently."

"I fear I still smell like a camel and a goat, and possibly of dung, and sour milk and cheese." Saul lifted one of his sinewy hands and sniffed at it consideringly. "Yes, it is true. There were times when I bathed as infrequently as my poor and simple companions, out of necessity. Too, it is not always wise to appear singular."

"It is also dangerous," said Joseph, meditating over what Saul had already told him. He saw that the winds and dusts of the terrible deserts had scoured Saul's flesh, had melted away any suggestion of fat and had reduced his body to leather and whips and sinews and ligaments and hard rope. Yet never had he appeared so young, no, not even in those days long ago when he had visited Jochanan ben Zachary in the wilderness, nor had there been this peace upon his countenance. It was not the placid peace of resignation to the will of God, not the peace of saintliness and gentle forbearance or mysticism, not the peace of withdrawal. His resolute chin was as sharp in contour as if a sculptor had made the line and had forebore to round and soften it, and his nose was thin and large, like a knife, and there were hollows under his cheekbones like dry blackened pits, and the cheekbones thrust out from his face. If ever a man had been seasoned and honed and tempered by God, Saul was such a man, and yet there was about him his very youthful humor—so missing for so many years—and a strong but not mawkish gentleness.

"And the Arabians hearkened to you, my son?" asked Joseph.

"They were courteous, like all dwellers of the desert, who must live or perish by courtesy. But they told me a seer had long foretold that they, the sons of Ishmael, would have their own revelation." For an instant his old impatience sparked in his eyes.

Joseph considered. Then he said, "I am old and forgetful, and so I cannot remember where once I learned that one could imagine God, blessed be His Name, as a wheel of infinitude, sparkling and turning in lightning and in thunder and luminous fire and incomprehensible power, and that while He was the wheel He was also the Hub, and all the spokes leading from the rim to the Hub were the prayerful hopes and faiths of all creation, and as the spokes were also God, as was the Rim and the Hub, they all led to the Center."

Saul himself considered and frowned thoughtfully. He said, "We have been given a New Covenant, as told to Jeremias centuries ago, and there is none else."

Joseph chewed soundlessly on nothing before he replied. "I believe Jeremias also related that one day all men would know the Lord, though perhaps He was, and is, called by a thousand different names, and He will not distinguish among His children. Ages before Moses brought to us the Commandments Egypt had a code of moral and religious laws not too dissimilar, and so did the Persians, and though the Greeks and the Romans based their moral and religious laws on ethics, merely, the Spirit shines through."

Saul moved restlessly. Was it for this that he had endured the dark hot years in the desert, and other sufferings, merely to listen to a senile old man who had lost the iron in his soul? While he was pondering Joseph gazed at him, and sighed, and realized that the new Saul was not truly new at all, but a man constantly wrestling with his own storms.

"We are a peculiar people," said Joseph. "God has chosen us from the ages, and will not depart from us, and that makes us peculiar."

Saul thought this extremely irrelevant and another sign of Joseph's senility, and he struggled again for the charity he was always proclaiming (though he frequently acknowledged that he had much need of it, himself).

Joseph said gently, "To each people God sends His revelation, in accordance with their nature and ability to understand in their own terms and in their own souls. Though it has been said that all men are the same, that is not entirely true, just as one man is different from his brother. We share the same flesh and the same being, and are of the same species, as Aristotle noted, but each people has its own arête. I have traveled. I have spoken long to the wise men of China and India, and to their people. Their minds are not our minds, nor do they contemplate creation as we contemplate it, nor are their mores ours, and they worship God in the Name they have given Him, and will He deny them His salvation? No. You have told me that one of the Apostles, Simon Peter of Galilee, told you that the Messias commanded him and his fellows to go forth and feed His sheep, in all nations. But how those nations will accept the message, and in what form, is their own, and we must not quarrel with it.

"The form given to us by the Messias is the form sympathetic with our natures and our minds, purely to be understood by the faithful of Israel and among the Gentiles of Greece and Rome, and even perhaps, the wildernesses of the barbarians of Gaul and Britain and the cold nations of the north. It is not alien to the minds of us of these places on the earth; the ground has already been prepared. Yet, to all nations and all peoples was the message given: 'Blessed is he who comes in the Name of the Lord!' But who shall quarrel with the Name, and what men herald it?"

He is truly wandering, thought Saul. But Joseph was smiling. He was remembering how he had heard that none in Damascus among the Jews would accept Saul's new and fervent teaching, saying to his face and among themselves: "Is this not the servant of the Romans, a fierce and ravening Jew, who imprisoned and flogged our brothers in Jerusalem because they believed that the Messias had been born to us? Shall we trust him? No! He is a spy of the Romans. He comes to us now in pretense, that he might trap us, and then bind us and imprison and slay us. Begone with him!" So, they had spoken, and had incited the cynical Greeks in Damascus against Saul, and others of the Gentile community, and to save his life Saul had had to be lowered in a basket at midnight over the walls of Damascus, and had fled to the desert. To one so proud that must have been a humiliating and disastrous experience; to be rejected was intolerable, especially when one believed he brought the truth. Ah, Saul, thought Joseph, with love, and smiled again. Seeing that smile, Saul thought he was being mocked.

The young man said with sternness, "The world is in bondage to the Roman. The world is oppressed by Rome. There is not a man who can today say, 'I am free, on my own earth, in my own house, safe from tyranny and taxes, free of government hirelings who torment me with inquisitive questions and puny malicious laws, a man free before the Face of God.' From this oppression and tyranny the Messias came to deliver us." He paused, with sudden angry impatience, for the old man was slowly shaking his head.

"My son," said Joseph, "the world of men has always been in bondage, oppressed by some powerful nation or even its own permitted government. No man has ever been truly free for long, safe from taxes and impudence and malicious bureaucrats and wars and massacres and seizures and outrages. It has been said by the Greeks that men deserve their government, and I have seen nothing in my lifetime to refute this. If men are now slaves, it was by their own complacent acquiescence, their own meek weakness, their own greed and slovenly character, their own pridelessness, their own envy. It has also been said that if a mouse accept a morsel from a tiger, in apparent amity and charity, the tiger will soon make a morsel of the mouse for himself. Was it not the Chinese who declared that governments are more to be feared than a tiger?

"So, the world of bondage today is no different from the world of bondage under the Egyptians and under Alexander of Macedonia, nor will it be changed tomorrow. It will always be in bondage. But if a man says in his soul, though his hands are manacled, 'I am a free spirit and the iron of man cannot manacle that spirit,' then he is not truly a slave. It was that freedom of the spirit which the Messias brought to us, and the nations who will hear Him, for did He not say, when taunted by the rigorous Pharisees and shown a coin with the head of Caesar upon it, 'Render unto Caesar the things which are Caesar's, and unto God things which are God's'? To Him, blessed be His Name, governments are forever oppressive and bloody and ambitious, and their nature cannot be changed, for men who receive power become devils. But only a man, himself, can make himself a slave in his soul. From that slavery He would deliver us. Caesar will eternally be Caesar. A man can only rise from his knees and know Caesar to be mad, and to refrain from giving Caesar all the power he covets."

In spite of himself something impelled Saul to listen, as he would not have listened some years ago, and again he pondered, and he rubbed his dark and seamed forehead. He murmured, "It is true: Only God can give us true liberty. Still, we should fight for freedom against bloody and ambitious and ravenous governments."

"That is also our duty," said Joseph. "It is a duty laid upon man from the beginning. Did not Moses shout, 'Proclaim liberty throughout the land, unto the inhabitants thereof?' Yes. But man forgets. Bread and ease and security are the tawdry prizes offered for his freedom as a man, and without fail, throughout the history of the ages, he will accept those prizes."

Saul thought of the insane Caesar now on the throne in Rome, and shuddered. Was it not rumored, with loud laughter, that he had made his horse a Consul of Rome? "We are on the eve of terrible events," said Saul.

"We always were. We shall always be," said Joseph, and in his weariness he fell asleep, and Saul rose in silence and left him, and he went to the Street of the Tentmakers where he had begun, again, to ply his trade, and to dream his great dreams and plot his fight.

Saul of Tarshish, called by the Greeks and Romans Paul of Tarsus, was almost incessantly consumed by the power and the glory of the revelations which had been given him, and which were still being given him. To himself, he appeared to walk in light, contemplating the beauty of the world with an overpowering ecstasy, and so filled with the love of the Messias that there were times when he almost fainted in his reflections and raptures. Now he loved man also, and felt pity for him—on most occasions when he did not feel his old passionate impatience—that man did not see the light as he saw it, or looked at him wonderingly or with skepticism, or turned away with indifference. Surely the truth was so clear, so omnipresent! Surely all men felt the presence of the Messias in their souls! What was more important to a man but his eternal destiny basking in the radiance of the Messias, and what was of less importance than the things of the earth, the dusty little things, the miserable little treasures, and the cares they created? Had the average man so small a mind that he could not encompass the incredible difference? It was as if a man entered on a tiny oasis and believed that that oasis was the entire world and resented even the thought that beyond that meager place existed enormous cities and mighty lands and the murmurous hum of endless life. He, little man, wailed when it was indicated that he must leave and go on to a larger existence, and clung to his ragged palm tree and his trampled plot of grass and little pool of murky water, and would not believe—nay, refused to believe—that a greater destiny called him and he must go on. (However, there were charitable moments when Saul reflected that man's soul was frail and vulnerable, and that what was familiar to him, however slight, was more preferable to him than vistas beyond his comprehension, and therefore he should be pitied rather than constantly chided, and led with tenderness and cheer and compassion rather than driven.)

To the turbulent young man, still so easily exasperated, many of the Nazarenes, who had accepted the Messias, were more than a "thorn in my flesh." They were a festering spear.

He saw them daily, near sunset, in the cool gardens of the Temple and in the Portico of Solomon, sitting with their fellow Jews and gently expounding, in—to Saul—their pompous simplicity and childish narrow faith. To them, Saul soon discovered, the Messias was not Lord of Lords, the mighty One of Sion, the Majesty of endless universes, armed not only with love and mercy but with terrible justice, King of angels and men and worlds, awful in His power, eternal and inflexible in the Law, crowned with lightnings, armed with thunders. He was "meek and mild," without sexual attributes, without masculinity, without force and terror, a mere gentle Shepherd clad in ragged garments and shorn of His stateliness and grandeur. Had He not said, they told Saul, gazing at the fuming young man with large childlike eyes, that a man should be humble and patient? Had He not abased Himself by washing the feet of His Apostles? Had He not submitted to shameful execution like the Lamb of God, killed for our sins? Had He not implied, by His whole life, that man should not resist evil, should withdraw himself from the world, should ignore Caesar and his governments, should disavow the whole fabric of man-made institutions, should "take no heed for the morrow, what you shall wear and what you shall eat?" His teachings, the innocent ones declared, emphasized no-resistance and passive deportment to exigent demands, and a man should spend his life merely adoring, merely exuding Love and smiling with gentle charity on others.

And was not His return expected hourly, perhaps the next moment? Had He not clearly said, "This generation shall not pass away" until His Second Coming had been consummated? Why, therefore, should a man labor and heap up treasure, or care for the morrow or the bread and milk and cheese and fruit for his family, or engage himself in the industry of more ignorant men? Had they not been told to "watch," as did the vigilant Virgins of His parable, for "who knew when the Bridegroom will come?"

So they watched all the hours permitted, in the Temple, gazing happily and hopefully at the skies over the gardens, when they were not softly exhorting their fellow Jews who paused to listen to them, and eating the bread of the industrious.

Almost worst of all to Saul, was not only their gently obstinate ignoring of the Jewish Law that a man must labor and earn his own bread, and their serene belief that the Lord was imminently to be expected, but these Nazarenes also believed that the neglect of bodily needs meant the neglect of the scrupulous daily bathing which was part of the Jewish Law. If some man, pitying them as they sat in unclean clothes in the Temple purlieus, offered in generous charity some bread and wine and meat, they ate the offerings with unwashed hands and without the customary prayer of thanks to God, accepting all things as their due—for were they not the followers of the Nazarene Who had despised the world, its laws, ordinances and customs? Besides, as the Messias was due any instant, of what use to the giver was his excess provender? They saw no charity in any living soul but those who had accepted the Messias. All else was cunning self-seeking.

Though a pious Jew was not permitted "to cut the corners of his beard," there was no prohibition that he refrain from keeping that beard clean and combed and free of vermin. The beard was, by tradition, a holy thing. But the Nazarenes, in their placid disregard for the customs of their fathers and the Law, no longer groomed their beards and their persons, and to Saul they "stank highly." When reproached by their fellows they tenderly quoted, "The soul is more than raiment," thus implying that a man should not wash.

Saul was an erudite man, a Pharisee, a citizen of Rome, a graduate of the University of Tarsus, familiar with the philosophies and poetry of the world, understanding of the history of nations, a traveler to far places. He had, by the mighty Grace of God, had a revelation. He had returned to Jerusalem, after the catastrophe at Damascus—that rainbowed, hot and fervid city—and after his sojourn in the desert—convinced that his fellow Nazarenes in the Holy City would be of more knowledge than the Jews of Damascus and other scattered places, and that they, so close to the past awesome events, would listen to him with understanding. Men near a volcano knew of thunderings and lightnings and the heaving of the earth and the roar of fiery rain.

Many of the Nazarenes of Jerusalem, alas, had dwelt near the volcano and had not understood the giant voice they had heard. Certainly, they were a few, but Saul had not as yet encountered many of them.

It was in vain that Saul told the Nazarenes he met in the Temple—who were more sedulous than their fellow Jews in their pious duties—that they were, most probably, misinterpreting the words of Yeshua of Nazareth. Had not God spoken sternly of the grasshopper who wasted the summer away and then expected the industrious ant to feed him, the ant who had worked the year? "He who does not work, neither shall he eat!" shouted Saul in anger. But the Nazarenes shyly informed him that they should "take no thought of the morrow," and besides the unbelievers fed them, and so did the indulgent priests of the Temple.

Saul had a dreadful inner vision of the total collapse of civilization and law and order and the Laws of God should the prevailing views of the Nazarenes spread among them all. Man was not only an eternal soul. He was a privileged denizen of this beautiful green and gold and purple world which God had made in His infinite love, and he shared his nature with the animals in the world, and had need of sustenance. The animals hunted and foraged diligently, and provided for their mates and their offspring. They built nests and cleaned caves; they marked their territories against invaders. They cared for their children and loved them and taught them stringently, so that they, in turn, could provide for themselves and their families. They cleansed themselves and groomed themselves strictly, that their health might be preserved. They lived by Law, given to their natures, and woe be to any who transgressed that Law! He surely died. Law applied to man, also, as a creature of this world.

This analogy, presented to the Nazarenes by Saul, was met with pitying smiles. Was not man more than an animal?

Saul was infuriated. The Lord had meant, surely, that they were not to destroy themselves and their tranquillity by fear of the morrow, for who knew what the morrow would bring? Perhaps death, perhaps greater duties, perhaps far calls to strange lands. A man, however, should certainly care for the problems and the duties of today! The Nazarenes gave him their wide shy smiles and merely shrugged, and stared at the skies, awaiting the Messias.

Saul shouted, "If your fellow Jews did not give you bread and oil and meat and cheese and wine, who then would feed you?" They replied, in a gentle whisper, "The Lord." "Not if you disobey His Law of work! Was He not a carpenter?" They answered, "That was only to display His humility."

Saul noted that the Nazarenes were making converts among the slaves of the Greeks and Romans and Egyptians and Persians and sundry others in Jerusalem, and he was dismayed that the perverted tenets of the simple were received with enthusiasm by those slaves. The Nazarenes were assuring them that, as slaves, they were superior to their masters, yet they must submit in all meekness, for was not the Messias expected hourly, and would He not exalt them as kings, and masters, above their owners? Would He not clothe them in gold and heap treasures about their feet, and give them the rule of the world? Verily. Hearing this, Saul despairingly clutched the red hair at his temples. In short, the Nazarenes were propounding that all men must not attempt to improve their fate, that they must submit to slavery and degradation, and not acquire dignity and manhood. "Proclaim liberty throughout the world, unto the inhabitants thereof!" he shouted as Moses had shouted.

His fellow Nazarenes said, "What is liberty?" and shrugged, and considered they had made a wise epigram.

If their fellow Jews were exasperated with them and their softness and their lack of fortitude and industry and courage, Saul was even more exasperated. It came to him, with fury, that he must not engage them in learned conversation, for though they could recite the ancient prayers with the addition of the new, and could slowly point out Hebraic characters on scrolls, they were only "Amaratzim." Did not God want able and intellectual and learned men among His servants? Saul would sometimes ask himself, wrathfully. And the reply came to him, "Indeed, for who then shall lead the people?"

As the Nazarenes were only men, it came to Saul, and men by nature hated responsibility and labor and toil and sweat, they had seized on the new sect as an excuse for indigence, sloth, idleness and self-indulgence, and lack of pride. Oh, they had pride! he would rage. They believed that by doing nothing they would inherit the earth! In a vision he foresaw the enormous perversion of the words of Yeshua of Nazareth spread throughout the world, and he knew despair. What was he to do?

"God," he said, in his endless exhortations to the meek smilers, "speaks in mysteries and in symbols. You have simplified the words of the Messias into a code justifying your indolence and self-abasement and aversion for labor, and reliance on the charity of others, who smile at you. Yet, the Law remains: Man must labor for his bread with the sweat of his brow. The Messias reminded you that He had not come to break the Law, but to fulfill it. You degrade the Law! It is not enough that you believe in Him. You must follow His example, and He was a mighty Man, acquainted with anger, and with a terrible Voice. He did not sit in the Temple and do nothing. He worked and He labored. You have known Simon Peter, and James and John, and others of His Apostles and disciples, and though they go abroad among the people and preach they also earn their own livings. Have they abjured you to sit here, among your stenches and the remnants of baskets of charity, and watch for the coming of the Messias? No, they were called to labor in the world. Get you hence, you idle, you perverters of the Word!"

Finally, in spite of their docile smiles he saw hatred in their eyes. Moreover, his fellow Jews who had not accepted the Messias became annoyed at his exhortations among them. "Are you not he who persecuted our brothers?" they asked him. "Did you not bind and imprison them? Are there not widows and bereft mothers and weeping sisters and brothers who suffer because of you? Are you a spy of the Romans? Once you were full of fervor against these Nazarenes. Now you preach to them! You are a man of moods and inconsistencies, and we are charitable to say only this of you. We do not trust you, Saul of Tarshish. Depart from among us. We have shut our ears against you, and will not hear you, for a man of passion is suspect, and he who blows cold one day and hot the next is to be doubted of his sincerity."

Why had the Messias revealed Himself to him, if only for this failure? He was failing among his own people, and his failure was beyond encompassing. It was useless to say, "I was wrong, and I was blinded. But God gave me His Revelation, which I would reveal to you in love and in joy, for my heart yearns over you, and I would give you the words of His Salvation. Let us reason together, for He has said, 'You are the salt of the earth; if the salt lose its savor' how then shall the bread of life be eaten? What man would partake of it? Hearken to me, for through you, as He has said, comes His Salvation. 'Salvation is of the Jews.' That He has said, and will you not listen, my people?"

But the Nazarenes feared him, for he exhorted them to labor as their Lord had labored, and they did not wish to labor, and the Jews hated him for his former persecutions and did not trust him.

Once the more extreme of the Zealots and the Essenes had alarmed their fellow Jews for their open and useless attacks on the Romans, which resulted in punitive measures against the more moderate. Now a fresh alarm seized them. Some Nazarenes, thinking they were emulating the divine Savior, deliberately incited the Romans by choking the streets of Jerusalem with their supine bodies, in mute protest, not against oppressive laws but because the Romans were not eagerly embracing the new Jewish sect. They said, "If the Roman become a Nazarene, then will he partake with us of the fruit of peace, the wine of amity, and all men will embrace each other, and when the Lord returns—as soon He must—He will discover a world awaiting it; full of lovingkindness and songs."

On the other hand when taxgatherers sought them those few who had some coins, or whose tolerant family supplied them with a pouch, gave the taxgatherers not only the due exacted, but more, with meekly tender faces, forgetting that the Lord had despised such bureaucrats as the lowest of men, needful of all the mercy divine justice could give them. When their exasperated brothers demanded of the Nazarenes why they did this dangerous thing, they replied that the Lord had bidden them to give the thief who stole their purse their cloaks also. The lesson of the parable was lost on them. They adhered only to the word, but not to the subtle substance, and this Saul found most intolerable of all.

The Romans lost patience in Jerusalem. They dragged away those unresisting men and women who clogged the streets with their prone or supine bodies, and thrust them into prison, and many of the imprisoned rejoiced in what they considered their martyrdom and implored that they be put to death as their Lord had been put to death.

Without avail Saul cried to them: "The Messias would have you live and labor for him more strenuously than ever before, but you weak cowards seek what He would have you avoid in good conscience! Has He not said that the harvest is heavy but the laborers are few?"

To Saul, the Faith was far more menaced by laughter and sloth and ridicule than by any possible sword wielded by the vexed Romans. The new procurator had mimes parody the Nazarenes, and the new legate in Syria wrote his colleague in amusement about these creatures, yet warned that they must not be permitted to disrupt orderly procedures and civilized life. Hearing of this, Saul felt shame for his fellow Nazarenes. They had forgotten that a Man had lived among them, with manly attributes. They thought of Him as a submissive and womanish Savior, who wished them to be as inert as themselves.

Therefore, Saul was confronted by the two opponents:

His fellow Jews who distrusted him and so rejected him, and some of the Nazarenes, his fellow Jews also, who thought him a savage fellow who had none of the charity of the Lord in his soul, and who harangued them with smarting words and called them pusillanimous and informed them that while awaiting the Second Coming they must bestir themselves and earn their own bread.

Saul, once certain that the Revelation on the road to Damascus would solve all his inner storms and impatiences and despairs and angers, now found himself assailed by fury and impotence, and by practically everybody. He was sure in his soul that God had ordained a path he must take—but where was that path? If no one listened to him, then better he speak to the jackals of the desert and the wild ass and the vulture!

He was beside himself. "Where shall I go, Lord?" he demanded with more passion than reverence, and awaited a reply. His powerful soul could not bear the waiting. The self-identity he had always known was more vehement than ever. His love for reality had increased, and now that he knew the Great Reality of the Messias it seemed incredible to him that none listened to him in Jerusalem, but avoided him as a violent man. Abandoned, he brooded alone in the Temple.

Chapter 36

SHEBUA BEN ABRAHAM had died while Saul had lingered in the deserts of Arabia. Rabban Gamaliel had died before his return, and so had the noble Roman lady, Clodia Flavius. David ben Shebua was now a rich and elderly man, as judicious and moderate as always. The sons of Shebua, Simon and Joseph, had embraced the new sect, but with a sturdy earthiness which Saul respected and understood. (However, they did not embrace him, for they remembered his passionate nature and now he seemed more passionate and dogmatic than before, and did they not have trials of their own and did they not, now in their old age, desire peace and the leisure to contemplate the Messias, and perform their religious duties? Their purses were open to their fellow Nazarenes who were in distress. They believed, not with wild exultation, but with common sense. Their souls were muscular and without incoherence. They were not enamored of Saul, their nephew, nor did they like his appearance at their houses in the rough garb he preferred, not in emulation of humility but because he disdained luxury.)

Therefore, there was left to Saul of the house of Shebua ben Abraham only his sister, Sephorah, whose husband had sickened and died but a few weeks ago. "We are a house of mourning," the lovely Sephorah said, weeping, "but those we loved died in the knowledge of the Messias, and they now rest in His bosom." Her children were gentle young things of no particular intellect, except for Amos ben Ezekiel, who had been raised from the dead by the Messias, and it was to this young man, now nineteen years of age but still unmarried, that Saul turned in his distress.

Amos was of a kind if adamantine spirit, quiet in speech, determined in action, just, reverent, devoted and patrician. Once decided upon a way, he could not be moved from it. He listened to Saul's impassioned diatribes against his fellow Jews, both Nazarene and unbeliever, with calm detachment. With something of his grandfather, David's, objective amusement—which he did not display, however—he understood exactly why Saul had been rejected, but no more than Saul did he know what the older man must do. "God will enlighten you concerning His Will," said Amos, trying to gentle that most ungentle man. To which Saul replied, "I have been seeking His will since I was born, and He has still not informed me! Am I to waste my life among fools or hostile men, who will not listen?"

"He will tell you," said Amos. Saul was about to burst out in imprecations when he saw Amos' golden eyes, shining like coins, and radiant, and it came to him in wonderment that Amos' words had suddenly struck on his hot heart like a cool cataract of healing water, and he said, "You are only a youth, with hardly a beard, and I am your uncle, and I know the world and have had a Revelation. Yet, something mysterious tells me that you have spoken words of wisdom, and I have sinned in my impatience."

Amos sighed. His uncle had always been excessive in emotion, though paradoxically he was a man embedded in reality. Was his fault that of an inability to endure fools gladly, or at least suffer their existence? All men were not called to arduous service. Why did Saul believe they were? He, Amos, had his own plans, which he did not divulge to Saul.

Saul's encounters with Simon Peter had not been the happiest of events. Simon Peter, a brawny fisherman, was not of Saul's subtle and colorful mind. He was as stubborn as Saul and frequently as obdurate, and often their voices had risen to acrimonious heights. Peter had explained his own vision that in the sight of the Lord there were no "common" men, nor unclean, and that he must not reject those among the Gentiles who came to him for learning and teaching and baptism. Saul had said with scorn, "But how obvious that is! Once I, too, despised the Gentile and avoided him, as an infidel and heathen, but now I know—not through a vision such as you have had—but with my intelligence, that God is the Father of all men. I did not need a vision!"

This offended Peter. Had Saul seen the Messias in the flesh? Had he walked with Him in the dust? Had he witnessed His crucifixion? Had the Messias imparted to him wondrous things over many days? (John had said, and truly, that if all that the Messias had said and done were recorded it would fill "many books.") Saul claimed to have seen the Messias on the desert, and Peter did not doubt this for an instant. But first he had persecuted the followers of the Messias as no Roman would persecute them. Who had slept with the Messias and broken bread with him, but Simon Peter? Had not he, Peter, washed the feet of the Messias? Had he not walked with Him for forty days after He had risen from the tomb? Yet this Saul of Tarshish, this Pharisee, this man of Greek and Roman knowledge and worldly ways, this man of haughty intellect, appeared to believe that he had more understanding of the Messias than those who had dwelt with Him! It was very vexatious.

Through Peter Saul had also met the umbrageous brothers, John and James ben Zebedee. They, like Peter, were industrious men acquainted with labor and toil, and somewhat younger, though all were young. However, they were more of Saul's own spirit, fiery, sometimes inclined to excesses of speech and gesture, unyielding and full of temper. Peter considered Saul's anger against the docility of many of the Nazarenes sinful, and urged him to look upon those who labored as diligently as ever, or more, and did not sit in the Temple purlieus in slothful attitudes with upturned and useless palms, not overly clean. He also told Saul that a man could not entirely blame the Jews for not accepting his teachings, because they feared and distrusted him.

"Are we not all imperfect men?" Peter asked him.

"Are we not to put on perfection?" demanded Saul.

Peter sighed. He was a man of quiet humor. "We can but try," he said, a remark which Saul thought frivolous. John and James listened to this with emotion racing across their darkly active faces, and Saul, to his pleasure, saw that they agreed with him and not with Peter. However, they also agreed with Peter that before a Gentile could become a Nazarene he must first become a Jew, be circumcised and learn all the sacred Scriptures. How else could he understand the Messias, who had been prophesied through the ages, and the signs of His coming?

John said, "When we were in Samaria, and the people therein rejected Our Lord and would not hearken to Him, I implored Him to call down fire on the city and destroy it."

"And what did the Lord reply?" asked Saul.

Peter's large brown eyes glinted again with humor. "The Lord rebuked John," he said, in a tone which implied that the rebuke had not been gentle. John flushed and pulled his cloak closer about his shoulders. James lifted his head in a most vigorous movement. It was obvious that they still believed that cities and nations which rejected the Lord deserved hell-fire. For some obscure reason this annoyed Saul. One should feel sorrow for the cities and the nations and seek to enlighten them, but certainly not to devour them in flames. That was hardly a good method of persuasion.

Their fellow Jews did not reject Peter and John and James with deaf contempt, but granted them the courtesy of listening to them, and thus they made many converts to the new sect. Moreover, they rebuked the docile

Nazarenes who would not work but simply awaited the imminent arrival of the Messias. "Who knows but what hour He comes?" asked Peter. "Let Him not find us idle, but engaged in honest toil and in prayer." And many were ashamed and resumed their labor.

This baffled Saul. He was rejected, but the other Apostles were given respectful attention. They even made converts among the Romans and the Greeks. But he had no offerings to give the Lord, no flowers to lay on His altar.

It came to him slowly and disastrously that with the exception of a few now, of his own house, no one spoke to him, all shunned him and averted their eyes, or stood at a distance silently derisive, that even the priests in the Temple had nothing to say to him, no, not even during the High Holy Days. Peter had left Jerusalem, and James and John had gone far away, and no Jew, orthodox or Nazarene, recognized his existence.

Chapter 37

To Saul's pathetic pleasure he received an invitation to dine with his old friend, Joseph of Arimathaea, who hinted that he might be happy to meet another guest. Saul, with a new humility consulted his nephew Amos, who advised a long tunic of deep red wool bordered with gold, a gold girdle and ring, and a cloak of dark blue and fine leather boots against the chill of autumn. "How sinful it is to garb one's person so when there is hunger in the land. The Messias scorned luxury," said Saul, who nevertheless thought his appearance vastly improved. He still could not grow a beard because his skin, though darkened by the sun, was extremely tender, but the long red curls before his ears were clean and polished and glistening with health and his hair was a shining red mane.

"All the gold of men in the world would not abolish poverty nor feed all the hungry," said Amos, who was as practical as his great-grandfather, Shebua ben Abraham. "And He smiled upon Mary of Magdala who bought sweet ointment for His feet, costly and fragrant, and He

rebuked those of His disciples who told her that it should
have been better had she spent the money on the poor.
There is a time for all things," said the handsome young
man glancing with amusement at his uncle, who was
surveying himself in a long mirror in Amos' chamber.
"There is a time to be poor and a time to be rich, a time
to cut a figure and a time to be inconspicuous. This is
your time to be a peacock, Saul."

Saul, even in the expensive raiment, was hardly a peacock, with his sun-darkened countenance and arms and
hands. Amos had thought of a single jeweled earring,
widely affected among young Jews in these days, or armlets of gold and jewels, or gemmed wristlets, or a slight
effusion of perfume, but he thought it injudicious to mention these things. He had struggled enough with his uncle
over a few matters.

"Hah," said Saul.

"You are a rich man," said Amos. "You have not
touched even the interest on your interest, according to
my mother."

"I think of other concerns," said Saul, with sudden
gloom. However, he let Amos persuade him to take one
of the family cars and he drove off with a flourish, seated
on velvet cushions, with a driver almost as well-clothed
as himself. Sephorah had clapped her hands at her
brother's "splendor," and innocently prayed that this occasion would be the beginning of his return to the house
of his family. Saul, holding to the gilded rail, did not
know why he felt a sudden hope and ease. After all, he
was only dining with a senile old man, and a stranger.

Joseph met him with embraces in the beautiful atrium
of his house, and then a young man with a pink and
merry face, a gleaming black and curling beard and
deep black waves of hair on his head, and wearing a cap
of the tribe of Levi, emerged from the shadows, and
Saul, with delight and amazement cried, "Barnabas!" He
fell into the arms of Barnabas and the young men embraced fervently, for this was Barnabas ben Joshua who
had saved his life in Damascus by lowering him over the
walls of the city in a basket. It was Barnabas who had
told him much of the Messias, for he had been one of
His disciples, and he had given letters to Saul to introduce

him to Simon Peter and the brothers, John and James
ben Zebedee.

Saul's weary face glowed and became young and un-
lined again as he embraced Barnabas over and over in
his joy, and then held him off to exclaim, "Is it really
you, you rascal?"

"It is surely I," said Barnabas. His features were plump
and highly colored; he had a mouth like a mischievous
boy, and eyes that danced with a black light. Nothing
could darken or sadden that cheerful spirit for too long,
and Saul had found him a solace during moods of
doubt, and a staff to help him over rough boulders of
thought, and a companion who loved to eat and drink fine
wine and jest to such effect that even Saul had reluctantly
found himself bursting into laughter, the old boisterous
laughter of his youth.

To Barnabas the Messias was not terrible, as He sometimes was to Saul, but a joyful and tender Comrade,
loving a jest also, and enjoying an excellent meal in the
houses of rich Pharisees. When Barnabas repeated some
parable, he did not do it solemnly in the way of Peter and
John and James, but with a twinkle, and at once Saul
could see the Messias smiling and His imperial blue eyes
shining with mirth. "Often He implied to us that Heaven
is full of laughter and gaiety," Barnabas would say, "and
humor both subtle and broad, and that merriment rings
from the battlements, for that which is good is happy
and blithe, but that which is evil is somber and dark and
laughs not at all. I admit some of us did not regard the
thought with pleasure, but you know how gloomy many
of us Jews are, alas."

Though Saul had sometimes suspected, as he studied
the ancient and holy Scriptures, that God would have
His joke occasionally, he had thrust the thought aside as
impious. But a laughing God now appealed to him, like a
refreshment in a smiling garden, and Barnabas had frequently called his attention to the fact that in some creatures there was immense humor, and fantasy and buoyant
invention and appearance, and the stormy dark heart of
the young Pharisee had been impressed: Until lately, in
Jerusalem, where he had found nothing to inspire his
humor, not even the acrid humor of his youth.

Barnabas, too, had encountered the apathetic and

sweetly smiling and docile Nazarenes in Damascus, who sat in sloth staring at the sky in hopes of seeing the Messias return immediately in clouds of glory. But he had not despised them as Saul despised them.

He would say to them, "It is true that the Messias told us not to tear our hearts in fear for the morrow, for today has its own miseries and evils and duties, and that is sufficient for the day, for man lives but one day at a time and the future is mysterious and not yet his own. He also taught us that anxiety is impious, for God our Father knows what we need and desire, and if we labor and are industrious and are prideful of our labor and do the best we can with the hands and minds He has given us, and forget Him never, and seek always His Kingdom, then all else will be added to us."

While this did not convince all those who preferred sloth and indigence and charity, it did shame the more intelligent among them and sent them hurrying to resume their labor and rejoin their families. Saul had succeeded not at all, except in inspiring the hatred of the shameless.

Joseph's old face was bright with pleasure at the sight of the young friends and he led them into the dining hall, where Barnabas, surveying the rich sauces and fine meats and good wines and the roast fowl and broiled fish, cried, "Ha! This is a feast for angels! Behold those opalescent grapes, with the dew upon them and the delicate frost, and those olives swimming in delicate oil, and those citrons like the sun, and those plums like a girl's mouth, and that spiced cabbage and beans in a delectable sauce, and that bread whiter than snow, not to mention the cheeses and the sweetmeats and many other things! Joseph, you are a pasha, a veritable Persian pasha!" He laughed with delight, and added, "Ah, if but the Messias were here with us now, as He was before! How He would rejoice in these viands, which even the richest of the Pharisees who invited Him to dine never served!"

A Messias who had enjoyed the delicious foods of the earth, and had savored the best wines with appreciation, was a new Messias to Saul. But he said to himself, "I am ridiculous. Why should He not have loved the bounty of God, for did He not create them? Why should not He, above all, relish their flavors and admire them?"

Barnabas might be merry and cheerful and he might

rub his hands in anticipation, but he was not obtuse. He saw the new thoughts fluttering over Saul's tired face like restless moths, and he saw the stern mouth beginning to smile faintly. Ah, Saul, Saul, he thought with deep love, the Messias brought enchantment to us, and not only raptures and faith and hard toil! For, was He not Joy, Itself, the glory and the jubilation? He was Man, as well as God, and had an affection for innocent pleasures, and never rejected a bright face. In truth, He had inveighed against the dolor of the more rigorous Pharisees, who thought that a melancholy countenance and grave and irksome ritual pleased God. They had thought that the lawful pleasures given to man to soothe and rest him were evil, and in that they most surely must have offended Him. Had He not spoken with approval of feasts and wines to the old prophets?

Seating himself and smiling with wider delight, Barnabas thought, "What patience God must have with us, that we despise His gifts, or interpret Him, the Unknowable, in the terms of our little minds, and bind the Incomprehensible to the measures of our small natures!"

Joseph was pleased that Saul, the austere, was actually enjoying this meal, goaded as he was by the laughing Barnabas, who was surely one of God's merriest saints. Saul even remarked on the flavor of the wine. Toward the end of the meal, which was leisurely and full of happy if inconsequential chatter—Barnabas' desire—Barnabas said to Saul, "I have a message for you."

For some reason Saul's heart bounded and his soul expanded, and he looked into the black and beaming eyes of his friend, and Barnabas nodded gaily. Immediately Saul began to tremble, and tears came into his eyes, and he bent his head over the jeweled cup he held and drank of it deeply to conceal his emotion, for he knew that Barnabas would tell him when he chose, and would not be pressed, and he also knew that the message was not trivial.

"It may not please you," said Barnabas, "but you have no choice. Yet, as you are Saul of Tarshish, it may indeed please you, for the reason you have no choice."

He then resumed his jests, and Joseph laughed and Saul forced himself to laugh. They returned to the atrium after dining, and then Joseph turned to Saul with a grave face and said, "You must forgive me, but we have another visitor who will be here. He demanded to see you at my house, and as he is an old friend and of many tribulations I could not refuse him."

He gazed hesitantly at Saul, as if imploring his pardon, and then the visitor was announced. Saul, to his anguish and shame and sorrow, saw that it was Tobias ben Samuel, and instantly his vision was suffused with moisture and it was as if a sword had struck him. Joseph embraced his friend, who replied absently. His cold and bitter eyes fixed themselves on Saul and he gazed over Joseph's shoulder, and Saul saw his silent hatred and suffering, and could feel no resentment.

Tobias did not greet him. He stood before the younger man and looked at him with slow and contemptuous reflection, as if studying and rejecting each feature, each hair, each limb and garment. The haughty Saul felt himself coloring in spite of his own pain, and he thought, I am of a nobler house than his, yet he surveys me as if I were the basest of slaves! Then at once his anguish and sorrow returned, and when Tobias had concluded his inspection Saul fell on his knees before him, clasped his hands and said in a voice shaking with torment, "Forgive me. I knew not what I was doing. My excuse is that I believed I was accomplishing the will of God—"

Tobias interrupted with such loathing and scorn that Saul winced: "Is it possible that one such as you could believe that God was working His will through you?"

"I believed. I was in error. But I believed." Never had Saul so abased himself before, in humiliation and remorse, and Joseph felt a pang for him and made a gesture to Tobias who, however, waved aside that gesture.

"You believed," said Tobias to the kneeling man whose head was bent over his clasped hands, "that you were just in murdering my son, my only son, my beautiful and beloved son, my gentle and devoted son? You believed that God desired that innocent blood? You believed He was as monstrous as you, Saul of Tarshish?"

Saul raised his proud red head but did not rise from his knees. He looked Tobias in his face, and controlled his voice. "Tobias ben Samuel, you know the ancient penalty for heresy. I believed Stephen was a heretic; I believed it with all my soul. I was wrong. I have wept and prayed for forgiveness. I would have spared your son; I attempted to spare him. No matter. I have spent years in the desert, contemplating the Messias and learning of Him, the Messias your son so loved, and for Whom he died—at my hand, yes. And now I know that God has forgiven me, for I did not do what I did in malice, but only what I thought was ordained in law. That is my only plea: That I believed I was an instrument of God—"

"And so you, in fervent pursuit of your wicked error, also bound and imprisoned and caused the death of others of the innocent, Saul of Tarshish?" Tobias' voice was so full of contempt that it was heavy and weighted.

"I did not believe it an error. I would that I had a thousand lives, that I might give up each one in torture to atone! God has accepted my penitence—"

"And, who informed you of that, Saul of Tarshish?" Tobias stepped back from him as if he carried a fetid contagion.

"I saw Him, on the desert floor, on the way to Damascus. If He had not forgiven me, if He had not known that what I had done I had done in honest and fervid error, and not in wantonness and cruelty, He would not have shown Himself to me."

Tobias regarded him for a long and bitter moment. Then he said, "It is my opinion that you are mad, Saul of Tarshish. You had no revelation. You did not see Yeshua ben Joseph, except, perhaps, in His lifetime. Your dream was your own demented conscience calling to you! That is, of a certainty, if you possess a conscience, which I believe you do not."

"I saw Him," said Saul, and struck his breast with his clenched fists, and his face became brilliant with both pain and ecstasy. "I saw Him! None can take that from me! And I have heard His voice, calling unto me, and it was not a voice of wrath!"

"Then surely you dream, for otherwise He would have struck you dead for your crimes against my son, and the other Nazarenes!" Tobias pointed his finger almost into Saul's face. "Do you know what you have done? I have tried to believe as my son believed. I have talked with many Nazarenes. But I cannot become one of them, for my son's murderer remains unpunished, and surely if Yeshua of Nazareth were the Messias He would not permit you to profane His Name, and claim that He had appeared unto you! The fact that you exist, and live, is proof to me that Yeshua ben Joseph was not the Messias!"

Saul's eyes became stricken and filled with tears and Tobias nodded with satisfaction. "So hundreds of others believed. You are anathema both to the Jews who do not believe in the Messias, and those who do. You are a calamity in this city, Saul ben Hillel. You bring doubt to those of the old Faith, and those of the New, for they say, 'Is this not the merciless persecutor of the innocent, and is he not a spy, who would destroy us? Even if he is sincere, then he is mad, for a man does not persecute one day and lift up and embrace the next. And who but the mad would listen to the mad?' "

Barnabas had been listening to all this also, at a little distance, and he felt deep sorrow both for the embittered and bereaved father, and for Saul, and he prayed that both might be comforted.

Tobias continued, "I believe that my son lives, for I have been offered proof, and none can deny that proof. But when I dream of him his eyes are tearful, though he smiles. He does not speak. I think he remembers how he was murdered, and would have me avenge him."

"Ah, no!" cried old Joseph. "Once you believed that he would have you join him in faith, and accept, and would have you know that he was happy in the company of the Messias!"

Tobias' pink lips thickened and paled with venom as he looked at Saul, though he replied to Joseph: "I know only that I hate this man, and will have no peace so long as he is in this city. And so I have paid scores of taunters, and have had them whisper among the people, and he will make no converts—or victims—here! He stands alone. Neither Nazarene or old Jew will hearken to him, no, not even a priest even in charity. He is without arms or armor. He is despised and rejected. His name is accursed, and it is a noble name and as a man of a noble house I am ashamed for him. Saul of Tarshish! Shake the dust of Jerusalem from your feet and leave the city of your people, for you are less than a rat in the gutter to us, and lesser than a jackal!"

"Forgive, forgive," prayed old Joseph, advancing on his friend and laying his hand on the other's silken arm.

"The Lord was crucified, and He was innocent, and His last words were addressed to the Father, that He pardon those 'who know not what they are doing.' Are you less forgiving than God, and is that not a blasphemy?"

Tobias flung out his arms in a gesture of hopeless despair and agony. "I am not the Messias! I am not God! I am only a suffering father, deprived of his only son by this monster, and before God, blessed be His Name, I will have his blood if he does not depart from this city which is cursed by his presence!"

"Tobias, Tobias," Joseph pleaded. But the agonized father could only weep and cover his face with his hands.

"Forgive me," said Saul, weeping also. "In the Name of God, forgive me, Tobias ben Samuel."

Tobias spoke from behind his fat, ringed hands, and his voice was muffled, "Let me have peace. Let me know you are no longer here, and I will strive to forgive, though I shall never forget. In the Name of God you have asked my forgiveness, and it is written that when an offender pleads so one must forgive or be accursed, himself. But, you must go. I must hear the name of my son's murderer no longer."

He turned, and though Joseph would have accompanied him he shook his head and left the atrium and was borne away in his litter.

Saul fell on his face and wept and uttered incoherent cries of torment and sorrow, and pleas for forgiveness. And Joseph and Barnabas were helpless against such tremendous pain. They could only pray. But finally Saul was more composed and he rose to his feet, staggering, and his face was ravaged.

It was then that Barnabas said, "Saul, my dear friend, I must give you the message, which Our Lord conveyed to me in a dream through one of His angels. You must depart from Jerusalem and return to your home in Tarshish, and there await His Will."

Saul started. He wiped away his tears frankly with his hands. "I must return to Tarshish?"

"Yes. There are Nazarenes there, but whether they will accept you or not I do not know, for alas, your fame has spread wherever the Nazarenes are spread, and also among the Jews. You must wait in patience. God has a great destiny for you."

"I feel He has abandoned me," said Saul, in the accents of his early youth and with the same anguish.

"No, never will He abandon those who love Him," said Barnabas, and put his arms about his friend. "He has accepted your penitence. You have gazed upon His transfigured Face. But you must leave Jerusalem, for your destiny is not here."

Two days later Saul stole from the city of his fathers at dawn, and looked behind him at the walls and the towers and the spires, and the golden dome of the Temple, and his pain was almost more than he could bear, for he was leaving behind him all that he loved and adored, and he knew not if he would ever see them again. Worst still, he had failed God.

Chapter 38

"I HAVE taught you since you incontinently dropped your feces and your urine in your father's garden," said old Aristo. "Shall the student now teach the teacher? Gods! What teachers must endure, and without true appreciation! We surely shall inherit the Blessed Isles! Or, there are no gods."

The face of Aristo resembled an old Pan's countenance, full of shrewdness and dry crevices and subtlety, and the eyes were as young as ever. "To me, you are still my childish student, as insistent as always, and as obstinate, and, I must admit, as belligerently eloquent. But, my Saul: I am an old man, and I have some wisdom, and I am a Greek, and I know the philosophies, and I find your determined teachings no more elevating nor wiser than the words of Aeschylus, Sophocles, Aristophanes, Cimon, Aristotle, Demetrius, or Theophrastus, or others I could name."

"I do not claim to be wiser nor nobler nor more intellectual than those men," said Saul. "I only attempt to speak the truth. I am not in competition with Socrates! I do not propound conundrums, nor present enigmas."

"Listen to me," said Aristo, as they sat in Saul's garden in the heat of the day, under striped awnings and drank cooled wine and ate small cakes. "Truth has a thousand faces and voices, and speaks through poets as well as through sages, and has many aspects. I believe that a miracle of some mystery was performed for my father-in-law in his lifetime, but I know neither the how nor the why. We say that it is safer not to be too inquisitive about the gods and their actions, for they can become petulant. My wife is a Nazarene, and I do not jest with her concerning it, nor object to her peculiar devotions and beliefs and practices. I only ask that your God's attention not be drawn to her too· minutely, for there is danger in that also! I am content to let the gods mind their own affairs, and hope that they will let me mind mine, in peace. If that seems to you the philosophy of an impudent man, and a lazy one, so be it.

"While there is a strange light in your eyes and frequently on your countenance, my dear Saul, you do not seem happier than in your youth. You fume; you appear restless and vexed. Ah, you have told me! You await the call of your God. Good. But do not force him upon me, and I shall refrain from mentioning Zeus, who seems to me handsomer and more robust.

"My childhood and youth, until I was rescued by your father, and may the gods not pursue him now as they pursued him in life, were not years of happiness and caperings. But since then I have known the pleasures of living such as only Greeks can know, in the contemplation of the world's beauty, in women, in poetry, in noble statues, in fine buildings, in harmony, in music, in painting and in textures and colors. Greeks are surely the wisest of men, for they love the day and the hour, and the felicity and glory of them, or even the dark sadness, and they do not ponder much concerning the gods, who are our invention. (You must admit, my Saul, that they are prettier than your God, who seems to me a dolorous Being concerned with duty.) We praise good viands and enjoy wine and song, and the loveliness of women and congenial companionship. I do not know who created this world, nor do I care. But to That which created it I give my obeisance, and I admire Him, for He is the greatest of Artists, surely, and all artists are pleased by appreciation. Greeks are the tasters of life, the rejoicers in it, the devotees of it, though sometimes we flog ourselves with meditations on tragedy, just as a man takes a laxative when his bowels are costive. Nothing so gives an edge to life as thinking about death, and that is why we have Greek tragedians.

"I have observed your Nazarenes in Tarsus. It is true that the majority of them are Jews, and that may partly explain their somber countenances. I have listened to them, unfortunately, and I have listened to you. I find nothing in your revelations, as you call them, which inspire me with joy, or give me fresher pleasure in the world, or a happier heart."

"You are an old lecher, and a voluptuary," said Saul, but he smiled.

"If I am those—and I do not deny the truth of it—then I have also done no man any harm. To be harmless is the greatest of virtues, Saul. I treat every man with as much justice as there is in my nature, and do not cheat, unless it is in the market place where all men are cheaters. I could wish nothing more than the epitaph: 'He enjoyed the world and loved it, and saw beauty in it as well as ugliness and pain, and he departed with regret yet with relief, for he was old and would sleep.'

"I do not question why we are here, nor how we arrived, nor the purpose, for I do not believe there is a purpose. Ah, you frown, Saul, in your old impatient manner. I am content to be here, to watch the banners of the seasons and the changing of the trees and the flowers, and to lie in the arms of my beautiful wife and stroke her hair, and dine, and read poetry and admire vases. You would say you know the purpose of our being, and you have explained it to me. I confess it bores me. Who would wish for eternal life except a ravenous fool who cannot satisfy his greed and his appetites? A man dies when he is surfeited, whether he is young or old. How long he lives is not important; it is only how he lives, in as much beauty as he can see with his eyes, touch with his hands, hear with his ears.

"Sometimes I remember the beliefs of the Indus, that we are endlessly born again. Is that not a frightful thing to contemplate? Lovely though the world is, one life is quite enough for any man, and then silence and darkness and rest. Thanos is a sweeter god than any other, and I await his call in tranquillity.

"Tell me, my Saul: Is your faith a happier one than mine?"

As he was obdurately honest, Saul hesitated. Then he said, "But we look for even greater happiness in an eternal noon, and a contentment beyond our present knowing, face to face with the Beatific Vision of God."

Aristo sighed and scratched his cheek thoughtfully and narrowed his eyes against the sun that struck like fire on the gardens. "I confess the thought wearies me. Who would wish to spend eternity glaring at any vision? Again, I have listened to your Nazarenes and their ecstatic accounts of their coming Heaven, and it does not tempt me. They seek to convince their fellow Jews, who usually repel them, and I find that very perspicacious of them—"

"Jew or Nazarene, we believe in the same God, and in the same Heaven, Aristo."

"How unfortunate. It does not appeal to me. Nor do spiritual raptures, except those incited by beauty. I hear rumors that the new Jewish sect is spreading like fire in dry corn. I think that is very sad, for too many reasons, many of which I have already confided to you. I do not love the Romans, but I admit that they have brought order and peace to the world, and they are the people of Law, and of a rigorous if unimaginative nature. They are also scientists and men of valor, though not famous for discrimination, and are gross materialists. However, they have built magnificent if heavy cities, and have established commerce and trade and amity and health among nations, and are rooted, more or less, like oaks. Can you imagine what disorder and confusion and catastrophe would occur in this world if the Romans ever embraced your God? All that they have established would vanish, and as Nazarenes do not love conquest or the sword nor harsh justice, the lusty barbarians would seize the world. If I could pray to any god I would pray that this disaster never come upon the Romans, though I have cursed them in my lifetime."

"It is useless," said Saul, and looked for a ripe fig and began to suck it. "We can never come to terms in our semantics."

"Why do not you Jews keep your Messias, as you call him, for yourselves alone, and let the rest of the world bask in peace?"

"It is commanded we feed all men the bread of truth," said Saul. "For the sake of their eternal souls."

Aristo held up his veined hands in mock horror. "Let me make a bargain with you: Attend to your own soul, and in gratitude I will attend to mine!"

"I love you," said Saul, in a low voice, "and so I would bring you to the Messias. I have told you how I saw Him, and His glorious appearance, and the utter joy that came to me on the desert near Damascus. I am not eloquent, though you have said I am, otherwise I should have convinced and awed you, and you would have come to Him, yourself."

Aristo was touched. He tapped Saul lightly on his knee. "Dear child," he said, "you are eloquent enough, and Ianthe is entranced by your words. But as all men would not desire to live in Rome, or even in Athens, so all men cannot desire your Heaven. Possess it for yourself, and may the gods not disappoint you."

"And you are not moved by the thought that you will see your beloved wife in the world hereafter, if you fall at the feet of the Messias and accept Him?"

Aristo laughed a little. "One life with a woman is quite enough, however loved, and I am certain that in her heart Ianthe would not desire to spend eternity with me, though she loves me. A repetition of feasts would be very Hades, itself, and so would be endless communication even with those who are of our hearts. Your Heaven must be a noisy place, and I prefer the waters of Lethe, and now, if you will forgive me, dear child, I will return to my house and sleep until the day has gone and the cool night has come. More than that, no man can desire."

There were but two households in Tarsus where Saul was welcomed, and those were the households of Aristo and the sons and grandsons of old Reb Isaac, dead these many years. In the latter house there dwelt the beauteous and childless young widow, Elisheba, who had once desired to marry Saul and whom he had rejected. The male relatives and descendants of Reb Isaac were cordial and kind to the lonely young man, partly in deference to the memory of the old patriarch, and partly to the fact that Saul was of a noble house and rich and unmarried.

All had become Nazarenes and Saul found comfort in the house where he had studied as a youth. None of the men had the intelligence and wisdom of the patriarch, but they were friendly souls and Saul curbed his impatience when they merely stared at him with embarrassment after he had made some obscure reference to some obscure prophet or commentator. At first he sought to teach them and brought them ancient tomes, but though they, in their efforts to please, accepted those books and promised to read them they, alas, were no more informed than before. Only their confusion grew.

Why had God limited the intelligence of the great majority of men? Then Saul suddenly remembered what Rabban Gamaliel had told him: "The world is a world of labor and physical necessities. If all men were born delicate scholars and men of intellect and artistry, who then would hew the wood, build the fires, draw the water, erect the houses, establish roads, manufacture goods for commerce, sail the ships, wash the walls, clean the sewers, plow and sow and reap? Not that," said the Rabban with a chuckle, "I would not like to observe some of the said scholars forced to do some of that labor, also! It might drive various of their dreams from their heads—dangerous dreams—and acquaint them with raw reality and put calluses where they dash perfume, and send them to bed, not to toss on soft pillows, but to sound sleep on straw. Beware of the man who denigrates those who labor. He is a fool, however learned. And one must consider if the man with skilled hands is not at least as valuable as a man with skilled brains, and has his own intelligence."

The table in the house of Reb Isaac, though no longer presided over by the dead and famous Leah, was excellent, and Saul was welcome at any time. The ladies of the household—the wives and daughters of the men, and Elisheba—cooked lustily and lavishly, and served fine wines. Modestly, they waited on the men, as they had been taught, their faces averted and their heads covered as becoming to Jewish matrons, but Elisheba's luminous dark eyes dwelt on Saul lingeringly, and her pale bright face became brighter, and for some careless reason a wing of her brilliant black hair would frequently escape her headcloth and lie over her rounded cheek. The same carelessness was sometimes evident in the tightness of the sash about her slender waist, and the smoothness of her garments over her rounded bosom and hips. The men did not reproach her, nor did their wives and daughters, and often Saul caught the fragrance of mint or rose or jasmine as she passed him meekly with the dishes or gave him another spoon or knife.

Obtuse in the ways of women, and unaware of a household conspiracy, it was some time before Saul became overtly aware of Elisheba. His aversion for women since Dacyl had not decreased over the years, and the yearnings and fevers of his flesh he ascribed to sinfulness and forbidden lust and he had quelled them. Now, after a year in Tarsus the yearnings and fevers were returning, and mortifications of his flesh and labor in his own gardens and endless studies and long stridings along the roads did little to suppress them. Women were a snare and an evil, though a necessary one for the propagation of the race, and they had wiles and were innately wanton, and therefore should be rigorously controlled by the men of the family and sternly kept in place, lest God be offended, and they should not be permitted to rule or raise their voices. And the urges men felt for them, apart from the marital bed where appetites should be judiciously indulged at specified times only, were the snares of Satan for the souls of hapless men. Had not the prophets so warned?

Nevertheless, Saul became more and more aware of Elisheba, and all his efforts to regard her as a trap for his unwary soul did nothing to abolish that awareness. Lately his heart had a curious way of bounding when she entered the dining hall with a dish for the table, her beautiful eyes lowered and her rosy lips held in a demure line, and when she left a brightness left with her. He was puzzled. Faint echoes of what he had felt for Dacyl began to haunt him. He did not recognize them for love, but told himself they were lust. Elisheba's dead husband had had no brothers, and so she was still a widow, which Saul thought unfortunate, and he wondered often why her male relatives had not sought another husband for her. It was very strange that when he considered reminding the men of their duty he felt fresh yearnings and umbrage.

Then one night when he dined at the house of Reb Isaac Elisheba did not wait on the table with her female relatives, nor did he see her in the halls, gliding gracefully and with bent head. It took some time before he, with an affectation of uninterest, inquired about her. His host informed him that she was visiting her sister in Tarsus, the sister having recently given birth. She would not return for some time. Saul did not notice the smiling glances exchanged among the men. He only was conscious, with a sudden aghast knowledge, that the absence of Elisheba devastated him.

How could he, who had given his life to God and His Messias, have been so betrayed by his own flesh? he asked himself in anguish for several days and nights thereafter. Was this another temptation, another snare, of Satan to draw him from his ordained dedication? Saul walked the dim roads at midnight and wept and wrung his hands. It horrified him when he discovered that without his conscious knowledge he was haunting the vicinity of the house where Elisheba lived, in the dark hours before dawn.

It was during one of these dark hours that he encountered her outside the walls and the gardens of her brothers' house.

At first he was affrighted, thinking her a shade, and then he was appalled at the shadow of a young woman creeping about alone in the darkness, and he advanced upon her, and then, by the faint light of the stars he saw Elisheba's shining countenance, mute, glowing, filled with helpless love for him. He stopped, struck and trembling. She raised her hands to him, and he saw her long uncovered hair and the whiteness of her neck and the quick lifting of her bosom.

At what moment she was in his arms he could never remember, but with an acute sensation of joy he felt the pressure of her young breasts against his chest, and the warmth of her body against his own, and then his head bent and their lips met in hot and tender passion. All his flesh shuddered with an anguish of rapture when she put her arms about his neck and her sleeves fell back and the warm roundness of her flesh was unimpeded. This was quite different from the raptures of the spirit which he had known, yet in some fashion it was not too dissimilar.

He held her tightly in his arms, as if afraid that she

might be turned into mist or vanish, and he heard her warm murmurings against his throat, and his heart rejoiced and his eyes melted in tears of happiness, and yet his mind roared against him. He was betraying God, to Whom he had pledged his miserable life in absolute service. He was betraying the Messias, Who had forgiven his monstrous sins and had condescended to rescue him and give him a mission—though the mission, after a year in Tarsus, still eluded him. Another thought shrieked in his brain: Was the Messias permitting this new temptation of him, this glorious temptation, from Satan, to test his worthiness?

But, how sweet was woman flesh, and the scent of a woman, and the softness of a woman! How could anything so desirable, so fulfilling, so lovable and so full of beauty, be sinful? Saul's head roared with mingled passion and horror at himself.

Now he could hear what Elisheba was whispering against his throat, and it was the love song of the Queen of Sheba, and never had it sounded so heart-shaking:

" 'As the apple tree among the trees of the wood, so is my beloved among the sons. I sat down under his shadow with great delight, and his fruit was sweet to my taste. He brought me to the banqueting house and his banner over me was love. Stay me with flagons and comfort me with apples, for I am sick of love! His left hand is under my head, and his right hand embraces me! The voice of my beloved—!' "

The whole spirit of Saul thrilled and leaped at these wondrous words and his lonely heart knew the heat of love and desire and total ecstasy, and he held Elisheba closer to him and murmured in reply, in the words of Solomon:

" 'You have ravished my heart, my sister, my spouse. You have ravished my heart with one of your eyes! How fair is your love, how much better is your love than wine and the smell of your ointments than all spices! Your lips drop as the honeycomb; honey and milk are under your tongue, and the fragrance of your garments is like the scent of Lebanon!' "

For an instant—terrible to him—a thought like fire flashed through his brain: Was not human love like this lovelier than love for God, and was not the touch of a beloved woman more complete and more comforting than all else?

Human love was not forbidden by God. In truth, it was blessed. He, Saul, had none to love him now but this girl, this delight in his arms, this fragrant sweetness against his throat, and he knew that she loved him not in wantonness but in truth and humility and joy. His loneliness overwhelmed him. The emptiness of his days was like a cold lake creeping to his heart. He had only to take this gift she offered and life would hum with color and scent and laughter and pleasure and contentment.

Then he saw the road before him, which he had accepted with reverence and rejoicing, and he knew he must travel that way alone. He could not take Elisheba and her distractions with him. His vows must be fulfilled. The road was bitter and hard, but at the end was a fulfillment beyond dreaming and imagining. While it was better to marry than to burn, some men must not marry, and he was convinced that he was one of these.

In the total service of God a man must deny himself all things, even human love and human yearning. A man so dedicated could bring nothing but sorrow and bewilderment and loss to another human being, for he could not give his whole heart to that being. Elisheba must not be hurt; she must not be wounded, or he, himself, would expire in his pain and his remorse that he could not give her his whole self and his whole spirit and life.

Gently then, and almost with despair but with resolution, he disengaged the clinging arms of Elisheba and led her to a spot of darkness near the walls of her brothers' house, and they sat down together, and she clung to him and rested her head on his shoulder, and in spite of his fierce resolve he could not put her away. The warm grass under them was bruised and a shower of jasmine blossoms fell over them like rain, and the great stars, scarlet, blue, white, golden, seemed to flame within reach. Somewhere a nightingale sang with so poignant a theme that the hearts of the young man and woman, listening, opened and quivered with mingled sadness and exaltation.

One of Elisheba's breasts leaned against Saul's arm, and he held her hand and thought how beautiful and peaceful it would be to die like this and never wander again, never search, never hunger, never know despair. He tried to speak, but his lips would not open. So it was with the prescience of love that Elisheba spoke softly:

"I have loved you long, my heart's glory and delight, since I was a child and you were but a youth with your books in my grandfather's house. I saw you before you saw me. I heard your voice before you heard mine. When I was a girl you were my dream of Paradise, the vision of an angel, a young Moses. Then you went away for many years, and I married, for it was my duty, but it was without love. Never was your face absent from my thoughts. It was you, and not my husband, who stood with me under the marriage canopy."

Elisheba drew a deep and crying breath, and then continued in her low and dulcet voice:

"No, never did I forget you, my beloved one, not for an hour. Yet always did I know, even as a child, that you could belong to none on earth, and only to God. My grandfather spoke of this, in comfort to me, but I had known always. You cannot take me with you, for the way you go must be taken alone, for One loves you more than I, and from His call you dare not retreat.

"I implore but one thing of you, my beloved. Do not deny me your presence after this night. Do not refrain from letting me gaze upon you. No glance of mine will disturb or distract you; no smile will cause you to falter. I ask only that I see you in my brothers' house, and that I bring you wine and meat and fresh linen and serve your bread. Your shadow falling upon me will be brighter than the sun to my eyes. The sound of your step and your voice will be my consolation, my contentment. I am only a frail woman. I could not live, henceforth, if you deprived me of the sight of your face."

She lifted his hand to her lips and humbly kissed it. Then she looked at him and by the light of the stars he saw that she was whitely smiling and that her eyes glistened and sparkled with tears.

He had thought all women weak and suspect and more than a little contemptible as well as dangerous, but now he saw a resolution and courage and self-denial that would have been glorious in the bravest man, and even in his agony he was awed and humbled, and his love for

Elisheba became reverent as well as dear and beautiful beyond speaking.

He took her slender face in his palms and bent and kissed her lips, and they were no colder nor saltier than his. Then he put her from him and rose and left her. She gazed after him until the night had taken him, and then with a little cry she fell on her face on the grass and moaned like a dying lamb, and she did not stir until the first gray light of dawn paled the east.

Chapter 39

THE fourth slow year turned at Tarsus, and Saul waited, and no sound came to him and no fresh revelation. He was like a ship thrown upon a beach and there left to dry and wither beneath the sun, useless and without a crew or captain, its sails flapping in the wind and no movement on its parched deck.

Had it all been a dream, a delusion? Had God forgotten at last, and left him to die here in this far spot? The spiritual leader of the Jews asked him, with hesitant compassion, not to speak in the synagogue any longer, for it angered the people who remembered that he had once persecuted his own. Nor was he welcome among the Nazarenes, who also remembered. I am friendless, he thought, save for those in the house of Reb Isaac, and the woman I dare not take, and my old tutor, Aristo, and his wife.

He walked in his gardens. He labored with the servants. He picked grapes for wine. He had a small shop in Tarsus where he sold the goat's hair he wove for tents, and he had few customers. I am like Cain, with a brand on my forehead, he would think. There was not the furious hostility toward him that he had encountered in Jerusalem, but it was deep enough to make him a pariah to his own people. He wrote letters to his cousin, Titus Milo, in Rome, and was grieved to hear of old Aulus' death and the death of his cousin, Hannah. Yet everything became as a dream to him at last, and he waited for the awakening, so long delayed.

His sister wrote him with news of the dwindled family, and she tried to make her letters gay and comforting, as if she suspected his misery. He wished to speak of his dryness of soul and the grayness of his spirit, but could not. Only one truly knew, and that was Elisheba, and more and more he went to the house where she lived for the consoling sight of her, and her soft smile, and the sound of her step. Then he could go no more, for her brothers were becoming sullen and casting reproachful glances at him and lifting their eyebrows, and so even this oasis in the desert was closed to him. Sometimes he cried to the night: "God has forgotten me, and so should I not forget Him also, and take my joy to my heart and live as other men, and beget children and sit under my own fig tree and rejoice in the sight of my wife?" He would then leave his house and go to the house of Elisheba and stand without the gates like a thief, crushed with desire and loneliness and love. But Elisheba, keeping a pact with him and God, did not come to him though he knew, with a strange knowing, that she was aware of his presence. Then he would return to his house, vaguely comforted, as if her hand had touched his in the darkness and her heart had lain on his own.

As he had done years before he argued, implored and wrangled with God. "I am like a steed, saddled and bridled, stamping his feet, and You do not call me to the battle! I am like a sword, rusting in the scabbard. I am a banner unraveling in the wind and the insignia upon it is fading. My helmet has dimmed; my armor is pitted. I am no longer young. Use my strength, O my Lord and my Savior! Use my years, or I will wither like the dried meat of a nut. Where is the altar to which You would call me? Why have You thrown me aside like the rind of a melon, like chaff, like useless straw? Here are my hands, my heart, my blood, my flesh! Take me before I die in old age, mumbling a forgotten dream!"

There was no answer. Distracted, he would pace the empty rooms of his house. Mourning as if they were freshly dead, he visited his parents' tombs. There he would speak to his father, imploring his intercession with the silent God. "You loved Him, my father," he would murmur at the stone of the tomb, "and surely you served Him, and He will hear you, though He is now deaf to my cries. How have I offended Him, that He keep His countenance from me? Touch His garment, the shining garment of the Messias, and remind Him I await His call, as once He told me."

One day, in his hapless wanderings in the cool of the early evening, he found himself passing a small cemetery where the Gentiles were buried, but Gentiles of humble station such as freedmen and servants. The wall was low and he saw the graves and the dark cypresses. Then suddenly he was shaken, for on several of the graves he saw rude wooden crosses twined with flowers or ribbons, and he opened the gate and went within, treading gently as if not to disturb the sleepers in the dust.

The graveled path led around a cluster of cypresses and he came upon more graves with the crosses upon them, and now he started and almost fell back. For a young man was kneeling with clasped hands before one of those crosses, and his red hair blazed like fire in the sun, and his face was the face of the younger Saul.

My son, thought Saul. He would have crept away but his slight movement caught the attention of the young man who lifted quiet blue eyes, as metallic as Saul's own, to his face. Boreas rose to his feet, still gazing at Saul, and the two confronted each other in silence. The sun glinted on the cypresses and the withering grass of the summer. The wind talked to the trees and a distant chariot clattered on the hot road.

"I know you," said Boreas, and his voice was the voice of Saul.

"Yes," said Saul. He tried to smile. He felt his heart cracking with the old pain. "I saw you as a child. You are Boreas, are you not, the son of—?"

Boreas did not answer. He stood, as stalwart as a young lion and did not move. A peculiar smile came to rest upon his mouth. A butterfly hovered near his shoulder. He surveyed Saul with penetration, and the odd smile increased.

"I never forgot you," said Boreas at last. "As the years passed, I remembered you more and more. And I have seen you in the marketplace, Saul ben Hillel, and I have heard you speak and harangue the people. I have followed you into the synagogues, for all it is unlawful," and the smile deepened with satire and irony, "and I have marveled at your eloquence."

Saul could not speak. He wanted to flee, but Boreas' look held him.

"I am a Nazarene, also," said the young man. "And so was the good man I called my father, who lies in this grave." He gestured at the larger cross. "I say he was good, for always must he have known I was not his son, yet he loved me and took me as his own. Was it because of the money? But the money did not come to him for several years after I was born, and I remember that he dandled me on his knee as a babe, and taught me to walk, long before there was money." The ironic smile became colder and harder. "The money of my grandfather, Hillel ben Borush."

Saul's face had paled to the color of clay, and his mouth opened as if he could not breathe. Yet he could not glance aside from that condemning and satirical young countenance, and the youth suddenly appeared amused.

"You thought I did not know how you would creep upon me when I was a child, after we had first met," said Boreas. "I pretended not to see you, and your peering through hedges or peeping over walls. Was I so dear to you, Saul ben Hillel, that you dared not speak to you, your son?"

Saul's eyes darkened with his sorrow and with the love that sprang at his throat like a tiger.

"Look at me!" said Boreas, and he advanced a pace. "Do you deny I am your son? Do you know what they say to me, those who have seen you and know me? They laugh, as if at a good-tempered jest, and they say, 'There is but one in all Tarsus besides yourself, Boreas, who has the color of your hair and your eyes, and your features, and that is Saul ben Hillel of the noble Jewish house. Perhaps, when your mother was carrying you in her belly she happened upon him, and he impressed himself upon her mind, and so marked you!' That is what they say, Saul ben Hillel, and they have said that since my earliest youth, and sometimes in the hearing of the good man who had taken me into his family."

His voice had risen and it lashed at Saul like a whip. Saul spread out his hands and he said, "Condemn me if you will, Boreas, but I loved your mother, and I was hardly fifteen when I begot you, years younger than yourself at your present age."

"And she was but a miserable slave, and you were a Jew of a great house!"

Saul shook his head. "No, no." He could not tell this young man that his mother had known other men besides himself, and was not an innocent virgin when she had given herself to him, and that she was his first encounter with a woman.

Boreas' eyes narrowed and his red lashes were like a flame across his hair and freckled face.

"I never knew my mother," said Boreas. "But I have heard she was very beautiful and kind and loving, and she was the favorite of her mistress who freed her when she married, and gave her a dowry. Were the stories lies?"

"No. They were not lies," said Saul. He gathered strength. "I have told you: I was not yet fifteen. I am a Jew. Your mother was not a Jewish—maiden. I could not have married her, for my father would not have given his consent, and I had duties to my people."

Boreas said, "I have heard of those duties, for your fame preceded your return, my father." Saul could not endure the words, nor the smile which accompanied them.

"I am not a child," said the young man. "I have lain with slave girls, as you lay with one of them. Why then do I condemn you? I do not know. Perhaps I have dreamed you would claim me, but that was a false dream, was it not? I am not a Jew."

Saul held out his arms in a vehement gesture, and he dropped his hands fiercely on Boreas' strong young shoulders, and he cried, "You are my son, my seed, and I did not claim you, fearing what has already come to pass, and desiring only your peace!"

Boreas started to recoil from him. He raised his hands to seize those of Saul to fling them from his shoulders. But as he touched his father's hands his own came to rest on them, helplessly, and they stood and gazed into each other's eyes, and slowly they began to smile at each other.

Then Saul took his son into his arms and embraced him hungrily and said, "I have not forgotten you, Boreas,

my son, as you know. I have longed for you through the
years. But I would not have you harmed, nor derided.
For your sake I did not seek you out. Condemn me for a
coward, if you will, but I was a coward in your behalf.
Oh, I would that my father had held you on his knee and
had kissed your cheek!"

"I visit his tomb, and the tomb of my grandmother,"
said Boreas, and his voice became husky. "I am proud
that I am of their flesh, and of yours also. Now I understand, and I implore you to forgive me."

Saul drew him closer and kissed his forehead, then his
cheeks. "You have come to me as the sun, brightening
my life," he said, his voice shaking. "I have none but
you, of my seed. All that I have shall be yours. For I am
a man without a home, without a land now, and without
a people, and perhaps even without a God."

It seemed to him when he left Boreas in the cemetery
that his flesh had been torn and that he had left a vital
member of it behind him. But he was also comforted. He
had arranged with Boreas that they meet in quiet places,
where they could speak together and where Saul would
teach him the ancient truths of his people. I am not
alone! Saul often exulted to himself. And he went to his
lawyers to consult with them secretly.

Chapter 40

BOREAS said, "But they will jest at you, my father, and
mock you, and that I will not endure."

Smiling, Saul replied, "Never in all my life have I
refrained from an action for fear of public comment, or
gibes." His face changed. "Alas, I was sometimes evilly
wrong. But in this matter I am correct, and you must
obey me."

So they went before the magistrates and Saul adopted
Boreas as his son, and named him publicly as Enoch ben
Saul, and the magistrates concealed their wonder and
their sidelong glances and kept their faces indifferent and
grave. They had not had to conjecture; the appearances
of the two men spoke the truth. But Saul was a rich man,

and he had adopted this young man, and the son would inherit and be rich in return, and magistrates do not smile obliquely at wealth.

Saul had intensively taught his son the faith of his fathers, and Boreas had a sharp and perceptive and humorous mind, and Saul was proud of him. At length Boreas said, "Now I must be circumcised and admitted to the congregation of Israel."

"Not so," said Saul. "I have argued this with Simon Peter, who remains adamant that a man must first embrace the ancient faith, be circumcised, and then only can he be truly called a Nazarene, before the Countenance of the Messias. For I have had thousands of revelations, and I know that the Messias, blessed be His Name, came also to the Gentiles, and it is sufficient for them to learn of the prophets and the patriarchs and all the Scriptures, and Moses, and know for themselves that the prophecies have been fulfilled concerning the Messias. It is true that without the ancient knowledge of the Commandments and Sinai, and the Covenant and the faith which God gave to our fathers it is impossible for a man to comprehend Him. But it is not necessary for him to be a Jew, and be admitted to the congregation of Israel. Ah! One of these days I will meet Simon Peter again, face to face, and we will have this out!"

Boreas had no doubt, looking at the flushed and kindling face of his father, that this would come to pass, and he smiled fondly at Saul.

Saul was thirty-eight years old, and Boreas was now twenty-three. It had been in Saul's mind to send his son to the great University at Alexandria. But Boreas said, "My heart is with the land, and I have been working the farms my—Peleus—left to his children, and my brothers and sisters work them with me, and I would not leave my home."

With harsh jealousy Saul exclaimed, "They are not of your blood!"

"In the memory of the good man, their father, they are more than of my blood," said Boreas, and his face became the stern face of Saul and Saul, seeing that, was touched as always he was touched at these manifestations. "That alone would keep me with them. But even more is the love for the land."

It was almost intolerable to Saul that his son, his only son, would not be a scholar. Father and son eyed each other implacably with the selfsame eyes, and it was Saul who finally glanced aside and was forced to smile. A few days later he bought much land adjoining Boreas' farms, with olive trees and orchards and cattle and meadows and pine forests, and gave them to his son, who accepted the gift in silence though with some tears of happiness, and embraces.

The fourth year of strange exile was almost over and spring was on the land again. Though Saul chafed now, and sighed, and entreated God, and stamped with furious impatience, he later knew that in these years he had been absorbing knowledge, not through the teaching of men but by the direct teaching of the Messias. The lessons came to him in the silence of the night, in dreams, in visions, in sudden marvelings and intuitions, in sudden quiet excitement when he cried out softly, "Of a certainty, that is true, though I did not understand before!" Then for hours, or days, he would be elevated and exultant, until his impatience overcame him again. Later he was to say, "I was taught by the Holy Spirit and not by the voice of men, and it is a great mystery."

One noon he was dining with his son, Boreas, in the cool dining hall, when the overseer came to him and said, "Lord, there are three strangers who desire to converse with you, and they await you in the atrium."

Saul frowned, then rose, and Boreas rose and accompanied him in the loving way of a son who fears for the safety of his father. Three men awaited Saul in the atrium, which was open to the blaze of the gardens, and Saul exclaimed, as he recognized two of them, "Amos! Barnabas!" and he ran to his nephew and embraced him and kissed him on both cheeks, and then he flung his arms about Barnabas of the merry face and black beard and dancing eyes. He could not believe it was they, and his joy almost overcame him, and then he seized their hands and was about to exclaim again when he remembered the stranger with them.

The man was vaguely familiar to him, tall and slender in dark blue robes, his face planed and composed, his large blue eyes fearless and dimly smiling, his hair, once pale gold, now gray and rolling in waves over his fine skull. Saul hesitated. The man wore no cap of any of the Tribes; his head was bare and his pale cheeks were slightly reddened by the sun, and he had no beard. Therefore, he was not a Jew. Nor was he a swarthy Roman, sturdy and overly assured, nor a soldier, nor a dark Egyptian or any other. Saul, studying his features, and trying to remember, felt a sick plunging of his heart, though he knew not why, and he thought with vague confusion, "He is obviously a Greek." The man had a youthful aspect but it was evident that he was near to fifty years of age.

The stranger said, and now his voice was recalled also, "Do you not remember me, Saul ben Hillel? We have met twice before," and his face became sad.

Saul had a flashing memory of sea and sails and the scent of hot tar and rope, and then a memory of agony and blood and screaming men and the heat of the wilderness. His mind staggered with the onslaught of memories, and then he knew. This was the Greek physician, Lucanus, met on the ship of Tarsus, met dolorously at the martyrdom of Stephen ben Tobias. It was all long ago. It was only yesterday, and the torturing pain assailed Saul, and he could not speak.

Barnabas, watching, and knowing, said, "Saul, this is our dear friend, Lucanus, who has taught your nephew, Amos ben Ezekiel, much, and Amos, as you know, is now a physician."

Amos, knowing also, said, "I am to take his place, as a healer, Saul, while he spreads the Good News, as he has been commanded, wherever men will hearken to him."

"He is my dear companion," said Barnabas, and placed his arm about the shoulders of Lucanus.

But Lucanus, his face even more sad than before, held out his hand to Saul, and said, "Greetings, my friend, my brother before God and His Messias."

Saul looked at that outstretched hand of brotherhood, and then he looked at his own, and to him it appeared that his fingers were wet with blood. He rubbed them on his tunic, then with downcast head he held out his hand and took the cool thin fingers of the physician.

"We have both come a long way," said Lucanus, as if consoling the other man.

"A long way," Saul muttered. Then Lucanus was embracing him like a father, and Barnabas and Amos—Amos of the golden hair and young beard—smiled at each other.

Boreas had watched in the shadow of a column with curiosity and interest, and he gazed at Amos intently, for now he knew him as his cousin, of whom Saul had often spoken, and Amos, feeling that gaze, turned his head quickly and stared incredulously at the other young man, recognizing in his face the young uncle of his, Amos', childhood and youth, and seeing, instant by instant, the amazing resemblance. Amos' fair cheeks began to color with embarrassment, and he saw that Barnabas was also observing Boreas, and Barnabas' black eyebrows were lifted and his mouth had opened in astonishment.

Saul suddenly recalled his son. He went to Amos and turned him fully in the direction of Boreas and said, "Amos, my nephew, this is my son, Enoch ben Saul, and he is your cousin, not only by blood but by adoption."

"Greetings to Amos ben Ezekiel," said Boreas, and he came forward with dignity and held out his hand. Amos looked quickly from father to son, and his color was higher, but with Boreas' own dignity he embraced the older young man and said, "Greetings to my cousin, Enoch ben Saul. Shalom, my cousin, Enoch."

Saul smiled his old brilliant smile and said, "Call him Boreas, for like the wind he loves the land and blows upon it solicitously from every direction," and he put his arm about his son and they stood side by side, while the others gazed at them.

Lucanus could hardly suppress his amusement. He had heard much of Saul over the years, and by the malicious tongue of rumor in Jerusalem and Damascus, and he had disbelieved much. He had even reserved opinion when Simon Peter had said, "Both Jew and Nazarene call him 'the great renegade,' and I do not wholly trust him, for he is a man of fierce passions and will always have his way, and he is impetuous and impatient and immoderate, and though he now strives for humility there is a hauteur about him and a condescension, in the presence of those of inferior birth, which ill becomes a follower of the Messias."

It is possible, thought Lucanus, that there is some truth in all the rumors of Saul ben Hillel, but he is a man of fearlessness and courage and a noble disregard of the opinions and strictures of others, for he stands beside his son proudly and acknowledges him.

Lucanus suddenly thought of one of his sister's sons, who was a farmer in the Campagna near Rome, and he recognized a similar farmer like that nephew in Boreas, for Boreas, though fair of skin had arms browned and blackened by the sun, and when Lucanus felt his hand in his the calloused palm and fingers were also familiar. The rays of the burning sun appeared about the eyes of Boreas, and there was that far still expression in those eyes which only the man of the land can reveal, that expression of peace and firmness and confidence, and a pure knowledge which the urban man can never know.

Barnabas had said to Saul, "Your exile, which was your school, is now over. You go with me and Lucanus to Antioch, where we will teach and bring men to the knowledge and the feet of the Messias."

Saul had rejoiced. His only regret was in leaving his son, Boreas. In truth, as the days passed, he began to feel a great and overpowering grief, for something whispered in his soul that never would he see this son again after he left Cilicia. He did not know how he knew, but long ago he had abandoned questing concerning his intuitions, and so he kept Boreas beside him as much as possible as he sat with his friends and his nephew in his house.

Boreas did not know why Lucanus, the aristocratic Greek physician, and Barnabas, the revered teacher, treated Saul with a most peculiar deference. It was not his house they revered, the astute Boreas soon discerned, nor his name, nor his wealth, for Boreas now understood that Lucanus, himself, was a man of riches. Boreas, jealous that all should treat his father with respect, was pleased and gratified, though he still did not know the source of the deference. The physician was as erudite, and Barnabas had as much fervor in the faith and was gentle and merry besides, which Saul was not. Yet, as it were, they sat at the feet of Saul, who was very eloquent and could converse without weariness by the hour, and his voice was commanding and impelling and resonant and none ventured to interrupt nor to argue. It was as if they listened to a sage.

Is it possible that he lay with my mother, a young slave girl whose origin no one knew, and begot me? Boreas would ask himself. To the young farmer this father, only fifteen years older than himself, became as a patriarch, a prophet, another Moses. He knew of the vision on the road to Damascus, for Saul never tired of exulting in it and speaking of it, but Boreas had considered that this was only another miracle on the part of One Who had, in His mercy and love, performed many miracles, and miracles were part of the deep faith of the Nazarenes, who accepted miraculous interventions as common signs granted to many of them. Some had walked with the Messias for forty days after His crucifixion, and even more had seen Him in His risen flesh. But Saul had not walked with Him; he had never spoken to Him in Jerusalem, as Barnabas had spoken. He had not learned patiently from Him in the dust of Israel, traveling the long and weary roads beside Him. Yet, these visitors accorded him the reverence and courtesy they would bestow on renowned sages. I am of his flesh and his blood! Boreas exulted, and was proud, though he did not know why he should be so proud.

One night Saul suddenly said to his son, when the visitors had retired to their chambers: "Before I leave with my friends, Boreas, you must marry. I have chosen the wife for you, the daughter of Judah ben Isaac, who is the son of my old mentor, Reb Isaac, may he rest in peace."

"I do not know the maiden, nor the family!" Boreas exclaimed.

"Pish," said Saul. "Of what moment is that?" He paused, and an unfathomable look of pain darkened his features for a moment. "I know the family. I have already spoken to Judah ben Isaac, though we are not friends any longer, for a reason I will not tell you. The maiden is named Tamara, and she is fourteen years old, and beautiful and modest. Her father, alas, is no scholar, but her mother has taught her the ways of rectitude and the wifely duties, and that is enough knowledge for a woman, for women are weak vessels and are not designed for wisdom. The girl has a handsome dowry, and dowries are not to be despised. Enough. It is arranged."

Boreas brooded for a moment. During the meetings of the Nazarenes women were permitted to sit among the men, unlike the women in the synagogues, and though they were gentle and silent they had dignity and the men did not treat them as inferiors, but as sisters equal in the love of the Messias. Many a pretty face had caught the eye of Boreas. It made him rebel that his father had chosen a wife for him, of whom he had never heard, and expected that his son would take that wife meekly and not even see her face until the day of their marriage. Boreas had also rebelled at the note of light or grave contempt that would steal into his father's fascinating voice when he spoke of women, even the Nazarene women.

Boreas said, "I will not take this girl to wife until I have looked upon her face, for I could not live with a woman who repelled me."

Saul said, "A woman is born to obey her father, her brothers and above all, her husband, and she is born to marry and produce sons for that husband. Are we Romans and Greeks, that our women are bold and infamous and go their own impudent way on the streets and byways and in the market places and banks and halls of commerce? No."

Boreas, who had Saul's own way of rushing into speech without due prudence, said with bitterness, "You are thinking of my mother!"

Saul paled with anger. Then he thought, "It is true, and I have offended my son." So after a moment, he said in a milder voice, "I will arrange for you to see the face of this maiden—at a distance—and you and I will speak with her father, though the prospective husband is not usually included in a conversation between fathers, and if she does, indeed, strike you as repulsive then you need not marry her, though I have wished it, and as your father I can command it."

For Saul was now thinking, with mingled pain and melancholy amusement, how he had defied his own father in the matter of Elisheba, though Hillel had commanded him to marry her.

So the matter was arranged, and Boreas lurked at a distance and gazed upon a young virgin with a face like a lily and eyes like dark stars and with a gay shy smile, and he had loved and had desired her at once. Later Boreas said to Saul, "I will marry the girl, if it is your wish, my father," and attempted to look resigned and obedient.

Boreas was accordingly espoused to Tamara bas Judah, and the marriage was arranged to take place before Saul's departure for Antioch. Boreas could not know the forebodings in the heart of his father, that never would they meet again, and that Saul wished his son to possess as much consolation as a wife and family could bestow on him.

"You will live in this house, which I have left to you in my will, with your wife," said Saul. "The house is yours, and all that I have."

There was a conversation Saul had with Lucanus and Barnabas which mystified Boreas, for it was the first time that Lucanus and Barnabas had looked coldly on Saul.

They were sitting in the gardens of the house of Saul ben Hillel in the late afternoon, after the heat of the day. The sky was no brighter nor more blue than the utterly still pond, in which it and its few little rosy clouds were perfectly reflected, as was the ebony carved and arching bridge with its dragon forms, and the white and black swans and ducks which sailed tranquilly over the water. A cypress or two was also reflected, sharp and black as if rigidly painted. The palms were already heavy with yellow clusters of dates, and the red pomegranates hung among their green leaves and the golden figs were fat in their hanging boughs and the citrons were like gilt amidst their glossy foliage. The fountains flashed like white fire in the sun, blinding the eye, and the walls broke into waves of red and white and purple flowers. The red-gravel paths sparkled like thrown rubies as they wound through grass and flower beds still vigorous for all the hot and passing summer, and an air of glittering peace shimmered over the gardens.

Saul and his son and nephew and the guests sat under the wide striped awnings with refreshments near their hands, and they discussed the spread of the Church into Greece, Rome, Africa and Asia Minor. "The Good News," said Lucanus, "travels on the wings of the morning and is carried on the plumes of night." The great Roman roads, which facilitated swift travel and rumor, were somewhat responsible for it, as well as the mighty commerce between east and west which had its center in Israel. "The moment of history was chosen," replied Saul, with that catch of joy and excitement at his heart so familiar to him now. He would go with Barnabas to establish more churches, to give heart and courage to the new young ones, to settle any disputes, to bring his revelations to all who would hear. (There were indeed disputes, even so early, for new interpreters rose up like locusts with dissensions and argumentations, and though Barnabas expressed his concern Saul was indulgent. "They need but correction and explanation," he said, with a hope that Barnabas fervently prayed would be granted.)

As Saul sat in his gardens he knew this would be for the last time, and each day was sorrowfully closer to the end. Because his sight had been so sharpened since he had seen the vision of the Messias he was now constantly overwhelmed by the beauty of the world and no longer found sin in the contemplation of it, but only prayerful reverence and marvelings.

Barnabas said, "As Elias was carried to Heaven in the fiery chariot and Our Lord ascended before our eyes, so Mary was also lifted when she died in the house of John. We were in his house when she died, and she was wrapped in the burial cloths and spices, and we knelt about her bed, praying, and suddenly there was a great noise, greater than any thunder, for it shook the little house, and there was a light more vivid than the sun, and we fell on our faces, mute and blind and fallen of senses. And when we lifted ourselves, dazed, the bed was empty and only a glimmer of light lay there, which faded before our eyes as we stared at it."

Instantly Saul was incredulous, though the others bowed their heads and their faces were illuminated. "What!" he exclaimed. "A mere woman to receive such a divine honor! I do not believe it. You were stricken with grief, and so looked for a miracle—"

Barnabas said, "Whence, then, disappeared her body?"

Saul shrugged. He replied, "Who knows? Those who sought a miracle, or wished to reveal prodigies, bore her away while you lay stunned."

He suddenly remembered that he had uttered similar words when his cousin, Titus Milo, had told him of the resurrection of the Messias. But he fumed. A woman, a mere woman, who had but given her virgin flesh to the Lord? Despite Leah and Judith and Rachel and Ruth and Sarah, there were few Mothers of Israel, and none of them, however worthy and beloved of God, had been granted such divine favors. He had prayed countless times at the tomb of Rachel in Jerusalem, and had thought that despite the obvious nobility and grandeur of Rachel she had died and rotted as had millions of women before her. It was true that Mary had been chosen from among all women to bear the Messias, and had clothed Him with her flesh and had given Him her blood and her milk, but she had only been, as Lucanus had related to him, "the handmaid of the Lord," a lowly Galilean girl if of the House of David. She had been but a woman, the weak vessel, the river on which Grace had traveled like a white ship. Who honors the waters which bear the sails and the Passenger? The river is but a helpless way.

It was then that a sad coldness spread over the faces of his guests.

Barnabas said, "You have forgotten. Even God waited on her consent—this little maiden just past puberty—to bear His Son! She had been announced from the ages, this virgin child. She nurtured God at her breast; she taught Him to walk; she heard His first childish words. She made His clothing; she rocked Him in her arms; she babbled to Him as only mothers tenderly babble, and infants listen with delight and trust. She cooked His meat and His fish; she made His bread. She milked the goats for Him, and gathered the fruit. She attended to the needs of His human flesh. For thirty years He was hers alone, and what wonders must have been revealed to her! And how she must have brooded and wept over His cradle, understanding that one day He must leave her and bring the holy tidings to mankind, and that He must die under frightful circumstances. The Apostles, and Lucanus, have told us of these things. The Lord performed His first miracle at her loving request. It was He who gave her as Mother to all men, as He hung dying on the infamous cross. She was present when the fire of Pentecost descended on His weeping Apostles and disciples. Did it carefully refrain from blazing upon the Mother?

"She was no 'mere woman,' Saul. She was the Mother of God. He loved her before He loved others in His human flesh. He ran beside her as a Child; He was helplessly dependent on her for nurture. We men love our mothers and reverence them. How much more, then, must God love and bless His Mother! Nothing is impossible with God. If He chose to lift her uncorrupted body to Him, as the Messias had been lifted, who shall dispute Him? Though," said Barnabas, the merriment gone from his face as he regarded Saul, "she was but a woman."

Saul reflected. He unwillingly granted all of the arguments of Barnabas. It was a mystery. Still, Mary had been only a woman, and women were not highly regarded by the prophets and the patriarchs, for all of the Mothers of Israel. They were prone to weaknesses of the flesh and the will. He thought of his own mother, and Dacyl and others he had known.

Then he remembered the one time he had seen Mary, when he had been a youth in Jerusalem, and she had dozed wearily near him, awaiting her Son. He recalled the tender reverence the Messias had given her; He had fed her with His own Hand. He had shown sorrow and concern for her. He had called her "Emi."* If the Lord could so honor and love His Mother, when then should men cavil? Had not she cried, "All generations shall call me blessed"? Saul shook his head.

"It is a mystery," he murmured, with uneasiness. "I must meditate upon it."

The Nazarenes received women among them with full equality and respect. They met in the houses of wives and mothers, to escape the exasperated wrath of their fellow Jews. They honored women because of the Mother of the Messias. Saul shifted in his chair. He must, indeed, "meditate upon it." Later he was to give reluctant acceptance to women, but it remained reluctant.

The marriage of Boreas, or Enoch ben Saul, to Tamara bas Judah, took place the day before Saul left Tarsus.

A Nazarene priest performed the ceremony in the

*Mother.

house of Judah ben Isaac, and only before Nazarenes. Saul had dreaded the hour when he must face Elisheba, the aunt of the bride, and yet had longed for the occasion, for the last sight of that beloved face.

But Elisheba was not among the family. She was not among the guests. Saul dared not ask of her, and no other spoke of her. It was as if she had no existence.

He welcomed his son and the bride and the guests to his house, and he looked upon them with heavy sorrow, and with new foreboding that never would he see them again. The road had finally been revealed to him, and he was a traveler forevermore. He was jubilant. But as a man, of human flesh, he was grieved also.

Chapter 41

THROUGH the lonely years of Tarsus it had come to Saul slowly and inevitably as the patient falling of rain, that his mission was to the Gentiles. A thousand times he had rejected the conviction. There were other evangelists, other missionaries, though it was to be admitted that their work among the Gentiles had borne but rare rewards, and few there were among the converted. The Jews would not listen to him, Saul ben Hillel, distrusting him, and the Jewish Nazarenes had similar aversions. They listened to the missionaries and evangelists, but not to him!

It was Barnabas, who had known nothing of the slow only half comprehended revelations to Saul over those four years of exile, who had told him, "You are to teach and convert the Gentiles. That is your mission. And that is why our fellow Jews, under mysterious promptings, will have naught to do with you. God, blessed be His Name, knows what is necessary."

Barnabas added, "The ways and the customs and the thoughts of the Gentiles are not familiar to me, as a Jew of modest life and quiet existence and narrow knowledge, as they are to you, Saul. Therefore, I have difficulty in speaking to them in terms they can understand and in metaphors congenial to their spirits, and in language familiar to them. I can speak and be comprehended by our fellow Jews, especially the humble and devout. (He did not add that Saul's natural impatience and erudition and learning made it almost impossible for him to speak to those humble ones of little worldly knowledge. He was too easily inflamed.)

"But you are a learned man, of Greek and Roman understanding, as well as a Pharisee Jew. The Gentiles will listen to you, as they will not listen to me, and others like myself. More and more do I understand why and how God chose you, Saul ben Hillel! How wondrous are His ways!"

Saul had never been in Antioch of Syria before, the birthplace of Lucanus, who would accompany him and Barnabas on frequent occasions. "My adoptive father," Lucanus had said with an affectionate smile, "loathed the city, called it a pestilential den, stinking with urine and gutters and rotten fruit and goats and camels and asses and unwashed hides of men and beasts. It was also too fervent, too hot, too alien to his Roman spirit. He had been sent there as legate, and despised every moment of what he called his exile. He was an able administrator, the noble Diodorus Cyranus, and a firm 'old' Roman, and a patriot, and a soldier above all, and adored the old gods and obeyed them, and was a man of justice and honor. For that he was respected by the inhabitants of Antioch, though hated by taxgatherers and not understood by the people of the city. To him, a matter was wholly right or wholly wrong, according to the law of old Rome. He was an anachronism in a world of hot confusion and a multitude of warring tongues. He had a simplicity and purity of nature not to be comprehended by men of compromise and veniality. Alas, the world is poorer that he died, and the world will grow poorer through the years that his kind is known no more."

"Surely God will raise up other generations like him," said Saul.

Lucanus shook his head. "Who knows? Rome is dying, and all the spirit of Rome."

Though Saul, all his life, had been given to deprecating men's opinions and impressions of the world—as too subjective—he found, to his dismay, that Antioch was somewhat worse than Lucanus had described, and he sympathized with the Roman Legate, Diodorus Cyranus.

The Romans, of course, were as ubiquitous there as they were in Israel, and their swarming bureaucrats were equally obnoxious. Everything was regulated, supervised, ordered and meanly inspected by those bureaucrats, and their minute records, as Lucanus had ruefully remarked, kept account of every man's defecations and every new tunic or animal. They had buildings heaped with orderly records, and the bureaucrats toiled among them like ants. To them, men were not men. They were sheets of parchment, a number in a book. "Imperial nations," said Lucanus, "become cumbersome and weighty, and finally fall under the sheer massiveness of their regulations. When a nation no longer has respect for individuals but only for masses, its day is done." He smiled his cold Grecian smile. "That is what my father always declared, and he was correct."

"We have the Roman bureaucrats in Israel also," said Saul. "However, they are cautious not to trespass too far. We are a people of temper."

"The people of Antioch prefer to brawl, feast and lie with women," said Lucanus, and his smile broadened somewhat as he regarded Saul. "Therefore, they do not openly fight the taxgatherers and other bureaucrats. It is a game: They choose, rather, to outwit them, and I find it a gayer custom."

He had encountered Saul but twice before, and on each occasion he had seen a different vivid aspect of him, and since his visit to Tarsus Saul had often baffled him by the presentation of still other aspects, many of them contrary to those once glimpsed. There was a protean quality to this man, apparently bold and courageous and open though he appeared, and without dissemblance. Leonine in appearance and in character, he was yet subtle and versatile, changeful and the same. In comparison with the merry and simple Barnabas, he was like a strong man beside an amiable and tender child. It was apparent that he loved Barnabas, but often when the three would be conversing together and Barnabas made an artless remark Saul did not appreciate the artlessness as did Lucanus and accept it as evidence of a gentle and crystalline nature. He would frown in quick irritability, which wounded Barnabas. Seeing then that he had hurt his friend, Saul would be immediately contrite, but he would change the subject hastily as if he thought the matter too obtuse for Barnabas, which further wounded the latter.

The three, so dissimilar in all things, were bound together with bonds stronger than flesh and blood or mere friendship or human affection. The bonds were invisible, but they were as mighty as rock and iron. They were evidence of a love greater than man's, and a faith more invincible than death. They lived and had their being in the Messias. As Saul was to write in a letter later he also said, "To me to live is Christ. —I have been crucified with Christ; it is no longer I who live but Christ Who lives in me, and the life I now live in the flesh I live by faith in the Son of God, Who loved me and gave Himself for me."* Therefore Lucanus and Barnabas were, to Saul, not men separate from himself but men inextricably joined with himself in the love and salvation of God. And so they regarded him also. To these men others who did not believe so deserved their tears, prayers and compassion, for did they not live in a darkness from which God intended them to be rescued?

For the first time, and in Antioch, were Nazarenes called "Christians," and they were so named by the bantering Greeks, for the word "Christus" in Greek means "the Anointed." The name was given not always with respect, but sometimes with Greek humor, for they considered that the Nazarenes took themselves and their mission too seriously, and Greeks regarded the gods as beautiful symbols, when they regarded them at all, and at the worst they considered them not only nonexistent but risible. As the Nazarenes in Antioch—as elsewhere—seemed concerned only with an everlasting life beyond the grave, and anxiously sought to draw others to them below the Crucifix—a dire symbol in itself—and did not appear to be happy in the way of ordinary men, and did not sensually pursue pleasure and beauty, the Greeks either pitied them as men without the capacity for enjoyment and delight or impatiently shrugged and left them. Moreover, they were almost invariably Jews, and the Jews had a reputation for staring beyond the limits of the world and contemplating God, a dreary occupation.

*Gal. 2:20.

With the same attitude, but with somewhat less tolerance, the pragmatic Romans also regarded the Christians. They, to the Romans, had but one virtue: They paid their taxes in full, an astonishing phenomenon which even Romans did not practice. Beyond the puzzling virtue they seemed passive, too gentle, too peaceful, to not only the Romans but to the myriad races in Antioch, including Persians, Syrians, Egyptians and Indus, and thousands of dark-skinned, fierce-featured men of unknown desert tribes and to barbarians. True, there were not many Nazarenes, or Christians, in Antioch, but in some incredible manner they also seemed to be everywhere at once, inoffensive but insistent—lovingly insistent—and concerned, not with themselves or trade or gain or feastings or laughter, but with unworldly matters too bizarre and strange for the mind of a sensible man to understand. Their very inoffensiveness, their very soft and tentative smiles, annoyed those about them. Therefore, they were often publicly insulted, or cheated openly in their poor little shops, or exploited in many other ways. A slave who was also a Christian served with eager humility, thus earning the detestation of fellow slaves and the greater contempt of the master. It was known that a man might impetuously strike a Christian and the wretch would not even defend himself!

But the gentle water was beginning, in some slight measure, to make a matrix in the stone of humanity.

To this eastern city, then, this lusty, noisy, clamorous, dirty and heated city, had come Saul of Tarsus, to inspire and encourage the infant Church. He was something new to the Romans, and to the Greeks. He was a Jew with an impetuous aspect, contained but visible, a man of hauteur and pride and impatience, with a blazing blue glance, beardless, emanating a mysterious strength, and he was not a man of the lowly places but a man of learning and riches and power and urban confidence. His mane of red hair, now streaked with gray, commanded attention, as did his manner and his voice. There was something military about him, in his abrupt gestures, and in his assurance. It was rumored that he was a tentmaker and a weaver of goat's hair, something which the Romans rejected as absurd, as did the Greeks.

Here was a man neither meek nor mild, a man who

would not retreat a foot from another aggressive man, a man who could roar, a man capable of his own violence of speech and act. He was a Christian, but, of a certainty, not the sort of Christian extant in Antioch!

The Romans and others were not the only ones of this opinion. The Christians discovered this for themselves also, and not with entire happiness.

He came to the young Church in Antioch—that urinous city, that motley city of thieves and wayfarers and rascals and riches and slaves and opulence, as filthy as it was uproarious—and it was evident that he intended to take charge of the Church, and not merely to preach. It was first in Antioch that he said to the Christian community, "Though you have countless guides in Christ, you do not have many fathers. For I became your father in Christ Jesus through the Gospel. I urge you, then, be imitators of me. What do you wish? Shall I come to you with a rod, or with love in a spirit of gentleness?"*

His first quarrel with the community came as a result of his insistence that Gentile converts need not become Jews to accept Christ. The Jewish Christians, vastly in the majority, were vocally outraged, and in the presence of Gentiles who were drawn to them. To these Gentiles Saul said, "I wish those who unsettle you would mutilate themselves!" He was not less sarcastic to those Christians who insisted that to be a true follower of the Christ one must live as meekly and as inoffensively as a slave, for, as he later often and furiously repeated, "You gladly bear with fools, being wise yourselves! For you bear it if a man makes slaves of you, or preys upon you, or takes advantage of you, or puts on airs, or strikes you in the face!"†

To Saul, many of the Christians of Antioch were even more exasperating than some of the Nazarenes of Jerusalem. Too, the elders of the Church were offended by his short manner of disposing of their dissensions and intense scrupulosities. Young though the Church was it was already beset by a multitude of interpreters who shouted that they had received divine inspiration and that their opinions must be accepted or the offender suffer

*I Cor. 4:15–21.
†II Cor. 11:19–21.

hell-fire. Saul attacked these with a passion as devastating as it was ruthless.

He said to Lucanus, on the eve of the Greek's departure for Philippi: "In Jerusalem many of the earlier Nazarenes were of distinguished family and learning and education and erudition, men of travel and intellectual stature. But in Antioch we draw but the simple and illiterate and the dully obstinate."

Lucanus had had much more experience than Saul with the ignorant and humble, and knew, more than did Saul, that once these were given a petty authority they were more arrogant than a man born to great authority. He was also more compassionate, though less inclined to uncritical love. When Saul roared, alone with his friends in their miserable little rooms in a poor inn, Lucanus said, "Speak more gently with more conciliation, my Saul. And more slowly and in less learned terms. The humble mind is easily offended and fragile and inclined to unreasonable rages, and does not follow an intricate and rapid argument. Rather, it resents and derides the speaker because it does not understand him. Speak as if to unlettered children, in simple language and with less haste."

It was rumored among the Christians that Saul and Lucanus were men of considerable riches. Why, then, did they live so meagerly? Lucanus was a Greek and a Gentile, and Gentiles were often incomprehensible, but Saul was not only a Jew but a Pharisee. Therefore, he baffled the other Christians. It was known that both men gave lavishly of their money to the young Church and sent tithes to the Church in Israel, which was doubtless exemplary. But the charity of Saul did not excite affection among the Christians, nor gratitude. They had a communal society, did they not, where every man shared with his brother, and were not the poor, by the mere fact that they existed, entitled to the treasures of a rich man, earned or unearned? They believed this in all righteousness, though it was contrary to the teachings of some of the elders. They took umbrage when Saul shouted at them, as he had shouted before, "He who does not work, neither shall he eat!" (The Christians of Antioch, however, were less inclined to sit and wait for the imminent arrival of the Messias, and were more inclined to earn their bread.)

As for Lucanus, they were awed by him and his cool and aloof manner, for he was a "stranger." Many of the Jewish Christians still harbored a conviction that a Gentile was to be treated with restraint and some wariness, even if he was a Christian, too. "Respect but suspect," their simple forefathers had said of the Gentiles, and those descended of them were inclined to agree, still. The few Greeks and Syrians and other "strangers" among them were, on the other hand, given to wondering if gentle contempt for their fellow Gentile, who was rich yet did not condescend to them, the poor, but gave them of his purse as well as of his skill. They recalled that in Christian love he was impelled to do this, but as they were human as well as Christians it was somewhat incredible to them. The poor shared with the poor, but for a rich man to do so unsettled the simple and naïve, and decreased their respect.

Antioch was not only a city of seemingly unending heat and sun, where the black cobbled streets were as hot as fire at noon, but it was a city of walls in the Oriental manner, and secluded gardens and courtyards, behind those walls, and winding roads and stinking gutters and blazing white skies and dogs and camels and sheep and goats loose even on the streets, accompanied by geese and doves. It was also a city of markets, even more so than Jerusalem, and the rabble here was more turbulent and blasphemous and ribald in a dozen tongues, and impudent beyond endurance. It never slept at night; the night clamored with the flutes and harps and zithers and drums and wild laughter and yells and shrieks and barkings, and the taverns never closed and roisterers roamed the street all night in garments of a score of other nations. Roman guards never walked alone; there were always two or three or four of them at least. The men of Antioch spat at them and cursed them, but cheerfully and in a comradely spirit, and if the Romans smiled indulgently they were often, and immediately, invited to visit the nearest tavern with those who had just insulted them, and all entered with arms over shoulders. It was also an important port, on its broad river, and ships of many countries were always at anchor there, loading and unloading.

"You must admit it is a colorful city, even zestful,"

said Barnabas, who was somewhat inclined to find mitigating features no matter how deplorable the man, the town or the customs.

"It stinks," said Saul.

"I have heard it does not stink worse than Rome," said Barnabas.

The Christians met in abandoned ruins, on the outskirts of the city in fields, in quarries, in barns, in miserable little houses. When Saul suggested a House of God some of the elders, careful now of his temper, mentioned that the Lord had spoken of "a Temple not built of hands." That was another source of Saul's vexation: These people confused metaphor with reality. When the Lord had said that those "who hunger and thirst for justice would be satisfied," that was the clear reality He had promised in the world hereafter and after His Second Coming. But when He spoke in mysterious parables— however simple they appeared on first hearing—and in metaphor, many were confused and it was only the wise who could interpret to them, sometimes to their mutiny. Saul had less trouble with his fellow Christian Jews, for they were acquainted with the mysteries and the symbols of the Scriptures and the elusive words of the prophets, which required commentators. It was the converted heathen who obstinately clung to the word and not the spirit.

"The Lord," Saul would explain over and over, "spoke in Aramaic, not in Greek or Latin or Syrian or Persian or Egyptian or Parthian. It is a subtle tongue, full of inner meanings and versatility and symbols."

So, he bought an old inn for the Christians and removed walls and made of it a Temple and with the elders he sanctified it, and set up an altar, and the women made a cloth of coarse white linen for the altar and embroidered it lovingly, and there on the altar Saul set a fine pair of seven branched candelabra, bought from a Jewish merchant who sold good silver, and behind the altar was hung a tall gilt Crucifix. The Christians were at first doubtful, then proud of their temple.

It had been explained to them, even before Saul, that the consecration of the bread and the wine made them purely the flesh and blood of the Messias. But many remained doubtful. Some of the elders argued, "The Lord said, 'Do this in commemoration of Me!'" They brightened. Ahah! They looked at Saul with triumph. "It is but a symbol!" They swelled with pride; they had this haughty man at last.

Saul shook his great red head. "You are ready to accept symbols when you decide they are symbols. But this is a reality. The bread and the wine are indeed of the substance of the Lord. When spoken in Aramaic, in which He spoke only, His words do not mean 'imitation' or symbol. They mean a repeated truth."

"That is true," said the Jewish Christians, nodding their heads. This immediately provoked a noisy argument between them and their fellow Christians who did not know Aramaic and, deplorably, there was some shaking of upraised fists. Saul found humor in the situation, and watched indulgently. They were good and harmless men. They would not actually strike each other—would they? When one did he banished the man for a period of five days, and the others were ashamed and prayed that he be forgiven.

While Saul was an organizer and an interpreter and the high priest, Barnabas was the teacher, happy and cheerful, loving and forgiving, gentle and kind. He often averted some transgression from coming to Saul's fierce attention, and some sinner given a harsh and crushing rebuke. Sometimes, in a mood of despondency, common with him, Saul would confess to Barnabas that the Law of God was perfect, but it was most evident that man is not capable of following it. Consider even me, he would say, who have had the ineffable Grace of a vision, a direct confrontation with the Messias, and have been taught directly by Him, and not through the words of men. I do not understand my own actions. "For I do not do what I want but I do the very thing I hate. I do not do the good I want, but the evil I do not want is what I do. For I delight in the Law of God, in my inmost self, but I see in my members another law at war with the law of my mind and making me captive to the law of sin which dwells in my members. Wretched man that I am! What will deliver me from this body of death?"*

"We are all sinners," said Barnabas, sadly.

"But we should not be sinners!" cried Saul. "Alas, that

*Rom. 7:15–25.

I reproach these poor creatures when I am worse than they! For I was mightily blest and saw with my own eyes."

"It is the conflict of our spirit with our flesh," Barnabas urged. "God, blessed be His Name, understands this. Our little victories are not small to Him. They are blessed and great and received with love, for He knows how dearly they have cost us.

"Baptism removed our inherited sin," said Barnabas. "We—"

"We continue to sin merrily," said Saul, that most unmerry man.

But the power of his voice, the marvelous eloquence of his teachings, his intuitive understanding, his vast sincerity and passion, and the fact that he was rich and learned, finally overcame the wariness of the Christians, gathered them together in a firm and enlightened body, drove lingering superstitions from them, enhanced their love of God and man, gave them courage and zeal. They never came to give him their confidences—those were reserved for the tender Barnabas—but they trusted Saul as they did no other man and when he urged them to go out among the heathen and bring them to the Messias they felt their spirits uplifted and their resolution exalted.

"Be just and kind and mild and loving, speak always with honor and truth, stand like a shining pillar in the darkness, be honorable and temperate of speech and manner, be joyful that others may know your joy, avoid open or private sin, pray always, and let your countenances speak of the miracle which Our Lord has wrought in your souls. So you will draw others to you, in wonder, to be enlightened, and to be saved. This is an evil world. He who can point the way to peace and justice and salvation and everlasting joy and love is a messenger of good tidings, a servant of God. For he comes, asking not for money or position or favor himself. He asks only happiness for the souls of others. This alone is a stupendous request, before which all men must stand in amazement and awe, for never was it offered before."

So in their labor, and in their leisure, the Christians zealously proselyted as they had not proselyted before, with a fervor and a persistence which pleased even Saul.

He thought of them as his children, and he as their father, and he loved them with all his heart:

Even when they vexed him, which was nearly always. Knowing his own imperfection, he could not endure the imperfections of others. He despised them in himself and in them.

Chapter 42

SAUL left his grim little shop where he sold the products of his loom and made his way through the riotous and clamorous city to the house of the famous Egyptian physician, Khefren, who was a friend and colleague of Lucanus. He had met the physician before, a tall and subtle man with a perpetually amused and sardonic expression, and a pale brown skin and mysterious slanted eyes, and thin black hair which appeared painted on his narrow skull. He had long and exotic hands and he colored the palms red and his nails were tinted and he gave the impression of being not only very wise but fastidious and rich, all of which he was. It was not possible to guess his age; he could have been forty and again, in some lights, he appeared old. His beard was short and pointed and sleek with perfumed oil.

Once Saul had discerned him in company with Lucanus when he, Saul, had preached in the new poor Temple which the Christians regarded so pridefully. He had stood among the sweating crowds and the red sunset light had streamed over his dark face but had revealed nothing except interest in his black eyes. He was dressed richly but quietly in deep crimson and gray robes with a sleeveless vest of intense and brocaded blue and a short coat of white silk embroidered with gold threads. Every finger bore a valuable ring and there was a fringed necklace of delicate gold about his throat and one jeweled earring in his right ear. Though he was an Egyptian he had placed a small turban of crimson, blue and white upon his head, and many were the timid glances, wary and tentative, cast on him by the poor Christians of Antioch gathered together to worship and to partake of the Body and the Blood of their Lord in communal love.

When the offering basket was passed among the congregation Khefren had carelessly dropped into it a costly jeweled ring and a handful of gold Roman sesterces. Those near him had gasped at this treasure. But he had stood like a preoccupied Pharoah in their midst, and appeared to muse upon what Saul had said. Then he had disappeared as the communicants had walked humbly and prayerfully to the altar to receive their blessing and the Sacrament.

Twice later he had appeared, and always he departed with that bemused expression.

Saul had said to Lucanus, "Your friend, the Egyptian physician, seems impressed by what I say, and the words of Barnabas. Is it possible he will become a Christian?"

"I think not," said Lucanus, with that pale cold smile of his which Saul could never understand. "He considers you a magnificent orator. You interest him. He is not only a physician but a student of many religions and the mind of man."

There was something in his manner which indicated that he would prefer not to discuss his friend, and Saul did not intrude. However, he heard frequently of Khefren's genius as a physician, and so tonight he made his way through the seething and noisy throngs to the house of Khefren, which was guarded by yellow stone walls and an iron gate and two men in livery who looked at his poor garb without favor and crossed spears barring him from the gate. The scarlet sunlight splashed on the walls and on the stony street and the air was rank and hot.

Saul said impatiently, "I know the illustrious physician, your master, and I beg of you to inform him that Saul of Tarsus wishes to consult him."

The guards were contemptuous. But one said, "He does not receive patients at this hour and only in the morning. Nor does he receive those who cannot pay."

Then Saul fixed them with his terrible blue eyes and coldly repeated his request and one guard scuttled away while the other, vaguely frightened, stood with his spear pointed warningly at Saul's breast. Then the second guard returned with a confused look, nodded to his companion, and they reluctantly opened the gate and admitted him to a beautiful cool garden with fountains and lanterns newly lighted and to the distant sound of a harp. He walked up the red gravel path to the portico, where the white columns glowed in the sunset, and there a slave awaited him who bent before him in the Eastern manner touching his forehead and then his lips and then his chest, as if Saul were an honored visitor. He conducted him to the wide atrium where a small fountain, exotically perfumed, splashed water like crystal into the air. Here Khefren met him, bowing, then holding out his hands. He smiled and said to Saul in Aramaic, "Shalom. Greetings and welcome to this house, Saul of Tarsus."

He clapped his hands and a slave appeared and he ordered wine and refreshments. Saul said, "I come as a patient, Khefren, not as a guest."

Khefren smiled. "But I receive you as a guest. Be seated, I pray you."

Saul sat in a Roman chair of ebony inlaid with nacre and ivory. He was hot and weary and dusty, and the luxury about him brought to his mind how arduous was his life. He drank of the spiced wine served to him in a silver goblet enameled in blue and gold and red, and ate a few sweetmeats and slowly his exhaustion left him. In the meanwhile Khefren spoke amusingly and lightly of Antioch and the news from Rome, which he found risible. His sardonic expression more and more detached him from the follies and stupidity of mankind and Saul uneasily thought of him as a spectator rather than a participant in life. In comparison with Khefren's garb his own seemed the miserable garments of a slave or a laborer in the country. Once he thought he saw, somewhat to his vexation, that Khefren was obliquely regarding him with satire.

"You have said, Saul ben Hillel, that you have come to me as a patient," said Khefren at last. "Is that not extraordinary? I have heard some of you Christians say that all illnesses are 'sins,' and that only evil men are subject to the torments of the body."

Saul's face became irascible. He put down his goblet on a fine lemonwood table. "They *will* misinterpret!" he exclaimed. "Because Our Lord, when performing a miracle, said to the sick, 'Rise and sin no more,' they believe that He meant that physicians were no longer needed and that a good man would not suffer the diseases of the flesh! They do not realize that He had performed a two-fold miracle, each separate from the other: Forgiveness of their sins as men, and a cure for their body. Each was a distinct marvel. Only last night a man covered with sores and in pain came to our Temple, and there were many who wished to drive him from the congregation, saying, 'He is a sinner, and therefore anathema, for other-wise the sores would not have afflicted him!' Yet I know him for a timid and gentle Syrian who has a blacksmith shop. I rebuked my people, but they glared at him sullenly and later three of the elders accosted me and disputed with me." Saul reflected. "I am afraid that I hoped that they, too, might be afflicted in some manner as a punishment for their presumption."

Khefren laughed lightly, then said, "If this new Jewish sect spreads, then woe to us physicians! We will be degraded to the status of mere servants, and hardly tolerated."

Dismayed, Saul contemplated this thought, and his red brows frowned and met over his eyes. He rubbed his chin. "Surely," he said, "men are not as stupid as that."

Khefren said, "My dear Saul. There is no limit to the stupidity of mankind, and to the results of that stupidity. All changes, but the nature of man. That is the great immutable. Nations may fall into rubble but out of the ruins comes man again, cursed or endowed with his ancient faults and character, and he sedulously builds once more to watch, once more, the fall of what he has built. I find that very amusing."

"A man's nature can be changed," said Saul, who found the conversation disturbing, "but only through the power of Christ Jesus, and the mercy of God, blessed be His Name. In his flesh man is divided from himself and from his brother. This is the spiritual death of which Our Lord spoke, for death is sin and sin is death. God did not intend this so; man willed it for himself, and Our Lord would save him from the corruption, and the tragedy."

"So I have heard you say," said Khefren. "The thought is not new. Before you were as a nation we Egyptians expounded that through our learned priests. So do the Indus. So did the Chinese and many others. Do you think it unique? God, or Ptah, as we Egyptians call Him, loves —it is said—all His children and would redeem them. It is our obstinacy and our dull souls which reject Him. You new Christians speak of the Golden Rule, but long before your Messias spoke that to you your Jewish fathers declared, 'What is hurtful to yourself, do not do to your fellow man.' We Egyptians say, 'That nature only is good when it shall not do unto another whatever is not good for its own self.' The Indus say, 'In five ways should a man minister to his friends and familiars—by generosity, courtesy and benevolence, by treating them as he treats himself.' Therefore, it is obvious that Ptah, the Father Almighty, Creator of heaven and earth and gods and men, loves and teaches all His creatures."

He smiled and continued, "Is it not true, then, that your Messias belongs to all men, who recognize Him dimly in all their religions, as well as you Christians?"

"True," said Saul, and frowned, reflecting. Then he said, "But we wish all men to recognize the Messias fully and come to Him for their salvation and their change of soul."

Khefren said, "What is it that ails you, Saul ben Hillel?"

Saul was vaguely affronted. He replied, "I have an itch of the body, and some boils on my back. I have had them for many weeks and they now interfere with my rest."

Khefren smiled again. "And you have not prayed them from your flesh?"

Saul gave his sharp boisterous laugh and rose and accompanied the Egyptian to his pharmacy. He stripped his clothing from his broad back and Khefren looked upon the bleeding and inflamed soreness on his skin and the oozing of it. He took a large jar of some golden powder from his shelf and dusted it over the inflammation. At once the itch and heat and pain subsided and Saul gave a deep sigh of relief. Khefren poured some of the powder into a pouch and laid it near Saul's hand.

"This will ease you. But it will not cure you," said the Egyptian. "The affliction is in your mind. Tell me. What is it in your life which so irritates and disturbs and exasperates you, that the heat of your thoughts and your anger torment your flesh? And destroy your hours of rest and appears in the form of pus?"

Saul was startled. He knew that Jewish physicians had

long expounded that the sores and agonies of the soul would often appear visibly in the flesh, and in madness. But he had forgotten. Slowly, he put on his garments, thinking. Then he said with that abrupt confiding manner of his, "My people vex me, for how often I explain, 'As in Adam all die, so also in Christ shall all be made alive,' they do not attempt to understand. Many believe that I mean that customary death of the body will not occur to them, if they profess the Messias and trust in His promises, and that they will live eternally in the world without first the intervention of normal expiring. Did not the Messias save them from the death of Adam? Therefore, they will not die! Oh, there are many such fallacies among my people, and I lose my patience and I brood and wonder if this generation will ever comprehend."

Khefren made a slight and indulgent gesture with his long and slender dark hand. "Why will you not accept the normal stupidity and blindness and obtuseness of man as part of his being? Why will you, yourself, not understand that few can comprehend you, and that others must be guided like little dull children? Did you think your Messias suddenly endowed all who listen to Him with extraordinary intelligence and understanding? Did you not say, yourself, that your Messias asked, 'Who, by taking thought, can add one cubit to his stature?' In short, a man is born with inherent capacities, and if those capacities are small and feeble no 'taking thought' will increase them."

"We Jews believe that a man can indeed increase his wisdom by learning," said Saul, uneasy again.

"He can only understand to the limit of his capacity, and in the majority of men that capacity is meager," said the Egyptian. "We, in Egypt, have a learned and aristocratic class of priests, for we are older than you and infinitely wiser, and for the simple we have amulets and prescribed invocations and gestures, but for the wiser by birth we have other words, and other rituals, and for the wisest we have introductions to the Mysteries. We, in mercy, understand that though all souls are equal before God, in the matter of the divine Law, every soul is unique and entirely different from all other souls, in stature, in wisdom, and in comprehension. Some souls remain children forever. Others grow, for they have the capacity to grow, given to them by Ptah, the Father Almighty. Woe to you Christians, Saul ben Hillel, if your teachers ever proclaim that all mēn are equal in measure of soul and understanding and intelligence! If that comes to pass, then your faith will disintegrate and confusion abound." He smiled his sardonic smile. "I believe you should hearken to your Messias rather than to your own hopes, Saul ben Hillel. Then perhaps your afflictions will disappear. Do not expect more of the ordinary man than he has the endowment to give."

He walked with Saul to the atrium again. "It is suffi- cient, surely," he said, "for a man to be harmless, and harmlessness is not an attribute of man. Rather, he is a wild beast. Teach him peace; teach him not to harm. That is a prodigious task in itself!"

"I pray I can bring you to the Messias," said Saul.

The physician was both astonished and amused. "My dear friend!" he exclaimed. "We Egyptians knew of Him long before the Israelites heard of Him through their prophets! Of a certainty, in your ages of exile in Egypt your wise men absorbed the knowledge of Him by way of our priests and our wise men. Does not our Osiris, mur- dered by intransigent man, not rise when the spring is in spate and speak again to his people? Does he not offer again his salvation and his peace? Jehovah has a thousand names, and through each He speaks to His children. I urge you once more: Speak of love and harmlessness and peace to your people, and however you name Him, He is One. To each generation, to each people, He speaks eter- nally."

The Egyptian looked through the white portals of the atrium to the purple twilight. He said, "He is but One, blessed be His Name, and to those who adore Him, no matter the name they give Him, He is forever the same."

Saul's heart swelled and he trembled. Before he could speak Khefren said, "Speak to the ignorant. Tell them of Him. For the world is full of Godless and wretched men, as always it will be, and take the slight harvest of men's hearts with rejoicing, for even that harvest is blessed to Him."

He looked at Saul and his eyes became opaque. "I am subject to visions," he said, "and often they are unwel- come. But I will tell you: There are races unknown to you now who will hear your voice through the ages, for never have they known the Holy One, and they live like beasts, worshiping animals and trees and stones, and the elements. To them will you bring your revelation, though they are not yet born. I tell you: The sun rises west."

Saul was tremendously moved. He said, "We are of the same people."

The Egyptian shook his head. "Ah, no. We Egyptians are of the Hebraic races. But you Jews are not. You are universal, and are of no race, or all. In that is your destiny and your despair and, perhaps, your ultimate triumph among those you call the heathen. For only the universal man can speak to all nations and to all races, and through you will men accept your Messias."

Seeing that Saul, dejected, shook his head the physician touched his shoulder with his hand. "Be not dismayed," he said gently. "What began obscurely in dust and blood you will make glorious in the sight of men."

Again Saul shook his head, and now he bit his lip, and then he exclaimed, "How they insist, the foolish ones, that the Lord is a small sniveling person like themselves, and how they emphasize His meekness! He is not masculine, strong, powerful, massive and terrible in His wrath, a monumental figure! Ah, that diminishes them! They will not understand that His meekness consisted in offering Himself as the Lamb of God, without resistance, in their behalf. They insist on their own meekness, and see it as holy stature instead of pusillanimity, because they lack strength of spirit. They make of their weakness a virtue, of their failings an offering, and they peek and peer modestly in what they believe is an imitation of the Divine Lord! Are these the warriors of God? No! They think servility is mildness, and timid speech praiseworthy, and lack of pride love. Above all, He desired to be adored by free men, free in their choice of Him, but these are not free!"

"Ah," said Khefren, "you are harsh," but lines of laughter deepened about his eyes. Then he become sober. "I should like to warn you, my friend. Jews, wherever they live, move discreetly, in the majority, about the Romans. They are wise. They do not dispute with the Romans, or any man, except in the courts of law. They avert their heads when passing alien temples, but they do not spit upon its steps, nor do they speak in public contempt of those who bring incense and offering to strange altars. They ask only that the same respect given by them to the religion of others be extended to them also, and few have challenged them. That, too, is wise.

"But I have heard that your Christians are beginning to denounce 'heathen gods' before the very temple porticoes. I have heard that some have entered those temples and have overthrown the statues, before the faces of the worshipers. They dispute with those worshipers and frighten women and girls. They call down the wrath of God upon those who adore 'false idols.' Out of their weakness, as you call it, has come arrogance, and is not that always the story of weak men?

"The Greeks laugh at their gods, but they feel that in the beauty and grace of their gods lies their own glory. The Romans do not believe in their gods, but the gods represent their country. A man's pride in his past and in his nation is a powerful thing, and woe to that man who belittles it. Even now the Romans have begun to eye your Christians with disfavor, and the disfavor of a Roman can become dangerous—and fatal. Do your people court death and torture and exile zealously? No sane man does that. Therefore, warn your people to be temperate in their zeal, and not to offend, and not to insult the gods of others. In short, let them practice what they preach, and exercise a measure of tolerance."

Saul stared at him in consternation. "I have not heard of these things!"

"Nevertheless, they are true. The Romans are inclined to tolerance of religions, as you know, and there are Romans among your Christians, and Greeks also, and many others. But these are now more aggressive than your Jewish Christians! They are offending men where their emotions lie the deepest and are the most primal."

Saul's back began to itch and heat again, and he moved his shoulders restlessly. "I have told them a thousand times or more that faith is a gift of God and that no man can force another to believe against his will. I have said to them, 'Though I speak with the tongues of men and of angels, and have not charity, I am become as sounding brass or a tinkling cymbal. And though I have the gift of prophecy, and understand all mysteries, and all knowledge, and though I have faith, so that I could move mountains, and have not charity, I am nothing. And though I bestow all my goods to feed the poor, and though I give my body to be burned, and have not charity, it profits me nothing. Charity suffers long and is kind. Charity envies not, charity vaunts not itself, is not puffed up. Charity does not behave itself unseemly, seeks not her own, is not easily provoked, thinks no evil. And now abide faith, hope, charity, these three, but the greatest of these is charity.' So I have spoken. Has it come to nothing?"

"You are dealing with men, alas," said Khefren.

"I forget, always," said Saul.

Dispirited again, and again with considerable despair, he returned to his lonely little chamber in the poor inn, and sat down, his hands hanging between his knees, his head bent. Occasionally his old fiery anger against mankind seized him and shook him. Only last night had he admonished several of his people not to boast that they had the gift of tongues, and had been touched by Pentecostal fire. Worse, they insisted they could prophesy. They had gazed at him mutinously, though with their usual fear. "God has given to men many gifts, blessed be His Name," he had said, "and none is poor in His sight. You who can teach are blest, those of you who can administer are also blest, and those who labor for God are blest, and some can only show in quiet lives and tender devotion and obscurity and love of neighbor Who has changed their hearts. But is not that the greatest of blessedness? We are members of each other, and not one member is the lesser."

He saw, alas, that many desired, above all else, to be singular, to stand before others for their awe, because of implied superiority in their faith. Could it be that it was these who were beginning to provoke the Romans and those of other religions in Antioch, and perhaps in many scattered nations where they had gone to live and to preach? Saul shuddered. When Barnabas returned from the Temple Saul questioned him. Barnabas' cheerful face changed, but he said at once, "We must not forget their humanity."

With bitterness Saul replied, "Their 'humanity' can cost them their lives, or at the least the tolerance of others, and what will that avail them and the Church? I tell you, I am filled with foreboding."

"Let us not be distressed," said the other man. But Saul had begun to smile grimly as he remembered, from far days, what Rabban Gamaliel had said, that God should be consulted before men offered martyrdom to Him, and that God did not seek victims, however devout, though He loved the intention. He, Saul, had felt rebellion at the Rabban's words. Now he understood.

He said to Barnabas, who was watching him anxiously, "I have medicine for my sores. Dust my back with it." He smiled at Barnabas then and said, "It is my anger and my impatience with our people that has given me the boils of Job. What a generation is this!"

Chapter 43

"I HAVE fought the good fight," said Saul to himself, "I have run the race."

He had just returned from a brief visit to Jerusalem where he had hotly engaged Simon Peter in the fulminating argument concerning heathen converts to the Faith. Simon Peter had insisted that "the heathen" must first become Jews before being admitted to Christianity, but Saul had prevailed in spite of the bitter antagonism of the Apostles, and their earlier open contempt of him. He saw that they still distrusted him, both Jews and Christians. To them he was still "the great renegade." But he called upon God to sustain him and with his eloquence and the power of his compelling voice he had finally convinced Simon Peter and the others, though not without some dark glances and sullen grimaces.

He wrote to a friend: "The Gospel of the uncircumcision was committed to me, as the Gospel of the circumcision was given to Peter, for He that·wrought effectually in Peter to the Apostleship of the circumcision the Same was mighty in me toward the Gentiles.—I withstood Peter to the same, because he was to be blamed, for he did eat with the Gentiles but when they were come to him he withdrew and separated himself, fearing them which were of the circumcision. I said to Peter, 'If you, being a Jew, live after the manner of the Gentiles, and not as do the Jews, why do you compel the Gentiles to live as do the Jews? We who are Jews by nature, and not sinners as the Gentiles.' "*

Faith, to Saul, was the only thing necessary for a man to have to be admitted to the worship of the Messias, and to the Law. For faith was a gift of God, and a man of faith had been marked as His own.

In Antioch he had at length prevailed on his people that they must not be intemperate in their actions and speeches to others, not antagonize men in an unseemly and unnecessary manner, in an effort to bring them to Christ. Zeal was splendid, but excess was dangerous both to the faith and to themselves. Rather, a man should labor diligently and speak kindly. By the time Saul had attained some success—but not until his own wild shows of anger and disgust—there were many in the Church of Antioch who were Gentiles of scores of races, and a considerable portion were men of learning and culture and wealth. They had come to listen to "the Jewish prophet," out of idleness or curiosity, and they had remained to pray with him. For the God of the Jews was not licentious, cruel, depraved and voluptuous, nor was He capricious and unstable, inclined to favor without reason and to revenge without reason. He was to be feared because He was the Almighty, and all things were in His hand, but He was not to be feared because He was intemperate and malicious and unpredictable or violent, as were their own gods. He could not be placated or cajoled by amulets, sacrifices or superstitions. He desired only contrition and a faith in Him, and on those who trusted Him—and even those who did not—He lavished mercy and loving kindness and eternal happiness and justice. A God whom a man could trust! A God who moved in light, and not in darkness! A God who was as simple as water and as mysterious as all life and death! A God who cared about men! Was not that astounding—that a God should care about that miserable little creature who lived one day and was destroyed the next, seemingly as the grass died? He listened to the whisper of a child as intently as He listened to the cry of a thousand men before His altar! None

*Gal. 2.

could escape His love and His salvation, if a man only accepted these treasures.

To men who feared and distrusted their own gods, who lived in terror of them, or who did not believe in them at all because of their wantonness and malice and cruelty toward each other and mankind, the message was unique, astonishing, dazzling, filled with hope, exhilarating, incredible.

But Saul made Him credible to them. Even the cultured and the wise became convinced, though not as early as did the credulous and the humble. The Church in Antioch prospered. Then Saul knew in his soul that he must leave the Church there, for the sandy soil had been replaced by rock, priests had been ordained, converts were sought with love and responded. Truly, in much less than twenty years since the Crucifixion the harvest had increased and the laborers also, and the Gospel had spread even to Rome and Athens, in little quiet colonies, and to Egypt, and other lands. It insistently crept like a small, unassuming plant filled with purple blossoms, and it covered the aridity of the soil of men's lives and made fragrant their arduous duties and more bearable their pain and their slavery under Rome and her taxes.

Here in Saul was a man who had, in a single moment, been lifted from persecution to adoration, and who spoke of it in a voice like a passionate and musical bell. It was impossible to doubt that he had seen what he had seen, whether he spoke in truth or in madness. If mad, it was a glorious madness, preferable to sanity. If truth—then the narrow horizon widened infinitely and brightened with the gold of hope and eternity. He cried to them, holding out his hands as if offering gifts, "If Christ be not risen, then our faith is in vain!" And they knew that He had died and had risen, and faith touched their hearts with a hot silver finger and they cried out in exultation, and in answer.

He appeared to have inexhaustible energy, though none guessed it was the energy of his spirit and not of his weary flesh. Even his afflicted eye possessed power and gave him an inscrutable expression at times when he was most eloquent. If his face was haggard, if the white streaks in his red hair broadened almost visibly from month to month, few saw it, for all were entranced by his commanding tones, his imperial if impatient gestures, and then his sudden wide smile which was at once knowing, satirical, amused, wry and jovial. His laughter to them was a leonine roar of hearty mirth, masculine and strong and as free as the wind. And when he rebuked or condemned, they trembled.

To the Greeks who said that the life of a Christian appeared dismal and self-denying to them, and not of humanity and of human joy, he would say, "Our faith not only rescues us from a spiritual death, but it gives us a greater joy in our present lives, an ecstasy of internal being not found in worldly delights or sensual experiences. To a man who loves God there is none else, and no greater rapture, for the world both within and without is transformed into glory and radiant color and music." To the pragmatic Romans who said that Saul's God did not appear to offer much in tangible gifts, he said, "He who did not spare His own Son but gave Him up for us all, will He not also give us all things with Him? —We are more than conquerors through Him Who loved us."* To a Roman centurion who laughed jocularly and who asked if Saul's God would give the Romans conquest over the infernal Parthians if they accepted Him, Saul replied, "He is the God of the Parthians also, and loves them," a reply which mystified the Roman and made him shake his head. Gods were participants in battles. They favored one side or the other, but not both simultaneously. Surely the gods were on the side of the Romans who brought order and law to the barbarians, and defended Rome, and not with the enemy who would destroy it all. "God is no Respecter of persons," said Saul. "He is concerned only with a man's heart and soul," a reply which made the centurion muse and shake his head. He was convinced the Jew was demented. He said to Saul, "You live poorly and miserably, though I have heard you are a rich man. Surely your life is painful, and your death will be wretched."

Saul answered that death had not simply been made acceptable but had been destroyed in a fire of Love. "This new life is not our own, but Christ's, and it is so for we are part of Him."

But to the Roman and other Gentiles like him life after death was a poor thing as a shade bereft of human sen-

*Rom. 8:31–39.

suality. Not one seer had reported that the manes of the dead appeared happy, but always gloomy and melancholy, even those allegedly from the Elysian Fields or the Blessed Isles. All longed to be men again. But the Christians gazed at this life not with pleasure and intense concentration, as was normal with men, but with eyes fixed eagerly on an unimaginable heaven. To many of the Gentiles they appeared madmen. Men who repudiated this world of delight could only be against it. So they began to regard the Christians with suspicion, as haters of men. Therefore, the Christians were dangerous. Whispers rose that they worshiped the head of an ass and had obscene rites, offensive to the gods, and that they performed criminal private ceremonies, and blasphemed and that they plotted some mysterious attack on their fellow men through evil incantations.

Saul heard some of this but with no misgivings until he received a letter from his cousin, Titus Milo Platonius, now General of the Praetorian Guards in Rome, and stationed and living on the Palatine.

Though the letter was importantly sealed with his own seal, and bound with silken threads, and brought to Saul by a personal messenger, Milo was cautious in his references to the reigning emperor, Tiberius Claudius Nero Germanicus Caesar, nephew of the now dead Tiberius Caesar, for it was Claudius who had such a respect for the Praetorians that he had greatly increased their numbers and had given them a large and rich reward for their fidelity. (But, after all, it was the Praetorians who had elected him, he not being of the Julian gens.) "He is not the fool the Augustales privately declare he is," wrote Milo, "and has much learning, which cannot be said of many of the Augustales. He has given importance to freedmen, who are haughty and disdainful in the very face of the patricians. I believe that the Emperor enjoys their discomfiture and silent wrath. He is married, for the fourth time, to Agrippina, his own niece, which further inflames the Augustales and some of the old-fashioned Romans, and it is whispered that she is attempting to prevail on him to put aside his own son, Britannicus, in favor of her son by a former marriage (to Gnaeus Domitius Ahenobarbus), a handsome fair youth called L. Domitius Ahenobarbus whom some refer to as Nero. Whether the Empress will succeed or not is the subject of gossip in Rome, for Britannicus is a youth of remarkable qualities and able leadership and virtues, and Nero, though beguiling and full of charm and of a sweet voice and with a face which even Apollo would envy, is not of the character of Britannicus nor with his fortitude. Ah, well, I suppose you have heard of these matters. As a soldier, I am prudent and serve the Emperor and do not spread scandal. To do otherwise is not to be a soldier, with a soldier's discipline.

"My dear cousin, you will remember that my dead Emperor, Tiberius, was not inclined to favor the Eastern religions, and destroyed a temple to Isis—which the present Emperor has rebuilt. However, there lingers in Rome a distrust of Eastern religions. The Jews were once quite zealous in proselyting in Rome, but on discovering Tiberius' displeasure they desisted in overt attempts at conversion. This was very wise.

"But now we have many Christians in Rome, poor gentle people in the majority, who live and work in the noisome sections of the Trans Tiber. Most of them are former Jews, though they have gathered about them and converted many barbarians, slaves, miserable freedmen, starveling shopkeepers and laborers and workers in the manufactories. They have lived quietly amid their teachers and the evangelists from Israel, and have been dutiful and meek and industrious, and, up to very recently they have aroused no antagonism though considerable amusement, and have been accused of worshiping an ass's head.

"As a Christian, myself, I have sent them large gifts of money as the majority live in desperate poverty, for even the Christian Jews do not have the vitality and independence and strength of spirit of the 'old' Jews. I send them these gifts through a trusted young Praetorian, for it would not be seemly for a Praetorian General to alleviate the sufferings of what are referred to as 'the Eastern rabble,' though the present Emperor is indifferent to them.

"But two weeks ago the Christians aroused great anger in Rome. Devotees of Cybele met at her temple and then carried the goddess through the streets in a gilded chair, arrayed in gold and crimson. Romans believe in no gods, except for the 'old' Romans and elderly patriots, but they are afraid of them, and superstitious, and placate all the gods they encounter in processions or when they pass their temples. The procession of Cybele was very impressive, with many devotees in the parade, and all playing on zithers, harps and lutes and flutes and strange Eastern instruments. Multitudes halted to watch in pleasure, if not in reverence.

"The procession was just approaching the Via Appia when suddenly there was a surge in the crowd and about a hundred men appeared, flaming with righteous anger and with fiery eyes, and they screamed, 'Woe, woe to the harlot, Rome, and her abominations and her wicked gods and idols! For she is accursed and the wrath of God is about to fall upon her!' The populace was astonished. The procession stopped short, and the music halted, and there was one vast indrawing of breath in amazement. Even Senators in their litters, on the way to the Senate, commanded that their bearers wait so that they could observe the confusion through their silken curtains.

"This would have been outrageous enough, but the Christians—for it was they—burst into the procession, seized the image of the goddess, Cybele, and smashed her in the running gutters, screaming the while, 'Let all idolatry be destroyed, and the Kingdom of God be proclaimed while there is yet time before Rome is leveled to the ground!' They trampled the gilded chair and the draperies in their gasping violence. Women and children screamed and men roared their fury. It happened in a twinkling. Then the Christians fled and seemingly dissolved into the very walls, and none could be found, though many pursued them with sticks and stones. The devotees of Cybele fell on their faces and their knees and wailed that their goddess would seek revenge for this outrage to her divinity, and that Rome, indeed, was in deadly danger. Thousands listened to them and shivered, and muttered imprecations on the 'blasphemers.'

"Were this but a single incident it would soon be forgotten, but others have occurred if not in so spectacular a fashion. The Roman mob is very excitable, and loves riots and confusions, for their lives, as the conquerors of the world, is very dull. They adore scandal and rumor. Scores have ranged through the Trans Tiber, and on finding Christians they have severely beaten them before the very faces of the guards, who look aside. After all, it is thought, it creates amusement, and diversion, and if Romans have a victim they will not be so rebellious before the taxgatherers.

"I have secretly talked to many of the elders among the Christians—having them brought to my house on the Palatine at midnight—and have expressed to them my alarm and dismay, and my own anger, for the rioters have endangered their fellow Christians. The elders agreed with me, and deplored the excessive zeal of their flocks and have promised to calm and discipline them. I trust they will be effective.

"As so many of the Christians are former Jews the Jewish community in Rome is greatly alarmed at these demonstrations, for they know that the Romans will not, if enraged, make any distinction between the 'old' Jews and the Christians. I sympathize with their apprehension and fear, and have attempted to soothe them and have talked to them in Aramaic. But unfortunately this has further alarmed them, for am I not a Roman Praetorian, and possibly am I not a spy? As an imaginative people, they see monstrous enemies about them, as in the past, and for a time many of them dared not leave their houses. Even the prominent citizens among them, and their rabbis, tremble with dread. Is it not deplorable that a few heedless zealots can bring calamity to their law-abiding fellows? And, is it not unjust and sorrowful? I fear for both the Christians and the Jews.

"I long to see you again, my dear cousin. Perhaps you might find it in your heart to visit Rome and calm our fellow Christians, and inspire them to more restraint."

Saul read this letter with horror and foreboding. Those who adored the Prince of Peace were proclaiming Him with violence, fury and turbulence! True, it was possible that they were not in the majority, but a few could bring disaster on the many and the innocent. (Saul thought of the Zealots and the Essenes in Israel who had brought down slaughter and massacres on their fellow Jews in the streets of Jerusalem, because they lacked control of their emotions and sought to reform a whole world in one act of immoderate ferocity.) Were they deliberately seeking martyrdom? If so, they were mad. Or were they trying to call universal attention to their faith, and their presence among the populace? If so, they were mad, indeed, for an attention which is enraged and bloodthirsty is worse than no attention at all.

He pondered for a long while, then wrote to the elders and deacons of the Church in Rome, rebuking them that they had lost control over several of their members. He wrote:

"Let every soul be subject to the higher powers. For there is no power but of God: *the powers that be are ordained of God.* Whosoever, then, resists the power, resists the ordinance of God, and they that resist shall receive to themselves damnation. For rulers are not a terror to good works, but to the evil. Will you then not be afraid of the power? Do that which is good and you shall have praise of the same. For he is the minister of God to you for good, but if you do that which is evil, be afraid, for he bears not a sword in vain. He is the minister of God, a revenger to execute wrath upon him who does evil.

"Therefore, you must need be subject, not only for wrath, but also for conscience' sake. For, for this cause pay you tribute also— Render therefore to all their dues, tribute to whom tribute is due, custom to whom custom, fear to whom fear, honor to whom honor.

"Owe no man any thing, but love one another, for he who loves another has fulfilled the law. —Love works no ill to his neighbor, therefore love is the fulfilling of the Law. —Let us walk honestly, as in the day, not in rioting and drunkenness, not in chambering and wantonness, not in strife—"*

It was not a letter the younger Saul, who had burned with hatred for the Romans and had rejoiced at the exploits of the Essenes and the Zealots, would have written. But now he saw that the evil which lives in man cannot be destroyed by an answering evil, and only by patience, faith, love and endless striving for peace and conciliation. The sword was no substitute for enlightenment and justice. The mission of the Christians was salvation, not violence, God, not secular affairs, spiritual joy, not physical force, an empire of the soul and not of human ordinances. That man who had not first conquered himself and his passions—however righteous he considered them—was a desperate danger to his own soul and the souls of his fellows.

*Rom. 13:1–13.

This did not mean that a good man should be as milk and water. He should be as fine wine, invigorating, consoling, brightening, thirst-quenching and inducing fellowship. Above all, he should transmit joy, and the love which is the heart of joy.

He left Antioch, with Barnabas, for Corinth, feeling that the Church in Antioch was flourishing and prosperous, and needed him no longer.

Chapter 44

SAUL, who had been born in a hot and fervid country and had lived and worked in others equally so, found Greece, that green, gold, purple and silvery country astounding not only for beauty but for freshness and climate. The lucent light, the incandescent blue skies, the grace and dignity, charmed him. He had vaguely loved the Greeks because of Aristo. He had suspected their hedonism and their subtly gay and cynical attitude toward life and institutions, and their humor and form and style, but now he remembered their poetry and their tragedians and their ineffable prose, and steeped himself in the grandeur of written and spoken words. Their influence upon the Jews in Israel had been an affront to him and to the other Pharisees. Now he saw that the purity of a faith is enhanced, not diminished, by the quickness of another's perception, and there was something singularly similar between the conceptual abstraction of the Greeks and the mystical utterances of the prophets in the Scriptures. Religion was not diminished by a new insight, provided it did not deny any proven truth. Rather, it enriched and revitalized it, and made it more poignant.

He was by nature a urban man, and the urbane Greeks he encountered were men, he thought reluctantly, of his own kind. Barnabas was shyly wary of the Greeks, and Saul said to him with irritation, "Our Lord loves the cultured man, of a certainty, as much as He loves the illiterate and the unlearned and the simple! We must not confine our efforts to the market rabble—though God knows they need taming and disciplining!—and to the farmer in his field. If we are to advance, as commanded, we do not appeal solely to the slave and the humble, for the Messias spoke with the power of universal wisdom and out of great learning and subtle abstraction, in symbols far more hidden and abstruse than a Homer or a Virgil or a Horace, or any of the great poets of Greece. Truly, as He said, we must be as wise as the serpent and as harmless as the dove, but we must walk amid the porticoes and on the acropolises and in the edifices of learning and culture, as well as in the gutter and the dust. I do not recall that the Lord overthrew one statue or denounced one heathen temple, nor offended the Gentiles in any manner with derision or contempt or accusation. Nor must we."

As learned Greek gentlemen liked disputations and argument and the Socratic dialogue, Saul soon found himself of interest to these men. They came to his poor inn in Corinth, where they found him, in the evening, sitting in the dying sun and filling his eyes and soul with the resplendent beauty about him. He found himself enjoying his conversations with these men. Unlike the people of Israel and the people of Antioch, they were not surprised that a rich sage should choose to dress roughly. They confided, with a smile, that ostentation and virtue and wisdom were incompatible, though they left Saul with the uneasy surmise that they considered him affected, or eccentric as all "sages" were. In short, he was wearing an approved uniform as a wise man, so he could be distinguished from the ordinary race of men. This irked him, but strangely it also amused him. I am becoming a Greek, he would say to himself. When he tried to impart the intricacies of Greek thought to Barnabas the latter was confused. He said, "We dress humbly because we are humble men," and Saul said no more.

The plain of Corinth was very fertile and darkly green, and here was indeed the breadbasket of Greece and her source of fruit and vegetables. The temple on the cypressed acropolis was a miniature jewel formed of silver gilt, its columns glowing all day and becoming scarlet at sunset, its winding gardens bursting with the various living murals of endless flowers, and all under a sky of such dazzling peacock-blueness that it stunned the eye. Corinth, itself, was as white as snow, the small square houses bearing trellises of grapes, the narrow streets clean and rattling with chariots and wagons, the shops tiny and teeming. Saul had seen the royal-purple Aegean Sea and the Ionian Sea, as he had passed over the isthmus, and he had seen, at a distance, the rosy and green isles of Greece in their circles of gold beaches, and he thought to himself that heaven must be so. The aromatic dry heat did not irritate him. It soothed not only his flesh but his spirit, and he recalled that Greece was a favorite winter haven for rich Romans who suffered rheumatism in the dank Italian climate. There was, in the air, not only stimulation but a soothing quality that hinted of timelessness and the gods and meanings beyond the understanding of man.

Barnabas, who was not an urban man and therefore not a cosmopolitan, was less easy in the atmosphere of Greece than Saul. He was insistent in his belief that all men were the same, and so cultivated the humble of Corinth, the slaves, the peasants, the less prosperous shop-keepers, the laborers in the fields, the wine-pressers, the vineyard tenders, the guardians of flocks, the freedmen. If the men of Greece appeared different to the men of the East, from whence he had come, Barnabas, in his simplici-ty, accused himself of prejudice and narrowness of mind. But Saul rejoiced in the difference between the men of Greece and the men he had known the greater part of his life, for it proved to him the marvelous variety that God had created in His wisdom and His love for beauty and diversity. Moreover, as a man of active mind and imagination, he was curious and excited by contrary opin-ions, and he loved debates.

He was often invited to the pleasant homes of wealthy Greeks and he found himself enjoying excellent dinners if not the resinous wines of Greece. The Jews in Corinth, in the majority merchants and traders and bankers, were urbane also though, recalling Saul's former persecution of their Nazarene brethren, they were less friendly to him. The rabbis in the synagogue were aware of his presence among them on the Sabbath, and they observed that no man responded more fervently than did Saul of Tarshish nor with more ecstasy and devotion—wearing his cap of the Tribe of Benjamin—but they were suspicious. They were prepared to dispute with him should he rise in the synagogue and attempt to speak to the congregation, for he was not only a Pharisee but a member of the new Jewish sect, who were called Christians by the Greeks.

The rabbis had no objection to the Christians appearing for worship in the synagogue, for was not Israel plagued by many sects? If they were temporarily convinced that Yeshua of Nazareth was the Messias, blessed be His Name, it would pass. But Saul of Tarshish was another matter. He spoke in Corinth of his surety that Yeshua was the Messias, and that men who rejected Him could not be saved nor partake of the world hereafter in the fullest measure, for had not God made a new Covenant with Israel? But Saul did not rise to dispute with the rabbis. He merely gazed about him with eyes blazing with fervent love and desire.

The Jewish Christians were no less suspicious of him, and so he knew, again, that his mission was to the Gentiles, though he confined his personal worship to the synagogue. He left the Jews to Barnabas, who did not have his reputation and who was soft of speech and in all manners a true Jew. It was Saul's deepest desire not to create divisions among the Christian Jews, and he knew that his very presence was a contention.

In the meantime another thorn was pricking his flesh, and it was a very large thorn. For he was joined in Corinth by John Mark, one of the Apostles, a man much younger than himself who had seen the Messias close at hand and had followed Him and had slept in the fields with Him, and had broken bread and drunk wine with Him, and had seen His Resurrection. Mark was a tall thin young man with immense soft brown eyes which amazingly could become cold and hard when he gazed at Saul, and his hair and beard were like brown silk and his hands and feet were pale and long and he spoke with a slow deliberation and positive emphasis which annoyed Saul from the very beginning. He was not only shyly suspicious of Saul—which Saul detected at once—for Peter had not had kind words to say of him even after their reconciliation, but suspected his mission to the Gentiles.

Though Mark, recognizing that the Lord had come to the Gentiles also, was not averse to having potential converts among the Christians in Corinth or any other city, he believed with all his soul that the Jewish Christians were the inner circle of Israel, the Elect, the only ones assigned the Messianic Message, the only true saints, and that in the future it would be these Christian Jews solely who would have the governance of the Kingdom, and not the Gentile converts, who would form only a small and select body. Therefore, he was embittered against Saul who offered the Messianic and mystic inner circle to the Gentiles. He said to Saul, "The Lord warned us not to cast our pearls before swine nor to throw that which is holy to the dogs."

"There is no limitation to the Kingdom of God," Saul replied, and in the beginning he was patient. "The Messianic Mission is for all, and is not exclusive nor does it bar any man touched with the Finger of God, Jew, heathen or Gentile." He smiled coldly at Mark. "The Jews require a sign and the Greeks seek after wisdom. But we preach Christ crucified, unto the Jews a stumblingblock and unto the Greeks foolishness. But to them which are called, both Jews and Greeks, Christ the power of God and the wisdom of God!"* He added: "For we are laborers together with God. You are God's husbandry. You are God's building." When Mark did not answer Saul said with his natural wild impatience at such obduracy, "For as the body is one and has many members, and all the members of that one body, being many, are one body, so also is Christ. For by one Spirit are we all baptized into one body, whether we be Jews or Gentiles, bond or free, and have been all made to drink into one Spirit."†

Mark looked at him with a glaucous veil over his eyes. He said, "But you were a Pharisee—and the Lord denounced the Pharisees— We still fear and suspect them."

Saul was infuriated at this non sequitur, and his pride inflamed. He cried, "Whatever anyone dares to boast of I also dare to boast of that! Are they Hebrews? So am I! Are they Israelites? So am I! Are they descendants of Abraham? So am I! Are they servants of Christ? I am a better one—with far greater labors. I have been beaten and have been near death. Once I was stoned. I have been in danger from rivers, danger from robbers, danger from my own people, danger from Gentiles, danger in the city, danger in the wilderness, danger at sea, danger from false brethren; in toil and hardship, through many

*Cor. 1:22–24.
†Cor. 12:12–14.

a sleepless night, in hunger and thirst, often without food, in cold and exposure. And apart from other things there is the daily pressure upon me of my anxiety for all the churches."*

To this Mark answered nothing, but left him. Barnabas was distressed. Between the quiet obstinacy of Mark and the haughty pride and certitude of Saul he felt himself caught between an upper and nether stone. However, his intuition convinced him that Saul was right and just and the younger Mark provincial, for all that he was an Apostle. But Barnabas' greater distress was that such dissension should arise in the Church, an outcry of protesting tongues. If the Church were so divided then it would be weakened and its mission delayed and distorted. There was always room for discussion, for discussion frequently clarified, but there was no room for war and revolt. When Mark said to him, "The Message should only be given in the synagogues, and not in the heathen market places and in the houses of the Greeks, who are idolators," Barnabas tried to explain, but Mark was as convinced as Saul, himself, that he was right.

"I will have no part of this!" exclaimed Mark, and without taking leave of Saul he left for Jerusalem, there to complain of the arrogant Pharisee to Peter. (It was not for many years that Mark finally knew that Saul was just and admitted, in his Gospel, that the mission was to the Gentiles also, without restriction.) He told Peter that Saul was perverting the Message of the Messias, that he was destroying the holy faith and adulterating it, that, as he was a cosmopolitan, he was admitting alien influences into the Church and condoning strange practices and preaching strange doctrines, to the scandal of the faithful.

"Let him flaunt what he calls his authority," said the elders in Jerusalem, while Peter listened in perturbed silence. "He has put aside the Law, he has flouted Jerusalem, he appoints his own elders, he has put himself outside the pale. This Pharisee, this hunter of the innocent and the mild! He says he has been appointed by God and the Messias: Let him continue! God will not be mocked, but will destroy this prideful, boastful man."

Mark enlarged on the subject. Barnabas was his uncle. Saul of Tarshish had perverted that gentle uncle's faith,

*Cor. 11:21–30.

and had endangered his soul. He was bringing hordes of ill-informed and casual and idolatrous Gentiles into the Church merely to enlarge his authority and impress by numbers. He did not search a man's soul diligently and sedulously to be certain that that man had indeed been given the gift of faith. He baptized that man on a mere and hasty profession! He was the new Jeroboam, and no doubt an apostate, if ever he were a Nazarene, which was open to doubt. "He will be our death!" cried Mark, in all sincerity. "He will delay the Coming of the Messias, and plunge us all into darkness and despair! We shall not, because of our tolerance, share in the Kingdom. Woe to us!"

Others, listening to Mark and nodding in distress, again recalled Saul's former persecution of the Nazarenes. Was it possible that he had become a Christian only with the intention of destroying the Faith?

Peter said, in a low and hesitant voice, "I, too, doubted him for many reasons. But I visited him in Antioch, and found nothing wrong there. The Gentiles he had converted—they astonished and edified me with their faith and their joy. I have told you of this before. He convinced me. I saw the shadow of the light of the Spirit on his countenance. You must believe me. Once I was like you, but I had a vision. Saul has his message; I have mine. Each of us is commissioned to do his part. Let there be no dissension. If Saul is ever in error, Our Lord will correct him, or cast him out. True, he is a proud man and at ease among the Gentiles, but do not those very qualities give him power among them?"

But one of the elders said, "We Jews stand in a glorified place with the Messias, for we have been taught the Commandments and the Covenant was given to our people. We are a holy nation, indeed. Our Lord was an Israelite and He obeyed the Laws of our fathers, and was circumcised. Therefore, those who would join us must become as He."

The old argument continued, Peter observed to himself with a sigh. Would the young Church survive these heated dissensions? He said to the others, "I trust Saul, so you must trust him also. What is not of God will be cast out. Had they not all questioned Saul before, in Jerusalem, and had been convinced by him? True, he had antagonized them with his barely concealed arrogance and impatience at their lack of formal learning. But he had denied the accusation that he was forming a new faith. He was only bringing the Gentiles into Israel, as he had said, himself. Israel was God's chosen nation; he had acknowledged this to the elders. But the Messianic community included all peoples. Had not the Lord so declared, Himself, and Isaias, and all the prophets? What man dared say to one eager to believe and join the Messianic community: 'You shall not enter, for you are uncircumcised and unclean?' That would be an offense to God, who loved all men and would have them join Him in Heaven. Should man arrogate to himself the decision who should be saved and who shall not? That was truly Phariseeism." At this, Peter smiled gently at the heated elders.

He said, "If Saul of Tarshish were a man more like ourselves, more obscure, more temperate, more humble, born where we were born, having lived as we have lived, and not a Pharisee of great and worldly learning, not a man of the cosmopolitan community—in short, if he were of our features and our status and our speech—then we should not so resent him and dispute with him. For he was not born in Israel, and is a Roman citizen and a lawyer of Rome, and was taught by a Greek, so we consider him an upstart and an alien and resent his teachings to our brethren. This is a human error, to suspect the stranger even when he comes to us in good will and sincerity. We prefer our own. But God prefers no man over another." He added that the prophet Hosea had said that God would number the Gentiles among His people in the latter days. "Look now toward Heaven and tell the stars, if you be able to number them."* So, added Peter, all men were the seed of the Messias.

The elders subsided, but they did not love Saul though they trusted in the words of Peter, for had not the Lord founded His Church upon him, and could the Church be in error? No. The plan of casting Saul out of the Messianic community was abandoned.

James rose up and said that in his judgment those among the Gentiles who turned to God were not to be molested or thrown out of the Messianic community and

*Gen. 15:5–6.

Message, but that henceforth they were to abstain from idols, from adultery and fornication, from eating strangled animals, and from bloodshed. The Gentiles were but to obey the primal laws as given by Moses, and if they wished to adhere to the Law more fervently they would be joyously accepted as part of the Israelite community, and the Elect.

Saul heard of this meeting, and again he was inflamed. He accepted the judgment of the elders, but he burned in his heart. The Jewish Christians called the Gentile converts "brethren," but still to them they were only Gentiles. They were not truly Israelites, as the Lord was an Israelite. They were tolerated, only. Saul said to them, "He who accepts the Messias is in the most holy way an Israelite, and he who rejects the Messias is not an Israelite."

Having fully established the Church in Corinth Saul was anxious to move on to the wilderness where the Name of the Messias had not yet been proclaimed, and into Christian communities which were still weak. Barnabas, in his gentle fashion, suggested to Saul that Mark be invited to join them. Saul looked at him with angrily sparkling blue eyes.

"No," he said. "He has caused me enough trouble, and has raised up dissension in the Church, where all should be harmony."

"If he did," said Barnabas, almost in tears, "he did it out of zeal."

"I have no patience with zealots," said Saul, that most zealous man. He despised Mark that he had attempted to interfere with him. Had not Mark's quiet contentions brought about seizures in Saul, which enfeebled him? He who enfeebled a messenger flouted God. Barnabas argued, but in vain. Saul was adamantly opposed to Mark, not only out of conviction but out of human incompatibility.

So when Mark arrived Saul refused to see him, remembering offenses. Barnabas, torn between the love he had for his nephew, and the love he had for Saul, his friend, finally departed with Mark for Cyprus. Saul, proud and unyielding as always, eager to give love yet seemingly rejecting it, made other plans.

His first emotion against Barnabas was that his friend had deserted him, had abandoned him for his nephew, considering Saul of less moment. But as Saul was a rational man in spite of his temper and his harsh speech he finally said to himself: I drive away what I would embrace. I stir anger in what I would love. I lie down with rage when I would desire to consummate my greatest passions. I would tolerate stupidity if it were not so authoritative! Alas, I am a venal man.

He sorely missed Barnabas, that soft voice of temperance and kindness and charity. He missed the concerned brown eyes, the touch of the consoling hand. But he could not ask Barnabas to return as yet. One day he would beg that return, though not as yet, he told himself. In the meantime, in a gesture of reconciliation, he agreed to certain terms of the Jerusalem community, advanced to him by Peter who was growing in his esteem.

Now his desire was to advance into Europe after a visit to Athens, and to Athens he journeyed, that seat of Western wisdom and poesy and profound philosophy, that throne of beauty, that crown of ethics and subtle reasoning.

Chapter 45

THE silvery dust and silvery hills of Athens entranced Saul. All was iridescent in the rays of the most ardent sun and under that deep blue and incredibly brilliant sky. He would walk through the Agora, scanning the shops, the merchants. He would pause before the temple of music to listen to the musicians practicing. He visited academies and law courts, where the disputations of lawyers excited and amused him and the wry magistrates made him laugh in sympathy. He visited libraries, established by Marcus Tullius Cicero long ago, and paused to glance through books. He would stand upon a hill to look at the purple water of the port of Pireus and watch the ships at anchor. Here, in this light, this vivacity, this humorous and sparkling atmosphere, even the Romans seemed to him more amiable and enlightened. Above all, the Acropolis fascinated him and the giant statue of Athena Parthenos before the Parthenon, and he climbed to the top to wander the marble floors between temples and fountains and colonnades and to look down on the white city below. He marveled and was reverent. For the first time he thought, "How noble the mind and soul of man when delivered of grossness and materialism and expediency! How fateful, how portentous, his very shadow on marble when he surmounts his nature! Here beauty has set her monumental foot on stone, and the beauty was evoked from man's own spirit. I have often considered him mean and filthy, malicious and cruel, foul and deceitful, wicked and lustful, traitorous and vicious, and in truth he is all these things. But I know also—and how deeply I know—that he is also divine in the Divinity of God and that immortality echoes in the chambers of his brain, and that nothing can be denied him if he surrenders to the Most Holy and becomes one with Him. Only God can set man free to be himself, if he desires that freedom, for captivity is self-ordained and all its ugliness and vileness."

The statues on the Acropolis did not vex him as once they might have done; he delighted in their loveliness, was entranced by the unbelievable majesty and detail of them. They were like gods to him, and he could understand how it was that men often worshiped what they had made with their own hands, recognizing in the mysterious dark and mystic places in them that what they had created had been inspired in them and was not wholly their own. The God of Light and Beauty had smiled on this steep hill and Phidias had been His tongue in stone to speak to that in man which craves, unendingly, perfection and excellence. Socrates who spoke only in words was less than Phidias, who doubtless had had angels at his elbow and as architects. Worship struck at Saul's vulnerable heart. He stood and looked through the immense white colonnades at the passionate blue of the sky, and at the flaming air, and he thought that not even in the Temple of Jerusalem had he felt such reverence, such awe, such overwhelming joy, such ecstatic comprehension.

Greece would pass away as all nations pass, but the memory of her wisdom and her glory and her beauty would linger forever as long as one man remained to celebrate them. A poet was greater than a king; a wise man transcended the rich; an empire could be immortal only in the quality of men she had conceived and brought forth. Greece, in poetry and wisdom and texture of mind, surpassed all other nations. There were more beautiful countries than this, Saul had heard, and larger and grander. Yet, out of Greece, by a mysterious dispensation, had emerged the uttermost form of Beauty in marble and in word.

But the Christian community in Athens, both Jewish and Gentile did not, alas, share his excitement and joy over the city. The Jews thought the mighty spectacle of the Acropolis "snares of the devil," to divert the eye and spirit of man from the everlasting verities, and Saul, about to rebuke them with his lashing tongue, recalled that in his youth he, too, had voiced such sentiments to Aristo. The Gentiles were poor men, former freedmen or laborers or peasants, heavy with dust and toil, and though Greeks they had no pride in their heritage nor could their eyes encompass what Saul saw. They looked at him with dull and wondering surprise. What had this to do with their present or future existence? The works of man, however splendid—though they did not see the splendor—were dust and ashes and unworthy of a Christian whose thoughts should be fixed only on eternity.

The Jewish Christians were men of more substance than their Gentile fellows, being merchants and shopkeepers and bankers as they were in Corinth. They could not understand Saul, though he was of their own heritage and blood and bone. They were good men, and they believed that as Christians it was their sole duty on earth to alleviate the lot of the poor, to elevate the distressed, to feed the hungry and the homeless, to rectify injustice, to proclaim freedom and to denounce slavery, to clamor in the courts of law—there were lawyers amongst them also —for compassion for the criminal and mercy for the wrongdoer. Their emotions and beliefs, they assured Saul earnestly, were liberal and kind and they suffered for the sufferers. Saul shook his head with his old impatience. Of a certainty a man should love his neighbor and assist him, for was that not God's own Commandment? But that love for neighbor and that assistance bloomed naturally out of faith and the duties of faith, as a rose naturally blooms from the root-stem of its being. Without faith and worship and the truth of God all service to neighbor was a mere self-righteous prattling.

Saul quoted Isaias to them: "The vile person shall no more be called liberal, nor the churl said to be bountiful, for the vile liberal will speak villainy and his heart will work iniquity, to practice hypocrisy, and to utter error against the Lord, to make empty the soul of the hungry. He will cause the drink of the thirsty to fail. The instruments of the churl are evil and he devises wicked devices to destroy the poor with lying words. The liberal devises liberal things, and by liberal things shall he stand!"*

They were horrified at his words, though Saul said, with a satirical smile, "I did not say them. The prophet Isaias said them. What! Do you not know your own sacred Scriptures?"

He continued: "The Lord has said that first we must seek His Kingdom, and all else will be added to us, even charity, even mercy for the afflicted. Let that search fill your days and your nights, and as water flows out of holy stone so will the water of your love flow from your souls to quench the thirst of the thirsty, and as manna fell from Heaven, so will the manna of your charitable gifts fall from your hearts."

The elders of the Church reproached him, calling his vision hard, saying his spirit was not touched by the prevailing misery, and that surely it was a man's deepest calling to engage in secular things and to change them for the better. Restraining his wrath, Saul said, "I will quote the prophet Ezekiel to you, and he spoke of this problem. 'The priests of Israel have done violence to My Law and have profaned My holy things, for they have made no distinction between the holy and the common, neither have they taught the difference between the clean and the unclean. —So, I have profaned them.' Your life, my friends, is in Christ Jesus, who said He was no divider of men and that His kingdom was not of this earth. Set the light of your faith before men and all dark shadows shall flee and the dungeon fly open, for it is faithless men who have created wretchedness and poverty and hunger and grief, and who have taken the roof from the widows and orphans. The man of faith is a shelter to the homeless, a filled larder to the hungry, a well to those who

*Isa. 32:5–8.

thirst, for out of his faith he is moved to alleviate torment."

They were awed, as multitudes before them had been awed, by his sonorous and compelling voice, his fascinating inflections and imagery, his sudden humor and tenderness following immediately after wrath, his eloquence, and by the mysticism of his being and appearance. But, like all men, they were enmeshed in their convictions and Saul began, again, the weary task of enlightenment. There was no life except in Christ Jesus, he would repeat over and over again, and that life was a Gift. There was no salvation in works, but in the faith which inspired those works.

After some weeks Peter in Jerusalem, doubtless inspired by the Holy Spirit, sent to Saul, as a companion, a young man named Timothy, whose father had been a Greek teacher, and his mother a Jewess. According to the Jewish law Timothy was therefore a Jew, even if uncircumcised. But he was an embarrassment to the Jews in the synagogues, which he frequented both as a Jew and a Christian, and Saul, remembering his agreement to the Jerusalem community—but sighing—told Timothy that he must be circumcised, "for we shall visit synagogues wherever we travel, to speak to our brethren, and it is sinful to humiliate others and to cause them offense and to force them to be rude. I have said, and taught, that it is not necessary for a Gentile to become a Jew and be circumcised in order to be admitted to the Christian community. But you, my dear Timothy, my young friend, are another pan of fish."

Saul had the quick thought that Peter, who had his own humor, was teasing him. However Timothy, who resembled a young Hermes, obeyed his suggestion with an alacrity which Saul found touching and consoling, remembering Mark. Saul, himself, performed the rite and the ceremony in the most scrupulous Israelite fashion, and was Timothy's godfather. Thereafter he was to refer to Timothy as "my dear child, my lawfully born child in faith." He conceived a love for the youth similar to his love for his true son, Boreas, whose wife, Tamara bas Judah, had now borne him two beautiful children, a son and a daughter. The son was named Hillel ben Enoch, the girl Dacyl bas Enoch, and on receiving the news Saul wept with mingled happiness and pain, happiness that Boreas had remembered his grandfather, and sad pain— yet pride in his son—that Boreas had honored his young mother, dead in her girlhood. Saul longed to see his grandchildren and his son with a longing that was an anguish and which haunted his nights, but he knew it was not to be. He confided his sorrow to Timothy, who quickly sympathized and with true emotion, and Saul wondered if Mark would have been so kind and intuitive. He decided he would not. I am always sighing these days, thought Saul, and that is a bad habit, indicating despair.

In some ways Timothy, the young man, was despairing, saying to Saul, "The heathen are Godless, corrupt, atheistic, libertines, lusters after the flesh and strong drink, full of laughter at the holy things, confirmed in wickedness, faithless. How can we bring these to God and the Messias?"

Saul replied, "You have not looked upon them with seeing eyes, my child. Contrary to your belief the Gentiles are not Godless, though they live and worship in error. The vast movement of religions from Egypt and the Orient over the west, yes, even to Rome, shows that the heart of man is ever ready to receive and adore the Truth. No tyrant, no madman, can stamp from the hearts of men the desire after God and the living waters, for it is born in the hearts of humanity. Corruption, faithlessness, lusts of the flesh, even wickedness, are symptoms of despair in the souls of men that they do not know God and know only the hunger in their spirits which no pursuit of pleasure or gain can satisfy. They accept the stones of vice and the poison of strong drink, to alleviate their agony and distress, not knowing that That which can console and heal and nourish them is waiting at hand. It is our duty to give them the bread of life and the living waters. When they accept these they will no longer accept vile and deceitful substitutes, mere illusions of wheat and meat and milk."

On the other hand Timothy was ebullient concerning the fate of the Church "in the future, when all dissensions will end and all men, like sheep, will be under the guardianship of the one Shepherd. Alas, that we shall not see this come to pass—but future generations will see it, and what has troubled the Church in these, our days, will no longer trouble her and peace will reign forevermore."

To this Saul wryly answered, "I do not denigrate optimism and hope, if they are based on the reality of human nature and probabilities. But to me optimism is cowardly, for optimistic men prefer fable to reality, and hope to the hard rock of fact—and hope is a liar, except when it is hope based on Our Lord. During the Roman Saturnalia men give gifts to their little children. But when children become men they must know that gifts do not fall from the skies under mysterious circumstances and without their own efforts and labor. To believe otherwise is not optimism; it is madness. True, faith is a gift from the hand of God only, but a man must seek that gift diligently and prepare his own soil for the seed. We, as appointed by Christ Jesus, must carry that seed; however, we can only offer it. We cannot even be optimistic, nor can we hope much. We can only pray.

"You speak of future ages when there will be no such dissension as today in the Church. Alas. My Timothy, preach the Word, be instant in season and out of season. Reprove, rebuke, exhort with all long-suffering and doctrine. For the time will come when they will not endure sound doctrine, but after their own lusts shall they heap to themselves teachers, having itching ears, and they shall turn their ears from the truth and shall be turned to fables. Therefore, watch yourself in all things, endure afflictions, do the work of an evangelist, make full proof of your ministry."* He added, more gently, "As men are men and prone to error and rebellion, we cannot expect that the Church will be free from dissension and strife and long and angry voices, disputing. We can only stand steadfast in the truth, not tolerant of false doctrine, not conciliators with liars and fools and the violent and those who would change for change's sake only. For, what is new in the world that men should lust after it? As Solomon said, 'There is nothing new under the sun,' nor will there ever be, and generations who will cry 'This is new, we are the new and what we say is new for today, and verity!' are foolish in their souls and not aware of history, nor are they men of learning and understanding. They are callow and ignorant and hysterical, and who will listen to them

*Tim. 4:2–5.

but goats like themselves? Nevertheless, they will be destructive and will confuse the faithful. But we have the promise of God that they shall not prevail against the Church."

He thought to himself, "The young demand absolutes. Did I not demand that, myself? But the only Absolute is God. The young demand solutions to all problems, pleasing to themselves, and never question if those solutions are satisfactory to Him, Who is the only Solution. Solutions built on theory and what the young deem 'good,' are chaff in the wind, blinding and choking, but never a nourishment. The wise young later understand that, but the young man grown old who still believes in solutions to all human problems without invoking God for wisdom and enlightenment, and believes men alone can find solutions, is a man of age but without comprehension. He is demented, and a danger to all men."

Saul, who was never deluded about his fellow men, had his periods of despondency. He could only hope in the ultimate triumph of God, which had been promised.

He had come to have a deep affection for the Athenians, not only because they received him with more respect than the Jewish Christians and the orthodox Jews but because he felt a kinship with them as worldly and cosmopolitan. He saw, however, that the intelligent and cultivated Athenians were interested in God as a philosophical hypothesis, not to be taken as an actuality in the prosaic affairs of men. God, as Aristotle had said, was the Prime Mover of all that was created, but the created, after having been touched by the divine Finger, was thereafter its own destroyer or its own savior. It seemed incredible to the majority of the enlightened Athenians that God would condescend, and with love, to be born of man and to walk among them to lead them from their error—which was self-ordained. The Prime Mover was surely more august than that, concerned as He was with the creation of universes and suns and planets and galaxies.

"He is concerned with the fall of a sparrow," said Saul, and they shook their heads, smiling. "He observes the fly who lives but for a day, and the beetle who busies himself with the laws of his own nature." The Athenians looked aside and smiled again, and thought that Saul profaned his own God by attributing to Him the pettiest of matters. Nature's laws, once set into motion by the Prime Mover, could not be altered, and woe to that man or insect or beast who foolishly set himself in the path of inexorable Destiny.

Saul, in his last days in Athens, spoke to the city on the Hill of Mars, on the Acropolis, in the aromatic heat of noonday, where the shadow of column and cypress cast sharp blue shadows. Above him soared the grand Parthenon and lesser temples, white and blazing as snow under the ardent sun, and nearby was the Rock of Justice, huge, gray, and the Roman Temple of Jupiter with colored friezes on pediments and porticoes, and before it his mighty gilded statue glittering in the light, seemingly helmeted in hot lightnings. Below Saul lay the theater of Dionysus, round as a bowl, filled with seats like narrow marble terraces, rising one above another to the very brim of the bowl, many gayly cushioned and waiting, and the walls ornamented by bas-reliefs of the utmost beauty, depicting gods and their fables and their exploits. The sides of the Acropolis glimmered with the enormous white marble steps leading to the top, and crowds teemed up and down, those climbing with arms full of flowers and other offerings for the temples, those descending conversing with that mingled seriousness and wit and laughter notable among Athenians. And Saul could see, far below in the city itself, the ruby-red roof of the immense market place, the Agora, and the crowded official buildings of gold and white, and the endless clusterings of pale and cube-shaped houses with their gardens and their vine-covered walls. Everywhere was color, vitality, vivacity, movement, life and clamor, the exuberance yet logic of the western mind. In spite of the seeming violence of tint and hue and shade, the seething comings and goings, the noise and the music and the roar of voices, the almost intolerable profusion of light, the burning blue of the sky, there was a certain order, a certain restraint.

And, in the distance Saul could see the humid purple sea, the dark green of wooded hills, the sepia land, the emerald meadows beyond the city, the glint of golden streams. To him Athens appeared like a glimpse of Paradise. For a fresh breeze, despite the heat, came from the sea, and the brilliance of the air and all that stood in the air held a deep and happy excitement. Even the traffic of wagons and carts and chariots and cars in the narrow streets below possessed a kind of joyous determination. No wonder, thought Saul, that my grandfather loved this city, though I despised him for it when I was young, thinking nothing more beautiful or significant than Jerusalem. Out of Sion came the Law, as he knew, but the Law also contained variety and beauty which were universal.

The Greeks had given Saul a humorous name: "The Jewish Socrates." Saul had discovered that the Greeks delighted in the word and its aptness, and they were as great in argument and disputations as the Jews and loved the precision of well-chosen language. He was not offended at the name given him. He looked down now at the colorful crowds gathered to hear him, at the rich in their litters and with their slaves, at the businessmen and the bankers and the lawyers and the physicians, all elegantly dressed, and at the poor and the laborers, the farmers and the drifters, the artisans, the toilers in the city and in the fields. All stood and sat on the steep high marble steps leading to the top of the Acropolis, and many tried to hide in the shadow of neighbors to escape the sun, and many held parasols over their heads in a multitude of rainbow colors. They talked endlessly, of course, in the manner of Athenians, but when Saul began to speak, in his eloquent loud voice, they gave him their attention, politely, for he had a reputation. Besides, it was possible that the gods—in whom they only abstractedly believed—were about to speak in him. Of a certainty, he had an aspect which other men did not possess, with that flaming mane of mingled red and white hair, and his lined and passionate leonine face and the wild blue of his eyes. He was dressed humbly, and in a long brown tunic such as a laborer in the manufactories would wear, and his girdle was only rope and his sandals were tied with rope. But he had a commanding presence, almost godlike, and inspiring, and his gestures were wide and awesome, and from him flowed a powerful and superhuman conviction. He was no ignorant demagogue such as they knew too well, no venal politician seeking office and votes, no self-server. He came to them, it was reported, out of love for his God, of Whom, as the God of the Hebrews, they had heard rumors. Not all the rumors inspired admiration, however.

He had appeared too much as a God of wrath and very little as a God of beauty, and His devotees were somber and seemed to despise life and laughter and gaiety, and talked with long faces. But here was a Jew who appeared joyous and joyously inspired and who looked down on their city with delight, and so he was a more interesting Jew, and his voice held the richness of rough humor, and his speech was in impeccable Greek.

"Men of Athens!" he cried, embracing them with his arms outheld, and with his voice and the sparkle of his eyes, vivid even in that vivid air. "You have heard me before, those of you who listened to me in the market places, and in the synagogues in the Court of the Gentiles, and in the streets, and so my message to you is not new to your ears. Many of you have said to me, with all reverence, 'Is your Jesu the Unknown God of Whom we have heard throughout the ages?' And I have answered you, 'Indeed, He is your Unknown God, and the Unknown God of all men, who have worshiped Him in darkness and hope and humility. But now I speak to you of Him Who is no longer unknown, but stands in resurrected light, and is finally revealed to the whole world, in splendor, dignity, awesome power, grandeur, love and tenderness and beauty. There is not a religion of man, dead or living, which has not held the golden seed of the Promise, and all men have awaited Him, though multitudes did not know for Whom they waited. They only hoped, but hope is enough for it has been fulfilled.'

"This I have said to you, and this have I preached, in many places in your city. Many have laughed, and have said, 'Who is this wandering Jew who speaks of intricate matters so simply, and is no philosopher but a man in humble garments and with dust on his feet?' But many more have listened in politeness and with courtesy and I thank them, though they have not accepted my witness."

He then recounted to them his vision on the road to Damascus, and now they were utterly silent, with the walls of noise beyond them merely concentrating the silence within their grouping. Some had heard this before, but it enthralled them to hear it again. Many had not heard it at all, and they were enchanted, for it seemed to them that Saul had not only become a poet—and they reverenced poets above all other men—but was somewhat godlike, himself. His descriptions, fired as if from the sun itself, and endowed with majesty and power, moved them to the heart if not in sudden faith then in veneration of beauty. It was as if a new Homer sang to them new and heretofore unrevealed poetry. Their eyes filled with tears at the vision of the Messias, so vividly brought before their eyes by Saul, and His glory and might, but they were tears of appreciation at such a mar-vel of perfection. Jesu was a new manifestation of Apollo or Zeus or Hermes, glorious of limb, scintillating of coun-tenance, endowed with authority and with a radiance greater than the sun, more terrible than a storm, more invincible than a whirlwind. They were caught up in tumultuous emotions; some sighed; some murmured; some clasped hands tightly together; some merely stared at Saul, rapt and trembling. They believed every word he said. They did not doubt that he had seen a god, probably even Zeus, himself. It was a vision that appeared to make the air about them golden and shaking with light. Even the most sophisticated and urbane, who were convinced that Saul had been struck by the divine and fearful mad-ness—of the gods, perhaps, or of his own poesy most probably—were stirred and exhilarated.

They gave him, mutely, the honor they would bestow on a poet whose cantos they had heard before but whose imagery was ineffable. It did not matter to them if the vision had been true, or untrue, or only imagined. It was Beauty, and was not their nation the very seat of Beauty, and was not Beauty her own logic and reason for being?

But some there were who listened—and not only the humble—and were touched with the finger of faith like a finger of flame on their hearts, and were moved by the Holy Spirit. Some of them said to themselves, "It is un-reasonable, and it is mad, and there is no logic in it, no argument, no revelation of a rational mind—yet I believe. I do not know why I believe, but I know in all my parts that what this man has told me is veritable truth, beyond all reasoning, all doubt, and that he has seen God and has spoken to Him, and that what he says I must accept lest I die. For my soul is alight with the grandeur of God, and what I see only darkly now is a vision that can expand into ineluctable delight, into a deliciousness beyond the senses, into an ecstasy which cannot be imagined but only endured and remembered."

To others, however, his redemptive gospel was too simple, too childlike, too uncomplicated for true wisdom, too easily to be grasped and held by the vulgar, too immature, and even somewhat maudlin. It was poetic, but as truth it was absurd. The man should publish his poetry and then he would be acclaimed, for were not poets endowed with the divine and a joy to the tired hearts of men? Even their absurdities and transports were lovely. However, in the business of daily living, in the intransigence of wives and children, in the competition of the market place and in banking and commercial affairs, what Saul of Tarshish was saying had no application. The gods ruled their realm. Men ruled theirs. There should be no blurring of borders. When gods intrude on the realms of men, and vice versa, then madness resulted. The men of Athens preferred rationality and hoped that the gods would keep their distance, for what did Olympus know of stock markets and banks and politicians and taxgatherers? Or, for that matter, of the desperate predicament of man?

Saul had no way of knowing whose heart was touched by the Holy Spirit and whose cool, urbane and rational heart remained untouched except for the poetry of his words. Near him, and behind him, stood young Timothy, the Hermes with the cherubic face, understanding both worlds and distressed by both, and with an urgent conflict in his heart. Timothy wanted to cry out, There is no Jew, no Gentile, no heathen, no division among men, no race, no Athenian, no Roman or Parthian or Persian or Egyptian, no barbarian, no obscurity! We are only men— and what Saul and I have brought to you is a truth pertaining to all. Listen, and let your hearts be moved. Those who divide us are enemies. Those who set brother against brother are murderers. There is but one truth, ordained for all men. Hearken to it. God is the Father of us all, and beyond that you need know nothing more!

Saul was startled, on the conclusion of his speech, to hear hearty and appreciative applause from the ranks who had listened to him, the same admiring applause they would have given to a fine actor whose performance they extolled, and whose words of tragedy and joy had moved their intellects and inspired their sense of beauty and grandeur. Saul understood at once, with both chagrin and an inner wry hilarity, but he consoled himself that the Messias had His own Wisdom and He knew whose hearts he wished to touch. I am a lion before men, thought Saul, though a worm before Him.

Saul left Timothy to talk to those few who wished to know more and who were considering baptism, and he descended the high marble steps wearily, for as always his own eloquence and passion exhausted him. Many touched him on the arm to congratulate him on an excellent presentation and his poesy and he saw they were not mocking him so he restrained a hasty answer. Then it was that he saw Lucanus, the physician, on the outskirts of the crowd, watching him with a pale and unreadable expression, and Saul's heart rose on a wing of joy and his weariness left him and he raced down the steps to embrace his friend.

Chapter 46

"OUR dear and glorious physician!" exclaimed Saul, and he could not have enough of embracing the Greek. "What a rapture to our eyes you are! When did you arrive? How goes it with you, my dearest friend? You appear tired, even ill. What! Have you been straining yourself too mercilessly among the heathen?"

His words rushed from him, so filled with happiness he was, and delight, and so he evidently failed to see that Lucanus' blue eyes were heavy with sorrow and that his face was drawn. Lucanus put his hands on the other man's shoulders and tried to speak, then could not. But Saul seemed not to see. He waved impatiently to Timothy high above him on the gleaming marble steps and shouted, "Come at once! We have Lucanus here with us, my dear friend!"

His own harassed face, so worn and sunburned and brownly sprinkled with freckles, and crowned by that thick and arrogant mane of red and white, glowed with joyous emotion. When Timothy started down the steps

Saul pressed and repressed Lucanus' arm, like a younger brother. The Greek, who was now in his early sixties, still possessed a tall slenderness, upright and proud, and his snowy hair curled over his fine skull and his eyes were those of a youth for all the pain-wrinkled flesh about his mouth. He was footsore and dusty. Saul exclaimed, "I will take you at once to my poor inn, which though humble is clean, and you must bathe and rest before all else, and then—though I am no lover of food—I will take you to a splendid inn where the viands are marvelous, it is alleged, and the wine and whiskey of the best!"

"Saul," began Lucanus in a low voice, then halted as Timothy joined them and the listeners began to stream past them with curious glances, recognizing Lucanus as a Greek. Some vaguely recalled him, from their younger years, as a physician who had lived in Athens from time to time, and saluted him politely, a gesture he returned. But he appeared both distraught and excessively tired. Young Timothy had never seen him before, though he knew him at once as a Greek and he looked back artlessly at Lucanus who gave him a brief though thorough examination with eyes that could not be deceived.

"Our Lucanus, the evangelist!" shouted Saul to his young friend, and Lucanus and Timothy embraced and said simultaneously, "May the peace of Christ Jesus be with you." And Saul stood and beamed at them, his weariness gone, and then he walked between them, linking his arms with theirs, and led them the long way down the Acropolis, past the many temples and the gardens and the fountains and the colonnades. He never ceased to utter cries of pleasure, and squeezed the arms he grasped, and laughed like a boy. An intensely intuitive man, his joy apparently prevented him from immediately knowing that Lucanus was silently distracted, but Timothy, less overwhelmed, began to become more and more quiet, and he would glance at Lucanus uneasily.

"It is not far to my inn," said Saul. "Yonder it is, beyond that grove of cypresses and that smaller grove of olive trees where the oil is pressed. I warn you, Lucanus, it is not a fine inn!"

"It does not matter," said the Greek, and his white brow seemed to shrivel with his sorrowful thought.

"But tell me!" cried Saul. "Where have you traveled!

What news do you bring! How is the Church faring in far places?"

"Let us first wash the dust from us, and have a cup of wine," said Lucanus, trying to smile. "Then we will sit where it is cool and I will tell you—" He shrank a little, and Timothy, who, though he walked on the other side of Saul, felt the shrinking of the physician, and his alarm grew.

The inn was indeed humble, and noisy, and its courtyard was filled with asses and horses and goats and fowl and stank lustily, and men shouted as they tended their animals and cursed in the heat and spat on the cobbled stones. Lucanus followed Saul into the dank darkness and odors of the interior, where Saul shouted for the innkeeper and demanded the best available room for the physician. The innkeeper, a foul fellow in a leather apron, squinted at Lucanus, bowed and said, "But the noble physician arrived but two hours ago and he already has a chamber, my very best, I assure you, Master, for did he not cure my poor mother thirty years ago and not charge her one drachma? He has but to command."

"Oh," said Saul, and looked foolish, and Lucanus smiled at him affectionately and said, "But I did not know this was your inn, my dear Saul, and too you have not allowed me to say a single word!"

"I am usually talking," said Saul. He looked at the innkeeper, and Lucanus said, "I am not hungry, I fear, so I should prefer a light meal and not go to another inn."

"The food," said Saul, staring with a hard expression at the innkeeper, "is unbelievably atrocious in this place."

"Lord," said the innkeeper, "it is your taste which is atrocious, and not my table, for you order but little, and the poorest. If the noble lord will but command I will set before him and his guests the finest of feasts, whiskey, beer, excellent wine from Italy—not the wine of the miserable Roman foot soldier but the wine of the captains—artichokes in oil, beef steeped in golden wine, a soup to make the gods envious, bread as white as snow, vegetables with dew still on them and the dressing concocted of wine, lemon juice, salt, honey and garlic, a fish still cold and wet from the sea and to be browned to crackling lusciousness as swiftly as possible, fruit tart and sweet and chilled from my cellar, cheeses which the throat hesitates to swallow for fear of depriving the mouth of delight, and pastries like ambrosia which melt like a snowflake on the tongue and cause tears of happiness to fill the eyes."

"Aha," said Saul, disbelieving, "and from whence will come these treasures?"

The innkeeper shrugged, winked and laid his dirty forefinger along his nose.

Timothy and Lucanus had been listening with slight smiles. Saul said, "I will pay anything for such a feast, but if one thing fails to meet the test I shall not pay for the dinner. Hence with you, rascal!" and he clapped the innkeeper heartily on the shoulder as the man turned away. "He is a liar, of course," said Saul. "He will send his scoundrelly sons to the best inn, with baskets, and will serve his embezzled dinner to us for an enormous price. No matter. It is not every day that you arrive, Lucanus."

He hurried away to bathe and to remove his dusty long tunic for something more suitable. Timothy would have followed him but Lucanus laid his hand on his arm.

"I have dire news for Saul ben Hillel," said Lucanus, "and I do not know what words I must choose, or when."

Timothy nodded and replied, "I suspected such, Lucanus. But my mother, may she rest in peace, always declared that a man can bear grief with more fortitude if his stomach is filled."

"As a physician, I do not recommend that you break evil news to a man with that full stomach, for it may give him a seizure of the heart. It is better that he drinks."

Timothy considered. "I have never seen Saul drunk, no, not even on the Passover or the New Year, when drunkenness is condoned as a celebration. He has attended weddings and drank but half a cup of wine. He is very austere."

"I have, in my pouch, something I will drop into his whiskey when you gain his attention for a moment," said Lucanus, "and another to follow in the wine which increases the desire to drink it. I know he is austere, so he will not eat to satiety. The pills will restrain his emotions for several hours, and then we will renew them."

Timothy's young light blue eyes moistened and he bent his head and went away, and, sighing, Lucanus went to his own chamber.

They met again very shortly and the innkeeper led them to a distant table in the clamorous dining room which smelled of the manure outside and sweat and vinegar and heat and dust. The fierce and brilliant sunlight streamed through the open windows. The party of three had a measure of privacy in this corner and here it was not so hot and not so bright. Saul seated himself between his friends and again his face glowed.

"Tell me all!" he commanded Lucanus. He looked suspiciously at the three small cups, tarnished and greasy, which the innkeeper put before them with a flourish. "The best Syrian whiskey, from a secret place in my cellar!" said the innkeeper.

"Excellent," said Lucanus, and lifted the cup. He glanced at Saul then at Timothy. "Timothy, you are the youngest here, so I beg of you that you give us a toast, for on this occasion we shall honor youth."

Timothy said, "We thank God, King of the Universe, for this meal."

A toast by the youngest was something new in Saul's experience, and he decided it must be a Greek custom on some special occasion. Timothy, who had never dissembled before, turned very red. He began to stammer, gazing at Saul. "I believe there are five whom we may baptize," he said. The little cup in his hand trembled. Saul smiled at him kindly. "I spoke to at least six score," he said, "but let us be happy for the smallest harvest, for these Greeks are very slippery men, indeed."

Timothy saw, out of the corner of his eye, that Lucanus had deftly dropped something in the whiskey before Saul. He murmured, trying to smile, "But Lucanus is a Greek, and so was my father, may he rest in peace."

"I regret my stupid remark," said Saul. He looked with distaste at the whiskey, began to put it beside the hand of Lucanus, but Lucanus said, "What! Are you refusing to drink this nectar with me? If I remember rightly you and I enjoyed such whiskey on board a certain vessel long ago. Drink, my dear friend. I command it. It is only courtesy."

"I do not dislike it," said Saul. "I grimace as a habit,

a foolish one, implying to others that meat and drink are beneath me," and he laughed loudly and roughly, like a boy, and others at a distance, hearing, turned and stared at him, then laughed also, for it seemed to them that Saul must be drunk. In their turn Timothy and Lucanus forced themselves to laugh, not entirely without true mirth, for Saul's ridicule of himself was disarming. He drank the whiskey, looked down into the cup and said, "This does not taste like Syrian whiskey, as that rascal averred. It was probably illegally distilled somewhere in the hills of Macedonia and the Roman customs stamp forged."

"A merry practice of my countrymen—forgery," said Lucanus. He poured another cup for Saul who drank it and said, "It improves."

"I have observed that about whiskey," said Lucanus. "Ah, here is the wine. Let us taste it and see if it is as promised." The innkeeper, with many gestures, wiped the inside of the cheap glass goblets with a fairly clean cloth and poured the wine as if pouring a libation on an altar, and the others watched, fascinated.

The wine, though hardly Bacchian, was tolerable, and the dinner, though hardly Lucullan, was not to be despised. Timothy observed that Lucanus magically dropped another pellet into the wine at Saul's hand, when Timothy asked a question of the physician and Saul looked intently at him, for the question was clumsy. Saul ate sparingly, as usual, but he drank more copiously and now a deep flush was on his face and his blue eyes opened wider as if the lids had relaxed. He said, "Lucanus, you have not told me what has brought you here, not where you have traveled, for I have not had a letter from you for over a year."

Lucanus said, "I have traveled in many climes and cities, and have found what you, yourself, have bewailed: Defectors, schismatics, dissenters, complacent fools, self-ordained oracles who interpret Our Lord to suit their thought or their position or their vices or their virtues— and often I do not know which is which! As Cicero has said, there is nothing so absurd but what some philosopher has said it, and this, alas, is notably true of the members of the Church. There is not a little obscure bishop in some dusty town who cannot tell you exactly what was meant by this parable or that, and smiles superbly when you mention the Jerusalem Community and Peter, who is the bishop of all. Our Lord did not abrogate the law of human nature, which remains as pigheaded and as egotistic as ever, and arrogates to itself the divine prerogative of defining divine law. One conjectures, at times, if these little men do not sometimes lecture God before permitting sleep to overcome them at night, and sternly call to His attention some error which they wish to be corrected at once."

Lucanus' expression was so dismal that Saul laughed. He did not know it but he was laughing at almost every remark now and Timothy watched him dubiously, wondering if Lucanus' pellets were not too efficacious.

"To paraphrase Caligula," said Saul, "I would that the troublemakers had but one neck."

"Fortunately," said Lucanus, "I am a physician, and nothing surprises me overmuch about man. We know that the Church will survive and the gates of hell will not prevail against her—for has not Our Lord so said? But it will not be with the aid of man! But I bring you a letter from your nephew, Amos ben Ezekiel, who is worthy of his uncle, and who is not only a better physician than I but far more eloquent. I was never a man of long-suffering, but Amos is not only patient—he has a sunny nature which wins hearts."

Saul's face brightened with pride and affection. "He resembles my father," he said.

He spoke fondly of his sister, the widow Sephorah, who now had only her children, and one of them an evangelist. "I shall visit her soon," he said, "for she is lonely and we are young no longer."

Lucanus spoke of his travels and of those he encountered, and the perils he had known, and Saul listened with avid sympathy. The harsh lines of his face melted away. He drank another glass of wine and ate of the cheese and fruit and bread, and listened with all his attention, and Lucanus watched him covertly as he spoke. Saul's weariness appeared to have been banished. A certain serenity and calm, foreign to his nature, had taken possession of him, a certain loose passiveness of hand and shoulder. He found remarks of Lucanus' amusing rather than irritating, when the Greek referred frequently to the obduracy and rebellion of the scattered churches, and the resentment of the elders when he, Lucanus, tried to correct them, and the knowing smirks of the deacons.

Then Lucanus, his face darkening, said, "It is very petty and very human, and can be borne. But what cannot be borne is the pompous and noisy pretension to supreme virtue and righteousness in some of our militant brethren in certain places, which arouses the anger of those not converted. If they did not display it overtly, nay, if they did not conspicuously and loudly seek occasions to be publicly overheard, it would not be so dangerous. It is not well for the weak to inspire the wrath of the strong; sweet reason and a gentle tongue are not cowardly, even in the mighty, and they are prudent in the defenseless. Truth should not blow a brassy trumpet nor write graffiti on the temples of others, for such trumpets do not incite admiration nor do such scribblings attract tolerant attention. The Jews learned that long ago, and learned to live in peace with their neighbors. But our little brothers remind me that Our Lord said we should bring the Gospel to all nations, and they are determined to do it immediately, at once, with fanfare, and all by themselves, no matter whose wrath they raise and whose sensibilities they offend."

"I know," said Saul, and his tone was not irascible as usual and Timothy stared at him. "Every man a little Moses, screaming from his own tiny Sinai. That is what comes of self-interpretation—a new Tower of Babel. I know it is dangerous, but men have so many religions now and so many temples and gods and so many insistent devotees and priests, that in the confusion it may be that the Christians are not too threatened."

Timothy was astonished. This was unlike Saul ben Hillel who could roar like a jungle beast at foolish and obstinate and opinionated men. But Saul was actually smiling benignly and leaning back in his chair in an attitude of happy lassitude and physical comfort. His eyes, however, were glazed and strange, and suddenly he yawned widely and shook his head as if in amusement at himself. Then he gave Lucanus a sudden and unfathomable look.

"The heat overwhelms me today, and the wine," he said in apology. "Too, I am young no longer."

Lucanus said, "Let us retire to our chambers and rest until the cool of the evening."

"Alas," said Saul, "I am to meet at the house of a few friends today, and it is already late. Do accompany me, Lucanus, and you also, Timothy. They are men of mind and culture and while they are not Christians as yet I am praying for this culmination, for they have influence in Athens."

He yawned again, so widely that all his big white teeth were visible, and tears came into his eyes. He shook his head and laughed once more.

"An hour's rest," said Lucanus. "Come. I am a physician. Will you not obey me, my dear friend, and grant me this concession?"

He stood up and his face was so earnest and grave and commanding that Saul said, "Very well. But only an hour." He too stood up, staggered, caught at the table, and forced himself upright. He was aghast. "Can it be I am drunk?" he asked, ashamed.

"No," said Lucanus, and took his arm, and the others in the dining room grinned and winked at each other. "You are weary. Come. I have something most serious to tell you, dear Saul, and this is not the place. When you are in your bed I will impart some news to you."

Saul's eyelids were drooping, and he shook his head over and over. Lucanus dropped a small pile of golden coins on the table, an act Saul was seemingly incapable of observing now. Then Lucanus motioned with his head to the pale, mute Timothy, and the young man took Saul's other arm and they led him from the room. There was loud laughter behind them, another thing which the sensitive Saul did not heed.

They climbed the dirty gritty stairs to the hot rooms above and Saul's legs were heavy and his feet seemed to sink into the floor and he said, "I have never been drunk. I did not drink much. Have I become ill? This cannot be! I have no time for illness!"

"You are not ill," said Lucanus, "but you are very tired, and even the warhorse must drop his head and slumber and listen to no drum until he has slept." —

"The corridor swims," murmured Saul, as if he had not heard. "The air is afloat with mist. Yet, I feel no sickness, no weakness. I wish only to sleep a little. Of a certainty,

I have never been so drowsy before, and the thought of my bed delights me."

He fell on his bed with a rich sigh of pleasure and a comfortable murmur. But Lucanus drew the one chair in the miserable room to the hardly less miserable bed with its soiled blankets, and sat beside Saul, who looked momentarily surprised in his drowsiness. Timothy, trembling, stood at the foot and clasped his hands hard together. Then, at the motion of Lucanus' head he drew the ragged woolen curtains across the glare of the high small window, and the chamber was immediately plunged into a hot dusk.

Then Lucanus bent over Saul, laid his hand on the other's flushed cheek and said, "Open your eyes, Saul, and look into mine, for I must have your attention."

Lucanus reached to the table on which stood a candle and he held it out to Timothy and said in a peremptory tone, "Go at once, do not delay, and light this candle at the fire in the kitchen, and bring it back with all haste!"

Saul heard this and partly raised his head off the pillow and stared at Lucanus. Lucanus held his hand tightly, as if forcing his own tired strength into Saul. In a moment the door opened rapidly and the panting Timothy returned with the lighted candle which blinked in the dimness like a painful red eye.

Lucanus moved the candle slowly back and forth before the dilated eyes of Saul. Saul was still half-raised in his bed. Lucanus murmured, "You will gaze intently at this flame and when I snap my fingers you will sleep. But you will hear all I say in your sleep and will awaken at my signal, and you will be calm, accepting all."

To his astonishment, Saul struck the candle with the back of his hand and sat upright and looked at his friend with eyes no longer slack and moist. They glowed like blue flame. He said, gently, "My dear Lucanus, I am no fool. I have seen hypnotism before, when Egyptian priest-physicians used it for the benefit of their patients. Though I gave no sign of heeding I have been aware since your arrival that you are burdened with sorrow, and so I know you bring dreadful news. I also saw you drop pellets in my whiskey and wine, and I am grateful for that, for I am weary, and I knew it was to calm me.

Am I a child or a man? Am I to be soothed by drugs and hypnotism, for fear I will not be able to bear another burden, another grief, another despair? If you think I am a child, then I will be offended. If you consider me a man, tell me all, and as quickly as possible."

Lucanus put aside the candle, and his whole ascetic face trembled, and Timothy quaked anew. "It is well," said Lucanus. "I regret that I thought to spare you, Saul, for indeed you are a man among men and not a weakling whose emotions must be dulled for fear of hysteria_and madness. But above all, I am a physician, and the habit of ministration is hard to overcome, and we are often of the opinion that it is best to spare others the sword of sorrow and anguish, and thus we denigrate mankind. We are men—or we are whimpering children."

He spoke quietly, but his large eyes filled with tears and he bent his head and began to speak in a low voice.

Lucanus had visited the Christian community in Tarsus two months before, which Peter had asked him to do because of defectors and quarrels arising there. An evangelist, too, was needed for the heathen. "The Christian community," Peter had written, "in Tarsus, has begun to question my authority and they are antagonizing the Gentiles and those not yet converted." So Lucanus had obeyed.

The Christians were still accepted in the Jewish community, for the majority were former Jews, and they worshiped together in the synagogues, keeping all the Holy Days as in the days of their fathers, and celebrating together. When the deacons and the priests spoke of Yeshua of Nazareth and His Resurrection, the unconvinced Jews listened politely and many finally accepted Him and His Mission, and among them were some rabbis. Those yet unconvinced watched with indulgent tolerance the consecration of the Host, and those who partook of the Sacrament, and when the Christians sang the Psalms of David in their native Aramaic, or even Hebrew, the Jews joined in with deep reverence. To them, still, the Christians were but an aberrant sect in Israel, which would survive or not survive, depending on the truth they proclaimed. Those who came in the Name of the Lord should be respected, even if their message were in error.

Though all was not completely calm between young Jewish hotheads of deeply traditional beliefs and the self-righteousness and equal hotheadedness of Jewish Christians, it was generally admitted that the Christians spoke in love and a desire to save the souls of men and so they should not be despised or attacked. But it was irritating to be told that unless even the most holy and pious of men accepted the proclaimed Messias they were doomed to spend eternity in hell, and that all their faithful forefathers were now burning in that dolorous place, including blameless infants and the prophets and King David, and virtuous maidens and dutiful matrons. All the devotion and faith and love and obedience to God which the Jews had observed over the centuries, they were told, availed them nothing. They were damned; they were still damned; they would continue to be damned. Their love and faith and obedience and devotion might just as well have been given to Devil or to Moloch. To the Jews this seemed outrageous and an insult to God. But the more wise among the Christian deacons soothed their ire, and so the Christians were still admitted to the synagogues.

The Gentile Christians were another matter. They were excessively zealous, and their zeal was in no wise reduced by the fact that they knew nothing of the Root from which their Faith had sprung. Therefore, they spoke of the words of the Messias as "mysteries" unaware of the Hebraic context in which He had spoken. When He had referred to Elias and Isaias and David and Moses and Solomon and Abraham, they thought these mighty men faintly mythical angels of glorious gods briefly inhabiting the earth to lift up the souls of men, very like their discarded sons of the gods and the goddesses, or their former sylvan deities. In truth, many of them blithely incorporated the beautiful deities in their new religion, and quite a number confused Mary of Nazareth with Artemis or Diana—for were not all these holy virgins? Jesus began to take on the adumbrance of Apollo, the aspects of Zeus. They could not understand the protests of the Jews and the Christian Jews, and were annoyed by them, and when the old gods and goddesses and dryads and nymphs were referred to as "demons" something uneasy stirred in them, born of past memories. Many had been adherents of Isis, and they were bewildered when the Christians refused to give her attributes to the Mother of the Messias.

Some of the Christian Jewish deacons and priests set themselves the laborious task—in love and tenderness—to enlighten the Christian Gentiles about the Faith from which the Messias had sprung, and told how He had declared that He came not to overthrow the Law but to fulfill it. Therefore, the converts must know about the Law or they certainly would never be able to encompass the teachings of the Messias. They must know about Moses and the patriarchs. But some of the new Christians said disdainfully, "That is past and gone. We need only the Messias." "But if you do not know of what He spoke, then how can you comprehend His words and His mission?" The deacons and the elders did not have notable success, for their words were incomprehensible to the converts who found it all a little tedious and had nothing to do with the immediate Second Coming, and their own glorification and their splendor and their rule over the earth, and the consignment of unbelievers to an eternal hell, which they would contemplate from the battlements of Heaven in happy justification and complacence. This made the priests and deacons shudder.

"But you know all these things. You have encountered them, yourself," said Lucanus to the intently listening Saul.

"Alas, yes," said Saul. "I often wonder if Peter were not wiser than I."

"Perhaps it is enough to accept the Messias as Lord and God and Savior," said Lucanus. "These poor ignorant people are faithful, at least, and I do recall hearing that not all the ancient Israelites honored the prophets, either," and he smiled ironically, and Saul smiled in answer.

"Shall only the wise and the cultured inherit Heaven?" asked Saul. "Heaven forbid! For the controversies they would provoke, even in Heaven, would make it a hell. No one is more insistent and intolerant than those who called themselves intellectuals, as I observed, myself, in Israel, among the Sadducees and the Pharisees."

In spite of his apparent calm, he was beginning to pant and his eyes had fixed themselves with mingled terror and fortitude on Lucanus, awaiting the blow of the sword.

He sat upright now in his bed, his arms embracing his knees.

The controversies would have remained in the Christian Tarsus community without danger—except from militants and defectors and self-interpreters and schismatics and dissenters—had it not been for the over zealous who were convinced that they had a mission to destroy every faith they encountered except theirs. They scorned the teachings and the persuasions and the reasonings of the mild and the gentle and the loving. The heathen world must be converted immediately, its idols overthrown, or God would not hold them guiltless. So, as had done their brethren in Rome, they openly attacked religious processions, rushed into temples and overthrew the statues of gods and goddesses, shouted on the street corners that all men were doomed if they continued to honor the ancient inhabitants of Olympus, and that those who did not accept the Messias immediately were accursed and condemned to everlasting torment—when He returned, which would probably be tomorrow—and that the obdurate were unclean, vile, anathema and to be avoided by all good men. Worse still, the laws and the lawgivers of Rome, or any other local authority, were to be disobeyed passively or openly, as a "sign" of the withdrawal of the Christian community from other men. "We are the Witness!" they cried in the market places and the fori and in "heathen" temples. "Believe us, or you must die and writhe forever in the flames of hell! Who is Caesar, that we must obey him? He represents the decadent, the past, the passing, the wickedness, the unjust, licentious, voluptuous, worldly, the depraved, the established evil. We bring to you freedom from Caesar and his monstrousness and his laws! We are another world, ruled by the Messias—who is surely expected even in the days in which we live!"

The Roman military, honoring the greatest of their generals, Augustus Caesar, and having conferred on him the mantle of divinity, raised a temple to him in Tarsus—as they had done in many other cities—and established therein a gigantic and glorified image of their dead Caesar, whom many accounted greater than Julius, himself, who had also been declared a deity. Priests had been appointed to serve him and to receive sacrifices, and retired captains and centurions and soldiers haunted his temple, sighing over these decadent days wherein military prowess was less honored than a mean politician with a snake's tongue and crafty businessmen and bankers and merchants and stockbrokers. Though many of them, being "old" Romans, did not believe in the divinity of Augustus Caesar, they delighted in honoring a symbol of integrity, arms, pride in Rome, Rome, herself, and the glorious days when Rome had stood among lesser nations like a Colossus of law and honor and order and probity.

It was into this temple that a number of Christians roared one sunset, when some of the rheumatic old captains and centurions were paying honor to Augustus and their nation, and not only screamed "Woe!" to those present before the altar, but seized and hurled down the statue of the dead Caesar. The translucent alabaster, beautifully chiseled, smashed to fragments on the gold and black marble of the floor, carrying the altar with it in the sound of thunder and destruction, and the altar lights leaped up amid the tangle of silk like veritable flames out of Hades, perfumed with incense and burning flowers. The priests rushed in horror to survey the ruins, and they lifted their hands and cried to the aghast worshipers, "Let this infamy be avenged, or we are not Romans, but only asses and dogs!"

The Romans, being tolerant and cynical toward their gods, had overlooked the former excesses of the Christians, despite protests from local inhabitants of Tarsus. Who cared about Isis and Cybele and Osiris and Horus and the multitude of other Eastern gods? But when Caesar Augustus had been attacked the patience and tolerance of the Romans came to a cold and vengeful end. Religion might be attacked, for every priest—as every one knew—believed that only he had the truth. But an attack on Augustus was an attack on Rome, herself, a flouting of her authority and rule and law, a display of enormous contempt for all that was Rome. The centurions and the generals and the captains and the soldiers came in a body to the legate and demanded justice and vengeance, on that "Jewish sect," including all the other Jews in Tarsus. Had they not wrought infamy on Rome? Were Romans meek donkeys that they should be openly defamed and ridiculed? Dishonor demanded to be washed out in blood. The noble history of Rome had been spat upon, reviled, and with it all her sons. Worse still, if the desecraters were not apprehended at once, and punished, then Rome might as well furl her banners and slink back behind her walls and surrender to the barbarians, and let the orderly world collapse into shrieking chaos.

The legate, a fat and peaceful man, hated controversy, so he deftly asked the soldiers what they would suggest. They suggested that the Jewish-Christian community be fined a sum sufficient to replace the holy statue, and that they then be commanded to adore it. This seemed eminently reasonable to the legate who called the leaders of the Jewish and Christian community to have an audience with him. He said to them, "Rome is a mighty and pacific city and her legions roam the world to maintain her Pax Romana and her law. Members of your sects have defiled and destroyed a sacred statue to the divinity, Augustus Caesar, in defiance of the ordinances of Rome that all religions must be respected and revered. You must pay in gold for the restoration of this statue and the other destruction wrought upon the temple, and then after that your people must adore the divinity one day a week, man, woman and child, cripple or aged, and make a just sacrifice in his name on the day designated."

The Jewish Community and the Christian agreed to the restoration of the statue. One rabbi and one elder pleaded, "These were delirious youths and we disclaim them and their shameful violence, and if they become known to us we shall punish them. It is very possible that these malcontents are not true believers, for if they were they would have honored the law of respect for others and their religion and their opinions. It is also possible that they are haters of mankind and wish to incite brother against brother for their own obscure and evil purposes."

"I have heard," said the legate, "that the Christians are haters of men."

"We are lovers of men," said the Christian elders, turning very pale. "It was so commanded by God, blessed be His Name, under the Mosaic Law, and by His Messias."

"We have lived in peace with Rome," said the Jewish

rabbis, turning even more pale. "It is true that we have our Zealots and our Essenes, as the Christians have their excessive malcontents, but we have not approved them."

The legate was becoming impatient. "I do not understand the Jewish sects, nor do I wish to understand," he said. "As a Roman, however, I honor your religion. But in turn you must honor mine. You must adore the statue of the divine Augustus Caesar when it has been procured with your money. I have spoken, and will speak no more."

The Jewish and Christian leaders frantically assured each other that with the restoration of the statue the legate would forget that he had commanded public adoration of it by the Jewish and Christian communities. But their hope was in vain, as all hope of man must be, for the Roman soldiers would not permit the legate to forget, for the honor of Rome must not be humiliated lest all subject nations should hear of this and be defiant also. So a day was proclaimed when the Jewish and Christian communities must adore the statue, and those refusing to do so would be severely punished as rebels against Rome, and traitors.

Those wealthy enough among both Jews and Christians quietly departed for long sojourns in other countries, for their health, and those who had no firm faith at all accompanied them, or decided that their religion was worth a simple reverence to the statue, with interior reservations, for the sake of peace and safety and tranquillity. "After all," they said to each other, "have we not been forced through the centuries to worship Baal and Moloch and other heathen gods, and have we not, on the Day of Atonement, disavowed those vows which we were forced to utter, and were forgiven by God, blessed be His Name?"

But the men of stronger faith, both Jews and Christians, declared that they would prefer death to the worship of false idols, and they let their resolution be well known throughout Tarsus. They were vehement in their public utterances, and in the synagogues. This inflamed the soldiers, and the populace also who had never loved the Jews and particularly despised the Christians, the alleged haters of joy and gods and life and men. To them there was no distinction at all between the orthodox Jews and the Christians. They were Jews together, and everyone knew that the Jews were a contentious people. That there were Christians who were Greeks and Syrians and Cilicians and Egyptians and Persians and even Romans was either ignored or unknown to the rabble.

So on one hot Sabbath evening when the nearest and largest synagogue was filled to the doors with both Jews and Christians, worshiping their one God together, the foot soldiers and scores of slavering incendiaries and lusters after blood gathered before the synagogue and set it afire, first barricading the doors so that none could leave. The windows were mere slits in the thick stone walls, so escape there was impossible. The dome of the synagogue became incandescent and from beneath it rose desperate cries and agonized prayers.

Lucanus, overcome, could not continue. He bent his head and wept, and there was only the sound of his weeping in the sweltering little chamber, and the weeping of Timothy. But Saul sat rigidly upright and stared at the cracked plaster wall and his face was the face of a dead man.

He said, "Continue. I know my son, Boreas, is dead, and that you came to tell me." His voice was calm and lifeless.

"It is true," said Lucanus, when he could control himself. "And his young wife, Tamara bas Judah, died also, and their little children, and all of the house of Judah ben Isaac, and the wife of your old tutor, Aristo, and two hundred others. Boreas—he attempted to save his infant daughter, and hoped that one outside would be merciful, and he thrust her through one larger slit—"

"And the child was murdered also," said Saul.

Lucanus could not speak. The silence in the room was like the silence of death. Then Lucanus faltered, "Your tutor, Aristo, was an old man. I must tell you all. When his wife died in that fire he hanged himself. All that you have loved in Tarsus, Saul, has perished."

Saul turned his great leonine head and gazed fixedly and without tears at the candle which fumed and burned redly on the table near his shoulder. He might have been reflecting or indifferent.

"I am a Christian, but I am also a man," said Lucanus, and now his voice was low and baneful. "One of those who perished was the beloved only daughter of the legate, himself. He had not known that the maiden and her mother were Christians, recently baptized. Four wives of the centurions and captains were incinerated. Their husbands had not known that the women were Christians. Those incendiaries and their inciters have been arrested, and they will die for their crimes."

Saul rose from his bed like a man hypnotized and he sought his dagger and he slashed his garments slowly and carefully. Then he sat down in a far corner and bent his head and began the long lamentation for the dead, uttering, "The Lord gives. The Lord takes away. Blessed be—" But he could not say the final words and could only rock on his buttocks, groaning like an animal that has been mortally wounded, until the very walls echoed his groaning.

"Blessed be the Name of the Lord," said Timothy in a broken voice, but Saul did not repeat it.

Then Lucanus rose and went to Saul and stood over him and said in a deep and shaking voice, " 'I am the Resurrection and the Life—' "

When Saul did not heed him the physician knelt before him and took him in his arms. But with a convulsive gesture, such as a dying man gives in his extremity, Saul pushed him from him. Then he fell face down on the floor as if he had died, and the dreadful groaning ceased.

Together Lucanus and Timothy lifted the unconscious man to his bed, and he lay there and the physician felt his weak and staggering pulse and wiped away the icy sweat which gathered on his face. And Lucanus remembered how he had stood outside the synagogue, listening to the screams of children and their mothers and had watched the walls finally fall in mercy upon them in a last and terrible explosion of scarlet flame. The physician found it in his heart to hate again, even more fiercely than he had hated on that appalling evening. He looked down at Saul and he questioned why this man, who gave all his life and heart to God, should have been made to suffer so, as if an evil punishment had crashed upon him.

Lucanus said to Timothy, "Would that he die before he awakens again to knowledge! But that, doubtless, will not be granted. He will continue to the end. He is a greater warrior than I, for I confess that if all that I have loved had died so, in innocence, and defenseless, I should turn away—"

"They live again, in the Vision of the Messias, blessed be His Name," said Timothy. "Only we are left to mourn, and to remember."

But Lucanus did not reply.

Chapter 47

LUCANUS stayed at the inn with Saul for many days, and for those days Saul lay on his bed, mute and still and almost motionless. Lucanus fed him like an infant, and Saul ate and drank a little as if only his body were present and his soul at a far distance. The physician bathed him and removed garments and replaced them. He bought the best of wine for the stricken man, and mixed with it certain potions and the beaten eggs of geese, and forced it gently through the clenched lips. Young Timothy was like a small son whose father had been struck down, and it soothed him to be sent on errands and to write letters. He would look at Saul with grief, wringing his hands.

Peter, having heard, wrote tenderly to the man whom he had once declared to be a thistle in his hand, a stone under his foot, a cinder in his eye. He reminded Saul of what the Messias had said, that men, though they die, will live again in the radiant shadow of His Being, and that those who perish in His Name will be assumed to Him at once. Sephorah wrote a tearful and loving letter, and so did many members of the Jerusalem Community, and elders and deacons who had once quarreled with him and now suffered with him. Lucanus read all these bountiful letters to Saul, who said nothing. Then members of the Christian community in Tarsus came in groups to console him, but he would not see them. They promised prayers for his alleviation of sorrow, and he did not answer them.

The cold bright winter came to Athens and Lucanus

bought a small brazier for Saul's chamber, and he now slept on a floor pallet near Saul's bed the better to hear him and attend him. Though Saul was so still and so silent, Lucanus guessed acutely at the agony he was enduring, too great for speech, for even the flicker of an eye, for tears, for mourning.

"He was a noble Apostle," said the Christians.

"He *is* a noble Apostle," said Lucanus, and they went away in silence.

"He is our brother, and though we do not accept what he has told us he is still our brother, a Jew among Jews. He has our prayers, and may God, blessed be His Name, infuse new life into him that he may live again," said the Jews.

"I pray with you," said Lucanus, "in the Name of Him Who was a Jew also."

One night Saul awoke from his lethargy and was instantly aware. He saw Lucanus sleeping wearily beside him. He saw the weak candle flame. Confused memories tried to return to him, but he shrank from them. Then he fell asleep again. He began to dream.

He dreamt that he was wandering in a vast garden, and the tremendous trees floated in a golden mist and all the flowers glittered with a silvery dew. There was the sound of singing waters, and the distant sight of ivory and golden hills, and fountains. It was warm, and the soft air was perfumed and the sky beamed in clear blueness. He wandered, and knew there was something he must remember which would cause him anguish, but it was sufficient now to walk in this bliss, this shining solitude, this calm joy, this assurance of love and companionship, though he saw no one. The grass under his feet was fresh and new and sparkling with greenness, and he saw glades offering blue cool shadow and many of the trees were flowering in myriad colors. How blessed this was, how full of peace. Who had said, "The peace that passes understanding?" Saul could not remember, but the words echoed in his heart and he knew that peace. A branch of a tree hung over his head and he saw it was heavy with scarlet globed fruit, and he took one and ate of it and it was like honey and wine, refreshing his soul.

Then he saw a young man approaching him across the

grass, and there were enormous wings of light palpitating from his shoulders, and his garments shimmered like moonlight and clung to his massive limbs and flecks of white fire radiated from his robe and his face was more beautiful than the face of any man, with locks glossy and dark and polished, and eyes deep and dark and bearing in them an expression which no human creature could understand. It was enigmatic, removed, kind and aloof. His feet, sandaled with silver, barely bent the grass and where he moved he left a fading brightness. A curious sword hung in its curious scabbard from his gemmed girdle, a sword shaped like a jagged bolt of lightning, and there was lightning on his brow.

Saul was not afraid, but he felt a pulsing deep within him and an awe. The young man came closer to him, and he was taller than the tallest man and his arms were clasped with jeweled armlets. He looked down at Saul reflectively, and his slight smile was not human though it remained gentle. Saul could see his strong pale throat and the throbbing in it.

"Saul ben Hillel," said the stranger in a voice which was both close and far, and filled the silent air. "I bear a message for you."

Saul knelt before him and clasped his hands, and waited, looking up into that unearthly countenance.

"There is a time for mourning, and that time has passed," said the stranger. "You have forgotten much, but it has been forgiven you, as all is forgiven to those who love. Now you must gird yourself like a man and resume what has been ordained for you, lest those who love you are grieved that their passing has ended your life and your mission. Multitudes have sorrowed before you, and multitudes will sorrow after you, but sorrow is vain, for only One can heal and you have not asked Him."

"My heart is only human," said Saul. "I sorrow with a human heart."

"He also has a human Heart," said the stranger with severity. "It has grieved, and is grieving still, as no other man could grieve. The humanity of His Heart surpasses yours, Saul ben Hillel, and His sorrow is as a mountain. Will you desert and betray Him, or will you rise and say, 'There is none else, O my Lord and my God'?"

Saul began to weep. The stranger continued, "God also has a Son, and He saw that Son offer up Himself for wretched mankind, saw His flesh bruised and nailed and torn, saw His humiliation and the fear and shrinking in that most human Heart, saw the malice which surrounded Him, and watched His death."

Saul lifted his tearful face and stretched up his arms and looked at the sky and said, "Forgive me, my Lord and my God, and strengthen me so that I may endure and not forget again, and spread Your Wings beneath my feeble flutter and carry me. For I am not God. I am only a man and You have fashioned me to suffer as a man."

When he looked for the stranger he was gone, and now a dark noisomeness closed about Saul and he awakened and saw it was cold hard morning and Lucanus was stirring the coals in the brazier.

Saul said in a weak but clear voice, "Dear friend, I have seen an angel, and he has reproved me." Now, in reality he wept the first tears, and Lucanus held him in his arms and did not restrain him, but comforted him in silence.

And now the long missionary journey began. Accompanied by Timothy and Luke, Saul resumed a colossal task which to him seemed endless, frequently frustrating, dolorous, desperate, harsh with opposition, resentment, persecution and ridicule and obduracy from members of the young Church. On receiving a letter from Corinth that he not visit that city again he answered sadly and tenderly: "I made up my mind not to make you another painful visit. For if I cause you pain, who is there to make me glad but the One whom I have always pained? And I wrote as I did so that when I came I might not be pained by those who should have made me rejoice.—For I wrote out of much affliction and anguish of heart and with many tears, not to cause you pain but to let you know the abundant love that I have for you."*

As time passed his afflicted eye began to darken, and his strength, which had, for years, been the strength and energy of heart and spirit and will, declined alarmingly.

*Cor. 2:1–4.

In vain Lucanus urged him not to strive so vigorously, and to rest between journeys. "If I am to bring order out of stubborn and doctrinal chaos then I must press on," he said. "There is a time to die and I would that death will not find me sleeping, in luxurious ease and forgetfulness. My task is not complete."

Sorrow and years had taken the last audacious red from his whitened hair and his brows, and his face was creviced with sorrow and pain and there was a faint but constant tremor about his wide firm mouth. But he walked upright and strongly on his bowed legs and his glance, despite his afflicted eye, was still leonine and commanding, and his voice held an imperious note still, and a fascination, which seized men's attention. None held a lukewarm opinion about him. He was fiercely and devotedly loved, or as fiercely and devotedly hated, in the Church. Rebuking, chastising, exhorting, condemning, praising, loving, explaining, teaching, converting, comforting, laughing or weeping, jesting or scorning, he journeyed apparently without fatigue, his eyes sparkling or blazing or tender, in accordance with the occasion, his manner abrupt, violent, impatient, conciliatory, depending on those he encountered. If he marveled often at the blind stupidity of man and the sin and error in which he appeared confirmed, embracing the death of the soul which so terrified him, himself, Saul also saw the piteous predicament of man, the hopeless sorrow, the bewilderment, the anxious pain, the infirmities, and he marveled anew that so frail a creature possessed also a fortitude and an endurance and a desire for truth and certitude which must move the hearts of angels.

Once he said to Lucanus, "If I were to be permitted but one word to describe a man I would say he is brave. For he is brave in spite of his intelligence which makes him aware of a hostile world and environment, and which seemingly is without hope and surety or help for pain, and is heavy with loss and sadness and disappointment. Animals are not aware of these things, so they have an animal courage for the day's needs. But a man knows the years and the memory of them, and he knows that the coming years hold out to him no promise of splendor and satisfaction but only a repetition of yesterday, and in spite of that he has the bravery to endure, and we must salute him."

His compassion grew as he journeyed to the harsh shores of Lystra, to golden Ephesus, to Macedonia, to Philippi of the gray stone mountains and the scarlet poppy plains. It was in Philippi that the Romans—becoming more and more exasperated by the Christians—and having heard that he was a turbulent man who insulted the gods, and desecrated their temples and aroused rebellion among slaves and freedmen and the rabble, and had commanded them to rise against Rome and their masters, seized him and threw him into prison, there to await trial and probable execution as a traitor. This was done on a day when Lucanus and Timothy were absent.

The Romans brought him before a magistrate to be cited before his trial. He said to the magistrate with his old pride, "I am a Roman citizen, not by purchase, but by birth, and I demand a jury of my peers. For I am blameless of the spiteful charges you have heard against me, the lies and the calumnies. I came in peace. I would depart in peace."

The magistrate was impressed both by Saul's manner and speech, and by his claim to Roman citizenship. So he had the manacles removed from his wrists and ankles—restraints but for slaves and subjects—and ordered a goblet of wine for him, and bread and cheese and meat, to be served to him three times a day in his cell, while awaiting his formal trial. The magistrate would have released him, but for a number of years the excesses of the more zealous among the Christians had vexed him, in spite of his Roman tolerance, and there were complaints from the people of Philippi against them, and the priests of the temples also complained that as so many were being converted to this Jewish sect they were losing revenue and the temples were full no longer. As the temples paid a portion of that revenue to Roman taxgatherers for the maintenance of the Roman garrisons in the city, this was a serious matter. There was also a rumor that some of the younger Christians, and the more passionate, had a disagreeable habit of openly scorning the gods of Rome, and refusing to do them honor.

And Saul was rumored to have come to Philippi to cause greater disturbances and more inflammatory rebel-

lion, and it was also rumored that he had written letters
to the Christian community to resist Roman laws and
ordinances even before his arrival. The magistrate, on
questioning Saul, came to the conclusion that all this was
lies, but as the feeling in the city was intense against him
he had no other choice but to incarcerate him and
remand him for trial.

"It is a mortifying thing for a Roman citizen to be
held in prison on the word of mere freedmen and rabble
who have no claim on Rome at all," said the magistrate
to his colleagues. "But we know how passionate the
rabble is, and how easily incited to riot and incendiarism,
and so we must pacify them, though the gods know
why! I do not. I only obey my orders from Rome."

"In less easy and decadent days we should merely have
set upon the rabble at the first sign of rebellious and
dangerous behavior," his colleagues said with a sigh.
"But now all is conciliation, understanding, smiling tolerance, excuses and a light hand on the sword. This will
mean the death of Rome. If law, and the authority of
law, is flouted, then barbarism follows, and chaos."

Saul sat in his cell and fumed. He was not afraid
for himself, but he was distressed that his mission was
delayed, and that it might even be destroyed. Lucanus, a
Roman citizen also, was permitted to visit him and to
bring him blankets and other small comforts, and the
Romans were struck by the aspect of the Greek and his
voice and his profession.

"Alas, that you find me here," said Saul, and immediately asked about the Christian community. Lucanus did
not tell him that it was like all the young Christian
communities, lacerated by dissensions and threatened
schisms and doctrinal quarrels, and even suits against
members in the Roman courts, and avid youths who
spoke of "the sword of God." Instead, he told Saul that
the community was large and flourishing—which it was
—and that many converts were being made among the
Gentiles. He assured his friend that he would soon be
cleared of false charges, and released, though he was
not certain of this, himself. As for Lucanus, he must
go alone now on his own journeys as an evangelist.

The two friends embraced, encouraging each other.
Saul, through the bars of his cell, watched Lucanus re-

treating down the wet stone corridor. He fell on the blankets and wept, and the passing Roman soldiers observed this and wondered, for Saul had impressed them with his courage and his calmness.

Saul was stricken anew by the thought that all he loved had died: His son, Boreas, the wife and children of Boreas, Elisheba bas Judah. Why should I, he thought, old and worn and tired and despairing, live and the young and beautiful die? For they have dreams and hopes that no longer haunt me, and lovely illusions spun of rainbows and moonlight and their eyes are sunlit and they carry banners with wonderful insignia and march to the sound of drums that never were, but which are glorious to their ears. What they have is illusion—but how sweeter it is than this bleak reality with its intimation of bones and imminent decay! Alas, when I think of my young beloved's deaths, Heaven, itself, seems less shining, less desirable, for what a child suffers in agony at the hands of man must mar the radiance of the hereafter eternally for him.

Alas, alas, he said to himself, I think and grieve as a man for I am nothing but a man and my heart is nothing but a wound. Would that I die tonight!

"The Christian rabbi weeps," said the soldiers to each other, "but for sorrow and not for himself."

Saul thought of his old wry teacher, Aristo, and even in his tears and in the midst of his pain he began to smile. "Ah, Aristo," he murmured aloud, "one day in my childhood you threatened me that I should find myself imprisoned because of my temper and other imperfections of character, and I laughed gleefully in your face, for in those glowing years the world was before me like an opal, filled with delicate shadows and fiery light and endless breathing colors, and set ablaze by the Presence of God. Yet you find me here now, dear friend. I cannot believe that you are not in Heaven, for all teachers must rise there at once, considering their pupils, so look down from the blue and blazing battlements and send me comfort—if you will."

The soldiers yawned at the end of the narrow stony corridor. Saul occupied one of the cells which had a high little window looking out upon the city, for he was a Roman citizen and so could not be consigned to the dungeons below, airless and black. He was also the only prisoner on this corridor. The soldiers squatted by the light of a lantern and torch and began to dice and to sing to pass the dull hours of the night. Some drowsed with their backs against the huge damp stones of the walls, wrapped in their cloaks. Some ate their rude military rations and drank their ordinary wine and talked of girls; a few engaged in boxing or wrestling matches. Saul could hear their young boisterous voices, their hoarse laughter, and he was filled with love for them, these youths who did not know as yet what it was to be old and tired and anxious and bereaved.

One or two strolled down to converse with him, for they found him witty and his laughter as rough and loud as their own, and he often had strange tales to tell, concerning his Deity who had died in Jerusalem on a cross for inciting the people to riot against the Romans. They listened in fascination to his account of his vision on the desert to Damascus, and were awed, but not touched by faith. They believed him without question. It was a magnificent story. The Jewish God was no less beautiful and puissant than their own, and no more to be believed. But, it was a magnificent story and they had awe for the man who had seen the vision. "He is a poet," they said. "A veritable Homer."

They told him they could not understand the Christians, who had no desire to be soldiers and did not lust after the things of the belly, nor after girls, and did not engage in the pleasant ways of barter and cheating in the marketplaces. Were they not men, and did they not have the parts of men? Or, did they hate the ways of men and so men, themselves, for disdaining the pleasures of the world? They listened to Saul, but shook their young heads. They had no hatred for the Christians, for who knew which god was the most powerful? But they were commanded to keep the peace, and the Christians were not always peaceful, but they openly denounced the gods as "idols" and refused, in the courts, to swear by Apollo that they would speak the truth and swore only by their own God, Who was not recognized among the hierarchy of the Divine as yet. So, who could trust their testimony and their promises? Saul explained, over and over, but as he spoke in a context totally strange to their ears and their minds—he was not successful. However, they were kind to him and gave him of their own wine and fruit. After all, a wise man, even though a prisoner, was not to be despised, particularly a Roman citizen.

They said to him tonight, "Why do you weep so loudly, Rabbi?"

They leaned against the bars of the cell and gazed between the bars at him with earnest youthful faces, for Saul had not seemed to them the kind of man who would weep.

He looked at them by the light of the dim lantern they held and he said gently, trying to halt his tears, "I had a son, and he had a son and a beautiful wife and a little daughter, and my son and all his family died—in a fire. Therefore, I weep."

"Ah," said one of the soldiers, with sympathy. He held his leather flask of wine to Saul, between the bars. Saul did not want the wine but he desired more not to hurt the feelings of the lad, so he thanked him and drank a little, restraining a grimace at the vinegary smart of it. The soldier said with the wisdom of youth, "It does nothing to weep for the dead. They have passed to Pluto's realm or they are in the Elysian Fields or on the Blessed Isles, and they know us not any longer nor care for us."

Saul said, "It is a good and worthy thing to pray for the dead, and to ask their prayers in return." As always, he baffled them. "Their prayers," said Saul, "are more efficacious than the prayers of the living, for they are closer to God."

The soldiers nodded gravely in polite affirmation but did not believe it in the least. These Jews were very curious. They wandered back to their companions. Saul watched their going. I have no power, he thought sadly. These lads listen to me each night and day yet I do not move them.

He sat on his blankets and listened to the noisy laughter and voices of the soldiers, and mourned in the darkest part of his soul for his dead. Then all at once he became conscious that there was utter silence beyond his cell, not even broken by the patrolling footsteps of the guard. He listened acutely. It was deathly quiet as if he were incarcerated in the blackest womb of the earth where no man lived but he. He rose achingly from his blankets and thrust his head as far as possible between the bars and looked down the corridor.

He saw an incredible sight. The soldiers were not sleeping but they were frozen like statues in the very acts and postures in which they had been engaging. Some sat rigidly against the walls; some were stilled in the movements of dicing, some were standing with their flasks to their mouths, others were caught in the very motion of chewing, others had been stilled, as if they had seen Medusa, herself, in the gestures of boxing and wrestling. One young soldier was immobilized in the air just above the back of his comrade, who had thrown him over his shoulder, and another stood, knees bent, helmeted head averted, with his fist against the mouth of another soldier.

Saul could not believe it. He saw that the soldiers were not unconscious, for he caught the dim glitter of their open, glaring, terrified eyes by the flickering red light of a torch thrust into the wall and the lantern attached to a stone. Only their eyes were aware and in motion, and their young faces were running with sweat as they strove to shake off the invisible stone that encased their bodies.

Then they, and Saul, saw the black iron door slowly opening. The soldiers had heard the creak of it, and they rolled their eyes in its direction, though this was the only part of them which could move. Their sweat fell over their cheeks like tears, dripped onto their leather-harnessed chests. Saul, as fearful and as fascinated as themselves, saw the dark aperture widening as the door opened. Then a young man in a long white tunic stood on the threshold, fair and stately as a god, and as serene and indifferent.

He glanced with aloof amiability at the transfixed soldiers, stepped over their legs easily and moved around them. He walked down the corridor to Saul's cell and there was no sound of his sandals on the wet stones. It was as if he walked on air just above the floor. He paused at the bars of Saul's cell, and looked into his face with that calm and remoteness which were more frightening than violence, and even more terrible than rage, for it was not human and what was human could not disturb him.

Saul could see the slight luminous aura about him, like pale and shifting gold. It illuminated his large features, his robe, his hands, his feet. He smiled slightly at Saul, but not with the friendship and concern of a man. He said, and his voice echoed along the corridor like the long sound of music: "Put on your sandals, Saul of Tarshish, and take up your cloak, for I have come to release you."

Saul, as if stricken like the soldiers also, could not stir for a moment or two. A chill and ambiguous fear came to him, and he thought, "Is he releasing me to death, though all my work is still before me?"

The young man said with stately peremptoriness, "Hasten," and his eyes had a glint of impatience.

Saul gathered up his blankets, his cloak and a scroll, and put on his sandals with trembling hands. He could not look away from his visitor during this, and he teemed with questions he knew would not be answered. Then he stood up.

The young man put his hands on the bars of the cell and shook them, not vigorously, but as a child would shake them with the slightest effort. And at that instant the earth roared in thunder, the floor rocked under Saul's feet so that he staggered and fell heavily against the wall of his cell, and his human heart was terror-stricken. The thunder echoed and beat through the air, and the walls swayed and the torch and lantern down the corridor blew as if a gale had seized them. The soldiers did not move, but Saul, running to the bars and gazing down the corridor to them, could not only see the dread on their young faces but the ghastly horror of their living eyes. They still had not moved, petrified into statues.

Saul heard a clanging. The door of his cell had flown open. It hung on its hinges, broken, and not by human hands. The visitor had vanished. Saul left his cell on shaking legs. He moved slowly down the corridor. He said to the young soldiers watching him, "Do not fear. You will soon be released." But they only stared at him, as motionless as their own shadows.

He passed from the prison into the dark of the city, which was illuminated only by the red flare of torches and restless lanterns which bobbed through the streets. The earthquake had done little harm, but there were agitated groups on the streets and alarmed soldiers. Saul made his way to his inn, and found Timothy there.

"Saul!" cried the young man, rising from his bed and falling upon Saul's neck with a groaning exclamation of joy and relief. "They have released you!"

"No," said Saul, "God did."

He put his hands on Timothy's shoulders and said, "I was mourning and I was lost and forgotten, and God sent his messenger to lead me out of prison."

But as a Roman and a lawyer he knew his duty. The next morning, after a brief and peaceful sleep, he went to the magistrate who had sent him to prison. The rumor, however, of what had transpired the night before had run before him and the magistrate regarded him gravely. "I have heard the soldiers," he said at once. "If the gods do not desire you to remain in prison and be tried, and punished, who is man to command that? If the gods believe you innocent of all charges, who am I to declare you guilty?"

Now there was fear in his eyes, and superstition. The soldiers had told him, in their own terror and excitement, that Apollo, himself, or at least Mercury, had caused an earthquake to free Saul of Tarshish, and that they had been unable to prevent his escape. The gods, it would seem, loved the Christians. The magistrate made a mouth. "I do not admire their taste," he said, and wrote on the records that Saul of Tarshish had been found innocent and had been delivered from prison.

Chapter 48

THE story of the miraculous deliverance exalted the Christian community, and they never tired of hearing about it and the heavenly messenger. If Saul had been so rescued and by such an ineffable personage, then surely the Messias' Second Coming was at hand.

"It does not follow," said Saul. "What if the laborers in the fields said, 'We believe the master will return home tonight and will ask us to feast with him, so why should we labor and exhaust ourselves and not stand at the gates and watch for his coming?' The master would return to discover that the grain had rotted because it had not been reaped, and woe to that man who had let his scythe remain idle! We do not know when He will return. But He must not find His harvest lost and the rats among the grain and the bread devoured by vermin."

It seemed to many that Saul was too harsh, and that he did not believe that the Lord would imminently arrive, and so there was much discontent. But Saul exhorted them and taught them like children, and after a long sojourn in Philippi he resumed his journeys. He rejoiced in the gathering multitudes of Gentile converts, whom he patiently taught and with a paternal love. He baptized them, guided them, enlightened them and brought them in, rejoicing, to the Christian community. The majority of Christians welcomed them with almost the deep love which Saul held for them, but there were also dark glances of suspicion and contention and whispers among the majority. These were sometimes quite valid, for some of the new Christians were at first exalted by the thought of the almost instantaneous arrival of the Messias in clouds of glory, to judge the quick and the dead, the sheep and the goats, and when He did not appear but the daily drudgery and weariness remained, and the same problems of taxes and food and shelter and discontented wives and intransigent children and wages and quarrels and ills of the flesh, the new Christians began to doubt, and frequently doubt was followed by defection and contempt and hatred and ridicule, and even malice and a desire for vengeance on the "deceivers."

In vain did Saul try to enlighten these men and women. They would look at him narrowly, and narrowly smiling. He had promised them ecstasy of soul and a seat in Heaven—but the world remained the same and the Messias tarried, if He ever intended to return at all, or if there was any truth in Saul's words. They had sought, he saw, not the rapture of the oneness with God, not the deliverance from sin and death, not the delight of service and virtue, but worldly affluence and comfort and triumph. "Did you not tell us of the words of Christ, that if we accepted the Kingdom of Heaven all else will be given to us? Yet, nothing has been given! The world remains the same and our misery and our hopelessness, in spite of our acceptance."

"His Kingdom is not of this world," Saul would repeat. But they contradicted him with his own quotations from the words of the Messias, and they resented his explanations and interpretations. So, they defected. Some of the Christian Jews said to him with gloomy satisfaction, "What other did you expect, Saul ben Hillel? They cannot comprehend the Messias, nor can they encompass His parables which echo the old Scriptures."

The more educated of the Gentile converts, in particular the Greeks, said, "They are ignorant and venal, low slaves or freedmen or peasants. Their old religions taught them only earthly joys and victories, if they pleased the gods, and they cannot understand spiritual rewards."

But Saul grieved over these wandering sheep and wept over them and prayed for them, and some returned for in the world they found no hope at all, no love or companionship, no friends, no concern for their welfare. At least in the Christian community they had friendship, and if they were hungry they were fed, and if they were thirsty they were given wine, and if they had no shelter a roof was found for them. "Let us not drive them forth, like intruding cattle, these poor little ones," said Saul, to the vexed Christians. "Did He not seek the lost sheep and bring them home? There is room in His House for the very meanest and the most humble and stupid, and His wings can cover all humanity. Let us be patient, and teach and bring light to those dark small minds, and who knows but one day they will shine suddenly like the sun?"

As Saul traveled in Asia Minor and in Europe he not only founded new churches but increased and heartened the established. He wrote always, endless letters full of eloquence and poetry and passion and faith and love, and especially to his dear friends in Corinth, the weaver Aquila and his wife, Priscilla, who had once sheltered him. His letters were cherished and treasured and guarded, but many were lost forever though their spirit remained. He suffered stonings, blows, floggings and shipwrecks on his journeys, for to the pious Jews he was still the "great renegade," and many of the Christians remembered his earlier persecutions of the Church, and priests of local religions resented his converts and their loss of revenue, and the Romans were suspicious of this white-maned man who spoke in cultured accents but lived like a slave. Such men were dangerous, as history had noted, for they did not love the things of the world and incited men against the world, and the world was the theater for law and order and Roman prosperity, and what else existed but the world of men—and perhaps of the gods? Besides, it was reputed that he spoke of "the conquest of the world," and that was treasonous.

Yet, multitudes of Romans also became converts, and soldiers and their officers, including those in Philippi who had spread the wondrous tale of Saul's deliverance from prison. As a number of these were rich the Church could expand her charitable endeavors and succor the sick and the dying and the abandoned, and the children left to die of exposure, and runaway slaves and the aged and former prisoners. Great ladies in various cities became Christians, and found in the new faith a rescue from boredom and fear, an inspiration beyond mere physical beauty and fleshly pleasures. Becoming Christians, they were charitable and their hearts, for the first time in their pampered lives, were moved by the misery of their fellow men whom they had once regarded as lower than vermin.

One day Saul said to Timothy who was now, himself, no longer young, "My time grows shorter. I have had a vision. I must return again to Jerusalem, and when I saw the vision I saw a darkening over the beloved city—and never again after that will I see her."

"You are weary," said Timothy. "Your tired flesh speaks, and not your soul."

But Saul had his premonitions. "I long to see my sister again, and her grandchildren, whom I have never seen," he said evasively. "I hear of my nephew, Amos, and his triumphs during his travels and ministrations, and I might encounter him in Jerusalem." He smiled at Timothy. "I am only a man, and I need human comforting, though none appears aware of that."

He received letters from Lucanus, and answered them, and they rejoiced in each other's victories and converts. "One day," wrote Lucanus, "there will not be a people or a nation that will be ignorant of His Name, and the triumph He foretold will have come to pass. Press on, dear friend, though you complain of bodily weakness and a weariness that will not lift! It is only our flesh, and it can be commanded and subdued, for He will give us sustenance for our souls and not let us die before we have accomplished our mission."

Saul sighed on receiving this letter. He had come on a period of dryness where the way was no longer plain and all inspiration had been removed. He knew the Truth, but his mind felt dulled and his volition was faltering. Sometimes he dreamt of his house in Tarsus, now sold to strangers, and he could smell the roses and the jasmine again and see the black carved bridge over the peaceful water, and the arbors and the grottoes. His whole being craved for surcease, for quiet loving voices and the touch of loving hands, and the sun setting on palm and cypress and pomegranate tree and sycamore, and gentle music in the atrium, and the smiles and voice of his dead son, whose children he had never seen. Sometimes he dreamt that he was a child again, laughing at Aristo and teasing his little sister, Sephorah. And sometimes he dreamt of Dacyl and her love for him, and his love for her no longer seemed lewd and wicked but the love of a young Adam for his Eve, and the place of the waterfall was the Garden of Eden.

And there were times when he was beset by evil agonies which he recognized but could only strive against, weakly, though knowing their source. Had it all been a phantom, a dream, his whole life? Sometimes he groaned like Job, "My eye is also dim by reason of sorrow, and all my members are as a shadow." In this dark confusion he would wander for days, and even weeks, and all that he said and did during that time was as if he struggled in manacles of iron. He found his followers tedious and dull; he found even his devoted Timothy to be obtuse. His native impatience, fed by illness and age, would be like a flame in his heart and his flesh would itch and he would scratch himself until he bled. All sought his comfort and learning and enlightenment; all believed he was more than man. If they saw his exhaustion they were dismayed and troubled, but felt little pity, for was he not the shepherd and they only the sheep, and must the sheep not be eternally comforted and sustained or the shepherd be held guilty? When he saw their faces Saul would arouse himself by sheer power of will, for if the sheep doubted or felt lost they might well stray. They were fragile and uncertain in the wilderness of their lives, and could stumble. So he would speak to them resolutely, with a smile on his ashen lips, and they were relieved.

Then one night he received the summons to return to Jerusalem, and he awoke, saying to himself, "The beginning of the end has arrived, and soon I will find rest."

Chapter 49

ALL had been the reverse of peaceful in Jerusalem during Saul's long and many absences.

The Christians—or the Nazarenes as their fellow Jews still called them in the city—and especially the young men, had joined with the Essenes and the Zealots, and were led into a desperate situation by the Zealot, Eleazar. He lured them into a turbulent and deadly struggle with the Romans, saying that the time had come to free their beloved country. Whether or not he was a true Christian Saul had not been able to learn from the letters he had received from Jerusalem, but it was evident that Eleazar was a violent man and was employing the Nazarenes "to take our people from bondage," as the Messias had promised. So fierce and savage was the uprising that nearly thirty thousand Jews, both "faithful" and Nazarene, were slaughtered bloodily in the Temple purlieus, and the Roman procurator declared a state of revolution and anarchy. Eleazar was found and publicly executed. And the bitterest of hatreds rose among the people.

The families of the Jews who were murdered blamed those deaths on the Nazarenes, and now considered the "heretics" to be their mortal enemies, who brought down slaughter and death and ruin on all Jews. They detested the "renegade" Jews more profoundly than they detested the Gentile Nazarenes, for were not the Christian Gentiles the humblest and generally the most peaceable of the workers in their midst? But the "heretics" included some of the more intelligent and wealthiest and educated members of the Jewish people, and therefore they should have restrained Eleazar and his Zealots and not made common cause with them against the Romans. "Revolutionaries! Brigands! Outlaws!" they cried to the Christians. "You betray your own people and lead them to the slaughter-house!"

Now it was said that all the churches established throughout the civilized world by the Apostles and evangelists were subversive and were instigating riots and upheavals against Rome. Once Saul had been denounced to the Romans in Jerusalem: "He is a plague-carrier, a fomenter of revolt among all the Jews of the Empire, which he detests." This had been taken so seriously by the Emperor in Rome that he had warned the Jews of Alexandria not to receive missionaries, unless they wished to be condemned as participants in "a pest which threatens the whole world now." To the Romans, there was no significant difference between the Nazarene Jews and the "faithful" Jews, for the new sect was "but a Jewish sect, now led by the most irresponsible and murderous of the Zealots and Essenes."

Saul had known of these things; he knew he was considered a Zealot by Jew and Roman alike. His appearance in Jewish synagogues throughout the world, during his travels, was greeted with dismay at first, then was tolerated, and later was cursed. He would bring fresh death and persecution and forced exile on his people—he must, therefore, be avoided at all costs. He had caused "the first Jewish war" against the Romans. The Jews were determined that he would not cause another. They heard with sorrow and despair that the synagogues in Rome, among the more prosperous, had been closed by the Emperor, "for fear of a mounting revolution." When the Nazarenes ceased their worship in the synagogues in Rome the Emperor permitted their reopening. But the bitterness and terror remained, and now the cleavage between the Nazarenes and their fellow Jews was complete. "The Nazarene youths," wrote the historian Josephus later, "are unkempt, savage, intolerant, lawless, alas, and their very appearance excites Roman animosity, for they appear as barbarians and not part of a civilized community. They walk and talk offensively, and with open sneers at authority and defy established government in all nations. They engage in pitched battles with guards in the cities, and hurl unmentionable weapons upon those guards, and the soldiers, shouting that the return of the Messias is at hand and they were in the vanguard of his army."

In Israel, the Essenes and the Zealots (so many of them now Nazarenes) became a particular object of the frightened hatred of the Jews. Therefore, they refused to listen to their message and all sympathy for them, as patriotic Jews opposed to the Roman, disappeared. In other parts of the world Saul was received with resentment and fury by his fellow Jews, as a potential troublemaker and revolutionary, and so a threat to their lives. In vain he pleaded that "His Kingdom is not of this world," and that "freedom from bondage" meant freedom of the soul from death and sin. They thought this a mere sophistry, and so did the Romans.

So Saul returned to Jerusalem to reconcile both Jews and Christian Jews, and to save the Church there. On the journey, he was often overcome by despair. He feared for the Christian community in Israel, and deplored the excesses of the Christian Zealots and Essenes. He had written to them while still in Athens: "While we proclaim the Messianic Age—for it has truly arrived—we insist that the Law is still in force, for it is immortal and was given by God, blessed be His Name. Alas, that the Zealots believe that the Messianic Age compels them to throw off all restraint and to engage in riot and incendiarisms and physical attacks and disobedience! For the Lord is the Prince of Peace, and not the Leader of violence and murder and hatred between brothers."

He had been even more disturbed at receiving information from Jerusalem that the Gentile converts were misinterpreting the Messias, and were using His very Name to incite trouble. As these converts were in the main former slaves, and freedmen, and of many random races, and artisans and malcontents and desirous of the riches "promised" by the Messias, they mischievously mocked the Roman military on the streets of Jerusalem and caused much disturbance and hostility.

The Romans felt themselves, and their Empire, threatened throughout the world, and were aghast at the incredible spread of the Messianic Message in every nation. Saul found matters in Israel much worse than even his vivid imagination had imagined. Simon Peter, the bishop of the Christian community, had left for Rome, with the desire to bring order and comfort to the Christians and to allay the terrors of his fellow Jews. Saul learned of all this in Joppa, the seaport, where he remained for a few days.

Joppa, though it stank as did all cities, was still swept by the winds of the sea, freshening and stimulating. The streets were like stairs, one above the other, and walled and paved with blocks of marble and sandstone, and wound precipitately, and were so narrow that overhanging balconies almost touched. The windows which looked out upon the streets were grilled and slitlike, and there were meager little shops set in the walls below. Huge flocks of gulls lifted like metallic gold shavings flung against the hyacinth skies, and glittered. And everywhere, where there was a spot of bare ground, rose the green clouds of tamarisk and sycamore trees, and the knifelike emerald blades of palms, and the counters of the little shops were heaped with citrons, green and yellow, and cakes and meats and fabrics and spices. Over all was the chuckling and wash of the sea and the strong sea-born winds, and the cries of children and the complaints of animals.

Saul found the house of Simon the Tanner and remained there for a space, while they discussed the precarious situation of the Jerusalem Community, beset within and without. Simon was a crooked little man with a satyrish grin and small dancing eyes and clever hands, and he made elaborate purses and pouches as well as sandals and boots, and exquisite ornaments of leather embossed with gold and silver. He was not a man to take life too seriously, as he explained to Saul. What came of a somber countenance and fears and premonitions and terrors? A bad digestion, and one knew that a bad digestion could cast gloom on the soul, and in that gloom the soul was cut off from the life-giving sun of God, blessed be His Name. To fear was to doubt God, for were not all things in His Hand? Saul looked at that small and malformed face and wondered if Simon were secretly jesting at him.

"I have loved greatly, and I have lost greatly," said Simon, in his shrill womanish voice. "But I endured, and

I survived. What avail is it to complain? The Jerusalem Community will survive, if God wills it, and it will not survive, if He wills it."

"God's 'failures' are really man's failures," said Saul, with bitterness. "It is easy to throw all onto the Shoulders of God and do nothing. But we are called to labor, even if the result is His own. What else can we do?"

Simon went to the door of his odorous little shop and looked at the sky and the gulls and then over the shelves of the street to the brilliant blue sea. Waves were coming in tall and rapid, and as they crashed on the beach they were a pure flash of white fire, hurtful to the eyes. Simon blinked.

"What else can we do?" repeated Simon. "We can do only our best, and if that fail it is not our failure, for it was ordained."

After a moment he said, "I have lost many I loved to the Romans. But I know that it is appointed for men to die once, as you have said, yourself, Saul of Tarshish. What matter when a man dies? Is life so beautiful, and so desirable, that we must strain all measures of juices from it, even from the seeds and the rinds and the gall, as women strain the juices of citrons or pomegranates? Let us not yearn for the pulp and the bitterness of the refuse, greedily like goats, unwilling to put down the cup. The sweet first juice is enough."

This seemed to Saul to echo the very words of his old teacher, Aristo, for they had a cynical overtone and a faint hint of laughter. But looking at Simon's gnarled face, and the dark deep sorrow in his eyes, Saul knew that he spoke out of wisdom and not in jest. Still, it was not consoling, and Saul soon took his leave. He journeyed to Jerusalem in a small car rented from an inn in Joppa, and on the way to the beloved city he brooded and thought.

His sister's house, where Sephorah's husband and her husband's father had been born, and all her own children, was like a rescue to Saul, like a loving refuge. Sephorah's once bright hair was almost as white as his own, and her grandchildren stood about her like saplings around an old parent tree. She embraced Saul with tears and laughter, and he found the kisses of the little ones pure and endearing, and many of the scars he carried on his soul became smooth and halted their aching.

"We are no longer young," he said to Sephorah, as they wandered in the calm and lovely gardens he remembered and paused by the very bench on which he had sat and wept dolorously when a youth, to be found there and comforted by his father, so long dead. Here he had crouched in anguish in the spring, and it was spring again, the Pentecostal Season. Nothing had changed except himself and the human world. Nature and nature's law went their way indifferently, as heedless of man as the clouds, themselves, and as remote.

"We are not old, unless we desire to be," said Sephorah, and her wrinkled face was sweet. "I feel in my heart that I am still a girl, joyful and expectant, eager for each newly minted day, and love is still ruler of my heart." She touched his hand gently, remembering how many he had lost, and how weary and dusty was his way, and how misunderstood, and how full of danger and wretchedness. But still he was Saul, her brother, and his eye still held passion and steadfastness, and his spirit shone forth, and so flesh was nothing.

He told her of the letters he had received from his cousin, Titus Milo Platonius, the Praetorian general in Rome, for no longer did he believe that all women were superficial and light and trivial and unable to understand important matters. He saw a maternal wisdom in Sephorah's golden eyes, which were immortally young and gay, and the intrepid valor of her soul, and he thought to himself that she resembled their dead father whom he had so misjudged.

"Milo," he said, "is most unhappy in Rome under the domination of that vile Commander of the Praetorian Guard, Tigellinus, who is his superior officer, and who, at the instigation of the wife of Caesar, Poppea, murdered the old Commander, Bursus. Ah, there is a wicked woman, truly the harlot of Babylon, for did she not incite Nero Claudius Caesar Augustus Germanicus to murder his mother Agrippina, out of jealousy and fear of the mother's influence? Tigellinus hates Milo, and Milo does not fear death, but his soldiers love him and so Tigellinus refrains from still another murder—though it may not be for long. Alas, that men like our cousin are becoming more rare each day, and rarer still are men like his father, Aulus. Milo is a reproach to the Roman court, and to Nero, for he is a man of virtue, and a Christian, though others do not know this. Can we not induce our cousin to return to Israel, where he was born, and on the night the Messias was born? He is old, too, but indomitable. If he remains in Rome he will surely die."

"I have written him so, also," replied Sephorah, "but he answers that his duty is in the city of his fathers, for is he not a Roman as well as a Jew?" She sighed, and smiled. "How he danced at my wedding! And how he drank!" She thought of the days of her girlhood and it seemed to her that it was the dream of another and not herself, and she had heard of it only by rumor. "Why do you not visit him, Saul, and implore him to return to us for at least a space?"

"I? Visit Rome?" Saul was incredulous. "That seat of vice and infamy and murder, of luxury and terror and unspeakable lewdness, of crime and degeneracy? God forbid!"

"But Simon Peter is there," said Sephorah. "Did you not know? He left but a month ago, for the Christian community in Rome is in disarray. The Roman populace has taken a dislike to the Christians of whom they tell vile lies and of whom they make the wickedest accusations. Jew and Christian—they are equally hated in Rome and are the jest of the people, who complain that Claudius Caesar had once expelled the Jews but Nero permitted them to return. I hear he is a most vicious and decadent man, for all his youth, and one wonders why he allowed the Jews to resume their home in Rome and regain a measure of their property."

"Perhaps," said Saul with gloom, "he wishes to make of them a scapegoat as have other rulers in other nations." His words, even to himself, seemed incredible, and then a cold wind touched him between the shoulder blades and he shivered. He said, "I knew Peter had gone to Rome. We never loved each other, for each of us believed that our way was the only way," and Saul smiled. "But, in His Name we were reconciled, in spite of Mark who never loved me, either."

Sephorah took his browned and calloused hand in hers and said, "My brother, you are as easily hated as loved, for never do you falter and your opinions are inflexible, and your judgment, alas, is usually correct."

Now Sephorah, sighing again, spoke of Jerusalem and of the people, whose despair increased hourly. The new procurator, Felix, hated the Jews even more than had Pontius Pilate, and conspired with the High Priest and his minions to oppress and steal from the people and to break their spirit. What they had endured under Pilate was nothing to what they endured now, for their own priests had turned against them, and plotted against them and reduced them to fearful anguish. They were robbed of their last substance in taxes, to be sent to Rome, and to support the Temple which the priests profaned by their very presence. The priests imposed enormous tithes even on the destitute, and woe to that man and his family if the money was not forthcoming on demand. Now assassins, nameless, roamed through the purlieus of the Temple, and left blood and dead bodies behind them, and no one knew what vengeance they were executing, whether on the worshipers or on their oppressors. It was said that King Agrippa was responsible, that he wished to reduce his people to the status of slaves, in order to please the Romans. Still others said that the assassins were Zealots or Essenes, and that they were revenging the insult to the Temple. And still others said they were Christians, or Nazarenes, as they were still called in Jerusalem, young men intent on overthrowing the government of Felix and of Rome, and of King Agrippa.

"I only know we all live in terror," said Sephorah. "The people pray to God in one voice, for deliverance from their tyrants, Jew and Nazarene together, and the longing for God in the hearts of our poor people is an agony. They see the priesthood living in luxury on the money stolen and wrested from them and see those closest to the High Priesthood reveling with the Romans in the most indecent of orgies and celebrations, and in blood spectacles in the circuses and in licentious plays at the theater." When the people periodically could endure no more there were mysterious murders of both Jewish priests and Romans, and then there were accusations that the excessive Zealots had accomplished these crimes, and the Zealots were hunted out and crucified and the people subsided in renewed terror and were quiet for a time.

"Never was our people and our nation in so desperate a plight," said Sephorah.

Saul gazed at the tender blue sky and then at the pink almond blossoms and the flowering palms and pomegranates and he thought how beautiful was the world, and how immeasurably evil was man, who created murder and hatred and ruin and ugliness out of his own heart, and delighted in the pain of the innocent and in their oppression, and made victims of his brothers. For him had the Messias come and had given up His blameless life!

"It is well, perhaps, that I have returned," said Saul. "I was commanded so, in a vision, but I am only one man and neither the Jews nor the Christians will hearken to me, here in my own nation and among my own people. I do not know why I am here. It is in the Hands of God, for I do not know where I must start and what I must say!"

He contemplated the modern world of blood and plunder, of monstrous Caesars and faithless priests, of debaucheries and wars, of hatred among the peoples, of despair and tears and terror, of mindless rage and cruelty, of exploitation and slavery, of imprecations on the weak and the glorification of the strong. Surely the world he had known as a youth had not been so wicked! Surely it had not been so depraved and heartless! It was as if the Messias had never been born, and that the legions of hell now ruled the earth.

Surely, he said to himself, when this age passes there will be peace and kindness among men. The present would pass like a direful dream, and future ages would bask in the sun of the Messias. For that, he worked and hoped and prayed. "And there shall be war no more." Nor would there be enmity and malice and lust and fury and hatred. All would pass, and men would rejoice in the new and celestial dispensation.

Chapter 50

"THE great renegade has cursed us again with his presence," said the Jews of the city.

"The man who persecuted and imprisoned us has returned," said the Nazarenes.

"The troublemaker," said the priests in the Temple, "is amongst us again, and what will he plot now, that Zealot?"

"He admonished and repudiated us," said the young Zealots and the Essenes, "though once he pretended to love us, so say our fathers. Has he returned to massacre us?"

Even the Roman procurator, Felix, spending the pleasant springtime season in Caesarea by the sea, heard of Saul of Tarshish, whom he called Paul of Tarsus. The news was brought to him by old soldiers who remembered Saul, and by many of the truckling priesthood. "He caused grave dissension in Jerusalem and throughout Judea," said the soldiers, "and his people hated him and reviled him, a Jew, himself." "It is he who has aroused the Nazarenes, or Christians, throughout Asia Minor and Europe, itself, against the rule of Rome," said the priests. "He has caused riots and upheavals and blasphemies wherever he has trod. It is whispered that he is a member of the Zealots and the Essenes, who live but to destroy."

"If all detest him," said Felix indolently, "why has someone not murdered him before this?" He thought the situation amusing, and dismissed Saul from his mind.

In the meantime Saul walked the streets of his city, wherein he had not walked for many years. He lingered in the walled space where he had first seen the Messias with His Mother, and he sat on the bench where he had sat and gazed at the empty bench opposite him. He wandered in the market place where he had heard his name called in that thunderous, masculine voice, "Saul! Saul of Tarshish!" He entered the Temple at an hour when it was not very crowded and stood on the very spot where he had felt the Presence of the Messias. He left the city for the wilderness where the youthful Zealots had been executed, and where Christ Jesus had comforted them, and they had known Him though others had not. He stood on the crossroads where he had heard the Messias address the Scribes and the Pharisees and the common people. He walked on the way the Messias had walked, with His cross, to the place of His shameful murder. He visited the tomb which Joseph of Arimathaea had given for the Messias' body, and from which He had risen. He went to the mount where the Messias had ascended to Heaven, and to the cave where His child-Mother had given Him birth.

And he marveled, with a marveling as new as if he had just heard it, that God had actually been present on these sacred spots, had deigned to be born as a Man, with all man's humiliations and animal functions of the body, with all humanity's common pains and griefs and hungers and yearnings. Saul touched the earth the sandals of Christ had touched, and said to himself, "Surely this is a holy place." Man, himself, had become holy through the Holiness of his Redeemer, though he merited nothing by his own efforts. Human life was holy because One had taken on the flesh of mankind, had redeemed man from sin and death. Sometimes, in contemplation at these places Saul would be seized by a rapture which held him immobile and trembling for moments at a time, and people passing would stop to stare at his illuminated face and wild fixed eyes, and would smirk at the sight of this workingman with his long tunic the color of the red earth, and his leonine white mane, and his strange appearance. But Saul, consumed by love and the passionate desire to see the Messias again, could only think, in the rapture: "Oh, surely men will never forget that He lived and walked in Israel and died here, and will forever hold this little land sacred and inviolate!"

And there were occasions when he felt no rapture and no hope, for all about him was confusion compounded by confusion, where men should be brothers in joy and delight and not mortal enemies. Sometimes it seemed to him that Israel was a cup from which poured violence, bewilderment and murder among brethren, and surely, he would say to himself, this was the greatest of all blasphemies, for Israel was holy beyond all other holinesses, and her people prophets. That there should be contentions, rivalries, disputes, hatreds, rebellions and betrayals in this holy land was an affront to God, Who had so blessed her through the ages and had protected her, and had given her His only Begotten Son. "If I forget you, O Jerusalem, let my eye be blinded and my right hand be withered!" Saul repeated from the prophets, and his heart would swell to bursting and his eyes would run with tears.

It was growing more and more incredible to him that

the new Church could be rent by doctrinal disputes, narrow little interpretations, self-glorification, anger, repudiation, dissent and quarrelings which led to actual violence, for the Way was so plain and simple. But then, he would also think, we are only men, if redeemed, and we carry into the Holy of Holies our imperfections and our vices and our egotism, alas. Often we will not surrender our souls and our lives to Him, to Whom they belong, because to do so would rob us of the delicious sins we love so much.

His soul wept for his beloved people and his beloved land, the seat of prophets and heroes, the halo of revelation, the holy mountains, the sacred earth, the land above all lands which had been so blessed, and he remembered that the Messias had wept also and for the same country.

I have been commanded to return here, he thought, yet I do not know why, for none will listen to me, either Jew or Christian, and I am accursed of both. I linger, waiting. In the meantime he played with Sephorah's grandchildren and walked in her gardens, and meditated impatiently, and sorrowed.

Then one Sabbath eve he was urgently moved to go to the Temple. He arrayed himself in his meager finery, his heart shaking, and put on his best plain sandals and his prayer shawl and his phylacteries and curled his earlocks. He came upon Sephorah sitting in the atrium with two of her grandchildren, and when she looked at him it seemed to her that he had a grave and unearthly aspect, and she rose dumbly and stared into his eyes. He took her in his arms and kissed her forehead, and suddenly she clung to him and still could not speak. But she felt his sorrow, deep and speechless. He put her from him and left the house with his head bent, for he knew that never again would he see his sister.

"Saul! Saul!" she cried after him, regaining her voice, and she ran to the portico. But he was far down the street and did not answer her. The red sunset had inflamed the mountains, the streets and the skies over the city, and it was as if a conflagration was devouring them all. Sephorah could not even weep. She put her hands to her mouth and she watched until her brother disappeared, then she leaned against a column and prayed and now her tears came. She began to shudder. She saw that the dull red shadows from the sky cast black shadows on the earth, and she remembered the prophecies that the Temple would be destroyed and Israel rendered desolate, and it was all mingled, in her quaking mind, with the image of her brother and the prophets, and woe filled her heart and it appeared to her that the whole world was burning.

If the Christian elders and deacons had been wary of Saul, and had consulted with him only briefly on a number of occasions, at night, and stealthily, and if the Jews had fearfully avoided him both as a "heretic" and an alleged and violent Zealot who would bring fresh trouble on Israel, and if they had all hoped that his presence would not be known to the Romans, they had reason for dismay, thousands praying that he would depart and leave them in peace. The Roman garrisons and officers were well aware of his presence, and spies, encouraged by the High Priest, Ananias ben Nebedaeus, knew each step he took and with whom he conversed. The High Priest was determined that Saul cause no more upheavals in Israel. He felt a particular hatred for this aging Pharisee, a personal hatred, for he had learned of Saul's contempt for the decadent High Priesthood and his denunciations of it in many cities. The Sanhedrin knew of his presence. If Saul sometimes had heard shufflings in the night, and had uneasily felt the eye of an enemy upon him during the day, and had seen shadows cast, he had attributed it to his imagination.

The priests knew that Saul, the pious Jew, would not long refrain from visiting the Temple, and they knew that he had a way of addressing the worshipers in synagogues, as was permitted by the Law. So, they kept a zealous watch on him, and on the night he dressed and began to walk to the Temple all were alerted, and in particular the Roman garrison which had been warned that Saul was dangerous to Rome. As he walked unhurriedly in the scarlet twilight he saw that others began to walk beside him too, in the crowded streets, men in cloaks and hoods, but he thought no evil. They were only Jews bent on his own mission, to worship at sundown, and on the Sabbath. That his death had been determined upon by the High Priesthood would have seemed the wildest absurdity, had it been communicated to him. He hated no man, except liars and hypocrites and evil-doers, and even for them he prayed each night with tears and hopes, that their hearts would be changed and their souls redeemed.

The priests had found none, not even amongst the most rigid and devout Jews, not amongst the Nazarenes or Christians, nor among the Zealots and Essenes, who would consent to appear in a body, in public, or in the Temple, to denounce Saul of Tarshish. All had been approached, and threatened, but all had resolutely refused. "If he be of God," said the Jews, "he must not be disturbed. If he be of the Devil, God will smite him." The Christian elders said, "He is one of us, and though he baptizes Gentiles who have not been informed of the Torah, and disputes with his own Pharisee sect, we find no wrong in him except excessive zeal." The Zealots and Essenes said, "He loves and honors our prophet, Jochanan ben Zachary, and speaks of him always, and knew him in his youth, and he loves his people and his country, and though we resent his denunciations of what he terms our 'excesses' and calls us 'extremists,' we have no complaint of importance against him. We feared his return, believing he would incite our people against us, but he has lived in peace." (They did not mention that many of the Zealots desired Saul's death, he having antagonized them.)

The High Priesthood seethed with wrath, for these very people had frequently complained to them of Saul ben Hillel in the past. Now they were willing that he be left in peace and not punished for some vague violation of some law. Without a public demonstration against Saul, which would inflame the Romans, Saul could not be apprehended and executed. Caiphas had warned the priests of this man, and the present High Priest had vowed to destroy him—and yet this pusillanimous and complaining people refused to do their duty! "I would," said Ananias ben Nebedaeus, "that a thunderbolt fall on Israel, for its cowardice!" As this was said only to his familiars the Jews did not hear of it.

There was but one thing to do: To gather a market mob and call them "Jews from Asia," and have them denounce Saul either in the Temple or on the street, and thus bring about his arrest. There were thousands among the rabble to do this, with bribes and with promise of excitement and violence. So long before Saul went to the Temple on the Sabbath the careful plan had been laid. It needed but the public appearance of Saul ben Hillel. Tonight, he had appeared, and was on the way to the Temple.

As Saul walked along the streets and descended them, he saw the Sabbath candles already lighted in the scarlet dusk and standing in windows, and he saw the people, streaming from side streets, arrayed in holiday garb and moving with him toward the Temple. The Queen of the Sabbath was presiding again over the hearths and the homes of the people of God, and Saul's heart was suddenly filled with happiness and expectation. If some pressed too closely to him, and some jostled aside from him and the jostlers moved nearer, he did not heed. He forgot his premonitions.

Now he saw the Temple, burning gold against the crimson sky, and the mounts like bronze beyond it. He saw the golden dome and the thin spires and the gardens and the colonnades, all so dearly familiar and beloved, and his heart was moved strongly as one who comes home after a far journey. The Temple was already crowded on the Sabbath, even the Court of Women and the Court of the Gentiles, so Saul was not aware for a few moments that he was unable to lift his arms and that he seemed to be sweeping in a tide. When he became aware he attempted to slow his pace, looking about him, in the Temple precincts, at the hooded men, and he saw fierce and sparkling eyes fixed upon him and teeth visible between stretched lips, like the teeth of wolves. His awakened instincts shouted to him that he was about to be killed, and he tried to halt in that mass of shoulders and heads and elbows and arms and legs and feet, but they pressed closer to him and moved him on, and now he heard that sound which affrights any man: The wolf growl of hatred and blood-lust. It echoed back and forth among the columns, low, intense, vicious and deadly.

The crowd was no longer moving. The mass was retreating to make him the center of a small tight circle, and his white mane rose on his head and the coldness of death raced over his body. He saw the flaming torches on the far walls and the lanterns, and the distant bronze doors standing open and the crowded pale faces beyond the doors, staring. Then he returned his attention to the panting throng near him and made his face firm and bold.

"What do you wish?" he asked, and now the snarling was silent and there was only the hissing of the torches in the immense quiet.

Then a man shouted, "You! Vile enemy of Israel, renegade, traitor, despoiler, heretic, blasphemer, betrayer of the people!"

The crowd roared, and fists were flung up into the warm dim air and many spat at Saul, who stood unmoved and apparently undismayed.

"Men of Israel," he said, when the last echo had died away, "you profane the Temple with your cries, your shouts, your imprecations!"

One man, with a loud sonorous voice, was evidently the leader, and the others only the chorus, so Saul knew this was no chance demonstration against him, but a prepared one, and if prepared, it would end in his death. His lips were icy and numb but his eyes looked at his enemies without apparent fear, and there was a blue kindling in them.

"You are the profaner, you are the profanation!" cried the man with the compelling voice, and again the crowd roared, and a sharp hot wind of fetid breath and sweat blew upon Saul and it revolted him. But he held his place.

Now he saw the leader, taller than the others, with a lean dark face and a thin black beard and fiery black eyes, his complexion brown from many suns. He had an avid excited appearance, a vicious countenance, and he whipped not only others to fury but himself, also. His garments were dark crimson and blue and Saul saw the dagger at his girdle, half-drawn.

It was this man who shouted to the other men now: "Men of Israel, help! This is the man that teaches all men everywhere against the people and the Law, and the Temple, and has polluted this holy place! He has brought Greeks into the Temple, and all manner of unclean men!"

The crowd screamed and yelled hungrily, and Saul quickly glanced about. Where were the Temple guards, the priests? Who had called them away so that he was left unprotected? Then he knew. It was the priesthood, itself, which had condemned him to death.

"Away with him, from this holy place!" shouted the leader. "For his blood must not pollute the stones of the Temple nor his head rest upon them! Away with him, to the streets!"

A dozen violent hands seized Saul and dragged him from the Temple precincts into the streets, where the alerted Roman soldiers and their captain awaited. The Romans had been warned discreetly not to enter the Temple, but if the disturbance erupted outside they were to act. Now the waiting soldiers saw the rush of men through the bronze doors, dragging Saul with them, and his mouth and nose ran with blood.

The disciplined Romans loathed all mobs, everywhere, for they threatened not only law and order but civilization, itself. The High Priest had broadly hinted to the captain that if Saul died, "at the hands of the unruly," it might be regrettable but it was only what he deserved, for did he not, himself, incite riots and incendiarisms wherever he journeyed? Had he not, many years ago, brought Jerusalem almost to the edge of chaos?

But the captain acted instinctively, and because of his years of discipline. The mob was now hurling Saul back and forth amongst themselves, and each time men struck him but would not let him fall and kept him flying between them on his feet, and beating him with fists and kicking him with their boots. The warm and darkening air of the Sabbath evening was alive with groans and grunts and thuds and imprecations and tossing arms and heads, and eyes that glowed like the eyes of animals in the dusk, and above it all roared the voice of the leader, hoarsely, pantingly, "Kill him! Kill the blasphemer, the heretic, the enemy of Israel!" And he tried to get closer to Saul to impale him with his dagger.

It was then that the Roman acted, and his legionnaires made a wedge and drove themselves into the mob, and the infuriated men spat upon them also and tried to kick them, fearful they would be deprived of their victim. But the Romans were stronger, and trained, and they struck the men with the sides of their drawn swords and their alien faces were terrible in the light of the torches. They hurled the would-be murderers of Saul to the ground and kicked the sides of their heads and trampled them, and used their shields as battering rams. Their polished helmets with the crests of horses' hair glittered in the torchlight, and their swords flashed, and they pressed like a phalanx toward Saul.

Now the captain caught his arm as he was hurled backward to the waiting and eagerly gasping punishers, and held him upright, bleeding and fainting. Even his white hair was stained with blood and his face was deathlike. The captain snapped manacles on his wrists, and pushed him into the arms of two of his soldiers. Then he faced the snarling and hating and frustrated mob, contemptuously noting the savage eyes, the inhuman froth on wet lips, the heaving breasts, the beards on which lusting saliva was dripping. A sudden silence fell, and then it began to hum as if giant bees had invaded the street.

It was Roman law that a man must not be punished or executed without a hearing, so the Roman captain said with cold anger, "What has this man done, that you should set upon him?"

A tumult as of hell broke loose then. The leader shrieked, "He is a blasphemer, a liar, a heretic, a destroyer of Israel!" Others screamed other accusations; grasping hands darted from sleeves toward Saul, who lay half-fainting in the soldiers' arms, as if to tear him limb from limb. The captain tried to sort out the howling accusations, but it was as if all the animals in the circus dens were yelling and shrieking and roaring simultaneously. He stood there, a young sturdy man, bare legs far apart, hands, in the Italian manner, perched on his hips, his broad face cynical and harshly fierce. He tilted his head, his lips curled. Then he raised his mailed hand, and the noise diminished to that deep humming again.

"Hearken to me," said the captain. "No mob, where I have jurisdiction, is going to slaughter any man, no matter who desires his death!" He raised his rough voice higher, so that any lurking priests might hear and thereafter scuttle to their masters with the report. "I will take this man to the Fortress Antonia, which is beside the Temple, and there confine him for a just trial. As for you, if you riot again you shall regret it—if you live."

He motioned with his head to his men, who lifted Saul in their arms and began to carry him to the Fortress

Antonia, adjoining the Temple. Other crowds had gathered curiously on the street, not Jews but men of other races, and they watched the procession of Roman soldiers, saw Saul carried high by two legionnaires, following the captain, and then the still infuriated mob which was hardly chastened by the captain's threats. Yet, they made no overt gesture but cursed loudly between their teeth. Now a tawny moon was rising over the tiered city and its light was golden on the stones and the walls.

"Away with him!" the mob screamed. The soldiers reached the steps of Fortress Antonia, and Saul turned his bloody face to the captain and said in a weak voice, "I pray you that you have me set down, for I would speak to them." He spoke in perfect Latin, and the captain stared at him, for he had been told that this man was an ignorant and unlettered peasant, a Zealot from the dead hills of Galilee. The captain motioned to the soldiers, who set Saul on his feet on the steps of the Fortress, above the heads of the crowds, and he said to Saul in his blunt voice, "Who are you? It is possible I have heard of you wrongly, and so speak and tell me the truth."

Saul said, and his wonderful voice began to return, "I am a Jew of Tarsus, of Cilicia, no mean city, a citizen thereof, and a citizen of Rome. I beseech you, let me speak to the people."

The captain stared incredulously, but Saul repeated, "I am indeed a citizen of Rome, and a Roman lawyer, of the University of Tarsus."

The captain said abruptly to his men, "Put him down, but protect him."

So they stood him on his feet and he swayed dizzily for a moment, and a soldier caught his arm to steady him. He gathered all his strength and looked down at the heaving mobs in the red light of the torches, and he beckoned to them like a father, that they might draw closer. Now he spoke in Hebrew, with resonant emphasis:

"Men, brethren, and fathers, hear my defense, which I will now make unto you. I am verily a man who am a Jew, born in Tarsus, a city in Cilicia, yet brought up in this city at the feet of Gamaliel—"

"Gamaliel! Gamaliel!" shouted many men, in astonishment, and they glanced at each other, for they had not known this, and their faces darkened and they drew closer to Saul.

"—and taught according to the perfect manner of the Law of the fathers, and was zealous toward God, as you all are this day."

"He lies!" cried the leader, fearful that his victim, for whom he had already been paid, might escape him, and vengeance fall on him, himself. But the crowd was suddenly very quiet, for Saul's voice, as usual, commanded attention and his words struck on their ears and they were bewildered, for they had been told he was not only a blasphemer but a malcontent and a friend of the Romans and an enemy of Israel.

Now Saul's voice, ringing, soaring, eloquent, narrated the story of his former persecution of the Nazarenes out of zeal and error, and his journey to Damascus. The vast mass of men did not stir; all eyes were fixed upwards on that blood-stained face, and none saw the soldiers and their armor about Saul. They were entranced by the story, which they had not heard before. He told how the Lord had commanded him to leave Jerusalem, after he had returned to the city.

"While I prayed in the Temple I was in a trance, and I saw the Lord again and He said to me, 'Make haste and get you quickly out of Jerusalem, for they will not receive your testimony concerning Me.' And I said, 'Lord, they know that I imprisoned and beat in every synagogue them that believed in You, and when the blood of Your martyr, Stephen, was shed I also was standing by and consenting to his death, and kept the raiment of them that slew him.' And He said unto me, 'Depart, for I will send you far hence unto the Gentiles.' "

Saul paused. The crowd muttered and murmured uneasily, and looked into each others' eyes. Some were bewildered, others baffled, still others incensed, and others again lusted after a victim. The soldiers, not understanding, scowled at the men below and shifted their iron-shod feet.

Then the leader shouted, "You have heard his own testimony, that he persecuted his people and deserted them for the Gentiles, whom he has brought into the holy places for a scornful profanation! Away with such a fellow from the earth, for it is not fit that he should live!"

The crowd screamed, and bent and lifted handfuls of dust into the air and flung them at Saul, and some tore their clothing in an excess of fury and renewed rage.

The captain, in disgust at all this undisciplined passion, which reminded him of the motley mobs of Rome, curtly ordered Saul to be taken to the prison within the Fortress. Then he sat, legs spraddled, while the still manacled man stood before him, the dried blood on his face, the eyes drooping in exhaustion. He narrowed his gaze disbelievingly on Saul. "I believe I will get the truth from you by scourging." And he waited for what Saul would say.

Saul was still gasping; he tried to steady himself. He wiped his bleeding hands on the side of his long tunic. He looked at the wet gray walls of the inner side of the Fortress, and the wet gray floor, and at the skeptical young captain who was eying him so sharply. The youth of the Roman, the gleam of his big bare knees, his broad unsubtle face and bristling black hair, moved Saul by the reason of his youth, and he smiled. He said, with gentle reason:

"Is it lawful for you to scourge a man that is a Roman, and uncondemned?"

The captain narrowed his eyes again in what he evidently considered a very shrewd expression, and cynical. "What is a Roman citizen doing, inciting the mobs to murder him?"

"I have done nothing which you could understand, for it is unbelievable yet true. It is a doctrinal matter, which would not interest you."

"You Jews are always aflame with doctrinal matters," said the captain, "while the gods laugh. Well, so you are a free-born Roman!"

He stood up and removed the manacles from Saul's wrists and tossed them with a clangor on the stone floor. "Had you spoken sooner, Paul of Tarsus, I should not have bound you, for it is unlawful to bind a Roman. This is no affair of mine, but only the affair of you Jews. I cannot release you, for fear that your own people will murder you, so you will remain in the Fortress tonight, and then you must appear before their own Sanhedrin.

As a Roman, that is outrageous, but you are also a Jew. It is a delicate matter."

He conducted Saul to a cell which was both dry and comfortable, for it was reserved for prisoners of distinction, and he ordered wine and meat and cheese and fruit for Saul, and clean blankets for his cot, and a lantern to light the darkness. "I trust you will understand my position," he said to Saul.

"Yes, and I thank you," said Saul, and the captain, who could have been disciplined for maltreating a Roman citizen, smiled for the first time.

Chapter 51

THE next morning Saul was brought before the Little Sanhedrin.

The morning was hot and dark and thunderous, but there was no rain. The judges sat, sweltering, in their tiers of chairs and regarded Saul with stern faces, closed and grim. Ananias the High Priest was there, a tall slender man whose figure, under his ceremonial robes, was distorted by an amazingly huge belly. Yet all his limbs were thin, and his face, and he wore his tall priestly hat and his garments were splendid and jeweled and his brown beard perfumed and there was the priestly ring on his hand, flashing in the hot gloom. His features were intelligent and alert, yet curiously weak and uncertain, and his eyes were baleful as they regarded the man he most hated in all the world.

Saul bowed to the Sanhedrin, touched his brow and then his lips and then his breast, and said, "Men and brethren, I have lived in all good conscience before God until this day."

Ananias made a sign to the two Temple guards standing beside Saul and one struck him violently in the mouth, and Saul staggered. But he did not take his eyes from the High Priest. He said, "God shall smite you, you whited wall, for sitting to judge me after the Law and command me to be smitten contrary to the Law!"

Some members of the Sanhedrin shouted, "Do you dare to revile the High Priest?"

Saul looked at them bitterly and said in a strong voice, "I would not, brethren, that he was the High Priest! For it is written, You shall not speak evil of the ruler of your people."

The Roman captain and several of his men had insisted that they be in the Chamber with Saul, and they stood at a distance near the tall gilded doors, and the captain smiled in approval of Saul's bold words. Truly, this was a Roman and not a meek Jew!

Saul, in the meantime, had been scrutinizing his judges, and he saw that many were Sadducees and many were Pharisees. Now he gave all his attention to his fellow Pharisees, for he still had a detestation of the worldly and atheistic Sadducees.

His voice was still stronger when he addressed the Pharisees only:

"Men and brethren! I am a Pharisee, the son of a Pharisee! Of the hope and the resurrection of the dead I am called in question!"

This was an astute appeal, for the Sadducees did not believe in any life hereafter nor did they believe in the resurrection of the dead, and the issue was still bitter between them and the Pharisees, whom they loathed. So the Pharisees glanced in consternation at each other, and one whispered, "He has preached the resurrection of the dead, in accordance with the teachings of his fathers, and for this should he be held guilty?"

Suddenly Saul and all that he was was of lesser importance to the Pharisees than the Sadducees, who believed in no life nor angel nor spirit, and the ancient enmity bristled up among the Pharisees. They glared at the Sadducees, who stared back in cold contempt. Why had this man been brought before the Sanhedrin? True, it was said he was a Nazarene, but he was also a Pharisee of a noble house, and had never repudiated his people nor his sect, but had merely tried to bring the truth to the misbegotten Gentiles. Was that so sore a crime? Had not the Pharisees for ages proselyted among the Gentiles, bringing thousands of them into the House of Israel, and had they refrained only now because the Romans had commanded them to refrain?

The Scribes among the Pharisees were suddenly enraged that Saul, who was a Pharisee, was being judged by these Sadducees, and that he had been attacked in the holy Temple by order of them and almost murdered by the market rabble, and that—shame of shames!—he had had to be rescued by the heathen Romans from his own people! And he had been thrust into prison. All the other charges made against Saul through the years in Israel were forgotten.

So the Scribes of the Pharisees, the intellectuals, who disdained brutality and violence, stood up with a great and angry cry, shouting, "We find no evil in this man! But if an angel or a spirit has spoken to him, let us not fight against God!"

Instantly, Saul was totally forgotten. The Sadducees rose from their seats and began a furious debate with the Pharisees, so loud and so full of gestures, that the captain was fearful again for the life of this Roman citizen who had shown no fear of those who could have ordered his death. So he advanced with his men and took hold, politely, of Saul and they led him from the Chamber. None saw them go, for now the disputants had come to blows, intellectual Scribes and all, gentlemen and scholars, and the captain glanced back once and grinned. The High Priest, himself, was being jostled by sharp elbows, and his stately hat had been knocked from his head.

When Saul was safely delivered to his comfortable cell in the Fortress the captain sat down on the table and ordered wine for both of them, and fruit and pastries. He simmered with amusement. He scratched his bristling pate; he shook his head. "What immoderate sages and judges!" he remarked. Saul laughed with him. His nose and one of his cheeks were still swollen from the blows he had received last night, and still sore, but he laughed.

"There is none so stupid as the wise, it has been written," he remarked. He drank the wine and ate thoughtfully of the fruit and pastries. He felt a comfort in the presence of the young Roman, and he began to talk to him of his journeys and his accounts were so fascinating that the captain was reluctant to leave and return to his duties. When the captain was alone, he thought: Why did a man of family and wealth leave his country to travel like a miserable slave among other nations, and to bring them a message of redemption? The young captain had been barely born at the time of the Crucifixion, and he had heard nothing of it until he had been sent to Israel. It was an awesome and beguiling story, and he did not believe in it at all, as he did not believe in the gods. From what should a man be redeemed? From sin and death, said the Nazarenes and this Paul of Tarsus, who was a lawyer and a Roman. The captain was baffled. It was obvious to him that Nazarenes died as easily and as frequently as other men; therefore, where was their deliverance from death? As for sin, the Jews, "faithful" and Nazarene, believed all pleasure was sin, and was that not an absurd doctrine and an insult to the gods who made pleasure their entire existence?

A great tranquillity came to Saul. He had not slept much the night before, because of the pain of his wounds, despite the unguents and lotions the captain had ordered to be put on them for healing. Now a sweet exhaustion came to him and he lay on his cot and began to dream.

He saw the Messias again, the mighty and puissant face, the triumphant and manly eyes, the heroic mouth and the brow radiating golden lightning. And He said to Saul, "Be of good cheer, Saul, for as you have testified of Me in Jerusalem so must you bear witness also at Rome."

The young captain, Claudius Lysias, was in a quandary. He could not keep Saul forever imprisoned, nor could he release him to the vengeance of the High Priest, Ananias. He was not accustomed to be faced with dilemmas, for life was simple to him. As he was ruminating in his room in the Fortress and drinking wine with melancholy determination, his centurion came to him and said, "Captain, there is a certain man who beseeches to speak with you, and his name is Amos ben Ezekiel, a man of distinction and family and of apparent wealth, for his garments are rich, and he declares that he is the nephew of Paul of Tarsus and had arrived in Jerusalem only last night. He is also a physician, and a citizen of Rome."

"Ha," said the captain, conjecturing that perhaps his dilemma was at an end. "Bring him to me at once."

The visitor entered and at his aspect the Roman captain rose slowly, for Amos was tall and dignified and clad in blue and scarlet silk and he wore jewels on his hands and his sandals were gilded. His hair and his beard were a mingling of soft gold and white, for Amos was no longer young but in his early middle age. His air of majesty and pride and assurance merited the young captain's respect, and he touched his forehead slightly in a quick salute, and offered his visitor a chair, and ordered wine.

Amos smiled at him gravely and seated himself, and the captain saw the nobility of his features and the quietness of his manner. "I thank you, Captain Lysias, for receiving me. I have heard that you have treated my uncle, Saul ben Hillel, with kindness and discretion and that twice you have saved his life. May I present you with a token of my esteem?" And he removed a beautiful jewel on his finger and laid it on the table. The captain flushed. "I did but my duty, lord," he said. Amos smiled again.

"But should not duty be rewarded? I beg of you to accept it. Otherwise I will be greatly insulted, and my uncle insulted, that you did not accept the sign of our gratitude."

Amos spoke in the most perfect Latin. The captain remembered that his visitor was a Roman citizen, and one did not insult Romans. So he said, "I accept, with answering gratitude," and in a twinkling the ring was in his pouch, and Amos repressed an indulgent smile.

"I have distressing news," said Amos, "and it must be told quickly. This morning I heard that a band of men, forty, have joined together—at whose behest you may conjecture—and have sworn a blood oath to the High Priest and the elders, saying, 'We have bound ourselves under a great curse, that we will eat nothing until we have slain Saul ben Hillel.' So, the High Priest has directed a messenger to come to you before sunset, requesting your prisoner to be brought before the Sanhedrin in the Temple early in the morning, to inquire something more perfectly concerning him. But my uncle will never reach the Temple, for the men are to lie in wait for him and murder him in the streets."

"But he is a Roman!" cried the captain, outraged, and laying his hand on his sword. "They would not dare murder a Roman before he is tried and condemned!"

Amos inclined his head and made a slight and eloquent gesture with his hand. "Nevertheless, that is what these cutthroats intend to do, and they will disappear like locusts after the field is bare, and none will dare claim to have seen them."

The captain flung himself into a chair, propped his elbow on the table, rested his chin on his fist and scowled at the wall, muttering under his breath. He could deal with simple military stratagems but not with villainous civilians. Amos cleared his throat. "Would it not be best to send my uncle to some safe spot, quickly and silently? In short, at once?"

"Ha!" said Claudius Lysias, and struck the table with the flat of his hand. He shouted for his centurion, who came immediately, and the captain demanded pen and parchment and wax for his seal and a candle. He began to write, slowly and laboriously, and with flourishes, and when he had finished and dusted sand over the ink and had shaken the parchment free, he gave the message to Amos.

"Claudius Lysias at Jerusalem to the most excellent Governor Felix sends greetings:

"This prisoner was taken of the Jews and should have been killed of them. Then came I with an army, and rescued him, having understood that he was a Roman. I would know the cause wherefore they accused him, and so I brought him forth to their court. I learned he was accused of questions of their Law, but to have nothing laid to his charge worthy of death or of bonds. Now I have learned that a band of murderers are lying in wait for him in the morning, and so I am sending him to you for safety, and will tell his accusers to appear before you to say what they have against him. Farewell."

Amos' mouth quirked a little at the youthful militarism of the message, but admitted to himself that it told the story, if bluntly. He said, "Captain Lysias, you are a noble Roman, indeed, and my cousin, who is also cousin to my uncle, and a general of the Praetorian Guard in Rome—Titus Milo Platonius—will hear of your acts and your precision by my own hand."

The captain's jaw dropped and he goggled at Amos. "Titus Milo Platonius? Why was I not informed of this before?" He turned violently red. "To think that that abominable High Priest dared to order the death of the cousin of that great and distinguished General, whose name is famous in Rome, as were the names of his fathers! This is an insult which must be washed out in blood!" He sprang to his feet. Amos had never seen a man foam before but he saw it now. He lifted his hand quickly, for bloodletting was not what he had had in mind.

"Captain Lysias," he said, "my cousin, for all he is a heroic man and a great soldier and a Roman of enormous pride, is also a man of discretion. You know how inflammable are my people, and how they are tormented these days by the High Priest and his minions. Any action taken against them, or even that disgusting Ananias, would cause my uncle, Saul ben Hillel, the greatest suffering, for these are his people despite all. So General Platonius would not command action to injure them, out of his love for Saul."

"I do not understand such a love!" shouted the captain, and struck the table again.

Amos bent his head in an attitude of affirmation. "Nor do I," he said, and prayed internally that God would forgive his mendacity. "Alas, but that is the situation."

The captain, still engorged with rage, gave Amos a dark glance, then sealed the letter with unnecessary vigor and summoned his centurion again and gave the letter to him. He said, "Make ready two hundred soldiers to go to Caesarea, and horsemen threescore and ten, and spearmen two hundred, at the third hour of the night, and provide them with horses, that they may take Saul ben Hillel whom we call Paul of Tarsus, our distinguished prisoner, and bring him safe unto Felix the Governor."*

Amos was awed by this tremendous protection of his uncle, and then begged to see Saul, and the captain took him to the cell and opened the door with a flourish. Saul started up from his cot and blinked at Amos, and did not immediately recognize him, for he had not seen him for many years. Then he uttered a great cry of joy and flung himself into Amos' arms, and they kissed and embraced, and wept together, and even the captain was moved. Surely this Paul of Tarsus was a great man, and a worthy Roman. The captain fingered the ring in his pouch. There was a certain little villa just outside the Equestrian Gate in Rome of which he had been dreaming, and a certain lovely girl.

*Acts 23:23–30.

The governor, or Procurator, Felix, was an impatient little man with a swart and active face and a more active body. Like many small men he was arrogant and belligerent. He had a detestation for intricacies and details, and would bluntly say to petitioners, "Yes, yes, but what is the central request? Why do you annoy me with trivialities and explanations?" As it was in Jewish nature to explain and elaborately explain again, so that no point of importance would be overlooked, and all subtleties arranged, Felix disliked the Jews no less than had done Pontius Pilate, though his wife was a Jewess. He would point to the water clock when a delegation was before him, assign a limit on it and declare that beyond that mark they would no longer be heard. At the appointed hour, even in the midst of an involved argument, he would rise and bustle to his girls, and return no more.

When Saul had been delivered to him he had frowned and scratched his hairy neck and had said, "Lysias can find no fault with you. But the Jews have complaints, and I have heard them long before you were brought to Caesarea. Therefore, as the Procurator, I am bound to hear them out, and I will hold you so that they may make an appearance before me. However, if you have violated no Roman law, as a Roman, I am not concerned with other charges which do not apply to you—as a Roman."

He took a liking to Saul for Saul had not immediately rushed into elaborate explanations and defenses, but had merely bowed as one reasonable man to another. So he confined him to Herod's Hall in Caesarea, and it was really a small but handsome house with gardens on a hillside overlooking the shining plain of the sea and the great twin harbors, one receiving cargo from the swinging ships and one loading with cargo. Saul had but one guard, an elderly subaltern, and one servant, an old woman of the town, a wise ancient Jewess who prepared his simple meals. Here he lived in peace and quiet and meditation, and waited, and found his depleted strength returning. He would sit for hours on the low stone wall that looked out to sea and watch the seething water traffic and it reminded him of Tarsus, and he sighed. He wrote many letters, in the little cool atrium, and Felix was good-natured enough to send them on their way, after he had scrutinized them with bewilderment. They were all to the multitude of churches which Saul had founded or expanded and the rapturous yet sensible language vaguely intrigued the Procurator, who liked poetry.

After some time, as Felix feared, the Jewish delegations from the High Priest began to arrive with long and detailed accounts of Saul's transgressions of the Jewish Law. Felix listened with his exaggerated air of long patience. He said, "Enough. My prisoner is a Roman, and your complaints are all ecclesiastical. Yet your own Sanhedrin has not condemned him with any specific charge. You are dismissed."

So the High Priest, Ananias came to Caesarea with a man of great eloquence, an orator named Tertullus. Felix said at once, "If these are more ecclesiastical complaints I will not hear them. If you have a charge against my prisoner concerning Roman law, then I will hear you, if you do not tax my patience with irrelevancies."

Tertullus bowed. He said, "Lord, I, too, am a Roman citizen as well as a Jew. I revere Rome. We desire to live in peace with her. My charges against Paul of Tarsus are concerned with Roman law."

Felix glanced at Ananias. He detested the High Priest, who was not only tall but had a patrician appearance, which he, Felix, did not. Moreover, Ananias did not hold Felix in high regard and this was evident in the cold gleam of his blue eyes and the expression about his mouth. Felix waited for the High Priest to speak, but Ananias waited for Tertullus.

Tertullus said, "Lord, since you came to Israel we have enjoyed great quietness, and very worthy deeds were done to this nation by your providence. We accept it always, and in all places, most noble Felix, with all thankfulness.

"I will not be tedious, and hope that in your clemency you will hear my few words. For we have found this man, Saul of Tarshish, a pestilent fellow, and a mover of sedition among all the Jews throughout the world, and a ringleader of the sect of the Nazarenes, who have also gone about to profane the Temple. We took him, and would have judged him according to our Law, but Captain Lysias came upon us and with violence took him out of our hands. He then commanded this man's accusers to come to you, by examining of whom you may have knowledge of these things."*

Felix motioned to Saul to speak, and Saul said, "Captain Lysias used no more violence than was necessary to save my life, lord." This pleased Felix, for it vexed him to have Roman soldiers criticized. He smiled at Saul and motioned him to continue. Saul denied the charges of sedition. He declared that no one had found him in the Temple disputing or quarreling with any man, nor did he incite the people nor had ever incited the people against Rome, nor had he profaned any law whatsoever, Jewish or Roman.†

Saul then challenged Ananias directly to deny these things, but Felix wearily raised his small dark hand and said, "He will only repeat what other delegations have said against you, Paul of Tarsus, and none of these things are relevant to a Roman."

Saul bowed and smiled. Then his worn face became serious and he said, "These men, including the one who calls himself the High Priest, have only doctrinal charges to bring against me, though these doctrines they claim are false are part of my sect, the Pharisees. For we believe in the resurrection of the dead, and the Sadducees do not, and I have proclaimed my faith, which is ancient and which was given to us by God, blessed be His Name, through His prophets. But the Sadducees, who now rule the holy city, consider that faith ridiculous, and wish to impose their secularism on a devout and prayerful people, saying that only man is important and is ruler of the universe, and that God is dead. But," and he looked at the High Priest directly, "we will oppose that edict of the Devil with our lives, if necessary, and if that is sedition so be it."

Felix yawned, glanced at the water clock. He said, in a virtuous tone, "Whosoever declares the gods dead is blasphemous, and a fool." He said suddenly to the High Priest, "Are you one of those Sadducees?"

Ananias' pale cheeks turned pink. He gave Saul a vicious glance, then returned to Felix. "Lord," he said, "the matter is not so simple."

"It never is with you Jews," said Felix. He scratched

*Acts 24:1–8.
†Acts 24:10–16.

his ear. "My own wife, Drusilla, can never state a case plainly, in a few words, and in this she is even worse than other women. They prattle for hours and say nothing, but my wife can talk for days and end with the very sentence she began. I think that all Jews, and all women, are born lawyers, and I dislike lawyers."

He knitted his black brows at Ananias, who was gazing with a martyred air at Tertullus, who seemed to have lost his eloquent talent of oratory. Felix said, "If you have only doctrinal matters to charge against this man— who denies even these charges—then I must hold him only on your charges against him concerning Rome, and we will judge of that later. It is now outside your province."

He said to Saul, "The charges of sedition against Rome are serious, and though these men have no proof, but only their sly opinions, which I do not trust, and no Roman has as yet charged you, I must hold you for a space, to consider the matter."

Chapter 52

THE wife of Felix, the Roman Procurator, was named Drusilla, and she was of the House or Tribe of Benjamin, like Saul, himself. Drusilla was short, resembling her husband, and was a fat and bustling little woman with an air of uncommon sense and capability, and she was childless, a woman in her middle-age. She was also astonishingly like Clodia Flavius, the mother-in-law of Sephorah, Saul's sister, except that her eyes were like little balls of black glass, knowing and disillusioned. She ruled her household vigorously, and was not disturbed by her husband's frolicking with slave girls; in truth, she approved of it, for he had a way of interfering in household matters and scrutinizing bank accounts and complaining over expenses, for he was a restless man. The girls kept him occupied and pleasantly tired, so Drusilla did not object. She loved the little violent Roman, and he loved and revered her, and was terrified of her, and complained of her to anyone who would listen. Hearing those com-

plaints, Drusilla would smile indulgently and herself prepare a special delight for his delectation at dinner.

She thought long about Saul ben Hillel, of her own
Tribe, in Herod's Hall, and she knew his history. Like herself, he was also a Pharisee. She had sent the old Jewess
to cook his meals and serve him, for the Pharisees were
very rigorous concerning food. She listened to Felix's
half-jesting stories of Saul's miraculous powers. It was
rumored that he had raised a dead man in Ephesus, and
had instantly restored hundreds to health again by the
mere laying-on of his hands. "It is not a strange story,"
she told her husband. "Many wandering rabbis throughout our history possessed such powers, given to them by
God, blessed be His Name."

"But they did not contrive to get themselves so generally hated as Paul of Tarsus," said Felix. "So it is possible
that he is not holy. Why are you Jews so obsessed with
your God?"

"I have told you many times," said Drusilla. "He
chose us. We did not choose Him."

"Hah," said Felix. "You Jews are not more virtuous or
worse, than other men, and you resemble all races! Why
did not your God choose us Romans? We already have an
Empire for Him, better-administered, it is obvious, than
your priest-ruled Israel."

It had long been Drusilla's hope that Felix would become a Jew, but he had made a certain lewd remark concerning this, including the fact that his favorite female
slaves might complain about the matter. Drusilla had
smiled comfortably, without offense. But she thought of
Saul for a long time. Then one day she went to Herod's
Hall, accompanied by two middle-aged women of her
household, and Saul received her with great courtesy.
"Greetings to the Lady Drusilla," he said, "and I am doubly
honored, for we are of the same Tribe, I am informed,
and you are also a Pharisee."

Drusilla explained in Aramaic that she wished to in-
spect his household and to order his comfort. She inquired about many small details, and in the meantime she
was shrewdly studying him with her small wise eyes.
Then she asked him to accompany her to his garden,
where she desired to see if the vegetables and flowers
were receiving the rightful care, and she left her slave

women behind. She walked beside Saul, panting in the
heat and frankly wiping her damp red face with her
headcloth, and heaving. Saul impressed her, though he was
not of great stature nor of a handsome appearance, but
was old and his thick hair was white and he wore no
beard because of his skin affliction, and she could discern
that he was bowed of legs even through his long tunic
of brown linen, and he had an afflicted eye. However,
when he spoke he immediately commanded attention and
Drusilla reflected that never had she heard before such a
strong and beautiful voice, persuasive and firm and eloquent.

"Rabbi," she said, after they had considered the garden,
"I trust you do not hold animosity toward my husband
for your confinement here."

Saul was surprised. He looked down at Drusilla and
said, gently, "Lady, your husband has been very just toward me, and I know his situation, and thank him. He
could do no other but what he has done. I have appealed
to Caesar, in Rome, for consideration of my case, as I
am a Roman citizen. The Procurator, Felix, dispatched
my appeal at once." He smiled at her. "I find here some
rest and peace, and have time for meditation, and my
health, sorely depleted, is being restored, so I know it is
God's Will that I be here, so that I will be worthy of the
battlefield again."

Drusilla nodded. "It is a sensible thought," she said.
She hesitated, and then said, "You are a Nazarene. Tell
me of your belief. Do you truly believe that the Messias
has already been on earth in our flesh, that He died for
our sins, and sits now at the right Hand of the Father?"

Saul's heart quickened. He led Drusilla to a bench under a great green tamarisk tree, where it was cooler, and
he sat down beside her. Again he told her the old story
of his vision, but to him it was eternally new, it had just
occurred, he was still in transports, still overcome with
joy and rapture and wonder. Drusilla had fixed her eyes
intently on his face as she listened, and then those eyes,
so hard and so shrewd, softened with tears as Saul spoke
—and it had been many years since her last tears—and
her soul was profoundly moved, and she said in herself,
"Truly, this man speaks truth."

He recounted to her his earlier persecutions of the

Christians, or Nazarenes, and then his missionary journeys, lightly jesting about his hardships, stonings and beatings. And she thought, "He is an intrepid man, of courage and valor, and such men are rare."

After he had fallen into silence Drusilla looked at the harbors, visible over the walls, and then at the incredible scarlet of the sunset filled with golden and green celestial sails and the red orb of Mars shining alone in the silent tumult of color. Looking with her, Saul said, " 'The Heavens declare His glory, and the firmament shows His handiwork!' "

"Blessed be His Name," said Drusilla. She wanted to weep and did not know why, and her heart, so realistic and so desiccated, swelled as if with spring moisture.

"Rabbi," she said in a voice her husband would not have recognized, "I must consider these strange things which you have told me." And then she wondered at herself, and why she was so shaken. She rose slowly and ponderously from the bench, and she walked to the walls in silence with Saul beside her, and they gazed together at the awesome spectacle of the sky and the sea, which was stained red by the sunset, and the vastness of the water. The huge tumbled rocks which divided the two harbors were wet, and the scarlet light made them run as if with blood. A wind arose from the land and it was scented with resin and dust and fertile fields and grapes.

Saul said in a low voice, quoting from the prophet, " 'For Sion's sake I shall not be silent. For Jerusalem's sake, I shall not rest.' "

Drusilla bowed her head—that round big head—and prayed also, as she had not prayed since she was a girl. Then she looked at Saul and said, "You must tell me more, on another occasion, and perhaps my husband will listen also, for he is inclined to good will toward you, Saul of Tarshish." Suddenly she smiled, and brilliantly, and her face was the face of a maiden, and her plain thick features became beautiful.

"It is nonsense," said Felix, yawning at the table expansively, for his wife had prepared the dinner herself with cunning and with spices and with wine sauces, to please him and to soften his belligerence. "But it is a very fair story, and full of mystery. I am not like many

Romans, denying the gods. But another god would be redundant."

"There is but one God," said Drusilla, deftly refilling his wine goblet. (As he was frugal and bought only the cheapest of wines, she had ordered a delicious old wine for him from the marketplace, and her own thrifty soul winced at the price.)

"Nonsense," repeated Felix and lifted the goblet to his lips, and he smacked them. "The local wine is improving. How could it be possible that one God could rule not only the world but all the universes beyond it? He would have to employ lesser gods, and goddesses, so you see how ridiculous it is when you claim there is but one God. He would never rest."

" 'He who guards Israel neither slumbers nor sleeps,' " quoted Drusilla.

Felix shook his head and chuckled. "I thought I had made a good Roman of you," he said. Drusilla gave him another sweetmeat of delicate pastry filled with poppy seeds and dates. Felix chewed on it thoughtfully and with appreciation. "Still, there is too much for one God."

"He has angels and archangels," said Drusilla.

Felix smacked his hand on the table with triumph. "So! Auxiliary gods and goddesses!"

"It is not the same," said Drusilla. "Your prisoner, Paul of Tarsus, has a wondrous tongue and is full of stories, like all Jews. Let your girls alone for an afternoon and talk with him, and it is as if another Jeremias—or Homer —speaks."

Felix uttered a rude and cynical word. Then he said, "I love poetry, for does not our Emperor, Nero, love it also?" He grinned at Drusilla. "I shall avail myself of the pleasure your poet, Paul of Tarsus, offers—if there are not spies about to report to that abominable High Priest, Ananias, who will not be satisfied with anything save Paul's death. Nor do I wish to incur the wrath of King Agrippa."

But that night the healthy and robust Drusilla became gravely ill, and fell into delirium. Frightened slave girls rushed to the Procurator in the morning, as did the two family physicians, one a Greek, one an Egyptian. "Lord!" cried the Greek, "we have tended the Lady Drusilla all through the night but now she is at the point of death and we can do no more!"

Important Jews and Romans from Jerusalem were consulting with Felix this morning, and his atrium was crowded with them, and there was also two letters from Rome, sealed with Imperial seals. His scribes were at hand, busily recording the meeting, and Felix had been in the midst of a diatribe when his slaves and the Greek and Egyptian burst in upon him, without warning. They knew of his burly devotion to the Lady Drusilla, and had not sent a messenger first, imploring an interview.

He started up, his full dark eyes aghast. He cried, "I did not know she was stricken!" He forgot the impatient visitors, who were glancing meaningly at each other.

"She begged us not to disturb you in the night," said the Greek, "and we obeyed, and then she became insensible." The household revered Drusilla and respected her, and many loved her for her abrupt kindnesses and justice. Both physicians began to weep and wring their hands. "Only the gods can save her now," said the Egyptian.

Felix uttered imprecations concerning the gods, and both Jew and Roman were appalled. Then the Procurator, as if throwing them off also, flung off his robes of office and ran from the atrium to the women's quarters of his beautiful house, which had been built for Pontius Pilate by King Herod.

Drusilla's bed chamber was hot and dim, for the velvet curtains had been drawn over the windows, and she lay sweating in her death agony on the bed, and her tangled black hair was strewn in feverish disarray over the pillows, which were silken and of many colors. She lay sprawled and heedless, her fat round body clothed only in a night garment of white linen; her thick white limbs were constantly convulsed. She breathed with a deep croaking, far down in her throat, and her enormous bosom struggled for breath, and her hands grasped and clutched at the blankets in torment. The big plain face was distorted with pain, and the black eyes stared blankly, or rolled, and her swollen tongue was thrust through her wet gray lips.

Felix fell on his knees beside the bed and tried to take one of his wife's hands, but she tore the hot flesh from his grasp. "Drusilla!" he cried. "My beloved wife, Drusilla!" The heat in the chamber was past bearing. Despite the scent of flowers in the room there was already the sickly sweet stench of death, and Felix, who had been a soldier, recognized it at once and the bristling hair on his head rose in terror and his heart seemed to stop. He burst into tears, and beat his forehead with his clenched fists, and then he glared at his physicians and almost screamed, "If you do not save her, you will die!"

"Lord," said the Egyptian, "I am a physician and so am a citizen of Rome. I am not a slave. The Lady Drusilla is in extremis, and we have done our best, and if that is not enough, it is the will of Ptah that she die."

"You and your accursed gods!" howled Felix. "What do I care for your gods, or mine? They do not exist! To whom can I appeal then, but to you, you worthless swine who cannot save my wife!" He was beside himself. He swung his head back and forth on the pillows beside his wife, and then he began to groan, and he flung his arm over the tossing body of Drusilla.

"Sweetheart," he said. "You are more to me than life, for all your tongue and your admonitions and your extravagance. You gave me no sons, but ten sons are not worth your life, Carissima. Do you not know me, your husband, Felix? Do you not love me? Will you leave me desolate? Have mercy, my beloved. Have mercy!"

It seemed to the Roman that Drusilla was not only his wife, but his mother and his daughter and, above all, his dearest friend, for did she not console him constantly and advise him wisely and with rough tenderness, and then hold him in her arms in sympathy?

Drusilla did not respond to his caresses and his words. The deep and vibrating croak in her throat and breast increased, and there was an ominous rattling. Felix, in spite of his disbelief, began to invoke Asclepius and his daughter, Hygeia, and Apollo and Mercury and Chilon, not to mention his patron, Mars, whom he loved above all the others. Around him stood the wailing slave women and the physicians. The Egyptian lifted Drusilla's fat wrist in his fingers, then bent and listened to her heart. He whispered to the Greek, "She is dying, or is dead." The heat in the chamber increased. Drusilla's sweat ran from her like gray water. Her eyes opened widely, and fixed themselves on the painted ceiling, and did not blink.

Felix uttered the wildest threats and imprecations, shaking his fists, as he knelt, and promising torture and death to those about him if Drusilla was not saved. The physicians shrugged, but they were uneasy. These Romans were capable of anything, in their unseemly wrath and arrogance.

It was then that a slave woman, bowing and terrified, approached the kneeling Felix and said in a quaking voice, "Lord, there is a rabbi in Herod's Hall, who is reputed to have raised the dead and to cure the desperately ill. Send for him at once, I implore you."

"That superstitious and condemned Jew?" cried the Egyptian, looking about him with umbrage and with lacerated pride. He drew himself up; his thin black beard pointed in the air.

"That Nazarene!" exclaimed the Greek. "Is he not already dead?" His rounded features expressed his contempt.

But Felix was gazing at the slave woman with stretched and glittering eyes. "Send for him at once!" he shouted. "Make haste! Call the overseer of the hall!"

The slave woman fled. The physicians approached Felix with pleading and outstretched hands. "No Jewish mountebank, with incantations, can save the Lady Drusilla," they said. "Let him not profane her deathbed. See! She is already moribund; she is drawing her last breath."

And then indeed Drusilla gave a last loud cry, shuddered in all her parts as if a decapitating ax had struck her, convulsed all her limbs, and then collapsed on the pillows and on the bed. Her flesh immediately seemed to dwindle, to become less, as the inhabitant within had left and there was nothing remaining but a shell.

Felix uttered a howling and discordant cry, and grasped her hand and kissed it madly, and wept with moanings, like a tortured child. He writhed; he clutched; he incoherently implored all the gods he had ever known or had heard of by repute. He threatened; he gasped; it was as if he were dying, himself.

The physicians dared not even approach the deathbed, for fear of an attack on them by Felix, in his ferocious despair. They wanted to close the dead woman's eyes, to compose her thrown limbs in a more seemly fashion, to draw the sheet over her head. But they were afraid of this mad man. The slave women began the long lamentation for the dead, kneeling about on the floor and bowing their heads. The physicians exchanged miserable glances. Only the unfortunate Drusilla was silent and motionless. A stabbing ray of hot sun struck through the aperture between the draperies, and it lay on Drusilla's quiet and staring face, and somewhere there was the ominous buzz of marauding flies, scenting death, and the murals on the walls, of many colors, appeared to move with a life of their own, crawling silently. Felix, weeping without restraint, dropped his head beside that of his wife, and embraced her fiercely, and called to her in many endearing words as if to halt her spirit. Over and over he implored her not to leave him. Of what use was his life without her? His voice, wheedling, coaxing, became that of a little boy, cajoling his mother, a frightened and terrified voice, and the physicians dropped their eyes or looked aside, in embarrassment. Men did not implore the dead. The Roman was lesser in their eyes now, yet more terrible, for his emotions were capricious, and they thought his grief both an exaggeration and excessive.

The silken curtains were thrown aside and Saul entered with the slave woman, and instantly Felix was upon him, grasping his arms and shaking him and uttering both maledictions and pleas together. Saul laid his hand on the Roman's shoulder and said loudly, "Let us be calm, lord. I have heard that the Lady Drusilla had been stricken in the night, and I came at once." He put aside Felix and approached the bed and the two physicians watched him come with affronted expressions. "The Lady Drusilla has suspired," said the Egyptian.

"I am no physician," said Saul, and touched his forehead briefly with his hand in token of respect. He then stood and gazed down at Drusilla, whose women had arranged her limbs and covered her body and closed her eyes. Saul was saddened. He had been the recipient of many kindnesses from this lady of his Tribe and blood. She had sent delicacies from her own kitchen and dainties she had prepared herself to hearten his spirit and to let him know that he was not entirely abandoned, and she had had numerous conversations with him since her first visit and always she had listened with respect.

Now she was dead, and suddenly. He took her cooling

hand in his, as if she were alive and he wished to comfort her. The heavy flesh lay in his fingers, and he opened his mouth to recite the prayers for the dead. The bereaved husband stood behind him, clutching his shoulders, but Saul did not feel the pressure.

Then Saul heard distinctly and loudly in his inner ear, "Bid the woman rise," and he knew that beloved Voice, and his whole body trembled. He said, and all heard him, "Yes, Lord, I obey."

His lips felt suddenly cold and numb and there were flashes of light before his eyes, and he was weakened as if his blood had drained from him to this woman. He held her hand tightly and said, and all could hear him, "Arise, Drusilla, and waken to the day, in the Name of Christ Jesus Who has power to raise from the dead!"

The physicians heard this incredulously, and they turned to each other at once, and the Greek whispered, "He is mad!" The Egyptian made a sound of both derision and disgust. But the Procurator gazed at his wife, and the slave women bent from the waist and stared at the woman on the bed, whose hand was held by this strange Jew.

Moment passed into moment, and there was a deathly silence in the chamber. Then Drusilla murmured a deep and distressful sigh and stirred a little. The physicians came at once to her bedside and their eyes widened and the Egyptian seized his beard in his hand, and the Greek turned very pale.

Then Drusilla, sighing more and more, slowly opened her eyes and her broad gray lips turned a faint rose and the fullness of her eyes lifted and they were bright and clear again. The Roman cried aloud with joy and rushed to his wife and half lifted her in his arms, but she looked only at Saul with a mournful look, and did not heed her husband's kisses and caresses and joyful words.

"Forgive me," said Saul. "I was bidden to recall you by One who is the wisest of the wise."

Tears swelled into her eyes. She pushed aside her tangled black hair, then she looked at her husband and took his head in her arms and held it to her breast, like a mother. Then she gave her attention to Saul again.

"You must do as you must do," she said, "but I would that I had not returned."

"Yes," said Saul, and bowed his head and grieved with her that she had been restored to the world. "But you returned, as a witness."

The physicians brushed by him and could not believe that this woman who had been dead was now alive, and that she spoke in sturdy accents, she who had been able to utter only groans all through the night, and the Egyptian touched her brow and it was cool, and the Greek felt her pulse and it was bounding with health. Confounded, they fell back, and the Egyptian said to Saul, "She was not truly dead."

"I am not a physician," he repeated, and smiled faintly. "But you declared she was dead, and I have seen the dead too many times to be deceived," and he thought of his nephew, Amos, who had died and had been restored, and how he, Saul, had said the same words that they had said. "She was restored that she might be a witness to Him Who conquered death and sin and redeemed our souls."

"I know that I had passed the way all men must pass," said Drusilla, "but what I saw and with whom I spoke it is forbidden for me to speak." She leaned her plump cheek, now ruddy with health, on the top of her husband's head and she closed her eyes and tears seeped between her short black lashes.

Saul left the chamber and none went with him and as he walked his strength returned and he was no longer trembling.

That evening, before Saul put on his prayer shawl and his phylacteries, he was visited by Felix and Drusilla, and the Roman led his wife by the hand, fearful of releasing her. But when he saw Saul he dropped the hand of his wife and fell on Saul's neck and embraced him. He exclaimed, "Ask anything I am able to give you, Paul of Tarsus, and it shall be yours! For you brought to me my wife who is dearer to me than all other creatures and dearer than treasure!"

"I did not do it," said Saul. "Only God can restore the dead, and He bade me raise up the Lady Drusilla as a witness to Him."

"I will sacrifice two milk-white oxen to Him, with golden collars about their necks and gold rings in their nostrils!" cried the Roman. "I will go to the temple of

Zeus to do this at dawn, for your God is greater than Zeus, and more merciful."

"He does not desire such sacrifices," said Saul, "but only a humble and a contrite heart. He desires only your love, lord."

Drusilla bowed her head over her clasped hands and said to Saul, "Teach us of Him, Who is the Messias of God and became Man for our sakes."

And as he reasoned of righteousness, temperance and judgment to come, Felix trembled—*

Chapter 53

MONTH drifted into month and the seasons changed. Saul was no longer confined to his house and his garden but could walk over the small town and go down to the harbor and watch the sea and the ships. He baptized Drusilla, but Felix was another matter. He was half convinced that the physicians were correct, and that his wife had not truly died but had been unconscious. Moreover, he was a Roman and though Saul had informed him that multitudes of Romans were now Christians Felix could not bring himself to accept their faith. He felt that in some way it would be an insult to Rome and his soldierly forebears who had honored the old gods. And he was hearing more and more turbulent stories of the Christians, which angered him. He did not wish to issue edicts and punishments against them, as Ananias urged in numerous letters, for he did not desire to offend Saul and sadden him. He came often to hear Saul converse of the Messias but faith did not touch his skeptical soul. He had a rational explanation for everything and did not refrain from advancing those explanations. Sometimes he wondered why Saul—if he did indeed possess miraculous powers—did not grow white pinions and rise into the heavens and be free, and far away from Caesarea and his enemies, instead of remaining as a prisoner waiting judgment from Rome.

One day he asked Saul concerning this matter, and

*Acts 24:25.

Saul smiled. "If the Messias willed it I should, indeed, rise like a stork and fly from this place. But He has not willed it, and I have not questioned. He has mysterious ways, and I await His plans. I was weary and old and tired and ill, when I was brought to Caesarea, but as each day passes and I see the waters and I walk to the harbors and through the city I sleep like an infant and enjoy my meals and have calm and tranquillity about me and time for meditation; my soul and my body are strengthened and it is as if youth had been granted to me again. I am like one waiting the call to the Great Games."

Felix went away and pondered on the matter. This was a very strange God, indeed, Who did not endow His worshipers with wealth and honors and beautiful women and power, as did the Roman gods when they chose to favor some mortal. Rather, He gave them pain and ignominy and humiliations and did not deliver them from their enemies. The old gods understood that life was reasonable and favors were exchanged for favors, and that is how it should be. Saul's descriptions of spiritual joys and peace of soul only made Felix impatient. He could not accept and was frank concerning it. "Your faith does not touch my spirit," he said to Saul. "I hear with these ears but my mind is closed to it."

Saul said, "It is possible that the Lady Drusilla, who has many virtues and loves the Messias, will lead you into His Presence as she would lead a child." At this, Felix laughed. "The religion of you Jews is very gloomy," he said, "nor does your Heaven entice me. I prefer my little slave girls and what is beyond the grave is of no moment."

As month melted into month and moons waxed and waned, Saul lost a measure of his tranquillity, for it seemed to him that he had spent too many years, as a youth and a man and now an old man, waiting. The harvest was heavy and the laborers were few. He received letters from the churches, and they were full of joy, and converts were confessing Christ Jesus in multitudes, and every faithful hand and voice was needed. "And I languish here!" Saul would exclaim aloud, fuming. He was full of health and vitality now, and his limbs were strong with energy—yet it was as if he had been forgotten.

He went to the synagogue in Caesarea, a small one but

like a perfect jewel, and many were the Christians worshiping among their fellow Jews, and many were Gentiles. The rabbi, on seeing him and recognizing him, came to him and pleaded that Saul not speak in the synagogue. "We live in peace with the Romans," he said, "and you have the reputation of—I implore your pardon!—an intemperate man who arouses controversies and dissensions."

"My reputation maligns me," said Saul. "I come in peace and love, and not with wild intentions. Nevertheless, I will do as you ask, and will not speak until you bid me."

The Christians surrounded him on the streets outside the synagogue, and he was gentle and tender with them, and he healed many. But, remembering the anxiety of the old rabbi, who trembled for his people, he did not address the congregation inside, as the Law permitted. And he was always conscious of the two Roman soldiers who followed him when he entered the little city, and he did not want reports reaching Felix that his trust in his prisoner had been violated and that Saul had caused quarrelings in the synagogue and on the streets. For many were the things said in the synagogue by the Christians which were in error, but Saul waited until they were about him beyond the doors and there corrected them, in a low voice of authority. The older Jews of the congregation resented the presence of the Gentile Christians among them in the synagogue but their sons and their daughters pleaded for tolerance, for did not these Gentiles study the the Torah zealously in order to understand Yeshua the Nazarene more fully? The rabbi said, "We have come on strange days," and fearfully reminded his people that Rome had commanded that the Jews do no more proselyting. "Yet the Nazarene Jews refuse to obey this edict, and this will be woe for us."

One day Felix charged into the atrium of Saul's house, and called for him irritably. The active little man sprawled in a chair, irascibly inspected a bowl of fruit, chose one and morosely chewed it. When Saul came in from the garden, where he had been picking the golden dates, Felix burst out: "You have been here nearly two years, and there is no word from Rome concerning you!"

Saul bowed and said, "I am sorry, noble Felix, that my enforced stay with you is unwelcome."

Felix uttered a filthy word, and chose another fig, inspected it with black suspicion then threw it on the white marble floor. "How you twist my words, Paul! As far as it concerns me, and the Lady Drusilla, you may remain here forever, for your company is fascinating. It is that High Priest, Ananias! Three days never pass without a letter from him concerning your abominable Christians—and you. And most especially, you. As Rome, he declares, is evidently not interested in you or your fate, and will let you rot before hearing your case, and officials imply that they cannot understand the charges against you, and King Agrippa, himself, is bored at the mention of your name, why do I not deliver you up to his merciful justice? I could release you at once, but it would be like releasing a net of tigers, in the opinion of Ananias, though I confess I find you a peaceable man enough."

"As your soldiers report," said Saul, smiling. Felix laughed loudly, and nodded. "It is so," he said. He glared at the fruit again. "Well? What am I to do with you? Will you promise me that if I release you—to escape that damnable priest's importunities—that you will leave Israel at once and relieve her of the delight of your presence forever?"

Saul said in a low voice, "I have seen the Messias in a vision and He has commanded me to go to Rome, to witness concerning Him."

"Excellent!" said Felix. "Go at once!"

"I have not received the summons," said Saul. "He will tell me when I must go."

"He has probably forgotten you, like Rome," said the cynical Procurator.

"There is another matter," said Saul. "You have forgotten King Agrippa, who is indebted to Ananias. If I should—disappear—Ananias will wail to Agrippa and Agrippa will scream to Rome, and I understand that the Emperor looks on him kindly—"

"If that is so, why does not Agrippa, himself, in the name of Rome, seize you and deliver you to Ananias, with a command from the Emperor?"

"Agrippa is also a Roman as well as a Jew, and he

reveres Roman law, and would not deliver a Roman to the loving mercies of Ananias."

Felix became very gloomy. "I must tell you that I fear for your life," he said. "My boys who follow you are not only my spies; they are to protect you. Or did you not know that?"

"No."

Felix suddenly shouted, his active face turning almost purple, "If I loved you less, and if I did not believe in my heart that you restored my wife to me, I should have you quietly poisoned or strangled and your body buried in my gardens or thrown into the sea, to relieve me of the embarrassment of your presence!"

"Ananias would be very distressed," said Saul, and laughed. "He would not be content with my murder, or my disappearance. He wishes to witness my death."

"So, you will remain here, and I shall continue to listen to Ananias' lamentations." He studied Saul thoughtfully. "I have an inspiration. I will have Ananias, himself, poisoned or strangled."

Saul was incredulous and then he saw that Felix was serious. He said, "Few love Ananias, except the Sadducees, and the Sadducees are very powerful now in Israel, and they have access to King Agrippa at any time. Ananias is a Sadducee, and therefore is a false shepherd, for he does not believe in the very words of God, Himself, blessed be His Name, concerning the resurrection of the dead and the life of the soul. You tempt me as a man, noble Felix, you, of a certainty, tempt me! But we are forbidden to murder, though you may scorn that, considering Ananias. The people loath the High Priest, yet his—murder—would arouse all of Israel, for the High Priest represents Israel to the people no matter how contemptible he is and worthy of death. And the Sadducees would be enraged, and they are not stupid men. They would denounce you to Agrippa."

"How you have complicated my life!" said Felix. "You are a veritable dilemma to me."

Saul said, "I have a cousin in Rome, and I have thought of appealing to him, but I am loathe to do this for fear of embarrassing him also, for that with which I am charged does not come under his jurisdiction."

Felix was immediately interested. "A banker? A stockbroker? A rich man?" He licked his lips and thought of a ransom. It could be done delicately, and money was not to be despised and he had treated Saul well, and it could be accomplished with good will on the part of all.

Saul could read his thoughts, and he smiled indulgently. He said, "Alas, he is none of these, though he is a rich man and of a noble name in Rome. Did not Captain Lysias tell you?"

"The captain uses as few words as possible and only those directly concerned with the subject." Felix sat up in his chair. "Who is this famous cousin of yours?"

"He is a general in the Praetorian Guards, under the command of Tigellinus—"

At that hated-name Felix shuddered and it was not for a moment that it forced itself into his mind that Saul had mentioned a cousin in the famed Praetorian Guards. Then he shouted, "His name, his name!"

"Titus Milo Platonius."

Felix sprang to his feet and stared at Saul. His small dark face became sallow as he lost color. "Titus Milo Platonius!" he repeated, almost in a whisper. "He is your cousin?"

Saul was puzzled by Felix's changed expression, which he could not read.

"Of a certainty, yes. We are of the same blood. He was born in Israel, and his father was a famed soldier."

Felix slowly seated himself again, but he did not take his restless black eyes from the other man's face. He appeared to be greatly shaken. Then in that whisper he said, "Aulus Platonius was the dearest friend of my father's." He looked sharply away from Saul. It was almost as if he were hiding his face, and Saul was suddenly alarmed and approached him closer, and his heart suffered a premonitory sickness.

He faltered, "If you have evil news to tell me, noble Felix, be quick about it!"

Felix did not answer for a moment, then he stood up again and faced Saul. He was not a man of tenderness and kindness, but now he put his hand on Saul's shoulder and looked into his eyes, and his own widened with sympathy.

"Have you heard of Faenius Rufus, the colleague of

Tigellinus, that poisoner and murderer, and Plautius Lateranus, Consul-elect of Rome?"

"No, I have not."

"They were both members of the Praetorian Guard, as was your cousin, and so were many centurions and a number of Tribunes." Felix's coarse mouth flattened. "They were discovered, it is said, in a conspiracy to murder Nero, about four months ago. They—and a number of other Praetorians—were executed."

Saul felt as though he would fall to the floor, and he grasped the edge of a table to prevent it. His face aged again, lost its youth. "And Milo was one of them?"

"It is true. If I had known, when I heard of the matter from Rome, I should have told you at once, but I did not know that Titus Milo Platonius was your cousin."

Saul cried out in despair, "Milo was a Christian, and no matter how heinous Nero is Milo could not have been induced to join a conspiracy to murder!"

Felix shook his head. "Nor were the others guilty. I have heard a rumor that Sabina Poppaea, Nero's wife, instigated the murders for reasons of her own. She is a Fury, for all her reputed beauty. She instigated the death of Claudius' son, Britannicus, and Claudius' lovely daughter, Octavia, who was married to Nero, and made him a matricide, also." He pressed Saul's shoulder. "Milo was not a young man, as I remember."

"True," said Saul, in a faint voice. "But the world is the lesser for the death of such a man as my cousin. It is infinitely poorer. And I did not know! I did not have even the smallest premonition, not even a dream!"

"It is possible that your God spared you as long as possible."

But Saul did not hear him. He said with tears, "He was the most honorable of Romans, and he died in dishonor!"

"Ha!" said Felix. "No one murdered by Nero is judged to have died in dishonor! In truth, it is a mark of honor." He shook his head again. "Rome is no longer Rome. She is a harlot."

Then he looked about him quickly, terrified that he had been overheard, and fearful even of Saul. But Saul had fallen into a chair and had covered his face with his hands and Felix drew a deep breath of relief. However he crept stealthily to the door of the atrium and looked onto the portico. No one was there. He moved without sound to the farther door leading into the body of the house and flung that door open. But none listened there. Felix wiped his face with the back of his hairy dark arm, and returned to Saul.

"Sacrifice three black oxen with silver collars to your God," he said, consolingly, "that your cousin be released from Hades and transported to the Blessed Isles."

Saul lifted his head. "I have no fear for the soul of Milo, for not only was he a Christian but he was the noblest and truest of men. Alas, I have not seen him for many years and he wrote to me often, but in my labors I was forgetful and I answered but a few!"

Felix was touched, and as this was a rare emotion for him he did not recognize it. He wished to strengthen Saul, so he stood up straightly as a soldier and said, "Paul of Tarsus, we are Romans!"

Even in his grief Saul almost smiled at the sight of this rigidly standing little man who had assumed a heroic expression. He stood also and repeated, "We are Romans."

They solemnly shook hands, and Felix departed, and Saul was left alone with his new sorrow, and he felt that the world had emptied for him and had been made desolate.

Saul awoke one morning to find a cypress, the sign of mourning, standing by the portico, and he was moved at this silent tribute to the grief of Saul on the part of Felix, and the gesture of honor to the noble dead.

He went to the synagogue to pray for the soul of his cousin, and he stood up with the mourners when the rabbi extolled "those who sleep in the dust—their memory is a blessing," and spoke of the peace of their spirits. Many were there who were curious at the sight of Saul standing, and his sorrow-ravaged face, and they wondered for whom he mourned. The rabbi said, "The dead are in the blessed Hands of God, and He is full of lovingkindness, and it is ourselves who are bereaved and not those who have gone before."

One evening Felix came to see Saul again, and he said, "I have been recalled to Rome, thank the gods! I shall depart with my wife within a few days. I am to surrender this house—and you—to Porcius Festus, who is expected daily at Caesarea."

"Alas, I lose another friend," said Saul.

Felix frowned. "It is possible he has news from Rome concerning you. I know him well. He is very stupid, but very amiable and inclined to good will, which is not very intelligent of him. I am leaving him a letter concerning you."

Drusilla came also to say farewell. She said, "Rabbi, as you have taught me, and my parents before you, it is all God's Will."

"Which I find incomprehensible at times," said Saul.

He had not known how much he would miss these friends until they had departed, and the house of Pontius Pilate awaited new tenants. For he had dined in that house often, listening with amusement to the bragging of Felix and his little bullying quarrels with Drusilla.

One morning there was a great bustling about the palace and Saul came close to observe that Porcius Festus had arrived with his family and entourage and guards.

Two days later Festus sent for Saul, and two soldiers accompanied him to the house of Pontius Pilate.

Chapter 54

PORCIUS FESTUS sat in the atrium in his robes of office. He was as short a man as Felix, but he was also enormously fat, with a bald and rosy head and a huge rosy face and several chins, and sharp little blue eyes like polished stones. Saul stood before him and he inspected Saul closely, rubbing one of his chins and humming like a bee under his breath. His meaty little hands were covered with sparkling rings, and he affected pure white clothing of the finest linen, and perfumes. He said at last, "So you are Paul of Tarsus, hated by your own people, who desire your death, and loved by Felix and his household."

Saul bowed and said, "I have done nothing to deserve the hatred of the High Priest, Ananias, and certainly I am not worthy of the affection of the noble Felix."

At this Festus smiled, and Saul thought that Felix had underestimated this man's intelligence, and perhaps even his good will. Festus said, "I have received a message from your bloodthirsty Ananias praying that you be delivered to him in Jerusalem, for judgment. But I have commanded him and his court to appear here so that I might hear them."

Saul sighed. "It is a weariness, lord, to hear the same ancient charges against me."

"Nevertheless," said Festus, "it is necessary for you to be here, for you are a Roman citizen and it is your right." His voice was like that of a friendly bull and Saul left him after another bow and retired to his house.

Within a few days Ananias and his court of Sadducees arrived in Caesarea and laid their complaints before the new Procurator. Festus disliked Ananias at once, for he had a remote and supercilious air and wore an expression of strained patience and resignation before the Roman. Saul was summoned. Ananias averted his head, as if confronted by an obscenity, and his court withdrew a little also and Saul was left in a wide circle alone before Festus. The small sharp blue eyes rested on Saul a moment, then moved to the High Priest and Festus commanded Ananias to state his complaints again before the accused.

Saul shut his eyes in deep weariness, and Festus was amused and rubbed his chins until they were crimson as he listened to Ananias. When Ananias had completed his complaints Festus said, "I am but an ignorant Roman and therefore not very clever. It would seem that Paul of Tarsus is guilty of certain Jewish doctrinal errors, which do not concern me. The charge of sedition is diffused and not sustained, against Rome." He turned his attention to Saul. "Speak, Paul of Tarsus, citizen of Rome! Answer if you are guilty."

As Ananias and his court were not Roman citizens their faces became like ice, and they were affronted and knew that Festus had deliberately affronted them. They kept their countenances averted as Saul began to speak:

"I stand at Caesar's judgment seat, where I ought to be judged. To my fellow Jews I have done no wrong, as you, lord, know. For if I be an offender, or have committed anything worthy of death I refuse not to die, but if there be none of these things whereof these accuse me no man may deliver me unto them. I appeal unto Caesar."*

Festus hummed like a giant bee in the silence of the

*Acts 25:10–11.

chamber, examined his rings, rubbed them on the linen which covered his knee, yawned, scratched his ear. Then he stood up with a gesture of dismissal and said, "You have appealed to Caesar. Therefore, unto Caesar shall you go."

Ananias and his court, who had expected quite another judgment on the part of the new Procurator, were outraged and tried to protest, but Festus heavily stepped down from his chair and left them without a backward look. Saul, accompanied by the two soldiers, returned to Herod's Hall. When alone in his garden he prayed, "Lord, how much longer must this farce be continued, and what is the purpose of it?"

One gold and scarlet evening he heard a noisy hubbub at the house of Pontius Pilate, and he came to his garden walls to discover the reason. He saw that King Agrippa and his entourages had arrived to do honor to Festus, and with the king was his Queen, the beautiful Bernice, and her many slave women and friends. The feastings and celebrations continued for several days and nights and the soft and nimble air of Caesarea rang with music and laughter and shouts and gaiety. Then days of sodden satiety and exhaustion set in and all slept and it was quiet again.

Festus and King Agrippa, the Jew, were old and roistering friends, and Festus, when he had recovered from the debauch and the celebrations he had prepared for Agrippa, told him of Saul. "I have sent another courier to Rome praying that this man be delivered before Caesar for a judgment, as he is a Roman citizen. In the meantime, your High Priest is clamoring that I give Paul of Tarsus into his gentle hands."

King Agrippa despised Ananias. Ananias treated him with a respectful hauteur that was like an insult, for Ananias was a Sadducee and Agrippa's family was of the comparatively humble Tribe of Dan. He said, "Ananias should be Master of the Gladiators in the circus, for he surely lusts for blood. Let us send for this Saul of Tarshish, whom you call Paul, and I will hear him for myself."

Festus yawned. "I have forgotten to tell you, my friend, that Ananias arrives tomorrow—again—with his court of accusers against my poor prisoner, so you will have to hear them also."

Agrippa was dismayed. "But I heard them in Jerusalem! I said to them, 'It is not the manner of the Romans to deliver any man to die, before that he which is accused have the accusers face to face, and have license to answer for himself concerning the crime laid against him.' I beg you, Festus, bring the man to me at once."

So Saul was summoned again to the atrium and he was astonished at the assemblage, for Agrippa's court was there and his Queen, Bernice, and the sunlight made moving color and light of the silken garments and the jewels. Saul's eyes flew to Agrippa, and he saw a florid and handsome man of a truly Semitic countenance, like a Phoenician, arrayed in scarlet and gold. His Queen had a lovely face with glowing gray eyes and she was dressed in the fashionable Egyptian manner, her dark curls braided with gems and ribbons and her bosom nearly entirely bared. Her court of ladies stood beside her chair and fanned her with ostrich plumes, and her face was as white as milk and her lips like a poppy.

When the large atrium was quiet, Festus said to Agrippa, "King Agrippa and all which are here present with us, you see this man about whom many Jews have dealt with me, both at Jerusalem and also here, crying that he ought not to live any longer. But when I found that he had committed nothing worthy of death and that he, himself, has appealed to Caesar, I have determined to send him. But I have no certain thing to write to Caesar. Therefore I have brought him forth before you, O King Agrippa, that, after examination I might have something to write, for it seems unreasonable to send a prisoner and not withal to signify the crimes laid against him."*

King Agrippa studied Saul thoughtfully, and he was disappointed, for he had thought to see a more imposing man, like the prophets, and kingly. But Saul seemed to him to be old and weary and juiceless, and unprepossessing, and dressed like a worker in the vineyards. Agrippa disdainfully lifted his fragrant kerchief to his eagle nose and sniffed of it, as if Saul smelled of the field and the barnyards, and his thick black lashes touched his brown-red cheek in indifference.

*Acts 25:24–27.

He said, "You are permitted to speak for yourself." (Why was he constantly annoyed with reports concerning this insignificant Jew, who was alleged by Ananias to possess the major attributes of Satan, and so deserved death?)

Saul stretched forth his hand to the king, and spoke, and at once everyone was transfixed by his voice, for it filled the great chamber and rolled back from the glittering marble walls. Even the ladies forgot to fan Bernice, who was leaning forward now to gaze at Saul, and Agrippa dropped his kerchief and Festus rubbed his chins.

"I think myself happy, King Agrippa," said Saul, "because I shall answer for myself this day before you, touching all the things whereof I am accused. I know you to be expert in all our customs and questions which are among us. Therefore, I beseech you to hear me patiently."

He then spoke of his family, his birth, his Tribe. He spoke of his, and his father's, long quarrel with the secular Sadducees. "Why should it be thought incredible that God should raise the dead?" he implored, and recalled to Agrippa that this was the teaching of the Pharisees, that on one day God will open all tombs.

Agrippa did not love the Sadducees, himself, and his wife was very devout though she arrayed herself like an Egyptian. He leaned his elbow on the gold arm of his chair and partly covered his handsome red lips and beard with his hand as he listened to Saul, and he thought, "So must the voices of the prophets have been, eloquent and trumpeting and filled with verity!"

Saul continued to speak, with passionate gestures, and his eyes burned like blue fire and his thin and weary figure seemed to attain great stature. He spoke of his whole life, and his searching and his seeking for God, and his persecution of the Nazarenes. Then he spoke of his journey to Damascus, and now there was not a single sound in the atrium and even Festus ceased his bee-humming and nothing could be heard but the rustling of trees in the garden and Saul's commanding and sonorous voice. And when he wept, as he related the Vision of the Messias, others wept with him though they did not know why, and Queen Bernice's rosy lips trembled and her gilded lashes were pearled with tears. But Festus looked amused.

Saul told of his mission to the Gentiles and Agrippa's

black brows drew together and his eyes never left Saul's trembling face. "For this, my mission, have I been condemned, for it is alleged I profaned the Temple and the synagogues, but Christ had shown a light to His people, and to the Gentiles, as was prophesied by Isaias." He paused, then said in a louder voice, "King Agrippa, do you believe the prophets? I know that you believe!"

Agrippa mused. There was a darkling light under his brows, and a gravity on his countenance. At last he looked at the doors of the atrium, as if pondering, then at the ceiling, then at the shining walls, then at his wife who gave him a long look of pleading and adoration.

The king said, "Almost do you, Saul of Tarshish, persuade me to be a Christian!"*

Festus stopped smiling, and all were still. Saul said in the gentlest voice, "I would to God that not only your Majesty, but also all that hear me this day were as I am!"

Agrippa motioned to Saul to stand apart and he and Festus stood and came together with counselors, and talked quietly among themselves. Agrippa said, "This man has done nothing worthy of death or of bonds! He might have been set at liberty, if he had not appealed unto Caesar."†

"If he had not so appealed," said Festus, with a broad smile, "Ananias would have had him murdered long ago!"

Chapter 55

AND now it was determined to send Saul to Rome, for Caesar's judgment, and he was to sail on the morrow.

The night before his departure he had an awesome and terrible vision. It was as if he stood on the highest battlements of earth and surveyed the world, and the city of Rome, and all was a vast and murmurous sound, and all was full of color and flashings and movements and armies and caravans and thunder and sudden bursts of human

*Acts 26:28.
†Acts 26:31–32.

terror, of lightning flaring on marble, of sunlight and flame and dust, of endless roads and looming mountains and waters as red as blood, of crashing walls and falling pillars. His eyes roved strange cities in one glance, but always they returned to Rome. And then as he regarded the mighty city he saw it gush with a tempest of fire and the white columns—like white forests—were illuminated in it, and roofs fell and the earth shook, and from a multitude of voices there rose a great cry: "Woe unto Rome!" Then a mightier chorus responded, as if from every corner of the world: "Woe unto all mankind!"

"Woe unto the world!" rose the holocaust of voices. "Woe, woe!"

Saul rose at dawn, trembling, drenched with his own sweat, and he fell on his knees to pray, that the awful vision would not come to pass, and that all men would come unto the Lamb of God for salvation. But a dark agony remained in his mind and his heart, and he said, aloud, "There is little time. I must make haste!"

A few hours later he was on a ship to Rome, in the harbor of Caesarea.

He leaned on the railing and surveyed the fervent and colorful little city. He saw the palace of Pontius Pilate, the house where he, himself, had spent four long years, the roads, the market places, the winding streets, the theaters and government buildings, the distant circus, and, all about him, the ships with rising sails, the scent of hot tar and resin, the shouts of sailors and the carriers of cargo, and the blinding blue water and the flat plain of the waiting horizon.

Then he knew that never again would he see his beloved country and his beloved countrymen, nor the golden Temple, nor the holy city, Jerusalem. He began to weep, and he whispered, "If I forget you, O Jerusalem, let my right arm wither—"

He moved across the deck for fear he would be too stricken with grief, and he stared across the plain of light which was the Great Sea and which would bear him to Rome. He was only a man. How could he endure it that never again would he see his kindred, nor hear the sounds of his country, but be forever an exile, going into an unknown future and to an unknown death? He would not be buried in this sacred soil. He knew that as surely as he knew that he was departing. What earth would hold his bones? What friends would mourn him? He looked at the sky which was too radiant to gaze upon, and he dropped his chin on his folded arms and it seemed to him that he had lived too long and was too weary. Of what use was he now, to God, an old man, when youth was needed? God deserved the young to witness for Him.

Then, as he leaned his arms on the railing and his head was bent upon them in a prostration of human sorrow, it seemed to him that he heard the voice of his father, Hillel ben Borush, as he had heard it in his youth, and the voice of Hillel was tender and strong and loving and prayerful:

> " 'O God, You are my God!
> Early will I seek You.
> My soul thirsts for You
> In a dry and thirsty land
> Where no water is;
> To see Your power and Your glory,
> So I have seen You in the Sanctuary,
> Because of Your lovingkindness,
> Is better than life!
> My lips shall praise You,
> Thus will I bless You while I live!
> I will lift up my hands in Your Name,
> My soul shall be satisfied
>   as with marrow and fatness.
> And my mouth shall praise You with joyful lips—' "

> " 'My soul follows hard after You—!' "

Saul lifted his head and took a last look at his land, for the ship was moving and the sails were filled with wind and light. His eyes welled with tears, but his lips smiled with love, and he lifted his hand and said,

"Hear, O Israel! The Lord our God, the Lord is One!"

His soul was strong again, and young. He saw his country drop below the curve of the world and he knew that the Messias would return again to His people and all the earth would rejoice, crying, "Hosannah!" For all nations were His own.

Bibliography

The Holy Bible

Reader's Digest Articles on the Apostles

Josephus *Antiquities,* etc.

Juvenal

The Vatican Libraries

Life Magazine, 1964, Series on the Bible

Museums, Athens and Israel

Philostratus

Pliny

St. Jerome, *Comments on Philippians*

W. P. Davies, *Paul and Rabbinic Judaism*

The Catholic Encyclopedia

A. Dreissman, *Paul.*

R. A. Knox, *St Paul's Gospel.*

W. M. Ramsay, *St. Paul the Traveler and Roman Citizen.*

J. Lebreton and J. Zeiller, *The History of Primitive Christianity.*

G. Ricciotti, *Paul the Apostle*

Max I. Dimont, *Jews, God and History.*

Henri Daniel-Rops, *The Heroes of God* and *Jesus and His Times.*

The Metamorphoses of Ovid

Tacitus *History.*

Aubrey de Selincourt, *The Early History of Rome*

Dr. Hugh S. Schonfield, *Those Incredible Christians.*

Aristotle's *Politics* and *Ethics*

Charles M. Bakewell, *Source Book in Ancient Philosophy.*

Phaedo of Plato

    And literally hundreds of other books concerning Roman, Greek and Jewish history, and the history of Christianity, too numerous to mention.